Creating Personal, Social, and Urban Awareness through Pervasive Computing

Bin Guo
Northwestern Polytechnical University, China

Daniele Riboni
University of Milano, Italy

Peizhao Hu
NICTA, Australia

A volume in the Advances in Human and
Social Aspects of Technology Book Series
(AHSAT) Book Series

Managing Director:	Lindsay Johnston
Editorial Director:	Myla Merkel
Production Manager:	Jennifer Yoder
Publishing Systems Analyst:	Adrienne Freeland
Development Editor:	Allyson Gard
Acquisitions Editor:	Kayla Wolfe
Typesetter:	Lisandro Gonzalez
Cover Design:	Jason Mull

Published in the United States of America by
Information Science Reference (an imprint of IGI Global)
701 E. Chocolate Avenue
Hershey PA 17033
Tel: 717-533-8845
Fax: 717-533-8661
E-mail: cust@igi-global.com
Web site: http://www.igi-global.com

Library of Congress Cataloging-in-Publication Data

Creating personal, social, and urban awareness through pervasive computing / Bin Guo, Daniele Riboni, and Peizhao Hu, editors.
    pages cm
 Includes bibliographical references and index.
    ISBN 978-1-4666-4695-7 (hardcover) -- ISBN 978-1-4666-4696-4 (ebook) -- ISBN 978-1-4666-4697-1 (print & perpetual access) 1. Ubiquitous computing. 2. Mobile computing. I. Guo, Bin, 1980- editor of compilation. II. Riboni, Daniele, 1977- III. Hu, Peizhao, 1981-
    QA76.5915.C74 2014
    004--dc23
                        2013025028

This book is published in the IGI Global book series Advances in Human and Social Aspects of Technology (AHSAT) (ISSN: 2328-1316; eISSN: 2328-1324)

British Cataloguing in Publication Data
A Cataloguing in Publication record for this book is available from the British Library.

All work contributed to this book is new, previously-unpublished material. The views expressed in this book are those of the authors, but not necessarily of the publisher.

For electronic access to this publication, please contact: eresources@igi-global.com.

Advances in Human and Social Aspects of Technology Book Series (AHSAT) Book Series

Ashish Dwivedi
The University of Hull, UK

ISSN: 2328-1316
EISSN: 2328-1324

MISSION

In recent years, the societal impact of technology has been noted as we become increasingly more connected and are presented with more digital tools and devices. With the popularity of digital devices such as cell phones and tablets, it is crucial to consider the implications of our digital dependence and the presence of technology in our everyday lives.

The **Advances in Human and Social Aspects of Technology (AHSAT) Book Series** seeks to explore the ways in which society and human beings have been affected by technology and how the technological revolution has changed the way we conduct our lives as well as our behavior. The AHSAT book series aims to publish the most cutting-edge research on human behavior and interaction with technology and the ways in which the digital age is changing society.

COVERAGE

- Activism & ICTs
- Computer-Mediated Communication
- Cultural Influence of ICTs
- Cyber Behavior
- End-User Computing
- Gender & Technology
- Human-Computer Interaction
- Information Ethics
- Public Access to ICTs
- Technoself

IGI Global is currently accepting manuscripts for publication within this series. To submit a proposal for a volume in this series, please contact our Acquisition Editors at Acquisitions@igi-global.com or visit: http://www.igi-global.com/publish/.

Titles in this Series

For a list of additional titles in this series, please visit: www.igi-global.com

User Behavior in Ubiquitous Online Environments
Jean-Eric Pelet (KMCMS, IDRAC International School of Management, University of Nantes, France) and Panagiota Papadopoulou (University of Athens, Greece)
Information Science Reference • copyright 2014 • 325pp • H/C (ISBN: 9781466645660) • US $175.00 (our price)

Innovative Methods and Technologies for Electronic Discourse Analysis
Hwee Ling Lim (The Petroleum Institute-Abu Dhabi, UAE) and Fay Sudweeks (Murdoch University, Australia)
Information Science Reference • copyright 2014 • 546pp • H/C (ISBN: 9781466644267) • US $175.00 (our price)

Advanced Research and Trends in New Technologies, Software, Human-Computer Interaction, and Communicability
Francisco Vicente Cipolla-Ficarra (Alaipo, Italy)
Information Science Reference • copyright 2014 • 361pp • H/C (ISBN: 9781466644908) • US $175.00 (our price)

New Media Influence on Social and Political Change in Africa
Anthony A. Olorunnisola (Pennsylvania State University, USA) and Aziz Douai (University of Ontario Institute of Technology, Canada)
Information Science Reference • copyright 2013 • 373pp • H/C (ISBN: 9781466641976) • US $175.00 (our price)

Cases on Usability Engineering Design and Development of Digital Products
Miguel A. Garcia-Ruiz (Algoma University, Canada)
Information Science Reference • copyright 2013 • 470pp • H/C (ISBN: 9781466640467) • US $175.00 (our price)

Human Rights and Information Communication Technologies Trends and Consequences of Use
John Lannon (University of Limerick, Ireland) and Edward Halpin (Leeds Metropolitan University, UK)
Information Science Reference • copyright 2013 • 324pp • H/C (ISBN: 9781466619180) • US $175.00 (our price)

Collaboration and the Semantic Web Social Networks, Knowledge Networks, and Knowledge Resources
Stefan Brüggemann (Astrium Space Transportation, Germany) and Claudia d'Amato (University of Bari, Italy)
Information Science Reference • copyright 2012 • 387pp • H/C (ISBN: 9781466608948) • US $175.00 (our price)

Human Rights and Risks in the Digital Era Globalization and the Effects of Information Technologies
Christina M. Akrivopoulou (Democritus University of Thrace, Greece) and Nicolaos Garipidis (Aristotle University of Thessaloniki, Greece)
Information Science Reference • copyright 2012 • 363pp • H/C (ISBN: 9781466608917) • US $180.00 (our price)

Technology for Creativity and Innovation Tools, Techniques and Applications
Anabela Mesquita (ISCAP/IPP and Algoritmi Centre, University of Minho, Portugal)
Information Science Reference • copyright 2011 • 426pp • H/C (ISBN: 9781609605193) • US $180.00 (our price)

www.igi-global.com

701 E. Chocolate Ave., Hershey, PA 17033
Order online at www.igi-global.com or call 717-533-8845 x100
To place a standing order for titles released in this series, contact: cust@igi-global.com
Mon-Fri 8:00 am - 5:00 pm (est) or fax 24 hours a day 717-533-8661

Table of Contents

Section 1
Introduction

Chapter 1
> *Bin Guo, Northwestern Polytechnical University, China*
> *Yunji Liang, Northwestern Polytechnical University, China*
> *Zhu Wang, Northwestern Polytechnical University, China*
> *Zhiwen Yu, Northwestern Polytechnical University, China*
> *Daqing Zhang, TELECOM SudParis, France*
> *Xingshe Zhou, Northwestern Polytechnical University, China*

Section 2
Personal Awareness

Chapter 2
> *Yunji Liang, Northwestern Polytechnical University, China*
> *Xingshe Zhou, Northwestern Polytechnical University, China*
> *Bin Guo, Northwestern Polytechnical University, China*
> *Zhiwen Yu, Northwestern Polytechnical University, China*

Section 3
Social Awareness

**Section 5
Conclusion**

Detailed Table of Contents

Section 1
Introduction

Chapter 1

    Bin Guo, Northwestern Polytechnical University, China

    Yunji Liang, Northwestern Polytechnical University, China

    Zhu Wang, Northwestern Polytechnical University, China

    Zhiwen Yu, Northwestern Polytechnical University, China

    Daqing Zhang, TELECOM SudParis, France

    Xingshe Zhou, Northwestern Polytechnical University, China

In the past decades, numerous research efforts have been made to model and extract the contexts of users in pervasive computing environments. The recent explosion of sensor-equipped mobile phone market and the phenomenal growth of geo-tagged data (Twitter messages, Foursquare check-ins, etc.) have enabled the analysis of new dimensions of contexts that involve the social and urban context. The technology trend towards pervasive sensing and large-scale social and community computing is making "Social and Community Intelligence (SCI)" a new research area that aims at investigating individual/ group behavior patterns, community and urban dynamics based on the "digital footprints." It is believed that the SCI technology has the potential to revolutionize the field of context-aware computing. The aim of this chapter is to identify this emerging research area, present the research background, define the general system framework, characterize its unique properties, discuss the open research challenges, and present this emerging research field.

Section 2
Personal Awareness

Chapter 2

Yunji Liang, Northwestern Polytechnical University, China
Xingshe Zhou, Northwestern Polytechnical University, China
Bin Guo, Northwestern Polytechnical University, China
Zhiwen Yu, Northwestern Polytechnical University, China

With the unprecedented sensing capabilities and the emergence of Internet of things, studies on activity recognition have been hot issues for different application areas, such as pervasive healthcare, industry and commerce, and recommendation systems. Much effort has been devoted to activity recognition using different sensors. Based on the differences of ubiquitous sensors, the authors classify the existing work into approximating sensing, wearable sensing, and video/audio sensing. Generally, methodologies for activity recognition are divided into logical reasoning and probabilistic reasoning. They illustrate the generalized framework and outline the advantages and disadvantages for each algorithm. Despite the research on activity recognition, activity recognition still faces many challenges in many aspects including nonintrusive data collection, scalable algorithms, energy consumption, and semantic extraction from social interaction. Towards those challenging research issues, the authors present their contributions to the field of activity recognition.

Chapter 3

Igor Bisio, University of Genoa, Italy
Alessandro Delfino, University of Genoa, Italy
Fabio Lavagetto, University of Genoa, Italy
Mario Marchese, University of Genoa, Italy

Human-machine interaction is performed by devices such as the keyboard, the touch-screen, or speech-to-text applications. For example, a speech-to-text application is software that allows the device to translate the spoken words into text. These tools translate explicit messages but ignore implicit messages, such as the emotional status of the speaker, filtering out a portion of information available in the interaction process. This chapter focuses on emotion detection. An emotion-aware device can also interact more personally with its owner and react appropriately according to the user's mood, making the user-machine interaction less stressful. The chapter gives the guidelines for building emotion-aware smartphone applications in an opportunistic way (i.e., without the user's collaboration). In general, smartphone applications might be employed in different contexts; therefore, the to-be-detected emotions might be different.

Web service descriptions with Semantic Web annotations can be exploited to automate dynamic discovery of services. The approaches introduced aim at enabling automatic discovery, configuration, and execution of services in dynamic environments. In this chapter, the authors present the service discovery aspect of MERCURY, a platform for straightforward, user-centric integration and management of heterogeneous devices and services via a Web-based interface. In the context of MERCURY, they use service discovery to find appropriate sensors, services, or actuators to perform a certain functionality required within a user-defined scenario (e.g., to obtain the temperature at a certain location, book a table at a restaurant close to the location of all friends involved, etc.). A user will specify a service request, which will be fed to a matchmaker, which compares the request to existing service offers and ranks these offers based on how well they match the service request. In contrast to existing works, the service discovery approach the authors use is geared towards non-IT-savvy end users and is not restricted to single service-description formalism. Moreover, the matchmaking algorithm should be user-aware and environmentally adaptive (e.g. depending on the user's location or surrounding temperature), rather than specific to simple keywords-based searches, which depend on the users' expertise and mostly require several tries. Hence, the goal is to develop a service discovery module on top of existing techniques, which will rank discovered services to serve users' queries according to their personal interests, expertise, and current situations.

Chapter 5

Recent years marked many smart environment solutions hitting the market and applying latest pervasive computing research advancements on an industrial scale. Context-aware smart environments are able to act accordingly to the immediate environment information in an intelligent, predefined, learned, or automatically inferred way, and are able to communicate to their users, thus increasing users' comfort and awareness level. Since the beginning of the 2000s, many projects have been designing and implementing smart environment systems. When looking post-factum at the architectures of these systems, one can notice a lot of similarities among them. With the same basic structure, the biggest differences usually arise at the level of individual components, aimed to satisfy different end-level requirements. Taking many successful and undergoing projects as case-studies, this chapter looks for the common structure, the common patterns, and the "best practices" that can help future projects to reduce the efforts spent on the general system frame, and redirect those efforts to more specific requirements that are unique in every project. It introduces several architecture layers that inevitably exist in one form or another, discusses the possible layer components and the common information flows, and mentions the most notable problems, such as scalability and fault tolerance. Several case studies of successful or undergoing smart building projects show that the presented pattern can be easily mapped to their architectures.

Vlasios Kasapakis, University of the Aegean, Greece
Damianos Gavalas, University of the Aegean, Greece

Pervasive games are a new type of digital games that combines game and physical reality within the gameplay. This novel game type raises unprecedented research and design challenges for developers and urges the exploration of new technologies and methods to create high quality game experiences and design novel and compelling forms of content for the players. This chapter follows a systematic approach to explore the landscape of pervasive gaming. First, the authors approach pervasive games from a theoretical point of view, defining the four axes of pervasive games design, introducing the concept of game world persistency, and describing aspects of spatially/temporally/socially expanded games. Then, they present ten pervasive game projects, classified in five genres based on their playing environment and features. Following that, the authors present a comparative view of those projects with respect to several design aspects: communication and localization, context and personal awareness aspects, information model, player equipment, and game space visualization. Last, the authors highlight current trends, design principles, and future directions for pervasive games development.

Section 3
Social Awareness

Zhu Wang, Northwestern Polytechnical University, China
Xingshe Zhou, Northwestern Polytechnical University, China
Daqing Zhang, TELECOM SudParis, France
Bin Guo, Northwestern Polytechnical University, China
Zhiwen Yu, Northwestern Polytechnical University, China

Due to the proliferation of GPS-enabled smartphones, Location-Based Social Networking (LBSNs) services have been experiencing a remarkable growth over the last few years. Compared with traditional online social networks, a significant feature of LBSNs is the coexistence of both online and offline social interactions, providing a large-scale heterogeneous social network that is able to facilitate lots of academic studies. One possible study is to leverage both online and offline social ties for the recognition and profiling of community structures. In this chapter, the authors attempt to summarize some recent progress in the community detection problem based on LBSNs. In particular, starting with an empirical analysis on the characters of the LBSN data set, the authors present three different community detection approaches, namely, link-based community detection, content-based community detection, and hybrid community detection based on both links and contents. Meanwhile, they also address the community profiling problem, which is very useful in real-world applications.

Intelligent Transport Systems (ITS) encompass sensing technologies, wireless communication, and intelligent algorithms, and resemble the infrastructure for ubiquitous computing in the car. This chapter borrows from social media, locative media, mobile technologies, and urban informatics research to explore three classes of ITS applications in which human behavior plays a more pivotal role. Applications for enhancing self-awareness could positively influence driver behavior, both in real-time and over time. Additionally, tools capable of supporting our social awareness while driving could change our attitude towards others and make it easier and safer to share the road. Lastly, a better urban awareness in and outside the car improves our understanding of the road infrastructure as a whole. As a case study, the authors discuss emotion recognition (emotions such as aggressiveness and anger are a major contributing factor to car crashes) and a suitable basis and first step towards further exploring the three levels of awareness, self-, social-, and urban-awareness, in the context of driving on roads.

Smart homes are equipped with multiple sensors and actuators to observe the residents and environmental phenomena, to interpret the situation out of that, and finally, to react accordingly. While the data processing for a single smart home is facile, the data processing for multiple smart homes in one smart building is more complex because there are different people (e.g., like several residents, administrators, or a property management) with different interests concerning the processed data. On that point, this chapter shows which kind of typical roles can be found in a smart building and what requirements and challenges they demand for managing and processing the data. Secondly, Data Stream Management Systems (DSMS) are introduced as an approach for processing and managing data in a smart building by presenting an appropriate architecture. Finally, the chapter discusses further concepts from DSMS and illustrates how they additionally meet and solve the requirements and the challenges.

Chapter 10

Zuo Yuchu, Sun Yat-sen University, China
You Fang, Sun Yat-sen University, China
Wang Jianmin, Sun Yat-sen University, China
Zhou Zhengle, Sun Yat-sen University, China

Sina weibo microblog is an increasingly popular social network service in China. In this work, the authors conducted a study of detecting news in Sina weibo microblog. They found the traditional definition for news can be generalized here. They first expanded the definition of news by conducting user surveys and quantitative analysis. The authors built a news recommendation system by modeling the users, classifying them into four different groups, and applying several heuristic rules, which derived from the generalized definition of news. By applying the new recommendation system, people got newsworthy information, while the funny and interesting tweets, which are popular in Sina weibo microblog, were put in the last ranking list. This study helps us achieve better understanding of heuristic rules about news. Some official organizations can also benefit from the work by supervising the most popular news around civilians.

Section 4
Urban Awareness

Chapter 11

Ali Diab, Al-Baath University, Syria & Ilmenau University of Technology, Germany
Andreas Mitschele-Thiel, Ilmenau University of Technology, Germany

It is well accepted that the physical world itself, including communication networks, humans, and objects, is becoming a type of information system. Thus, to improve the experience of individuals, communities, organizations, and societies within such systems, a thorough comprehension of collective intelligence processes responsible for generating, handling, and controlling data is fundamental. One of the major aspects in this context and also the focus of this chapter is the development of novel methods to model human mobility patterns, which have myriad uses in crucial fields (e.g. mobile communication, urban planning, etc.). The chapter highlights the state of the art and provides a comprehensive investigation of current research efforts in this field. It classifies mobility models into synthetic, trace-based, and community-based models, and also provides insight into each category. That is, well-known approaches are presented, discussed, and qualitatively compared with each other.

Alaa Almagrabi, Latrobe University, Australia & King Abdulaziz University, Saudi Arabia

Seng W. Loke, Latrobe University, Australia

Torab Torabi, Latrobe University, Australia

Responding to a disaster is a process that should take the least time with high-level information. It requires human decisions that could delay the whole process, thus putting more lives at stake. However, recent technological developments improve this process by facilitating decisions within the domain. Discovering the spatial relationship can help to clarify the spatial environment for the domain. In this chapter, the authors give an overview of using spatial modelling and spatial relations for context-aware messaging with emphasis on emergency situations. They utilize various existing spatial relations recognized within the field of spatial computing such as RCC8 and Egenhofer relations. The RCC8 and Egenhofer relations are examined besides a range of spatial relations using English phrases in Mona-ont emergency ontology. The Mona-ont emergency ontology is used to describe emergency scenarios. The Mona-ont emergency ontology is employed by the Mona Emergency System (MES) that generates alert messaging services to actors within a disaster area. The authors demonstrate the validity of the Mona-ont spatial relations in describing a (fictitious) flood situation in the Melbourne CBD area. They also prescribe the structure of such context-aware messages (i.e. their content and target description) for the MES system.

Lin Sun, TELECOM SudParis, France

Chao Chen, TELECOM SudParis, France

Daqing Zhang, TELECOM SudParis, France

The GPS traces collected from a large taxi fleet provide researchers novel opportunities to inspect the urban dynamics in a city and lead to applications that can bring great benefits to the public. In this chapter, based on a real life large-scale taxi GPS dataset, the authors reveal the unique characteristics in the four different trace stages according to the passenger status, study the urban dynamics revealed in each stage, and explain the possible applications. Specifically, from passenger vacant traces, they study the taxi service dynamics, introduce how to use them to help taxis and passengers find each other, and reveal the work shifting dynamics in a city. From passenger occupied traces, they introduce their capabilities in monitoring and predicting urban traffic and estimating travel time. From the pick-up and drop-off events, the authors show the passenger hotspots and human mobility patterns in a city. They also consider taxis as mobile GPS sensors, which probe the urban road infrastructure dynamics.

Chapter 14

Pervasive computing was envisioned by pioneers like Mark Weiser but has yet to become an everyday technology in our society. The recent advances regarding Internet of Things, social computing, and mobile access technologies converge to make pervasive computing truly ubiquitous. The key challenge is to make simple and robust solutions for normal users, which shifts the focus from complex platforms involving machine learning and artificial intelligence to more hands on construction of services that are tailored or personalized for individual users. This chapter discusses Internet of Things together with Social Computing as a basis for components that users in a "digital city" could utilize to make their daily life better, safer, etc. A novel environment for user-created services, such as social apps, is presented as a possible solution for this. The vision is that anyone could make a simple service based on Internet-enabled devices (Internet of Things) and encapsulated digital resources such as Open Data, which also can have social aspects embedded. This chapter also aims to identify trends, challenges, and recommendations in regard of Social Interaction for Digital Cities. This work will help expose future themes with high innovation and business potential based on a timeframe roughly 15 years ahead of now. The purpose is to create a common outlook on the future of Information and Communication Technologies (ICT) based on the extrapolation of current trends and ongoing research efforts.

Section 5
Conclusion

Chapter 15

The "big data" explicitly produced by people through social applications, or implicitly gathered through sensors and transaction records, enables a new generation of mining and analysis tools to understand the trends and dynamics of today's interconnected society. While important steps have been made towards personal, urban, and social awareness, several research challenges still need to be addressed to fully realize the pervasive computing vision. On the one hand, the lack of standard languages and common semantic frameworks strongly limit the possibility to opportunistically acquire available context data, reason with it, and provide proactive services. On the other hand, existing techniques for identifying complex contextual situations are mainly restricted to the recognition of simple actions and activities. Most importantly, due to the unprecedented quantity of digital traces that people leave as they go about their everyday lives, formal privacy methods and trust models must be enforced to avoid the "big data" vision turning into a "big brother" nightmare. In this chapter, the authors discuss the above-mentioned research issues and highlight promising research directions.

Foreword

In the early 1990s, Mark Weiser articulated a dream of ubiquitous computing (i.e., pervasive and invisible computing that is embedded in objects of everyday life and becomes a utility providing access to information and computing services anytime and anywhere). Since then, a large number of ubiquitous and pervasive computing research teams around the world have made substantial progress in changing this dream into reality. Over the past 20 years, this research community has developed models, technologies, and also applications based on these models and technologies. This progress is reflected not only in research publications but also in an increasing number of commercial pervasive computing applications. Pervasive computing applications need to be context-aware – they may need to encompass a variety of computing devices, ranging from small sensors, through phones to workstations, and also heterogeneous network technologies, while providing users with services that adapt to the users' current circumstances and needs.

Many would consider research on pervasive computing as mature because of a proliferation of models and prototypes for augmenting work and everyday user environments with sensing and computing to provide required information and services. There are, however, many facets of pervasive and ubiquitous computing that are still very challenging for the research community. These challenging areas include the three aspects that the editors of this book address: personal awareness, social awareness, and urban awareness. Addressing such challenges will lead to the next generation of pervasive computing applications.

Research on pervasive computing technologies encompasses a variety of research areas, including digital design, distributed computing, mobile computing, computer networks, machine learning, human-computer interactions, social science disciplines, and psychology. Pervasive computing researchers from my generation had a background in two or three of these research areas and sometimes struggled to see the need for considering other areas to achieve comprehensive solutions to the research challenges they were addressing. We now have a new generation of researchers in pervasive computing – they started their professional life by carrying out PhD research in pervasive computing and learned very early the multidisciplinary nature of research in this area. They easily embrace new social media and have a very good understanding of the possible impact of social media on future pervasive computing applications. The editors of this book belong to this new generation of pervasive computing researchers – their whole professional life is related to pervasive computing, including their doctoral dissertations, their research projects, their journal and conference publications, and high quality pervasive computing conferences that they help organize. They are well equipped to develop the next generation of pervasive computing, and this book is a step towards this goal.

Jadwiga Indulska
University of Queensland, Australia

Jadwiga Indulska *is a Professor of Pervasive Computing in the School of Information Technology and Electrical Engineering at the University of Queensland, Brisbane, Australia. Her research interests are in the areas of computer networks, distributed computing, and pervasive computing. Over the last 15 years, her research has addressed many problems in pervasive and autonomic computing, including context information models for context-aware applications, autonomic management of context information, privacy of context information, software engineering of context-aware applications, balancing user control and software autonomy, and autonomic, rapidly deployable mesh networks. She has led research projects on interoperability of distributed applications, mobile computing, pervasive computing, and autonomic networks at the DSTC, an Australian Government funded Collaborative Research Centre on Distributed Systems Technology (1992-2005), and at NICTA (National Centre of Excellence in Information and Communication Technology). She has served on editorial boards of journals on pervasive computing including the Elsevier Journal of Pervasive and Mobile Computing and on numerous conference program committees. She has been a very active member of the PerCom organizing committee (IEEE International Conference on Pervasive Computing and Communications).*

Preface

INTRODUCTION OF THE BOOK

Over the last few years, several research efforts have been made to model, extract, and manage the context data of users, devices, and the surrounding environment in order to enhance the user experience. The recent emergence of social network applications, the prevalence of sensor-equipped mobile devices (e.g., GPS, accelerometers), and the availability of large amounts of geo-referenced data (Twitter messages, Foursquare check-ins, etc.) have enabled the analysis of new context dimensions that involve individual, social, and urban contexts. Data available include not only people's mobility patterns but also emotional status and activities; these data are massively produced and shared in real time by users. Extracting the collective intelligence process that generates those data is a fundamental research issue with important applications, which could improve not only the experience of single users but also the community, organizations, and societies. In order to exploit these massive data sets, novel methods must be devised to model and understand the way in which people interact and behave in the environment.

OBJECTIVE OF THE BOOK

With the development of sensor-enhanced mobile phones, the prevalence of sensing devices in buildings and urban facilities, as well as the growth of social network services, pervasive computing is stepping out of lab environments and into our daily lives. The "big data" obtained from real environments presents unprecedented opportunities to understand human life, organizations, and societies. With this background, the objective of this book is to make a thorough exploration of the emerging research trends of pervasive computing, more specifically defined as personal awareness, social awareness, and urban awareness. We will provide an overview of the theories, state-of-the-art techniques, and practical applications that are related to the three dimensions of context awareness, and remark on how far we are from the new era of context-awareness.

TARGET AUDIENCE

The title covers a new era of context-aware computing, with a focus extension from personal awareness to social and urban awareness. It discusses topics overlapping a number of disciplines and fields in computer science: context-awareness (context gathering, modeling, and management), pervasive and ubiquitous computing, activity recognition, social and urban intelligence, data mining, etc. Therefore, the most typical audience is from the field of context-awareness and pervasive computing research. We believe the proposed title will aid the prospective audience (e.g. university lecturers and professors, students, researchers, and developers of the context-aware applications). With a focus on the current theme of "big data," industry practitioners can also benefit from the latest development in the field of context-aware and pervasive computing and understand how "big data" contribute to the realization of personal, social, and urban awareness.

STRUCTURE

The structure of this edited book is organized as follows. The introduction chapter gives an overview of the emerging research direction towards personal, social and urban awareness. This is followed by a selection of 13 high quality chapters covering the three themes: personal, social, and urban awareness, with topics including context gathering, modeling, middleware design,and applications. Finally, we conclude the book by sharing a view of the research challenges for personal and collective awareness.

Section 1: Introduction

Chapter 1: Towards Personal, Social, and Urban Awareness

In the past decades, numerous research efforts have been made to model and extract the contexts of users in pervasive computing environments. The recent explosion of sensor-equipped mobile phone market and the phenomenal growth of geo-tagged data (Twitter messages, Foursquare check-ins, etc.) have enabled the analysis of new dimensions of contexts that involve the social and urban context. The technology trend towards pervasive sensing and large-scale social and community computing is making "Social and Community Intelligence (SCI)" a new research area that aims at investigating individual/group behavior patterns, community and urban dynamics based on the "digital footprints." It is believed that the SCI technology has the potential to revolutionize the field of context-aware computing. The aim of this chapter is to identify this emerging research area, present the research background, define the general system framework, characterize its unique properties, discuss the open research challenges, and present this emerging research field.

Section 2: Personal Awareness

Chapter 2: Activity Recognition Using Ubiquitous Sensors – An Overview

Human activities are a fundamental aspect to characterize the contextual situation occurring in a pervasive computing environment. The diffusion of low-cost sensing devices has enabled new methods to recognize activities based on streams of sensor data. This chapter reviews the most prominent proposals and illustrates the strong and weak points of the different approaches. Finally, the authors identify open challenges and present their ongoing work.

Chapter 3: Opportunistic Detection Methods for Emotion-Aware Smartphone Applications

The human voice carries rich information about the emotional status of the speaker, which could be exploited to improve the user experience in a series of pervasive computing applications, including human-machine interaction, teleconferencing, and multimedia adaptation. In this chapter, the authors illustrate this intriguing research field and present guidelines to build emotion-aware smartphone applications in an opportunistic way.

Chapter 4: Service Discovery with Personal Awareness in Smart Environments

Complex pervasive computing applications may be obtained by the composition of simpler components, and may need context data acquired on the fly based on the current situation. In this chapter, the authors illustrate how the Semantic Web service paradigm can be used to support these applications by introducing Mercury, a service discovery platform to find appropriate sensors, services, or actuators to perform a certain functionality as required by the user based on the current context and goal.

Chapter 5: Architecture Pattern for Context-Aware Smart Environments

Smart environment is one of the hot topics under the theme of "big data." Context-aware computing is often adopted as a technique to augment the smartness in ordinary environments. There are many attempts over the last decade to develop a system, which supports user activities in these smart environments. Most of these systems focus on aspects of what users need, resulting in the problem-specific design of the systems. In this chapter, the authors analyze a variety of context-aware smart environments described in the literature and show that while each of these systems was designed from scratch, their approaches to context gathering, evaluation, dissemination, and reasoning have some common functionalities. The authors then propose a generalized architecture that outlines the requirements for designing and developing such smart environments.

Chapter 6: Design Aspects and Context Awareness in Pervasive Games

This chapter explores pervasive games, a new type of digital games, which combine game and physical reality, introducing unprecedented research and design challenges for developers. After systematically classifying pervasive games based on their social- and context-aware features, the authors survey the most prominent projects and discuss them with respect to different design aspects. Finally, they highlight current trends, design principles, and future directions for pervasive game development.

Section 3: Social Awareness

Chapter 7: Community Detection and Profiling in Location-Based Social Networks

Due to the proliferation of GPS-enabled smartphones, Location-Based Social Networking (LBSNs) services have been experiencing a remarkable growth over the last few years. Compared with traditional online social networks, a significant feature of LBSNs is the coexistence of both online and offline social interactions, providing a large-scale heterogeneous social network that is able to facilitate lots of academic studies. One possible study is to leverage both online and offline social ties for the recognition and profiling of community structures. In this chapter, the authors attempt to summarize some recent progress in the community detection problem based on LBSNs. In particular, starting with an empirical analysis on the characters of the LBSN data set, the authors present three different community detection approaches, namely, link-based community detection, content-based community detection, and hybrid community detection based on both links and contents. Meanwhile, they also address the community profiling problem, which is very useful in real-world applications.

Chapter 8: Social Cars – Sensing, Gathering, Sharing, and Conveying Social Cues to Road Users

Intelligent Transport Systems (ITS) encompass sensing technologies, wireless communication, and intelligent algorithms, and resemble the infrastructure for ubiquitous computing in the car. This chapter borrows from social media, locative media, mobile technologies, and urban informatics research to explore three classes of ITS applications in which human behavior plays a more pivotal role. Applications for enhancing self-awareness could positively influence driver behavior, both in real-time and over time. Additionally, tools capable of supporting our social awareness while driving could change our attitude towards others and make it easier and safer to share the road. Lastly, a better urban awareness in and outside the car improves our understanding of the road infrastructure as a whole. As a case study, the authors discuss emotion recognition (emotions such as aggressiveness and anger are a major contributing factor to car crashes) and a suitable basis and first step towards further exploring the three levels of awareness, self-, social-, and urban-awareness, in the context of driving on roads.

Chapter 9: Challenges for Personal Data Stream Management in Smart Buildings

Nowadays, sensors and actuators are embedded in smart-homes, allowing the observation of residents and environmental phenomena, in order to interpret the situation and react accordingly. The presence of multiple people in a smart building introduces several challenges in terms of data processing and interpretation. In this chapter, the authors introduce this research problem, and propose "Data Stream Management Systems" (DSMS) as an approach for processing and managing data in a smart building. They present an architecture for DSMS and illustrate how it fulfills the requirements and challenges.

Chapter 10: News Recommendation for China Sina Weibo Micro-Blog Service Based on User Social Behaviors

Sina Weibo has become a popular micro-blogging service in China. In this chapter, the authors conduct a study of detecting news from the data collected from Sina Weibo. They first expand the definition for news by conducting user surveys and quantitative analysis. A news recommendation system is then presented. The authors classify users into four different groups and apply several heuristic rules for recommendation. By applying the recommendation system, people can retrieve popular tweets from Sina Weibo according to interest. This study helps us achieve better understanding of heuristic rules for news recommendation. Business organizations can also benefit from this work to fit user preferences.

Section 4: Urban Awareness

Chapter 11: Human Mobility Patterns

It is well accepted that the physical world itself, including communication networks, humans, and objects, is becoming a type of information system. Thus, to improve the experience of individuals, communities, organizations, and societies within such systems, a thorough comprehension of collective intelligence processes responsible for generating, handling, and controlling data is fundamental. One of the major aspects in this context and also the focus of this chapter is the development of novel methods to model human mobility patterns, which have myriad uses in crucial fields (e.g. mobile communication, urban planning, etc.). The chapter highlights the state of the art and provides a comprehensive investigation of current research efforts in this field. It classifies mobility models into synthetic, trace-based, and community-based models, and also provides insight into each category. That is, well-known approaches are presented, discussed, and qualitatively compared with each other.

Chapter 12: Spatial Relations in Contextual Information for Mobile Emergency Messaging

When mapping from a physical environment to its digital representation, the spatial relations of objects become an important topic. This chapter provides an overview of techniques in the modeling of spatial relations with a focus on messaging in emergency situations. The authors study a number of representative solutions in the field of spatial computing. The Mona-ont emergency ontology is proposed as an alternative to model the spatial relation in disaster scenarios. A prototype system, Mona Emergency System (MES), demonstrates the use of this ontology to disseminate evacuation messages to citizens in the scenario of flooding.

Chapter 13: Understanding Urban Dynamics from Taxi GPS Traces

The huge collections of GPS traces collected from urban taxis implicitly contain rich information about the dynamics of a city. In this chapter, the authors aim to exploit passenger behaviors and urban dynamics from large-scale taxi GPS traces. First, they show how to infer taxi service dynamics, such as taxi-business dynamics and work-shifting dynamics, from passenger-vacant traces. Second, the authors derive traffic dynamics and anomaly passenger delivery dynamics from passenger-occupied traces. Based on the recorded pick-up and drop-off events, they present how to extract the hotspots and community dynamics from taxi traces in urban environments. Finally, the authors propose a new way to detect the road network changes by considering taxis as roaming GPS sensors.

Chapter 14: User-Centric Social Interaction for Digital Cities

Within the last decade, many services and ordinary objects have become "Internet enabled" (from social networking to our TV and refrigerators). As a result of the "Internet of things" trend, many of these services and connected devices have become sources of information, which contributes to the theme of "big data." With the ease of access to open information sources (through well-defined APIs), citizens will have the ability to "program the cities" for their social needs. This chapter studies these topics and shares an insight of how we should approach the problem of giving ordinary people the ability to mash-up apps for the digital cities.

Section 5: Conclusion

Chapter 15: Research Challenges for Personal and Collective Awareness

Important steps have been made towards personal, urban, and social awareness. However, several research challenges still need to be faced to fully realize the pervasive computing vision. The opportunistic acquisition of available context data and the possibility of reasoning with them are strongly limited by the lack of standard languages and common semantic frameworks. The recognition of complex contextual situations is further limited by different technical issues and deficiencies of existing approaches. Moreover, the unprecedented quantity of digital traces left by people calls for novel trust models and formal privacy methods. In this chapter, the authors discuss the above-mentioned research issues and highlight promising research directions.

Bin Guo
Northwestern Polytechnical University, China

Daniele Riboni
University of Milano, Italy

Peizhao Hu
NICTA, Australia

Acknowledgment

The idea for this book grew over two years with the support of many people from the pervasive computing community, especially the ones from our advisory board.

We would like to extend our thanks to all the folks at IGI Global Publishing, especially Kayla Wolfe, whose initial belief in the project made it all possible. Thanks are also due to Monica Speca and Allyson Gard (our Editorial Assistants), whose patience and whip kept us in line and writing throughout the entire process.

A special thanks to Prof. Jadwiga Indulska, for her gentle guidance during the book editing process and providing the foreword of this book.

Bin Guo
Northwestern Polytechnical University, China

Daniele Riboni
University of Milano, Italy

Peizhao Hu
NICTA, Australia

Section 1
Introduction

Chapter 1
Towards Personal, Social, and Urban Awareness

Bin Guo
Northwestern Polytechnical University, China

Zhiwen Yu
Northwestern Polytechnical University, China

Yunji Liang
Northwestern Polytechnical University, China

Daqing Zhang
TELECOM SudParis, France

Zhu Wang
Northwestern Polytechnical University, China

Xingshe Zhou
Northwestern Polytechnical University, China

ABSTRACT

In the past decades, numerous research efforts have been made to model and extract the contexts of users in pervasive computing environments. The recent explosion of sensor-equipped mobile phone market and the phenomenal growth of geo-tagged data (Twitter messages, Foursquare check-ins, etc.) have enabled the analysis of new dimensions of contexts that involve the social and urban context. The technology trend towards pervasive sensing and large-scale social and community computing is making "Social and Community Intelligence (SCI)" a new research area that aims at investigating individual/ group behavior patterns, community and urban dynamics based on the "digital footprints." It is believed that the SCI technology has the potential to revolutionize the field of context-aware computing. The aim of this chapter is to identify this emerging research area, present the research background, define the general system framework, characterize its unique properties, discuss the open research challenges, and present this emerging research field.

INTRODUCTION

With the technological advances in sensing, computing, storage, communication and Internet, a lot of research areas have emerged such as sensor network, pervasive computing, Internet of Things,

social network, to name just a few. From those emerging areas, there is a clear trend of augmenting the physical devices/objects with sensing, computing and communication capabilities, connecting them together to form a network, and making use of the collective effects of networked things. As a

DOI: 10.4018/978-1-4666-4695-7.ch001

result of the recent explosion of sensor-equipped mobile phone market, the phenomenal growth of Internet and social network users, and the large deployment of sensor network in public facilities, private buildings and outdoor environments, the digital traces left by people while interacting with cyber-physical spaces are accumulating at an unprecedented breadth, depth and scale, and we call all those traces left by people the "digital footprints".

Leveraging the capacity to collect and analyze the "digital footprints" at community scale, a new research field called "social and community intelligence (SCI)" (Zhang, Guo, & Yu, 2011) is emerging that aims at revealing the patterns of individual, group and societal behaviors. The scale and heterogeneity of the multimodal, mixed data sources present us an opportunity to compile the digital footprints into a comprehensive picture of individual's daily life facets, radically change the way we build computational models of human behaviors. Numerous innovative services will be enabled, including human health, public safety, urban planning, environment monitoring, and so on. The development of SCI will greatly expand the scale and depth of context-aware computing, from merely personal awareness to the understanding of social interactions (e.g., social relations, community structures) and urban dynamics (e.g., traffic jams, hotspots in cities).

Different from other closely related research areas such as sensor-based activity recognition and mobile social networking, the unique characteristics of this new SCI research area can be embodied in the following aspects:

- **Infrastructure:** The scale of the SCI system goes beyond single smart space and reaches the level of a community. An infrastructure is required to integrate large-scale and heterogeneous devices, data processing tools, and provide systematic support for rapid application development, deployment, and evaluation.

- **Data and Contexts:** The data sources are multi-modal and heterogeneous. The social and community intelligence can be inferred from three main data sources: *mobile/wearable sensors*, *the infrastructure-bound sensor networks*, and *the social data from social networks and Internet applications*. While each data source independently shows one facet of the user's daily life, the combination of the three data sources can reveal unforeseen human-centric contexts, i.e., the awareness of personal activities, social interactions, as well as urban dynamics.

- **Technology:** The core technologies for SCI are data mining, machine learning and AI. The major technical challenge is how to mine higher-level social and community contexts from large-scale raw sensor data (e.g., from talking to meeting; from driving slowly to traffic jam), faced with problems such as scalability of algorithms, heterogeneous data processing, correlation analysis among geo-social properties, and so on.

In this chapter, we intend to explore the characteristics of SCI, its application areas, potential research challenges, and our ongoing efforts to this emerging field. The rest of this chapter is organized as follows. Section 2 presents the research background of SCI. The general framework and characters of SCI systems will be presented in Section 3. Potential applications and research issues of SCI will be elaborated in Section 4 and 5, respectively. In Section 6, we present our ongoing efforts regarding to SCI. Finally, we conclude this chapter by proposing some promising research directions.

RESEARCH BACKGROUND

Research on SCI is still at its early stage. However, as a result of the convergence of several research disciplines such as ubiquitous computing, social networking, urban computing, and data mining, SCI has its deep roots in the following three recent fast-growing research fields.

Activity Recognition

With the prevalence of wearable and mobile sensors (GPS devices, sensor-equipped phones, accelerometers), activity recognition has become a hot research area in ubiquitous computing. The purpose of activity recognition is to collect and analyze various sensing data in real life and predict human daily activities. Most of the early work on sensor-based activity recognition was motivated by applications in elderly care (Pollack, 2005), and healthcare (Tentori & Favela, 2008). Some of them have also been applied to habitat monitoring with sensor networks (Szewczyk, Osterweil, Polastre, Hamilton, Mainwaring & Estrin, 2004), and human interaction tracking in offices (Connolly, Burns & Bui, 2008).

Sensor-based activity recognition can be roughly divided into two categories based on where the sensors are deployed: *human body* or *object*. Wearable sensors that attached to human bodies can generate various signals when they perform different activities, which are rich sources to extract human physical movements, such as *walking*, *running*, *scrubbing*, and *exercising* (Tapia, Intille & Larson, 2004). Object-based activity recognition is rooted from the observations that many activities can be characterised by the associated physical objects. Activities that are rich in interactions with the environment, e.g., *grooming*, *cooking*, *toileting*, *washing hands*, and so forth, can be recognized through this approach (Philipose, Fishkin, Perkowitz, Patterson, Fox, Kautz & Hahnel, 2004). The key idea behind sensor-based activity recognition is to build or train a mathematical model of activity based on a series of raw sensor readings. By feeding new sensor readings into the learned model, human activities can be predicted.

Recently, with the prevalence of sensor-enhanced mobile phones, a few researchers initiated the research in individual or group activity mining with mobile phone sensing data. For instance, The MetroSense project (Campbell, Eisenman, Lane, Miluzzo & Peterson, 2006) from Dartmouth Colleague explores sensor-embedded mobile phones to support personal and public sensing. The Reality Mining project (Nathan, Alex & David, 2009) from MIT investigates the social behaviors of individual users and organizations by analyzing the large-scale mobile phone data. Based on the communication records of 100,000 mobile phone users, researchers from Northeastern University discovered that human trajectory has a high degree of spatial-temporal regularity (Gonzalez, Hidalgo & Barabasi, 2008).

Social Networking

Humans are social by nature. People constantly participate in social activities to interact with others and form various communities. Social activities such as making new friends, forming an interest group to exchange ideas, sharing knowledge with others are constantly taking place in human society. The analysis of the social community interactions has been studied by social scientists and physicists for couple of decades (Freeman, 2004). An excellent introduction to the concepts and the mathematical tools for social networks analysis can be referred to (Wasserman & Faust, 1994). In the early stage, efforts on social network analysis are mostly based on the relational data obtained by survey.

During the last two decades, we have observed an explosive growth of social applications such as chatting, shopping, experience sharing, etc. These applications, along with traditional e-mail, instant messaging, have changed the way we communicate with each other and form social communities. Corresponding to this trend, a large amount of work on social network analysis and knowledge discovery springs up, including Email communication networks (McCallum, Wang & Corrada-Emmanuel, 2007), scientific collaboration and co-authorship network (Barabasi, Jeong, Neda, Ravasz, Schubert & Vicsek, 2002), etc.

More recently, as the internet stepped into the era of the Web 2.0, which advocates that users interact with each other as contributors to the websites' content, researchers turned their attention to the online social utilities, such as Facebook, Twitter, and Blogs. For example, ArterMiner (Tang, Jin & Zhang, 2008) seeks to harvest personal profile information from a user's homepage. Amit Sheth's research group has done much work on summarization of event information like space, time and theme from social web resources for building public services (Sheth, 2010). Twitter has been reported to support real-time mining of natural disasters such as earthquakes (Sakaki, Okazaki & Matsuo, 2010) and the moods of citizens (Bollen, Pepe & Mao, 2009).

Urban Computing

Understanding human movement in urban environments has direct implications for the design of public transport systems (e.g., more precise bus scheduling, improved services for public transport users), traffic forecasting (e.g., hotspot prediction), and route recommendation (e.g., for transit-oriented urban development). A number of studies have extracted citywide human mobility patterns using large-scale data from smart vehicles, mobile phones, and smart cards used in public transportation systems. The Real Time Rome project of MIT uses aggregated data from buses and taxies to better understand urban dynamics in real-time (Calabrese & Ratti, 2006). Liu, Biderman and Ratti (2009) claimed that the spatio-temporal patterns of taxi trips are essential for a more refined urban taxi system, which enables the control of taxi supply according to travel demands in space and time. Morency, Trépanier and Agard (2007) investigated the spatio-temporal dynamics (e.g., examining the effects

of weather on transit demand) of public transit networks, leveraging the 10-month bus boarding records collected from a city in Canada. The learned human mobility patterns are also useful for urban planning. For example, Nicholson and Noble (2008) have studied how to leverage the learned human movement dynamics to improve the distribution of cell infrastructure (e.g., to have a better load-balance among cell towers) in wireless communication networks.

THE CHARACTERS AND FRAMEWORK OF SCI APPLICATIONS

In this section, we first characterize the key features of SCI, and then present a generic framework for developing SCI applications.

Characterizing SCI

Aggregated Power of Heterogeneous Data Sources

SCI aims to extract individual/group behaviors, and community dynamics from three important data sources: Internet and Web services, static sensing infrastructure, mobile devices and wearable sensors. The three sources have distinct attributes and strengths:

- **Internet and Web Service:** Is a major source to extract static or slowly changing information, such as user profile, organization structure, user relationship in a community.
- **Static Infrastructure:** Enables the detection of indoor and urban user activities, group activities, and space context in sensor-enriched environments.
- **Mobile Devices and Wearable Sensors:** Are always user-centric, thus great at sensing individual activities, interpersonal in-

teractions, significant user locations, and public environment contexts.

Due to the diverse features, aggregation and fusion of data from those three different sources provides unique opportunities to social and community intelligence extraction. This can be elaborated from at least two aspects. (*i*) *We can leverage the knowledge obtained from one domain to enhance the applications in the other domain.* For example, social relationship from the Web can be used to assist social activity recognition in the physical world. For a detected social gathering, if it is in the evening and the participants are all friends, it is more likely to be a party; if it occurs in a weekday morning and the participants are managers and subordinates, it is more likely to be a meeting. There are many more that can be explored. (*ii*) *We can merge the data from different sources to better characterize a situation.* Data from different sources often characterizes the specific facet of a situation, thus the fusion of several distinct data sources can often draw a better picture of the situation. For example, by integrating the mined theme from user posts and the revealed location information from GPS-equipped mobile phones, Twitter has been exploited to support near real-time report of earthquakes in Japan (Sakaki, Okazaki & Matsuo, 2010).

Interplay between Online and Offline Behaviors

Human is involving in heterogeneous communities in the hyper world, and we often traverse and switch our roles among them in daily life. Therefore, human behaviors in different communities (online or offline) are not isolated, but interweaving. Different social networks have distinct features in terms of geographical coverage, infrastructure support, function time, and so on. This also leads to distinct human interaction patterns (e.g., comment/like in online communities, co-location in offline communities) and implicit

social knowledge (e.g., friendship/trustworthy in online communities, social popularity/movement patterns in offline communities) that can be extracted from them. Study of the interaction between online and offline social networks (e.g., how does online social network data mirror physical events), as well as merging their complementary features and fully combining their merits (e.g., connecting the two forms of social networks to enhance data dissemination/sharing), however, has become an important yet challenging research direction of SCI.

So far, researches on online and offline communities follow two separate research lines. The interaction/collaboration of the different communities has yet little been explored. There have been studies about social network analysis across heterogeneous networks. For example, Tang, Lou and Kleinberg (2012) developed a framework for classifying the type of social relationships by learning across different networks (e.g., email network, mobile communication network). Researchers from CMU study the relationship between the users' mobility patterns and structural properties of the online social network, to identify the implicit social link between physical interaction and online connection (Cranshaw, Toch, Hong, Kittur, & Sadeh, 2010). Lee, Wakamiya and Sumiya (2011) proposed a geo-social event detection method by mining unusually crowed places (e.g., reporting social events such as festivals or protests) from geo-tagged Twitter posts. However, numerous open issues remain unexplored, such as the aggregated/collaborative effects of distinct social networks, data dissemination over heterogeneous social networks, and so on.

A Generic Framework

A general architecture for a SCI system is shown in Figure 1, which consists of five layers: pervasive sensing layer, data anonymization layer, hybrid learning and inference layer, knowledge management layer, and application layer.

Figure 1. The generic framework of SCI

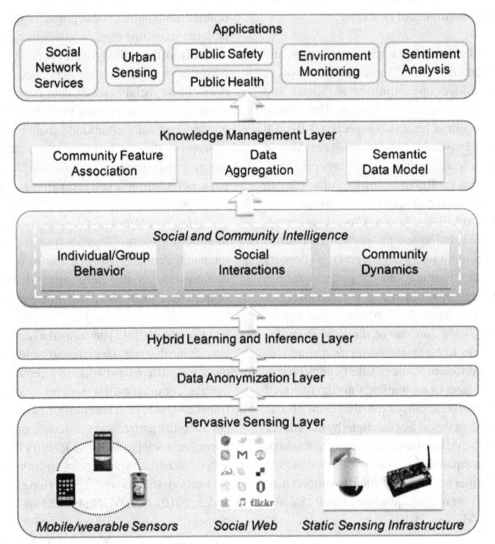

Layer 1: The large-scale pervasive sensing layer involves the three major information sources: *mobile and wearable devices, static sensing infrastructure, social web and Internet services.*

Layer 2: As privacy is a major concern for private and organizational data sharing individually, our proposed framework incorporates an anonymization layer before the data releasing and processing. All the data released must be sufficiently anonymized, and different anonymization algorithms can be applied for privacy protection.

Layer 3: The hybrid learning and inference layer applies diverse machine learning and data mining techniques to converting the low-level, single-modality sensing data into high-level social and community intelligence.

Level 4: The knowledge management layer consists of three components. The *community feature association* component analyzes the association among spatial and social features of heterogeneous communities. The aggregated power of heterogeneous data sources is handled by the *data aggregation* component. The semantic data model uses semantic Web and ontology techniques to represent the complex association among the obtained facts/features and provide standardized model for knowledge sharing.

Layer 5: The application layer includes a variety of potential services that can be enabled by the availability of SCI. An application might be installed directly on the mobile device, or run on remote servers (such as a Web application) but communicate with the mobile device via wireless gateways.

APPLICATION AREAS

SCI applications are mainly driven by the needs to (1) develop better social software to facilitate interaction and communication among groups of people; (2) predict the real-time change of real world to benefit human life. Here we can foresee at least the following four major SCI application areas.

Mobile Social Networking

Forging social connections with others is at the core of what makes us human. Mobile social networking (MSN) aims to improve social connectivity in physical communities (i.e., helping people stay in touch anytime, anywhere; recommending new connections) by leveraging information about people, places, and interpersonal interactions. Social Serendipity is one of the earliest MSN studies, which signals matching interests between nearby people who do not know each other to cue informal, face-to-face interactions (Nathan & Pentland, 2005).

When people connect, they influence and persuade. In MSN, peer influence becomes more important than ever, which offers a wealth of new business opportunities. Bottazzi, Montanari & Toninelli (2007) have proposed a place-dependent viral marketing solution that supports product advertisement distribution (e.g., forwarding promotional messages like coupons) among customers and their encounters in stores, following the word-of-mouth model. It can be imagined that when all these MSN applications are at their disposal, businesses will bring the tools of direct-response marketing to physical places.

Healthcare and Well-being

SCI brings new opportunities for public health monitoring and personal well-being improvement.

1. **Public Health:** SCI can facilitate the anticipation and tracking of disease outbreaks across large-scale populations. For example, epidemics of seasonal influenza are a major public health concern, causing tens of thousands of deaths worldwide each year. Its impact can be reduced by early detection of the disease activity. The Google researchers have shown that by mining indirect signals from millions of geographically localized health-related search queries, one can estimate the level of influenza-like illnesses in regions of the United States with a reporting lag of just 1 day (Neil, Derek, Christophe, James, Philip & Donald, 2006). It is faster than the estimates provided by government agencies, which publish regional data weekly based on virology and clinical statistics.

2. **Human Well-Being:** With community sensing, we can log personal physical activity trajectory, track the food intake, sense the mental status in real-time, and record the social activities we attend each day, which can be used to improve human well-being management. For example, the Neat-o-Games system detects human movements (e.g., walking, running) by using a wearable accelerometer, and uses the computed

quantity of motion to control the avatar of the user in a virtual community race game (Fujiki, Kazakos, Puri, Buddharaju, Pavlidis & Levine, 2008). Nutrition Monitor, a mobile application, can track user food consumption and trends over time, and warn the user against unhealthy food choices (Dorman, Yahyanejad, Nahapetian, Suh, Sarrafzadeh, McCarthy & Kaiser, 2010).

Environment Monitoring

The nomadic, participatory, and in-situ experience nature of community sensing provides new opportunities for environment monitoring and natural resource protection.

1. **Nature Preservation:** With the help of human volunteers, the Great Backyard Bird Count project reports the cumulative counts of birdwatchers from across American in its website (http://www.birdsource.org/gbbc/). The MIT Owl project (http://web.mit.edu/newsoffice/2008/tracking-0822.html) is more interesting, which aims at leveraging the network of smart phones equipped with GPS, compasses, and directional microphones, to lessen human efforts in assessing owl populations.
2. **Pollution Measurement:** With the aid of portable pollution sensing devices, there have also been several projects targeting environment pollution measurement. The BikeNet application measures several metrics to give a holistic picture of the cyclist experience, including the CO_2 level along the path. It facilitates public sensing and sharing by letting multiple users merge their individual data, for example, to create pollution and noise maps of their city (Eisenman, Miluzzo, Lane, Peterson, Ahn & Campbell, 2007). In the PEIR project, GPS-enabled phones are used to detect user transportation mode (e.g., driving, walking), which is then used to assess an individual's environmental impact and exposure, like carbon footprints and exposure to air pollution (Mun, Reddy, Shilton, Yau, Burke, Estrin, Hansen, Howard, West & Boda, 2009).
3. **Disaster Reporting:** The real-time user contributed data is helpful for emergent or dangerous event detection and reporting. For example, Twitter has been reported to support rapid response to the social or natural disasters such as terrorism attack in Bombay (Sheth, 2009) and earthquakes in Japan (Sakaki, Okazaki & Matsuo, 2010). Comparing to traditional media, community sensing is more vigilant.

Public Safety

Public safety involves the prevention of and protection from events that could endanger the safety of the general public, these events can be crimes or disasters. The combined power of surveillance cameras widely deployed and networked in a city can help solve a series of public security challenges, such as crime prevention. For instance, Memphis in the US uses the CRUSH system, developed by IBM, to monitor the hotspots around the city and predict crimes (http://www.memphispolice.org/). CRUSH works using a series of crime patterns learned from historical crimes and arrest data, in combination with other factors such as weather forecasts, economic indicators, and information on events, such as paydays and concerts.

RESEARCH CHALLENGES

To facilitate the development of SCI applications, there are still several open issues to be explored, such as activity recognition, heterogeneous data processing, understanding of human mobility, community detection, and evaluation methods.

Activity Recognition

Understanding of human activities has become an important research area of SCI. However, it is a non-trivial problem and still faces numerous issues.

1. **Large-Scale Modeling:** Human behavior modeling at a large-scale under real-world conditions is still a challenging problem. For example, existing classification models do not always perform well on a diverse population (e.g., people have different characteristics such as age, gender, life style). Training personalized models that incorporate different contexts and user characteristics are effective in addressing this challenge. However, this approach burdens the users with collecting and manually labeling their own training data which is not scalable. To address this problem, Lane, Xu, Lu, Hu, Choudhury, Campbell and Zhao (2011) have proposed CoCo, a new approach to personalizing classification models by leveraging social networks. It lowers the amount of training data required from every user by sharing training data and classification models within social networks.

2. **Energy Consumption:** For applications such as healthcare, the recognition of human activities is a continuous process. However, long-term sensing of human activities usually leads to a high cost on energy-consuming. For example, the battery lifetime of Samsung i909 is about 30 hours when all applications and sensors are turned off, but this value declines to 5.5 hours, when a single 3-D accelerometer is invoked (Liang, Zhou, Yu, Guo & Yang, 2012). Therefore, energy consumption is a practical and critical issue for the success of long-term activity recognition.

3. **Understanding of Group Activities:** Many human activities are conducted in groups. Understanding of group activities is thus also important. There have been numerous studies about personal activity recognition, however, quite few studies address the extraction of semantic information from group activities. Our previous work studied the recommendation of groups using contexts and social graph mining in real-world settings (Guo, He, Yu, Zhang & Zhou, 2012). Garg, Favre, Salamin, Dilek & Vinciarelli (2008) proposed an approach to recognize participant roles in face-to-face meetings. However, both group organization and social interaction in group activities are complex, and there are still many issues unexplored.

Heterogeneous Data Processing

The data producers in the SCI system can be very different in terms of modality (e.g., mobile phones, fixed cameras, Web services), their connectivity to the Internet (e.g., constant, intermittent, or affected by a firewall), their sharing willingness or privacy sensitivity, and resource capabilities for processing data locally. The information consumers are also heterogeneous in terms of running environments (applications that run locally or at community-level remotely), and data needs (some might need only high-level context information while others might need raw sensor data). The heterogeneity leads to several challenges on data management:

1. **Multi-Modal:** Different type of sensors have different attributes and capabilities, they might have different accuracy in sensing the physical and virtual world. Integrating information from diverse data sources adds difficulty to SCI mining. Raw data from different sensor sources need to be transformed

to the same metrics and represented by a shared vocabulary/ontology to facilitate the learning and inference process (Guo, Zhang & Michita, 2011).

2. **Inconsistency:** The same sensor may sense the same event under different conditions (for example, sensing one's voice in a quiet office or noisy restaurant). However, for the same event, user context often leads to different inference results (good or poor). Due to environmental differences, a group of co-located sensors running the same classification algorithm and sensing the same event in time and space could compute different inference results, and thus leads to the issue of system inconsistency. Miluzzo, Cornelius, Ramaswamy, Choudhury, Liu and Campbell (2010) have proposed a collaborative approach to dealing with this inconsistency problem and more solutions are needed.

Human Mobility Patterns

With the increasing availability of digital footprints, the study of human mobility patterns has become a research direction of SCI. There are several sources to obtain human geo-trajectories, such as GPS devices, location-based services (e.g., Foursquare, Twitter), or GPS-enhanced mobile phones. Based on the unprecedented sensing ability of large-scale human trajectories, they try to find hot spots for service recommendation (Zheng & Xie, 2011), investigate the temporal-spatial patterns of human mobility (Giannotti, Nanni, Pinelli & Pedreschi, 2007), and mine the social ties based on the geo-trajectories (Cranshaw, Toch, Hong, Kittur, & Sadeh, 2010).

One common character of the above studies is that they are mainly conducted at the macroscopic view. To understand human mobility at a fine-grained level, it is important to understand what are the driving forces that lead to the regularity and variability of human movements? For

example, it is important to investigate the impact factors of human mobility, such as user age, time, occupation, income level, etc. These impact factors, which link people and geo-trajectories, can be leveraged in many application areas such as urban planning, location prediction, targeted advertising, etc. By analyzing the Nokia mobile phone dataset (http://research.nokia.com/page/12000), we have investigated the correlation between several factors (time, job and age) and human mobility (Liang, Zhou, Guo & Yu, 2012). It can be a starting point for the study of human mobility at the microscopic level. The links between individuals have been proved to be another important factor that impacts human mobility (Cho, Myers & Leskovec, 2011).

Community Detection

The community structure of social networks is important in SCI. Community detection is the process of partitioning the network into a number of groups, by which we will find many interactions within groups while few interactions among them. Even though different community detection approaches have been proposed (Michele, Fosca & Dino, 2011; Xie, Stephen & Boleslaw, 2013), there are still several challenges in this area.

1. **Time Complexity and Precision:** Community detection is a time-consuming process, especially when dealing with large-scale networks which allow multiple community memberships. One widely adopted overlapping community detection approach is *link-centric clustering* (Ahn, Bagrow & Lehmann, 2010), which chooses to cluster links rather than nodes. Generally speaking, the amount of links is usually much more than the amount of nodes in a given network, making the link-centric clustering approach even more time consuming. To solve this problem, many heuristic community detection algorithms have been proposed to reduce the time complexity (Wakita & Tsurumi,

2007; Lu, Wen & Cao, 2013), leading to the decrease of precision. Therefore, the design of efficient and accurate community detection algorithms becomes the first challenge.

2. **Community Detection in Dynamic Networks:** Network topologies and node attributes might be time-varying, which lead to dynamic networks where communities may evolve over time (Nguyen, Dinh, Tokala & Thai, 2011; Gong, Zhang, Ma & Jiao, 2012). Detecting and tracking communities in a dynamic network where changes arrive as a stream is another challenging issue in real-world applications. Instead of mining communities on each snapshot independently, algorithms that incrementally update communities (Ning, Xu, Chi, Gong & Huang, 2007) are very useful when applied to real-time monitoring of huge data streams, such as the Internet traffic or online social interactions. Therefore, another challenge of community detection is the design of incremental data mining algorithms.

Evaluation Standards

Another challenge of enabling SCI is the missing of standards for evaluating different techniques and approaches, which mainly lies in the following aspects:

1. **Lacking of Standard Datasets:** Scientifically solid comparisons of different learning methods are only possible if we can guarantee equal test conditions. To this end, many machine learning-related communities rely on standard benchmark datasets. Unfortunately, social and community intelligence extraction, so far, has not relied on such datasets.

2. **Reproducibility of Results:** Most context-awareness work published so far is inherently difficult to replicate, and the reproducibility of context-recognition research has long been a difficult issue. There have been attempts to define relevant evaluation standards in pervasive computing (Scholtz & Consolvo, 2004; Connelly, Siek, Mulder, Neely, Stevenson & Kray, 2008), but the scientific community still hasn't reached a consensus.

3. **Lacking of Ground Truth:** In some cases, we are not aware of the corresponding ground truth of the revealed SCI, making the evaluation difficult. For example, the actual community structure of a large-scale dataset is usually unknown. Then, how can we estimate the quality of the detected communities? Even though researchers have proposed many indirect ways to evaluate the detected communities, there was no widely acknowledged evaluation mechanism yet.

TOWARDS SCI: OUR EFFORTS

Awareness of personal activities, social interactions, and urban dynamics brings new potentials in many application areas. We make a summary of our ongoing work in the following and provide insights on how we address the issues discussed in last section.

Energy-Conservation in Activity Recognition

With the prevalence of sensor-equipped mobile phones, awareness of personal activities via mobile phones has become a hot research area. However, it is still a challenge due to the constraints of resources on mobile phones, such as battery limitation, computational load, and so on. To address these issues, we have proposed a scalable user awareness algorithm based on the Hybrid Data Processing (HDP) strategy (Liang, Zhou, Yu, Guo & Yang, 2012; Guo, Zhang, Yu, Liang, Wang & Zhou, 2012). In HDP, to reduce communication cost, raw sensor readings are processed by lightweight feature extractors (time features, frequency features) running on the phone, the extracted features are then transmitted to backend servers for user activity recognition and routing mining. The HDP solution significantly reduces the communication cost between clients and backend servers, and increases the resilience of the entire network.

To demonstrate the effectiveness of the HDP strategy, we developed the Activity Recognition application on the Samsung i909 Android platform. Figure 2 (left) illustrates the data collection and training process of the application, while the classification process is shown in Figure 2 (right). The battery lifetime is used as a metric to measure the resilience of the system. We measured the battery lifetime when 1) only feature extraction is executed on the phone and 2) both feature extraction and the classifier (based on the decision tree algorithm) are executed on the phone. We find that when the classifier is mounted from the phone to the backend server, the mobile phone battery lifetime increases from 6.3 hours to around 10

hours (the sampling frequency was set to 10 Hz), which indicates that the classifier consumes much higher power than feature extraction. This result also indicates that the HDP strategy can improve the energy-conservation performance of mobile phone sensing systems.

Community-Aware Computing

As a promising research direction, we have studied the enhancement of social and community interaction using SCI through two projects: *Social Contact Manager* and *Hybrid Social Networking*.

1. **Social Contact Manager:** Integration of data from heterogeneous networks. The ability to use the power of a network of social contacts is important to get things done. However, as the number of contacts increases, people often find it difficult to maintain their contact network using human memory alone. People are frequently beset

Figure 2. Screenshots of the human activity recognition: training (left) and classification (right)

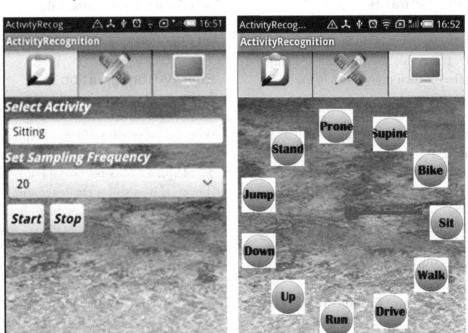

with questions like *"Who is that person? I think I met him in Tokyo last year."* Existing contact tools make up for the unreliability of human memory by storing contact information in digital format; however, manually inputting contact data can burden the users. To address this issue, we develop SCM (Social Contact Manager), an intelligent social contact management system (Guo, Zhang & Yang, 2011). It supports the auto-collection of rich contact data (e.g., profile, face-to-face meeting contexts) from online and offline (ad hoc) networks, leveraging the aggregated power of pervasive sensing and Web intelligence techniques.

Our solution is inspired by the general contact acquaintance process. In social occasions, our connection with a new contact usually starts from exchanging *business cards*. After obtaining basic information from *business cards*, people gather more information about the contact from the Web. An interesting phenomenon is revealed, in which

the "business card" plays a key role, triggering and leading the contact data gathering process. SCM explores techniques to automate this process, as illustrated in Figure 3. We employ a mobile card-scanner to extract basic information from the collected business cards (forming an opportunistic network). The scanned basic information is then used to obtain other contact information from the Web (i.e., the online network) using an information extraction method based on a hybrid of heuristic rules and Conditional Random Field (CRF) (Guo, Zhang & Yang, 2011). The collected information can be leveraged to manage their contacts better, especially for efficient contact retrieval in name-slipping situations.

2. **Hybrid Social Networking:** Interlinking heterogeneous social networks to facilitate data dissemination. People now connect to, interact with and transit over heterogeneous social communities (e.g., online/offline, interest/professional groups) in the cyber-physical space. In the past few years, sig-

Figure 3. Social contact manager: data integration from heterogeneous networks

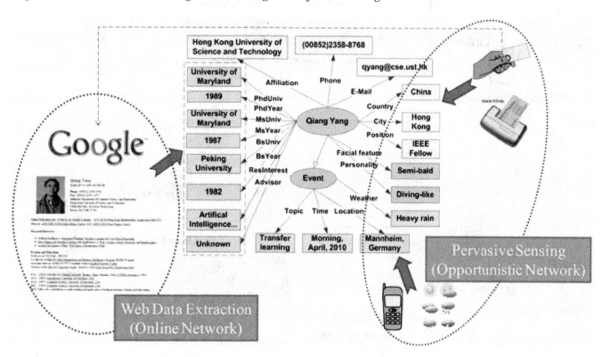

nificant research efforts have been made on facilitating information sharing in online and offline communities. However, they follow separate research lines, and the interlinking of the two forms of communities has little been explored. We have thus proposed the *hybrid social networking* (HSN) infrastructure (Guo, Zhang, Yu & Zhou, 2012), which is inspired by the multi-community involvement and cross-community traversing nature of modern people. For example, at one moment, *Bob* is staying at a place with Internet connection and he can communicate with his online friends (in the *online community*); later, he may travel by train with merely ad hoc connection with nearby passengers (forming an *opportunistic community*). Here we use HSN to indicate the smooth switch and collaboration between online and opportunistic communities.

One of the key features enabled by HSN is the popularity-based online broker selection protocol. Different from existing protocols, the online broker selection approach we proposed allows users to choose brokers *online* from his social connections, while not requiring direct contacts with others in the real world. Users advertise their predicted popularity in the online community, and a publisher can choose the ones with highest-popularity among them. Online broker selection also decreases the time cost on task allocation: the dissemination task can be allocated to the selected nodes with no delay if they are online, while offline brokers can be informed of the allocated task once they are within an environment with Internet connection (hotspots, wired network, etc.) Experiment results indicate that the interlinking of distinct social networks can enhance data dissemination among people.

Figure 4. The hybrid social networking infrastructure

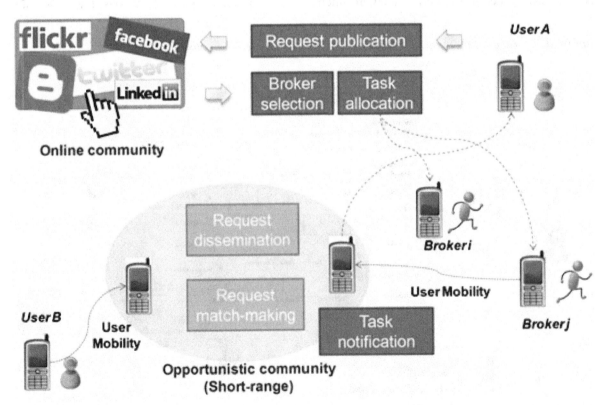

The Smart Campus

The university campus is a typical socially-active environment. To assist and enhance social interaction among students and staffs, we have designed and implemented a Smart Campus prototype (Yu, Liang, Xu, Yang & Guo, 2011) under a collaboration project with Microsoft Research Aisa. The smart campus aims to benefit social interactions based on participatory sensing and mobile social networking. We have implemented two typical applications: *Where2Study* and *I-Sensing*.

The main purpose of *Where2Study* is to find a suitable place to study by using Wi-Fi positioning technology. It not only presents the navigation map of a building to help students find classrooms (Figure 5a), but also shows the status of all classrooms (full or free seats available), as shown in Figure 5b. Furthermore, *Where2Study* is also a mobile social networking application, which supports students to query the status and locate their friends in the university campus.

People are often interested in the information about a place while they are not there. For instance, Bob is in the library and wonders whether the tennis court is occupied. *I-Sensing* is a campus-scale information sharing system based on participatory sensing, which allows users to share the status of public infrastructures in a university campus, such as play yards, libraries, coffee shops, and so on. Once a user posts a space-query to *I-Sensing*, the task manager of *I-Sensing* will deliver the sensing task to a selected number of "observers" who are locating near that space (based on their GPS readings). Local observers can answer the query by either authoring text messages or simply taking pictures (as shown in Figure 5c). To encourage users to participant in more social interactions, social competition is also incorporated (see Figure 5d). In the future, we will analyze the interaction data from *I-Sensing* and estimate inter-personal relations (e.g., based on their common point of interests, such as tennis court) and recommend friends to university users. To summarize, by leveraging the mobile and static sensing devices in the campus, the Smart Campus will provide university users with the awareness of their living environment and their social links.

Figure 5. Screenshots of Where2Study and ISensing

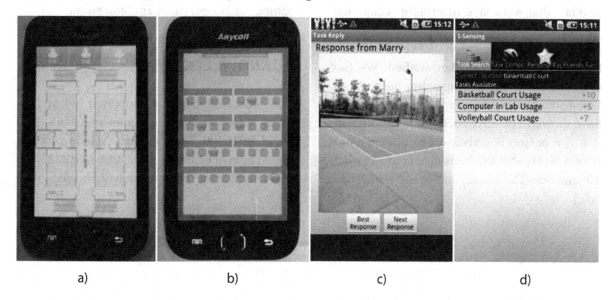

a)   b)   c)   d)

Mobile Phone-based Social Behavior Mining

In physiology, social behavior is behavior directed towards society, or taking place between members of the same species. Understanding of human social behaviors has long been a fundamental scientific problem, where data preparation is of most important. In traditional social science, data is collected majorly by self-reporting and interviewing with subjects, thus the scale of the data obtained is often limited. The popularity of smart phones, however, opens a new window to study large-scale social behaviors.

In our previous work (Li, Wang, Guo & Yu, 2012), we have explored human social behaviors by analyzing the large-scale data (including data from GPS, call-logs, Bluetooth, and Wi-Fi records) collected from off-the-shelf smart phones. The work is also based on the Nokia mobile phone dataset. Since social behaviors present in different forms, in this work, we try to understand human social behaviors from three aspects: *online interaction patterns, face-to-face interaction patterns*, and *mobility patterns*. For example, we find that people have more outdoor activities at night than daytime, and more online interactions (with phone calls) on holidays than weekdays. In terms of occupation, we find that workers are often more active than students. The correlation between different behavior patterns is further studied. We find that human activities during online interactions, face-to-face interactions and mobility patterns have showed a positive correlation. This means that if a person is active in one dimension, it is very likely that he/she is also active in other dimensions. The results and observations help us understand human social behaviors via a novel way: computation and real-world data (mobile phone data) mining.

CONCLUSION

Social and Community Intelligence (SCI) represents a new interdisciplinary research and application field, presenting opportunities to various application areas, such as mobile social networking, healthcare, environment monitoring, and so on. We have identified the new features of SCI: the aggregated effects of heterogeneous data sources, and the interplay of online and offline activities. As we have discussed, the prevalence and development of SCI still face numerous challenges, such as activity recognition, heterogeneous data management, evaluation standards, and so on, which are expected to nurture a series of new research opportunities for academic and industrial. We have also presented our efforts to this promising research area, as well as our insights on addressing the challenges faced by SCI, such as energy-conservation in activity recognition, computing over heterogeneous communities, deployment and usage of SCI applications in a campus-scale environment, and so on.

ACKNOWLEDGMENT

This work was partially supported by the National Basic Research Program of China (No. 2012CB316400), the National Natural Science Foundation of China (No. 61103063, 61222209), the Natural Science Foundation of Shaanxi Province (No. 2012JQ8028), the Program for New Century Excellent Talents in University (No. NCET-12-0466), the Basic Research Foundation of Northwestern Polytechnical University (No. JC20110267).

REFERENCES

Ahn, Y. Y., Bagrow, J. P., & Lehmann, S. (2010). Link communities reveal multi-scale complexity in networks. *Nature, 466*(7307), 761–764. doi:10.1038/nature09182 PMID:20562860.

Barabasi, A. L., Jeong, H., Neda, Z., Ravasz, E., Schubert, A., & Vicsek, T. (2002). Evolution of the social network of scientific collaborations. *Statistical Mechanics and its Applications, 311*(3–4), 590–614. doi: 10.1016/S0378-4371(02)00736-7

Bollen, J., Pepe, A., & Mao, H. (2009). *Modeling public mood and emotion: Twitter sentiment and socio-economic phenomena*. Paper presented at the meeting of WWW 2009 Conference. Madrid, Spain.

Bottazzi, D., Montanari, R., & Toninelli, A. (2007). Context-aware middleware for anytime, anywhere social networks. *IEEE Intelligent Systems, 22*(5), 23–32. doi:10.1109/MIS.2007.4338491.

Calabrese, F., & Ratti, C. (2006). Real time Rome. *Networks and Communications Studies, 20*(3-4), 247–258.

Campbell, A. T., Eisenman, S. B., Lane, N. D., Miluzzo, E., & Peterson, R. A. (2006). *People-centric urban sensing*. Paper presented at the 2nd Annual International Workshop on Wireless Internet. Boston, MA.

Connelly, K., Siek, K. A., Mulder, I., Neely, S., Stevenson, G., & Kray, C. (2008). Evaluating pervasive and ubiquitous systems. *IEEE Pervasive Computing/IEEE Computer Society [and] IEEE Communications Society, 7*(3), 85–88. doi:10.1109/MPRV.2008.47.

Connolly, C. I., Burns, J. B., & Bui, H. H. (2008). *Recovering social networks from massive track datasets*. Paper presented at the Meeting of the IEEE Workshop on Applications of Computer Vision. Copper Mountain, CO.

Cranshaw, J., Toch, E., Hong, J., Kittur, A., & Sadeh, N. (2010). *Bridging the gap between physical location and online social networks*. Paper presented at the Meeting of ACM Conference on Ubiquitous Computing. Copenhagen, Denmark.

Dorman, K., Yahyanejad, M., Nahapetian, A., Suh, M., Sarrafzadeh, M., McCarthy, W., & Kaiser, W. (2010). Nutrition monitor: A food purchase and consumption monitoring mobile system. *Mobile Computing, Application, and Services, 35*. doi:10.1007/978-3-642-12607-9_1.

Eisenman, S. B., Miluzzo, E., Lane, N. D., Peterson, R. A., Ahn, G.-S., & Campbell, A. T. (2007). *The bikenet mobile sensing system for cyclist experience mapping*. Paper presented at the Meeting of ACM Conference on Embedded Networked Sensor Systems. Sydney, Australia.

Freeman, L. C. (2004). *The development of social network analysis: A study in the sociology of science*. Empirical Press.

Fujiki, Y., Kazakos, K., Puri, C., Buddharaju, P., Pavlidis, I., & Levine, J. (2008). NEAT-o-games: Blending physical activity and fun in the daily routine. *ACM Computers in Entertainment, 6*(2). doi:10.1145/1371216.1371224.

Garg, N. P., Favre, S., Salamin, H., Dilek, H. T., & Vinciarelli, A. (2008). *Role recognition for meeting participants: An approach based on lexical information and social network analysis*. Paper presented at the Meeting of ACM International Conference on Multimedia. Vancouver, Canada.

Giannotti, F., Nanni, M., Pinelli, F., & Pedreschi, D. (2007). *Trajectory pattern mining*. Paper presented at the Meeting of ACM SIGKDD International Conference on Knowledge Discovery and Data Mining. San Jose, CA.

Gong, M., Zhang, L., Ma, J., & Jiao, L. (2012). Community detection in dynamic social networks based on multiobjective immune algorithm. *Journal of Computer Science and Technology, 27*(3), 455–467. doi:10.1007/s11390-012-1235-y.

Gonzalez, M. C., Hidalgo, C. A., & Barabasi, A. L. (2008). Understanding individual human mobility patterns. *Nature, 453*(5), 779–782. doi:10.1038/nature06958 PMID:18528393.

Guo, B., He, H., Yu, Z., Zhang, D., & Zhou, X. (2012). *GroupMe: Supporting group formation with mobile sensing and social graph mining*. Paper presented at the Meeting of International Conference on Mobile and Ubiquitous Systems: Computing, Networking and Services (MobiQuitous'12). Beijing, China.

Guo, B., Zhang, D., & Michita, I. (2011). Toward a cooperative programming framework for context-aware applications. *Journal of Personal and Ubiquitous Computing, 15*(3), 221–233. doi:10.1007/s00779-010-0329-1.

Guo, B., Zhang, D., & Yang, D. (2011). *Read more from business cards: Toward a smart social contact management system*. Paper presented at the Meeting of IEEE/WIC/ACM International Conference on Web Intelligence (WI-11). Lyon, France.

Guo, B., Zhang, D., Yu, Z., Liang, Y., Wang, Z., & Zhou, X. (2012). *From the internet of things to embedded intelligence*. World Wide Web Journal. doi:10.1007/s11280-012-0188-y.

Guo, B., Zhang, D., Yu, Z., & Zhou, X. (2012). *Hybrid SN: Interlinking opportunistic and online communities to augment information dissemination*. Paper presented at the Meeting of IEEE International Conference on Ubiquitous Intelligence and Computing. Fukuoka, Japan.

Lane, N. D., Xu, Y., Lu, H., Hu, S., Choudhury, T., Campbell, A. T., & Zhao, F. (2011). Enabling large-scale human activity inference on smartphones using community similarity networks (CSN). Paper presented in the Meeting of Ubiquitous Computing. Beijing, China.

Lee, R., Wakamiya, S., & Sumiya, K. (2011). Discovery of unusual regional social activities using geo-tagged microblogs. *World Wide Web (Bussum), 14*(4), 321–349. doi:10.1007/s11280-011-0120-x.

Li, M., Wang, H., Guo, B., & Yu, Z. (2012). *Extraction of human social behavior from mobile phone sensing*. Paper presented in the meeting of International Conference on Active Media Technology (AMT-12). Macau.

Liang, Y., Zhou, X., Guo, B., & Yu, Z. (2012). *Understanding the regularity and variability of human mobility from geo-trajectory*. Paper presented at the Meeting of the 2012 IEEE/WIC/ACM International Conference on Web Intelligence (WI-12). Macau.

Liang, Y., Zhou, X., Yu, Z., Guo, B., & Yang, Y. (2012). *Energy efficient activity recognition based on low resolution accelerometer in smart phones*. Paper presented at the Meeting of GPC 2012. Hong Kong.

Liu, L., Biderman, A., & Ratti, C. (2009). *Urban mobility landscape: Real time monitoring of urban mobility patterns*. Paper presented at the 11th International Conference on Computers in Urban Planning and Urban Management. Hong Kong.

Lu, Z., Wen, Y., & Cao, G. (2013). *Community detection in weighted networks: Algorithms and applications*. Paper presented at the Meeting of PerCom'13. New York, NY.

McCallum, A., Wang, X., & Corrada-Emmanuel, A. (2007). Topic and role discovery in social networks with experiments on Enron and academic email. *Journal of Artificial Intelligence Research, 30*(1), 249–272.

Michele, C., Fosca, G., & Dino, P. (2011). A classification for community discovery methods in complex networks. *Journal of Statistical Analysis and Data Mining, 4*(5), 512–546. doi:10.1002/sam.10133.

Miluzzo, E., Cornelius, C. T., Ramaswamy, A., Choudhury, T., Liu, Z., & Campbell, A. T. (2010). *Darwin phones: The evolution of sensing and inference on mobile phones.* Paper presented at the Meeting of MobiSys '10. San Francisco, CA.

Morency, C., Trépanier, M., & Agard, B. (2007). Measuring transit use variability with smartcard data. *Transport Policy, 14*(3), 193-203. doi: 10.1.1.156.2090

Mun, M., Reddy, S., Shilton, K., Yau, N., Burke, J., & Estrin, D. … Boda, P. (2009). *PEIR: The personal environmental impact report as a platform for participatory sensing systems research.* Paper presented at the Meeting of MobiSys. Krakow, Poland.

Nathan, E., & Alex, P. (2005). Social serendipity: mobilizing social software. *IEEE Pervasive Computing/IEEE Computer Society [and] IEEE Communications Society, 4*(2), 28–34. doi:10.1109/MPRV.2005.37.

Nathan, E., Alex, P., & David, L. (2009). Inferring social network structure using mobile phone data. *Proceedings of the National Academy of Sciences of the United States of America, 106*(36), 15274–15278. doi:10.1073/pnas.0900282106 PMID:19706491.

Neil, M. F., Derek, A. T. C., Christophe, F., James, C. C., Philip, C. C., & Donald, S. B. (2006). Strategies for mitigating an influenza pandemic. *Nature, 442*(7101), 448–452. doi:10.1038/nature04795 PMID:16642006.

Nguyen, N. P., Dinh, T. N., Tokala, S., & Thai, M. T. (2011). *Overlapping communities in dynamic networks: Their detection and mobile applications.* Paper presented at the Meeting of Mobile Computing and Networking. Las Vegas, NV.

Nicholson, J., & Noble, B. D. (2008). *Bread crumbs: Forecasting mobile connectivity.* Paper presented at the Meeting of Mobile Computing and Networking. San Francisco, CA.

Ning, H., Xu, W., Chi, Y., Gong, Y., & Huang, T. (2007). *Incremental spectral clustering with application to monitoring of evolving blog communities.* Paper presented in the Meeting of SIAM International Conference on Data Mining. Minneapolis, MN.

Philipose, M., Fishkin, K. P., Perkowitz, M., Patterson, D. J., Fox, D., Kautz, H., & Hahnel, D. (2004). Inferring activities from interactions with objects. *IEEE Pervasive Computing/IEEE Computer Society [and] IEEE Communications Society, 3*(4), 50–57. doi:10.1109/MPRV.2004.7.

Pollack, M. E. (2005). Intelligent technology for an aging population: The use of AI to assist elders with cognitive impairment. *AI Magazine, 26*(2), 9–24.

Sakaki, T., Okazaki, M., & Matsuo, Y. (2010). *Earthquake shakes Twitter users: Real-time event detection by social sensors.* Paper presented at the Meeting of WWW 2010 Conference. Raleigh, NC.

Scholtz, J., & Consolvo, S. (2004). Toward a framework for evaluating ubiquitous computing applications. *IEEE Pervasive Computing/IEEE Computer Society [and] IEEE Communications Society, 3*(2), 82–88. doi:10.1109/MPRV.2004.1316826.

Sheth, A. (2009). Citizen sensing, social signals, and enriching human experience. *IEEE Internet Computing, 13*(4), 87–92. doi:10.1109/MIC.2009.77.

Sheth, A. (2010). Computing for human experience – Semantics-empowered sensors, services, and social computing on the ubiquitous web. *IEEE Internet Computing, 14*(1), 88–97. doi:10.1109/MIC.2010.4.

Szewczyk, R., Osterweil, E., Polastre, J., Hamilton, M., Mainwaring, A., & Estrin, D. (2004). Habitat monitoring with sensor networks. *Communications of the ACM, 47*(6), 34–40. doi:10.1145/990680.990704.

Tang, J., Jin, R. M., & Zhang, J. (2008). *A topic modeling approach and its integration into the random walk framework for academic search.* Paper presented at the Meeting of 2008 IEEE International Conference on Data Mining. Pisa, Italy.

Tang, J., Lou, T., & Kleinberg, J. (2012). *Inferring social ties across heterogeneous networks.* Paper presented at the Meeting of Web Search and Data Mining. Seattle, WA.

Tapia, E. M., Intille, S. S., & Larson, K. (2004). Activity recognition in the home using simple and ubiquitous sensors. *Pervasive Computing, 3001,* 158–175. doi:10.1007/978-3-540-24646-6_10.

Tentori, M., & Favela, J. (2008). Activity-aware computing for healthcare. *IEEE Pervasive Computing/IEEE Computer Society [and] IEEE Communications Society, 7*(2), 51–57. doi:10.1109/MPRV.2008.24.

Wakita, K., & Tsurumi, T. (2007). Finding community structure in mega-scale social networks. Paper presented in the meeting of WWW'07. Alberta, Canada.

Wasserman, S., & Faust, K. (1994). *Social network analysis: Methods and applications.* Cambridge, UK: Cambridge University Press. doi:10.1017/CBO9780511815478.

Xie, J., Stephen, K., & Boleslaw, K. S. (2013). Overlapping community detection in networks: The state of the art and comparative study. *ACM Computing Surveys, 45*(4). doi:10.1145/2501654.2501657.

Yu, Z., Liang, Y., Xu, B., Yang, Y., & Guo, B. (2011). *Towards a smart campus with mobile social networking.* Paper presented at the Meeting of IEEE International Conference on Internet of Things. Dalian, China.

Yu, Z., & Xie, X. (2011). Learning travel recommendations from user-generated GPS traces. *ACM Transactions on Intelligent Systems and Technology, 2*(1). doi: doi:10.1145/1889681.1889683.

Zhang, D., Guo, B., & Yu, Z. (2011). The emergence of social and community intelligence. *IEEE Computer, 44*(7), 21–28. doi:10.1109/MC.2011.65.

Section 2
Personal Awareness

Chapter 2
Activity Recognition Using Ubiquitous Sensors:
An Overview

Yunji Liang
Northwestern Polytechnical University, China

Bin Guo
Northwestern Polytechnical University, China

Xingshe Zhou
Northwestern Polytechnical University, China

Zhiwen Yu
Northwestern Polytechnical University, China

ABSTRACT

With the unprecedented sensing capabilities and the emergence of Internet of things, studies on activity recognition have been hot issues for different application areas, such as pervasive healthcare, industry and commerce, and recommendation systems. Much effort has been devoted to activity recognition using different sensors. Based on the differences of ubiquitous sensors, the authors classify the existing work into approximating sensing, wearable sensing, and video/audio sensing. Generally, methodologies for activity recognition are divided into logical reasoning and probabilistic reasoning. They illustrate the generalized framework and outline the advantages and disadvantages for each algorithm. Despite the research on activity recognition, activity recognition still faces many challenges in many aspects including nonintrusive data collection, scalable algorithms, energy consumption, and semantic extraction from social interaction. Towards those challenging research issues, the authors present their contributions to the field of activity recognition.

1. CONTEXT AWARENESS AND ACTIVITY RECOGNITION

The vision proposed by Mark Wiser is unfolding with the significant breakthroughs in sensing and communication. Especially, with the explosion of sensor-equipped mobile phones, broader utiliza-tion of the Global Positioning System (GPS), the emergence of lots of ubiquitous sensors offers an opportunity to seamlessly monitor contexts based on lots of digital traces that people leave while interacting with web applications, static infrastructure, and mobile and wearable devices (Zhang, Guo & Yu, 2011; Guo et al., 2012). Meanwhile,

DOI: 10.4018/978-1-4666-4695-7.ch002

the popularity of Location Based Services (LBS) facilitates the collection of large-scale digital interaction records, which provides the opportunity for the nonintrusive and transparent data collection. The unprecedented accumulation of sensing data makes it possible for the construction of context-aware applications. Context awareness refers to the idea that computers can both sense, and react based on their environment.

Human activity, one kind of the most important contexts, not only describes the current states of objects, but also indicates user intents. Activity could be applied into the field of healthcare to provide proactive services according to ongoing activities, to trigger reminders and recommendations; activity control has been employed in the industry and commerce, like industry manufacturing and commercial games. Meanwhile, the social attribute of activity has been explored. The social attribute may facilitate the communication efficiency and information sharing. The multi-facet nature of human activity makes the activity recognition a hot issue in the field of pervasive computing.

Even though there is lots of work about the activity recognition (Chen & Hoey, 2012), many applications pose new challenges for existing researches. In this chapter, we summarize the existing work in this field from many aspects including sensing devices, recognition algorithms, and applications; on the other hand, we analyze challenges faced with the introduction of ubiquitous sensors. Meanwhile, our undergoing work is presented to demonstrate the feasibility of the proposed solution.

The rest of this chapter is organized as follows. We will summarize the work of activity recognition based on the differences of ubiquitous sensors in Section 2. Section 3 presents methodologies involved in the activity recognition, including logical reasoning, fuzzy reasoning, probabilistic reasoning and transfer learning. We not only present the generalized framework for activity recognition, but outline the advantages and

disadvantages for each algorithm. In Section 4, the application areas of activity recognition are elaborated, including healthcare for the elderly or the disabilities, industry and commerce etc. Even though there are lots of progresses in the field of activity recognition, some challenging research issues are presented in Section 5 followed by our efforts for the activity recognition in Section 6. At last, we conclude this chapter and point out the future work in Section 7.

2. CLASSIFICATION OF ACTIVITY RECOGNITION BASED ON UBIQUITOUS SENSORS

There is lots of work in the field of activity recognition. They may differ from each other in terms of activity types, sensor types, or algorithms. To benefit the summarization of existing work, in this section, we first provide the method about how to classify the work in the field of activity recognition. Then we focus on the classification of activity recognition based on sensor types.

2.1. Classification of Activity Recognition

The researches on the activity recognition could be classified according to different metrics, such as size of users, sensors types, and relationships among target activities. Based on the size of user, the research on activity recognition could be classified into single-user and multi-user. For the single user activity recognition, it focuses on the statuses for the single object. On the contrary, the multi-user activity recognition simultaneously detects multi-activities for more than one object. Compared with the single user activity recognition, the multi-user activity recognition is more interesting and challenging. The smart meeting room (Koike, Nagashima, Nakanishi & Sato, 2004; Yu, Yu, Aoyama, Ozeki & Nakamura, 2010; Ahmed, Sharmin & Ahmed, 2005; Sumi &

Mase, 2001) is an example of multi-user activity recognition. Charif and Mckenna (2006) tried to track and annotate the activities of participants based on the trajectory of head using the particle filters. Based on the trajectory of head in the video clip, multi-activities for multi users could be recognized simultaneously.

In addition, according to relationships among activities, it also could be classified into sequential, interleaved and concurrent activities. The differences of three kinds of activities are illustrated in Figure 1. For the sequential activities, only one activity could be performed at each time slot. And another one will not begin until the former one was completed or finished. As shown in Figure 1a, the activity of washing hands consists of three steps: to open tap, washing hand and to close tap. The three steps are absolutely not overlapped.

Different from the sequential activities, multiple activities could be performed at the same time slot for concurrent activities. An example of concurrent activities has been illustrated in Figure 1b. When we are brushing tooth, we may listen to some music. Similarly, when we are preparing for the breakfast, we may also listen to music. Certain activities are interleaved. For example, while cooking, if there is call coming from a friend, people pause cooking for a while and after answering the phone, they will continue to cook (see Figure 1c).

Due to the differences of sequential, concurrent and interleaved activities, some solutions have been proposed to address the issues for the different activities. For the sequential activities, Hoey, Bertoldi, Poupart and Mihailidis (2010) designed a prototype system to assist persons with demen-

Figure 1. Sequence diagrams for different types of activities: (a) presents the sequential activities; (b) presents the concurrent activities; (c) illustrate the interleaved activities

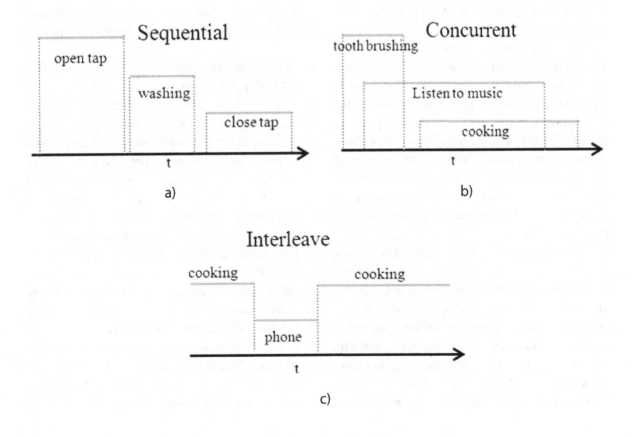

tia during hand washing. Furthermore, a prompting system, named COACH (Mihailidis, Boger, Craig & Hoey, 2008) was implemented to help older adults with cognitive disabilities such as Alzheimer's disease by reminding of the proper sequence of hand washing that need to be completed. With the interleaved activities, Gu elaborated how to recognize the interleaved activities (Gu et al., 2011).

In this chapter, we mainly focus on the activity recognition based on ubiquitous sensors. As amounts of different sensors such as accelerometers, camera have been utilized for the monitoring of user activity, the activity recognition based on the sensors could be detailed into three types: proximity sensing, wearable sensing and the video/audio sensing.

2.2. Activity Recognition Based on Ubiquitous Sensors

Generally, there are a large amount of ubiquitous sensors utilized for activity recognition including accelerometers, cameras, gyroscopes etc. Due to the features of sensors, lots of prototype systems were developed. Based on the sensor types, all those prototype systems could be classified into 3 types: proximity sensing, wearable sensing and video/audio sensing. In this section, we will present the workflow for each kind of systems.

2.2.1 Proximity Sensing

With the broader utilization of radio frequency identification (RFID) technique in the many applications such as asset tracking, supply chain management, it is possible to identify an object or person within proximity space. We name the detection of nearby entities as proximity sensing. The key idea of the activity recognition based on proximity sensing is that user activities usually lead to changes of object states, which not only imply the users' goals, but also indicate activity patterns. Generally, there are two solutions for the activity

recognition based on the proximity sensing. First, by analyzing the approximate objects, it is reasonable to infer the user activities due to the relationship among user activities and the nearby objects. Another one is that activity leads to changes of environment such as the signal strength of radio frequency. Based on the changes of environment, we may infer the potential activities.

Most of existing work (Krahnstoever, Rittscher, Tu, Chean & Tomlinson, 2005; Inomata, Naya, Kuwahara, Hattori & Kogure, 2009; Patterson, Fox, Kautz & Philipose, 2005; Buettner, Prasad, Philipose & Wetherall, 2009; Bouchard, Bouchard & Bouzouane, 2011; Yang, Lee & Choi, 2011; Chen, Nugent, Cook & Yu, 2011) follows the first solution. Patterson, Fox, Kautz and Philipose (2005) designed an RFID glove (shown in Figure 2), by which to recognize the daily activities using the probabilistic graphical model. Buettner, Prasad, Philipose and Wetherall (2009) designed the UHF RFID tags to detect user activities based on the traces of object usage. The activity recognition based on this methodology highly depends on the pre-deployment of RFID tags. To achieve the seamless detection of user activity, the RFID tags should be bided with every entity.

Different from the first solution, the second solution depends on the detection of patterns of environment. The ActiviTune, which relies on changes in an environment impact the propagation of radio waves, is proposed. The changes of the radio waves implicitly contain different information with respect to distinct environmental situations. By extracting suitable features from the raw dataset and recognizing activities, environmental awareness can be realized. It is demonstrated that the ActiviTune can distinguish among 'the empty room', 'the opened door' and 'a walking person' with an average accuracy of over 90%.

The proximity sensing facilitates the activity recognition for indoor situations. With lots of sensors embedded in the smart space, it provides the opportunity to detect fine-grained user activities. However, the deficits of proximity sensing

Figure 2. RFID tag types and the RFID gloves (Patterson, Fox, Kautz & Philipose, 2005)

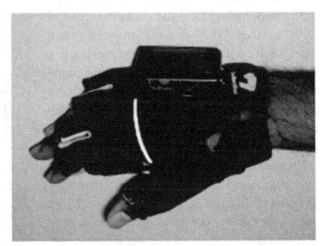

are obvious. First, it is difficult to be utilized for the seamless monitoring in the open space due to its pre-deployment and human mobility. Second, the poor scalability is another challenge. Usually, a probabilistic model, which describes the probabilistic relationship among user activities and objects, is built based on the machine learning algorithms. However, it is difficult to make sure the pre-learnt model could cover all situations; on the other hand, the cold-start problem exists for a new activity.

2.2.2. Wearable Sensing

With advantages of the wireless communication and the IT manufacture, more sensors are portable and support wireless communication, which contribute to the emergence of the wearable computing. Generally, a body area network consisted of lots of wearable sensors is constructed to monitor the user activities (Mizuno, et al., 2007; Cho, Nam, Choi & Cho, 2008; Lukowicz, et al., 2004; Ward, Lukowicz, Gerhard & Starner, 2006; Inooka, et al., 2006, Choudhury, et al., 2008). The generalized framework for activity recognition based on the wearable sensing is presented in Figure 3. Lots of sensors such as accelerometers, microphone, and pressure sensor etc. are deployed on human body,

and collaboratively collect the raw data. All those sampled data is delivered to the computing center such as computer or workstation via the wireless communication. Finally, the offline data model is utilized to distinguish user activities.

For the activity recognition based on the wearable technology, accelerometers play important roles for the data collection. Numerous studies have been conducted about the activity recognition based on accelerometers. A survey of the work towards the activity recognition based on accelerometers is presented in Table 1.

First, the activity recognition based on multi-accelerometer sensors is conducted (Gyorbíró, Fábián & Hományi, 2009; Kern, Schiele & Schmidt, 2003; Bao & Intille, 2004; Mannini & Sabatini, 2010; Krishnam, Juillard & Colbry, 2009; Ruch, Rumo & Mader, 2011). Gyorbíró, Fábián and Hományi (2009) implemented an activity recognition system by using a wristwatch-like device, named MotionBand, which contains an accelerometer, a magnetometer and a gyroscope. Three MontionBand devices are attached to the wrist, hip and ankle to collect the sensory data of user activities. Then all those sensory data is sent to a mobile phone by Bluetooth and is classified using the feed-forward back-propagation neural networks. Although lots of sensors are

Figure 3. Generalized framework for activity recognition based on wearable sensors

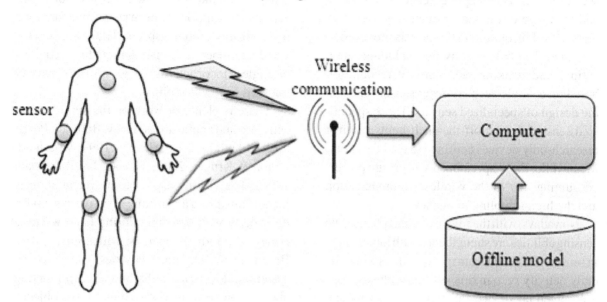

Table 1. Survey of activity recognition based on accelerometer sensors

Work	Range	Num	Hz	Activities	Algorithms
Gyorbíró et al. (2009)	±6g	3	50	Resting, Typing, Gesticulating, Walking, Running, Cycling	Artificial Neural Network (ANN)
Kern et al. (2003)	±2g	12	92	Sitting, Standing, Walking, Writing, Typing	Bayesian Classification
Bao et al. (2004)	±10g	5	76.25	Stretching, Scrubbing, Reading, Vacuum, Drinking, etc.	Decision Tree (DT)
Khan et al. (2010)	±6g	1	20	Lying, Sitting, Walking, Running, Standing, Lie-Stand, etc.	Linear Discriminant Analysis (LDA) and ANN
He et al. (2008)	±3g	1	100	Jumping, Still, Running, Walking	Support Vector Machine (SVM)
Ravi et al. (2005)	±4g	1	50	Standing, Walking, Running, up stairs, down stairs, sit down, Vacuum, Brush teeth	DT, K-Nearest Neighbors (KNN), SVM, Naïve Bayes
Mathie et al. (2004)	±10g	1	45	Fall, Walking, Sitting, Standing, Lying	DT
Krassing et al. (2010)	±1.5g	1	512	Walking, Running, Sitting down, Standing up, Standing, Sitting, Bending forward, Lying	DT, ANN, Hybrid Classifier
Kwapisz et al. (2010)	±2g	1	20	Walking, Jogging, Ascending stairs, Descending stairs, Sitting	DT, ANN, Logistic Regression

employed to benefit the recognition, sensors fixed on human body are barriers for users. On one hand, users are confined to the laboratory environment due to constraints of wearable sensors, which reduces the practicability of the prototype in our daily life. On the other hand, users are distracted from their tasks. This is contradicted with the vision of pervasive computing for less attention taken from users.

Second, single accelerometer sensor is utilized to benefit the activity recognition (Khan, Lee, Lee & Kim, 2010; He, et al., 2008; Ravi, Dander, Mysore & Littman, 2005; Lee, et al., 2010). Khan, Lee, Lee and Kim (2010) carried out experiments to monitor physical activities based on a tri-axial accelerometer. The sampling frequency was 20Hz and the range of the sensor outputs was ±6g. A hierarchical recognition scheme was proposed to recognize 15 kinds of activities including lying, sitting, and walking etc. Activity recognition based on a single accelerometer sensor relies on the design of specialized sensors. Those specialized sensors are not off-the-shelf items and just research-only devices confined to the laboratory. Meanwhile, those specialized sensors are power-consuming due to the wireless communication and the high sampling frequency.

Nowadays, with the advent of smart phones, the sensing abilities are strengthened with lots of built-in sensors. Different from most previous work, the daily activity recognition on smart phones uses a commercial device rather than experimental devices, and employs a single device conveniently kept in the user's pocket rather than multiple devices distributed across the body (Kwapisz, Weiss & Moore, 2010; Mathie, Celler, Lovell & Coster, 2004; Krassing, Tantinger, Hofmann, Wittenberg & Struck, 2010). Kwapisz, Weiss and Moore (2010) employed the accelerometer in the smart phone to recognize 6 kinds of activities including walking, jogging, ascending etc. However, the power consumption of recognition scheme is not considered in the previous work. For the resource-limited devices, the power-consumption and the computation workload pose challenges to the activity recognition on smart phones. The existing recognition algorithms are time-consuming and heavyweight for the mobile phone.

However, the wearable system is intrusive as it poses a barrier for daily life and distracts user attentions from their activities. Furthermore, the power consumption of wireless communication is vitally important, which poses a challenge on the long-term monitoring of daily activities.

2.2.3. Video/Audio Sensing

Video sensing facilitates the context-aware systems to monitor user behaviors and environment changes with camera. The research on vision-based activity recognition has been performed for a long period from different aspects. They have investigated a number of scenarios including activities of single actor or activities of group users, activity tracking from video clips.

There is plenty of work on the single object activities and applications (Hoey, Bertoldi, Poupart & Mihailidis, 2010; Gavrila, 1999; Moeslund, Hilton & Kruger, 2006; Yilmaz, Javed & Shah, 2006). The vision-based activity recognition is incorporated into a real-time assistive system for the elderly with dementia during hand washing (Hoey, Bertoldi, Poupart & Mihailidis, 2010). Based on the ongoing activities, the proposed system could provide verbal and visual prompting about to be performed activities for the objects. Meanwhile the group-level activities have been researched (Charif & Mckenna, 2006; Khan & Shah, 2005; Chang, Krahnstoever & Ge, 2011; Lin, Sun, Poovendran & Zhang, 2010; Antonakaki, Kosmopoulos & Perantonis, 2009). Charif and Mckenna (2006) proposed a vision system to tracking the activities of participants in a meeting based on a head model which models the head trajectories. Based on the proposed solution, user activities including entering, exiting, going to the whiteboard, getting up and sitting down could be recognized. Khan and Shah (2005) detected complex activities characterized by the collective participation of several individuals such as people parades, airplane flight formation with rigidity of formation. Different from the activity recognition for group with fixed size, the group event detection with a varying number of group members is still a challenge. Chang, Krahnstoever and Ge (2011) elaborated the recognition of group activities in unconstraint surveillance environments with the agglomerative hierarchical clustering. Lin, Sun, Poovendran and Zhang (2010) proposed to use a group representative to handle the recognition with a varying number of group members.

While computer vision corresponds closest to the way humans perceive their environment, it has many problems of its own. This includes sensitivity to light conditions, expensive costs for equipment and background clutter as well as large computational complexity. More importantly, privacy is a controversial issue of vision-based activity recognition. Therefore, sound analysis is utilized into many application areas such as behavior recognition, location detection, and auditory scene recognition etc.

With regard to the behavior recognition based on sound sensors, Istrate, Castelli, Vacher, Besacier and Serignat (2006) proposed the utilization of sound to deal with medical tele-monitoring of the home. Microphones placed in every room of the apartment are used to spot events which will cause an alarm (breaking of glass, falling of objects or screams) out of everyday sounds like ringing phones, footsteps, moving chairs or slamming doors. Lukowicz et al. (2004) integrated the microphone into their wearable system to recognize wood workshop activities such as hammer, saw, and drilling etc. The combination of microphone and acceleration benefits the improvement of recognition rate. Yatani and Truong (2012) proposed BodyScope to detect fine-grained activities such as eating, drinking, and coughing by acoustic sensor placed nearby the user's throat area. The low-power issue of activity recognition

based audio sensing is concerned in the work of Mathias (2006).

In summary, there are lots of sensors and sensing technology utilized into the field of activity recognition. To recognize user activity continuously, we need a nonintrusive, lightweight, and real-time recognition scheme. The popularity of smart phones makes it possible. Smart phones are equipped with lots of sensors including the accelerometer, digital compass, microphone, camera, etc. However, activity recognition on smart phones is still a challenge due to constraints of available resources, such as battery capacity, computational load, etc.

3. METHODOLOGIES FOR ACTIVITY RECOGNITION

With regard to the issue of activity recognition, lots of methodologies are proposed to address challenges from many different application backgrounds. It is very difficult to summarize all those algorithms. In this section, we briefly elaborate the optional algorithms for activity recognition.

As shown in Figure 4. The overview of the activity recognition algorithms could be roughly divided into two classes: Logical reasoning and

Figure 4. Overview of the recognition algorithms

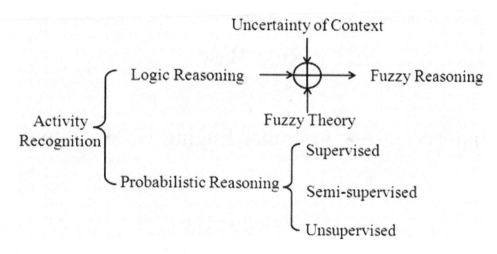

probabilistic reasoning. The logical reasoning is very common and we utilize it to learn about the unknown information. Logical reasoning is the process of using a rational, systematic series of steps based on sound mathematical procedures and given statements to arrive at a conclusion. With the development of Fuzzy theory, the fuzzy reasoning is established to deal with the uncertainty of data. For probabilistic reasoning, it is classified into three types: supervised algorithms, unsupervised algorithms and semi-supervised learning.

3.1. Logical Reasoning

Logical Reasoning depends on the logical operators such as the ∧ (AND) and ∨ (OR). In logical reasoning, an if-then statement (also known as a conditional statement) is a statement formed when one thing implies another and can be written p→q. The simple example for the logical reasoning is present in the Figure 5. See more details for the logical reasoning in work of Badder and Nutt (2003).

As shown in Figure 6, the general framework for the logical reasoning consists of 5 components. Knowledge base describes the properties for entities and also establishes the relationships among entities. Rule base defines all the causal relationships, based on which new knowledge could be

Figure 5. Example for logical reasoning

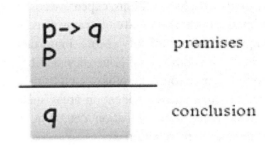

extracted. The inference engine is the executor, which performs the logical reasoning based on the inputs, knowledge base and the rule base.

Based on the logical reasoning, we built a smart pillbox based on the RFID to improve the medication adherence for the elderly (Tang, et al., 2011; Liang, Zhou, Yu, Wang & Guo, 2012). For the smart pillbox, each medicine bottle is tagged with a RFID tag, and a RFID reader is deployed at the bottom of pillbox. When a bottle is taken out of the pillbox, the RFID reader can detect the state changes of medicine (e.g., taken out of the pillbox or put back). To detect whether the user is taking medicine, we employ user contexts such as user location and approximating entities to infer user activities.

We design the device ontology, user ontology and medicine ontology for representing the contexts of user, device and medicine respectively.

Figure 6. The general framework for logical reasoning

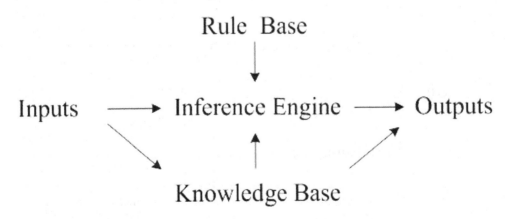

All those knowledge are stored in the knowledge based. The reasoning for medicine intake behavior is shown in Figure 7 (Liang, Zhou, Yu, Wang & Guo, 2012). We use the Web Ontology Language (OWL) for ontological model and representation. OWL is based on the well-developed knowledge representation formalism for Description Logic (DL) (Badder & Nutt, 2003). More importantly, DL supports the reasoning of concepts and infers the relationships between concepts. Rule Bases are definitions of relationships amongst concepts and provide criterion for new knowledge. Generally, the Rule Bases not only contain the predefined rules in the SWRL domain, but also support the rule customization. Through rules defined in the Rule Bases, new knowledge could be inferred from existed knowledge. To facilitate the process of matching, the rule customization is necessary. Readers can refer to our previous work (Liang, Zhou, Yu, Wang & Guo, 2012; Yu, Zhou, Yu, Park & Ma, 2008) for more details about reasoning.

Furthermore, the logical reasoning could be utilized to infer fine-grained activities with the lots of sensors. Chen, Nugent and Wang (2012) elaborated a knowledge-driven system to detect daily activities in smart home. A model that describes the semantic of sensors and mutual relationships among sensors is constructed. Based on this model, the contexts are integrated and formalized according to model. Then the semantic reasoning is utilized to infer activities (Figure 8). With the rich of context, the proposed system is characterized by the coarse-grain and fine-grain activity recognition.

3.2. Fuzzy Reasoning

There are lots of sources of uncertainty in data including imprecision in numerical measurement and ambiguous terms. With the development of fuzzy theory, the combination of logical reasoning and the fuzzy theory, named the fuzzy reasoning, is proposed to handle the uncertainty of knowl-

Figure 7. The medicine intake behavior reasoning based on ontology

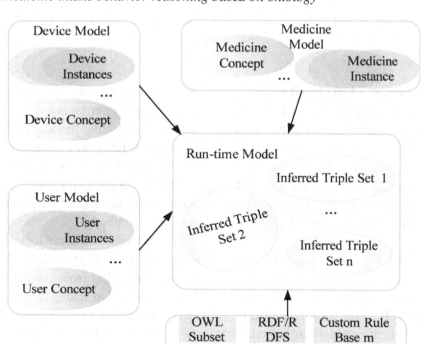

Figure 8. The system interface for activity reasoning (Chen, Nugent & Wang, 2012)

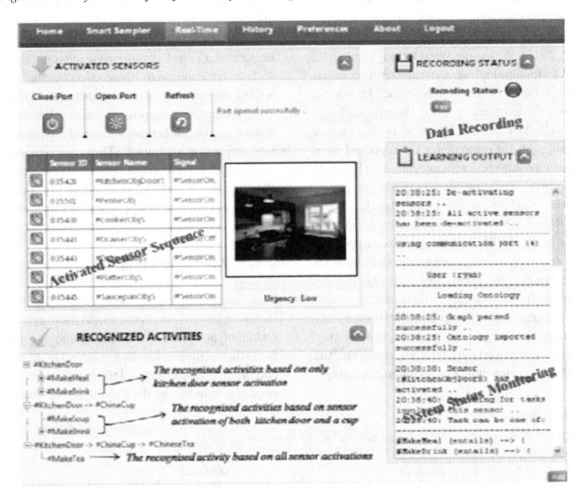

edge. The fuzzy logic is a logic based on fuzzy sets and membership functions. The elements in the fuzzy set are characterized by truth-values in the [0,1] interval rather than crisp 0 and 1, as in the conventional set theory. While the function that assigns a number in [0,1] to each element of the universe of discourse of a fuzzy set is called membership function (Siler & Buckley, 2004; Pappis & Siettos, 2005; Ross, 2004).

The workflow for the fuzzy reasoning is illustrated in Figure 9. First, the fuzzification takes inputs and determines the degree to which these inputs belong to each of the appropriate fuzzy sets. After the fuzzification, the fuzzy inference engine incorporates the fuzzy rules and the fuzzified inputs to infer knowledge. The last step in the fuzzy reasoning process is defuzzification. Fuzziness helps us to evaluate the rules, but the final output of a fuzzy system has to be a crisp number. The input for the defuzzification process is the aggregate output fuzzy set and the output is a single number.

The differences between logical reasoning and fuzzy reasoning are presented in Table 2. For the rules in the logical reasoning, they describe the casual relationship among different concepts. As shown in Table 2, the conclusion D depends on the conditions A, B, and C. Only when the multi

Figure 9. Generalized workflow of fuzzy reasoning

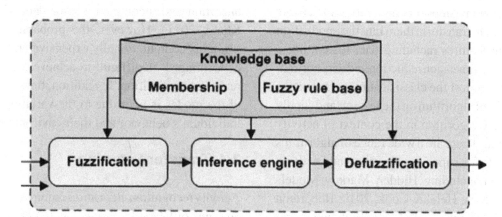

Table 2. Examples of rules for logical and fuzzy reasoning

Types	Examples
Rule	*IF* A *AND* B *AND* C *THEN* D
Fuzzy Rule	*IF* A is High *AND* B is High *AND* C is High *THEN* D is High

conditions are satisfied, the statement will be true. However, for the rules in the fuzzy reasoning, each concept is fuzzified by the membership functions. The membership functions classify the continuous or digital variables into discrete states (such as high, medium, and low for temperature) defined in fuzzy set.

Due to the uncertainty of contexts, the fuzzy reasoning is introduced into the field of activity recognition. There is lots of work on the activity recognition based on the fuzzy reasoning. A fuzzy reasoning system is elaborated (Perianu, et al. 2008) to support a production or maintenance worker by recognizing the worker's actions and delivering information about activities to be performed. RFID sensors are placed on the human body and the on the car to detect the assembly steps. And the assembly modeling is designed to track the performed steps. In order to properly deliver a reminder in an appropriate time and way,

Zhou, Chu, Yu and Kim (2012) investigated when and how to prompt the reminding message to the elderly based on the fuzzy linguistic model.

3.3. Probabilistic and Statistical Reasoning

Probabilistic & statistical reasoning can be broadly divided into three strands: supervised, semi-supervised and unsupervised learning. The supervised learning algorithms depend on the labeled dataset by which the parameters could be learned for each category. The offline trained parameters are applied to classify unknown data. On the contrast, the unsupervised learning algorithms don't require the labeled dataset and try to find hidden structure in unlabeled data. Semi-supervised learning falls between the supervised leaning and unsupervised learning. Semi-supervised learning makes use of both label and unlabeled data for training – typically for the sparse of labeled data.

For the supervised learning, its general procedure consists of offline data training and online activity recognition. The offline data training includes several steps: (1) to collect sensor outputs and label them; (2) data preparation including data cleaning and data filtering; (3) feature extraction from the labeled data and learning of parameters.

For the online activity recognition, it composes of the following steps: (1) integration of sensors outputs; (2) to transform them into the application dependent features including data fusion, noise elimination, dimension reduction and data normalization, (3) to test the classification performance of the trained algorithm on the test set; and finally to apply the algorithm in the context of activity recognition. There are a wide range of algorithms and models for supervised learning and activity recognition including Hidden Markov Models (HMMs) (Kim, Helal & Cook, 2010; Robertson & Reid, 2006; Fusier, et al., 2007), dynamic and naive Bayes networks (Kern, Schiele & Schmidt, 2003), decision trees (Bao & Intille, 2004; Mathie, et al., 2004), nearest neighbors (Ravi, et al., 2005) and support vector machines (SVMs) (He, Liu, Jin, Zhen & Huang, 2008).

Unsupervised learning tries to directly construct recognition models from unlabeled data. The basic idea is to manually assign a probability to each possible activity and to predefine a stochastic model that can update these likelihoods according to new observations and to the known state of the system (Chen & Khalil, 2011). Such an approach employs density estimation methods, i.e., to estimate the properties of the underlying probability density or clustering techniques, to discover groups of similar examples to create learning models (Chen & Khalil, 2011). The limitation of the unsupervised learning probabilistic methods lies in the assignment of these handcrafted probabilistic parameters for the computation of the activity likelihood.

However, in real activity recognition systems, labeled samples are usually difficult or expensive to obtain as they require the efforts of human annotators (Chen & Khalil, 2011). In such cases, the semi-supervised learning is proposed, which makes use of a small amount of labeled data combined with a large amount of unlabeled data to classify unknown data.

A major strength of the activity recognition algorithms based on probabilistic and statistical learning is that they are capable of handling noisy, uncertain and incomplete sensor data (Chen & Khalil, 2011). However, the probabilistic reasoning is computationally expensive and energy consuming. It is difficult to achieve the goal of real-time recognition. In addition, the scalability of the modes is poor due to the variation of the individual's behavior and their environments.

3.4. Transfer Learning

Activity recognition algorithms require substantial amounts of labeled training data to perform well under very diverse circumstances. As a result, researchers have been designing methods to identify and utilize subtle connections between activity recognition data sets, or to perform transfer-based activity recognition (Cook, Feuz & Krishnan, 2012). Transfer learning is the study of dependency of human conduct, learning or performance on prior experience, which leverages experience from previous tasks into improved performance in a new task which has not been encountered before (Kasteren, Englebienne & Krose, 2010). Different from the supervised algorithms, the assumptions about the same feature space requirement, the same underlying distribution requirement and the same label space requirement don't hold on for activity recognition based on transfer learning.

The benefits of transfer learning are numerous; less time is spent on learning new tasks, less information is required from experts (usually human), and more situations can be handled effectively (Cook, Feuz & Krishnan, 2012). These potential benefits have lead researchers to apply transfer learning techniques to many domains with varying degrees of success. Kasteren, Englebienne and Krose (2010) studied activity recognition across different sensors. To address the differences of feature space, a meta-feature space is utilized, which describes the properties of the actual features. Each sensor is described by one or more meta-features. However, the construction of the meta-feature space manually is the key limitation. To relax the assumption of same feature space, same label space as well as same underling distribution, the authors proposed a transfer learning framework based on the assumption that distributions of sensors may be similar (Hu & Yang, 2011; Hu, Zheng & Yang, 2011). Cook, Feuz and Krishnan (2012) summarized the undergoing progress in the field of activity recognition based on transfer learning.

4. APPLICATION AREAS OF ACTIVITY RECOGNITION

Activity is one of the most important contexts for many applications. Based on recognizing activities, user statuses could be extracted to monitor or evaluate user activities. Meanwhile, activities also play important roles for intelligent decision making. In this section, we summarize the dominating application areas of activity recognition.

4.1. Pervasive Healthcare

Activity is one of the most important contexts for the implement of pervasive healthcare system, and is utilized for proactive service provision, real-time interactive system (reminder) and other intelligent system. In the field of pervasive healthcare, especially for the adult older, a number of assisting systems were designed to provide assistances in the form of proactive services and reminders. Mihailidis et al. (2008) proposed an interactive system, named COACH to help the elderly during the hand washing. It real-timely detects user activities with the video-content and reminds of the proper sequence of hand washing that need to be completed. A smart pillbox (Tang, et al., 2011) is designed to detect whether the medication has been taken according to the prescription. Every pill bottle is attached with a RFID label. The logical reasoning methodology is utilized to monitor user activities. Meanwhile, the pillbox provides multimodal interactions including video and audio assistance for the elderly. Ni et al. (2012) applied

pressure sensors to detect the sleep postures, which provide proofs for the evaluation of sleep quality.

In addition, the activity recognition contributes to the evaluation of metabolic energy expenditure (Kawahara, Ryu & Asami, 2009; Ryu, Kawahara & Asami, 2008; Rothney, et al., 2007) and improvement of efficiency of hospital staff (Sánchez, Tentori & Favela, 2008). Both Kawahara et al. (2009) and Ryu et al. (2008) use the accelerometer signals to assess the daily energy expenditure, which provides proof for the health evaluation. The iHospital (Sánchez, Tentori & Favela, 2008) is proposed to map contextual information to a user activity. A hidden Markov model uses contextual information to recognize user activities and provide opportunistic services for hospital staff.

4.2. Commercial Games

Activity is regarded as an interactive interface for the control of games. More exactly, it is the body movement that is widely employed to control the game. Currently, there are lots of devices supporting the movement-aware interaction, which contributes to the improvement of the user satisfaction. The Sega Activator, the first controller to allow full-body motion sensing, was released in 1993. Later, a new kind of controller, called the Wii Remote, appeared. It uses accelerometers to detect its approximate orientation and acceleration and an image sensor. In 2010, Microsoft has also released the Kinect, which uses cameras to detect the player's motions and translates them into inputs for the game. Furthermore, the eye movement is utilized to control games (Smith & Graham, 2006; Headon & Curwen, 2002). Through the eye movement, it provides a more natural interface to game control.

Different from the movement-aware control, Guo, Fujimura, Zhang and Imai (2012) presented a pervasive game, named treasure, which introduces the concept of "design-in-play" that allows the customization of the game according to the user contexts including user activities. For example, players can specify a multimedia action in the game when they physically interact with a given entity distributed in the smart space.

4.3. Recommendation Services

Traditionally, the recommendation services employ the user profiles and item information to provide candidate items. However, according to some studies of the psychology and sociology of music, users' short-term needs are usually influenced by the users' context, such as their emotional states, activities, or external environment. The importance of contextual information has been recognized to improve the user satisfaction for the recommendation system. Therefore, contexts including the user activities are incorporated into the recommendation system. (Refer to (Adomavicius & Tuzhilin, 2011) for more details about context-aware recommendation system).

Wang, Rosenblum and Wang (2012) present a context-aware mobile music recommendation based on daily activities such as working, sleeping, running and studying. The paper presented a ubiquitous system built on the off-the-shelf mobile phone to detect user's daily activities in real-time. To facilitate the collaborative work in the hospital operating rooms, a recommender system, which recommends virtual actions such as retrieval of information and initiation of communication with other staff, is presented (Doryab & Togelius, 2012). The recommender system recognizes ongoing operations based on the embedded sensors in the operating rooms. Yu et al. (2006) proposed a context-aware media recommendation platform using an NxM dimensional model to organize contexts including user activities.

4.4. Manufacturing

Activity recognition is also employed in the manufacturing, and contributes to the improvement of efficiency (Stiefmeier, et al., 2008; Zappi,

et al., 2007). Some scenarios have been given in (Hartmann, 2011), including maintenance scenario and quality assurance. A context-aware wearable computing system is elaborated by Stiefmeier et al. (2008) to support a production or maintenance worker by recognizing the work's actions and delivering information about activities to be performed. RFID sensors are placed on the human body and the on the car to detect the assembly steps. And the assembly modeling is designed to track the performed steps. Lukowicz et al. (2004) and Ward et al. (2006) present multimodal wearable systems to recognize the activities in the wood workshop. Different from previous work, this paper integrates accelerometers and micro-phone to detect the performed activities. It is demonstrated that the proposed solution could recognize activities in a wood shop with 84.4% accuracy. Further, a vision based system is presented for the recognition of manual assembly tasks. The method of this work is demonstrated by means of a fictive manual assembly scenario, in which screw and put actions are detected.

4.5. Enhancement of Social Interaction

Social factors are important in the design of healthcare services, which make the healthcare services more user-friendly and acceptable. Furthermore, social interaction with others benefits health for the elderly. MoviPill (Rodrigo, Cherubini & Oliver, 2010) is a mobile phone-based game that persuades patients to be more adherent to their medication prescription by means of social interaction. Playful bottle, a mobile social persuasion system, was designed to motivate the healthy water intake among social community. The social reminders from friends help to enhance the social interaction.

Human activities always are incorporated with semantics, such as user attitude, user intension etc. Extraction of social semantics from basic activities may facilitate the service provision based on user fine-grained social context, and enhance the social interaction among group members. Yu & Yu et al. (2010) present a smart meeting room prototype for capture, recognition and visualization of human interaction with multimodal sensors, such as video camera, microphones and motion sensors. The proposed system on one hand provides visualizing interaction; on the other hand, it also offers real-time feedback for improving participants' meeting skills.

5. CHALLENGING ISSUES ON ACTIVITY RECOGNITION

Even though there are many progresses in the field of activity recognition, we still face lots of challenges for the wide utilization of the activity recognition. In this section, we present the new challenges for activity recognition, especially for the large-scale users.

5.1. Nonintrusive Data Collection Based on Large-Scale Users

With the accumulation of digital footprints, a large amount of contexts are collected, ranging from the location, acceleration, speed etc. The emergence of Internet of Things (IoT) provides the opportunity for the seamless sensing with ambient intelligence. However, the nonintrusive data collection on the large-scale objects is necessitated for activity recognition.

Most of researches on the human activity recognition so far are based on small number of subjects and lab-created private data. Based on the dataset collected from small number of subjects, it is difficult to tell the reasonability of the proposed algorithm. Second, it is difficult to compare the proposed algorithms due to the differences of datasets. More importantly, the existing datasets were not collected in nonintrusive way. Specifically, in the data collection process, many details such as sensor types, sampling frequency,

and position of sensors are predefined. It is demonstrated that the position of accelerometers pose significant impacts on the outputs of sensors. On the other hand, although some datasets have been collected from the real world, the size of objects is small. To the best of my knowledge, almost 200 candidates were recruited for the Nokia Mobile Data Challenge (Kiukkonen, Blom, Dousse & Laurila, 2010); 136 for the HASC Challenge (Kawaguchi, et al., 2012).

Therefore, the nonintrusive data collection based on large-scale community is necessitated. On one hand, it doesn't distract user from their daily activities and provides dataset without human intervention. On the other hand, it provides the benchmarks for the algorithm evaluation.

5.2. Configurable Recognition Algorithm

Even though activity recognition has been introduced into some recommender systems, they are still running in demo instead of off-the-shelf services. Why? That is because existing algorithms don't work well for the activity recognition on large-scale persons (Lane, et al., 2011).

There are lots of algorithms involved for the activity recognition. However, those algorithms don't take user properties into the model. For the probabilistic reasoning algorithms, they rely on the training models between the sampled data and activities labels. This leads to the poor scalability of proposed algorithms. In fact, user properties, such as age, height, and health states etc. have direct impacts on the user activity patterns. For example, the gait patterns of elderly women are significant from that of young (Byrne, et al., 2002). Is it possible to integrate those user properties into the recognition algorithm? Guo, Zhang and Imai (2010) proposed a meta-design approach, which enables user-oriented management for intelligent system. Based on the meta-approach, the end user could customize the system according to preference individually; on the other hand, it benefits the design of the intelligent system without concerning about the multi-user management. Maybe this solution could enlighten the design of activity recognition algorithm. Based on those user properties, a configurable algorithm could be designed. The configurable algorithm could automatically select parameters according to user properties. It may provide the solution to address the poor scalability of existing algorithms.

5.3. Energy Consumption

The long-term sensing with the full working load of sensors is energy-consuming. For example, the battery lifetime of Samsung i909 reaches up to over 30 hours when all applications and sensors are turned off. But that declines to 5.5 hours (50 Hz) and 8 hours (20 Hz) respectively, when the single 3-D accelerometer is monitored with different sampling frequencies. Therefore, the energy consumption is a crucial issue for the success of long-term activity recognition.

Wang et al. (2009) designed a scalable framework of energy-efficient mobile sensing system (EEMSS) for automatic user state recognition. The core component of EEMSS is a sensor management scheme which defines user states and state transition rules by an XML configuration. The sensor management scheme allocates the minimum set of sensors and invokes new sensors when state transitions happen. Zappi et al. (2008) selected the minimum set of sensors according to their contributions to classification accuracy as assessed during data training process and tested this solution by recognizing manipulative activities of assembly-line workers in a car production environment. Li, Cao, Chen and Tian (2012) applied machine learning technologies to infer the status of heavy-duty sensors for energy-efficient context sensing. They try to infer the status of high energy consuming sensors according to the outputs of lightweight sensors. Existing solutions extend

the battery life by the collaboration of multiple sensors and the reduction of sensor active time.

5.4. Semantic Extraction from Group Activities

The social interaction among group members benefits the social collaboration and information sharing. Therefore, understanding and recognizing the group activities are significantly important. Some work explored the group-level activity recognition. However, little research has been conducted on social aspects. A few systems attempted to analyze semantic information of group-level activities. Hillard Ostendorf and Shriberg (2003) proposed a classifier for the recognition of an individual's agreement or disagreement utterances using lexical and prosodic cues. Garg et al. (2008) proposed an approach to recognize participant roles in meetings.

However, group activities usually encapsulate a large amount of communicative statements and semantic relationships between them that form an interaction network. To enrich knowledge about a meeting with social group dynamics, we need to analyze not only physical interactions such as turn-taking and addressing (who speaks to whom) between participants, but also semantic meanings behind the physical actions. Human semantic interactions are defined as social behaviors among participants. Various interactions imply different user roles, attitudes, and intentions about a topic during a discussion.

6. UNDERGOING EFFORTS ON ACTIVITY RECOGNITION

We still face lots of challenges in the field of activity recognition, especially for large-scale users. In this section, we present some our undergoing work for those questions.

6.1. Semantic Extraction from Pervasive Environment

Human activities always are incorporated with semantics, such as user attitude, user intension etc. Extraction of social semantics from basic activities may facilitate the service provision based on user fine-grained social context, and enhance the social interaction among group members. We design a prototype system for capture, recognition and visualization of human interaction with multimodal sensors, such as video camera, microphones and motion sensors (Yu & Yu, et al., 2010).

To extract the semantics interactions in meetings, a smart meeting system was built to capture, recognize and visualize the user interaction with multimodal sensors. The architecture of prototype system is illustrated in Figure 10. For the interaction capture system, the physical layer to collect raw context, multimodal sensors are utilized to capture the user interactions including sound and video records and head tracks. Based on those multi-dimensional heterogeneous contexts, a multimodal classifier was adopted to classify human interactions. In addition, we testified the reusability of trained data. Our experimental results indicate that our model can be trained once and used to test other meetings. Furthermore, we provide a social interaction browser named MMBrowser to efficiently review and understand the human interactions in the meeting. Figure 11 is an example to show the utilization of the MMBrowser, which helps meeting in the organization and improves people's meeting participation skills. Based on the proposed prototype system, we further investigated the interaction patterns

Figure 10. Smart meeting system architecture

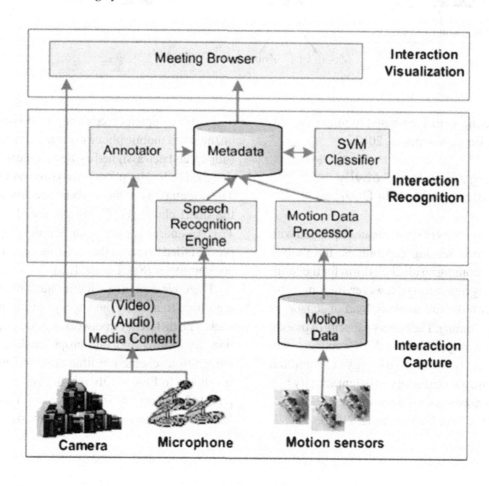

Figure 11. Meeting Browser overview

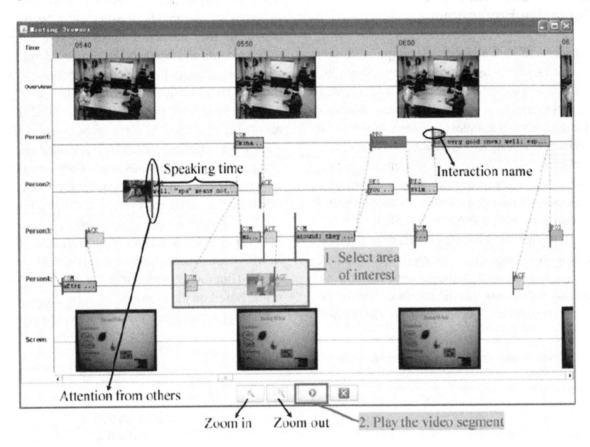

in the meeting with Tree-based mining (Yu, Yu, Zhou, Becker & Nakamura, 2012).

6.2. Energy Efficient Activity Recognition on Mobile Devices

With the popularity of smart phones equipped with unprecedented sensing capabilities, the mobile phone is becoming an ideal platform for the long-term activity monitoring. However, the long-term sensing with the full working load of sensors is energy-consuming. The battery capacity of mobile phones is a major bottleneck of context-aware applications. To address the energy consumption issue, we propose an energy-efficient activity recognition algorithm feasible on the mobile devices (Liang, Zhou, Yu, Guo, & Yang, 2012).

First, we implemented an application deployed on the smart mobile phone to collect dataset. Each subject has been assigned a smart phone where our designed android application has been preinstalled. The orientations of the tri-axial accelerometer in the smart phone (HTC) are presented in Figure 12a. An android application was developed and pre-installed to record the real-time outputs of the accelerometer (See Figure 12b).

Then, we designed a hierarchical recognition algorithm to address the energy consumption issues. The differences between classic classification algorithms and our proposed hierarchical recognition scheme are illustrated in Figure 13. As shown in Figure 13b, advantages of our proposed algorithm are in two aspects. Firstly, the feature extraction is completed in two steps, which

Figure 12. (a) Orientation of accelerator on the target mobile phone. (b) Experimental interfaces on mobile phones to collect acceleration data

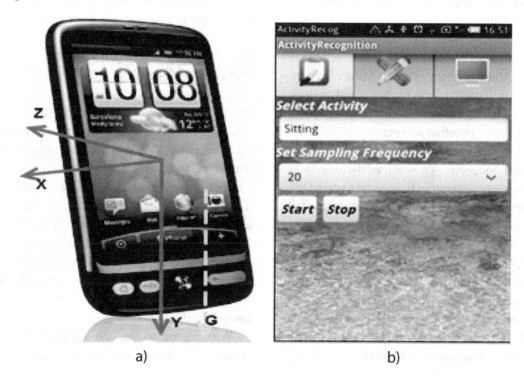

a)   b)

Figure 13. (a) Workflow of existing classification algorithm, such as decision tree, support vector machine etc. (b) Workflow of the hierarchical recognition algorithm.

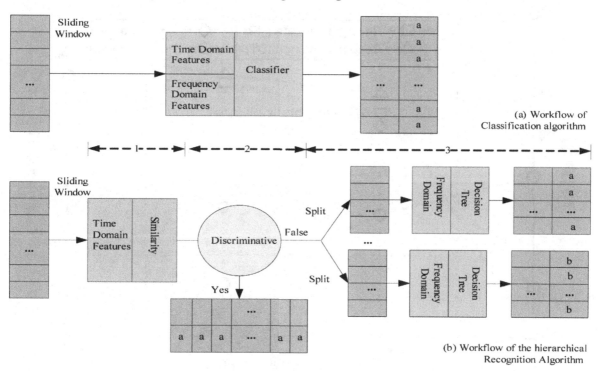

reduces the opportunity of utilization of the time-consuming frequency-domain features. Secondly, the size of sliding window is adjusted according to the similarity. When it is indiscriminative, the sliding window is split into small segments equally. And frequency-domain features are introduced to classify user activities based on decision tree. The algorithm with adjusting step length benefits the recognition accuracy.

To test the battery lifetime under different sampling frequencies, we measured the time spans with changes of sampling frequencies when 90% of battery power is consumed. The experimental results are illustrated in Figure 14. It is obvious that the battery life declines with the increasing of sampling frequencies. Also, it demonstrates that the recognition rates increase with the growth of the sampling frequencies. Additionally, the hierarchical recognition scheme (HR) and decision tree (DT) are compared in terms of time span and the recognition accuracy. As shown in Figure 14,

although the decision tree outperforms our proposed algorithm in recognition accuracy, the battery life is longer in our solution.

6.3. Activity Recognition for Pervasive Gaming

Pervasive games, a new genre in the field of entertainment, integrate many contexts to enhance the user experience. We designed a pervasive game, named treasure, which introduces the concept of "design-in-play" that allows the customization of the game according to the user contexts including user activities (Guo, Fujimura, Zhang & Imai, 2012). For example, players can specify a multimedia action in the game when they physically interact with a given entity distributed in the smart space. The composition of the treasure game is illustrated in Figure 15.

With regard to the activity recognition, we utilized the rule-based context reasoning, the

Figure 14. Time Span and Recognition rate vs. sampling frequencies

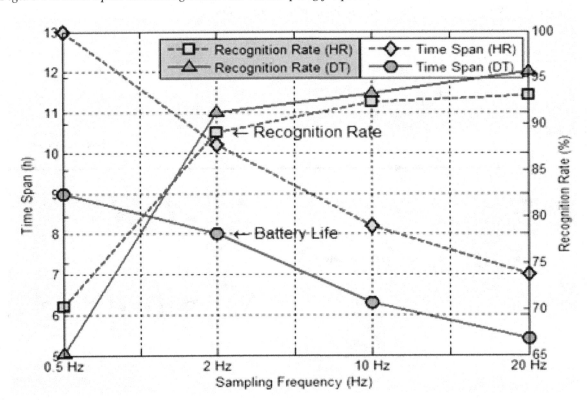

Figure 15. Workflow of context-aware game

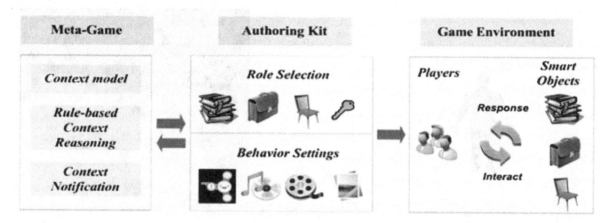

generalized frame of which is described in Section 3.1. We first design the context model, which presents the attributes of physical objects and the mutual relationship among different objects. Based on the predefined the rule or common knowledge, the rule-based reasoning is performed on receiving the notification of context update.

In the prototype of treasure game, there are lots of sensing are utilized to capture user contexts. As shown in Figure 16, the ultrasonic location sensors are utilized to locate entities distributed in the smart environment. Every entity is labeled with a unique U3D tag. Based on the updates of location coordinates, we could infer the movement of an object, such opening/ closing drawers, entering / leaving the room and hidden/found status of an object. Based on those multimodal sensors embed-

ded in the smart environment, we are capable of detecting the status of objects, which facilitates the fine-grained inference of user activities.

6.4. Sleep Pattern Recognition for HealthCare

Sleep quality is an important evidence to evaluate an individual's health state, especially for the old people. It is reported that in an aging study of over 9000 subjects aged 65 and older, more than 50% of older adults are subject to sleep problems such as insomnia, difficult waking or waking too early, or needing to nap and not feeling rested (Foley, Ancoli-Israel, Britz & Walsh, 2004). To evaluate the sleep quality for an individual, we focus on the design of an unobtrusive sleep posture detection

Figure 16. Sensors utilized in the context-aware game

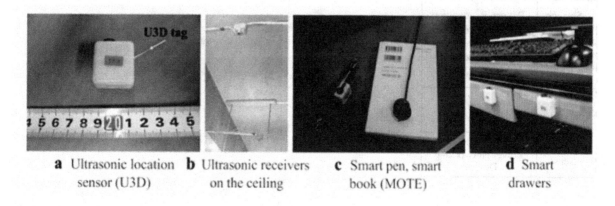

a Ultrasonic location sensor (U3D)   **b** Ultrasonic receivers on the ceiling   **c** Smart pen, smart book (MOTE)   **d** Smart drawers

Figure 17. The prototype for sleep pattern detection

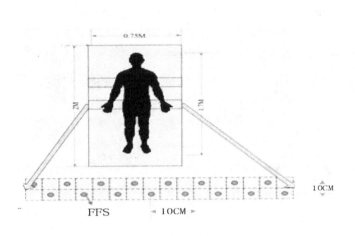

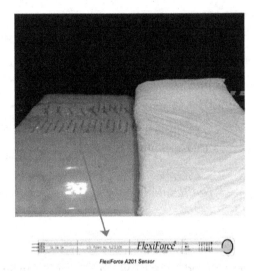

system (Ni, et al., 2012), which recognizes the body behavior during the sleep unobtrusively. Different from the existing work, we designed an unobtrusive sleep detection system with lots of embedded sensors and recognized four sleep postures with high accuracy. The prototype system is presented in Figure 17.

In the sleep detection system, we design a smart mattress with lots of pressure sensors embedded (as shown in Figure 17). To achieve the long-term monitoring of sleep, we chose a novel type of pressure sensor named FlexiForce, which is ultra-thin, low-cost and flexible. Based on the smart mattress, we implement our sleep detection

system. The framework of sleep pattern detection system consists of four levels, including physical sense level, data acquisition level, posture detection level, and service provision level (as shown in Figure18).

In the physical sensing level, pressure sensors and a Driving Power Unit (DPU) are utilized to sense the body pressure. The data acquisition unit (DAU) transmits the analog signals as digital data. The posture detection level recognizes sleep movement based on the real-time digitized data stream from DAU; meanwhile, the logging system records those sampled data. Finally, based on the sleep postures and their duration, we can infer the

Figure 18. Framework of the sleep pattern detection

Service Provision	Pattern Recognition Healthy Reminder
Posture Detection	Feature Extract Posture Classify
Data Acquisition	Data Transform Preprocessing
Physical Sense	Sensors/Driving Power/Networking Devices

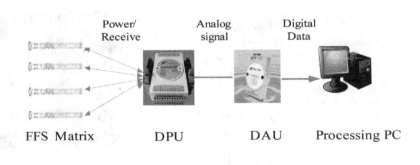

elderly user's sleep pattern, and evaluate the quality of sleep. In our work, we try to distinguish 5 kinds of sleep postures, including left-lateral sleep, right-lateral sleep, supine sleep, prone sleep (PS) and getting up (GU). In comparison with many classification algorithms, Random Forest method is the most stable solution with accuracy ranging from 98% to 86%. Based on the trained dataset, we could timely recognize the user posture during sleep. Meanwhile, for each subjects we record the turn-over patterns, which could be utilized to evaluate the sleep quality under the guideline of professional doctors.

7. CONCLUSION

With the unprecedented sensing capabilities and the emergence of internet of things, the researches on activity recognition have been hot issues for different applications areas, such as pervasive healthcare, industry and commerce, and recommendation systems. In this chapter, we summarize the existing work about activity recognition. We classify the work about activity recognition based on the different sensors. An overview of algorithms involved for activity recognition is presented. We briefly describe the advantages and disadvantages for each algorithms, and the generalized workflow are presented as well. Although activity recognition has been applied into many applications, we present some research issues that have not yet been address well, including nonintrusive data collection for large-scale persons, energy consumption, configurable recognition algorithm and semantic extraction from social interaction. Finally, our efforts on the activity recognition have been introduce, including smart meeting for semantic extraction, hierarchical algorithm for energy consumption, implement of activity-based pervasive game and the sleep pattern recognition for the elderly.

ACKNOWLEDGMENT

This work was partially supported by the National Basic Research Program of China (No. 2012CB316400), the National Natural Science Foundation of China (No. 61222209, 61103063), the Program for New Century Excellent Talents in University (No. NCET-12-0466), the Specialized Research Fund for the Doctoral Program of Higher Education (No. 20126102110043), the Natural Science Basic Research Plan in Shaanxi Province of China (No. 2012JQ8028), the Doctorate Fundation of Northwestern Polytechnical University, and the Basic Research Foundation of NPU (No. JC20110267).

REFERENCES

Adomavicius, G., & Tuzhilin, A. (2011). Context-aware recommender systems. In F. Ricci, L. Rokach, B. Shapira, & P. B. Kantor (Eds.), *Recommender Systems Handbook* (pp. 217–253). Berlin: Springer. doi:10.1007/978-0-387-85820-3_7.

Ahmed, S., Sharmin, M., & Ahmed, S. I. (2005). A smart meeting room with pervasive computing technologies. In *Proceedings of SNPD/SAWN.* SNPD/SAWN.

Antonakaki, P., Kosmopoulos, D., & Perantonis, S. J. (2009). Detecting abnormal human behavior using multiple cameras. *Signal Processing, 89*(9), 1723–1738. doi:10.1016/j.sigpro.2009.03.016.

Badder, F., & Nutt, W. (2003). Basic description logics. In F. Badder, D. Calvanese, D. McGuinness, D. Nardi, & P. Patel-Schneider (Eds.), *The Description Logic Handbook: Theory, Implementation, and Applications* (pp. 41–90). New York: Cambridge University Press.

Bao, L., & Intille, S. S. (2004). Activity recognition from user-annotated acceleration data. *Lecture Notes in Computer Science*, *3001*, 1–17. doi:10.1007/978-3-540-24646-6_1.

Bouchard, K., Bouchard, B., & Bouzouane, A. (2011). Qualitative spatial activity recognition using a complete platform based on passive RFID tags: Experiments and results. In *Proceedings of 9th International Conference on Smart Homes and Health Telematics (ICOST)*. Montreal, Canada: ICOST.

Buettner, M., Prasad, R., Philipose, M., & Wetherall, D. (2009). Recognizing daily activities with RFID-based sensors. In *Proceedings of the 11th International Conference on Ubiquitous Computing (Ubicomp)*. Ubicomp.

Byrne, J. E., Stergiou, N., Blanke, D., Houser, J., Kurz, M. J., & Hageman, P. A. (2002). Comparison of gait patterns between young and elderly women: An examination of coordination. *Perceptual and Motor Skills*, *94*(1), 265–280. doi:10.2466/pms.2002.94.1.265 PMID:11883574.

Chang, M., Krahnstoever, N., & Ge, W. (2011). Probabilistic group-level motion analysis and scenario recognition. In *Proceedings of IEEE International Conference on Computer Vision (ICCV)*. Barcelona, Spain: IEEE.

Charif, H. N., & Mckenna, S. (2006). Tracking the activity of participants in a meeting. *Machine Vision and Applications*, *17*(2), 83–93. doi:10.1007/s00138-006-0015-5.

Chen, L., Hoey, J., Nugent, C., Cook, D., & Yu, Z. (2012). Sensor-based activity recognition. *IEEE Transactions on Systems, Man, and Cybernetics. Part C*, *42*(6), 790–808. doi: doi:10.1109/TSMCC.2012.2198883.

Chen, L., & Khalil, I. (2011). Activity recognition: Approaches, practices and trends. In L. Chen, C. D. Nugent, J. Biswas, & J. Hoey (Eds.), *Activity Recognition in Pervasive Intelligent Environments* (pp. 1–31). Atlantis Press. doi:10.2991/978-94-91216-05-3_1.

Chen, L., Nugent, C. D., Cook, D., & Yu, Z. (2011). Knowledge-driven activity recognition in intelligent environment. *Pervasive and Mobile Computing*, *7*(3), 285–286. doi:10.1016/j.pmcj.2011.05.001.

Chen, L., Nugent, C. D., & Wang, H. (2012). A knowledge-driven approach to activity recognition in smart homes. *IEEE Transactions on Knowledge and Data Engineering*, *24*(6), 961–974. doi:10.1109/TKDE.2011.51.

Cho, Y., Nam, Y., Choi, Y., & Cho, W. (2008). SmartBuckle: Human activity recognition using a 3-axis accelerometer and a wearable camera. In Proceedings of HealthNet. HealthNet.

Choudhury, T., Consolvo, S., Harrison, B., Hightower, J., Lamarca, A., & LeGrand, L. et al. (2008). The mobile sensing platform: An embedded activity recognition system. *IEEE Pervasive Computing / IEEE Computer Society [and] IEEE Communications Society*, *7*(2), 32–41. doi:10.1109/MPRV.2008.39.

Cook, D., Feuz, K. D., & Krishnan, N. (2012). *Transfer learning for activity recognition: A survey*. Retrieved from http://eecs.wsu.edu/~cook/pubs/kais12.pdf

Doryab, A., & Togelius, J. (2012). Activity recognition in collaborative environments. In *Proceedings of IEEE World Congress on Computational Intelligence (WCCI)*. Brisbane, Australia: IEEE.

Foley, D., Ancoli-Israel, S., Britz, P., & Walsh, J. (2004). Sleep disturbances and chronic disease in older adults: Results of the 2003 national sleep foundation sleep in America survey. *Journal of Psychosomatic Research, 56*(5), 497–502. doi:10.1016/j.jpsychores.2004.02.010 PMID:15172205.

Fusier, F., Valentin, V., Bremond, F., Thonnat, M., Borg, M., Thirde, D., & Ferryman, J. (2007). Video understanding for complex activity recognition. *Machine Vision and Applications, 18*(3), 167–188. doi:10.1007/s00138-006-0054-y.

Garg, N. P., Favre, S., Salamin, H., Tur, D. H., & Vinciarelli, A. (2008). Role recognition for meeting participants: An approach based on lexical information and social network analysis. In *Proceedings of the 16th ACM International Conference on Multimedia (MM)*. Vancouver, Canada: ACM.

Gavrila, D. M. (1999). The visual analysis of human movement: A survey. *Computer Vision and Image Understanding, 73*(1), 82-98. doi: 10.1.1.131.2072

Gu, T., Wang, L., Wu, Z., Tao, X., & Lu, J. (2011). A pattern mining approach to sensor-based human activity recognition. *IEEE Transactions on Knowledge and Data Engineering, 23*(9), 1359–1372. doi:10.1109/TKDE.2010.184.

Guo, B., Fujimura, R., Zhang, D., & Imai, M. (2012). Design-in-play: Improving the variability of indoor pervasive games. *Multimedia Tools and Applications, 59*(1), 259–277. doi:10.1007/s11042-010-0711-z.

Guo, B., Zhang, D., & Imai, M. (2010). Enabling user-oriented management for ubiquitous computing: The meta-design approach. *Computer Networks, 54*(16), 2840–2855. doi:10.1016/j.comnet.2010.07.016.

Guo, B., Zhang, D., Yu, Z., Liang, Y., Wang, Z., & Zhou, X. (2012). *From the internet of things to embedded intelligence*. World Wide Web Journal. doi:10.1007/s11280-012-0188-y.

Gyorbíró, N., Fábián, Á., & Hományi, G. (2009). An activity recognition system for mobile phones. *Mobile Networks and Applications, 14*(1), 82–91. doi:10.1007/s11036-008-0112-y.

Hartmann, B. (2011). *Human worker activity recognition in industrial environments*. (PhD thesis). KIT. Retrieved from http://uvka.ubka.uni-karlsruhe.de/shop/download/1000022235

He, Z., Liu, Z., Jin, L., Zhen, L., & Huang, J. (2008). Weightlessness feature - A novel feature for single tri-axial accelerometer based activity recognition. In *Proceedings of 19th International Conference on Pattern Recognition (ICPR)*. Tampa, FL: ICPR.

Headon, R., & Curwen, R. (2002). Movement awareness for ubiquitous game control. *Personal and Ubiquitous Computing, 6*(5-6), 407–415. doi:10.1007/s007790200045.

Hillard, D., Ostendorf, M., & Shriberg, E. (2003). Detection of agreement vs. disagreement in meetings: Training with unlabeled data. In *Proceedings of HLT-NAACL*. HLT-NAACL.

Hoey, J., Bertoldi, A., Poupart, P., & Mihailidis, A. (2010). Assisting persons with dementia during handwashing using a partially observable Markov decision process. In *Proceedings of the 5th International Conference on Computer Vision Systems (ICVS)*. ICVS.

Hu, D. H., & Yang, Q. (2011). Transfer learning for activity recognition via sensor mapping. In *Proceedings of the 22nd International Joint Conference on Artificial Intelligence*. Barcelona, Spain: IEEE.

Hu, D. H., Zheng, V. W., & Yang, Q. (2011). Cross-domain activity recognition via transfer learning. *Pervasive and Mobile Computing, 7*(3), 344–358. doi:10.1016/j.pmcj.2010.11.005.

Inomata, T., Naya, F., Kuwahara, N., Hattori, F., & Kogure, K. (2009). Activity recognition from interactions with objects using dynamic bayesian network. In *Proceedings of ACM International Workshop on Context-Awareness for Self-Managing Systems (CASEMANS)*. Nara, Japan: ACM.

Inooka, H., Ohtaki, Y., Hayasaka, H., Suzuki, A., & Nagatomi, R. (2006). Development of advanced portable device for daily physical assessment. In *Proceedings of SICE-ICASE International Joint Conference*. Busan, Korea: SICE-ICASE.

Istrate, D., Castelli, E., Vacher, M., Besacier, L., & Serignat, J. (2006). Information extraction from sound for medical telemonitoring. *IEEE Transactions on Information Technology in Biomedicine, 10*(2), 264–274. doi:10.1109/TITB.2005.859889 PMID:16617615.

Kasteren, T. L. M., Englebienne, G., & Krose, B. J. A. (2010). Transferring knowledge of activity recognition across sensor networks. In *Proceedings of the 8th International Conference on Pervasive*. IEEE.

Kawaguchi, N., Terada, T., Inoue, S., et al. (2012). HASC2012corpus: Large scale human activity corpus and its application. In *Proceedings of International Conference on Information Processing in Sensor Networks (IPSN)*. Beijing, China: IPSN.

Kawahara, Y., Ryu, N., & Asami, T. (2009). Monitoring daily energy expenditure using a 3-axis accelerometer with a low-power microprocessor. *International Journal of Human-Computer Interaction, 1*, 145–154.

Kern, N., Schiele, B., & Schmidt, A. (2003). Multisensor activity context detection for wearable computing. *Lecture Notes in Computer Science, 2875*, 220–232. doi:10.1007/978-3-540-39863-9_17.

Khan, A. M., Lee, Y., Lee, S. Y., & Kim, T. (2010). A triaxial accelerometer-based physical-activity recognition via augmented-signal features and a hierarchical recognizer. *IEEE Transactions on Information Technology in Biomedicine, 14*(6), 1166–1172. doi:10.1109/TITB.2010.2051955 PMID:20529753.

Khan, S. M., & Shah, M. (2005). Detection group activities using rigidity of formation. In *Proceedings of the 13th Annual ACM International Conference on Multimedia (MM)*. ACM.

Kim, E., Helal, S., & Cook, D. (2010). Human activity recognition and pattern discovery. *IEEE Pervasive Computing / IEEE Computer Society [and] IEEE Communications Society, 9*(1), 48–53. doi:10.1109/MPRV.2010.7 PMID:21258659.

Kiukkonen, N., Blom, J., Dousse, O., & Laurila, J. K. (2010). Towards rich mobile phone datasets: Lausanne data collection campaign. In *Proceedings of 7th ACM International Conference on Pervasive Service (ICPS)*. Berlin: ICPS.

Koike, H., Nagashima, S., Nakanishi, Y., & Sato, Y. (2004). Enhanced table: Supporting a small meeting in ubiquitous and augmented environment. In *Proceedings of 5th Pacific Rim Conference on Multimedia Information Application (PCM)*. Tokyo, Japan: PCM.

Krahnstoever, N., Rittscher, J., Tu, P., Chean, K., & Tomlinson, T. (2005). Activity recognition using visual tracking and RFID. In *Proceedings of IEEE Workshop on Applications of Computer Vision*. Breckenridge, CO: IEEE.

Krassing, G., Tantinger, D., Hofmann, C., Wittenberg, T., & Struck, M. (2010). User-friendly system for recognition of activities with an accelerometer. In *Proceedings of 4th International Conference on Pervasive Computing Technologies for Healthcare (PervasiveHealth)*. Munich, Germany: PervasiveHealth.

Krishnan, N. C., Juillard, C., & Colbry, D. (2009). Recognition of hand movements using wearable accelerometers. *Journal of Ambient Intelligence and Smart Environments, 1*(2), 143–155.

Kwapisz, J. R., Weiss, G. M., & Moore, S. A. (2010). Activity recognition using cell phone accelerometers. *ACM SIGKDD Explorations Newsletter, 12*(2), 74–82. doi:10.1145/1964897.1964918.

Lane, N. D., Xu, Y., Lu, H., Hu, S., Choudhury, T., Campbell, A. T., & Zhao, F. (2011). Enabling large-scale human activity inference on smartphones using community similarity networks (CSN). In *Proceedings of the 13th International Conference on Ubiquitous Computing (Ubicomp)*. Beijing, China: UbiComp.

Lee, M., Khan, A. M., Kim, J., Cho, Y. S., & Kim, T. S. (2010). A single tri-axial accelerometer-based real-time personal life log system capable of activity classification and exercise information generation. In *Proceedings of 2010 Annual International Conference of the IEEE Engineering in Medicine and Biology Society*. IEEE.

Li, X., Cao, H., Chen, E., & Tian, J. (2012). Learning to infer the status of heavy-duty sensors for energy efficient context-sensing. *ACM Transactions on Intelligent Systems and Technology, 3*(2). doi:10.1145/2089094.2089111.

Liang, Y., Zhou, X., Yu, Z., Guo, B., & Yang, Y. (2012). Energy efficient activity recognition based on low resolution accelerometer in smart phones. In *Proceedings of 7th International Conference on Grid and Pervasive Computing (GPC)*. Hong Kong: GPC.

Liang, Y., Zhou, X., Yu, Z., Wang, H., & Guo, B. (2012). A context-aware multimedia service scheduling framework in smart homes. *EURASIP Journal on Wireless Communications and Networking, 67*. doi: doi:10.1186/1687-1499-2012-67.

Lin, W., Sun, M., Poovendran, R., & Zhang, Z. (2010). Group event detection with a varying number of group members for video surveillance. *IEEE Transactions on Circuits and Systems for Video Technology, 20*(8), 1057–1067. doi:10.1109/TCSVT.2010.2057013.

Lukowicz, P., Ward, J. A., Junker, H., Stager, M., Troster, G., Atrash, A., & Starner, T. (2004). Recognizing workshop activity using body worn microphone and accelerometers. In *Proceedings of Pervasive Computing (Pervasive)*. Vienna, Austria: IEEE. doi:10.1007/978-3-540-24646-6_2.

Mannini, A., & Sabatini, A. M. (2010). Machine learning methods for classifying human physical activity from on-body accelerometers. *Sensors (Basel, Switzerland), 10*(2), 1154–1175. doi:10.3390/s100201154 PMID:22205862.

Mathias, S. (2006). *Low-power sound-based user activity recognition.* (PhD thesis). Swiss Federal Institute of Technology, Zurich, Switzerland. Retrieved from http://e-collection.library.ethz.ch/eserv/eth:29348/eth-29348-02.pdf

Mathie, M. J., Celler, B. G., Lovell, N. H., & Coster, A. C. (2004). Classification of basic daily movements using a triaxial accelerometer. *Medical & Biological Engineering & Computing, 42*(5), 679–687. doi:10.1007/BF02347551 PMID:15503970.

Mihailidis, A., Boger, J. N., Craig, T., & Hoey, J. (2008). The COACH prompting system to assist older adults with dementia through handwashing: An efficacy study. *BMC Geriatrics, 8*(28). doi:doi:10.1186/1471-2318-8-28 PMID:18992135.

Mizuno, H., Nagai, H., Sasaki, K., Suginoto, C., Khalil, K., & Tatsuta, S. (2007). Wearable sensor system for human behavior recognition. In *Proceedings of 4th International Conference on Solid-State Sensors, Actuators and Microsystems*. Lyon, France: IEEE.

Moeslund, T. B., Hilton, A., & Kruger, V. (2006). A survey of advances in vision-based human motion capture and analysis. *Computer Vision and Image Understanding, 104*(2), 90–126. doi:10.1016/j.cviu.2006.08.002.

Ni, H., Abdulrazak, B., Zhang, D., Wu, S., Yu, Z., Zhou, X., & Wang, S. (2012). Towards non-intrusive sleep pattern recognition in elder assistive environment. *Journal of Ambient Intelligence and Humanized Computing, 3*(2), 167–175. doi:10.1007/s12652-011-0082-y.

Pappis, C. P., & Siettos, C. I. (2005). Fuzzy reasoning. In E. K. Burke, & G. Kendall (Eds.), *Search Methodologies* (pp. 437–474). Springer. doi:10.1007/0-387-28356-0_15.

Patterson, D. J., Fox, D., Kautz, H., & Philipose, M. (2005). Fine grained activity recognition by aggregating abstract object usage. In *Proceedings of the 9th International Symposium on Wearable Computers (ISWC)*. Osaka, Japan: ISWC.

Perianu, M., Lombriser, C., Amft, O., Havinga, P., & Troster, G. (2008). Distributed activity recognition with fuzzy-enabled wireless sensor networks. In *Proceedings of the 4th IEEE International Conference on Distributed Computing in Sensor Systems (DCOSS)*. Santorini Island, Greece: DCOSS.

Ravi, N., Dander, N., Mysore, P., & Littman, M. L. (2005). Activity recognition from accelerometer data. In *Proceedings of the 17th Conference Innovative Applications of Artificial Intelligence (IAAI)*. Pittsburgh, PA: IAAI.

Robertson, N., & Reid, I. (2006). A general method for human activity recognition in video. *Computer Vision and Image Understanding, 104*(2), 232–248. doi:10.1016/j.cviu.2006.07.006.

Rodrigo, O., Cherubini, M., & Oliver, N. (2010). MoviPill: Improving medication compliance for elders using a mobile persuasive social game. In *Proceedings of 12th International Conference on Ubiquitous Computing (Ubicomp)*. Beijing, China: UbiComp.

Ross, T. J. (2004). Properties of membership functions, fuzzification and defuzzification. In T. J. Ross (Ed.), *Fuzzy Logic with Engineering Applications* (2nd ed., pp. 90–119). New York: John Wiley & Sons.

Rothney, M. P., Neumann, M., Beziat, A., & Chen, K. (2007). An artificial neural network model of energy expenditure using noninte-grated acceleration signals. *Journal of Applied Physiology, 103*(4), 1419–1427. doi:10.1152/japplphysiol.00429.2007 PMID:17641221.

Ruch, N., Rumo, M., & Mader, U. (2011). Recognition of activities in children by two uni-axial accelerometers in free-living conditions. *European Journal of Applied Physiology, 111*(8), 1917–1927. doi:10.1007/s00421-011-1828-0 PMID:21249388.

Ryu, N., Kawahara, Y., & Asami, T. (2008). A calorie count application for a mobile phone based on METS value. In *Proceedings of 5th Annual IEEE Communications Society Conference on Sensor, Mesh and Ad Hoc Communications and Networks(SECON)*. IEEE.

Sánchez, D., Tentori, M., & Favela, J. (2008). Activity recognition for the smart hospital. *IEEE Intelligent Systems, 23*(2), 50–57. doi:10.1109/MIS.2008.18.

Siler, W., & Buckley, J. J. (2004). *Fuzzy expert systems and fuzzy reasoning*. Hoboken, NJ: John Wiley & Sons, Inc. doi:10.1002/0471698504.

Smith, J. D., & Graham, T. C. N. (2006). Use of eye movements for video game control. In *Proceedings of ACM SIGCHI International Conference on Advances in Computer Entertainment Technology (ACE)*. ACM.

Stiefmeier, T., Roggen, D., Tröster, G., Ogris, G., & Lukowicz, P. (2008). Wearable activity tracking in car manufacturing. *IEEE Pervasive Computing / IEEE Computer Society [and] IEEE Communications Society, 7*(2), 42–50. doi:10.1109/MPRV.2008.40.

Sumi, Y., & Mase, K. (2001). Digital assistant for supporting conference participants: An attempt to combine mobile, ubiquitous and web computing. In *Proceedings of International Conference on Ubiquitous Computing (Ubicomp)*. Atlanta, GA: UbiComp.

Tang, L., Zhou, X., Yu, Z., Liang, Y., Zhang, D., & Ni, H. (2011). MHS: A multimedia system for improving medication adherence in elderly care. *IEEE System Journal, 5*(4), 506–517. doi:10.1109/JSYST.2011.2165593.

Wang, X., Rosenblum, D., & Wang, Y. (2012). Context-aware mobile music recommendation for daily activities. In *Proceedings of the 20th ACM International Conference on Multimedia (MM)*. Nara, Japan: ACM.

Wang, Y., Lin, J., Annavaram, M., Jacobson, Q. A., Hong, J., Krishnamachari, B., & Sadeh, N. (2009). A framework of energy efficient mobile sensing for automatic user state recognition. In *Proceedings of 7th International Conference on Mobile Systems, Applications, and Services (MobiSys)*. Kraków, Poland: ACM.

Ward, J. A., Lukowicz, P., Gerhard, T., & Starner, T. E. (2006). Activity recognition of assembly tasks using body-worn microphones and accelerometers. *IEEE Transactions on Pattern Analysis and Machine Intelligence, 28*, 1553–1566. doi:10.1109/TPAMI.2006.197 PMID:16986539.

Yang, J., Lee, J., & Choi, J. (2011). Activity recognition based on RFID object usage for smart mobile devices. *Journal of Computer Science and Technology, 26*, 239–246. doi:10.1007/s11390-011-9430-9.

Yatani, K., & Truong, K. N. (2012). BodyScope: A wearable acoustic sensor for activity recognition. In *Proceedings of the ACM Conference on Ubiquitous Computing (Ubicomp)*. Pittsburgh, PA: ACM.

Yilmaz, A., Javed, O., & Shah, M. (2006). Object tracking: A survey. *ACM Computing Surveys, 38*(4). doi:10.1145/1177352.1177355.

Yu, Z., & Nakamura, Y. (2010). Smart meeting systems: A survey of state-of-the-art and open issues. *ACM Computing Surveys, 42*(2). doi:10.1145/1667062.1667065.

Yu, Z., Yu, Z., Aoyama, H., Ozeki, M., & Nakamura, Y. (2010). Capture, recognition, and visualization of human semantic interactions in meetings. In *Proceedings of Pervasive Computing and Communications (Percom)*. Mannheim, Germany: Percom. doi:10.1109/PERCOM.2010.5466987.

Yu, Z., Yu, Z., Zhou, X., Becker, C., & Nakamura, Y. (2012). Tree-based mining for discovering patterns of human interaction in meetings. *IEEE Transactions on Knowledge and Data Engineering, 24*(4), 759–768. doi:10.1109/TKDE.2010.224.

Yu, Z., Zhou, X., Yu, Z., Park, J. H., & Ma, J. (2008). iMuseum: A scalable context-aware intelligent museum system. *Computer Communications, 31*(18), 4376–4382. doi:10.1016/j.comcom.2008.05.004.

Yu, Z., Zhou, X., Zhang, D., Chin, C., Wang, X., & Men, J. (2006). Supporting context-aware media recommendations for smart phones. *IEEE Pervasive Computing / IEEE Computer Society [and] IEEE Communications Society, 5*(3), 68–75. doi:10.1109/MPRV.2006.61.

Zappi, P., Lombriser, C., Stiefmeier, T., Farella, E., Roggen, D., Benini, L., & Troster, G. (2008). Activity recognition from on-body sensors: Accuracy-power trade-off by dynamic sensor selection. In *Proceedings of 5ᵗʰ European Conference on Wireless Sensor Networks (EWSN)*. Bologna, Italy: EWSN.

Zappi, P., Stiefmeier, T., Farella, E., Roggen, D., Benini, L., & Troster, G. (2007). Activity recognition from on-body sensors by classifier fusion: Sensor scalability and robustness. In *Proceedings of the 3ʳᵈ International Conference on Intelligent Sensors, Sensor Networks and Information (ISSNIP)*. Melbourne, Australia: ISSNIP.

Zhang, D., Guo, B., & Yu, Z. (2011). The emergence of social and community intelligence. *IEEE Computer*, 44(7), 21–28. doi:10.1109/MC.2011.65.

Zhou, S., Chu, C., Yu, Z., & Kim, J. (2012). A context-aware reminder system for elders based on fuzzy linguistic approach. *Expert Systems with Applications*, 39(1), 9411–9419. doi:10.1016/j.eswa.2012.02.124.

KEY TERMS AND DEFINITIONS

Accelerometer: A device that measures proper acceleration.

Activity Recognition: Aims to recognize the actions and goals of one or more agents from a series of observations on the agents' actions and the environmental conditions.

Pervasive Computing: A brand-new model of human-computer interaction in which information processing has been thoroughly integrated into everyday objects and activities. More formally, pervasive computing is defined as "machines that fit the human environment instead of forcing humans to enter theirs."

Semantic Reasoning: To infer logical consequences from a set of asserted facts or axioms. The notion of a semantic reasoner generalizes that of an inference engine, by providing a richer set of mechanisms to work with. The inference rules are commonly specified by means of an ontology language, and often a description language. Many reasoners use first-order predicate logic to perform reasoning; inference commonly proceeds by forward chaining and backward chaining.

Smart Phone: The cell phones integrated with various sensors and programmable.

Ubiquitous Sensing: The capability of capturing a huge amount of information from the environment through many kinds of embedded devices, and sending them to a processing unit able to build a representation of the context that would catch all elements necessary for the specific application.

Wearable Computing: Different from the conventional mobile systems the interaction is based on a modified version of a desktop human computer interface (HCI), wearable computing is a new model of human computer interface, which is human-centric. There are six attributes of wearable computing. (1) Unmonopolizing of the user's attention: it does not cut you off from the outside world like a virtual reality game or the like. (2) Unrestrictive to the user; (3) Observable by the user; (4) Controllable by the user; (5) Attentive to the environment; (6) Communicative to others.

Chapter 3
Opportunistic Detection Methods for Emotion-Aware Smartphone Applications

Igor Bisio
University of Genoa, Italy

Fabio Lavagetto
University of Genoa, Italy

Alessandro Delfino
University of Genoa, Italy

Mario Marchese
University of Genoa, Italy

ABSTRACT

Human-machine interaction is performed by devices such as the keyboard, the touch-screen, or speech-to-text applications. For example, a speech-to-text application is software that allows the device to translate the spoken words into text. These tools translate explicit messages but ignore implicit messages, such as the emotional status of the speaker, filtering out a portion of information available in the interaction process. This chapter focuses on emotion detection. An emotion-aware device can also interact more personally with its owner and react appropriately according to the user's mood, making the user-machine interaction less stressful. The chapter gives the guidelines for building emotion-aware smartphone applications in an opportunistic way (i.e., without the user's collaboration). In general, smartphone applications might be employed in different contexts; therefore, the to-be-detected emotions might be different.

INTRODUCTION

In recent years the computational capabilities of mobile devices, such as smartphones, has exponentially increased, giving the possibility of a more personal human-machine interaction. Moreover, smart portable devices, such as smartphones, can collect a lot of data from the surrounding environment opportunistically, i.e. without needing any collaborative behavior by the user, and exploit the so obtained information to adapt its behavior to the context, enabling the development of the

DOI: 10.4018/978-1-4666-4695-7.ch003

so-called Context-Aware applications. The fastest and most personal method of interaction is the speech, furthermore, the speech is a signal that the smartphone can exploit opportunistically. Through the speech the mobile device can identify the speaker, its gender and, if there is more than one speaker, the number of the speakers (Agneessens, Bisio, Lavagetto, Marchese, & Sciarrone, 2010). Currently human-machine interaction is performed by devices such as the keyboard, mouse, the touch-screen and, especially in new generation smartphones, by speech to text applications, software which allow the device to translate the spoken words into text. These kinds of tools translate explicit messages but ignore implicit messages, such as the emotional status of the user, filtering out a portion of information available in the interaction process. Automatic emotion detection can be used in a wide range of applications. In teleconferences adding an explicit reference of the emotional state of the speaker can add useful information that can be lost due to the reduced naturalism of the medium. An emotion aware device can also interact more personally with its owner and react appropriately according to the user mood, making the user-machine interaction less stressful. For example, it has been proven (Burkhardt, 2005) that often users get frustrated by talking to machines and hang up without having the possibility to express their anger in some way, an emotion aware system can recognize user's mood and handle this problem. The smart device can also automatically adapt a playlist in order to play the better suited song for the particular mood detected in the user (Sandor Dornbush, 2005). In life-simulation videogames,

where the user have to control one or more virtual lifeforms the experience can be enhanced with an automatic emotion sensitive system capable to detect the emotional state of the player.

During the next years, several experts predict a significant growth in the market for converged mobile devices that simultaneously include voice-phone function with multimedia, PDA and game applications. These devices will allow expanding the current market by adding new types of consumers. In facts, they will employ these devices for activities very different with respect to classical mobile phone calls. This new trend will drive both Original Equipment Manufacturers (OEMs) and Carriers to meet this growth by providing smart devices and new services for the new class of users.

In more detail, in 2003 converged mobile devices, also termed smartphones, were forecast to make up three percent of worldwide mobile phone sales volume. Nowadays, the smartphone market is continuing to expand at triple digit year-over-year growth rates, due to the evolution of voice-centric converged mobile devices, mobile phones with applications processors and advanced operating systems supporting a new range of data functions, including application download and execution.

In practice, smartphones will play a crucial role to support the users' activities both from the professional and private viewpoint.

Operatively, the emotion recognition is a statistical pattern classification problem; a general speech emotion recognition procedure is shown by the flowchart in Figure 1. The speech is recorded by the microphone of the smartphone and the raw audio data is passed to the Feature Extraction block. Feature extraction consists in simplifying

Figure 1. Scheme of a general emotion recognition procedure

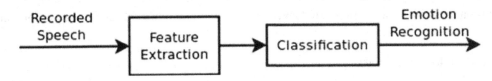

the amount of resources required to describe a large set of data accurately. In the classification stage machine learning methods are applied on the selected speech feature to recognize the emotional states in the speech.

Speech emotion detection has some limitations, one of the most important is the lack of emotional speech database. There are only few public databases containing emotion examples and each of them is made of only one or, in some sporadic cases, two languages. Emotion is strongly multimodal, emotions can be expressed through various different channels. Some emotions, like, for example, the disgust, can be easily detected from the facial expressions while they are very difficult to detect from the voice.

Smartphones

From the hardware viewpoint, the first generation of analog cell phones was composed of devices consisted of a discrete single CISC-based microcontroller (MCU) core. Its task concerned the control of several analog circuits. The migration from analog to digital technology created the necessity of Digital Signal Processor (DSP) core.

In facts, recent architectures include it, creating a Dual-core system consisting of an MCU and a DSP, which are currently integrated in a single ASIC. Actually, the aforementioned dual-core architectures did not support the feature requirements of converged devices because they were designed only to support communications tasks. As a result, today's smartphone architecture requires additional processing resources. Currently, a discrete application processor is included in the architecture together with the discrete dual-core cellular baseband integrated circuit. All processors require their own memory system including RAM and ROM, which complete the computation architecture of a smartphone.

Together with the above described architecture, recent mobile device include wireless networking interfaces, such as Wi-Fi and Bluetooth technol-

ogy. Each added communication interface, in several cases very useful also to provide Context-Aware services, requires additional modules for each function, including radio transceivers, digital base-bands, RAM and ROM components within the module.

In practice, modern smartphones are system architectures having a minimum of three, or as many as six, processors, each with its own dedicated memory system, peripherals, clock generator, reset circuit, interrupt controller, debug support and inter-processor communications software. Obviously, all the architecture needs of a power supply system.

A logical scheme of the described smartphone architecture is reported in Figure 2.

Concerning the software, the Cellular Baseband block reported in Figure 2, typically divides its tasks in the same way, in particular the DSP performs signaling tasks and serving as a slave processor to the MCU, which runs the upper layers (L2/L3) functions of the communication protocol stack.

On one hand, the Layer 1 signal processing tasks, handled by the DSP, include equalization, demodulation, channel coding/decoding, voice codec, echo and noise cancellation. On the other hand, the MCU manages the radio hardware and moreover realizes the upper layers functions of the network protocol stack, subscriber identity, user interface, battery management and the nonvolatile memory for storage for the phone book.

The Application Processor block, equipped by an MCU, manages the User Interface and all the applications running on a smartphone.

In this Hardware/Software architecture, it is worth noticing that performance conflict between the communication protocol tasks and multimedia workloads may have performance conflicts because they share the smartphone resource. In more detail, this problem, only mentioned because out of the scope of the chapter, requires a sophisticated internetworking approach and, in particular, advanced inter-processor communica-

Figure 2. Logical scheme of smartphones' hardware architecture from (Bisio, 2011)

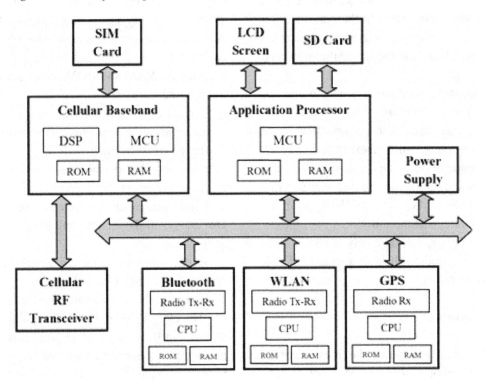

tions approaches aimed at increasing processing availability and at reducing overheads, and power consumption, which results in reduced battery life and usage time for the end user.

A possible low-cost solution to solve such problem may be to merge the Application Processor and the Cellular Baseband blocks into a single ASIC consisting of two or three cores. This approach eliminates the performance conflict between the communication protocol and multimedia tasks but the complexity of the inter-processor communication is not reduced, significantly.

In the recent few years, mobile network providers and users will have the new opportunity to come up with more advanced and innovative context-aware services based on the real-time knowledge of the user's surroundings. In facts, context data must be acquired from the smartphone's audio environment. In general, the classification of an audio environment or the correspondence between two or more audio contexts and the number and

the gender of active speakers near the smartphone together with other possible context features, can be useful information employed to obtain helpful contents and services directly by the mobile users' devices.

Description of Emotions

Human beings and animals have to deal with emotions in everyday life. People often use expressions like "I'm happy!", "It's sad but true" or "I love you" in order to express a sensation that is generally called "emotion". Every one of us knows the great impact that a statement such as those reported may have on our interpersonal relations or social life. Our emotional state often affects our way of approaching people and, more generally, animals or things. Furthermore, the externalization of this interior state can change the way in which other people approach to us. In addiction, is well known that "emotions" have great influence on our actions and opinions. For example, a scared person rarely is able to control itself in front of a danger or a threat. Despite its socio-cultural importance, the concept of "emotion" represents a particularly thorny problem. Even though the term is used very frequently, the question "What is an emotion?" rarely generates the same answer from different individuals, scientists or laymen alike. One of the most challenging issues of emotion detection is the description of what an emotion is and how it can be classified. Since the emotional state of a person is highly subjective, it is operatively very difficult to find an objective and universal definition of "emotion". The emotion classification problem was scientifically addressed for the first time by Descartes in the treatise Passions of the Soul in 1649. In this work Descartes defines six basic emotions called "primitive passions": wonder, love, hatred, desire, joy and sadness. Along with these primary emotions Descartes also accepts "an unlimited number" of further, specific passions, called secondary passions, which are combinations of the six primitive passions in different proportions. The secondary emotions are blend of the innate basic emotions much in the way that different colors can be created by mixing red, blue and green, for this reason this classification is known as palette theory. This kind of classification was also adopted in the 19th century when Charles Darwin's (Darwin, 1872) and William James' (James, 1884) theories of emotions have been proposed. Darwin, in his work, highlights the universal nature of expressions: "...the young and the old of widely different races, both with man and animals, express the same state of mind by the same movements". On this assumption Darwin classifies the emotions that are innate and can be recognized in each human culture population, and calls them "basic". Six basic emotions are distinguished: happiness, surprise, fear, disgust, anger and sadness. This type of classification had been widely used by the scientists, Ekman in 1972 (Ekman P., 1971) codified six basic or primary emotions in facial expressions: anger, disgust,

fear, happiness, sadness and surprise. A similar widely accepted classification is the one provided by Plutchik (Plutchik, 2001). He defines 8 basic emotions and provides a graphic representation of them, which is the wheel shown in Figure 3.

The emotions defined by Plutchik are: anger, anticipation, joy, trust, fear, surprise, sadness and disgust. Plutchik's wheel representation is formed by 4 couple of bipolar emotions, joy is opposed to sadness, anger to fear, anticipation to surprise and disgust to trust.

A tree-structured list was proposed by Parrot in 2001 (Parrott, 2001), where the first level is composed by six primary emotions (love, joy, surprise, anger, sadness, fear). The first two layers of Parrot's classification are shown in Figure 4. This classification differs from the others previously described because the secondary emotions are derivation of the primary ones instead of being combination of them.

Some scientists refused to engage this irresolvable dispute on the number and type of emotions, producing an alternative to the categorical classification: the dimensional classification, a more flexible solution to the problem of the representation of the emotional states. These dimensions include evaluation, activation, control, power, etc. In particular a 2-D representation of emotions called activation-evaluation space (Cowie, et al., 2001) has a long history in psychology, Figure 5. Research from Darwin forward has recognized that emotional states involve dispositions to act in certain ways. A basic way of reflecting that theme turns out to be surprisingly useful. States are simply rated in terms of the associated activation level, i.e., the strength of the person's disposition to take some action rather than none. The axes of activation-evaluation space reflect those themes. The vertical axis shows activation level and the horizontal axis evaluation.

The most recent classification merges the categorical and the dimensional classification: the cube representation proposed by Hugo Lövheim (2011) (Lövheim, 2012). In this repre-

Figure 3. Plutchik's Wheel of Emotions

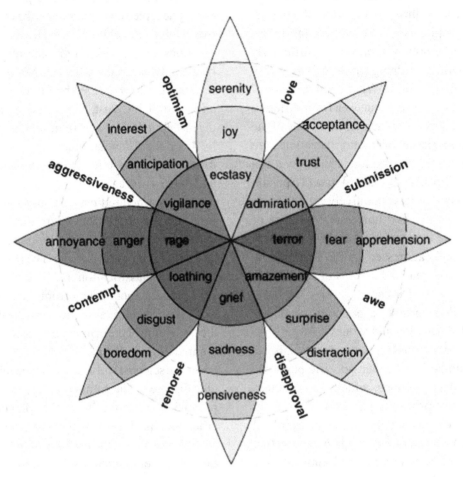

sentation eight basic emotions are ordered in an orthogonal coordinate system of the three main monoaminergic axes. The axes represent serotonin (5-HT, 5-hydroxytryptamine), dopamine (DA) and noradrenaline (NE), and each end of the arrows represents low and high levels of signaling respectively. Serotonin, noradrenaline and dopamine are the most important monoamine neurotransmitters. Many studies from different research fields support the belief that all three of the monoamines, serotonin, dopamine and noradrenaline are essential in the control of behaviors and emotions, and each of them is involved in a different behavior or emotion. The serotonin axis seems to represent aspects such as self-confidence, inner strength and satisfaction. The dopamine axis

has been found to be involved in reward, motivation and reinforcement. Noradrenaline has been coupled to the fight or flight response and to stress and anxiety, and appears to represent an axis of activation, vigilance and attention. From this the 3-D representation shown in Figure 8 is derived. The basic emotions which label the axis are derived by Tomkins affect theory (Tomkins, 1962).

Speech Emotions

Speech carries two different kind of emotion information: one refers to what is said and it is the task of recognizing the emotion from the explicit message of the speech, the second is the implicit message and it consists on how it is said and it

Figure 4. First two layers of Parrot's emotion classification

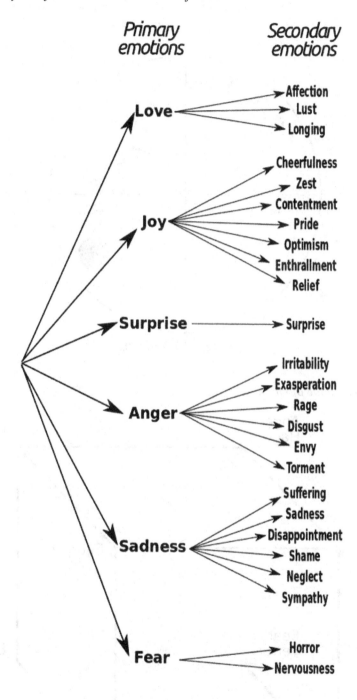

is the task of detecting the emotion by the pitch, the intonation and the prosody of the speaker. The emotion recognition from explicit part of the speech can be brought back to a text-based emotion detection problem (Kao, Liu, Yang, Hsieh, & Soo, 2009) applying speech to text algorithms. Problems of recognizing emotions in text can be divided in three categories: 1) Keyword-based detection: the emotions are detected by the presence of some keywords in the input text; 2) Learning-

Figure 5. Activation-evaluation space

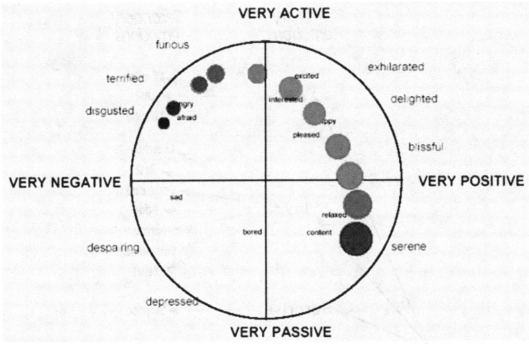

Figure 6. Hugo Lövheim cube of emotions

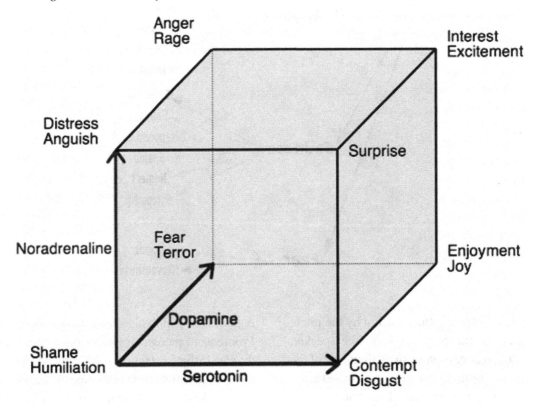

based detection: emotions are detected based on previous training results which permit to collect specific statistic through learning methods; 3) Hybrid detection: emotions are detected exploiting the combination of detected keywords, learned patterns, and other supplementary information.

Keyword-based emotion detection serves as the starting point of textual emotion recognition. Once the set of emotion labels (and related words) is constructed, it can be used exhaustively to examine if a sentence contains any emotions. This type of emotion detection has the pro that it is very straightforward and easy to use but it has some limitations: the definition of the keywords meaning can be ambiguous, the same word could change its meaning according to different usage and context; a keyword-based detector can not recognize sentences which do not contain keywords. This kind of approach is totally based on the set of emotion keywords. Therefore, sentences without any keyword would imply they do not contain any emotions at all; another limitation is that the keyword-based approach does not take into account of linguistic information.

Learning-based approach consists in classifying the input texts into different emotions using a previously trained classifier. This approach has some limitations, though learning-based methods can automatically determine the probabilities between features and emotions, learning-based methods still need keywords, but just in the form of features. The cascading problems would be the same as those in keyword-based methods. Moreover, most learning-based detector can classify sentences into two classes, positive and negative.

Since keyword-based methods and naive learning-based methods could not acquire satisfactory results, some systems use a hybrid approach by combining both or adding different components, which help to improve accuracy and refine the categories. Semantics and attributes are extracted from the text and then associated to the emotions. These emotion association rules replace the keywords as features in the learning-based methods.

However, the most challenging part is the detection of the implicit message of the speech, the emotions that the speaker expresses using prosody, intonation, pitch, etc., following sessions focus on it.

Emotional Databases

The main problem in emotion detection is that there is not a unique commonly recognized database but many different databases. As previously said, the definition of emotions is not unique, therefore the number and type of emotions labeled for each database differs. Works of emotion detection have been proposed by researchers from all over the world, producing databases composed by speakers of different languages (Ververidis, 2003). Database containing emotion-labeled utterances in English and German languages are the most common but there are also databases composed by Spanish, Japanese, Dutch, French, Hebrew, Sweden, Danish, Slovenian, Chinese and Russian utterances. Another important difference among the database is the way the emotions are collected: the emotions can be natural or simulated. Database of spontaneous emotions are rare because authentic affective expressions are difficult to collect and, also, labeling them is not a trivial operation. Database of acted emotions are the most common, they can be composed in two ways: cutting particularly emotional movies' parts or directly recording an actor simulating a certain emotion. Since the way to express the emotions varies from an individual to another, the databases are composed by many speakers' utterances. For the same reason emotional speech databases usually contain both genders recordings.

For choosing an existing database or for developing a new one is necessary to consider four main issues (E. Douglas-Cowie, 2003): scope, naturalness, context and used descriptors.

Scope includes several kind of elements like notably number of different speakers, spoken language, type of dialect (e.g. standard or vernacular), gender of speakers, considered types of emotional state, tokens of a given state, social/functional setting. These kinds of variation are potentially important for any attempt to generalize, and their importance depends on research goals. There do seem to be facial signs of emotion that are effectively universal (P. Ekman, 1994), and there are reasons to expect that the same is true of at least some vocal signs (Stevens, Emotions and speech: Some acoustical correlates, 1972). A recent review of the literature (Cowie, et al., 2001) shows that although some features are remarkably consistent across studies, others are quite variable. Gender is recognized as a key socio-linguistic variable (Trudgill, 1983). Hence, considering the importance of gender-dependency in the emotion recognition, several studies use two different databases: one containing only the sentences recorded by males, and the other containing only the sentences recorded by females (J. Rong, 2009). Some studies used also a third database containing only the sentences recorded by children. The same is true for social setting, i.e. the relationship that governs interaction between speaker and listener. These observations suggest that the emotional scope of databases needs to be thought through carefully. Since standard lists contain more than a hundred words for (non-basic) emotions (Cowie, et al., 2001), the scope may have to be very large. It is presumably possible to work with a smaller number of 'landmark' states and interpolate, but establishing a set of landmarks that is appropriate for speech research is an empirical task, which itself depends on access to data that spans the known range of emotional states. The number of subjects studied has tended to be small, so that it is difficult to gauge the extent of inter-subject variability. The possibility of gender effects compounds the problem. It is also difficult to gauge how many of the relationships that the literature describes may be specific to single relatively homogeneous cultural milieu.

Naturalness refers to the way the utterances are collected, sentences can be natural, simulated or acted, and elicited or induced. Natural expressions are spontaneous sentences collected from a real-world situation where users are not under obvious observation and are free to express emotions naturally, as they would in an everyday situation. Simulated expressions are sentences expressed by professional or non-professional actors and actresses. Elicited expressions are sentences in which naive users are presented with scenarios that induce the required emotional response. Acted speech from professionals is the most reliable for emotional speech recognition because professionals can deliver speech colored by emotions that possess a high arousal, i.e. emotions with a great amplitude or strength. It is empirically apparent that acted emotions are quite different from natural emotions as they measure significantly differently on the use of various analytical tools (as well as by human judgment). Moreover authentic affective expressions are difficult to collect because they are relatively rare and short lived. The easiest way to collect emotional speech is then to have actors simulate it. The difficulty with that approach is that strikingly little is known about the relationship between acted data and spontaneous, everyday emotional speech. Increasing evidence suggests that deliberate behavior differs in visual appearance, audio profile, and timing from spontaneously occurring behavior (Z. Zeng, 2009). For example, Whissell (Whissel, 1989) shows that the posed nature of emotions in spoken language may differ in the choice of words and timing from corresponding performances in natural settings. There are many reasons to suspect that there are systematic differences between acted and natural emotional speech. Acted speech is often 'read', not spoken, and read speech is well known to have distinctive characteristics (Johns-Lewis, 1986). Neither the words nor the phrasing are typically chosen to simulate emotional speech. The typical form is a non-interactive monologue, and so interpersonal effects are not represented. It would therefore be unsurprising if attempts to express emotion under these very atypical circumstances had very atypical features. The price of naturalness is lack of control. Emotion has an unpredictability that makes it difficult to collect samples of people in a target state, whether it is induced or spontaneous. Particularly if it is spontaneous, identifying the emotion that is being expressed becomes a substantial issue. A long-term solution to these problems may well be 'bootstrapping', i.e. using truly natural material to guide the production of material that is acted, but genuinely close to nature, as used in (S. Abdennadher, 2007). Research has relied relatively heavily on material that is acted and involves read, non-interactive material. However, there are also datasets that include fully natural speech in emotion-related states. A considerable proportion of the work involves intermediate strategies, i.e. use actors to read material that lends itself to the required emotion. The studies that use data with elicited emotion making recordings while the subject faces a machine, e.g. during telephone calls to Automatic Speech Recognition (ASR) call centres (C. M. Lee and S. S. Narayanan, 2005), or when the subjects are talking to fake-ASR machines, which are operated by a human (Wizard-Of-OZ method, WOZ) (Fischer, 1999). Giving commands to a robot is another idea explored (A. Batliner, 2004). Speech can be also recorded during imposed stressed situations. For example when the subject adds numbers while driving a car at various speeds (R. Fernandez and R. Picard, 2003), or when the subject reads distant car plates on a big computer screen (Hansen H. J., 1999). In the video kiosk settings (A. J. O'Toole et al., 2005)(Bartlett, 2007) (N. Sebe, 2004) the subjects' affective reactions are recorded while the subjects are watching emotion-inducing videos. The data with natural emotion can be instead recorded from radio or television (C. Clavel, 2004)(B. Schuller, 2005), or from human-human conversation scenarios include face-to-face interviews (M. S. Bartlett, 2005)(E. Douglas-Cowie, 2003)(J. Hirschberg, 2005) (G. I. Roisman, 2004), phone conversations (Vasilescu, Reliability of Lexical and Prosodic Cues in Two

Real-Life Spoken Dialog Corpora, 2004), and meetings (S. Burger, 2002). Furthermore, speech from real life situations such as oral interviews of employees when they are examined for promotion can be also used (Hansen M. R., 2002). Parents talking to infants, when they try to keep them away from dangerous objects can be another real life example (McRoberts, 2003). Interviews between a doctor and a patient before and after medication were used in (D. J. France, 2000).

Context is important for listeners because they use it to determine the emotional significance of vocal features (Cauldwell, 2000)(D. R. Ladd, 1986). Hence if research aims to understand human performance, or to match it, it needs databases that contain evidence on the way vocal signs relate to their context. Emotion is strongly multimodal in the sense that signs may appear in various different channels. However, not all types of sign tend to be available together, because context will affect the signs that are relevant or accessible. Four broad types of context can be distinguished: semantic context (emotionally marked and significant words), structural context (structural characteristics of the utterances like long or short phrases, repetitions, and interruptions), intermodal context (data from other sources in addition to the speech), temporal context (emotion ebbs and flows that speech involves over time). Much of the existing material is singularly devoid of context: purely audio recordings of short utterances with neutral semantic content and a preset linguistic structure. However, several projects have addressed context-related issues directly or indirectly, and they help to highlight significant issues. The issue of temporal context is not often considered explicitly, but the way naturalistic studies select units for coding implies intuitions about the patterns that need to be considered.

Constructing a database requires techniques for describing the linguistic and emotional content on one hand, and the speech on the other. The requirements for accurate labelling of emotional content may interact with naturalness. In terms of speech descriptors, two issues stand out. First, coding needs to acknowledge the full range of features involved in the vocal expression of emotion, including at least voice quality, prosody and non-linguistic features such as laughter, crying, etc. Second, it needs to describe the attributes that are relevant to emotion. As previously said, three main types of scheme could reasonably be used to describe the emotional content of a database: categorical, continuous, and appraisal-based. Categorical schemes involve assigning terms like anger, happiness, fear, and so on (O'Toole, 2005)(Piccardi, 2006)(A. Batliner, 2004) (G. I. Roisman, 2004), or only two labels (e.g. Positive, Negative) depending on the future application (Devillers, 2005)(S. Burger, 2002)(C. M. Lee and S. S. Narayanan, 2005). Numerous teams have tried to label relatively naturalistic material using schemes based on established psychological lists of emotions. It seems fair to say that the most used option is to consider a relatively small set of 'basic' emotions. It reflects the popular theory that a few universal types of emotions underlie all the emotions that a person can feel every day. A more radical alternative is to use the long-established psychological concept of emotion dimensions (E. Douglas-Cowie, 2003). Statistically, most of the information contained in verbal labelling can be expressed in terms of two dimensions, activation and evaluation. A finer theoretical tool comes from appraisal theory, which offers a descriptive framework for emotion based on the way the person involved experiences the events, things, or people at the focus of the emotional state. The relative merits of the three types remain to be resolved. Speech descriptors vary enormously with different studies. As a result, it is difficult to form a cohesive summary of the dimensions on which speech varies.

FEATURE EXTRACTION

Due to the physiology of the human vocal tract, human speech is highly redundant and possesses several speaker-dependent parameters, such as pitch, speaking rate and accent. An important issue in the design of a speech emotion recognition system is the extraction of suitable features that efficiently characterize different emotions. Although there is plenty of works on automatic speech emotion detection (Moataz El Ayadi, 2011), there is not a feature believed to be the best for this aim. The speech signal is not stationary, it is very common to divide the signal in short segments called frames, within which the speech signal can be considered as stationary. The speech process can be considered stationary for intervals of 10-20ms. If a feature is calculated on each frame is called local, otherwise, if it is calculated on the entire utterance is named global. There is not agreement between researchers on which of local and global features are more suitable for speech emotion recognition. Speech features can be grouped into four categories: i) continuous features, ii) qualitative features, iii) spectral features, iv) Teager Energy Operator (TEO) based features. Among continuous features can be distinguished pitch-related, formants, energy-related, timing and articulation features. Qualitative features are global features and are related to the quality of the speaker's voice, these features can be grouped in four sub-categories: voice level; voice pitch; phase, phoneme, word and feature boundaries; temporal structures. Spectral feature can be global or local and they can be extracted by Linear Predictor Coefficients (LPC), One-Sided Autocorrelation Linear Predictor Coefficients (OSALPC), Mel-frequency Cepstrum coefficients (MFCC). TEO is a nonlinear operator originally developed with the supporting evidence that hearing is the process of detecting energy. TEO based features are local feature that are proven to have good performances when the aim is to detect high energy emotions such as angry.

Continuous Features

Most researchers believe that prosody continuous features such as pitch and energy convey much of the emotional content of an utterance. Much information about the emotional state of the speaker can be inferred through the tone of his voice or its volume.

Pitch-Based Features

Speech consists of pressure waves created by the airflow through the vocal tract. The vocal folds in the larynx can open and close quasi-periodically, the result is that the voiced speech is quasi-periodic. This relative periodicity is often referred to as pitch. Strictly speaking the term pitch refers to the tone perceived by auditory. The fundamental frequency (F_0) of a periodic signal is defined as the reciprocal of its period and is well correlated with the perceived pitch. The F_0 contour (i.e., the temporal evolution of the pitch inside one utterance (J. Ang, 2002)) has been shown to vary depending on the emotional state being expressed. Cowan (Cowan, 2006) discovered that neutral or unemotional speech has a much narrower F0 range than that of emotional speech, and found that as the emotional intensity is increased, the frequency and duration of pauses and stops normally found during neutral speech are decreased inducing alteration on the pitch (Arnott, 1993). More specifically, angry speech typically has a high median, wide range, wide mean inflection range, and a high rate of change (Pronovost, An experimental study of the pitch characteristics of the voice during the expression of emotion, 1939). Nogueiras et al. (A. Nogueiras, 2001)sustain that the pitch has information about emotion, because it depends on the tension of the vocal folds and the sub glottal air pressure. The glottal volume velocity denotes the air velocity through glottis during the vocal fold vibration. High velocity indicates speech like joy or surprise. Fear was discovered to have a high pitch median, wide range, medium inflection range (E. Douglas-Cowie, 2003) (Pronovost, An experimental study of the pitch characteristics of the voice during the expression of emotion, 1939) (Stevens, Emotions and speech: Some acoustical

correlates, 1972), and increased pitch level is also apparent (Fonagy, A new method of investigating the perception of prosodic features, 1978). Conversely to fear exhibiting a wide range, there are reports that fear instead has a narrow F0 range (Magdics, Emotional patterns in intonation and music, 1963) and low speech rate (E. Douglas-Cowie, 2003). Contrasting these more excited emotions are sadness and disgust which typically have lower physiological activation levels. Sadness is shown to yield lower pitch mean and narrow range (Skinner, 1935)(Davitz, Personality, perceptual, and cognitive correlates of emotional sensitivity, 1964.)(Fonagy, Emotions, voice and music, 1981)(W. F. Johnson, 1986). More recently, Pereira has report that there are cases where there is no change in these features (Pereira, 2000,). Other studies have shown that pitch frequency also affects the number of harmonics in the spectrum. Less harmonics are produced when the pitch frequency is high. More harmonics are expected when the pitch frequency is low. It seems that the harmonics from the additional excitation signals due to vortices are more intense than those caused by the pitch signal (D. Cairns, 1994). Williams and Stevens (Stevens, Emotions and speech: Some acoustical correlates, 1972) discovered vowels of angry speech to have the highest F0. Fonagy (Fonagy, A new method of investigating the perception of prosodic features, 1978) found that angry speech exhibits a sudden rise of F0 in stressed syllables and the F0 contour has an "angular" curve. Frick (Frick, 1986) postulated that frustration, which has similar but less extreme physiological causes as anger, has a higher fundamental frequency than neutral speech. Scherer (Scherer K. R., Adding the affective dimension: a new look in speech analysis and synthesis, 1996) describes anger as having "an increase in mean pitch and mean intensity". Downward slopes are also noted on the F0 contour. In a number of studies, Scherer and his collaborators have made use of speech re-synthesis to systematically manipulate F0 level, contour variability and range, intensity, duration, and accent structure of real utterances. They discovered narrow F0 range signaling sadness and wide F0 range being judged as expressing high arousal, negative emotions such as annoyance or anger. Breazeal and Aryananda (Aryananda, 2002) found that prohibitions or warnings directed at infants are spoken with low pitch and high intensity in "staccato pitch contours". Cowan (Cowan, 2006) and Fonagy and Magdics (Magdics, Emotional patterns in intonation and music, 1963) found that happiness expressed in specch, like anger, has an increased pitch mean and pitch range. Additionally, studies of disgust report both an increase in mean F0 and a decrease in mean F0 (E. Douglas-Cowie, 2003).

Many values related to F_0 variations have been used for emotion recognition, as shown in Table 1.

There is a wide variety of algorithms for F_0 estimation, basically divided in two families: time-domain algorithms, which operate directly on the speech audio samples, and frequency-domain algorithms, which operate on the spectrum of the speech signal. Fundamental frequency estimators are strongly context-specific, algorithms that work efficiently with music may have poor performance with speech and vice-versa.

There are many ways to estimate the fundamental frequency of a signal, with different complexity and accuracy (Gerhard, 2003). Below a summary of F_0 detectors is presented.

Time-Event Detection

The idea behind time-event detectors is that, if the signal is periodic, there are some kinds of periodic events that can be counted. The frequency of these events in a second is an estimation of the fundamental frequency.

The simplest event to count is when the waveform crosses the zero line. This measure is called Zero-Crossing Rate (ZCR). ZCR is very easy to implement and has a very low computational complexity but has some evident limitations: if the spectral power of the signal is concentrated around its fundamental frequency the waveform crosses the zero line twice per period, but if higher spectral frequencies are present there may be more than two zero-crossing per cycle, leading, therefore, to a wrong F_0 estimation.

Another time-event based way to estimate the fundamental frequency is counting the number of positive (or negative) peaks of the waveform per second. The theory behind this detector is that the waveform has one maximum (or minimum) value each cycle, counting the rate of these values will determine F_0. This approach has the same limitations of the ZCR, it is possible that a waveform can have more than a local maximum per cycle, especially when the spectral power is not concentrated around its fundamental frequency.

If a waveform is periodic also its slope is periodic, sometimes ZCR and peak rate are more informative if counted on the waveform slope or their calculation may be more robust.

Time-event rate methods present some positive aspects: they are easy to understand and to implement and, crucial for their application on mobile devices, their complexity is very low, so requiring very low power consumption. The main limitation of these algorithms is their weakness. A waveform can have more than one zero-crossing or peak per cycle misleading this algorithm to a wrong F_0 estimation. If the nature of the signal is known these methods can be tailored in order to be more robust, for example, inserting a low pass filter before the estimator in order to cut off the unwanted harmonics.

Autocorrelation

The cross-correlation is a measure of similarity between two functions. The similarity is measured for each time shift between the beginnings of the two waveforms. The autocorrelation of a sequence $x(n)$ is a measure of similarity between a function and its all possible delayed replicas (1).

Table 1.

Feature	Papers
F0 mean	*(Vasilescu, Reliability of Lexical and Prosodic Cues in Two Real-Life Spoken Dialog Corpora, 2004)(Litman, 2004)(J. Ang, 2002) (F. Dellaert, 1996) (Scherer K. R., Vocal Affect Expression: A Review and a Model for Future Research, 1994)(M. Lugger, Robust estimation of voice quality parameters under real world disturbances, 2006)(Pieraccini, 2002)*
F0 maximum	*(Vasilescu, Reliability of Lexical and Prosodic Cues in Two Real-Life Spoken Dialog Corpora, 2004) (Litman, 2004) (J. Ang, 2002) (F. Dellaert, 1996) (Pieraccini, 2002)*
F0 minimum	*(Vasilescu, Reliability of Lexical and Prosodic Cues in Two Real-Life Spoken Dialog Corpora, 2004) (Litman, 2004) (J. Ang, 2002) (F. Dellaert, 1996)(Scherer T. J., 2000)(Pieraccini, 2002)*
F0 range (F0 maximum – F0 minimum)	*(Vasilescu, Reliability of Lexical and Prosodic Cues in Two Real-Life Spoken Dialog Corpora, 2004) (Izard, 1977)(F. Dellaert, 1996) (Pieraccini, 2002)*
F0 median	*(Litman, 2004) [2.110] (Pieraccini, 2002)*
F0 standard deviation	*(Litman, 2004) (J. Ang, 2002) (F. Dellaert, 1996) (M. Lugger, Robust estimation of voice quality parameters under real world disturbances, 2006) (Pieraccini, 2002)*
F0 variability	*(Scherer T. J., 2000)*
Medium Frequency Ratio (MFR)	*(J. Ang, 2002)*
Low Frequency Ratio (LFR)	*(J. Ang, 2002)*
High frequency ratio (HFR)	*(J. Ang, 2002)*
Average pitch slope	*(J. Ang, 2002)*
F0 first quartile	*(Litman, 2004) (M. Lugger, Robust estimation of voice quality parameters under real world disturbances, 2006)*
F0 third quartile	*(Litman, 2004) (M. Lugger, Robust estimation of voice quality parameters under real world disturbances, 2006)*
F0 regression coefficient	*(Litman, 2004)*
F0 slope in the voiced segments	*(Litman, 2004) (Scherer K. R., Vocal Affect Expression: A Review and a Model for Future Research, 1994)*
Maximum cross-variation of F0 between two adjoining voiced segments	*(Litman, 2004) (F. Dellaert, 1996)*
Maximum cross-variation of F0 with each voiced segment	*(Litman, 2004)*
First derivate of F0	*(Wei, 2005)*
Second derivate of F0	*(Wei, 2005)*
Amplitude variation in correspondence of F0	*(M. Lugger, Robust estimation of voice quality parameters under real world disturbances, 2006)*
Amplitude in correspondence of an integer multiple of F0	*(M. Lugger, Robust estimation of voice quality parameters under real world disturbances, 2006)*

$$R_x(k) = \sum_{n=-\infty}^{+\infty} x(n) \cdot x(n+k) \qquad (1)$$

The autocorrelation function of periodic signals has an interesting property: the autocorrelation function is itself periodic. When the time shift increases to half of the period of the signal the autocorrelation function present a minimum because the waveform is out-of-phase with its delayed replica, but after this point the autocorrelation function rises reaching a maximum as the time shift equals its period. The first peak of the autocorrelation function ($k > 0$) indicates the period of the signal and is an estimation of its fundamental frequency.

This method presents some problems when higher harmonics are present: the autocorrelation presents lower peaks in correspondence of the higher harmonic period and a higher peak at the fundamental period. It would be necessary distinguish between "high" and "low" peaks. From (1) the autocorrelation computation complexity might seem high, but it can be calculated in the frequency domain saving a lot of operations. This can be done because the cross-correlation of two functions is the convolution between the first function and the conjugate complex of the overturned second function. The convolution of two functions equals to the product of their Fourier transform. This brings the complexity of the autocorrelation computation, basically, to the Fast Fourier Transform (FFT) theoretical complexity which is:

$$O\left(\frac{N}{2}\log_2 N\right),$$

denoting with N the length of the sequence on which the FFT is performed. This makes it suitable for its implementation on smartphones.

YIN

The YIN estimator tries to solve the autocorrelation methods problem that peaks occur in correspondence with the sub-harmonics and is operatively difficult to distinguish between the sub-harmonics peaks and the fundamental frequency peak. YIN method is based on minimizing the difference between the waveform and its delayed replica instead of maximizing the product. The difference function is the following (2):

$$d_t(k) = \sum_{j=1}^{W} (x_j - x_{j+k})^2 \qquad (2)$$

In order to reduce the occurrence of sub-harmonic errors, YIN employs a cumulative mean function (3) which de-emphasizes higher-period dips in the difference function:

$$d_t'(k) = \begin{cases} 1, & k = 0 \\[2ex] \dfrac{d_t(k)}{1/k \sum_{j=1}^{k} d_t(j)}, & otherwise \end{cases} \qquad (3)$$

Other improvements in the YIN fundamental frequency estimation system include a parabolic interpolation of the local minima, which has the effect of reducing the errors when the period estimation is not a factor of the window length used.

Component Frequency Ratios

This method was first introduced by Martin Piszczalski in 1979 within a work for automatic music transcription. His system would extract the pitch of the signal (assuming that a single note was present at each point in time) and then find note boundaries, infer pitch key, and present a score. Piszczalski's original procedure began with a spectral transform and identification of the partials in the signal, using peak detection. For each pair of these partials, the algorithm finds the "smallest harmonic numbers" that would correspond to a harmonic series with these two partials in it.

Filter Based Methods

It is possible to estimate the fundamental frequency of a waveform by applying different filters with different center frequencies, and comparing their output.

A comb filter has many equally spaced pass-bands. In the case of the optimum comb filter algorithm, the locations of the pass-bands are based on the location of the first passband. For example, if the center frequency of the first passband is 10 Hz, then there will be narrow pass-bands every 10 Hz after that, up to the Shannon frequency, which usually is 8 kHz for voice signals.

Comb filter F_0 estimator is robust but it does not fit well with mobile devices needs, it is a computationally intensive algorithm.

A more recent filter-based is the method which exploits the tunable IIR filters. This method consists of a narrow user-tunable band-pass filter, which is swept across the frequency spectrum. When the filter is in line with a strong frequency partial, a maximum output will be present in the output of the filter, and the F_0 can then be read off the center frequency of the filter.

Cepstrum

Cepstral features were originally invented to distinguish between earthquakes and underground nuclear explosions but they have many applications in speech processing. The name cepstrum, which is the reversal of the first four letters of the word spectrum, was adopted by its inventors because they realized that they were performing operations in a transform domain that were more often performed in the time domain. The theory behind this method relies on the fact that the Fourier transform of a pitched signal usually has a number of regularly spaced peaks, representing the harmonic spectrum of the signal. When the log magnitude of a spectrum is taken, these peaks are reduced, their amplitude brought into a usable scale, and the result is a periodic waveform in the frequency domain, the period of which (the distance between the peaks) is related to the

fundamental frequency of the original signal. The Fourier transform of this waveform has a peak at the period of the original waveform. There is a complex cepstrum, a real cepstrum, a power cepstrum, and phase cepstrum, speech processing applications often use the power spectrum, defined as the squared magnitude of the Fourier transform of the logarithm of the squared magnitude of the Fourier transform of a signal (4):

$$C_P(q) = F\{\log(F\{f(t)\}^2)\}^2 \tag{4}$$

where $F\{\}$ denotes the Fourier transform operand.

Cepstrum features work well for speech processing because speech signals are spectrally rich and have evenly spaced partials.

Multi-Resolution

If the accuracy of a certain algorithm at a certain resolution is somewhat suspect, it is possible to confirm or deny any estimator hypothesis by using the same algorithm at a higher or lower resolution. Thus, use a bigger or smaller time window to calculate the spectrum. If a frequency peak shows up in all or most of the windows, this can be considered a confirmation of the estimator hypothesis. However, each new analysis resolution means more computational expense, which is why multi-resolution Fourier analysis is slower than a dedicated multi-resolution transform such as the discrete wavelet transform.

These methods may be useful in variable performance mobile applications because they give a settable trade-off between computational complexity and accuracy.

Neural Networks

Connectionist models, of which neural nets are an example, are self-organizing pattern matchers, providing a classification output for messy or fuzzy input. Logically, they consist of a collection of nodes, connected by links with associated weights. At each node, signals from all incoming links are summed according to the weights of these links, and if the sum satisfies a certain transfer function, an impulse is sent to other nodes through output links. In the training stage, input is presented to the network along with a suggested output, and the weights of the links are altered to produce the desired output. In the operation stage, the network is presented with input and provides output based on the weights of the connections.

Maximum Likelihood

F_0 estimation can be done exploiting the maximum likelihood algorithm. An observation O consists of a set of partials in a short-time Fourier transform representation of a sound. Each observation is assumed to have been produced by a sound with a particular fundamental frequency F_0, and each spectrum contains other information including inharmonic and non-sinusoidal partials (noise). This model is a simplification of the general sound model, assuming that a sound consists primarily of harmonic partials at integer multiples of F_0, with a minority of inharmonic partials and noise. For a set of candidate fundamental frequencies, the algorithm computes the probability (likelihood) that a given observation was generated from each F_0 in the set, and finds the maximum. The choice of the set of fundamental frequencies is important, because theoretically, the observation could originate from any F_0.

Formants Features

In the frequency domain, the location of vocal tract resonances depends upon the shape and the physical dimensions of the vocal tract. Since the resonances tend to "form" the overall spectrum, speech scientists refer to them as formants (E. Douglas-Cowie, 2003). Each formant is characterized by its center frequency and its bandwidth. Tolkmitt and Scherer found that subjects during stress or under depression do not articulate voiced sounds with the same effort as in the neutral emotional state (Scherer F. J., 1986) (D. J. France, 2000). Then, the formants can be used to discriminate the improved articulated speech from the slackened one. The formant bandwidth during slackened articulated speech is gradual, whereas the formant bandwidth during improved articulated speech is narrow with steep flanks. Neutral speech typically displays a "uniform formant structure and glottal vibration patterns", contrasting the "irregular" formant contours of fear, sadness, and anger (D. Morrison, 2007). Scherer (Scherer K. R., Vocal communication of emotion: a review of research paradigms, 2003) lists predictions of the formant frequencies along with several emotion classes. For happiness, it is noted that the F1 mean is decreased while the F1 bandwidth is increased. For anger, fear, and sadness, the F1 mean is increased while the F1 bandwidth is decreased. F2 mean is decreased for sadness, anger, fear, disgust. Williams and Stevens (Stevens, Emotions and speech: Some acoustical correlates, 1972) found that anger produced vowels "with a more open vocal tract" and from that the researchers inferred that the first formant frequency would have a greater mean than that of neutral speech. It was also noticed that the amplitudes of F2 and F3 were higher with respect to that of F1 for anger and fear compared with neutral speech. Formants are the distinguishing or meaningful frequency components of human speech and of singing and are defined as the spectral peaks of the sound spectrum $|P(f)|$. Formants are directly influenced by the shape of the individual vocal tract. The formant with the lowest frequency is called F_1, the second F_2, and the third F_3. The locations of the first two formants are sufficient to distinguish between vowels. Formants are often measured as amplitude peaks in the frequency spectrum of the speech.

Typically the values related to formants used as features for emotion recognition are as shown in Table 2.

Table 2.

Feature	Papers
Formants position	*(Litman, 2004)(M. Lugger, Robust estimation of voice quality parameters under real world disturbances, 2006)*
Formants bandwidth	*(Litman, 2004)(M. Lugger, Robust estimation of voice quality parameters under real world disturbances, 2006)*
Difference between third and second formant	*(Litman, 2004)*
Difference between first and second formant	*(Litman, 2004)*
Fi amplitude (i =1,2,...)	*(M. Lugger, Robust estimation of voice quality parameters under real world disturbances, 2006)*

Energy Related Features

Energy, often referred to as the volume or intensity of the speech, is also known to contain valuable emotional information (R. Huber, 1998)(R. Nakatsu, 1999)(Waibel, 2000)(S. McGilloway, 2000). According to the studies performed by Williams and Stevens (Stevens, Emotions and speech: Some acoustical correlates, 1972), the arousal state of the speaker affects the overall energy, energy distribution across the frequency spectrum and the frequency and duration of pauses of speech signal. Several studies have confirmed this conclusion. In their research, Fonagy (Fonagy, Emotions, voice and music, 1981) found that angry speech had a noticeably increased energy envelope. Happiness showed similar characteristics, as reported by Davitz (Davitz, Personality, perceptual, and cognitive correlates of emotional sensitivity, 1964.) and Skinner (Skinner, 1935). Sadness was associated with decreased intensity (Davitz, Personality, perceptual, and cognitive correlates of emotional sensitivity, 1964.)(Fonagy, Emotions, voice and music, 1981) and disgust had reduced loudness (Magdics, Emotional patterns in intonation and music, 1963). Scherer (Scherer

K. R., Vocal communication of emotion: a review of research paradigms, 2003) notes that in fear, joy, and anger there is an increase in energy. Recent study (Scherer T. J., 2000) (Cornelius, 2003) have confirmed that with the emotions of joy, anger, and fear the resulting speech is correspondingly loud, fast and enunciated with strong high-frequency energy while with the arousal of the parasympathetic nervous system, as with sadness, producing speech that is slow, low-pitched and with little high-frequency energy. These characteristics follow with what is expected of the emotional state. Those with high activation levels such as anger, surprise, and happiness generally have a higher intensity, while fear, sadness, and disgust have lower intensity (T. Nwe, 2003). The arousal state of the speaker is directly related to the energy of the vocal signal. For this reason many works try to infer the emotional state of an individual by features related to the energy of his voice. The energy of a sequence of length N is defined as follows:

$$E = \sum_{n=1}^{N} x(n)^2 \qquad (5)$$

The energy-related values used as feature to discriminate the emotional state of an individual are as shown in Table 3. The computation complexity of these features is very low.

Timing Features

As previously said, voiced speech is quasi-periodic. The presence of this periodicity permits to distinguish between voiced and unvoiced sounds. The duration of the voiced speech signal and the length of the pauses are other significant cues to the emotion expressed by the speaker. Properties of rhythm-based characteristics include pauses between voiced sounds, lengths of voiced segments, and rate of speech (that is usually calculated by measuring the number of syllables per second).

Table 3.

Feature	Papers
Energy mean	*(J. Ang, 2002)(Litman, 2004) (Scherer K. R., Vocal Affect Expression: A Review and a Model for Future Research, 1994)*
Energy median	*(Pieraccini, 2002)*
Energy maximum	*(J. Ang, 2002) (Litman, 2004) (Scherer K. R., Vocal Affect Expression: A Review and a Model for Future Research, 1994)*
Energy minimum	*(J. Ang, 2002) (Litman, 2004) (Scherer K. R., Vocal Affect Expression: A Review and a Model for Future Research, 1994)*
Energy range	*(J. Ang, 2002) (Litman, 2004) (Pieraccini, 2002)*
Energy standard deviation	*(Litman, 2004) (Pieraccini, 2002)*
Intensity	*(Scherer T. J., 2000)*
High-frequency energy	*(Scherer T. J., 2000)*

Speaking rate has been used in many researches (F. Dellaert, 1996) (R. Huber, 1998) (Petrushin, 2000) (J. Ang, 2002). From these studies emerge that fear, disgust, anger, and happiness often have a higher speaking rate, while surprise has a normal tempo and sadness a reduced articulation rate. Fonagy (Fonagy, Emotions, voice and music, 1981) found that anger has an increased speech rate, and "pauses forming 32% of total speaking time". Happiness has been shown to have either a slower tempo (Risberg, 1986), a "regular" rate (Davitz, Personality, perceptual, and cognitive correlates of emotional sensitivity, 1964.) and even a high rate (Fonagy, Emotions, voice and music, 1981). Disgust has a very low speech rate, increased pause length, with pauses typically comprising 33% of speaking time. For sadness, contrarily, it has been generally agreed that the tempo is slower (Risberg, 1986) (Davitz, Personality, perceptual, and cognitive correlates of emotional sensitivity, 1964.) (Fonagy, Emotions, voice and music, 1981) and the speech contains "irregular pauses" (Davitz, Personality, perceptual, and cognitive correlates of emotional sensitivity, 1964.). Additionally, researches concerning human emotions recognition have been demonstrate that fast speech led to inferences of joy, with slow speech judged as a mark of sadness (Scherer F. J., 1986).

Table 4.

Feature	Papers
Speaking rate	*(Litman, 2004) (J. Ang, 2002) (F. Dellaert, 1996) (Scherer T. J., 2000)*
Ratio of speech to pause time	*(Litman, 2004) (J. Ang, 2002)*
Total turn duration	*(Litman, 2004)*
Duration	*(Davitz, Personality, perceptual, and cognitive correlates of emotional sensitivity, 1964.) (Fonagy, A new method of investigating the perception of prosodic features, 1978)(Magdics, Emotional patterns in intonation and music, 1963)*
Duration of pause prior to turn	*(Litman, 2004)*
Duration of the articulation period	*(M. Lugger, Robust estimation of voice quality parameters under real world disturbances, 2006)*
Duration of the voiced period	*(J. Ang, 2002) (Scherer K. R., Vocal Affect Expression: A Review and a Model for Future Research, 1994)(M. Lugger, Robust estimation of voice quality parameters under real world disturbances, 2006)*
Duration of the longest pause	*(J. Ang, 2002)*
Number of long pauses inside an utterance	*(J. Ang, 2002)*
Pause ratio	*(J. Ang, 2002)*
Position on the time axis when F0 is maximum	*(Litman, 2004)*
Position on the time axis when energy is maximum	*(Litman, 2004)*
Number of silences	*(Litman, 2004)*
Length of silences	*(Litman, 2004)*
Zero Crossing Rate (ZCR)	*(Pieraccini, 2002)*

Qualitative Features

According with Abercrombie: "The term voice quality refers to those characteristics which are present more or less all the time that a person is talking: it is a quasi-permanent quality running through all the sound that issues from the mouth" (Abercrombie, 1967). Instead, Laver views the voice quality "as the characteristic auditory coloring of an individual speaker's voice, and not in the more narrow sense of the quality deriving solely from laryngeal activity. Both laryngeal and supralaryngeal features will be seen as contributing to voice quality." (Lavier, 1968). Then, "voice quality" is a confusing term. Sometimes it refers to laryngeal qualities or a specific phonation type, e.g. breathy voice, and sometimes it is used in a broad sense as the total vocal image of a speaker, including for instance pitch, loudness, and phonation types. In emotions recognition studies, "voice quality" is used in the latter sense. It is believed that the emotional content of an utterance is strongly related to its voice quality (Cowie, et al., 2001) (Davitz, The Communication of Emotional Meaning, 1964) (Scherer K. R., Vocal Affect Expression: A Review and a Model for Future Research, 1994). Experimental studies demonstrated a strong relation between voice quality and the perceived emotion. Scherer (Scherer K. R., Vocal Affect Expression: A Review and a Model for Future Research, 1994) suggested that tense voice is associated with anger, joy, and fear; and lax voice is associated with sadness. On the other hand, Murray and Arnott (Arnott, 1993) suggested that breathy voice is associated with both anger and happiness; sadness is associated with a "resonant" voice quality. Voice quality seems to be described most regularly with reference to full-blown emotions; i.e. emotions that strongly direct people into a course of actions (Cowie, et al., 2001). A wide range of phonetic variables contributes to the subjective impression of voice quality. The perceived emotion is related to the voice quality, especially full-blown emotions, i.e. emotions that are clearly expressed by the speakers. These kinds of emotions are opposed to underlying emotions, which influence positively or negatively a person's actions and thoughts without seizing control. In contrast to other spectral features, the voice quality parameters (VQP) describe the properties of the glottal source. The most common method is fitting a glottal pulse model to the inverse filtered speech signal. Since the VQP are derived by the fundamental frequency of the speech, its formants position and bandwidth the computational complexity required for their calculation is of the same order.

Open Quotient Gradient

The glottis is the combination of the vocal folds and the space between the folds. The open quotient is the part of the glottal cycle during which the glottis is opened. Men have a shorter pulse than women, this leads to a smaller open quotient. The Open Quotient Gradient (OQG) calculation is done by the equation:

$$OQG = \frac{\tilde{H}_1 - \tilde{H}_2}{F_0} \tag{6}$$

where $\tilde{H}_1$ and $\tilde{H}_2$ are the corrected spectral amplitudes of the first and second harmonics. F_0 is the fundamental frequency.

Glottal Opening Gradient

The Glottal Opening Gradient (GOG) is defined, similarly to OQG, by the following equation:

$$GOG = \frac{\tilde{H}_1 - \tilde{A}_{1p}}{F_{1p} - F_0} \tag{7}$$

where, $\tilde{A}_{1\mathrm{p}}$ is the corrected peak amplitude near the first formant and $F_{1\mathrm{p}}$ is the frequency of the spectrum peak near the first formant.

Skewness Gradient

Skewness is a measure of asymmetry. The equation used to measure the skewness of the glottal pulse, called the SKewness Gradient (SKG), is defined as follows:

$$SKG = \frac{\tilde{H}_1 - \tilde{A}_{2\mathrm{p}}}{F_{2\mathrm{p}} - F_0} \tag{8}$$

where, $\tilde{A}_{2\mathrm{p}}$ is the corrected peak amplitude near the second formant and $F_{2\mathrm{p}}$ is the frequency of the spectrum peak near the second formant.

Rate of Closure Gradient

The partial or complete closure of the glottis is called glottalization and is realized during the pronunciation of vowels and other sonorants. The Rate of Closure Gradient (RCG) is defined by the equation:

$$RCG = \frac{\tilde{H}_1 - \tilde{A}_{3\mathrm{p}}}{F_{3\mathrm{p}} - F_0} \tag{9}$$

$\tilde{A}_{3\mathrm{p}}$ is the corrected peak amplitude near the third formant and $F_{3\mathrm{p}}$ is the frequency of the spectrum peak near the third formant.

Incompleteness of Closure

The first formant bandwidth B_1 is correlated with the Incompleteness of Closure (IC) of the glottis. For this reason the IC computation is done by the following equation:

$$IC = \frac{B_1}{F_1} \tag{10}$$

Spectral Features

It is recognized that the emotional content of an utterance has an impact on the distribution of the spectral energy across the speech range of frequency (T. Nwe, 2003). For example, in(Scherer R. B., 1996) (Kaiser L., 1962) is reported that utterances with happiness emotion have high energy at high frequency range while utterances with the sadness emotion have small energy at the same range. Additionally, in(Scherer R. B., 1996) (Kaiser L., 1962) is shown that utterances with happiness emotion have high energy at high frequency range while utterances with the sadness emotion have small energy at the same range. Then, these empirical studies permit to conclude that emotional content of an utterance have a relevant impact on speech signal's spectral distribution. To take in account this fact, in addition to time-dependent acoustic features such as pitch and energy, spectral features are often selected as a short-time representation for speech. Spectral features consists substantially in a set of parameters extracted from raw voice signal segment (about 20-30 ms (M. Benzeghiba, 2007)) or on one non-linear filtered version which values vary in relation to the speech signal's spectral distribution. Linear Predictive Coding Coefficients (LPCCs) (Atal, 1974) and Mel-Frequency Cepstrum Coefficients (MFCC) (Mermelstein, 1980) are the popular choices as features representing the phonetic content of speech (Schafer, 1978). Emotion recognition has often been performed exploiting spectral features as short-time representation of the speech signal. The human perception of the audio signal does not follow a linear scale, therefore, often, the speech signal is passed through a bank of band-pass filters which model the Human Auditory System (HAS) frequency response. The most used frequency scale for modeling HAS is the Bark scale. The Bark scale is a psychoacoustic scale which models the ear

Table 5.

Features	Papers
Linear Predictive Coding Coefficients (LPCCs)	*(T. Nwe, 2003) (Hansen S. B.-G., 2000)*
Mel Frequency Cepstrum Coefficients (MFCCs)	*(T. Nwe, 2003)*
Mel Energy spectrum Dynamics Coefficients (MEDCs)	*(Wei, 2005)*
Log Frequency Power Coefficients (LFPC)	*(T. Nwe, 2003)*
One-Sided Autocorrelation Linear Predictor Coefficients (OSALPC)	*(Nadeu, 1997)*
Cepstral-based OSALPC (OSALPCC)	*(Hansen S. B.-G., 2000)*
Log-Frequency Power Coefficients (LFPC)	*(T. Nwe, 2003)*
Modified Mel Frequency Cepstrum Coefficients (M-MFCC)	*(Hansen S. B.-G., 2000)*

response to a sinusoidal tone. It ranges from 1 to 24 and it is composed by the 24 critical bands of hearing. The bandwidth of these auditory filters increases with higher frequencies and the precision of the frequency perception decreases.

Teager Energy Operator

Teager energy operator (TEO) is a useful tool for analyzing single component signals from the energy point of view. TEO is defined for a discrete sequence $x(n)$ by the equation:

$$\psi\big(x(n)\big) = x^2(n) - x(n-1)x(n+1) \qquad (11)$$

TEO was introduced by (Kaiser J., 1993) (Teager, 1990) arguing that linear speech model were inaccurate and can not model the nonlinear processes involved in the speech production. TEO-based features have been employed for detecting stress in speech because the TEO of multi-frequency signal reflects interaction between individual frequency components. The TEO-based features that can be used for recognizing the emotions:

- Teager energy profile of the pitch contour;
- Normalized TEO autocorrelation envelope area;
- TEO decomposed FM variation;
- Critical band-based TEO autocorrelation.

Feature Selection

A crucial problem for all emotion recognition system is the selection of the best set of features for characterizing the speech signal. The purpose of this stage is to appropriately select a subset of features from the original set in order to optimize classification time and accuracy. In real-time application is necessary to reduce the number of used feature in order to also reduce the computational complexity and the time required for completing the emotion recognition. Moreover, normally one would expect an increase in classification performance when more features are used. Nevertheless, the performance can decrease for an increasing number of features if the number of patterns is too small. This phenomenon is known as the curse of dimensionality. This stage aims then to reduce the size of the speech features set by selecting the most relevant subset of features and removing the irrelevant ones, or by generating few new features that contains most of the valuable speech information. The safest strategy to get the best feature set is an exhaustive search which is, often, computationally impractical, therefore, many sub-optimum algorithms have been proposed.

Sequential Forward Selection (SFS): it is a technique for data selection that begins with an initially empty set. A single feature is added at each step. Each unique feature set is tested with a subset evaluator. Each feature set is then ranked by classification accuracy and recorded. The selection of features stops when adding a new one does not increase the overall correct classification rate or when the number of the selected features reached a previously set number. SFS is not necessarily finding the best possible combination of features since it only considers the performance of individual features acting alone. Moreover, this algorithm is subjected to nesting problems.

Sequential Floating Forward Selection (SFFS): it is an iterative method to find a subset of features that is near the optimal one, and an improved version of the SFS. At each iteration, a new feature is added to the previous feature subset (forward step). Afterwards, the least significant features are excluded as long as the resulting subset is better in terms of the recognition rate than the previous subset with the same number of features (backward step). This conditional exclusion step is motivated by the fact that a new included feature may carry information that was already present in the set carried by other features previously selected.

Sequential Backward Selection (SBS): it is similar to SFS except that it works in the backward direction. It begins with a set containing all the features and then excludes poorly-performing features all the time that the recognition rate is increasing monotonically.

Genetic Search: a genetic search of the feature space mimics biological evolution by "mutating" chromosomes (feature sets). Genes (individual features) make up the chromosomes which are initially randomly turned on or off (set to "0" = off or "1" = on). Beginning with an initial population of randomly generated chromosomes, each chromosome is passed through a fitness function which ranks each member of the current generation according to its fitness, the classification accuracy. Those chromosomes with the greatest fitness are "selected" and mated, with a mutation probability that introduces or removes one or more genes. When a stopping criteria has been met, such as a maximum number of generations, the process stops and ideally an optimal feature set is produced.

The most used sub-optimum algorithms for feature reduction are:

Principal Component Analysis (PCA): the central idea is to reduce the dimensionality of a data set consisting of a large number of inter-related variables, while retaining as much as possible of the variation present in the data set. This is achieved by transforming it to a new set of variables, the Principal Components (PCs), which are uncorrelated, and which are ordered so that the first few retain most of the variation present in all of the original variables.

Multi-Dimensional Scaling (MDS): it is a linear method that starts with a matrix of items, containing the "similarity" of each element of each row column element. Then assigns a location to each item in N-dimensional space, where N is a priori specified. This technique starts with a system with as many dimensions as many elements of the system, and reduces the size up to N.

Independent Component Analysis (ICA): it is extension of PCA with the addiction that the Principal Components must be also independent.

ISOMap: it is a non linear method that provides a simple method for estimating the intrinsic geometry of a manifold data. It is based on a rough estimate of each data point's neighbors on the manifold. ISOMap is highly efficient and generally applicable to a broad range of data sources and dimensionality.

Self-Organizing Map (SOM): it is a non linear method that produces a low-dimensional discrete representation of the input space, preserving its topological properties.

CLASSIFICATION

Classification is the task of identifying to which category belongs a new observation. In the emotion detection problem the categories are the speaker emotions and the observations are the feature extracted from the speech. The key task of this stage is to choose an appropriate method which can provide an accurate recognition of the emotion expressed by the speaker. Each classification method has advantages and shortfalls, there is not a classification method which has been proved to work better for the task of speech emotion recognition, therefore, various type of classifiers have been adopted for the task of speech emotion detection, the most common are: Hidden Markov Model (HMM), Gaussian Mixture Model (GMM), Artificial Neural Networks (ANN) and Support Vector Machine (SVM). Hidden Markov Models have been often used in speech applications. The HMM is a doubly stochastic process which consists of a first-order Markov chain whose states are hidden from the observer. GMM is a density estimation method using a convex combination of multi-variate normal distributions. It is proven that GMMs work better when coupled with global features. ANN is another common classifier, it has been proved that ANNs are more effective than HMMs and GMMs in modeling nonlinear mappings. The Support Vector Machine classifier is widely used in many pattern recognition problems, it has some advantages with respect of HMM and GMM such as the optimality of the training algorithm.

Hidden Markov Model

The Hidden Markov Model (HMM) is a mathematical formalism that allows modeling of a stochastic system, which may undergo characteristic changes at uncertain times. It is often called a doubly stochastic process in which a Markov chain governs the characteristic change of the system and each state of the Markov chain is associated with a stochastic process or distribution, which supports the random nature of the observation. The Hidden Markov Model classifier has been extensively used in speech applications such as isolated word recognition and speech segmentation because it is physically related to the production mechanism

of speech signal. In affect recognition field, it is a statistical signal model trained by sequences of feature vectors that are representative of the input signal. In the training phase, the HMM parameters are determined as those maximizing the likelihood. This is commonly achieved using the Expectation Maximization (EM) algorithm. HMM generally have many interesting properties such as the ease of implementation and their solid mathematical basis. The basic theory of Markov chains has been known to mathematicians and engineers for close to 100 years, but it is only in 1980s that it has been applied explicitly to problems in speech processing. However, it has some drawbacks, such as the need of a proper initialization for the model parameters before training and the long training time often associated with them.

Mathematically, for modeling a sequence of observable data vectors, $\{x_1, .., x_T\}$, by an HMM, we assume the existence of a hidden Markov chain responsible for generating this observable data sequence. Let K be the number of states, π_i, $i = 1, ..., K$ be the initial state probabilities for the hidden Markov chain, and a_{ij}, $i = 1, ..., K$, $j = 1, ..., K$ be the transition probability from state i to state j. Usually, the HMM parameters are estimated based on the ML principle. In order to classify an utterance, a probability measurement is constructed. Assuming the true state sequence is $s_1, .., s_T$, the likelihood of the observable data is given by:

$$
\begin{aligned}
&p(x_1, s_1, ..., x_T, s_T) \\
&= \pi_{s_1} b_{s_1}(x_1) a_{s_1, s_2} b_{s_2}(x_2)...a_{s_{T-1}, s_T} b_{s_T}(x_T) \qquad (12) \\
&= \pi_{s_1} b_{s_1}(x_1) \prod_{t=2}^{T} a_{s_{t-1}, s_t} b_{s_t}(x_t)
\end{aligned}
$$

where $b_i(x_t)$ is the observation density of the i-th state:

$$
b_i(x_t) = P(x \mid s_t = i) \qquad (13)
$$

There are many design issues regarding the structure and the training of the HMM classifier. The topology of the HMM may be a left-to-right topology as in most speech recognition applications or a fully connected topology. The assumption of left-to-right topology explicitly models advance in time. However, this assumption may not be valid in the case of speech emotion recognition since, in this case, the HMM states correspond to emotional cues such as pauses. An extension of the single IIMM classifier is the Multi-Channel Hidden Markov Models (MC-HMM) classifier, that combines the benefits of emotional speech classification with a traditional single-channel HMM for speech recognition. The MC-HMM consists of states s_{cv}, $v = 1,...,V$, $c = 1,...,C$. Transitions are allowed from left to right as in a single-channel HMM, across emotional states within the same disc, and across emotional states in the next disc.

Gaussian Mixture Model

Gaussian Mixture Model (GMM) is a probabilistic model for density estimation using a convex combination of multi-variate normal densities. It can be considered as a special continuous HMM which contains only one state. GMMs are commonly used as a parametric model of the probability distribution of continuous measurements or features in a biometric system, such as vocal-tract related spectral features in a speaker recognition system. GMM parameters are estimated from training data using the iterative Expectation-Maximization (EM) algorithm or Maximum A Posteriori (MAP) estimation from a well-trained prior model. The use of a GMM for representing feature distributions in a biometric system may also be motivated by the intuitive notion that the individual component densities may model some underlying set of hidden classes. For example, in speaker recognition, it is reasonable to assume the acoustic space of spectral related features cor-

responding to a speaker's broad phonetic events, such as vowels, nasals or fricatives. These acoustic classes reflect some general speaker dependent vocal tract configurations that are useful for characterizing speaker identity. This is also the reason why GMMs are widely used in the field of emotion recognition.

Mathematically a GMM is a weighted sum of M component Gaussian densities as given by the equation:

$$p(x|\lambda) = \sum_{i=1}^{M} w_i g(x|\mu_i \Sigma_i) \tag{14}$$

where x is a D-dimensional continuous-valued data vector (i.e. measurement or features), w_i, $i = 1,...,M$ are the weights of the mixture and $g(x|\mu_i \Sigma_i)$, $i = 1,...,M$ are the component Gaussian densities. The mixture weights satisfy the constraint that $\sum_{i=1}^{M} w_i = 1$. Each component density is a D-variate Gaussian function of the form,

$$g(x|\mu_i \Sigma_i)$$
$$= \frac{1}{(2\pi)^{D/2} |\Sigma_i^{1/2}|} \exp(-\frac{1}{2}(x - \mu_i)'\Sigma_i^{-1}(x - \mu_i)) \tag{15}$$

with mean vector μ_i and covariance matrix Σ_i. The complete Gaussian mixture model is parameterized by the mean vectors, covariance matrices and mixture weights from all component densities. These parameters are collectively represented by the notation, $\lambda = \{\mu_i \Sigma_i w_i\}$, $i = 1,...,M$.

Artificial Neural Networks

Artificial Neural Networks are a classification method based on a mathematical model inspired by biological neural networks. A neural network consists of an interconnected group of artificial neurons, and it processes information using a connectionist approach to computation. In most cases a neural network is an adaptive system that changes its structure during a learning phase. Neural networks are used to model complex relationships between inputs and outputs or to find patterns in data. This technique is used for emotion classification due to its ability to find nonlinear boundaries separating the emotional states. The most frequently used class of neural networks is that of feed-forward ANNs, in which the input feature values propagate through the network in a forward direction on a layer-by-layer basis. Typically, the network consists of a set of sensory units that constitute the input layer, one or more hidden layers of computation nodes, and an output layer of computational nodes. The number of input nodes corresponds to the number of features and the number of output nodes corresponds to the number of emotional categories. Almost all ANNs can be categorized into three main basic types:

MultiLayer Perceptron (MLP): it is a feed-forward ANN model that maps sets of input data onto a set of appropriate output. An MLP consists of multiple layers of nodes in a directed graph, with each layer fully connected to the next one. It can distinguish data that is not linearly separable.

Recurrent Neural Networks (RNN): it is an ANN where connections between units form a directed cycle. This creates an internal state of the network which allows it to exhibit dynamic temporal behavior. Unlike feed-forward neural networks, RNNs can use their internal memory to process arbitrary sequences of inputs.

Radial Basis Functions Networks (RBFN): it is an ANN that uses Radial Basis Function (RBF) as activation functions. A radial basis function is a real-valued function whose value depends only on the distance from the origin.

Support Vector Machine

Support Vector Machine (SVM) is a relatively new machine learning algorithm introduced by Vapnik and derived from statistical learning theory in 1990s. Its main idea is to transform the original input set to a high-dimensional feature space by using a kernel function, and then achieve optimum classification in this new feature space, where discriminative training is achieved by optimal placement of a separation hyperplane under the precondition of linear separability.

Mathematically, given training data $\{x_{1,}.., x_n\}$ that are vectors in some space $X \subseteq \mathbb{R}^d$. To each training data labels $\{y_{1,}.., y_n\}$ are associated, $y_i \in \{-1, 1\}$. In their simplest form, SVMs are hyperplanes that separate the training data by a maximal margin. All vectors lying on one side of the hyperplane are labeled as -1, and all vectors lying on the other side are labeled as 1. The training instances that lie closest to the hyperplane are called support vectors. More generally, SVMs allow one to project the original training data in space X to a higher dimensional feature space F via a Mercer kernel operator K. In other words, we consider the set of classifiers of the form:

$$f(x) = \sum_{i=1}^{n} \alpha_i K(x_i, x) \qquad (16)$$

k-Nearest Neighbors (k-NN)

This algorithm has proved popular with vocal emotion recognition due to its relative simplicity and performance comparable to other methods. It estimates the local posterior probability of each class by the weighted average of class membership over the k Nearest Neighbors (k-NN). It assigns an utterance to an emotional state according to the emotional state of the k utterances that are closest to the u_{ae} in the measurement space. It uses the Euclidean distance in order to measure the distance between u_{ae} and the neighbors.

The disadvantages of k-NN are that systematic methods for selecting the optimum number of the closest neighbors and the most suitable distance measure are hard to find. In the latter case, the optimality is not feasible for a finite number of utterances in the data collection.

SUMMARY AND FUTURE WORK

In literature, many different approaches have been developed in order to accomplish the task of detecting the speaker's emotion. It is impossible to find the best emotion detector since the performance of the detector depends on many different factors such as the type of database, the emotion representation or the emotions that the application wants to detect. It is important to remark, also, that smartphone applications have to deal with the limited battery lifetime, and therefore the developed emotion-aware application must detect the wanted emotion performing the less operation as possible. For this reason the chapter has given an overview of the field in order to permit the smartphone application programmers to focus on the features which are better suited for their aim. The development of emotion aware application on smart portable devices will permit a more effective human-machine interaction.

ACKNOWLEDGMENT

The authors want to thank Dr. Angelo Cirigliano and Dr. Fabio Patrone for their precious suggestions and support.

REFERENCES

Abdennadher, S. M. A. (2007). BECAM tool a semi-automatic tool for bootstrapping emotion corpus annotation and management. *European Conference on Speech and Language Processing (EUROSPEECH '07)*, (pp. 946–949).

Abercrombie, D. (1967). *Elements of general phonetics*. Chicago: University of Chicago Press.

Agneessens, A., Bisio, I., Lavagetto, F., Marchese, M., & Sciarrone, A. (2010). Speaker Count application for smartphone platforms. *Wireless Pervasive Computing (ISWPC), 2010 5th IEEE International Symposium on*, (pp. 361-366). Modena.

Ang, J. R. D. (2002). Prosody-based automatic detection of annoyance and frustration in human computer dialog. *Proc. Int. Conf. Spoken Language Processing (ICSLP '02)*, (pp. 2037-2040).

Arnott, I. M. (1993). Toward the simulation of emotion in synthetic speech: a review of the literature on human vocal emotion. *The Journal of the Acoustical Society of America, 93*, 1097–1108. doi:10.1121/1.405558 PMID:8445120.

Aryananda, C. B. (2002). Recognition of affective communicative intent in robot-directed speech. *Autonomous Robots, 2*, 83–104.

Atal, B. S. (1974). Effectiveness of linear prediction characteristics of the speech wave for automatic speaker identification and verification. *The Journal of the Acoustical Society of America, 55*(6), 1304–1312. doi:10.1121/1.1914702 PMID:4846727.

Bartlett, M. P. (2007). Machine Analysis of Facial Expressions. In K. D. Grgic, Face Recognition (pp. 377-416). I-Tech Education and Publishing.

Bartlett, M. S. G. L. (2005). Recognizing Facial Expression: Machine Learning and Application to Spontaneous Behavior. *Proc. IEEE Int'l Conf. Computer Vision and Pattern Recognition (CVPR '05)*.

Batliner, A. C. H. (2004). "You stupid tin box" - children interacting with the AIBO robot: A crosslinguistic emotional speech corpus. *Proc. Language Resources and Evaluation (LREC '04)*. Lisbon.

Benzeghiba, M., R. D. (2007). Automatic speech recognition and speech variability: A review. *Speech Communication, 49.*

Bisio, I. F. (2011). Context-Aware Smartphone Services. In *Pervasive Computing and Communications Design and Deployment: Technologies, Trends, and Applications.* IGI Global. doi:10.4018/978-1-60960-611-4.ch002.

Burger, S. V. M. (2002). The ISL Meeting Corpus: The Impact of Meeting Type on Speech Style. *Proc. 8th Int'l Conf. Spoken Language Processing (ICSLP).*

Burkhardt, F. v. (2005). *An emotion-aware voice portal.* Proc. Electronic Speech Signal Processing ESSP.

Cairns, D., J. H. (1994). Nonlinear analysis and detection of speech under stressed conditions. *The Journal of the Acoustical Society of America, 96*(6), 3392–3400. doi:10.1121/1.410601.

Cauldwell, R. (2000). Where did the anger go? The role of context in interpreting emotion in speech. *Proceedings of the ISCA ITRW on Speech and Emotion,* (pp. 127–131).

Clavel, C. I. V. (2004). Fiction database for emotion detection in abnormal situations. *Proc. Int. Conf. Spoken Language Process. (ICSLP '04),* (pp. 2277–2280). Korea.

Cornelius, R. C. (2003). Describing the Emotional States that are Expressed in Speech. *Speech Communication, 40,* 5–32. doi:10.1016/S0167-6393(02)00071-7.

Cowan, M. (2006). *Pitch and intensity characteristics of stage speech.* Arch. Speech.

Cowie, R., Douglas-Cowie, E., Tsapatsoulis, N., Votsis, G., Kollias, S., Fellenz, W., & Taylor, J. (2001, Jan). Emotion recognition in human-computer interaction. *Signal Processing Magazine, IEEE, 18*(1), 32–80. doi:10.1109/79.911197.

Darwin, C. (1872). *The Expression of the Emotions in Man and Animals.* John Murray. doi:10.1037/10001-000.

Davitz, J. R. (1964). *The Communication of Emotional Meaning.* New York: McGraw-Hill.

Davitz, J. R. (1964). Personality, perceptual, and cognitive correlates of emotional sensitivity. In J. R. Davitz (Ed.), *The Communication of Emotional Meaning.* New York: McGraw-Hill.

Dellaert, F. T. P. (1996). Recognizing emotion in speech. *Proceedings of the International Conference on Spoken Language Processing (ICSLP '96),* (pp. 1970–1973). Philadelphia, PA.

Devillers, L. V. (2005). *Detection of real-life emotions in call centers* (pp. 1841–1844). Proc. Eurospeech.

Douglas-Cowie, E., N. C. (2003). Emotional speech: Towards a new generation of databases. *Speech Communication, 40*(1–2), 33–60. doi:10.1016/S0167-6393(02)00070-5.

Ekman, P. F. W. (1971). Constants across cultures in the face and emotion. In Journal of Personality and Social Psychology. Elsevier.

Ekman, P. (1994). Strong evidence for universals in facial expressions: A reply to Russell's mistaken critique. *Psychological Bulletin, 115,* 268–287. doi:10.1037/0033-2909.115.2.268 PMID:8165272.

Fernandez, R., & Picard, R. (2003). Modeling drivers' speech under stress. *Speech Communication, 40,* 145–159. doi:10.1016/S0167-6393(02)00080-8.

Fischer, K. (1999). *Annotating emotional language data.* Tech. Rep. 236, Univ. of Hamburg, Hamburg.

Fonagy, I. (1978). A new method of investigating the perception of prosodic features. *Language and Speech, 21,* 34–49. PMID:692241.

Fonagy, I. (1981). Emotions, voice and music. In J. Sundberg, Research Aspects on Singing (pp. 51–79). Royal Swedish Academy of Music no. 33

France, D. J., R. G. (2000). Acoustical properties of speech as indicators of depression and suicidal risk. *IEEE Transactions on Bio-Medical Engineering, 7*, 829–837. doi:10.1109/10.846676 PMID:10916253.

Frick, R. W. (1986). The prosodic expression of anger: differentiating thread and frustration. *Aggressive Behavior, 12*, 121–128. doi:10.1002/1098-2337(1986)12:2<121::AID-AB2480120206>3.0.CO;2-F.

Gerhard, D. (2003). *Pitch extraction and fundamental frequency: History and current technique.* Technical Report TR-CS.

Hansen, H. J. (1999). Speech under stress conditions: Overview of the effect of speech production and on system performance. *Proc. Int. Conf. Acoustics, Speech, and Signal Processing (ICASSP '99), 4*, pp. 2079–2089. Phoenix.

Hansen, M. R. (2002). Frequency band analysis for stress detection using a Teager energy operator based feature. *Proc. Int. Conf. Spoken Language Processing (ICSLP '02)*, (pp. 2021–2024).

Hansen, S. B.-G. (2000). A comparative study of traditional and newly proposed features for recognition of speech under stress. *IEEE Transactions on Speech and Audio Processing, 8*(4), 429–442. doi:10.1109/89.848224.

Hirschberg, J. S. B. (2005). Distinguishing Deceptive from Non-Deceptive Speech. *Proc. 9th European Conf. Speech Comm. and Technology (INTERSPEECH '05)*, (pp. 1833-1836).

Huber, R. E. N. (1998). You beep machine–emotion in automatic speech understanding systems. *Proceedings of the Workshop on Text, Speech, and Dialog*, (pp. 223–228).

Izard, C. E. (1977). *Human emotions.* New York: Plenum Press. doi:10.1007/978-1-4899-2209-0.

James, W. (1884). What Is an Emotion? *Mind.* doi:10.1093/mind/os-IX.34.188.

Johns-Lewis, C. (1986). Prosodic differentiation of discourse modes. In *C. Johns-Lewis, Intonation in Discourse* (pp. 199–220). San Diego: College-Hill Press.

Johnson, W. F., R. N. (1986). Recognition of emotion from vocal cues. *Arch. Gen. Psych, 43*, 280–283. doi:10.1001/archpsyc.1986.01800030098011 PMID:3954549.

Kaiser, J. (1993). Some useful properties of Teager's energy operators. *Acoustics, Speech, and Signal Processing, 1993. ICASSP-93., 1993 IEEE International Conference on*, (pp. 149-152).

Kaiser, L. (1962). Communication of affects by single vowels. *Synthese, 14*, 300–319. doi:10.1007/BF00869311.

Kao, E.-C., Liu, C.-C., Yang, T.-H., Hsieh, C.-T., & Soo, V.-W. (2009). Towards Text-based Emotion Detection A Survey and Possible Improvements. *Information Management and Engineering, 2009. ICIME '09. International Conference on*, (p. 70).

Ladd, D. R. K. S. (1986). An integrated approach to studying intonation and attitude. In C. Johns-Lewis, Intonation in Discourse (pp. 125–138). San Diego: College-Hill Press.

Lavier, J. D. (1968). Voice Quality and Indexical Information. *Department of Phonetics and Linguistics. University of Edinburgh, 3*(1), 43–54.

Lee, C. M., & Narayanan, S. S. (2005). Toward detecting emotions in spoken dialogs. *IEEE Transactions on Speech and Audio Processing, 13*(2), 293–303. doi:10.1109/TSA.2004.838534.

Litman, K. F.-R. (2004). Predicting Emotion in Spoken Dialogue from Multiple Knowledge Sources. *Proc. Human Language Technology Conf. North Am. Chapter of the Assoc. Computational Linguistics (HLT/NAACL).*

Lövheim, H. (2012, Feb). A new three-dimensional model for emotions and monoamine neurotransmitters. *Medical Hypotheses, Elsevier, 78*(2), 341–348. doi:10.1016/j.mehy.2011.11.016 PMID:22153577.

Lugger, M. B. Y. (2006). Robust estimation of voice quality parameters under real world disturbances. *Proc. IEEE ICASSP.*

Lugger, M. B. Y. (2006). Robust estimation of voice quality parameters under real world disturbances. *Proc. IEEE ICASSP.*

Magdics, I. F. (1963). Emotional patterns in intonation and music. *Z. Phonetik, 16*, 293–326.

Magdics, I. F. (1963). Emotional patterns in intonation and music. *Z. Phonetik, 16*, 293–326.

McGilloway, S. R. C.-C. (2000). Approaching automatic recognition of emotion from voice: A rough benchmark. *Proc. ISCA Workshop Speech Emotion*, (pp. 207-212).

McRoberts, M. S. (2003). Babyears: A recognition system for affective vocalizations. *Speech Communication, 39*, 367–384. doi:10.1016/S0167-6393(02)00049-3.

Mermelstein, S. D. (1980). Comparison of Parametric Representations of Monosyllabic Word Recognition in Continuously Spoken Sentences. *IEEE Transactions on Acoustics, Speech, and Signal Processing, 28*(4), 357–366. doi:10.1109/TASSP.1980.1163420.

Moataz El Ayadi, M. S. (2011, March). Survey on speech emotion recognition: Features, classification schemes, and databases. *Pattern Recognition, 44*(3), 572–587. doi:10.1016/j.patcog.2010.09.020.

Morrison, D., R. W. (2007). Ensemble methods for spoken emotion recognition in call-centres. *Speech Communication, 49*(2), 98–112. doi:10.1016/j.specom.2006.11.004.

Nadeu, J. H. (1997). Linear prediction of the one-sided autocorrelation sequence for noisy speech recognition. *IEEE Transactions on Speech and Audio Processing, 5*(1), 80–84. doi:10.1109/89.554273.

Nakatsu, R. N. T. (1999). Emotion recognition and its application to computer agents with spontaneous interactive capabilities. *Proceedings IEEE workshop on multimedia signal processing*, (pp. 439–444).

Nogueiras, A. A. M. (2001). Speech Emotion Recognition Using Hidden Markov Models. EUROSPEECH-2001, (pp. 2679-2682).

Nwe, T., S. F. (2003). Speech emotion recognition using hidden Markov models. *Speech Communication, 41*, 603–623. doi:10.1016/S0167-6393(03)00099-2.

O'Toole, A. J. (2005). A Video Database of Moving Faces and People. *IEEE Transactions on Pattern Analysis and Machine Intelligence, 27*(5), 812–816. doi:10.1109/TPAMI.2005.90 PMID:15875802.

O'Toole, A. J. et al. (2005). A Video Database of Moving Faces and People. *IEEE Transactions on Pattern Analysis and Machine Intelligence, 27*(5), 812–816. doi:10.1109/TPAMI.2005.90 PMID:15875802.

Parrott, W. (2001). *Emotions in Social Psychology.* Psychology Press.

Pereira, C. (2000,). Dimensions of emotional meaning in speech. *Proceedings of the ISCA ITRW on Speech and Emotion*, (pp. 25–28). Newcastle, Belfast.

Petrushin, V. A. (2000). Emotion recognition in speech signal: Experimental study, development, and application. *Proceedings of 6th international conference on spoken language processing (IC-SLP '00).*

Piccardi, H. G. (2006). A Bimodal Face and Body Gesture Database for Automatic Analysis of Human Nonverbal Affective Behavior. *Proc. 18th Int'l Conf. Pattern Recognition (ICPR '06),* (pp. 1148-1153).

Pieraccini, C. L. (2002). Combining acoustic and language information for emotion recognition. *Proceedings of the ICSLP, 02,* 873–876.

Plutchik, R. (2001). The nature of emotions (Vol. 89, No. 4. ed.). American Scientist.

Pronovost, G. F. (1939). An experimental study of the pitch characteristics of the voice during the expression of emotion. *Speech Monograph, 6,* 87–104. doi:10.1080/03637753909374863.

Pronovost, G. F. (1939). An experimental study of the pitch characteristics of the voice during the expression of emotion. *Speech Monograph, 6,* 87–104. doi:10.1080/03637753909374863.

Risberg, A. O. (1986). The identification of the mood of a speaker by hearing impaired listeners. *Speech Transmission Lab.* [Stockholm.]. *Quarterly Progress Status Report, 4,* 79–90.

Roisman, G. I., J. L. (2004). The Emotional Integration of Childhood Experience: Physiological, Facial Expressive, and Self-Reported Emotional Response during the Adult Attachment Interview. *Developmental Psychology,* 40. PMID:15355165.

Rong, J., G. L.-P. (2009). Acoustic feature selection for automatic emotion recognition from speech. *Information Processing & Management, 45,* 315–328. doi:10.1016/j.ipm.2008.09.003.

Sandor Dornbush, K. F. (2005). XPod a human activity and emotion aware mobile music player. *Proceedings of the International Conference on Mobile Technology, Applications and Systems.*

Schafer, L. R. (1978). *Digital Processing of Speech Signals.* Englewood Cliffs, New Jersey: Prentice-Hall.

Scherer, F. J. (1986). Effects of experimentally induced stress on vocal parameters. *Journal of Experimental Psychology. Human Perception and Performance, 12*(3), 302–313. doi:10.1037/0096-1523.12.3.302 PMID:2943858.

Scherer, K. R. (1994). *Vocal Affect Expression: A Review and a Model for Future Research.* Psychology and Biology of Emotion.

Scherer, K. R. (1996). Adding the affective dimension: a new look in speech analysis and synthesis. *Proceedings of the International Conference on Spoken Language Processing (ICSLP 1996).* Philadelphia, PA.

Scherer, K. R. (2003). Vocal communication of emotion: a review of research paradigms. *Speech Communication, 40,* 227–256. doi:10.1016/S0167-6393(02)00084-5.

Scherer, R. B. (1996). Acoustic profiles in vocal emotion expression. *Journal of Personality and Social Psychology, 70,* 641–636.

Scherer, T. J. (2000). Vocal communication of emotion. In J. H. M. Lewis (Ed.), *Handbook of emotion* (pp. 220–235). New York: Guilford.

Schuller, B. S. R.-H. (2005). Speaker independent speech emotion recognition by ensemble classification. *IEEE International Conference on Multimedia and Expo (ICME '05),* (pp. 864–867).

Sebe, N. M. S. (2004). Authentic Facial Expression Analysis. *Proc. IEEE Int'l Conf. Automatic Face and Gesture Recognition (AFGR).*

Skinner, E. R. (1935). A calibrated recording and analysis of the pitch, force and quality of vocal tones expressing happiness and sadness. *Speech Monogr.*, 2, 81–137. doi:10.1080/03637753509374833.

Stevens, C. W. (1972). Emotions and speech: Some acoustical correlates. *The Journal of the Acoustical Society of America, 52*(4), 1238–1250. PMID:4638039.

Stevens, C. W. (1972). Emotions and speech: Some acoustical correlates. *The Journal of the Acoustical Society of America, 52*(4), 1238–1250. PMID:4638039.

Teager, H. a. (1990). Evidence for Nonlinear Sound Production Mechanisms in the Vocal Tract. In W. J. Hardcastle, Speech Production and Speech Modelling. Springer Netherlands.

Tomkins, S. S. (1962). *Affect, Imagery, Consciousness.* Springer.

Trudgill, P. (1983). *Sociolinguistics: An Introduction to Language and Society.* London: Penguin.

Vasilescu, L. D. (2004). Reliability of Lexical and Prosodic Cues in Two Real-Life Spoken Dialog Corpora. *Proc. 4th Int. Conf. Language Resources and Evaluation (LREC).*

Vasilescu, L. D. (2004). Reliability of Lexical and Prosodic Cues in Two Real-Life Spoken Dialog Corpora. *Proc. 4th Int. Conf. Language Resources and Evaluation (LREC).*

Ververidis, D. K. (2003). A review of emotional speech databases. *PCI 2003, 9th Panhellenic Conf. on Informatics*, (pp. 560-574). Thessaloniki, Greece.

Waibel, T. P. (2000). Emotion-sensitive human-computer interfaces. *Proc. ISCA Workshop Speech and Emotion*, (pp. 201–206). 2000.

Wei, Y. L. (2005). Speech emotion recognition based on HMM and SVM. *Proc. of Int. Conf. on Machine Learning and Cybernetics, 8*, pp. 4898- 4901.

Whissel, C. M. (1989). *The dictionary of affect in language.* New York: Academic.

Zeng, Z., M. P. (2009). A survey of affect recognition methods: audio, visual and spontaneous expressions. *IEEE Transactions on Pattern Analysis and Machine Intelligence, 31*(1), 39–58. doi:10.1109/TPAMI.2008.52 PMID:19029545.

Chapter 4
Service Discovery with Personal Awareness in Smart Environments

Kobkaew Opasjumruskit
Friedrich Schiller University Jena, Germany

Birgitta König-Ries
Friedrich Schiller University Jena, Germany

Jesús Expósito
Friedrich Schiller University Jena, Germany

Andreas Nauerz
IBM Germany Research and Development GmbH, Germany

Martin Welsch
Friedrich Schiller University Jena, Germany
& IBM Germany Research and Development GmbH, Germany

ABSTRACT

Web service descriptions with Semantic Web annotations can be exploited to automate dynamic discovery of services. The approaches introduced aim at enabling automatic discovery, configuration, and execution of services in dynamic environments. In this chapter, the authors present the service discovery aspect of MERCURY, a platform for straightforward, user-centric integration and management of heterogeneous devices and services via a Web-based interface. In the context of MERCURY, they use service discovery to find appropriate sensors, services, or actuators to perform a certain functionality required within a user-defined scenario (e.g., to obtain the temperature at a certain location, book a table at a restaurant close to the location of all friends involved, etc.). A user will specify a service request, which will be fed to a matchmaker, which compares the request to existing service offers and ranks these offers based on how well they match the service request. In contrast to existing works, the service discovery approach the authors use is geared towards non-IT-savvy end users and is not restricted to single service-description formalism. Moreover, the matchmaking algorithm should be user-aware and environmentally adaptive (e.g. depending on the user's location or surrounding temperature), rather than specific to simple keywords-based searches, which depend on the users' expertise and mostly require several tries. Hence, the goal is to develop a service discovery module on top of existing techniques, which will rank discovered services to serve users' queries according to their personal interests, expertise, and current situations.

DOI: 10.4018/978-1-4666-4695-7.ch004

INTRODUCTION

Context-aware pervasive computing has become a prevalent topic over the last decade. With the upcoming of ubiquitous mobile devices, which provide heterogeneous sensors and facilitate internet access to users, we are close to realising the idea of the "Web of Things" (Mattern & Floerkemeier, 2010). In the Web of Things world, physical things are becoming smart web connected devices. Not only can they create, store and share data, they can even be programmed to make decisions based on these data. In addition to these concepts, things have become not only remotely controllable and able to communicate with each other, but also able to automatically adapt themselves to the demands of the user. By measuring the context of users and preferences, things (in particular resources) can be altered or configured to match the requirements of each user. For example, a user may want to receive an alert, if a weather advisory that concerns him (i.e., refers to a region where he will be when the advisory becomes active) is published. To achieve this functionality, a weather advisory service needs to be combined with information obtained from the user's calendar or his flight reservation service or another service that provides information about his whereabouts.

Even though various works have been devoted to the above concepts, none of them can relieve the painful integration nor ease the complexity of the usage for the non-technical user. Therefore, the major goal of the MERCURY project is to equip the non-IT-savvy users with the user-context adaptive service in order to utilize resources in their own environments. MERCURY is able to support both, generic everyday tasks, like, "set my to-do-task for working out when my daily calorie intake is above the limit", and sophisticated tasks involving several sensors, services and actuators. An example for such a sophisticated task is, "Monitoring medical sensors, such as glucose meters, electrocardiogram (EKG) sensors, respiratory

sensors, etc. When there is any sign of unusual condition, send an alarm to a caregiver or a nearby physician". While maintaining a user-friendly interface, another crucial gap that has not been efficiently addressed in any existing solution is – how to utilize information retrieved from mobile devices or social web in order to provide the user with an automation and recommendation system. Therefore, in order to cover the challenges mentioned above, we continue focusing on the service discovery requirement based on the work proposed in Opasjumruskit, Exposito, Koenig-Ries, Nauerz, and Welsch (2012).

The remainder of this chapter is organized as follows: First, we will review related work, which our assumptions and ideas are based on. We then review the existing approaches for discovering services and carve out the most important aspects of successful and thus most promising solutions. Afterwards, the Background section briefly presents an overview of MERCURY and motivates the relation to the service discovery topic. We present how service discovery fits into MERCURY and provide tangible use cases. Next, we make basic assumptions, which define the scope of our research, elaborate the implementation of the user-context adaptive service recommender. Finally, we describe our proposed architecture.

In section Building Blocks, we explain, in more detail, the request converter along an exemplary use case. In this building block, the service discovery results are improved by involving personal awareness. Next, the result integrator, which is used for merging ranked results from several service matchmakers, is described. We then conclude the chapter and finally, point out the remaining challenges for our future work.

RELATED WORK

Several works have followed the concept of the Internet of things (Mattern & Floerkemeier, 2010), where the Internet extends into the real world embracing physical objects, so that they can be controlled remotely and can be accessed via internet services. For instance, works like SenseWeb (Grosky, Kansal, Nath, Liu, & Zhao, 2007), Web Mashups (Guinard, 2009), SemSor-Grid4Env (Gray et al., 2011), Actinium (Kovatsch, Lanter & Duquennoy, 2012) and Bo et al. (2012) enable users to control smart devices through a web-based application. However, most projects are geared towards a few specific use cases and devices. Morcover, the user interfaces presented do usually not allow users to construct a customizable application on their own. Attempts to address such a problem like iCAP (Dey, Sohn, Streng & Kodama, 2006), Phuoc and Hauswirth (2009) aimed towards a non-programming user-defined context sensing application. However, the result is still not sufficiently user friendly and does not support heterogeneity of services. The approach presented by Guo, Zhang, and Imai (2011) supports different types of users, which are categorized by their programming skills. Thus, users can build a complicated application if they are expert users or simple applications if they have no programming skills. However, such user classification is difficult since the definitions are rather diffuse and we believe that the adaptive user interface and the possibility to share one's own applications/scenarios are attractive and tangible in this social network age.

However, we are not the only one who realizes the gap of improving on the internet of things. There are several products already, such as Cloud Business Apps Integration – CloudWork (2013), Cosm - Internet of Things Platform Connecting Devices and Apps for Real-Time Control and Data Storage (2012), Evrythng (2012), IFTTT - If this then that (2013), Paraimpu - The Web of Things is more than Things in the Web (2012), On{X} – automate your life (2012), and the list keeps going on. However, none of them quite meets the requirements outlined above: For Cloudwork and IFTTT, it is obvious that they provide a limited set of web services, which are mostly social network applications. While Cosm, Evrything, Paraimpu and on{X} offer a broader range of sensors and services, they require some programming and hardware skill from users in order to connect building blocks, e.g. sensors and services.

Assuming that systems like MERCURY or the ones described above become successful and that a large number of sensors, services and actuators become accessible via these systems, a major challenge will be to actually find the best fitting sensor, service or actuator among the large number of possible candidates. In the web service community, several attempts have proposed to make services discoverable. Typically, this happens by embedding a machine interpretable description into the service, based on a domain-specific ontology, as described in Maleshkova, Kopeck, and Pedrinaci (2009). A matchmaking service like for instance, SAWSDL-iMatcher (Wei, Wang T., Wang J., & Bernstein, 2011) and OWLS-MX (Klusch, Kapahnke, & Zinnikus, 2009) can then search for appropriate services. Other courageous approaches using collaborative techniques like WSColab (Gawinecki, Cabri, Paprzycki, & Ganzha, 2010) and Ding, Lei, Yan, Bin, and Lun (2010), also return promising results. Talantikite, Aissani, and Boudjlida (2009) and Martin, Paolucci, and Wagner (2007) discuss all the techniques for semantic annotations of web services, such as OWL-S, WSMO, WSDL-S and SAWSDL. Since the descriptions of web services currently in use are diverse and incompatible, we expect that MERCURY will need to support several of them to achieve best results.

In MERCURY, we have deployed the concept of the Internet of things in the way that users can exploit sensors and devices without programming skills. Even though there are several systems working on the similar direction, we will distinguish our project from the other competitors with a simple integration of sensors and devices. The automatic discovery of sensors with user context awareness could ease users while there are ubiquitous sensors and services spread all over the internet.

BACKGROUND

In this section, we first describe the architecture of MERCURY. Then, we motivate the necessity of automated service discovery we have perceived in our work. Finally, we explain how we use the service discovery in MERCURY.

MERCURY System Architecture

MERCURY offers a service implemented on a WebSphere Portal server (IBM, 2013), which allows users to access MERCURY from any location using any suitable device. In our previous work (Koenig-Ries, Opasjumruskit, Nauerz, & Welsch, 2012) we illustrated the possible architecture of MERCURY, as depicted in Figure 1. On the client side, a *sensor/actuator management* allows the user to add his devices to the system, to publish their descriptions and to define access rights to those devices. After the registration process, a

scenario modelling allows the user to select and combine devices. Finally, a *runtime UI* will be responsible for displaying events and the status of defined scenarios to the user.

The heart of the system consists of a *sensor/ service discovery* module, which manages the sensor's description repository and performs matchmaking of requests from the scenario modelling and descriptions. An *execution environment* obtains the script-like results of the scenario modelling and then accesses sensors, actuators via web services. A *user management* component stores user models (expertise, preferences, etc.) and access rights to devices.

In the bottom part of the architecture, sensors and actuators are either individually or as a network accessible via *gateway* components. These help overcome technical heterogeneity. Gateways are also responsible for bridging sensor networks to web services, so that the sensor/service discovery can access sensors and actuators.

Figure 1. The architecture of MERCURY

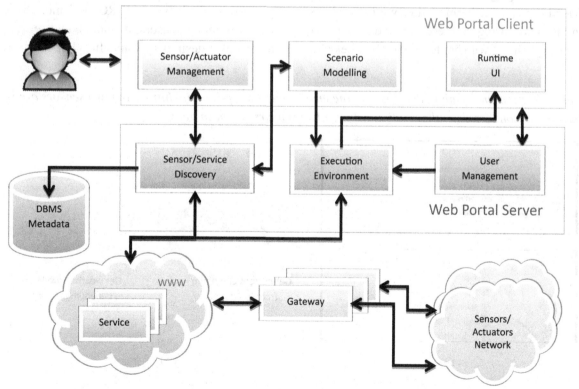

The first prototype (Opasjumruskit et al., 2012) demonstrated that MERCURY could aid the user to accomplish the desired task exploiting environment-adaptive capabilities. For example, a user can assign the location detection service to track her own current position and then automatically choose the appropriate sensor device nearby her, as Figure 2 depicts, and before executing her planned task. In other words, depending on the user's environment or context, MERCURY can perform the assignment with the appropriate selection of resources available at the specific time and place.

The service offered by MERCURY can be categorized into three main modules: device registration, device management and scenario modelling. The following example can describe the whole usage flow: Imagine an example user, Lea, has decided to go jogging regularly. If there is no rain in the morning, Lea would like to be woken up at 6 A.M. to go jogging. Otherwise, she prefers to receive an alarm message at 7 A.M., and have her calendar updated automatically with an event to go jogging in the evening with her friend instead. Furthermore, Lea works and lives in Stuttgart during the weekdays and spends her time in Freiburg with her family on the weekend.

Hence, she would like to maintain the same schedule for jogging at both places. Events and jogging partners will be updated accordingly.

To realize this scenario, a GPS locator, rain sensors close to Lea's living places and her calendar need to be registered via the device registration module. Afterwards, the parameters of these services and devices can be set in the device management module, e.g. update rates or privacy settings. Finally, Lea can wire services and devices to achieve the desired functionality via the scenario modelling module. For the scenario "Jogging plan", she can define several situations, such as, "if it rains" and "set the alarm clock" situations, so that the user can alter and reuse the scenario easily. A situation like "if it rains" can be composed of a GPS locator and a weather forecast service. On the other hand, an "if it does not rain" situation can be realized by adding the "if it rains" situation and a negation operation to the scenario. Each situation can be saved as a template for later use, the template can be shared among users and, eventually, each situation can be altered individually.

As described above, MERCURY allows flexibly combining sensors, actuators, and services to model a desired functionality. For the work

Figure 2. First prototype to demonstrate the environment-adaptive capabilities (a) two sensors are selected and connected (b) the relation between two sensors has been defined

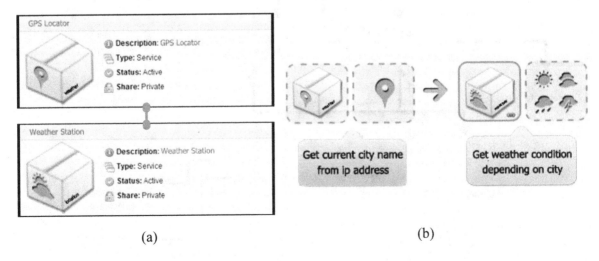

(a)   (b)

described in this chapter, we assume that sensors and actuators are wrapped as services, so that everything can be accessed via web service interfaces. In order to achieve maximum flexibility, we do not make any assumptions whether a given service wraps one individual sensor, an entire sensor network, or some combination of sensors and actuators.

Automated Service Discovery

In order to facilitate the user in searching for a service she needs, the automated service discovery plays an important role here. The basic idea behind the automated service discovery is to annotate services with machine interpretable descriptions. Usually, when a human user or an application is looking for a service she will provide a service request in a predefined format specifying the capabilities of the service she is interested in. A matchmaking component then compares available service descriptions and the request and returns the service(s) that best match the user's request.

For our work, we assume that the minimum information available for any web service is its WSDL description. The Web Services Description Language (WSDL) (Christensen, Curbera, Meredith, & Weerawarana, 2001), a World Wide Web Consortium (W3C) recommendation, is a syntactic description of a web service's interface. In our context, however, a WSDL description alone is not helpful, since it is meant mostly for human consumption and does not contain sufficient information for automated service discovery. The latter aim was first addressed by the AI (Artificial Intelligence) community which developed a number of ontology based techniques, such as OWL-S (Web Ontology Language for Web Services) (Martin et al., 2004) and WSMO (Web Service Modelling Ontology) (Roman et al., 2005). These rather heavyweight approaches describe a service's capability in terms of its preconditions and effects in addition to the service's interface. The descriptions use powerful logic languages,

which allows for the application of reasoning techniques. However, providing these descriptions requires significant efforts. Thus, up to now, uptake outside of research projects has been rather slow.

In an attempt to ease the way into semantic service descriptions, SAWSDL (Semantic Annotations for WSDL) was created. SAWSDL allows for semantic annotations of WSDL descriptions using arbitrary ontologies (Hobold & Siqueira, 2012). SAWSDL is a hybrid description that provides both syntactic and semantic discovery of services. Another lightweight option to support service discovery is the usage of community-provided tags as described, e.g., in Gawinecki, Cabri, Paprzycki, and Ganzha (2012).

For all of these service description approaches mentioned above, different matchmakers have been proposed, as Tran, Puntheeranurak, and Tsuji (2009) and Ngan, Kirchberg, and Kanagasabai (2010) have reviewed. There exist several initiatives to evaluate the respective merits of the different description formalisms and matchmaking algorithms, among them, according to Blake, Cabral, König-Ries, Küster, and Martin (2012), are the Semantic Web Services Challenge (Harth & Maynard, 2012), the Web Service Challenge (Blake, Bleul, Weise, Bansal, & Kona, 2009) and the S3 Contest (Klusch, 2012).

Since we want to be able to integrate arbitrary services available over the Internet, we cannot make any assumptions about the description framework used. Therefore, in our solution, we try to support several different description formalisms, including OWL-S, SAWSDL, and tag-based. For matchmaking, we will rely on those matchmakers that the S3 contest has ranked best.

In order to exploit existing service descriptions and to perform matchmaking as described above, appropriate service requests are needed. Quite obviously, ordinary users will not be able to provide such requests in one of the formal languages. Therefore, we rely on an approach similar to the one proposed in WSColab (Gawinecki et al., 2010), a tagging based solution: Gawinecki (2009) proposed the collaborative tagging with structure technique as a solution. To create a collaborative tagging description, we can use a structure based on WSColab system tags (Gawinecki, et al., 2012).

Crucial information about the service descriptions has been categorized into three categories: input (information the service needs), output (information the service provides), and behavior tags (description of the operation of the service). Afterwards, the request message will be converted to WSDL, SAWSDL, OWL or tagging format and be forwarded to the matchmaker module. The in-depth detail and example for the conversion are explained in the Building Blocks section.

In addition to the service discovery aspect, user profiles and context should be taken into account. Soylu, Causmaecker, and Desmet (2009) presented in the context of Pervasive Computing the idea to react to environmental conditions and adapt accordingly. However, automatic actions can easily lead to undesired results. Thus, users should be involved in resolving conflicts of priorities or desired behavior. MERCURY should only suggest appropriate and compatible services relevant in the given context. This way the user can make decisions easier without being overwhelmed by numerous irrelevant services. Additionally,

Breslin, Passant, and Decker (2009) presents the idea to derive user context from their social activities, e.g. from their interest, their expertise and their friend's activities. They consider social networking activities as an important aspect of user context.

In MERCURY, we define the situation as an event to identify specific outcome from sensor(s), or specific action to actuator(s), while the scenario performs as a whole application that is composed of several situations. Therefore, each situation is reusable and each scenario is easier to customize. We envision four main use cases of the service discovery module in MERCURY as shown in Figure 3: Service Registration, Situation definition, scenario definition, and scenario execution.

Usage of Discovery in MERCURY

1. **Service Registration:** Before a user can utilize sensors, actuators, or services in her situations or scenarios, she needs to register them with MERCURY. While this approach makes sense, e.g., it is not realistic to register all of the potentially relevant services available via the Internet. Therefore, we complement the manual registration with

Figure 3. Process flow of Sensor discovery in MERCURY

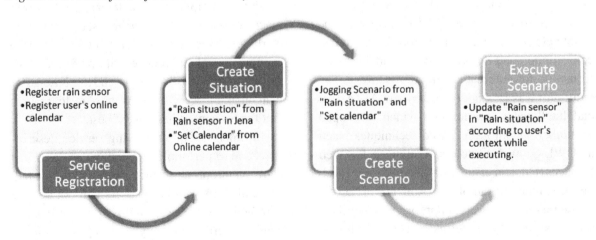

an automated service discovery approach. Figure 4 shows how the automated service discovery performs in service registration.

2. **Situation Definition (Create):** When a user creates a new situation, either from scratch or from a template, she might use the discovery module to find appropriate services to add to this situation. Consider, e.g., a user defining a "Rain in Jena" situation is looking for an appropriate sensor to implement this situation.

We can create a situation by two approaches.

a. **From Scratch:** A user searches for sensors one by one and adds them to a situation.

b. **From Existing Situation:** A previously created situation can be treated as a template. The description available for each situation can be defined by a user or automatically created from sensors' descriptions used in that situation.

Thus, service discovery plays a role as a sensor or service search engine. A user can search for existing services in order to model a situation. For example, she could use the service discovery module to discover weather sensors and sprinkler actuators in her backyard.

A service control panel in the Mercury modelling module is shown in Figure 5. There are two ways of discovery here: implicitly and explicitly. Figure 5(a) shows MERCURY implicitly recommends situations. Users can create, edit or delete situations easily via a control panel. Once a service has been added to the situation canvas, a service request is created implicitly and the resulting services are put in the recommendation panel. From Schafer, Frankowski, Herlocker, and Sen (2007), the recommendation can be based on collaborative filtering, such as rating from other users who have the same behavior, or based on content-based filtering, which does not need other users' efforts, but rather depends on services' descriptions.

Apart from the implicit recommendation, MERCURY also provides users an advanced search function, where a service request is created from explicit user inputs. Users can search for the service with specific inputs, outputs and functionalities as shown in Figure 5 (b). Moreover,

Figure 4. The automated service discovery offered in service registration module of MERCURY

Figure 5. Prototype for Modelling Module searching for a service or sensor (a) service recommendation (b) advance search in modelling module

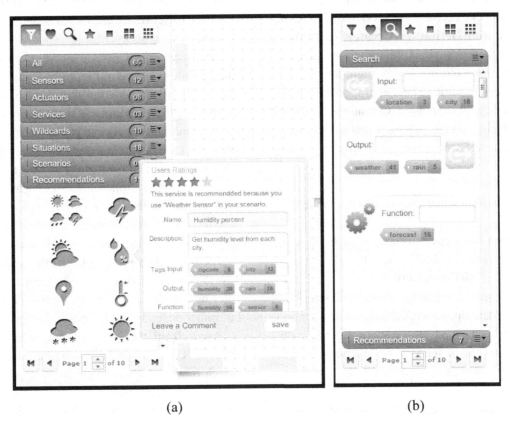

(a)   (b)

if a service description contains semantic annotations; more services that are relevant can be discovered.

After all services have been connected, the situation can be saved and the user will be prompted to specify a name and a description of this situation. From the user's definition of the description, MERCURY will create a description file (like SAWSDL or collaborative tagging, for example) so that the service matcher can discover the situation later.

3. **Scenario Definition (Create):** Similarly, when a user creates a new scenario from existing situations, she may want to use the discovery module to find appropriate situations to include in the scenario. The discovery process can be done implicitly based on the user's contexts or explicitly from the user's inputs as in the situation definition. Consider, as an example, a user aiming to define: if "Rain in Jena" then "set my calendar later as - I won't go jogging". Hence, she might look for a previously defined "Rain in Jena" situation.

Figure 6 displays an example in which a user created the situation called "Is it raining?" It will notify the user if a precipitation phenomenon occurs during a specific time frame of a day. The situation is triggered once it is raining or snowing at this time, let say early in the morning. Addi-

Figure 6. Prototype for Modelling Module creating the situation

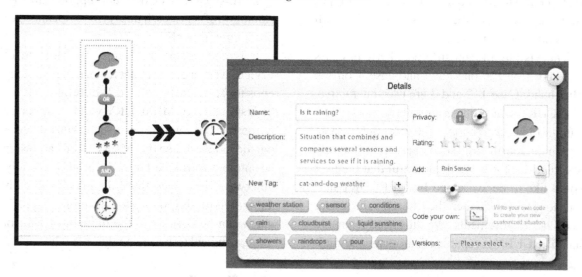

tionally, the situation can be tagged, shared and rated for the sake of community distribution and recommendation.

The situation template can be selected and edited to serve a particular user's need. For example, a user can select an existing template named "Turn on the light, if anyone enters the room". She can edit a parameter in the situation from "anyone" to "me" by changing the movement detector service to an RFID service that identifies a person who enters the room. To achieve this, the sensor discovery module will play two roles: discovering an existing situation and discovering an appropriate service.

4. **Scenario Execution (Dynamic Discovery of Sensors):** Users may also want to define generic situations that are automatically instantiated with appropriate services at runtime. Consider, e.g., a user who travels a lot. She might decide to replace the condition in the scenario above by a "Rain where I am" situation. Assume further, that for some reason she does not trust the web-based weather services, but would like to rely on

readings of "real", physical sensors in her vicinity. In this case, the situation would need to be changed, so that, first, a location sensor (maybe the GPS sensor in her cell phone) determines her current location. Next, a service request enables the run-time discovery of a rain sensor close to that location, which results in the discovery, configuration, and ultimately execution of the service.

For standard scenarios, there is no need to rediscover the service again. However, if the user needs to change the service automatically with respect to his or her current context, Mercury needs to use the "on-the-fly" service discovery. For instance, we have a situation says "Detect if there is a post office nearby my current location".

From the sensor discovery, the user selected a GPS sensor to provide a parameter "mylocation". During an execution of this situation, the rain sensor service should be re-run according to the value from "mylocation". At runtime, MERCURY will construct a request message for dynamic discovery of the service. The parameter "mylocation" is used as a keyword in service behavior, a service input is left blank and a service output can be an address of the nearest post office with approximate distance.

There is a significant difference between cases 1, 2 and 3 on the one hand and case 4 on the other hand: Case 1, 2 and 3 are user-interactive. MERCURY will propose suitable sensors, but it is up to the user to choose the most appropriate one. In the fourth case, such interaction is hardly possible, since it is highly doubtful that the user would like to be awakened by MERCURY at 5 a.m. to decide whether the chosen rain sensor meets her requirements. We thus need to ensure that MERCURY is capable of automatically finding the best sensor.

SERVICE DISCOVERY TECHNIQUES

In this section, we describe how we envision service discovery to work in MERCURY and how the discovery technique can be made aware of personal contexts and preferences in order to provide the proper recommendation or desirable result. We start with some assumptions to define the scope of this topic. Then, we present an architectural model of service discovery that can fulfil the previously mentioned requirements.

Initial Assumption

In MERCURY, as briefly mentioned above already, we assume that all sensors and actuators are available as web services. We do not make any assumptions whether a web service represents a single sensor/actuator or provides access to an entire sensor net. We do assume that all these web services are described using WSDL. In addition to these WSDL descriptions, which are necessary for the invocation of the services, the services may possess additional descriptions. These additional descriptions may be, e.g., OWL-S, SAWSDL, hRESTS or Micro-WSMO and/or "social" descriptions gained from user-provided

tags. MERCURY itself does not support semantic annotation of services. It does provide an interface for tagging, though.

It is compulsory to specify the domain of services we can discover here, since the ontology repository needs to be defined. We also assume that the installation of MERCURY will be supported by a certain business purpose, such as insurance or logistic industries, so that MERCURY can assign the ontology to a request from a user automatically. Otherwise, the request that contains semantically ambiguous descriptions, for example, "apple", which can be defined in the domain of fruit or brand, can lead to wrong analysis results.

Architecture

Figure 7 shows the architecture of the MERCURY service discovery module. First, a request needs to be created. To achieve this, the user needs to give the input via the Request UI, which requires input keywords or output keywords or service behavior keywords (MERCURY needs at least one keyword, it is not necessary to provide them all. The more keywords are provided, the higher the matching quality will potentially be). The same methodology is used to support automatic filtering, i.e. proposing only matching components when working with the modelling UI. In this case, the input is derived from state and context of the modelling module depending on the current content of the scenario.

Imagine a user who needs to look up the weather forecast service, which is indicated by zip code or city name. In this case, the service that the user is looking for should accept zip code or city name as inputs, return weather details as outputs, and, optionally, the behavior (in the other name, operation description) of the service can be described as "weatherByZipcode" or relevant terms (such as "cityWeatherForecast", etc.). Therefore, we can construct a request message as depicted in Algorithm 1.

Figure 7. MERCURY Service Discovery Architecture

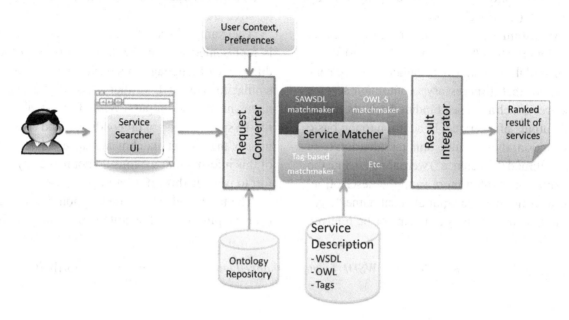

Algorithm 1. Service request formatted message constructed in MERCURY

```
<request>
        <message name="input">
                <element name="zipCode" type="string"/>
                <element name="cityName" type="string"/>
        </message>
        <message name="output">
                <complexElement name="weatherForecast" type="string">
                        <subElement name = "date"/>
                        <subElement name = "weatherDetail"/>
                </complexElement>
        </message>
        <message name="behaviour">
                <element name="weatherByZipcode" type="string"/>
                <element name="weatherByCityName" type="string"/>
        </message>
</request>
```

Optionally, input and output can be restricted to terms from a controlled vocabulary or ontology. This will improve match results. We will explain the technical details underlying the request converter in section Building Blocks. From these user inputs and possibly user context or prefer-ences, service requests are created. Since we do not know which description formalisms were used by the service providers, we convert the user input into requests following different formalisms. For the proof-of-concept implementation, these will be SAWSDL, OWL-S (input/output only), and tag-based following the model proposed by WSColab (Gawinecki, 2009).

Algorithm 2 shows the example of a service description in SAWSDL format. It was constructed from WSDL format, which contains service's information that are necessary for automatic service discovery, such as names, binding methods, inputs and outputs of a service. In addition to the basic description, the semantic annotations (notate in "sawsdl:modelReference") were added so that the machine can exploit more from the description. Considering that, the input element name "city" without semantic annotation cannot be referred to its super classes, such as "place" or "administrative area".

The example for an OWL-S service description is represented in Algorithm 3. Apart from the difference of languages, its basic construction is similar to SAWSDL in that it contains service name, inputs and outputs. While OWL-S allows for the specification of preconditions and effects, none of the current matchmakers takes advantage of this information; we thus do not make any effort to provide this information.

The tag-based service description in Table 1 (a) exemplifies how the collaborative tagging is

Algorithm 2. Service description in WSDL format, enhanced with semantic annotations (SAWSDL)

```
<wsdl:description ...>
        <wsdl:types> <xsd:schema ...>
                        <xsd:element name="WeatherServiceRequest"
type="xsd:string"
                        sawsdl:modelReference="http://.../ontosem.owl#city"/>
                        <xsd:complexType name="WeatherServiceResponse"
                        sawsdl:modelReference="http://.../ontosem.
owl#weather">
                                <xsd:sequence>
                                        <xsd:element name="date"
type="Date"/>
                                        ...
                                        <xsd:element name="weatherDesc"
type="String"/>
                                </xsd:sequence>
                        </xsd:complexType>
        </xsd:schema> </wsdl:types>
        ...
        <wsdl:interface name="WeatherServiceInterface">
                <wsdl:operation name="WeatherService">
                        <wsdl:input element="WeatherServiceRequest" />
                        <wsdl:output element="WeatherServiceResponse" />
                </wsdl:operation>
        </wsdl:interface>
        <wsdl:service name="WeatherService" >...</wsdl:service>
</wsdl:description>
```

Algorithm 3. Service description in OWL-S format

```
<rdf:RDF  …>
        <owl:Ontology rdf:about="">…</owl:Ontology>
        <service:Service rdf:ID="WEATHER_FORECAST_SERVICE">…</service:Service>
        <process:Input rdf:ID="_CITY">
                <process:parameterType> http://…/ontosem.owl#city</
process:parameterType>
        </process:Input>
        <process:Output  rdf:ID="_WEATHER">
                <process:parameterType> http://…/ontosem.owl#weather</
process:parameterType>
        </process:Output>
        …
</rdf:RDF>
```

stored. Each service contains tags for behavior, input and output of the service. In addition, each tag contains the number of users who tagged the service with the same keyword. Table 1 (b) shows the example of a service request that can be constructed from message in Algorithm 1.

We will use existing service matchers, such as, SAWSDL-iMatcher (Wei, Wang, T., Wang, J., & Bernstein, 2011), OWLS-MX (Klusch, 2009), etc. Each service may have more than one type of description (e.g. SAWSDL and tagging). In such a case, the user would not need to specify the type of description for the service he or she is looking for. The matcher will compare the request message with description files, which are already known by matchers.

Finally, the results returned from each matcher will be merged and rearranged again using weight parameters, which will be described in more details in section Building Blocks. The weight param-

Table 1. (a) Service description and (b) service request format for collaborative tag-based method described in WSColab

(a)	(b)

`<service name="Weather_Forcast_Service.xml">`
`<behaviour>`
`<annotation users="3" tag="weather_forecast"/>`
`<annotation users="2" tag="city_weather"/>`
`<annotation users="2" tag="weather_service"/>`
`</behaviour>`
`<input>`
`<annotation users="4" tag="city_name"/>`
`<annotation users="1" tag="city"/>`
`</input>`
`<output>`
`<annotation users="3" tag="weather_condition"/>`
`<annotation users="2" tag="temperature"/>`
`<annotation users="1" tag="weather"/>`
`</output>`
`</service>`
	input:city
	output:weather
	behaviour:weather_forecast_service

eters are configurable and can be determined as described by Klusch (2012). Match results from matchmakers with good evaluation results will be weighed more heavily than those from matchmakers with poorer performance.

The service discovery module acquires user's request from a text-based search, and separated between operation, input and output terms, and converts them into formatted structures. There is no specific service matching technique for our approach, since each service can be described in different forms. We also cope with all possible (and prominent) matching techniques by converting the request into required formats. Finally, the results from each service matchmaker are needed to be sensibly ranked. Therefore, we will discuss the necessary building blocks further in detail.

BUILDING BLOCKS

From the architecture of the MERCURY service discovery module we describe the two main building blocks, namely the request converter and the result integrator. The request converter section shows how the service request works with service matchmakers, which have various formats.

The result integrator section explains how MERCURY can rank the returned result from the service matchmakers, according to the relevance, and how the user context can manipulate the recommendations of services.

Request Converter

After a user submits a request, this data should be converted into an appropriate form for service matchers. As shown in Figure 8, the request converter will retrieve information from a configuration file for the name and the directory of

Figure 8. Data flow diagram of Request Converter and Service Matcher

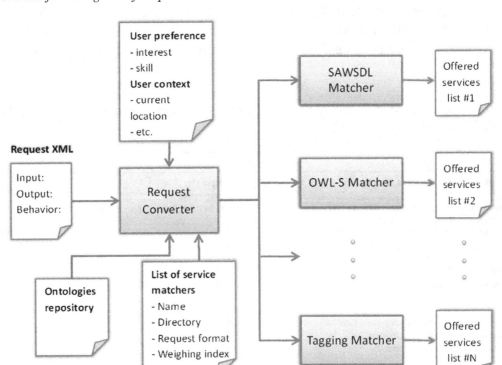

service matchers, so it can execute them. The request format is the key parameter for the request converter, since the request will be reformatted again according to this information. In addition to the service description, MERCURY will enhance it with semantic annotation. Thus, text analysis within the specific domain should automatically assign the ontology to the request. Currently, our implementation is using OWL ontologies following the test collection in Klusch (2012). The weighted index will be used in the result integrator, which is described in the next section.

A request message is converted to a compatible format of each matcher following a mapping schema. For example, to convert a request message shown in Algorithm 1, the request converter will look for a mapping schema for OWL-S, which is specified in a configuration file. The mapping schema, as Algorithm 4 shows, will specify the element and attribute of the request message to OWL-S format. Additionally, the semantic annotations of the input and output context can be automatically defined before the conversion. The request converter will look up for the semantic description of the word "weather" in an ontology repository. The result will be returned as URIs, which are defined as ontology attributes of an element.

In addition, user preference and user context are optional inputs, whenever they relate to the service being requested. Otherwise, this information will not be added to the request.

To exemplify how the request would look like before being processed by the service matchmaker, we use the SAWSDL based matchmaker as an example, as presented by Klusch (2009). Please note that we have omitted some information in the service request for the sake of simplicity. For other types of matchers, the same concept is applied.

From Table 2, the request for a service is matched with the offers in the service repository. As an example, the service request defines that the required service should provide two types of operations, both offer the weather forecast description as outputs, but one accepts a zip code as an input, and the other accepts a city name as an input. The first service offer provides both operations. Even though it contains different keywords from the request, the vocabulary problem can be resolved with the semantic annotations. The second service offers only one type of operation, which accepts only a zip code as an input. Thus, this service meets only half of the initial requirements. The third service accepts a city name as an input, thus also meeting half of the requirements for the input. However, since the operation of the third service is to get a zip code from a city name, the output and operation requirements are not fulfilled. If the service description repository contains only these three service offers,

Algorithm 4. Mapping schema example for OWL-S

```
[input]
                element(name) -> process:Input (rdf:ID)
                element(ontology) -> process:parameterType (node value)
[output]
                element(name) -> process:Output (rdf:ID)
                … // in this example, this part is similar to the input
[behaviour.request]
        element(name) -> grounding:wsdlInputMessage (node value)
[behaviour.response]
        element(name) -> grounding:wsdlOutputMessage (node value)
```

Table 2. Sample service request and offer for SAWSDL Matcher

Service Request	Service Offer (1)
<types><schema...> <simpleType name=" **zipCode**" modelReference ="http://... #ZipCode"> </ simpleType > <simpleType name=" **cityName**" modelReference ="http://... geographydataset.owl#City"> </ simpleType > <complexType name=" **weatherForecast**" modelReference ="http://... #weather"> <sequence> <element name="**date**" /> <element name="**weatherDetail**" /> </sequncc> </complexType> </schema></types> <message name=" **WeatherByZipCodeRequest**"> <part name=" **zipCode**"/> </message> <message name=" **WeatherByZipCodeResponse**"> <part name=" **weatherDetail**"/> </message> <message name="**WeatherByCityNameRequest**"> <part name=" **cityName**" </message> <message name=" **WeatherByCityNameResponse**"> <part name=" **weatherDetail**"/> </message> <portType name="**WeatherForecast**"> <operation name="GetWeatherByZipCode"> <input message=" WeatherByZipCodeRequest"/> <output message=" WeatherByZipCodeResponse"/> </operation> <operation name="GetWeatherByCityName"> <input message=" WeatherByCityNameRequest"/> <output message=" WeatherByCityNameResponse"/> </operation> </portType>	<types><schema...> <simpleType name=" **ZipCode**" modelReference ="http://... #ZipCode"> </ simpleType > <simpleType name=" **PlaceName**" modelReference ="http://... geographydataset.owl#City"> </ simpleType > <complexType name="**Precipitation**" modelReference ="http://... #precipitation"> <sequence> <element name="**date**" /> <element name="**weatherDetail**" /> </sequence> </complexType> </schema></types> <message name=" **GetWeatherByZipCodeHttpGetIn**"> <part name=" **zipCode**"/> </message> <message name=" **GetWeatherByZipCodeHttpGetOut**"> <part name=" **weatherDetail**"/> </message> <message name="**GetWeatherByPlaceNameHttpGetIn**"> <part name=" **cityName**" </message> <message name=" **GetWeatherByPlaceNameHttpGetOut**"> <part name=" **weatherDetail**"/> </message> <portType name="**WeatherForecastHttpGet**"> <operation name="GetWeatherByZipCode"> <input message=" WeatherByZipCodeRequest"/> <output message=" WeatherByZipCodeResponse"/> </operation> <operation name="GetWeatherByCityName"> <input message=" WeatherByCityNameRequest"/> <output message=" WeatherByCityNameResponse"/> </operation> </portType>
Service Offer (2)	**Service Offer (3)**
<types><schema...> <simpleType name=" **ZipCode**" modelReference ="http://... #Zip-Code"> </ simpleType > <complexType name="**WeatherDescription**" modelReference ="http://... # weather"> <sequence> <element name=" **WeatherID**" /> <element name=" **Description**" /> </sequence> </complexType> </schema></types> <message name=" **GetCityWeatherByZIPHttpGetIn**"> <part name=" **ZIP**"/> </message> <message name=" **GetCityWeatherByZIPHttpGetOut**"> <part name=" **WeatherDescription**"/> </message> <portType name=" **WeatherHttpGet**"> <operation name=" GetCityWeatherByZIP"> <input message=" GetCityWeatherByZIPHttpPostIn"/> <output message=" GetCityWeatherByZIPHttpPostOut"/> </operation> </portType>	<types><schema...> <simpleType name=" **ZipCode**" modelReference ="http://... #ZipCode"> </ simpleType > <complexType name="**ArrayOfAnyType**" > <sequence> <element name=" **anyType**" /> </sequence> </complexType> </schema></types> <message name=" **CityStateToZipCodeMatcherHttpGetIn**"> <part name=" **City**"/> </message> <message name=" **CityStateToZipCodeMatcherHttpGetOut**"> <part name=" **Body**"/> </message> <portType name=" **AddressLookupHttpPost**"> <operation name=" CityStateToZipCodeMatcher"> <input message=" CityStateToZipCodeMatcherHttpPostIn"/> <output message=" CityStateToZipCodeMatcherHttpPostOut"/> </operation> </portType>

the most relevant service would be the first service. The second service is ranked in the second place, and the third service will be omitted from the matching result.

The level of likeliness between requests and offers is determined by similarity values. When a similarity value is greater than a threshold value, then this offer and request are considered as "matched". The threshold level of similarity is adjustable. A higher threshold results in a potentially better match between the offer and the request. This may yield a better quality of results, but also reduces the number of potentially successful matches. Which threshold level should be chosen depends among other factors on the level of human involvement: If the results of the matchmaking process are used as recommendations or suggestions to human users, a lower threshold value might be advisable. If the matchmaking process results in direct invocation of matched services, a higher threshold is safer.

Considering the example of the weather forecast service discovery, users might be interested in one specific city or any city they are currently staying. The request can be tailored to get results that are more specific. By using the current location information of the user instead of direct input from the request interface, MERCURY can make the result more specific and useful for the user.

Result Integrator

The results returned from service matchmakers, as presented in Klusch (2012), can be sorted according to the similarity score that is assigned to each web service. For example, the score of result from SAWSDL-iMatcher (Wei, Wang T., Wang J., & Bernstein, 2011) could be WSSAWSDL-MX = [WS1, WS2, WS3, WS4, WS5] = [0.9, 0.7, 0.6, 0.85, 0.93], where the elements in the array represent the similarity level of each service with respect to the request.

When there are more than one service matchmakers, the result integrator needs weighing

parameters for each matchmaker. The weight parameter will be written and read from a configuration file. The default value will be "1" for all matchmakers. All similarity scores of each web service from all service matchmakers will be accumulated and normalized, so that we can rearrange the ranking according to the final score.

Once again, the user context can play an important role here, in order to match the relevance of service recommendation to the need of users in each circumstance. Considering the following scenario, a user who resides in the USA would prefer to use the weather forecast service with a description "US Weather Service" rather than the one with a broader description like "Global Weather Forecast". Furthermore, a service with a description like "European Weather Service" can be neglected or moved to the lower rank since it does not match with the user context.

FUTURE RESEARCH DIRECTIONS

Previously, we have proposed a prototype implementation of MERCURY. To accomplish the goal of "device and service smart integration", we need to integrate this module to MERCURY and exploit it along a practical use case. In addition, security concerns that may arise in particular with the personal awareness need to be addressed. We also consider the collaborative sharing, recommending and rating of "situation/scenario" templates among users. This can help to ease MERCURY accessibility for both personal and commercial use. Currently, we focus on the health insurance domain application for our next use case. We would like to deploy sensors and services such as blood sugar level sensors, training schedules, and nutrition advisors. We have a foresight that the health condition tracking application would help the users and boost up service' values for the health insurance company.

CONCLUSION

The MERCURY project aims to realize the seamless integration of devices and services with a user-friendly interface. In this paper, we mainly focused on the service discovery aspect exploiting personal awareness in order to improve the discovery results. We introduced a discovery module composed of a situation definition, a scenario definition and a scenario execution module. In order to address the requirements, we assumed that the service description contains at least a WSDL file. We also assumed that the application domain should be restricted, so that we can semantically analyse the request message properly.

The architectural overview described the main building blocks. The request converter reformats request and user context into compatible forms for service matchers. To improve the evaluation result, several service matchers may be used and the result integrator may merge the results. Finally, we reviewed related and existing work. At the moment, we are working on a proof-of-concept implementation.

ACKNOWLEDGMENT

This research is accomplished under the framework of the Mercury project and is supported by IBM Deutschland Research & Development GmbH, Foundation "Gran Mariscal de Ayacucho" and DAAD.

REFERENCES

Blake, M. B., Bleul, S., Weise, T., Bansal, A., & Kona, S. (2009). *Web services challenge*. Retrieved February 21, 2013, from http://ws-challenge.georgetown.edu/wsc09

Blake, M. B., Cabral, L., König-Ries, B., Küster, U., & Martin, D. (2012). *Semantic web services: Advancement through evaluation*. Berlin: Springer. doi:10.1007/978-3-642-28735-0.

Bo, C., Xiuquan, Q., Budan, W., Xiaokun, W., Ruisheng, S., & Junliang, C. (2012). *RESTful web service mashup based coal mine safety monitoring and control automation with wireless sensor network*. Paper presented at IEEE 19th International Conference on Web Services (ICWS), (pp. 620-622). IEEE.

Breslin, J. G., Passant, A., & Decker, S. (2009). *The social semantic web*. Berlin: Springer. doi:10.1007/978-3-642-01172-6.

Christensen, E., Curbera, F., Meredith, G., & Weerawarana, S. (2001). *Web services description language (WSDL)*. Retrieved February 21, 2013, from http://www.w3.org/TR/wsdl

Cloud Business Apps Integration – CloudWork. (2013). Retrieved February 21, 2013, from https://cloudwork.com/

Cosm - Internet of Things Platform Connecting Devices and Apps for Real-Time Control and Data Storage. (2012). Retrieved February 21, 2013, from https://cosm.com

Dey, A. K., Sohn, T., Streng, S., & Kodama, J. (2006). iCAP: Interactive prototyping of context-aware applications. []. Berlin: Springer.]. *Proceedings of Pervasive Computing*, *3968*, 254–271. doi:10.1007/11748625_16.

Ding, Z., Lei, D., Yan, J., Bin, Z., & Lun, A. (2010). *A web service discovery method based on tag*. Paper presented at International Conference on Complex, Intelligent and Software Intensive Systems (CISIS). New York, NY.

Evrythng. (2012). Retrieved February 21, 2013, from http://www.evrythng.com

Gawinecki, M. (2009). *WSColab: Structured collaborative tagging for web service matchmaking.* Retrieved February 21, 2013, from http://www.ibspan.waw.pl/~gawinec/wss/wscolab.html

Gawinecki, M., Cabri, G., Paprzycki, M., & Ganzha, M. (2010). WSColab: Structured collaborative tagging for web service matchmaking. In *Proceedings of the 6th International Conference on Web Information Systems and Technologies (WEBIST 2010),* (pp.70-77). Valencia, Spain: INSTICC Press.

Gawinecki, M., Cabri, G., Paprzycki, M., & Ganzha, M. (2012). Evaluation of structured collaborative tagging for web service matchmaking. In *Semantic Web Services Advancement through Evaluation* (pp. 173–189). Berlin: Springer. doi:10.1007/978-3-642-28735-0_11.

Gray, A. J. G., Castro, R. G., Kyzirakos, K., Karpathiotakis, M., Calbimonte, J. P., Page, K., et al. (2011). A semantically enabled service architecture for mashups over streaming and stored data. In *Proceedings of the 8th Extended Semantic Web Conference on the Semantic Web: Research and Applications,* (pp. 300-314). Berlin: Springer.

Grosky, W. I., Kansal, A., Nath, S., Liu, J., & Zhao, F. (2007). SenseWeb: An infrastructure for shared sensing. *IEEE MultiMedia, 14*(4), 8–13. doi:10.1109/MMUL.2007.82.

Guinard, D. (2009). *Towards the web of things: Web mashups for embedded devices.* Paper presented at 2nd Workshop on Mashups, Enterprise Mashups and Lightweight Composition on the Web MEM 2009. Madrid, Spain.

Guo, B., Zhang, D., & Imai, M. (2011). Toward a cooperative programming framework for context-aware applications. *Personal and Ubiquitous Computing, 15*(3), 221–233. doi:10.1007/s00779-010-0329-1.

Harth, A., & Maynard, D. (2012). *Semantic web challenge.* Retrieved February 21, 2013, from http://challenge.semanticweb.org

Hobold, G. C., & Siqueira, F. (2012). *Discovery of semantic web services compositions based on SAWSDL annotations.* Paper presented at IEEE 19th International Conference on Web Services (ICWS). New York, NY.

IBM WebSphere Portal. (2013). Retrieved February 21, 2013, from http://www-01.ibm.com/software/websphere/portal/

IFTTT - If This Then That. (2013). Retrieved February 21, 2013, from https://ifttt.com

Klusch, M. (2012). *Semantic service selection (S3) contest.* Retrieved February 21, 2013, from http://www-ags.dfki.uni-sb.de/~klusch/s3/index.html

Klusch, M., Kapahnke, P., & Zinnikus, I. (2009). SAWSDL-MX2: A machine-learning approach for integrating semantic web service matchmaking variants. In *Proceedings of Web Services* (pp. 335–342). IEEE. doi:10.1109/ICWS.2009.76.

Koenig-Ries, B., Opasjumruskit, K., Nauerz, A., & Welsch, M. (2012). *MERCURY: User centric device & service processing.* Paper presented at Mensch & Computer Workshopband (MKWI). Braunschweig, Germany.

Kovatsch, M., Lanter, M., & Duquennoy, S. (2012). Actinium: A RESTful runtime container for scriptable internet of things applications. In *Proceedings of the 3rd International Conference on the Internet of Things (IoT),* (pp. 135-142). IoT.

Maleshkova, M., Kopeck, J., & Pedrinaci, C. (2009). Adapting SAWSDL for semantic annotations of RESTful services. In *Proceedings of the Confederated International Workshops and Posters on On the Move to Meaningful Internet Systems,* (pp. 917-926). Berlin: Springer.

Martin, D., Paolucci, M., Mcilraith, S., Burstein, M., Mcdermott, D., Mcguinness, D., et al. (2004). Bringing semantics to web services: The OWL-S approach. In *Proceedings of the First International Workshop on Semantic Web Services and Web Process Composition (SWSWPC 2004)*, (pp. 26-42). Berlin: Springer.

Martin, D., Paolucci, M., & Wagner, M. (2007). Bringing semantic annotations to web services: OWL-S from the SAWSDL perspective. In *Proceedings of the 6th International the Semantic Web and 2nd Asian Conference on Asian Semantic Web Conference*, (pp. 340-352). Berlin: Springer.

Mattern, F., & Floerkemeier, C. (2010). From the internet of computers to the internet of things. *Lecture Notes in Computer Science, 6462. On{X} –Automate Your Life*. (2012). Retrieved February 21, 2013, from https://www.onx.ms

Ngan, L. D., Kirchberg, M., & Kanagasabai, R. (2010). *Review of semantic web service discovery methods*. Paper presented at IEEE 6th World Congress on Services (SERVICES-1). New York, NY.

Opasjumruskit, K., Exposito, J., Koenig-Ries, B., Nauerz, A., & Welsch, M. (2012) *MERCURY: User centric device and service processing – Demo paper*. Paper presented at 19th Intl. Workshop on Personalization and Recommendation on the Web and Beyond, Mensch & Computer 2012. Konstanz, Germany.

Paraimpu - The Web of Things is More Than Things in the Web. (2012). Retrieved February 21, 2013, from http://paraimpu.crs4.it/

Phuoc, D. L., & Hauswirth, M. (2009). Linked open data in sensor data mashups. In *Proceedings of the 2nd International Workshop on Semantic Sensor Networks (SSN09) in Conjunction with ISWC 2009*, (pp. 1-16). ISWC.

Roman, D., Keller, U., Lausen, H., Bruijn, J. D., Lara, R., Stollberg, M. et al. (2005). Web service modeling ontology. *Applied Ontology, 1*(1), 77–106.

Schafer, J. B., Frankowski, D., Herlocker, J., & Sen, S. (2007). Collaborative filtering recommender systems. *The Adaptive Web, 4321*, 291–324. doi:10.1007/978-3-540-72079-9_9.

Soylu, A., Causmaecker, P., & Desmet, P. (2009). Context and adaptivity in pervasive computing environments: Links with software engineering and ontological engineering. *Journal of Software, 4*(9), 992–1013. doi:10.4304/jsw.4.9.992-1013.

Talantikite, H. N., Aissani, D., & Boudjlida, N. (2009). Semantic annotations for web services discovery and composition. *Computer Standards & Interfaces, 31*(6), 1108–1117. doi:10.1016/j.csi.2008.09.041.

Tran, V. X., Puntheeranurak, S., & Tsuji, H. (2009). *A new service matching definition and algorithm with SAWSDL*. Paper presented at 3rd IEEE International Conference on Digital Ecosystems and Technologies (DEST '09). New York, NY.

Wei, D., Wang, T., Wang, J., & Bernstein, A. (2011). SAWSDL-iMatcher: A customizable and effective semantic web service matchmaker. *Web Semantics: Science. Services and Agents on the World Wide Web, 9*(4), 402–417. doi:10.1016/j.websem.2011.08.001.

KEY TERMS AND DEFINITIONS

Adaptive Computing: A computing system that can adjust to the environmental factors during the runtime. An adaptive system may change the behavior or functionality according to individual users or situations.

Collaborative Description: An effort to share service descriptions among users in the same system. Therefore, the services, which may or may not contain descriptions from service providers, can be discovered and recommended to the other users, with a minimum cold-starting problem.

Context Awareness: A property of a device, especially mobile devices, to sense the surrounding information, such as, location, temperature, etc. This term is coined from ubiquitous computing, since it is the bridge connecting between computer systems and physical environment.

Semantic Service Description: A service description, normally provided by the service provider, describes the functionality and instructs how to use the service. Not only consumable by machines, but human can also get benefits from the description. When the semantic service description is extended with semantic annotations, textual information will be enhanced with meanings derived from ontologies.

Service Discovery: An ability of automatically detecting physical devices and services, which are available on the computer network. Users are able to query for a service provider, then further access and exploit the required service.

Service Recommendation: In the context of MERCURY, once a service has been registered to the system, though by the other users, a user can receive a suggestion to add a service that is relevant to the contexts, preferences and expertises of the user.

User Centric: A stage of users being more powerful and able to take control over the devices or systems, in contrast to the traditional device centric technology. Thus, the users can exploit more from devices and systems regardless of operating systems, hardware or locations.

Chapter 5
Architecture Pattern for Context–Aware Smart Environments

Viktoriya Degeler
University of Groningen, The Netherlands

Alexander Lazovik
University of Groningen, The Netherlands

ABSTRACT

Recent years marked many smart environment solutions hitting the market and applying latest pervasive computing research advancements on an industrial scale. Context-aware smart environments are able to act accordingly to the immediate environment information in an intelligent, predefined, learned, or automatically inferred way, and are able to communicate to their users, thus increasing users' comfort and awareness level. Since the beginning of the 2000s, many projects have been designing and implementing smart environment systems. When looking post-factum at the architectures of these systems, one can notice a lot of similarities among them. With the same basic structure, the biggest differences usually arise at the level of individual components, aimed to satisfy different end-level requirements. Taking many successful and undergoing projects as case-studies, this chapter looks for the common structure, the common patterns, and the "best practices" that can help future projects to reduce the efforts spent on the general system frame, and redirect those efforts to more specific requirements that are unique in every project. It introduces several architecture layers that inevitably exist in one form or another, discusses the possible layer components and the common information flows, and mentions the most notable problems, such as scalability and fault tolerance. Several case studies of successful or undergoing smart building projects show that the presented pattern can be easily mapped to their architectures.

DOI: 10.4018/978-1-4666-4695-7.ch005

INTRODUCTION

The ability of pervasive systems to perceive the context of the surrounding environment and act accordingly proves to be an enormously powerful tool for raising immediate users' satisfaction and helping them to increase their own awareness and act in a more informed way. Therefore, recent years marked many smart environment solutions hitting the market and applying latest pervasive computing research advancements on an industrial scale.

Magnitude of context-aware smart spaces applications is enormous: it stretches from telephones that redirect the call to the room where the recipient is currently located, e.g. the Active Badge system (Want, Hopper, Falcão, & Gibbons, 1992), and simple coffee machines with the possibility to schedule the time of coffee preparation exactly to the time when you wake up to whole building automation systems with complex rules of behavior and planning techniques that are just waiting for your wink to launch the complex artificial intelligence reasoning that will understand and fulfill your unvoiced demands.

Going even further, smart environments matter not only on the Personal and the Social scale, but on the bigger Urban scale as well. Sometimes whole neighborhoods can be considered as smart spaces, as shown by many Smart Grid enabling projects (Georgievski, Degeler, Pagani, Nguyen, Lazovik, & Aiello, 2012), (Capodieci, Pagani, Cabri, & Aiello, 2011). By introducing small scale energy generating facilities, such as wind turbines or solar panels, it is possible for individual buildings to produce more energy than they consume at certain points of time. To avoid losing this precious energy (which becomes even more precious considering its "green" sustainable origin), peer-to-peer-like energy transfer connections are introduced between buildings, with full featured automated negotiation techniques that enable one building to sell excessive energy to another neighboring building. First field-testing projects, such as PowerMatching City project in the Netherlands (Bliek, et al., 2010), which features 25 interconnected households, show that not only such energy comes with a cheaper price, but also the "transfer overhead" is severely reduced, as now the average energy travel distance is much shorter.

As can be seen, context-aware smart environments come in many different faces and on many different scales, but underlying idea remains the same: the system is aware of its context, i.e. the environment around, is able to act accordingly in an intelligent, predefined, learned, or automatically inferred way, and is able to communicate to its users, thus increasing their comfort and awareness level as well. Seng Loke in his book (Loke, 2006) defines the three main elements of the context-aware pervasive system: sensing, thinking, acting.

In just a few years after the first introduction of smart environments, the topic became booming, and many projects both in research and in industry were dedicated specifically to advancements in this area. As happened in many other research fields where a big number of different research groups and industrial companies started to work separately on the same topic, in the context-aware environments area the problems that the groups face are to a large extent similar, and some of them were solved several times, sometimes in a similar manner.

One of such problems, and an important one, is the high-level architecture design of smart context-aware systems. Since the beginning of the 2000s, many projects have been designing and implementing smart environment systems from scratch. However, when looking post-factum at the architectures of these systems, one can notice a lot of similarities among them. With the same basic structure, the biggest differences usually arise at the level of individual components, aimed to satisfy different end-level requirements.

Naturally appeared the idea to unify the architecture design for such smart environments projects. Taking many successful and undergoing projects as case-studies, we tried to find the common structure, the common patterns, and in some sense the "best practices" that can help future projects to reduce the efforts spent on the general system frame, and redirect those efforts to more specific requirements that are unique in every project. The work of Preveneers and Novais (Preveneers & Novais, 2012) surveys similar efforts to find and study best practices on different levels of smart pervasive applications that were already done in previous studies, including requirements engineering, context modelling, development acceleration and code reuse. In this chapter, on the other hand, we focus on a pattern for architecture design of smart environment systems.

We will introduce several layers of the architecture that inevitably exist in one form or another, and discuss the possible components that may be parts of these layers. We will then discuss the common information flows within such architecture and mention the most notable problems, such as scalability and fault tolerance. Finally, we will present several case studies, successful or undergoing smart building projects, and show that the presented pattern can be easily mapped to their architectures.

SMART ENVIRONMENTS

During the last years a lot of projects were dedicated to intelligent buildings automation. Though in this chapter we do not aim to provide an exhaustive review of such projects and for more thorough surveys the reader can refer to (Cook & Das, 2007) and (Nguyen & Aiello, 2012), the history of the most influential smart environment projects can be presented as follows.

It all started with the Active Badge (Want, Hopper, Falcão, & Gibbons, 1992) as early as in 1992. Though Active Badge most commonly cited as the beginning of the general context aware computing area, it can be seen that the main part of the project was concerned with making the environment (particularly, stationery phones) smarter.

Thus Active Badge is as well the first project that was concerned with the smart environments, and implemented them.

One of the earliest projects aimed at full building automation was MavHome (Youngblood, Cook, & Holder, 2004) (MavHome, 2003), which started in 2000. The project was oriented at discovering patterns of device usage and occupants' behavior by utilizing different learning algorithms. The project produced a lot of datasets of activities, sensor data, etc., which were used to provide predictions on future usage. The conclusion of the MavHome project was also a starting point for the currently ongoing successful CASAS Smart Home project by the same university (CASAS, 2008).

iSpace, which started as iDorm in 2002 (Callaghan, Clarke, Colley, Hagras, Chin, & Doctor, 2004) (iDorm, 2002), project features a room in a dormitory of the University of Essex (United Kingdom) campus fully equipped with sensors and actuators. The project uses full range of devices, featuring temperature, humidity, and light sensors, door locks, infrared sensors, video cameras, as well as HVAC system, motorized blinds, window openers, and light dimmers. The system can remember user's habits and automatically adjust its behavior accordingly, so that explicit requests for actions from the user can be minimized, unless, of course, the user changes his or her habits.

The SmartLab Research Laboratory (López-de-Ipiña, et al., 2008) (SmartLab, 2006) was constructed in 2006 to create a model of interactions between people and the context aware environment that surrounds them. This laboratory is used in several research projects, including Assistive Display, ubiClassRoom, and Eldercare.

The CASAS (Center for Advanced Studies in Adaptive Systems) Smart Home project (Kusznir & Cook, 2010) (CASAS, 2008) started in 2008 and has since produced a lot of publications both in academic press and in mass media. The smart environment for the project is a duplex apartment at the premises of the Washington State University. The apartment is equipped with a grid of sensors, including motion, temperature, power meter. The project heavily relies on Artificial Intelligence techniques such as Machine Learning in order to automatically recognize patterns of occupants behavior and automate the building to provide help and increase occupants' comfort.

As a part of Smart Homes for All (SM4All) project (Aiello, et al., 2011) (SM4All, 2008), which also started in 2008, a smart apartment was constructed in Rome, Italy. The project implemented sophisticated AI planning techniques, which produce a set of actions to adapt the house to user's needs in every possible situation. The breakthrough of the project was the application of the Brain-Computer Interface, a great help for many disabled people, which features the ability to read brain impulses of a smart home user and transform them into a certain desire about the smart home state, which in turn can be transformed into a set of actions for smart home actuators.

The e-Diana project (e-Diana, 2009) started in 2009 and was concerned with creation of a unified platform for all possible sub-systems of a smart building, such as security, lighting, power consumption, HVAC, etc. The project also aimed to improve energy consumption efficiency of such buildings and to provide better situation awareness for infrastructure owners.

The GreenerBuildings project (GreenerBuildings, 2013) started in 2010 and implements the intelligent office, constructed on premises of the Technical University of Eindhoven, The Netherlands. The project features the ability of users to modify the rules of office's behavior, which will then automatically adapt itself to their needs based on the context information. The project gives special attention to such issues of smart solutions as fault tolerance and scalability, which are essential for realization of smart solutions on a large scale, given hundreds of separate offices per building, or thousands of smart homes within a combined smart city.

2010 is also the start year of the ThinkHome project (Reinisch, Kofler, & Kastner, 2010),

aimed at optimization of the energy efficiency while maintaining user comfort. The project uses knowledge ontologies for reasoning about the home states, and plans to provide a comprehensive knowledge base for evaluation of control strategies based on relevant building data.

There are also many specialized projects, for example EnPROVE (EnPROVE, 2013) or Bey-Watch (Beywatch, 2008) that mostly deal with energy saving part of the smart environments, however, we mentioned here only some of the general broad-purpose context-aware smart environments.

We now will go into details and introduce components that are common for such projects.

ARCHITECTURE OVERVIEW

In this section we will present the design pattern of the smart environment architecture. The overview of the pattern is shown in Figure 1. We will show that the full architecture may be split into four layers, with several distinct components in every layer. Most component patterns arise from the architecture design similarities due to requirements that are common for all context-aware smart environments. It is important to note that components, which will be described below, are not exhaustive in terms of components' availability to the system. The components here are the backbone, but it is often the case that the actual implementation dictates for some support components, which either establish communication between other components, or act as watchdogs, proxies, monitors, etc. Also, if the system features a certain specific ability, such as a specific handling of heating mechanisms, or a special support for disabled users, more often than not this will require a separate component. Thus the system that is described in this chapter should be viewed as extendable, with the ability to plug-in more components, if needed. And, to the opposite, some presented components and flows are sometimes simplified, combined, or

Figure 1. Smart System Architecture Pattern

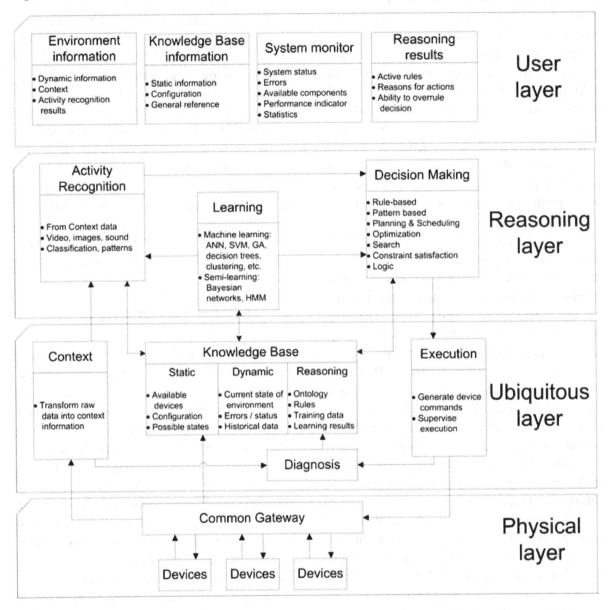

removed altogether in projects of smaller scale. This possibility will be highlighted at the level of components.

The Physical layer contains all hardware parts of the system, which include all wired and wireless sensors, actuators, network layout, low-level protocols associated with them, etc. One of the main tasks of the Physical layer is to collect information about the environment and transfer it to higher layers. Low-level protocols may be implemented to provide a common gateway, which allows to unify interfaces, hide the specific hardware differences, and/or reduce bandwidth requirements by bundling the information. The second main task of the Physical layer is to invoke actuators in the environment based on commands, sent from higher layers.

The Ubiquitous layer acts as an intermediary to the system components, and has several distinct responsibilities. First of all, the layer contains system's data storage, which means it collects and stores all the current and historical information about the environment, system configuration, system capabilities, user preferences, etc. The layer also should contain an information processing component, capable of detecting simple sensor errors or faults, transform information from low-level sensor values to high-level logical state of the environment, etc. On the actuation side the Ubiquitous layer is responsible for transforming commands from the Reasoning layer to low-level commands that the Physical layer is capable to execute, and making sure they are passed to the Physical layer in a concurrent non-blocking way.

The Reasoning layer is the layer where system's logic resides. It contains all components that are responsible for decisions on system's actions, be it a simple logic defined through strict if-then rules, or sophisticated AI techniques, such as planning or scheduling actions. The layer may also contain activity recognition or learning components, which should improve the automated system's response.

The User layer presents information about the system to its users. It contains two main parts. The first one presents information about the environment, current user preferences, reasons for certain decisions that the system makes, and allows a user to modify the configuration of the system according to her or his needs, enter new rules of execution, or overrule system's decisions. The second part provides meta-information about the system itself, such as the status of all components, whether they are working properly, statistics, resources consumption, etc.

We will now describe each layer in details.

Physical Layer

The main part of the Physical layer is, as the name hints, physical, i.e. devices that are implanted in the environment. All groups that decide to implement a smart home environment face an unavoidable issue from the very beginning: the heterogeneity of the devices they plan to use. Even now, while some companies started to specialize on providing combined sets of sensors and actuators, there are still a lot of special devices tailored to a particular need with distinct and possibly proprietary interfaces and communication protocols.

Thus it is essential to unify the interface and data gathering before sending the data further into the system. Not only such unification follows the famed low-coupling architecture principle, and makes it easy to add, remove, or change devices both individually, and as a whole type, but it also keeps all other parts of the system device-insensitive, so in its pure form the change of a device will not require a single line of code to be changed anywhere past the Physical layer.

Thus the essential part of the Physical layer is the Gateway, the component that initially collects data from devices and applies low-level transformation to it in order to send it further into the system in a uniform way. Note that the Gateway is highly hardware dependent, and will usually require changes in case of any changes of device types.

Of course, conceptually some other parts can be also treated as physical devices, especially information-providing ones, such as person's agenda, a call event over VoIP, or some electronic message from outside the system. Often such events are initially processed and entered into the system from the "top", i.e. from the User layer, or even via some other distinct entrance point, directly into the Ubiquitous or the Reasoning layer. But we argue that with a good level of abstraction, which a well-implemented Gateway provides, adding such events to the system from the "bottom", i.e. from the Physical layer, is also a perfectly viable solution that serves well to the unification of the event processing and information flows. In this case such event generators are commonly viewed and regarded as virtual or logical sensors.

Ubiquitous Layer

The Ubiquitous layer is the backbone of the whole system, the main support of all other components. It also contains main channels of information flow and storage, and in some sense the layer connects and helps in the interpretation of two different worlds: the device-level Physical layer and the domain-abstracted Reasoning layer.

There are several main components of the layer, and it is almost inevitable for all of them to be present in every smart environment system in one way or another.

Knowledge Base

We start with the Knowledge Base component. The database of the system belongs to this component, and for some systems the component will also be synonymous to the database. However, there is much more to it, first and foremost with respect to the types of information it handles. There are at least three types of information that are usually stored in the Knowledge Base, Figure 1 summarizes them.

The first type is the static information about devices. This includes the types of devices the system has, their communication protocols, whether they are sensors or actuators, the structure of readings they provide or states they can be set into. For configurable devices it also contains the configuration information. Though the name "static" implies that the information does not change frequently, it is nevertheless possible that the information will change automatically in the course of system's operation. For example, the SM4All smart home environment (Aiello, et al., 2011) provides the automatic device discovery feature.

The second type of the Knowledge Base information is the dynamic one, and this represents the information that changes with high frequency, for example the current state of the environment, devices, or executed commands. Many systems prefer to send this type of information directly to relevant components (for example in the Reasoning layer) instead of sending them to the Knowledge Base and letting the Knowledge Base handle further distribution. This makes sense,

since direct communication is also the fastest, and time of reaction is of utmost importance for the intelligent environment. However, the need for historical data collection is almost always a requirement, whether it is to update the training of a learning mechanism, to diagnose errors, or to show the history to a user. This means that even if the direct link for dynamic information transfer is outside the Knowledge Base, there should be a duplicate link which sends the data also to the Knowledge Base for storage and further retrieval and processing.

Finally, the last type of information in the Knowledge Base is almost exclusively used by the Reasoning layer, as it contains all the information, required for high-level reasoning. The exact model of information here depends heavily on what kind of reasoning the system uses. For ontology-based systems such as ThinkHome (Reinisch, Kofler, & Kastner, 2010), this will be the ontology of the system and the environment. For rule-based behavior the reasoning rules will be stored. Training data and learning results will be present for all systems that use machine learning in one way or another.

Context

The next component of the Ubiquitous layer is the Context. The main task of the context is to transform low-level raw data gathered from devices into a higher-level information, usable by the Reasoning layer.

One type of such processing is data packaging. Some sensors, for instance an acoustic sensor, send information with a very high frequency. It may be the case that the higher level components do not need such detailed information. Some simplified systems may only need to know, if there is a sound, or not, or the volume of sound, thus a lot of data transfers may be avoided by combining the information on the Context level and only sending the results higher into the system. Not only the bandwidth is saved, but also it removes the need for the Reasoning level to have a lower level representation of the device, and allows it to think in "domain-level" terms. Other examples include simple error filters that work nicely for such sensors as motion or light sensors, which for the most part send correct readings, but may occasionally send faulty ones. Such outliers are easily detectable by comparing them with neighboring readings.

It should be pointed out here that the Context component in its pure form does not involve any kind of domain level reasoning, such as activity recognition. The Context instead must prepare the data for the high-level reasoning by abstracting some devices and transforming the data from other devices. As an example, let us take the presence detection. Though in its basic form it is a simple mapping with the motion sensor, the recognition of presence in the room already reasons and operates in domain level terms. To increase the sophistication level, other sensors may be used in later versions of the system in order to get better recognition rate (such as RFIDs on entering people, video stream, etc.). This will change trivial mapping into intricate reasoning system. Thus from the beginning such reasoning should be placed into the Activity Recognition component of the Reasoning level.

Execution

The Execution component is in some sense the exact opposite to the Context. The task of the Execution is to transform action goals received from the Reasoning layer into executable actions that can be sent to devices. An important addition to the task is also to oversee the correct execution of the commands by devices.

It should be noted that the Execution in its pure form, as well as the Context, has absolutely no domain-level reasoning, i.e. it should not decide which command to execute out of several pos-

sibilities (any form of such reasoning belongs to the Reasoning layer). A good example is that the command to the Execution to "turn on a lamp" should also specify exactly, which lamp should be turned on in case there are several of them. If, on the other hand, the command is general, as in "turn on anything that provides light", the Execution then also assumes some responsibilities of the Reasoning layer components as there may be several ways to satisfy the request (e.g. turning any one out of several available lamps in a room), and the Execution component must be able to choose one of these several available executions by using some criteria. On practice it still may be a viable solution, in order to reduce the complexity or simplify the architecture, but the system architect in this case should always be aware of this mixing of responsibilities, understand the reasons for them, and evaluate alternatives.

Even with this being said, the Execution still has (and must have) some form of reasoning, on the level of particular devices. For example, it must be able to match the correct execution action with the desired end-state of the device. Also, if some command always involves actuation of several distinct devices in a uniform manner, such a command can be abstracted on the Reasoning layer to a single atomic action, and only inside the Execution component it will be transformed into a series of commands applicable to each device.

Diagnosis

Finally, the last component of the Ubiquitous layer is the Diagnosis component. This component is optional, i.e. some systems choose not to implement it explicitly, especially at the early stages of smart environment development.

The task of the component is to monitor readings from sensors and execution results, check the correctness of the devices, and detect any anomalies, if possible. For example, many battery-powered devices tend to send erratic data when the battery is low. This may cause large problems at the reasoning level, if not detected earlier.

The diagnosis may also have its counterpart at the reasoning level, which will use domain data together with the information from the Diagnosis to forbid the usage of faulty devices, until fixed, thus restricting the available domain.

Reasoning Layer

The Reasoning layer contains the domain-level logic of the system. This is the most diverse layer as well, as every smart environment project has its own ideas on how the environment should reason and make decisions about the actions it should perform.

Over the years of context-aware systems research many different ways to model the domain-level information were devised, some general, some more specific to a particular task that the system was designed to solve. Among the most known high-level context representations are Resource Description Framework (RDF) (Lassila & Swick, 1998), W4 (Who, What, Where, When) Context Model (Castelli, Rosi, Mamei, & Zambonelli, 2006), RDF-based Web Ontology Language (OWL) (Antoniou & Harmelen, 2009), and Context Modelling Language (CML) (Bettini, et al., 2010).

An extensive survey of different context representation models is presented in (Bettini, et al., 2010). The choice of the exact context representation model influences heavily the capabilities for system's learning, activity recognition, and decision making, thus it is among the most important choices to be done during the early design of the smart environment system.

We split this layer into three components, however, smart environment projects history shows that projects may have any combination of these components intertwined in many different ways.

Learning

The Learning component is responsible for automatic learning of the best possible decisions and actions based on input data, which can either be a real-time data, or previously gathered training data.

The Learning component has a bit special place among all other components of the system. On the one hand, this component is optional, i.e. it is possible to construct a smart environment system without any learning incorporated, for example if it is a rule-based system. On the other hand, if the component exists, it takes one of the most important central places in the system.

Machine learning methods are numerous: artificial neural networks, support vector machines, decision trees, genetic algorithms, reinforcement learning, different clustering techniques, etc. They all are applicable for usage in smart environment systems.

Of course, when we speak about the learning capabilities of the system, usually it implies that the system has the ability to re-learn and re-train automatically when initial data changes, e.g. a user develops a new habit. However, there is also another possibility, a "semi-learning" system, so to say. In such a system the Learning component is not an integral part of the day-to-day system operation. Instead, the learning is performed using a standalone learning module at the beginning on some initial existing data, and results are entered to the system as unalterable rules. They are often represented by Bayesian networks or hidden Markov models. In such cases the Learning component may often be omitted from the operational architecture, as it indeed is not involved in the operational flows. When the need arises to relearn or retrain the system due to considerable changes in the outside world, the standalone learning module may be launched again, and the new operational rules will be entered to the system to replace the obsolete ones.

Activity Recognition

The Activity Recognition component does exactly what the name suggests: it gets the information about the current state from the Context, and applies internal knowledge to classify and define more high-level information about the environment. For example, while the Context may send a reading from a motion sensor that there is motion in the room, the Activity Recognition will recognize that it corresponds to someone's presence in the room. Given the stream of video from the Context, the Activity Recognition may define a whole set of the new domain-level information, such as whether a person is working with PC, thinking, eating, moving around, etc.

Theoretically this component is not obligatory, as it is possible to make decisions directly based on the information from the Context. However, without the Activity recognition the complexity of decisions is severely limited, as they lack a big part of high-level domain information.

The activity recognition may include sound, video, or image recognition. Often it uses results obtained from the Learning component in order to classify and recognize the activity. Sometimes activity recognition may contain stricter definitions of what a certain activity means (such as a certain state of sensors will correspond to a certain activity), in which case the recognition itself checks the correspondence of the definition to the current state of environment.

The results of the Activity Recognition component will go into the Decision Making component, where, combined with the information directly from the Context, they will depict the full knowledge about the current state, which in turn will be used to make decisions.

Decision Making

The Decision Making component is what turns the intelligent environment from a silent observant into a resolute actor: it decides, which actions should be performed in a given situation with a given knowledge.

As with the Activity Recognition and the Learning components, the Decision Making component comes in many different forms, at least as many as there are fields in artificial intelligence and systems automation research areas. Some usable techniques include optimization theory, planning and scheduling, constraints satisfaction, search techniques, logical reasoning, ontological reasoning, reasoning under uncertainty, and many more.

The important difference to note is that decision making may be split into two types: instant and continual. Instant decision does not mean instant execution. However, it means that the decision, once it is made and sent to the Execution component, cannot be revisited and changed. Instead, the new feedback from the environment (even if it is a feedback about errors in execution) goes to the "new cycle" of decision making, and requires new decisions to be made. The instant decision making is easier from architectural point of view, particularly it goes well with stateless components, because every new decision can be made independently from previous ones.

However, sometimes instant decisions are not enough. Continual decision making usually involves several steps of execution within one decision. It also involves remembering the decision and revisiting it after receiving new feedback, possibly alternating some steps. Unlike instant decisions, continual ones usually require stateful components, thus are more demanding with respect to fault tolerance and general architectural cleanness.

User Layer

Though many projects opt not to give particular attention to interfacing with users, instead specifying UI as a part of some other architecture layer or component, we argue that it deserves a separate dedicated layer in the architecture.

The User layer provides a view of the system to the user, and, which is even more important, it gives the ability to change and fine-tune the system, to debug errors, to override system's decisions and much more.

In this section we will specify different parts of the system that require separate monitoring and control mechanisms.

The first component of the layer is the environment information. This is a monitoring component, which receives its information from two sources: the Context and the Activity Recognition. First of all, the component provides an important hint to the user about the view of the environment within the system, as generally it may be different from the actual state of the environment. Causes of this may be numerous: an erroneous reading of the sensor, a mistake of the Activity Recognition, missing information due to hidden changes that are not detected, etc. If the view within the system differs from the actual environment state, the decision may be incorrect or not optimal as well. Thus it is important for a user to be able to see the view within the system in order to be able to compare it with the actual state.

There is another important benefit of the environment information component: the increased user's awareness. Many studies show (Weiss & Guinard, 2010) that just by increasing users' awareness about the amount of energy they consume at certain times and when using certain devices, it is possible to reduce the total energy consumption, because users are more likely to decrease their usage of heavy-consuming devices.

Second component of the User layer is the knowledge base information and update. The static information about devices, their configuration, possible actions, etc., is a great reference to a user about the capabilities of the system. Whether or not the component should provide the ability to update static information depends on the general architecture of the system, particularly on where the entry point of such information to the system is located. For example, if the system should be able to automatically detect and configure the device for work, it may be wiser to restrict the ability to tamper with the device parameters through the user layer. More often than not incorrect detection may highlight deeper problems or bugs with device detection, which should be fixed, instead of just concealed by the manual correction.

The next component of the layer is the reasoning and decision making results. This information helps to understand the origins of system's actions, thus cannot be underestimated. It will show the reasons, why a particular decision was made by the system. For example, if the system decides to perform a certain action, this component will highlight, which rules exactly were activated. It is important to note that this includes information from all components of the Reasoning layer: the Decision Making, the Learning, and even the Activity Recognition. There is, however, no duplication of information with the environment information component, as the meaning of the information in these two cases is completely different. The environment information component must show the results of the activity recognition, in order to show, how the system perceives the state of the environment. The reasoning results component, however, explains how and why the decision was made. Therefore it will show in details, why the recognition algorithm classified the original information into exactly this activity, and not some other one. This knowledge will help the user to tweak the recognition algorithms if needed.

Finally, the last component of the User layer is the system monitor. Contrary to all previous components, instead of showing the information about the domain and the environment, this component shows the information about the system itself: health status of all components, their performance indicator, any detected status changes and/or errors, etc. This also includes detected errors in devices, which may require user's intervention in order to check if device is working properly or indeed needs to be changed or repaired.

OPERATIONAL FLOWS

Intelligent building systems are reactive, i.e. their behavior is a direct consequence of the information they got from outside. There are three general operational flows within the system, and every flow corresponds to a single information entrance point.

Of course, in our description it is assumed that all components are present in the system, which is not true for the general case, as many components are optional. If some component is missing, then every piece of information that should pass through the component is passed as it is (so we may assume that the transformation is the identity), and the component generates no new information.

Environment-Generated

This flow is the most common one, as it starts with any registered change in the environment, and partially even with every new sensor reading.

The sensor reading is generated on the Physical layer and is sent to the Common Gateway, where it is converted to a uniform format. From the Gateway the transformed reading goes to two places: to the Knowledge Base for storage and further retrieval as historical data, and to the Context for immediate processing.

In the Context the reading is assessed and transformed from a raw reading data into a higher-level state. It may be the case that the reading corresponds to no changes in a state, in which case, depending on the system, the flow may either stop here (if further components are only interested in changes), or go further as usual. Either a state or a raw reading data (depending on the system) is also sent to the Diagnosis component, where it is checked for correctness.

The state is further sent from the Context to the Reasoning layer, starting with the Activity Recognition component, where recognition is performed to generate domain level knowledge. Then it is sent to the Decision Making component, where it is combined with all other available information and the system decides, whether a certain action should be performed.

In case there is a need for a certain action, the action is sent from the Reasoning layer to the Execution, where it is transformed to a set of device-level commands. And finally, those commands are sent to the Common Gateway in order to be distributed between the corresponding devices. They are also sent to the Diagnosis component for further checks.

Of course, in parallel with the flow described above, the information is sent to the User layer to be displayed in a timely manner. As soon as the Knowledge Base receives the new state, it is reflected on the corresponding dashboard. The environment information dashboard shows the results of the Context and the Activity Recognition components, and the reasoning dashboard shows the decisions made.

User-Generated

The alternative flow is the user-generated one. This flow starts when a user shows the desire to change something in the way the system currently operates. For example, a user may override a certain decision, or change the priority of rules, or manually change a state of the environment, in case it was recognized incorrectly, etc.

The flow starts from one of the informational components of the User layer. When a user enters the change, it is processed and is sent to the respective component. For a manual change of the environment it would be either the Context, or the Activity Recognition, for a rule change it will be the Reasoning component, for a decision override it will be either the Reasoning, or the Execution component, etc. From there the flow goes further normally.

System-Generated

The first type of the system-generated flows concerns the normal system operation, for example, when executing scheduled events. In such a flow, on earlier stages a plan or a schedule has been generated that required certain actions to be performed in the future. In such a case the internal clock is set, and when the time comes, the action is automatically launched. The event usually starts from the Reasoning component, and goes further to the Execution normally.

Another type of the system-generated flows concerns the re-learning and re-training mechanisms. Usually the Learning component is updated during the course of system's operation, in order to correspond to changing conditions and requirements. Updating after every state change may be too cumbersome, especially for computationally expensive machine learning methods. Thus, re-learning happens either at some intervals of time or when a certain condition is met (such as a threshold for amount of changes is achieved).

ADDITIONAL CHALLENGES

For an intelligent environment that features a single room or a few rooms with no more than a couple of dozens of devices, the already described architecture will normally satisfy all demands of the architects and users combined. However, when a system becomes larger and grows to include several floors, a whole apartment or office building, or even several houses, new issues emerge that may render the intelligent environment almost nonoperational until properly solved.

The scalability of the system is the first such issue. First of all, a single server's CPU or storage power will be quickly outgrown, thus for any more or less large system several servers is a requirement. Currently many efforts are spent in the area of database systems on development of distributed fault tolerant databases, such as Hadoop (White, 2012), MongoDB (Chodorow & Dirolf, 2010), Redis (Sanfilippo & Noordhuis, 2011), Cassandra (Lakshman & Malik, 2009), etc. Such databases make a good base for extendable intelligent environments, as they already solve distribution, data replication, fault tolerance, and availability problems out of the box. However, not only the Knowledge Base needs proper scalability. The amount of sensor data grows with the number of devices as well, and at some point concurrency, queue processing speed and bandwidth issues may stop the system from further expansion. Thus it is also important to use proper solutions not only for data storage, but also for high-volume fast data processing. Such solutions as Twitter Storm (Twitter Storm, 2013) or RabbitMQ (Samovskiy, 2008) provide reliable ways for sending and processing large streams of data.

The Reasoning layer, however, is the one that may suffer most from system's expansion. The reason is that most of the machine learning, search and reasoning algorithms within the layer may be computationally expensive, with at least exponential solving time. While the parallelization and distribution on several servers may partially alleviate the problem, sometimes more fundamental changes to the algorithm will be required. One of possible changes is the usage of approximate algorithms (for example, greedy algorithms, or genetic algorithms) instead of exact ones for the search optimization reasoning. Another possible change is the splitting of the system into several independent subsystems of smaller size, and applying the algorithms within subsystems. While with this approach some dependency between parts from different subsystems may be permanently lost, if the subsystems have only weak and not important dependencies between each other this may be a big improvement in terms of system's reaction time with only minor consequences in terms of the optimality of reasoning results.

Another direct consequence of scaling the system onto several distributed servers is the need to increase the fault tolerance level. If the system works only in one room and on one server, crashes and other unrecoverable faults are rare and restarting the system is an unpleasant, but fast procedure that has overall light consequences. However, when servers become numerous, the rate of errors and crashes increases as well. The system should be designed in such a way that any single error will cause only a minor outage. So, for example, the system should be fully operational on fifth floor of the building even if the server that manages the second floor crashes.

This may be achieved through addition of special system-level components, i.e. components that manage the system itself. Monitoring and configuration component may keep track of all running instances of components and their servers, check their health status through heartbeats, and keep track of their configuration.

In case a component dies, the configuration component will automatically restart it either on the same server, or on a different one, and reconfigure other components so that now they contact a new instance. The configuration component may also perform load balancing and other utility tasks. As with databases and data streams, there are solutions that may come handy for such component implementation, such as Apache Zookeeper (Apache Zookeeper, 2010) or Doozer (Doozer, 2011).

CASE STUDIES

Finally, in this section we want to showcase several smart environment projects as case studies and discuss, how their architecture maps to the general pattern, described in previous sections.

Except for small differences, it can be seen that the general architectures of the presented projects have many things in common. These projects are chosen due to several factors. First of all, their focus is on creation of a fully featured general intelligent building, which influences all aspects of building's operations, as opposed to specifically targeted projects, such as those that aim to create a smart lighting system, or those that only target efficient system's infrastructure, etc. Secondly, all chosen projects have constructed, implemented and tested an actual real environment, thus the architectures of these projects have proved their feasibility and validity. And finally, they mostly feature clear distinction of architecture modules, as opposed to several smaller projects, where some modules can be seamlessly combined, or removed altogether, due to their reduced functionality.

Even though the presented pattern is the most commonly used one for smart buildings, sometimes specific requirements may induce other constraints on the project and its architecture. For example, an emerging view of smart home architectures is viewing smart building environments as multi-agent. Cook in (Cook, 2009) defines four different directions in multi-agent research of smart environments: (a) multi-intelligent software agents, (b) tracking multiple residents, (c) profiling multiple residents, (d) multi-agent negotiations. The first direction usually assumes viewing every module of the system as a separate agent, with communication protocols guiding interactions between them. Surprisingly, such a view of multi-agent architecture can be very well combined with the pattern, presented here. In fact, in the same work Cook uses the MavHome project, which is one of our case studies as well, to describe how the agents can be organized in a hierarchical layered configuration. Other research directions view as agents either different people (in which case the smart system itself remains unified, but has to incorporate additional intelligence for distinguishing people), or different devices. In the latter case, especially if devices are highly mobile and autonomous, thus may be viewed as a complete system by themselves, the proposed pattern may be inapplicable or sub-optimal, and other agent based architectures may be explored, for example as described in (Spanoudakis & Moraitis, 2006).

To avoid confusion, when referring to layers of respective projects and the layers of the architecture pattern, which is described in this chapter, we will refer to the former as "the project architecture", and to the latter as "the pattern architecture".

MavHome

Managing An Intelligent Versatile Home (MavHome) (Das, Cook, Battacharya, Heierman III, & Lin, 2002) project was one of the first scientific projects to create a functioning smart environment. The home system in the project acted as a rational agent, whose goal was to maximize comfort of its users and minimize costs of operation. The project used learning and prediction techniques heavily, to predict mobility patterns of the inhabitants and adapt to them in a timely manner.

The architecture of the project as described in (Youngblood, Cook, & Holder, 2004) is shown in Figure 2. Here we will briefly compare it to the pattern in the Architecture section of this chapter.

The Physical layer of MavHome exactly maps to the Physical layer as described in the pattern: it contains devices and device interfaces to higher components, reminiscent of the Common Gateway.

The Communication layer contains a lot of utility components that help to make the system operational, such as device drivers, operating system, proxies, and middleware. When comparing to the pattern, the Execution component is a part of this layer of MavHome. As we mentioned at the beginning of the Architecture Overview section, the implementation details are very specific

to every system, so we avoid to include support components into the pattern, however they may very well be present in the high-level architecture overviews of particular projects, as can be seen in the Middleware sub-layer of the MavHome project example, where they take an important place in the implementation. There is one thing to note, however, that all device and hardware related utility software, such as drivers, operating system, proxies, etc. may also be conceptually viewed as a part of the Physical layer of the pattern.

The Information layer of MavHome contains aggregator, prediction, data mining and database services. It can be seen that it combines into a single layer parts of both the Ubiquitous and the Reasoning layers of the pattern. Namely, the Knowledge Base and the Context from the Ubiquitous layer, and the Learning and the Activity Recognition from the Reasoning layer.

Finally, the Decision layer of the MavHome project corresponds to the Decision Making component of the pattern.

It should be noted that in the MavHome architecture there is no specific component or layer, responsible for interfacing with user, even though such interfaces (including mobile interface on PDA) actually exist. In case of their inclusion into the architecture picture, they may constitute the next layer, similar to the User layer of the pattern.

SmartLab

SmartLab is another project that has created a functioning smart environment (López-de-Ipiña, et al., 2008). The uniqueness of the project lies in the fact that the project itself features hardware and middleware parts of the environment (the Physical and the Ubiquitous layers in the pattern), with common interfaces for other projects to use and to create their own reasoning on top of it (the Reasoning layer of the pattern). The SmartLab

Figure 2. MavHome Architecture. © 2004 Youngblood, Cook, & Holder. Used with permission.

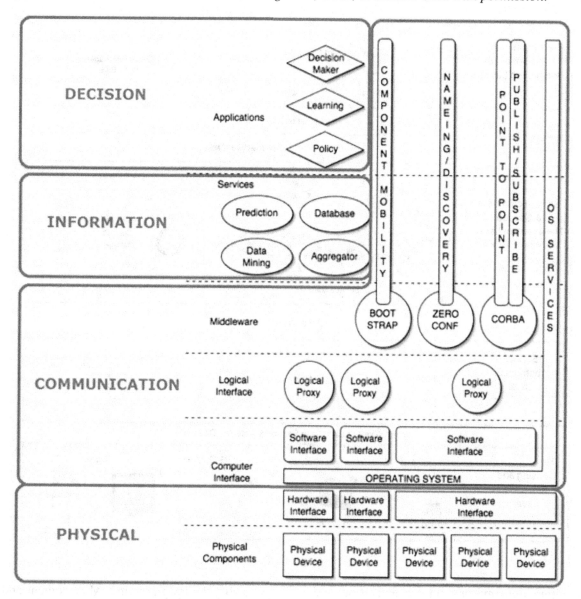

environment was already used as a base for several other research projects, including Assistive Display, ubiClassRoom, and Eldercare.

The architecture of the project as described in (López-de-Ipiña, et al., 2008) is shown in Figure 3.

The Sensing and Actuation layer contains all devices within the environment. They include EIB/KNX bus for lightning, HVAC, presence, temperature and motors on doors and windows,

VoIP and VideoIP, Indoor Location System, etc. The next layer is the Service Abstraction layer, which transforms functionality of the devices from the first layer into software services. Together these two layers represent the Physical layer of the pattern, with the second layer representing the Common Gateway.

The Semantic Context & Service Management layer contains the Service Manager, which

Figure 3. SmartLab Architecture. © 2008 López-de-Ipiña, et al. Used with permission.

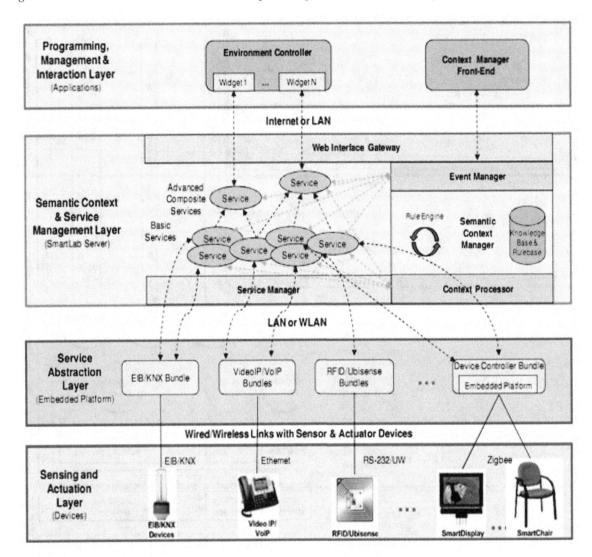

monitors the environment for activation and deactivation of devices thus for availability of services, the Semantic Context Manager, which stores knowledge about device in the common ontology, and the Web Gateway Module, which produces interfaces for third-party programs wishing to interact with the environment. This layer corresponds to the Ubiquitous layer of the pattern, with the Service Manager behaving as the Context component, the Semantic Context Manager behaving as static storage of the Knowledge Base component, and the Web Gateway behaving as the Execution component.

Finally, the Programming, Management and Interaction layer provides web-based interface for users of the SmartLab laboratory. The Environment Controller allows a user to manually operate the environment through a set of widgets, while the Context Manager Front-End offers a web interface for management of devices configuration, ontology, rule behavior, and tracking the system log and statistics. As can be seen, the layer closely resembles the User layer of the pattern.

Note that there is no layer similar to the Reasoning layer. As we already mentioned, the project provides capabilities for external programs to use the environment and middleware while applying their own reasoning. Thus such external programs will represent the Reasoning layer, when attached. Instead, the Semantic Context & Service Management layer provides all interfaces needed for external programs.

Smart Homes for All

Smart Homes for All (SM4All) (Aiello, et al., 2011) was a European-wide research project that had created a smart apartment in Rome, Italy. The project featured several innovative ideas within smart environments, including usage of the Brain Computer Interface for issuing the commands,

using planning techniques for finding a set of actions for a complex commands, and sophisticated execution mechanisms to avoid concurrency issues when executing the commands.

The architecture of the project as described in (Aiello, et al., 2011) can be seen in Figure 4.

There are three main layers. The Pervasive layer contains all devices and gives the possibility for devices to be added or removed dynamically through the usage of the common Universal Plug and Play (UPnP) protocol. As can be seen, the layer has the direct correspondence to the Physical layer of the pattern.

The Composition layer contains five major components. The Repository represents the

Figure 4. SM4All Architecture. © 2011 Aiello, et al. Used with permission.

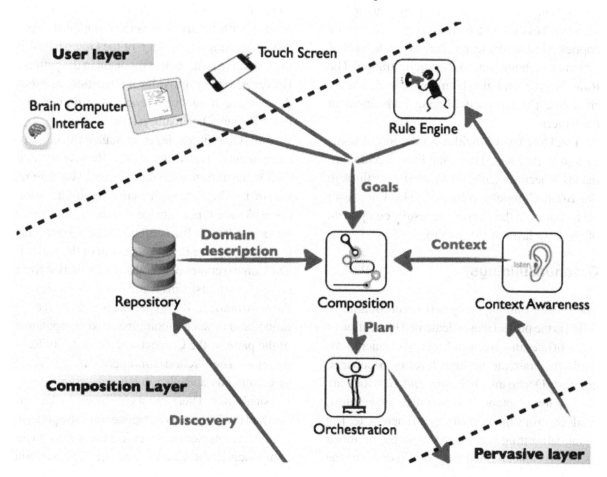

Knowledge Base component of the pattern, and contains a database, which includes registry of current devices and their abstract types, description of available services, and information about the layout of a house. The Context Awareness collects sensed data and represents the logical image of the environment, thus being the Context component of the pattern. Though there is no specific Activity Recognition component from the pattern included in the SM4All architecture, some parts of it are also included in the Context Awareness. The Orchestration component controls the execution, i.e. it invokes the physical services and receives feedback about the status of invocations. As such it corresponds to the Execution component of the pattern. The Rule Engine component contains rules of the environment behavior and constantly checks, based on information from the Context Awareness component, whether those rules are satisfied; if so, it invokes the Composition component, which applies AI planning techniques to create a set of actions which are sent to the Orchestration. The Rule Engine and the Composition combined constitute the Decision Making component of the pattern.

The User layer provides access to the home system to its users. They may issue direct commands either through the touch interface or through the Brain Computer Interface. The User layer corresponds to the Reasoning results component of the User layer of the pattern.

GreenerBuildings

The GreenerBuildings project (GreenerBuildings, 2013) is the project that is dedicated to creation of smart offices in a green and energy-efficient way, while maintaining the high level of occupants' comfort. Occupants' behavior and activities are the key for adaptation to maximize the comfort, while choosing the most energy efficient state. The living lab setting is constructed on the premises of the Technical University of Eindhoven, the Netherlands. The project puts a lot of effort into the creation of a scalable, distributed, and fault tolerant solution.

The architecture of the project is shown in Figure 5.

The Physical layer of the project contains all devices connected to the Sensors and Actuators Gateway, which sends the values further into the system. As such the Physical layer of the project resembles closely the Physical layer of the pattern. Note that the project layer contains one more component: the Interconnection with Smart Grid. Since the project puts a lot of effort in energy saving, the Smart Grid component provides the energy consumption and energy costs information. It also provides prices of energy from different energy providers, so that it is possible to choose the best price and the best time of task executions when the prices are the cheapest. The Interconnection with Smart Grid is the component, specific to the implementation of the GreenerBuildings, so there is no such component in the pattern. However, since it provides information, as other devices do, it can be viewed as a part of the usual Physical layer subsystem.

The Ubiquitous layer contains three main components: The Context, the Repository and the Orchestration, each having more subsystems within it. The Repository contains information about device types, device instances, and saves historical data for further retrieval. It corresponds to the Knowledge Base component of the pattern. The Context component collects information from sensors and transforms it into a consistent view of the environment. It also performs activity recognition, and as such it combines two components of the pattern: the Context and the Activity Recognition. The Orchestration performs execution of commands and also diagnoses errors on the Physical layer. Therefore it combines the Execution and the Diagnosis components of the pattern.

The Composition layer contains two main components: the Control and the Composition

Figure 5. GreenerBuildings Architecture. © 2013 GreenerBuildings. Used with permission.

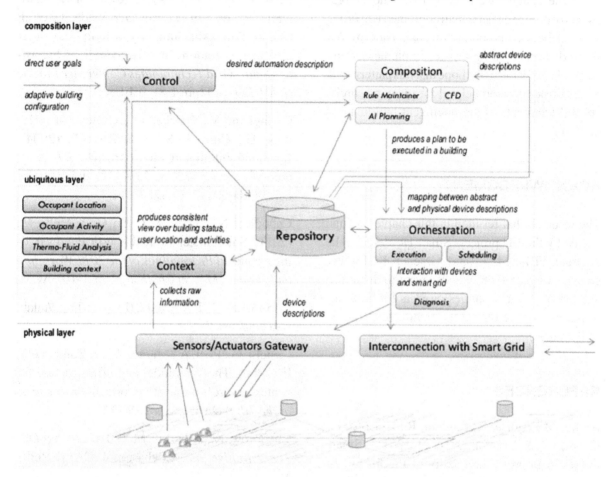

component. The Composition component contains the reasoning of the system. The Rule Maintenance system within the component uses constraint satisfaction techniques to constantly check all rules that users have added to the system, and finds the state of the environment which satisfies all the rules. Planning component creates a set of actions to be executed by the Orchestration, and the CFD is the special system for optimal handling of the heating mechanisms and air quality within the rooms. Thus the Composition component is the Decision Making component of the pattern.

The Control component is the main system interface to a user. It shows system's parameters, and allows a user to issue direct commands or overrule decisions of the system. It also collects

information about the users' satisfaction levels. As such it partially corresponds to the User layer of the pattern.

CONCLUSION

As we showed in this chapter, nowadays there are a lot of different initiatives which aim to create smart automated environments. For many of them, the architecture of the system is the first challenge they face, and as we showed, independently constructed architectures of many project still share similar component ideas, as a result of the inevitable process of finding the best solution and the best system design.

In the chapter we collected the knowledge, created by those projects, and combined it in order to describe a common architecture pattern. We showed, how existing project implementations resemble the pattern. We hope that this pattern will be of further use and helpful for many researchers and architects of the intelligent buildings in the future.

ACKNOWLEDGMENT

The research that resulted in this chapter is supported by the EU projects Smart Homes for All, contract FP7-224332 and Greener Buildings, contract FP7-258888. We also want to thank the authors of the case studies projects for granting us permissions to reprint the architecture figures of the projects.

REFERENCES

Aiello, M., Aloise, F., Baldoni, R., Cincotti, F., Guger, C., & Lazovik, A. et al. (2011). Smart homes to improve the quality of life for all. In *Proceedings of Engineering in Medicine and Biology Society* (pp. 1777–1780). IEEE. doi:10.1109/IEMBS.2011.6090507.

Antoniou, G., & Harmelen, F. V. (2009). Web ontology language: Owl. In *Handbook on ontologies* (pp. 91–110). Berlin: Springer. doi:10.1007/978-3-540-92673-3_4.

Apache Zookeeper. (2010). Retrieved 2013, from http://zookeeper.apache.org/

Bettini, C., Brdiczka, O., Henricksen, K., Indulska, J., Nicklas, D., & Ranganathan, A. et al. (2010). A survey of context modelling and reasoning techniques. *Pervasive and Mobile Computing*, 6(2), 161–180. doi:10.1016/j.pmcj.2009.06.002.

Beywatch. (2008). Retrieved 2013, from http://www.beywatch.eu/

Bliek, F., van den Noort, A., Roossien, B., Kamphuis, R., de Wit, J., van Der Velde, J., et al. (2010). PowerMatching city, a living lab smart grid demonstration. In *Proceedings of Innovative Smart Grid Technologies Conference Europe (ISGT Europe)* (pp. 1-8). IEEE.

Callaghan, V., Clarke, G., Colley, M., Hagras, H., Chin, J. S., & Doctor, F. (2004). Inhabited intelligent environments. *BT Technology Journal*, 22(3), 233–247. doi:10.1023/B:BTTJ.0000047137.42670.4d.

Capodieci, N., Pagani, A., Cabri, G., & Aiello, M. (2011). Smart meter aware domestic energy trading agents. In *Proceedings of the 2011 Workshop on E-Energy Market Challenge* (pp. 1-10). ACM.

CASAS. (2008). Retrieved 2013, from http://ailab.wsu.edu/casas/

Castelli, G., Rosi, A., Mamei, M., & Zambonelli, F. (2006). The W4 model and infrastructure for context-aware browsing the world. In *Proceedings of the 7th WOA Workshop*. WOA.

Chodorow, K., & Dirolf, M. (2010). *MongoDB: The definitive guide*. Sebastopol, CA: O'Reilly Media.

Cook, D. J. (2009). Multi-agent smart environments. *Journal of Ambient Intelligence and Smart Environments*, 1(1), 51–55.

Cook, D. J., & Das, S. K. (2007). How smart are our environments? An updated look at the state of the art. *Pervasive and Mobile Computing*, 3(2), 53–73. doi:10.1016/j.pmcj.2006.12.001.

Das, S. K., Cook, D. J., Battacharya, A., Heierman, E. O. III, & Lin, T.-Y. (2002). The role of prediction algorithms in the MavHome smart home architecture. *IEEE Wireless Communications*, 9(6), 77–84. doi:10.1109/MWC.2002.1160085.

Doozer. (2011). Retrieved 2013, from http://github.com/ha/doozer

e-Diana. (2009). Retrieved 2013, from http://www.artemis-ediana.eu/

EnPROVE. (2013). Retrieved 2013, from http://www.enprove.eu/

Georgievski, I., Degeler, V., Pagani, G. A., Nguyen, T. A., Lazovik, A., & Aiello, M. (2012). Optimizing energy costs for offices connected to the smart grid. *IEEE Transactions on Smart Grid*, *3*, 2273–2285. doi:10.1109/TSG.2012.2218666.

GreenerBuildings. (2013). Retrieved 2013, from http://www.greenerbuildings.eu/

iDorm. (2002). Retrieved 2013, from http://cswww.essex.ac.uk/iieg/idorm.htm

Kusznir, J., & Cook, D. J. (2010). Designing lightweight software architectures for smart environments. In *Proceedings of the 6th International Conference on Intelligent Environments* (pp. 220-224). IEEE.

Lakshman, A., & Malik, P. (2009). Cassandra: A structured storage system on a P2P network. In *Proceedings of the 21st Annual Symposium on Parallelism in Algorithms and Architectures*. ACM.

Lassila, O., & Swick, R. R. (1998). *Resource description framework (RDF) model and syntax specification*. World Wide Web Consortium.

Loke, S. (2006). *Context-aware pervasive systems: Architectures for a new breed of applications*. Auerbach Publications. doi:10.1201/9781420013498.

López-de-Ipiña, D., Almeida, A., Aguilera, U., Larizgoitia, I., Laiseca, X., Orduña, P., et al. (2008). Dynamic discovery and semantic reasoning for next generation intelligent environments. In *Proceedings of the 4th International Conference on Intelligent Environments* (pp. 1-10). IET.

MavHome. (2003). Retrieved 2013, from http://ailab.wsu.edu/mavhome

Nguyen, T. A., & Aiello, M. (2012). Energy intelligent buildings based on user activity: A survey. *Energy and Buildings*.

Preuveneers, D., & Novais, P. (2012). A survey of software engineering best practices for the development of smart applications in ambient intelligence. *Journal of Ambient Intelligence and Smart Environments*, *4*(3), 149–162.

Reinisch, C., Kofler, M. J., & Kastner, W. (2010). ThinkHome: A smart home as digital ecosystem. In *Proceedings of the 4th IEEE International Conference on Digital Ecosystems and Technologies (DEST)* (pp. 256-261). IEEE.

SM4All. (2008). Retrieved 2013, from http://sm4all-project.eu/

Samovskiy, D. (2008). *Introduction to AMQP messaging with RabbitMQ*.

Sanfilippo, S., & Noordhuis, P. (2011). *Redis*. Retrieved from http://redis.io

SmartLab. (2006). Retrieved 2013, from http://www.smartlab.deusto.es/

Spanoudakis, N. I., & Moraitis, P. (2006). Agent based architecture in an ambient intelligence context. In *Proceedings of the 4th European Workshop on Multi-Agent Systems (EUMAS'06)* (pp. 1-12). Lisbon: EUMAS.

Twitter Storm. (2013). Retrieved 2013, from http://storm-project.net/

Want, R., Hopper, A., Falcão, V., & Gibbons, J. (1992). The active badge location system. *ACM Transactions on Information Systems*, *10*(1), 91–102. doi:10.1145/128756.128759.

Weiss, M., & Guinard, D. (2010). Increasing energy awareness through web-enabled power outlets. In *Proceedings of the 9th International Conference on Mobile and Ubiquitous Multimedia* (pp. 20). ACM.

White, T. (2012). *Hadoop: The definitive guide*. Sebastopol, CA: O'Reilly Media.

Youngblood, G. M., Cook, D. J., & Holder, L. B. (2004). *The MavHome architecture*. Arlington, TX: Department of Computer Science and Engineering University of Texas at Arlington.

Chapter 6
Design Aspects and Context Awareness in Pervasive Games

Vlasios Kasapakis
University of the Aegean, Greece

Damianos Gavalas
University of the Aegean, Greece

ABSTRACT

Pervasive games are a new type of digital games that combines game and physical reality within the gameplay. This novel game type raises unprecedented research and design challenges for developers and urges the exploration of new technologies and methods to create high quality game experiences and design novel and compelling forms of content for the players. This chapter follows a systematic approach to explore the landscape of pervasive gaming. First, the authors approach pervasive games from a theoretical point of view, defining the four axes of pervasive games design, introducing the concept of game world persistency, and describing aspects of spatially/temporally/socially expanded games. Then, they present ten pervasive game projects, classified in five genres based on their playing environment and features. Following that, the authors present a comparative view of those projects with respect to several design aspects: communication and localization, context and personal awareness aspects, information model, player equipment, and game space visualization. Last, the authors highlight current trends, design principles, and future directions for pervasive games development.

INTRODUCTION

Games have been a key motivator in the development of many new technologies and techniques, particularly in the areas of computer graphics and artificial intelligence. Although computer games have been on the spotlight for quite a while,

new forms of gaming, such as web, mobile and pervasive games have recently emerged and attracted academic attention both from design and technological viewpoints (Chalmers et al., 2005).

The most successful paradigm of web games are the Massively Multiplayer Online Games (MMOGs) which enable thousands of players

DOI: 10.4018/978-1-4666-4695-7.ch006

to simultaneously interact in persistent, online, multiplayer-only worlds (Hsiao & Yuan, 2005). Through incorporating highly customizable/detailed avatars, objects, and actions, some MMOGs evolved into MMORPGs (Massive Multiplayer Online Role Playing Games) (Childress & Braswell, 2006). As for mobile games, those are broadly defined as games played on mobile platforms such as cell phones, PDAs and dedicated gaming devices (Davidsson, 2004).

Pervasive computing environments integrate networked computing devices -spanning from tiny sensors to highly dynamic, powerful devices- with people and their ambient environments (Zhu, Mutka, & Ni, 2005). Computers in pervasive environments shift from being localized/static tools to constant companions, enabling continuous interaction and promoting unstructured activities without clear starting or ending points. Pervasive games implement this new role of computational technology to enhance computer game design and computer-gaming experience. Pervasive technology offers three particularly promising dimensions on computer game play:

- Mobile, place-independent game play.
- Integration between the physical and the virtual worlds.
- Social interaction among players (Jegers & Wiberg, 2006).

Pervasive games represent an exciting and commercially promising new form of computer games that builds upon a combination of hybrid interfaces, wireless networking, and context-sensing technologies (Benford, Magerkurth, & Ljungstrand, 2005). Through a combination of personal devices, positioning technologies and other multimedia sensors, combined with wireless networking, a pervasive game can respond to players' movements and context and enable them to communicate with a game engine and with each other (Capra et al., 2005).

As in classic computer gaming, pervasive games may be classified in sub-genres, mainly based on their playing environment and features. The most known pervasive games sub-genres are the following: pure location-based games (IAD, 2011; Kiefer, Matyas, & Schlieder, 2006), mobile games(Chatzigiannakis et al., 2010; Lavín-Mera, Torrente, Moreno-Ger, & Fernández-Manjón, 2009; Peitz, 2006; PK, 2011; Walther, 2005a), trans-reality games (Benford et al., 2004; Benford et al., 2005; Chcok, Sreekumar, Lei, & Thang, 2006; C. A. Lindley & Eladhari, 2005; C.A. Lindley, 2004), augmented reality games (Fischer, Lindt, & Stenros, 2006; Guo, Fujimura, Zhang, & Imai, 2012; C.A. Lindley, 2004; Wetzel et al., 2009) and mixed-reality games (Cheok & Khoo, 2006; C.A. Lindley, 2004). Their corresponding definitions and representative prototypes are discussed later on in this chapter.

The main objective of this chapter is, firstly, to approach pervasive gaming and its design aspects from a theoretical viewpoint (defining the four axes of pervasive games design, introducing the concept of game world persistency and describing aspects of spatially/temporally/socially expanded games). Then to investigate in detail a representative set of pervasive games from several technical angles, so as to highlight the trends and challenges and extract design principles inherent in pervasive gaming (see Figure 1).

- Communication and localization refer to communication facilities (either among players or between players and some kind of game management engine) and localization techniques, which represent a fundamental requirement for pervasive games (Broll, Ohlenburg, Lindt, Herbst, & Braun, 2006).
- Context and personal-awareness criteria deal with gaming environmental and social aspects captured by the games as a means of linking changes in the environment with

Figure 1. Design and evaluation aspects of pervasive games

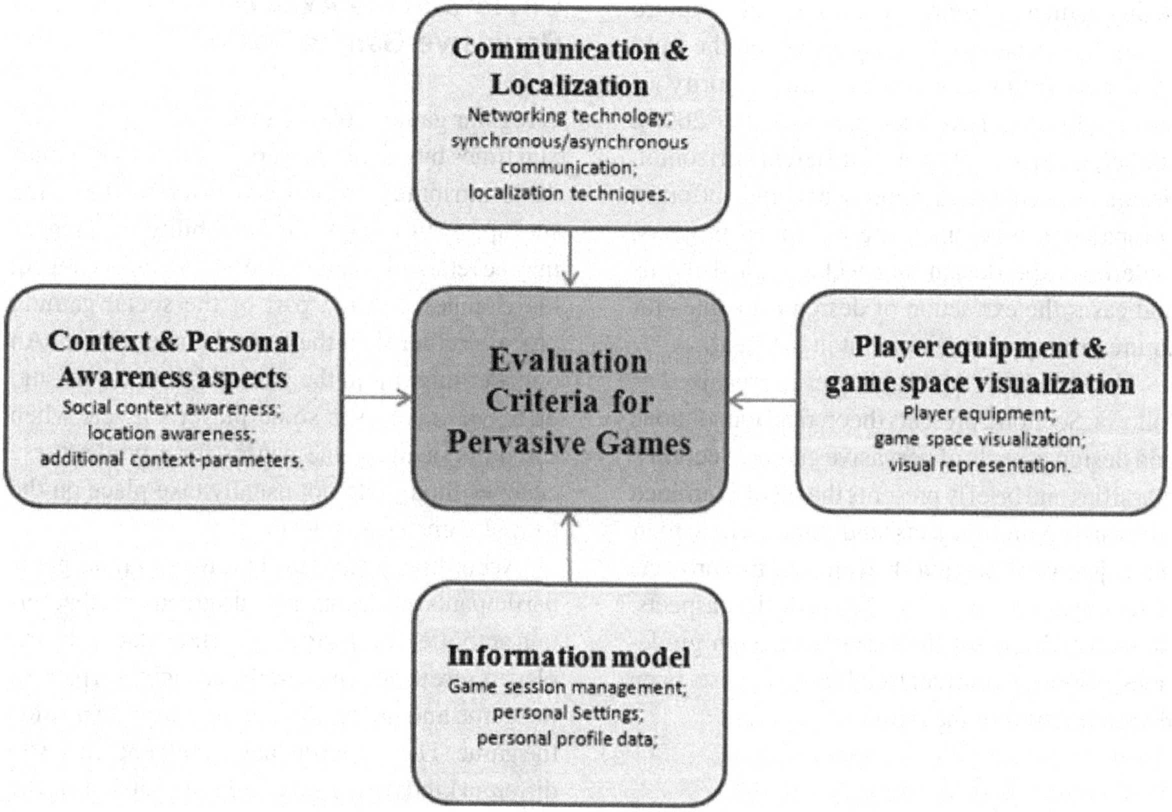

computer systems, which are otherwise static (Baldauf, Dustdar, & Rosenberg, 2007).

- Information model criteria aim at examining the informational and architectural models adopted in these games to assist users in satisfying their needs (Schuette & Rotthowe, 1998).
- Player equipment and I/O modalities criteria aim at evaluating the devices used by players and the means for providing input and perceiving the output of games (Jaimes & Sebe, 2007).

Our survey is based on the review and comparison of ten (10) pervasive games: Urban Defender (PhysicalComp, 2009), Parallel Kingdom Age of Emergence (PK, 2011), Insectopia (Peitz & Björk, 2007), Hot Potato (Chatzigiannakis et al., 2010),

Capture The Flag (Cheok et al., 2006), Uncle Roy All Around You (Benford et al., 2004), Age Invaders (Cheok & Khoo, 2006), TimeWarp (Herbst, Braun, McCall, & Broll, 2008), Treasure (Guo et al., 2012) and Epidemic Menace II (Fischer et al., 2006). While several other pervasive game prototypes currently exist (e.g., (Benford et al., 2006; Benford et al., 2007; PM, 2011; Sotamma, 2002; Stenros, Montola, Waern, & Jonsson, 2007)) we have chosen the abovementioned projects as a compromise between a fairly sized games' sample and achieving a balanced representation of prototypes with respect to their generation, genre and utilized technologies.

It is noted that a relevant survey has been published in 2005 (Magerkurth, Cheok, Mandryk, & Nilsen, 2005), wherein pervasive games are surveyed based on a vertical classification in smart toys, affective gaming, augmented tabletop games, location-aware games and augmented reality games. Herein, we do not only capture recent trends and provide an update on the field of pervasive gaming (in fact, the majority of surveyed games have been released after 2005). Rather, we take a completely different horizontal, design aspects-based approach which offers a comparative view upon the examined projects, underlines the design and technological trends and eases the extraction of design principles for future prototype development in the field.

The remainder of this chapter is organized as follows: Section 2 presents theoretical foundations and design aspects of pervasive games. Section 3 classifies and briefly presents the set of examined pervasive game projects and summarizes their main features. Section 4 evaluates the projects with respect to the above listed design aspects. Section 5 discusses the extracted design guidelines, highlights current trends and suggests open research issues in the field.

THEORETICAL FOUNDATIONS AND DESIGN ASPECTS OF PERVASIVE GAMES

A significant body if research has focused on establishing the theoretical foundations of pervasive games. A concept often encountered in the literature is the "soap bubble", referring to the game world with respect to the environment "outside" it. The "magical circle", a term coined by the Dutch historian Johan Huizinga, describes the game world as a "temporary world within the ordinary world, dedicated to the performance of an act apart". This idea was picked up and applied to digital games by Salen and Zimmerman, who refined this concept to denote "... where the game takes place. To play a game means entering into a magic circle, or perhaps creating one as the game begins" (Salen & Zimmerman, 2004).

The Concept of the 'Magic Circle' and the Axes of Pervasive Games Design

A regular game is played in certain spaces at certain times by certain players. In the classic games these attributes are defined prior to the game startup, even though the possibility of changes may be retained. When these features are changed, the changes become part of the social gaming process rather than the formal game system. An outsider might join the game while it is running, or maybe take over some player's assets when she quits or the game pauses for a while; these changes though do not usually take place on the formal game system level.

According to the idea of the magic circle, game participants make contractual agreements that certain activities, performed in certain places (by the players) are to be considered as meaningful parts of the game and not as parts of ordinary life outside the game. These contractual agreements make up different kinds of game boundaries, separating the structures and context of play from the ordinary life surrounding the game (Jegers, 2009).

In an attempt to approach the basic formalisms and most fundamental aspects of pervasive games, Walther (2005b) proposed a theoretical framework for pervasive gaming, specifying four axes of game design, which frame the domains of pervasive games. The four axes, detailed later in this section, provide the foundation for a somewhat broad definition of pervasive games: "pervasive games imply the construction and enactment of augmented and/or embedded game worlds that reside on the threshold between tangible and immaterial space, which may further include adaptronics, embedded software, and information systems in order to facilitate a "natural" environment for game-play that ensures the explicitness of computational procedures in a post screen setting" (Walther, 2005a).

The above definition focuses on essential qualities of pervasive computing, materialized in pervasive game systems. These qualities are (Walther, 2005b): (1) the explicitness of computational tasks (actions carried out in ways that go beyond the traditional screen-based environment through utilizing embedded computational technologies) and the metaphorical data manipulation (as in the case with screen-based interaction) are complemented and eventually replaced by simulated and natural interaction and manipulation of things and physical objects. (2) The overall importance of physical space, meaning that objects obeying the laws of physical space become open to digital manipulation and, as a consequence, takes on a double meaning; they are both objects residing outside the game world and at the same time objects within the game world. So far, the theory is rather robust and it mostly reflects what can already be understood as consensus in the area of pervasive game research (Jegers, 2009).

In order to support the above definition Walther (2005b) refers to four axes that together mark the main features and design aspects of pervasive gaming (PG).

- **Distribution:** Pervasive computing devices are frequently mobile or embedded in the environment and linked together within an increasingly ubiquitous network infrastructure composed of a wired core and wireless edges. This combination of embedded computing, ad-hoc networking, and discrete information sharing clearly affects and strengthens the distributed computing paradigm. One example of a distributed system designed to work in huge networks is the so-called Twine resource discovery system. It uses a set of resolvers Twine nodes that organize themselves into an overlay network to route resource descriptions to each other for storage and to collaboratively resolve client queries (Walther, 2007).

- **Mobility:** New challenges of pervasive computing further encompass mobility, i.e. computing/network/user mobility, as well as context awareness and devices heterogeneity. Particularly relevant to the field of PG is the developments in mobile 3G technologies, Bluetooth, and LAN-LAN Bridging.

- **Persistence:** The persistence factor touches upon the notion of temporality. Persistence means total availability all the time (Walther, 2007) A persistence virtual world is the one that cannot be paused. It continues to exist and function after the participant has left. This persistence changes the way people interact with other participants and the environment. A participant has a sense the systems in the space (environment, ecology, economy) exist with or without a participant's presence (Bell, 2008).

- **Transmediality:** Relates to modes of media consumption that have been profoundly altered by a succession of new media technologies, which enable average citizens to participate in the archiving, annotation, appropriation, transformation, and recirculation of media content. No medium in the present day can be defined as a self-sufficient application based on partial groupings. The junction of multiple media spread out over huge networks and accessible through a range of devices is rather a nice instance of how media commune in circular, not linear, forms.

Walther (2005b) also notes that by combining distribution, mobility, persistence, and transmediality we embark upon the 'PG possibility space'. This refers to a virtual space dealt with in networking given the focus on non-locality, non-metric systems and constant accessibility. It is a space that celebrates the freedom of device – games can be played on anything; game devices may also trigger anything, anywhere, anytime. Further, it is a space that favors non-closure; although pervasive games still cling to the law of goal-orientation (closure) they open up new ways of collaborative world building as well as inviting continuous structural expansion. Finally, the PG possibility space embraces circular storytelling as the norm of mediated entertainment (Walther, 2005b). The PG possibility space is illustrated in Figure 2.

Game World Persistency

As defined by Bell (2008), a persistent game world is a virtual world that cannot be paused. It continues to exist and function after the participant has left. Game worlds enabling persistency contain the seed of temporal expansion. Although it may not be the aim of the designers, players may start playing the game even when they are not playing officially. Especially role-playing games tend to do this. Series of live-action role-playing games are set in the same diegetic continuum, sometimes prompt the players to start playing between games (Montola, Stenros, & Waern, 2009). Persistence as such is not difficult to implement in a game, since a game without a pause or ending is persistent by definition. When designing a persistent game, one possible approach is to make a totally separated game world that does not have any actual connection to the physical world. A basic MUD (Multi User Dungeon) is an example of a separate dimension that mostly exists without direct links to physical world. An opposite approach is to link the physical environment to the game using information or context gathered from the physical environment (Lankoski et al., 2004); pervasive games take this approach to exploit the richness of the physical world as a resource for play by interweaving digital media with our everyday experience (using sensors capture information about a player's current context) (Capra et al., 2005).

Designing Spatially, Temporally and Socially Expanded Games

A pervasive game based on its spatial, temporal and social expansion "is a game that has one or more salient features expanding the contractual magic circle of play socially, spatially or temporally" (Montola, 2005).

Spatial expansion allows social playing in many locations simultaneously, taking games to places where they are not usually supposed to be. Ideologically, it can be seen as a way of reclaiming public spaces for people (Montola, 2005). Montola et al. (2009) also argues that playing in public always requires a good understanding of the local cultural and political environment. The most powerful tool for telling a location-based

Figure 2. Pervasive games Possibility Space

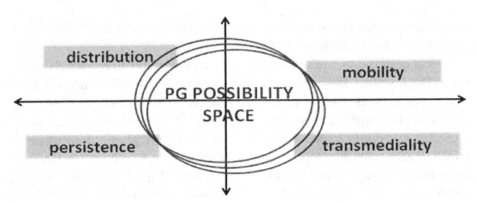

story is through the authentic physical space and physical game content. This can be achieved by embedding sights and local history into the game. Therefore the designer has to choose if the game will be site-specific and be localized and adapted to each new setting or a site-adaptable so as to adapt easily to a new setting by relying on types of places commonly found in most cities. Pervasive games can be played in urban, suburban and rural areas. The designer needs to choose the area type the game will be played on. Because spatial expansion requires a player to move, a player's body becomes a de facto game token, the flesh avatar of the player. This brings an important physicality to playing. One way of building highly physical games is through indexicality, using an indexical environment where every physical object in the game represents itself. Also, urban exploration strongly motivates voyaging and discovery, which are highly appealing game experiences. Adding web content and expanding the game online is the easiest step toward cyber spatial expansion. Perhaps the best-known approach to spatial expansion is to create a Mixed Reality Game and to use positioning technology to place virtual content at specific locations in the real world (Montola et al., 2009).

Temporal expansion ties in with social expansion, as the temporal span of the game is often obfuscated to the point where even the players might be unaware of whether they are actually playing at a given moment. For instance, when the game is able of calling the player without a warning, the player answering her cell phone does not know if that answering comprises a game action or not (Montola, 2005). A designer of a temporal expanded game has to choose among several styles of temporal expansion (dormant, ambient, asynchronous and temporally seamless game expansion) (Montola et al., 2009). Also the designer has to decide and design the game duration taking into account several issues like the moment the game is scheduled to start, the existence of a tutorial mode that will introduce the

player to the game environment and mechanics, the way the rules will change as the game time passes and how she will manage the late arrivals and early leavers of the game. The designer finally has to create ways of managing the stress which temporal expanded games may cause to the players (Montola et al., 2009).

Social expansion is achieved in several ways ranging from straightforward to revolutionary. The pervasive game might use outsiders as game elements. One planned (but unfortunately not implemented) way of doing so was sending an actor to interact with bystanders before the game, so that the players might get additional clues on their where about by discussing with the eyewitnesses (Montola, 2005).

When designing pervasive games, it is central to understand how the game awareness of participants fluctuates during the game. There are three rough levels of personal game awareness. Participants in the 'unaware' state do not notice anything strange going on, even though they are witnessing play or unknowingly even have a role in a game. Participants in the 'ambiguous' state notice that something is going on but fail to realize that the weird occurrences constitute a game. Finally, participants in the 'aware' state understand that there is a game going on and can usually tell who are playing and who are not. The personal awareness level of a player may change during the game. Often this journey from unaware to aware participation can intensify the overall game experience.

Changes in personal awareness take place through invitations, which represent another important issue a designer has to take into account is playership. One way of structuring tiered playership is using a layered 'onion' model with outer and inner modes of participation. An outsider could first be invited to spectate, then to participate in an alternate reality game, then treasure hunt in the physical world and, finally, a reality television show. Each layer of participation is more engaging, demanding and exclusive than the previous one: Players have to struggle to move through the layers, which also provides them with the invitation to refuse the inner layers. Encouraging social expansion in a game usually requires that players feel that interactions with bystanders (or players appearing as bystanders) will give them some benefit in the game. This can be achieved by giving the players missions where they need to engage with bystanders. Another way of encouraging interaction is to cater for random player-to-player encounters so that players never know when interacting with someone is relevant for the game. A useful way of creating the illusion of a live and densely populated game world is to make use of instructed non-player participants. These actors, plants and non-player characters are central tools for game designers and game masters. Whenever even more subtlety is needed, the designers can employ informed outsiders. These are people who do not know much about the game but have agreed to perform a certain task.

Playing pronoial inducing games in public spaces tends to create emergent interaction with outsiders. If the game design succeeds in instilling players with a feeling that it is safe to talk to anyone in order to enlist their help, the game world comes alive socially. From the players' point of view it is not relevant whether a game event was truly apophenic or if it was intended and designed by the game organizers. Apophenia can be a cornucopic source of meaningful game content and fostering it can result in a game much thicker with meaning than could be designed economically (Montola et al., 2009). As argued by Gaver et al. (2003), similar effects can be achieved by consciously using ambiguity as a design resource (Gaver, Beaver, & Benford, 2003). Design strategies that cater for apophenia include giving players goals but not telling how to achieve them, providing too much information for no apparent reason, encouraging extrovert character role-play, forcing players to ask for help from bystanders and pushing players to speculate, question, and tolerate uncertainty. A designer has to consider

about the way she will design the social play side of the game. The easiest and most common way to encourage social expansion is by designing a game that is fun and, more importantly, looks like fun. If the game is attractive to bystanders, they may stop to take a look—and if participating in the game has been made sufficiently easy, they might even join in.

Many players feel comfortable with the fact that they are not really doing a weird thing, but performing it. Embarrassment is created to a large degree by the fear that spectators will perceive the player as strange. The player prefers that spectators understand that she is playing, as they then realize that her behavior is sensible. Sometimes the easiest way is to state explicitly that a game is in progress, using signposts, player T-shirts, or by announcing the game in the local press. The game must still be designed in a way that makes joining it without preparation possible. What is expected of a new participant must be either obvious or easily explainable, and she cannot be required to have any specific equipment. Refusing or leaving the game must also be relatively easy (Montola et al., 2009).

CLASSIFICATION AND PRESENTATION OF PERVASIVE GAMES

To ensure a methodological presentation, we have classified ten representative pervasive gaming projects based on their genre, i.e. in augmented/mixed reality, pure location-based, mobile and trans-reality games. This section compares the surveyed games with respect to several technical viewpoints.

Augmented/Mixed-Reality Games

Augmented reality games enable views of a physical, real-world environment augmented by computer-generated sensory input such as sound, video, graphics or 3D models, using head-mounted displays (HMD), images projected on real-world surfaces and hand-held devices (Magerkurth et al., 2005). Below we present three augmented reality pervasive game research prototypes.

TimeWarp

TimeWarp (see Figure 3a) (Herbst et al., 2008) is played by two players as a team in the old town of Cologne. Players travel to different time periods in the history of Cologne to stabilize the time space continuum. This is endangered by little robots that the players meet throughout the game (Wetzel et al., 2009).

Treasure

Treasure is a pervasive game played in the context of people's daily living environments. Unlike other pervasive games, Treasure is not based on predefined game content and proprietary devices; instead, it exploits the "design-in-play" concept to enhance the variability of a game in mixed-reality environments (Guo et al., 2012).

Epidemic Mecane II (EM II)

EM II (see Figure 3b) is a cross media multiplayer social adventure game with strategy and action elements. The game is built upon the story of a humankind-threatening virus epidemic. Players participate both in the physical and a virtual world fighting against 3D viruses roaming around in the real world using augmented-reality technology (Fischer et al., 2006).

Pure Location-Aware Games

Pure location-aware games are supported by some short of localization technology and integrate the position of (one or several) players as main game element into their rules (Kiefer et al., 2006).

Urban Defender

Urban Defender is a location-aware game acted in the real world using a ball as main interface. The goal and main rule of the game is: try to conquer as many quarters as possible, reinforce these quarters and defend them against other players (IAD, 2011). By throwing the ball against a wall, the player acquires ownership on the containing quarter (PhysicalComp, 2009).

Mobile Games

Mobile games are played through a handheld device, like a mobile phone or a PDA, adapting the game rules based on the players' physical position (Walther, 2005a). Below we present three representative mobile games.

Figure 3. a) TimeWarp b) Epidemic Menace II

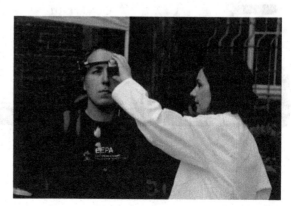

a)   b)

Parallel Kingdom Age of Emergence (P.K AoE)

The P.K AoE (see Figure 4a) is a GPS-based online role playing game for Android (Gavalas & Economou, 2011) devices by PerBlue. This game uses Google Maps for the background and puts a whole new virtual world upon it, wherein the user's location determines where she may go. The user needs to explore the game world in a circular area (within a radius around her current position) to find other players, monsters and items (PK, 2011; Whitney, 2010).

Insectopia

Insectopia (see Figure 4b) is a mobile phone game in which players compete in building, maintaining and trading insect collections (Peitz & Björk, 2007). Players roam the cityscape searching for and catching various insects. Insects can be found anywhere where Bluetooth devices are available (Peitz, 2006).

Hot Potato

Hot Potato (see Figure 4c) is played by a group of players gathered at a specific place (Chatzigiannakis et al., 2010). Each player holds a device (sensor node) that is likely to generate a "Hot Potato" after the game begins. Each such hot potato maintains a decreasing counter that ticks for a certain length of time until it "booms". Players try to "survive" by passing the potato on to another player (through gesturing, when in proximity to the co-player), thus eliminating the danger of the potato "exploding" on their device.

Trans-Reality Games

Trans-reality games take full advantage of pervasive, location-based and mixed-reality technology infrastructures to deliver new modes of game play experience, wherein the different staging contexts are integrated within a unified game space that crosses over technical borders (C.A. Lindley, 2004). Two representative trans-reality game prototypes are presented below.

Figure 4. a) Parallel Kingdom Age of Emergence b) Insectopia c) Hot Potato

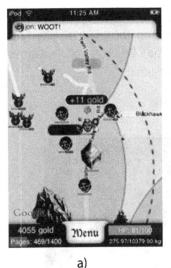
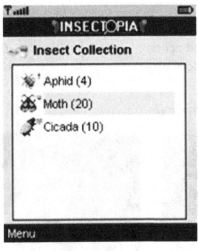

a) b) c)

Capture The Flag (CTF)

CTF (see Figure 5a) is based on the original 'Capture The Flag', a popular outdoor game. Real and virtual-world players are called 'knights' and 'guides', respectively. Any knight can occupy a castle by dropping his/her team's physical flag at a selected place. Then the knights try to physically pick up and carry the opponents' flag to their place. Meanwhile, guides can use traps and potions to help knights. The game terminates when a team successfully captures its enemy's flag and carries it to its base. The game may also end if one team's knights all fail to escape from an opponent trap or warrior (Cheok et al., 2006).

Uncle Roy All Around You (URAAY)

URAAY (see Figure 5b) (Flintham et al., 2003) is a mixed reality game that mixes online and street participants, physical and virtual worlds, and programmed game-play with live performance (Benford et al., 2004). In URAAY, players take action both on the streets and online. Street players tour through a city in search of an elusive character

named Uncle Roy, guided both by location-based clues from the game engine and also by remote online players who are able to track their progress in a parallel virtual model of the city and search for useful information such as the location of Uncle Roy's office (Benford et al., 2005).

Mixed Reality Games

Mixed reality games are played in spaces featuring both physical and virtual components (Montola, 2005). Below we present Age invaders, a mixed reality game research prototype (Cheok & Khoo, 2006).

Age Invaders

The concept of the Age Invaders (see Figure 6) is that two children are playing with two grandparents in an interactive physical media space while two parents can join into the game via the internet as virtual players, thus increasing the inter-generational interaction. The game offers adaptable game parameters to suit the simultaneous gaming of elderly and young. Adjustments

Figure 5. a) Capture The Flag b) Uncle Roy All Around You

a)

b)

Figure 6. Age Invaders

of game properties automatically compensates for potential elderly disadvantages, for example slower reaction time and slow movement (Cheok & Khoo, 2006).

Table 1 summarizes the main features of surveyed games (concept, shipping date, creator, whether they call for the participation of single or multiple players, genre, game space, unique features and status).

A DESIGN ASPECTS-BASED EVALUATION OF PERVASIVE GAMES

In this section we examine the above reviewed games with respect to several design aspects: communication and localization, context and personal awareness aspects, information model, player equipment and game space visualization.

Communication and Localization

The use of networking technologies is a fundamental requirement for pervasive games as they enable the communication among players or between a player and a centralized game management facility (Kaiser, Achir, & Boussetta, 2009).

The majority of the examined games utilized Bluetooth, WLAN and 2G/3G wireless technologies. Wireless technologies are better suited to pervasive environments as they free players' movement; hence, they dominate the networking landscape of pervasive games.

Bluetooth has been a common networking choice among many games (Cheok & Khoo, 2006; Cheok et al., 2006; Fischer et al., 2006; Hannamari, Kuittinen, & Montola, 2007; Wetzel et al., 2009) to enable short-range connectivity among players and communication between players and stationary game entities/side-equipment. In most

Table 1. Main features of the reviewed pervasive games

Game	Concept	Shipping Date/ Creator	Single/ Multi Player	Genre	Game Space	Unique Features	Current Status
TimeWarp (Wetzel et al., 2009)	Item hunt/ Puzzle	2007/iPcity	Multi/Single player	Augmented reality	City streets		Research prototype
Treasure (Guo et al., 2012)	Item hunt/ Puzzle	2011/Keio University	Multi/Single player	Mixed reality	Indoors	Dynamic and personalized role design and allocation by players	Research prototype
EM II (Fischer et al., 2006)	Item hunt/ Puzzle/ LARP	2006/ Fraunhofer FIT, University of Tampere	Multiplayer	Augmented reality	Indoors/ Outdoors (in a predefined area)		Research prototype
Urban Defender (PhysicalComp, 2009)	Chase	2009/Zurich University of Arts Department of Interaction Design	Multiplayer	Pure location-Based	City streets		Research prototype
P.K AoE (PK, 2011)	Item hunt/ puzzle/ strategy/ role playing	2010/PerBlue	Multiplayer	Mobile game	Outdoors/ indoors	Massive amount of players simultaneously; persistent game world	Publicly available / Commercial product
Insectopia (Peitz & Björk, 2007)	Item hunt	2006/Johan Peitz (Interactive Institute, Göteborg, Sweden)	Multi/Single player	Mobile game	Outdoors/ indoors		Publicly available
Hot Potato (Chatzigiannakis et al., 2010)	Chase	2010/University of Patras (Greece)	Multiplayer	Mobile game	Outdoors/ indoors	Allows operation in connected/ disconnected mode; persistent game world	Research prototype
CTF (Cheok et al., 2006)	Chase	2006/National University of Singapore	Multiplayer	Trans-Reality	Indoors/ City streets		Research prototype
URAAY (Benford et al., 2004)	Item hunt/ Puzzle/ LARP	2003/Blast Theory, Mixed Reality Lab, University of Nottingham	Single Player	Trans-Reality	Indoors/ City streets	Encourages players to cross boundaries between physical and virtual worlds	Research prototype
Age invaders (Cheok & Khoo, 2006)	Chase/ puzzle	2006/ Mixed Reality Lab	Multiplayer	Mixed reality	Indoors/ Floor Board	Compensation for elderly players' disadvantages	Research prototype

cases, Bluetooth has been supplemented by GPRS (Cheok et al., 2006; Fischer et al., 2006; Hannamari et al., 2007) and WLANs to allow for accessing web content, and communicate with web users as well as with a centralized game management server (or game engine). The rest of the games use a single network technology. TimeWarp uses Bluetooth adhoc technology to connect the two UMPC devices used by the players during game sessions. In contrast, URAAY used GPRS, while Hot Potato and Treasure were based on the interaction of devices with IEEE 802.4.15-compliant radios. In P.K AoE, users can choose among various network technologies (GPRS, 3G, WLAN) to establish an internet connection and remain online during the game session. In Urban Defender the system reads sensory data measured by the ball and uploads the information to the Arduino Nano using ZigBee.

A major challenge for almost all types of pervasive games is to identify players' position. As game content and action typically depend on the current location of individual players, pervasive games employ some short of tracking technology (Broll et al., 2006). The use of sensors is widespread for obtaining the orientation and acceleration status of the users and occasionally for detecting a gesture pattern or the touch of an object or player. Many of the games maintain game history records, typically fed as implicit input to the game engine.

Most games utilize user location information to navigate the user in real time, to provide transparent location-based information when she approaches a specified setting/landmark, and visualize co-players positions (Benford et al., 2004; Broll et al., 2006; Cheok & Khoo, 2006; Fischer et al., 2006; Hannamari et al., 2007; PhysicalComp, 2009; PK, 2011). GPS technology has been a reasonable choice for outdoor user positioning in most projects (Cheok et al., 2006; Fischer et al., 2006; PhysicalComp, 2009). However, in practice many users reported frustration due to GPS serious coverage and accuracy problems, especially in urban landscapes that accentuate GPS uncertainty (Benford et al., 2004; Cheok et al., 2006; Fischer et al., 2006; Herbst et al., 2008).

The coverage problems of GPS motivated the use of supplementary positioning technologies. TimeWarp makes use of computer vision technology (players' position is determined via small cameras attached to their PDAs and marked-based computer vision software running on the PDAs). Similarly, P.K AoE employs a combination of GPS and Wi-Fi cell identification to determinate users' position.

Only a few games make no use of GPS technology. Insectopia uses Bluetooth to check if the players are collocated for team play. The Age Invaders tracks players' positions in real time using RFID tags embedded in players' shoes. Hot Potato does not involve players' localization; its scenario only requires information of players' position relative to others (i.e. proximity awareness). In Treasure the designers used a U3D location system, including U3D tags to calculate an indoor object position. Finally, URAAY players explicitly define their position on a map interface (that design decision was made to account for GPS uncertainty, as experienced in CYSMN?) (Benford et al., 2004).

Context and Personal Awareness Aspects

Personal and context awareness are integral parts of pervasive games, enhancing the experiential engagement of players in the game action.

Peitz et al. (2007) explored several aspects of personal awareness. Firstly, the awareness of technology penetration as the user slowly understands the technological hidden context around her that supports the game and is motivated to play around that context. Secondly, the fact that people can remember the above context if they interacted with it in the past. For instance, in Insectopia many player remembered from past searches people or devices that contained valuable insects. Playing a game for a significant amount of time makes players realize the surrounding technological and physical context of a game. This event may cause the players to raise awareness for their personal habits as they may visit same places every day, ride the same bus everyday etc. All the above events influence the player's perspective about familiar locations, as she becomes aware of the context included within them. For instance, a player in Insectopia claimed that she played the game in her favorite library because she knew there were many laptop (hence, Bluetooth-enabled) devices there.

Almost all surveyed games incorporate some short of players' location awareness. The position of users appears to be the most common input to game engines, as it is used to trigger application events and game actions, make actions available depending on the current user position, etc (Benford et al., 2004; Cheok & Khoo, 2006; Cheok et al., 2006; Fischer et al., 2006; Hannamari et al., 2007; PhysicalComp, 2009; PK, 2011; Wetzel et al., 2009).

In several games only online players and the game engine are aware of street players' positions (Benford et al., 2004; Cheok & Khoo, 2006; Cheok et al., 2006; Fischer et al., 2006; Wetzel et al., 2009). In a few games only the central engine is location-aware (Peitz & Björk, 2007; PhysicalComp, 2009). Hot Potato does not communicate player's position to the game server. In P.K AoE both the players and the game engine are aware of players' positions.

Apparently, all the games take into account some kind of social context. Many of them are aware of co-players activity in addition to their location (Cheok & Khoo, 2006; Cheok et al., 2006; Fischer et al., 2006; Guo et al., 2012; Hannamari et al., 2007; PhysicalComp, 2009; PK, 2011; Wetzel et al., 2009). In Treasure the players are aware of other players' activity, as represented by the animation pattern of their remotely controlled avatar.

Several games capture additional contextual parameters such as orientation or acceleration (Gellersen, Schmidt, & Beigl, 2002), useful to the game engine (Cheok et al., 2006; Fischer et al., 2006; Guo et al., 2012; PhysicalComp, 2009; Wetzel et al., 2009).

Players Equipment and I/O Modalities

Interestingly, pervasive game players commonly use more than one device type as player equipment. In many cases players use mobile phones as part of their equipment (Cheok et al., 2006; Fischer et al., 2006; Hannamari et al., 2007; PK, 2011). Players also make use of UMPCs and PDAs (Fischer et al., 2006; Flintham et al., 2003; Wetzel et al., 2009), and sensor nodes (Chatzigiannakis et al., 2010) to complete tasks during the game sessions. Last, PCs represent also a common type of equipment (Cheok & Khoo, 2006; Cheok et al., 2006; Fischer et al., 2006; Flintham et al., 2003; Guo et al., 2012). Other types of equipment used in some projects are documented in Table 2.

Regarding the utilized means of game space visualization, virtual reality (generated upon various end devices) is a popular visualization instrument, used in eight games projects. Some games make exclusive use of virtual reality representation (Cheok et al., 2006; Hannamari et al., 2007; PK, 2011), while some use a combination of augmented reality and virtual reality (Fischer et al., 2006; Guo et al., 2012; Wetzel et al., 2009). A few use virtual reality integrated with sound (Flintham et al., 2003; Guo et al., 2012; Wetzel et al., 2009). Urban Defender is the only game that uses vibration (combined with audio) as a means of game space visualization (PhysicalComp, 2009).

As for position visualization, several games use exclusively 2D maps (Fischer et al., 2006; PK, 2011; Wetzel et al., 2009) while others provide both 2D and 3D map representations (Cheok et al., 2006; Flintham et al., 2003). Similar is the case in the use of graphics as visual modalities, while sound has been used as output modality in a few projects (Flintham et al., 2003; Guo et al., 2012; PhysicalComp, 2009; Wetzel et al., 2009). The surveyed games enable user input either explicitly (e.g. specific choices made by players through pressing buttons) or implicitly (e.g. through moving around the game space). The explicit input modalities vary considerably among the examined games. A common type of implicit input modality used in nine games is user position (Cheok & Khoo, 2006; Cheok et al., 2006; Fischer et al., 2006; Flintham et al., 2003; PhysicalComp,

Table 2. Synopsis of the reviewed games Communication and localization; Context and Personal Awareness aspects; Player equipment and game space visualization; Information model

	TimeWarp	Treasure	EM II	Urban Defender	P.K AoE	Insectopia	Hot Potato	CTF	URAAY	Age Invaders
Communication and Localization										
Networking technology	Bluetooth	WLAN / IEEE 802.15.4	LAN / Wireless LAN / Bluetooth / GPRS	ZigBee	Wireless LAN / 3G (EDGE, UMTS)/ GPRS	Bluetooth, GPRS	IEEE 802.15.4	GPRS, Bluetooth	GPRS	Bluetooth
Synchronous / Asynchronous	Asynchronous	Asynchronous	Asynchronous	Asynchronous	Synchronous	Asynchronous	Synchronous/ Asynchronous	Synchronous	Asynchronous	Synchronous
Localization	GPS, Computer Vision (CV)	U3D	GPS	GPS	GPS, Wi-Fi Cell ID	Bluetooth	Proximity metric (IEEE 802.15.4 radio range)	GPS	Players declare their position by clicking their location on a virtual map	RFID
Usage of user position information	Real-time navigation (visualization on map), transparent location-based information provision	Indoor objects positions	Real-time navigation (visualization on map), transparent location-based information provision, visualization of co-players positions	Checking the building status that the ball hits on	Real-time navigation (visualization on map), transparent location-based information, visualization of co-players positions	Check co-player proximity to enable multi hunting	Check co-player proximity to enable passing of 'hot potato'	Real-time navigation (visualization on map), visualization of co-players positions	Real-time navigation (visualization on map), transparent location-based information provision, visualization of co-players positions	Visualization of co-players positions
Context and Personal Awareness Aspects										
Social context awareness	Other players location and activity	Other players activity	Other players location and activity	Other players location and activity	Other players location and activity	Other players location and activity	Proximity of co-players	Other players location and activity	Other players last known location	Other players location and activity
Location awareness	✓	-	✓	✓	✓	✓		✓	✓	✓
Additional context-parameters	Orientation	Crossbow Mote sensor (object orientation, sound level)	Orientation	Acceleration	Cities founded and neighborhoods controlled by other players	-	Gesturing (acceleration)	Human touch (tactile sensor)	-	-

continued on following page

Table 2. Continued

	TimeWarp	Treasure	EM II	Urban Defender	P.K AoE	Insectopia	Hot Potato	CTF	URAAY	Age Invaders
Player Equipment and Game Space Visualization										
Player equipment	UMPC, headset, Bum bag with audio transmitter	PC, Prot device (combination of a projector, an ultrasonic speaker, a webcam, and a 3-DOFs rotating base)	LCD touch screen, PC, Mobile phone, PDA Augmented Reality device, Bluetooth aerosol can device	Customized Ball	Mobile Phone	Mobile Phone	Sensor node (SunSPOT)	PC, smart phone, Bluetooth-based GPS receiver, Linux-based Bluetooth device, Linux-based Bluetooth embedded flag	Handheld computer, PC, Web-Camera	Bluetooth toy gun, LED blocks floor, PC, shoes with embedded RFID tags
Game space visualization	Augmented reality, virtual reality	Augmented reality, virtual reality	Augmented reality, virtual reality	Vibration	Virtual reality	Virtual reality	-	Virtual reality	Virtual reality	Virtual reality
Visual representation (maps/graphics)	2D/3D	2D	2D/3D	-	2D	-	-	2D/3D	2D/3D	2D/3D
Information Model										
Game session management	Stores players' score and their trajectory	-	Stores viruses killed and total score	Stores into beagle board PC info about conquered buildings	Stores information about the last player's participation, duration of play, avatar's gender, current lifetime stats in gold, flags, oil wells, and levels earned; the user can resume the game at any time.	Stores the users collection in a web-server; the user may view and manage the insects of her collection and resume the game any time	Stores a countdown counter value, devices that hold hot potatos, number and IDs of active players	-	Stores the declared player position	-

continued on following page

	TimeWarp	Treasure	EM II	Urban Defender	P.K AoE	Insectopia	Hot Potato	CTF	URAAY	Age Invaders
Personal Settings	-	-	Players personalize a backpack with equipment	-	Personal settings and avatar customization	-	-	-	-	Age difference calculation, adjustable game settings by the online web player
Personal profile data	-	-	-	Players' names	Players names and flag color, current status message, city name	Players' names	-	-	Players names, gender, brief profile description and photograph	Players' names and age

Table 2. Continued

2009; PK, 2011). A detailed analysis of implicit and explicit input modalities is given in Table 2.

Information Model

Some of the game projects allow users to adjust their personal settings (Cheok & Khoo, 2006; Fischer et al., 2006; PK, 2011). In a few, users may also customize their avatar (PK, 2011). In order to play EM II the player has to set a personal backpack with equipment. Only a few games provide personalized services based on user profile. Age Invaders provides a semi-automatic setting adjustment using the user age as input and calculating the respective reaction time. It also allows online players to adjust game settings like speed at real time. In P.K AoE players' avatar is represented by a male or female 2D graphic face, based on user gender.

Many of the games support only basic, explicitly stated profile information, like name and gender (Cheok & Khoo, 2006; Flintham et al., 2003; Hannamari et al., 2007; PhysicalComp, 2009; PK, 2011). Most also maintain information implicitly specified like scores, walked routes, etc (Benford et al., 2004; Cheok & Khoo, 2006; C.A. Lindley, 2004; Peitz & Björk, 2007; PhysicalComp, 2009; PK, 2011; Wetzel et al., 2009). A few of the games allow the user to save his current game state and continue playing afterwards by resuming the game state (Hannamari et al., 2007; PhysicalComp, 2009; PK, 2011).

DESIGN GUIDELINES, TRENDS AND RESEARCH CHALLENGES IN PERVASIVE GAMING

The proliferation of mobile platforms, the fast evolution pace of wireless networking and the increasing availability of sensing devices have shaped a favorable technology landscape for the adoption of pervasive gaming. The shipping and adoption of mobile games (at the beginning, practically mobile versions of full-fledged desktop video games) has been the first major step towards the vision of pervasive gaming. Soon after, several games specifically designed for mobile platforms appeared (Fischer et al., 2006). Such games take advantage of the mobile features like network connectivity, portability and game context, enabled by the emergence and commercial availability of pervasive computing technologies. Coupled with the augmented reality technology, which allowed the mix of physical and virtual playscape and enabled the participation of online and 'street' players, pervasive games succeed in creating innovative and exciting game experiences.

Wireless communication represents a fundamental requirement for pervasive game design. Among others, latency, transfer speed, coverage, user capacity, billing and deployment are the most important factors for choosing a networking technology. Of course, those need to be examined in connection with the particular game scenario and user requirements. For instance, WLANs offer low user cost, low latency and high transfer speeds enabling prompt data updates of the user devices and the game servers. On the other hand, WLANs cannot satisfy requirements for wide coverage and may be expensive and difficult to deploy in large scale. While 3G communication appears an obvious solution for outdoor games, it may considerably increase the cost for mobile players, unless billing policies change radically. To this end, middle-range networking technologies like WiMAX may offer an attractive alternative in the near future, especially for urban-scale playscapes.

When direct player-to-player (peer-to-peer) communication is required, Bluetooth has been so far the obvious choice. However, mainly due to its limited range, Bluetooth is inappropriate for large-scale adhoc networking (Hay & Harle, 2009; Vergetis, Guerin, Sarkar, & Rank, 2005). Emerging short-range solutions such as UWB and ZigBee overcome many of the Bluetooth techni-

cal restrictions2 and could serve as an effective substitute, especially as these standards become adopted by smartphones (TexasInstr, 2011). As for localization techniques, GPS is the definite choice for outdoor game developers, although in some urban environments it is known to have connectivity, latency and accuracy problems. WiFi/3G cell ID techniques may also be considered in cases that high localization accuracy is not important, while Bluetooth (or alternative short-range communication technologies) may act as a proximity measurement tool (e.g. in games wherein players chase each other). In games that use augmented reality content, developers may use additional localization technologies in conjunction with GPS (like DRM III or CV) to ensure improved precision and allow the projection of AR content at the right display position, and also eliminate game flow interruptions due to GPS unavailability. For indoor games, developers may choose among available indoor localization systems (Varshavsky & Patel, 2010). RFID and NFC technologies may also act as supplementary tools for indoors/outdoors location tracking, especially since smartphones shipped with RFID and NFC readers become increasingly common (Intrepidus, 2010).

Notably, in most of the above-reviewed games, pervasive game developers commonly refer to uncertainty induced by technological infrastructure failures (e.g. inaccuracy of GPS-based positioning). The approaches used to tackle such problems, though, are likely to raise new concerns (e.g. the use of GPRS instead of WLAN to improve network availability may raise latency problems) (Benford et al., 2004; Cheok et al., 2006; Wetzel et al., 2009).

According to Montola et al. (2009), the personal awareness level of a player may change during the game as she slowly understands the hidden technological context around her that supports the game. Thus, the uncertainty raised from technology usage is crucial to the player personal awareness; on the other hand, technological failures may interrupt the player's immersion and cause a feeling of 'disconnection' from the game world, hindering awareness on hers and other players' game state. Therefore design choices as regards adopted game technologies are critically important because their well-known limitations (e.g. WLAN disconnections or GPRS latency) may severely impact the player's personal and social awareness.

In most games scenarios position visualization is a necessity, using 2D/3D maps. Google Maps will likely dominate among alternative map representation tools due to specialized API support in all major mobile platforms.

Simulation modalities (including virtual and augmented reality) represent a key feature in most games scenarios to enhance game experiences. As mobile devices evolve they become smaller and more flexible than the equipment players used in many of the surveyed games. This will likely motivate developers to incorporate these technologies that fuse physical and virtual content, in pervasive games.

As for contextual features, most game scenarios should benefit by incorporating the location and social context of players (e.g. ongoing activity and location of co-players). Additional context parameters (such as acceleration, orientation, proximity, gesturing, time, light intensity, temperature, weather conditions) may be useful to be taken into account and comprise alternative modes of implicit input in future game projects scenarios. Some of the abovementioned contextual parameters may be captured by dedicated wireless sensor network installations (Chatzigiannakis et al., 2011; Yick, Mukherjee, & Ghosal, 2008); the emergence of robust, programmable, 802.15.4-compliant sensor node platforms will likely influence the design decisions of pervasive game developers as those could reliably feed a multitude of environmental, social and activity context data. Even more so, smartphones and PDAs that commonly integrate GPS receivers, sensors, compasses and RFID readers are expected to play a significant role in providing contextual input in future game developments. Context parameters may also be provided by publicly available web services (e.g. weather status and forecast, public transportation schedules, etc.).

Privacy is an important consideration in pervasive gaming, although not as important as in other application areas of pervasive computing, as players are mostly aware that their game activity and behavior is recorded and utilized within the game logic. However, Montola (2005) argues that when a game is played constantly, privacy considerations become an issue. Two commercial pervasive games, Mogi and Botfighters, raise privacy issues; however, due to their commercial nature, neither their design details nor any user evaluations are available (Peitz, Saarenpää, & Björk, 2007). Privacy issues are subject to trade-offs: to be aware of other player's state you have to tell something about yourself; to access personalized services you need to disclose personal profile information, and so on. Still, the case of personal real time location information is troublesome since so far people have little experience on the issue. In this context Sotamaa (2002) makes the following suggestion: Games can offer a functional testing ground for potential users of such location-based services that take advantage of personal real time location. In a setting with commonly accepted rules, people can experiment what it feels like when other people are able to locate you. Being able to unsubscribe the game whenever one wants to, prevents the game becoming too scary.

Another promising research topic relates with user (player) modeling, which has not yet been thoroughly investigated. For instance, innovative game scenarios with dynamic establishment of user groups (teams) with similar interests or behavior could possibly appear. Such grouping could be realized through applying efficient clustering methods (Xu & Wunsch, 2005). Along this line, several game scenarios could incorporate intelligent game engine's recommendations to mobile players (Ricci, 2011) (e.g. player route or team establishment recommendations); such recommendations could take into account the actions/ behaviors of peer players (i.e. use collaborative filtering techniques (Herlocker, Konstan, & and Riedl, 2000)), or even the current game context (e.g. use context-aware collaborative filtering methods (Chen, 2005; Gavalas & Kenteris, 2011)).

Finally, future research should aim at gaining deep understanding in questions concerning methods, theories and techniques that address the concept of usability, in the context of pervasive gaming. The question of how the notion of usability can be defined and evaluated in this particular field, needs to be answered (Jegers, 2004). Having resolved this, formal usability trials could help to reveal the main usability issues appearing in pervasive game exercises and possibly extract directions for enhancements and transparent use of pervasive technologies. Even more so, understanding what makes players enjoy a game is perhaps the most important issue for successful pervasive game design (Jegers, 2007). From a research perspective, perception of player enjoyment enriches the evaluation of experimental pervasive game prototypes and concepts and allows developers to appreciate user experiences derived from use of pervasive technology in general. Interestingly, none of the relevant studies address player enjoyment explicitly; hence this topic also represents an open research subject.

CONCLUSION

This chapter provided an introduction to the field of pervasive gaming. Firstly, we approached pervasive games from a theoretical point of view,

defining four axes of pervasive games design, introducing the concept of game world persistency and describing aspects of spatially/temporally/ socially expanded games. Then we presented ten representative pervasive games, classified in five popular games genres, based on their playing environment and features. In the sequel, we examined the reviewed games with respect to several design aspects (communication and localization, context and personal-awareness, information model, player equipment and I/O modalities). Based on that discussion, we highlighted current trends, design principles and proposed future directions for pervasive games design and development.

REFERENCES

Baldauf, M., Dustdar, S., & Rosenberg, F. (2007). A survey on context-aware systems. *International Journal of Ad Hoc and Ubiquitous Computing*, *2*(4), 263–277. doi:10.1504/IJA-HUC.2007.014070.

Bell, M. (2008). Toward a definition of ``virtual worlds''. *Journal of Virtual Worlds Research*, *1*(1), 1–5.

Benford, S., Crabtree, A., Flintham, M., Drozd, A., Anastasi, R., & Paxton, M. (2006). Can you see me now? *ACM Transactions on Computer-Human Interaction*, *13*(11).

Benford, S., Flintham, M., Drozd, A., Anastasi, R., Rowland, D., Tandavanitj, N., & Sutton, J. (2004). *Uncle Roy all around you: Implicating the city in a location-based performance*. ACM Advanced Computer Entertainment.

Benford, S., Magerkurth, C., & Ljungstrand, P. (2005). Bridging the physical and digital in pervasive gaming. *Communications of the ACM*, *48*(3), 54–57. doi:10.1145/1047671.1047704.

Broll, W., Ohlenburg, J., Lindt, I., Herbst, I., & Braun, A. K. (2006). *Meeting technology challenges of pervasive augmented reality games.* Paper presented at the 5th ACM SIGCOMM Workshop on Network and System Support for Games (NetGames'06). New York, NY.

Capra, M., Radenkovic, M., Benford, S., Oppermann, L., Drozd, A., & Flintham, M. (2005). *The multimedia challenges raised by pervasive games.* Paper presented at the 13th Annual ACM International Conference on Multimedia. New York, NY.

Chalmers, M., Bell, M., Brown, B., Hall, M., Sherwood, S., & Tennent, T. (2005). *Gaming on the edge: Using seams in ubicomp games.* Paper presented at the 2005 ACM SIGCHI International Conference on Advances in Computer Entertainment Technology. Valencia, Spain.

Chatzigiannakis, I., Mylonas, G., Akribopoulos, O., Logaras, M., Kokkinos, P., & Spirakis, P. (2010). The hot potato case: Challenges in multiplayer pervasive games based on AdHoc mobile sensor networks and the experimental evaluation of a prototype game. *CoRR abs/1002.1099.*

Chatzigiannakis, I., Mylonas, G., Kokkinos, P., Akribopoulos, O., Logaras, M., & Mavrommati, I. (2011). Implementing multiplayer pervasive installations based on mobile sensing devices: Field experience and user evaluation from a public showcase. *Journal of Systems and Software.* doi:10.1016/j.jss.2011.06.062 PMID:21532969.

Chen, A. (2005). *Context-aware collaborative filtering system: Predicting the user's preference in the ubiquitous.* Paper presented at the International Workshop on Location and Context-Awareness. New York, NY.

Cheok, A. D., & Khoo, E. T. (2006). Age Invaders: Inter-generational mixed reality family game. *The International Journal of Virtual Reality, 5*(2), 45–50.

Cheok, A. D., Sreekumar, A., Lei, C., & Thang, L. M. (2006). Capture the flag: Mixed-reality social gaming with smart phones. *IEEE Pervasive Computing / IEEE Computer Society [and] IEEE Communications Society, 5*(2), 62–63. doi:10.1109/MPRV.2006.25.

Childress, M., & Braswell, R. (2006). Using massively multiplayer online role-playing games for online learning. *Distance Education, 27*(2), 187–196. doi:10.1080/01587910600789522.

Fischer, J., Lindt, I., & Stenros, J. (2006). *Final crossmedia report (part II) – Epidemic menace II evaluation report.* Integrated Project on Pervasive Gaming.

Flintham, M., Anastasi, R., Benford, S., Drozd, A., Mathrick, J., Rowland, D., & Sutton, J. (2003). *Uncle Roy all around you: Mixing games and theatre on the city streets.* Paper presented at the 1st International Conference on Digital Games Research Association (DIGRA'03). New York, NY.

Gavalas, D., & Economou, D. (2011). Development platforms for mobile applications: Status and trends. *IEEE Software, 28*(1), 77–86. doi:10.1109/MS.2010.155.

Gavalas, D., & Kenteris, M. (2011). A pervasive web-based recommendation system for mobile tourist guides. *Personal and Ubiquitous Computing, 15*(7), 759–770. doi:10.1007/s00779-011-0389-x.

Gaver, W., Beaver, J., & Benford, S. (2003). *Ambiguity as a resource for design.* Paper presented at the SIGCHI Conference on Human Factors in Computing Systems. Ft. Lauderdale, FL.

Gellersen, H. W., Schmidt, A., & Beigl, M. (2002). Multi-sensor context-awareness in mobile devices and smart artefacts. *Mobile Networks and Applications, 7*(5). doi:10.1023/A:1016587515822.

Guo, B., Fujimura, R., Zhang, D., & Imai, M. (2012). Design-in-play: Improving the variability of indoor pervasive games. *Multimedia Tools and Applications, 59*(1), 259–277. doi:10.1007/s11042-010-0711-z.

Hannamari, S., Kuittinen, J., & Montola, M. (2007). *Insectopia evaluation report*. Integrated Project on Pervasive Gaming.

Hay, S., & Harle, R. (2009). *Bluetooth tracking without discoverability*. Paper presented at the 4th International Symposium of Location and Context Awareness (LoCA'2009). New York, NY.

Herbst, I., Braun, A.-K., McCall, R., & Broll, W. (2008). *TimeWarp: Interactive time travel with a mobile mixed reality game*. Paper presented at the 10th International Conference on Human Computer Interaction with Mobile Devices and Services. New York, NY.

Herlocker, J. L., Konstan, J. A., & Riedl, J. (2000). *Explaining collaborative filtering recommendations*. Paper presented at the ACM Conference on Computer Supported Cooperative Work. New York, NY.

Hsiao, T., & Yuan, S. (2005). Practical middleware for massively multiplayer online games. *IEEE Internet Computing, 9*(5), 47–54. doi:10.1109/MIC.2005.106.

IAD. (2011). *Urban defender*. Retrieved from http://iad.zhdk.ch/en/node/157

Intrepidus. (2010). *NFC and RFID-enabled smartphones and mobile devices are coming*. Retrieved from http://intrepidusgroup.com/insight/2010/12/nfc-rfid-enabled-smartphones-and-mobile-devices-are-coming/

Jaimes, A., & Sebe, N. (2007). Multimodal human-computer interaction: A survey. *Computer Vision and Image Understanding, 108*(1-2), 116–134. doi:10.1016/j.cviu.2006.10.019.

Jegers, K. (2004). *Usability of pervasive games*. Paper presented at the 1st International Workshop on Pervasive Gaming Applications (PerGames'2004). New York, NY.

Jegers, K. (2007). Pervasive game flow: Understanding player enjoyment in pervasive gaming. *Computers in Entertainment, 5*(1).

Jegers, K. (2009). Pervasive GameFlow: Identifying and exploring the mechanisms of player enjoyment in pervasive games. Umea, Sweden: Department of informatics, Umeå University.

Jegers, K., & Wiberg, M. (2006). Pervasive gaming in the everyday world. *IEEE Pervasive Computing / IEEE Computer Society [and] IEEE Communications Society, 5*(1), 78–85. doi:10.1109/MPRV.2006.11.

Kaiser, A., Achir, N., & Boussetta, K. (2009). *Multiplayer games over wireless ad hoc networks: Energy and delay analysis*. Paper presented at the International Conference on Ultra Modern Telecommunications & Workshops (ICUMT'09). New York, NY.

Kiefer, P., Matyas, S., & Schlieder, C. (2006). *Systematically exploring the design space of location-based games*. Paper presented at the 4th International Conference on Pervasive Computing (Pervasive'2006). New York, NY.

Lankoski, P., Heliö, S., Nummela, J., Lahti, J., Mäyrä, F., & Ermi, L. (2004). *A case study in pervasive game design: The songs of north.* Paper presented at the Third Nordic Conference on Human-Computer Interaction. Tampere, Finland.

Lavín-Mera, P., Torrente, J., Moreno-Ger, P., & Fernández-Manjón, B. (2009). *Mobile game development for multiple devices in education.* Paper presented at the 4th International Conference on Interactive Mobile and Computer-Aided Learning. New York, NY.

Lindley, C. A. (2004). *Trans-reality gaming.* Paper presented at the Annual International Workshop in Computer Game Design and Technology. New York, NY.

Lindley, C. A., & Eladhari, M. (2005). *Narrative structure in trans-reality role-playing games: Integrating story construction from live action, table top and computer-based role-playing games.* Paper presented at the Digital Games Research Conference (DiGRA'2005). New York, NY.

Magerkurth, C., Cheok, A. D., Mandryk, R. L., & Nilsen, T. (2005). Pervasive games: Bringing computer entertainment back to the real world. *Computers in Entertainment, 3*(3), 1–19. doi:10.1145/1077246.1077257.

Montola, M. (2005). *Exploring the edge of the magic circle: Defining pervasive games.* Paper presented at the Digital Arts and Culture (DAC'2005). New York, NY.

Montola, M., Stenros, J., & Waern, A. (2009). *Pervasive games: Theory and design.* San Francisco, CA: Morgan Kaufmann Publishers Inc..

Peitz, J. (2006). Game design document - Insectopia. *Integrated Project on Pervasive Gaming, Deliverable D9.8B.*

Peitz, J., & Björk, S. (2007). INSECTOPIA using the real world as a game resource. In *Space Time Play* (pp. 294–295). Basel: Birkhäuser.

Peitz, J., Saarenpää, H., & Björk, S. (2007). *Insectopia: Exploring pervasive games through technology already pervasively available.* Paper presented at the International Conference on Advances in Computer Entertainment Technology. Salzburg, Austria.

PhysicalComp. (2009). *Physical computing: Urban defender.* Retrieved from http://iad.projects.zhdk.ch/physicalcomputing/seminare/embodied-interaction-hs-2009/projektgruppen/nino-dondi-philipp/

PK. (2011). *Parallel kingdom.* Retrieved from http://www.parallelkingdom.com

PM. (2011). *Pac Manhattan.* Retrieved from http://www.pacmanhattan.com/about.php

Ricci, F. (2011). Mobile recommender systems. *Information Technology & Tourism, 12*(3), 205–231. doi:10.3727/109830511X12978702284390.

Salen, K., & Zimmerman, E. (2004). *Rules of play: Game design fundamentals.* Cambridge, MA: MIT Press.

Schuette, R., & Rotthowe, T. (1998). *The guidelines of modeling – An approach to enhance the quality in information models.* Paper presented at the 17th International Conference on Conceptual Modeling (ER'98). New York, NY.

Sotamma, O. (2002). *All the world's a botfighter stage: Notes on location-based multi-user gaming.* Paper presented at the Computer Games and Digital Cultures Conference. New York, NY.

Stenros, J., Montola, M., Waern, A., & Jonsson, S. (2007). Momentum evaluation report. *IPerG Deliverable D11.7.*

TexasInstr. (2011). *Texas instruments brings ZigBee home automation to smartphones & tablets*. Retrieved from http://www.cocoontech. com/portal/articles/news/17-zigbee/432-texas-instruments-brings-zigbee-home-automation-to-smartphones-a-tablets

Varshavsky, A., & Patel, S. (2010). Location in ubiquitous computing. In J. Krumm (Ed.), *Ubiquitous Computing Fundamentals* (pp. 285–319). Boca Raton, FL: CRC Press.

Vergetis, E., Guerin, R., Sarkar, S., & Rank, J. (2005). Can bluetooth succeed as a large-scale Ad Hoc networking technology? *IEEE Journal on Selected Areas in Communications*, *23*(3), 644–656. doi:10.1109/JSAC.2004.842544.

Walther, B. K. (2005a). Atomic actions -- Molecular experience: Theory of pervasive gaming. *Computers in Entertainment*, *3*(3), 1–13. doi:10.1145/1077246.1077258.

Walther, B. K. (2005b). *Notes on the methodology of pervasive gaming*. Paper presented at the 4th International Conference on Entertainment Computing. Sanda, Japan.

Walther, B. K. (2007). Pervasive game-play: Theoretical reflections and classifications. *Matrix (Stuttgart, Germany)*, 1.

Wetzel, W., Blum, L., McCall, R., Oppermann, L., Broeke, T.S., & Szalavári, Z. (2009). Final prototype of timewarp application. *IPCity*.

Whitney, A. (2010). *Traverse a fantastic virtual world within the real world with parallel kingdom-age of emergence*. Retrieved from http://www. examiner.com/video-games-in-wichita-falls/ traverse-a-fantastic-virtual-world-within-the-real-world-with-parallel-kingdom-age-of-emergence

Xu, R., & Wunsch, D. (2005). Survey of clustering algorithms. *IEEE Transactions on Neural Networks*, *16*(3), 645–678. doi:10.1109/ TNN.2005.845141 PMID:15940994.

Yick, J., Mukherjee, B., & Ghosal, D. (2008). Wireless sensor network survey. *Computer Networks*, *52*(12), 2292–2330. doi:10.1016/j. comnet.2008.04.002.

Zhu, F., Mutka, M. W., & Ni, L. M. (2005). Service discovery in pervasive computing environments. *IEEE Pervasive Computing / IEEE Computer Society [and] IEEE Communications Society*, *4*(4), 81–90. doi:10.1109/MPRV.2005.87.

KEY TERMS AND DEFINITIONS

Augmented Reality: Augmented reality is a variation of virtual reality that draws virtual objects into a real-world environment.

Context-Awareness: A property of computing devices which allows the adaptation of their behavior according to changes sensed within their environment.

Game World Persistency: A virtual world that continues to exist even after a player exits it, and to whose state player-made changes are to some extent permanent.

Magic Circle: The metaphorical magic circle of play is a voluntary, contractual structure that is limited in time and space.

Pervasive Computing Environments: Environments that integrate networked computing devices -spanning from tiny sensors to highly dynamic, powerful devices- with people and their ambient environments.

Pervasive Games: An exciting and commercially promising new form of computer games that builds upon a combination of hybrid interfaces, wireless networking, and context-sensing technologies.

PG Possibility Space: Refers to a virtual space dealt with in networking given the focus on non-locality, non-metric systems and constant accessibility.

ENDNOTES

[1] Pronoia in games refers positive paranoia of the players when they become, in a way, paranoid, suspecting that everything relates to the game.

Section 3
Social Awareness

Chapter 7
Community Detection and Profiling in Location-Based Social Networks

Zhu Wang
Northwestern Polytechnical University, China

Daqing Zhang
TELECOM SudParis, France

Xingshe Zhou
Northwestern Polytechnical University, China

Bin Guo
Northwestern Polytechnical University, China

Zhiwen Yu
Northwestern Polytechnical University, China

ABSTRACT

Due to the proliferation of GPS-enabled smartphones, Location-Based Social Networking (LBSNs) services have been experiencing a remarkable growth over the last few years. Compared with traditional online social networks, a significant feature of LBSNs is the coexistence of both online and offline social interactions, providing a large-scale heterogeneous social network that is able to facilitate lots of academic studies. One possible study is to leverage both online and offline social ties for the recognition and profiling of community structures. In this chapter, the authors attempt to summarize some recent progress in the community detection problem based on LBSNs. In particular, starting with an empirical analysis on the characters of the LBSN data set, the authors present three different community detection approaches, namely, link-based community detection, content-based community detection, and hybrid community detection based on both links and contents. Meanwhile, they also address the community profiling problem, which is very useful in real-world applications.

DOI: 10.4018/978-1-4666-4695-7.ch007

1. INTRODUCTION

The recent surge of location-based social networks (LBSNs, e.g., Foursquare and Facebook Places) driven by the increasing popularity of smart phones is bringing a new set of opportunities for research scientists and application developers. Compared with traditional online social networks (e.g., Facebook, Twitter), a distinct characteristic of LBSNs is the co-existence of both online and offline social interactions, as shown in Figure 1. On one hand, LBSNs support typical online social networking facilities, e.g., making friends, sharing comments and photos. On the other hand, LBSNs also support offline social interactions, e.g., checking in places. In other words, LBSNs are heterogeneous social networks which consist of both online and offline social links (Guo, Zhang, Wang, Yu & Zhou, 2013). Meanwhile, vertices in LBSNs usually have multiple attributes, e.g., attributes of a user might include number of followers, number of followings, and number of check-ins; a venue might have attributes such as category, number of check-ins and number of visitors.

One fundamental issue in social network analysis is to detect user communities. A community is typically thought of as a group of users who are densely interconnected compared to the other users in the network (Newman & Girvan, 2004; Fortunato, 2010). Specifically, discovering communities of LBSN users who visit similar physical places are able to facilitate many applications, such as direct marketing, friend recommendation, and community sensing (Zhang, Guo & Yu, 2011). However, unlike social networks (e.g., Flickr, Facebook) which provide explicit groups for users to subscribe or join, the notion of community in LBSNs is not well defined. In order to capitalize on the huge number of potential users, quality community detection and profiling approaches are needed.

Firstly, unlike social networks which only contain a single type of social interaction, the co-existence of online/offline social interactions

Figure 1. An example of LBSN

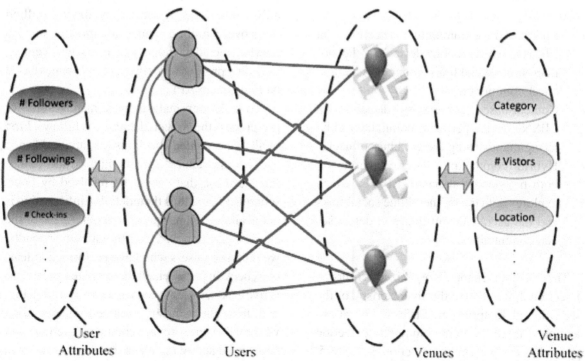

and user/venue attributes in LBSN makes the community detection problem much more challenging.

Meanwhile, it has been well understood that people in social networks are naturally characterized by multiple community memberships. For example, a person usually belongs to several social groups like family, friends and colleagues; a researcher may be active in several areas. Thus, it is more reasonable to cluster users into overlapping communities rather than disjoint ones.

Finally, we believe that it's important to characterize communities in a semantic manner to effectively support real-world applications. However, due to the limitation of available information, not much work has been done to address community profiling. The rich user and venue metadata available in LBSNs provides us the possibility to characterize the identified communities semantically.

In this chapter, we will present some of the recent progress in community detection and profiling on LBSNs. Based on the used information for LBSN community discovering, we classify existing community detection approaches into three categories:

- Link-based community detection in LBSNs, which mainly leverages the online/offline social links among users to discover communities.
- Content-based community detection in LBSNs, which performs community clustering mainly using the attributes of users.
- Hybrid community detection based on both links and contents in LBSNs, which explores both the online/offline social links and the user/venue attributes to detect social communities.

The rest of this chapter is organized as follows. In Section 2, we analyse the characteristic of the user's digital footprints in LBSNs. The above mentioned three different community detection approaches are presented in Section 3, 4 and 5,

respectively. Finally, we conclude this chapter by proposing some promising research directions.

2. DATA ANALYSIS

Foursquare, which is launched in March 2009, is a popular LBSN which has more than 20 million registered users till April 2012, and about 3 millions of check-ins are performed per day (https://foursquare.com/about). In this section, an empirical study is conducted based on the collected Foursquare dataset, which aims to reveal the characteristics of LBSN data on one hand, and shed lights to the design of community detection approaches on the other hand.

2.1 Data Collection

Foursquare API provides limited authorized access for retrieving check-in information, therefore we resort to Twitter streaming API to get the publicly shared check-ins. Our data collection started from October 24th, 2011 and lasted for 20 weeks, which results in a dataset of more than 30 million check-ins performed by about 1 million users over 3 million venues. Meanwhile, we also crawled metadata related to users and venues, including profiles for both users and venues based on Foursquare API.

To make our analysis more manageable, we pre-process the collected dataset as follows. First of all, we excluded check-ins that are performed over invalid venues. Specifically, invalid venues refer to those that cannot be resolved by Foursquare API, and thus their detailed information is not available. Consequently, about 7.52% of the check-ins are removed from the dataset. Secondly, we only keep users who have performed at least one check-in per week on the average (referred as active users), which means inactive users together with their check-ins are excluded. Finally, users who used agent software conducting remote and large scale automatic check-ins (with a check-in speed faster than 1,200 km/h, which is the common airplane speed) are defined as sudden move users (Cheng, Caverlee, Lee & Sui, 2011) and check-ins from these users are eliminated. We observed a total number of 9,276 sudden move users, which occupy about 4.04% of the active users. After the above data cleansing, the remained dataset includes 220,592 users and 16,652,839 check-ins which were performed over 3,088,945 venues.

2.2 User Characteristics

In this section, we will introduce and analyse several import attributes of LBSN users, including number of followers, number of check-ins and the user's radius of gyration.

Number of Followers

In Foursquare, users can follow each other to form a social network, and make use of their mobile phones to check in venues at their location and notify their followers. Figure 2 shows the cumula-

tive distribution function (CDF) of the follower number of Foursquare users. Accordingly, about 90% users have less than 200 followers, and only quite a small part of users have more than 1,000 followers (1,000 of 220,592, i.e., less than 0.5%). Particularly, the average number of followers of Foursquare users in our data set is 97.33.

Number of Check-Ins

The cumulative distribution function of the check-in frequency of Foursquare users is illustrated in Figure 3, based on which we can get the following observations. First, more than 90% users took less than 200 check-ins within 20 weeks, i.e., less than 10 check-ins per week. Second, the number of super-active users is very small, and only 195 users had performed more than 1,000 check-in during the data collection period. Specifically, the average number of check-ins of Foursquare users in the data set is 75.49, which means that their average check-in frequency is 3.78 check-in per week.

Figure 2. CDF of number of followers

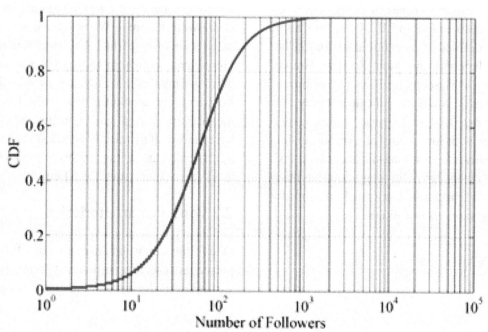

Figure 3. CDF of number of check-ins

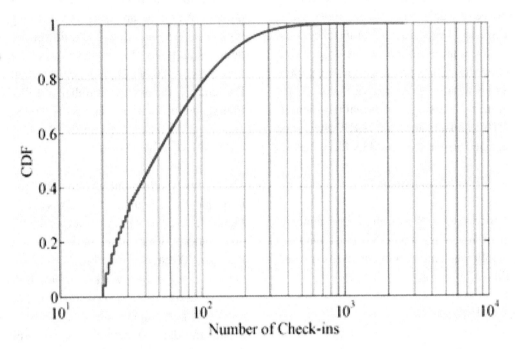

Radius of Gyration

Radius of gyration is an important metric that can be used to distinguish the life style of different users, which is usually defined as the standard deviation of distances between a user's check-ins and her home location. In LBSNs, a user's home location is defined as the centroid position of her most popular check-in region (Scellato, Noulas, Lambiotte & Mascolo, 2011). The radius of gyration metric is able to indicate not only how frequently but also how far a user moves. Generally, a user with low radius of gyration mainly travels locally (with few long-distance check-ins), while a user with high radius of gyration has many long-distance check-ins. The formal definition for radius of gyration is as follows:

$$r_g = \sqrt{\frac{1}{n}\sum_{i=1}^{n}(r_i - r_h)^2},$$

where n is the number of check-ins made by a user, and $(r_i - r_h)$ is the distance between the geographic coordinate r_i of a particular check-in and the user's home location r_h.

Based on the above formula, we calculated the home location of users in our data set, which is shown in Figure 4. We observe that the radius of gyration of more than 80% users is within 200 kilometres, indicating most of the Foursquare users mainly travel locally. Meanwhile, there do exist a certain amount of users who have many long-distance travels, e.g., more than 10,000 users have a radius of gyration beyond 1,000 kilometres. Specifically, the average radius of gyration of the users in our data set is 220.64 km.

2.3 Venue Characteristics

One of the important characters of LBSN is the presence of user location traces, thus in this section we will describe some of the useful venue-mode

Figure 4. CDF of the radius of gyration

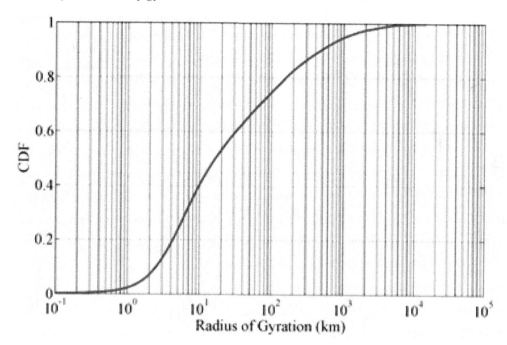

Number of Visitors

During daily lives, people continually move around in the physical world. Specifically, the users of LBSNs opportunistically visit and check in different venues. In other words, each venue may have a certain number of visitors. The dotted green line in Figure 5 presents the number of visitors of different venues. We find that more than 60% of the venues have only one visitor from our data set, and only a very small proportion of venues (3,199 of 3,088,945) have attracted more than 100 visitors during the data collection period of 20 weeks.

Meanwhile, Foursquare classifies venues into 9 different categories, i.e., Arts & Entertainment, College & University, Food, Great Outdoors, Nightlife Spot, Professional & Other Places, Residence, Shop & Service, and Travel & Transport. The inset of Figure 6 shows the number of visitors of different venue categories, in which the digits 1~9 on x-axis represents the above 9 venue categories respectively. We find that the difference between visitor numbers of different venue categories is not very significant. Specifically, the most popular venue category is Food which has 211,512 visitors (i.e., about 95.88% of the entire population of our data set), and the least popular venue category is College & University which has 107,399 visitors.

Number of Check-Ins

While each venue usually has multiple visitors, it also has a certain number of check-ins left by its visitors (each visitor may leave one or several check-ins over a particular venue). We give the check-in frequency of different venues in Figure 5 using the solid blue line, and its distribution pattern is quite similar to that of visitor numbers of different venues.

Meanwhile, we also show the check-in frequency of the 9 different venue categories in

Figure 5. CDF of the visitor/check-in frequency of venues

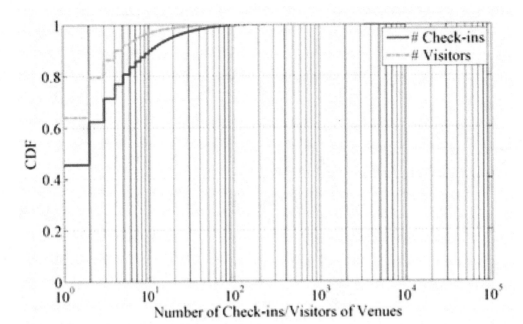

Figure 6. Number of visitors/check-ins of 9 different venue categories

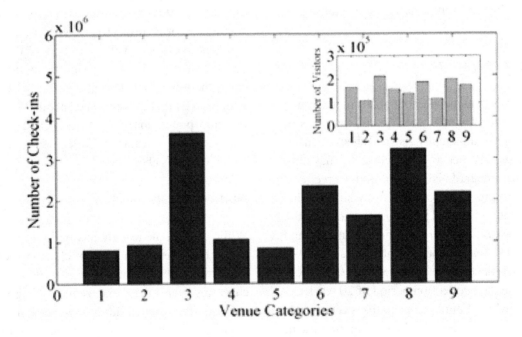

Figure 6. An interesting finding is that, while the visitor numbers of different venue categories vary a little, their check-in frequencies do differ from each other significantly. In particular, the most attractive venue category (*Food*) has more than 3.6 million of check-ins which is about 21.76% of the total number of check-ins, while the ratio for the least attractive venue category (*Arts & Entertainment*) is only 4.84%.

Temporal Check-In Pattern

In general, people visit and check in different kind of venues at different time, such that different venue categories might be distinguished according to their temporal check-in patterns (Ye, Janowicz, Mulligann & Lee, 2011). We divide a week into 168 (7×24) time slots and each time slot corresponds to one hour in a certain day of the week, reflecting the temporal feature of each user check-in. In such a way, we can build a weekly temporal check-in band for each venue category at the hour granularity, which means each temporal band corresponds to a vector of 168 dimensions (7×24). For example, Figure 7 plots the check-in patterns of two different venue categories: the bar and the museum. We can see that, according to the temporal check-in patterns, museums are most popular during the daytime of weekends while bars are extremely busy on Friday and Saturday evening.

The empirical analysis is not only able to help us understand some basic characters of LBSNs, but also capable of serving as the foundation for the investigation of community detection methods, which is reflected in two aspects. On the one hand, some of the above features can be directly used for community detection, for instance, Li and Chen (2009) leveraged a set of user attributes to discover communities in LBSNs, including num-

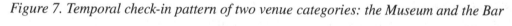

Figure 7. Temporal check-in pattern of two venue categories: the Museum and the Bar

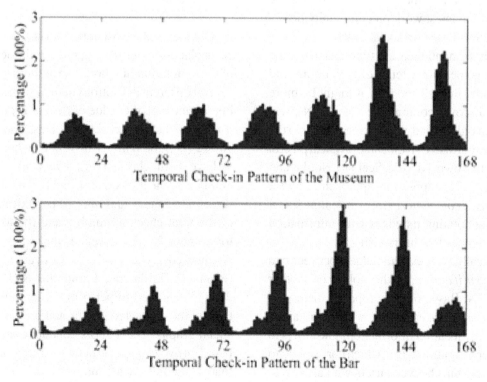

ber of friends, number of check-ins, radius of gyration, etc. On the other hand, these features could also be utilized to design more dedicated metrics for community recognition, for example, Wang, Zhang, Yang, Yu and Zhou (2012) proposed two metrics, namely user geo-span similarity and venue temporal similarity, based on radius of gyration and venue temporal check-in pattern, respectively.

3. LINK-BASED COMMUNITY DETECTION IN LBSNs

In social networks, a community is typically thought of as a group of users with more and/ or better *interactions* amongst its members than between its members and the remainder of the network (Newman & Girvan, 2004; Fortunato, 2010). Specifically, the most widely accepted concept of *interaction* is the social *links* among users, therefore communities that aggregate closely connected users should be detected by maximizing the intra-community modularity. In this section, we present the latest work on community detection in LBSNs based on social links.

As we have mentioned, a distinct characteristic of LBSNs is the co-existence of both online and offline social links. Therefore, it might be more useful to discover communities of LBSN users who are not only socially close to each other in the cyber space but also visit the same physical places. To this end, Brown, Nicosia, Scellato, Noulas and Mascolo (2012) proposed an approach to reveal *place-focused communities* from the online social graph by annotating its edges with information about the venues that users visit.

Specifically, there exists an edge e_{ij} between two users u_i and u_j *if and only if* they follow each other in the LBSN. Based on the proposed method, a weight is assigned to each edge, which is obtained by leveraging location information. The aim is to give higher weights to edges which correspond to online friendships between users who also go to

same physical places. Edges whose weights are not high enough to a place-focused community are excluded from the social graph, and users who are not connected to any edges with high enough weights are also removed.

Consequently, the LBSN can be represented as an weighted, undirected graph $G(U, E)$, which contains a set of venues V, and a list of user check-ins L. An annotation function f is introduced to assign weights to the edges, which is defined as $f: E \rightarrow \Re_{\geq 0}$. The annotation function f assigns a weight $f(e_{ij})$ to each e_{ij} in E by leveraging the check-in information of user u_i and u_j. Then, the detection of place-focused communities is formulated as follows:

- Assign to each edge e_{ij} in E a weight $f(e_{ij})$ based on the check-ins of u_i and u_j;
- Remove all edges with weight lower than a threshold $t > 0$ from the social graph;
- Exclude all users with no incident edges from the social graph;
- Apply a standard community detection algorithm.

Obviously, the most important issue of discovering place-focused communities is the definition of the annotation function. The authors proposed several different definitions in their work, including *binary* (i.e., the value of $f(e_{ij})$ is 1 *if and only if* u_i and u_j have co-checked at least one venue), *places* (i.e., the number of venues where u_i and u_j have both checked in), *check-ins* (i.e., the number of check-ins that u_i and u_j have left over the same venues), and *ratio* (the maximum ratio of the total check-in number and the total visitor number for all the venues that u_i and u_j have co-checked). Afterwards, the Louvain algorithm (Blondel, Guillaume, Lambiotte & Lefebvre, 2008) is adopted to perform community detection on the annotated graphs and on the original social graphs. The authors conduct experiments based on two large-scale network traces, and show that community detection using only the online links may fail to reveal groups of friends who visit the same places. Specifically, based on two evaluation measures named *colocation density* and *colocation fraction*, the approach is proved to be able to discover communities connected not only by online social ties but also by physical places. Here we quote the experimental results of Brown et al. (2012) in Figure 8 as an example, which illustrates the average colocation density and the average colocation fraction for communities of a given size.

Accordingly, the communities discovered by annotating the online social graphs based on *places*, *check-ins* and *ratio* have consistently higher values for both measures than the results achieved using *binary* and *unannotated* graph. The authors conclude that the proposed annotating mechanism is able to remove spatially unimportant edges from the social graph and reveal meaningful place-focused communities.

4. CONTENT-BASED COMMUNITY DETECTION IN LBSNs

While link-based approaches aim to discover groups of users who are densely interconnected compared to the other users in the network, another family of approaches is based on user attributes (i.e., contents) similarity measures (Orman & La-

batut, 2012). Such a measure allows translating the topological notions of maximum intra-community modularity in terms of maximum intra-community similarity. In other words, a community is defined as a group of users who are similar to each other, but dissimilar from the rest of the network. By introducing a user-to-user similarity measure, communities can be discovered by applying a similarity-based classic clustering algorithm (Gan, Ma & Wu, 2007). In this section, we will present some of the studies on community detection methods in LBSNs based on content information.

Li et al. (2009) propose two different similarity-based clustering approaches to identify user groups in Brightkite, which is a commercial LBSN website. One approach exploits the update (i.e., check-ins, photos and tips) of users to classify them into four disjoint groups based on the similarity of users' mobility patterns, which are *home*, *home-vacation*, *home-work* and *others*. Specifically, the authors use four metrics to calculate the mobility pattern similarity between two users. The first two metrics focus on the number of "hops" of users, which include the *number of uniquely visited places* and the *length of movement path*. The length is defined as the total number of visited places on the path, which might contain duplicates. The other two metrics are the user's *movement diameter* and *total travel distance*. The concept of movement diameter is

Figure 8. Colocation-based measures for the place-focused community

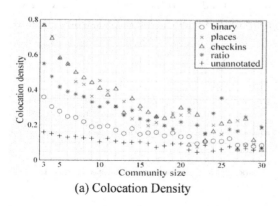

(a) Colocation Density

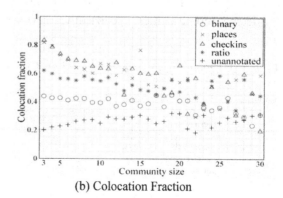

(b) Colocation Fraction

similar to that of radius of gyration, and is defined as the maximum distance between any two places visited by the user. The total travel distance is defined as the summation of the distances of all links on the path. Based on these four metrics, the authors adopt an unsupervised clustering algorithm X-Means (Pelleg & Moore, 2000) to discover user communities, which is an extended K-means algorithm with efficient estimation of the number of clusters.

The second approach clusters users based on the similarity of a set of user attributes, and lead to the identification of five disjoint groups, namely, *inactive*, *normal*, *active*, *mobile* and *trial* users. Specifically, 8 different user attributes are leveraged, including the number of friends, the number of updates, the number of active days, retained user (a binary value that indicates whether the user updated Brightkite in two continuous weeks), the number of uniquely visited places, the path length, the mobility diameter, the total travel distance. Afterwards, the expectation-maximization (EM) clustering algorithm is used to extract user clusters. We quote the experimental result in Figure 9, which presents the profiles of the detected five communities.

Noulas, Scellato, Mascolo and Pontil (2011) investigated the community detection problem in LBSNs based on Foursquare by exploring the similarity of user check-in patterns. A spectral clustering algorithm (Shi & Malik, 2000) is employed to group users based on the categories of venues they had checked in, aiming at identifying communities and characterizing the profiles of the detected communities. Specifically, each user

is represented using a check-in feature vector based on both the categories of venues one has checked in and the corresponding check-in frequency. Obviously, the dimensionality of such a vector is same as the number of different categories and the value of each feature is normalized over the total check-in number of each user. Afterwards, the similarity between two users is defined as the cosine similarity between their corresponding check-in feature vectors. Based on the above user-to-user similarity measure, a weight matrix W and a degree matrix D are constructed to enable the detection of user communities. We quote the experimental results in Figure 10, which presents the communities of Foursquare users from New York and London, and each community is characterized by two or three principal venue categories.

By analyzing the detected communities of both New York and London, the authors come out with some interesting findings, which are able to reveal the characteristics of different cities. For instance, users who are members of Cluster 3 of New York and Cluster 1 of London, demonstrate identical activity behaviors. Not only the ranking of the cluster features is very similar to each other, but also the respective average values are close to each other (*Nightlife, Food, Home*). A similar case is observed for Clusters 1 (New York) and Cluster 5 (London) of the two cities, with users performing more than 50% of their check-ins over places that belong to the *Home/Work/Other* category. A community profile however, that is not being observed in both cities, is the existence of a group of 223 users in New York whose princi-

Figure 9. Communities detected based on EM clustering

Cluster	User Type	Proportion %	Total Updates	Active Days	Retained %	Unique Places	Path Length	Mobility Diameter	Total Distance	Friends Number
	average	N/A	22.25	8.52	56.94	5.41	9.58	388.49	835.05	8.23
1	inactive	30	7.19	4.56	90.29	2.87	3.57	119.46	173.63	6.47
2	normal	16	47.10	22.07	99.30	10.00	19.02	226.33	624.00	15.69
3	active	6	197.73	47.25	99.60	34.97	77.95	1126.22	3747.30	36.26
4	mobile	8	20.43	10.37	90.90	9.06	12.22	3868.47	7304.41	11.77
5	trial	41	1.23	1	0	1.06	1.06	0.40	0.04	2.35

Figure 10. Community detection result based on spectral clustering of New York (Top) and London (Bottom). Some categories are abbreviated (e.g., Home is short for Home/Work/Other, and Parks denotes Parks & Outdoors).

Cluster 1(268)	Cluster 2(479)	Cluster 3(202)	Cluster 4(339)	Cluster 5(701)	Cluster 6(223)	Cluster 7(221)
Home (0.51)	Food(0.34)	Nightlife(0.53)	Food(0.41)	Food(0.26)	Shops(0.37)	Food(0.62)
Food(0.15)	Nightlife(0.29)	Food(0.19)	Nightlife(0.13)	Home (0.23)	Food(0.26)	Shops(0.11)
Nightlife(0.1)	Arts (0.08)	Home (0.07)	Shops(0.12)	Nightlife(0.12)	Home (0.08)	Nightlife(0.08)
Shops(0.07)	Shops(0.07)	Shops(0.05)	Home (0.08)	Shops(0.09)	Nightlife(0.08)	Home (0.04)
Travel(0.05)	Home (0.06)	Travel(0.04)	Parks (0.07)	Travel(0.08)	Travel(0.06)	Travel(0.03)
Other(0.12)	Other(0.16)	Other(0.12)	Other(0.19)	Other(0.22)	Other(0.15)	Other(0.12)

Cluster 1(62)	Cluster 2(95)	Cluster 3(72)	Cluster 4(66)	Cluster 5(95)	Cluster 6(119)	Cluster 7(31)
Nightlife(0.61)	Nightlife(0.35)	Home (0.35)	Food(0.58)	Home (0.59)	Food(0.22)	Travel(0.62)
Food(0.18)	Food(0.32)	Nightlife(0.29)	Nightlife(0.13)	Food(0.12)	Travel(0.18)	Food(0.12)
Home (0.06)	Arts (0.09)	Food(0.18)	Shops(0.08)	Travel(0.11)	Shops(0.17)	Home (0.1)
Travel(0.04)	Home (0.07)	Travel(0.07)	Home (0.06)	Nightlife(0.08)	Home (0.14)	Nightlife(0.06)
Parks (0.03)	Travel(0.06)	Shops(0.05)	Travel(0.06)	Parks (0.04)	Nightlife(0.14)	Shops(0.05)
Other(0.08)	Other(0.11)	Other(0.06)	Other(0.09)	Other(0.06)	Other(0.15)	Other(0.05)

pal check-in preference is the *Shop* category, which might reflect the presence of a fundamentally different shopping culture between the two cities.

5. HYBRID COMMUNITY DETECTION BASED ON BOTH LINKS AND CONTENTS IN LBSNs

While the aforementioned two kinds of community detection approaches (i.e., link-based and content-based) offer important insights into the community structure of LBSN users, none of them worked on overlapping community detection based on both online/offline social links and user/venue attributes. To fill in this gap, Wang et al. (2012) propose a multi-mode multi-attribute edge-centric clustering framework to discover profilable overlapping user communities in LBSNs, which leverages both link and content information.

The observation that each check-in on LBSNs reflects a certain aspect of the user's preferences or interests enlightens us to cluster edges instead of nodes, as the detected clusters of check-ins will naturally assign users into overlapping communities with connections to venues. Specifically,

we define a community as a cluster of bipartite edges (i.e., check-ins) with user and venue as two modes, where the attributes of users and venues characterize the properties of the community. Specifically, after obtaining edge clusters, overlapping communities of users can be recovered by replacing each edge with its vertices, i.e., a user is involved in a community as long as any of her check-ins falls into the community. In such a way, the obtained communities are usually highly overlapped.

5.1 Problem Formulation

We use $U = (u_1, u_2, \ldots, u_m)$ to represent the user set, and $V = (v_1, v_2, \ldots, v_n)$ to denote the venue category set, a community $C_i (1 \leq i \leq k)$ is a subset of users and venue categories, where k is the number of communities. On one hand, the check-in relationship between users and venue categories form a matrix M, where each entry M_{ij} corresponds to the number of check-ins that u_i has performed over v_j. Therefore, each user can be represented as a vector of venue categories, and each venue category can be denoted as a vector of users. On the other hand, users and venue categories might have several independent attributes, denoted as $(a_{i1}, a_{i2}, \ldots, a_{ix})$ and $(b_{j1}, b_{j2}, \ldots, b_{jy})$, respectively. Normally, every attribute reveals a certain social aspect of users or venue categories. For instance, as shown in Figure 1, a user has a certain number of followers and followings. Therefore, both user mode and venue mode have two types of representations: an inter-mode representation as well as an intra-mode representation.

Based on the above notations, the overlapping community detection in LBSNs can be formulated as a multi-mode multi-attribute edge-centric coclustering problem as follows:

Input:

- A check-in matrix $M_{(|U| \times |V|)}$, where $|U|$ and $|V|$ are the numbers of users and venue categories;
- A user attributes matrix $M_{(|U| \times |A|)}$, where $|A|$ is the number of user attributes;
- A venue category attributes matrix $M_{(|U| \times |B|)}$, where $|B|$ is the number of venue category attributes;
- The number of communities k.

Output:

- k overlapping communities which consist of both users and venue categories.

5.2 Multi-Mode Multi-Attribute Edge-Centric Clustering

As stated in the above section, we define a community in LBSNs as a cluster of bipartite edges (i.e., check-ins) of high similarity. Thereby, communities that aggregate similar users and venues together should be discovered by maximizing the intra-cluster similarity rather than maximizing modularity. This objective function is formulated as:

$$\text{Obj} = \arg\max_C \sum_{j=1}^{k} \sum_{e_c \in C_j} sim(e_c, C_j),$$

where k is the number of communities, $C = \{C_1, C_2, \ldots, C_k\}$ is the detected community set, e_c denotes an edge of community C_j, and $sim(e_c, C_j)$ is the similarity between e_c and C_j. With this formulation, the key is to characterize the similarity between a pair of edges. To this end, we introduce two inter-mode features, namely, *user-venue similarity* (i.e., characterizing a user based on a vector of venue categories) and *venue-user similarity* (i.e., characterizing a venue category by using a vector of users); and three intra-mode features which are *user social similarity, user geo-span similarity* and *venue temporal similarity*.

Based on the introduced inter-mode/intra-mode features, feature normalization and fusion are performed to calculate the similarity between a pair of edges. Afterwards, we put forward an edge-centric clustering algorithm named $M^2 Clustering$ to discover overlapping communities, which is a variant of k-means. We present the detected overall community structure of Foursquare users in Paris in Figure 11 based on Wordle (www. wordle.net). To make the result more clear, we cluster the detected communities into ten groups based on the venue categories.

According to Figure 11, we can see the size of a community (as shown by the number), the main activities of a community (from the tag size) and the overlapping degree between any two communities (from the links). For example, the biggest community in Paris is Office (362 users), which has more than 30% overlapping users with the Bar community (129 users), the French Restaurant community (187 users), as well as the Food and Drink Shop community (152 users). Apparently, it depicts the life style of the white-collar workers. Assume there are two highly overlapping communities and one of them is a mature market, the

Figure 11. Overall structure of the detected overlapping communities of Foursquare users in Paris. Each tag cloud represents a community; the number at the top right corner of a tag cloud denotes the user number of the community; two communities are linked if the overlapping degree is larger than 30% (thick links) or 20% (thin links). The overlapping degree is calculated as the ratio of the size of the intersection and the union of two communities.

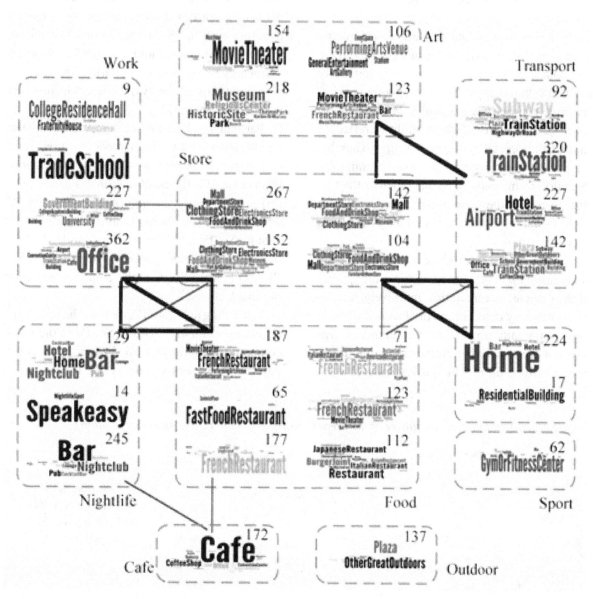

advertisers can then penetrate the other community by using the existing marketing channels.

5.3 Evaluating the Quality of the Detected Communities

Since the Foursquare data we use does not have the ground truth (Girvan & Newman, 2002) about the real community structure, we resort to indirectly evaluating the quality of the detected communities. Intuitively, users visiting similar venues tend to share similar interests, which might be reflected through the topics they discuss (i.e., tips). Thereby, we choose to estimate the proposed community detection framework by testing whether the tips that posted by the same community are also of high similarity, just as the community member's check-in patterns.

To this end, we introduce a measure named *community tip similarity* to evaluate the quality of the detected communities. Intuitively, a quality community detection method should achieve high community tip similarity, even though tips have not been used when clustering communities. Specifically, a tip t_k, which is left by user u_m at

venue category v_n, falls into community C_j *if and only if* there is an edge $e(u_m, v_n)$ that belongs to C_j. To compute the similarity between a pair of tips, we first project each tip to a latent topic space by using Latent Dirichlet Allocation (LDA), which helps to quantify the similarity between tips by denoting each tip as a topic vector (McCallum, 2002). Then, the community tip similarity can be defined by using cosine similarity. The average community tip similarity of different feature sets is shown in Figure 12.

Particularly, Feature Set I corresponds to the combination of two inter-mode features (i.e., *user-venue similarity* and *venue-user similarity*), Feature Set II is the combination of Feature Set I and *venue temporal similarity*, Feature Set III adds *user social similarity* into Feature Set II, Feature Set IV adds the other user-mode feature (i.e., *user geo-span similarity*) into Feature Set III, and Feature Set V is the combination of all the five features.

According to Figure 12, we have the following observation. Firstly, Feature Set IV is the most competitive feature set while Feature Set V is the next most competitive one, where the user geo-

Figure 12. Community tip similarity of different feature sets (Foursquare users in London)

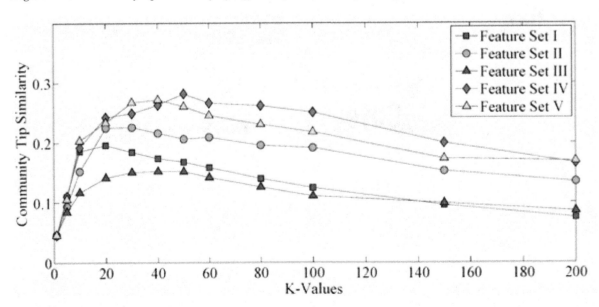

span feature has been leveraged. This indicates that users who have similar geo-spans are most likely to discuss similar topics. Meanwhile, while most of the introduced intra-mode features are able to increase the community tip similarity, the user social-status feature will lower the performance, i.e., the performance of Feature Set III is worse than the baseline method which only leverages inter-mode features for community detection (i.e., Feature Set I). The reason might be that there is no correlation between people's social statuses and their tip topics.

5.4 Community Profiling Based on Metadata

We characterize a community using the metadata of important users and venues that fall into the community, e.g., the member's average radius of gyration, and venue categories. To profile a community, we first compute the importance of each user and each venue-category based on their involvement degree. Afterwards, a community is represented as a feature vector, which depicts its characteristics. Specifically, the importance of a user u_m in community C_j is quantified by the percentage of u_m's check-ins that fall into C_j; the importance of a venue category v_n in community C_j is defined as the percentage of C_j's check-ins that is of category v_n. A user or venue category is a significant entity of a community *if and only if* its importance exceeds a predefined threshold θ. In such a way, we can obtain a list of important users as well as a list of important venue categories for each community, which serve as the basis of community profiling. Afterwards, a community can be represented as follows:

$$P_{C_J} = \{< f_{u_1}, e_{u_1} >, ..., < f_{u_m}, e_{u_m} > \\ , ..., < f_{v_1}, e_{v_1} >, ... < f_{v_n}, e_{v_n} >, ...\}$$

where each tuple $<f_{um}, e_{um}>$ or $<f_{vn}, e_{vn}>$ denotes either a user mode feature or a venue mode feature and the corresponding value. Particularly, on one hand, the value of a user mode feature is calculated based on the metadata of important users in community C_j. For example, the geo-span of C_j is defined as the average radius of gyration of its important members. On the other hand, venue mode features of a community C_j mainly refer to the significant venue categories in C_j, where each venue mode feature corresponds to a venue category v_n and its value is the same as the importance of v_n.

CONCLUSION

Community structure is an important feature of social networks, and lots of efforts have been made to devise methods for discovering communities. However, due to the limitation of available information about people's history locations, little work has leveraged both online and offline information for community detection. The recent surge of location-based social networks, which allows the user to check in places, write tips, and share locations and experiences with others, provides us the right data for performing cross-domain community discovering. In this chapter, we review the recent progress in community detection of LBSN users from three aspects, i.e., the link-based approach, the content-based approach, and the approach which explores both links and contents.

Even though a certain number of studies have been done on community detection in LBSNs, there still exist several problems that are worth further exploring. A thorough study on how to fuse the online and offline social links is one meaningful direction. Providing a framework to guide the selection and fusion of different features is another direction to work on.

ACKNOWLEDGMENT

This work is partially supported by the National Basic Research Program of China (No. 2012CB316400), the EU FP7 Project SOCIETIES (No. 257493), the National Natural Science Foundation of China (No. 61222209, 61103063), the Specialized Research Fund for the Doctoral Program of Higher Education (No. 20126102110043), the Natural Science Basic Research Plan in Shaanxi Province of China (No. 2012JQ8028),the Scholarship Award for Excellent Doctoral Student Granted by the Ministry of Education of China, and the Doctorate Foundation of Northwestern Polytechnic University (No. CX201018).

REFERENCES

Blondel, V. D., Guillaume, J. L., Lambiotte, R., & Lefebvre, E. (2008). Fast unfolding of communities in large networks. *Journal of Statistical Mechanics*. doi:10.1088/1742-5468/2008/10/P10008.

Brown, C., Nicosia, V., Scellato, S., Noulas, A., & Mascolo, C. (2012). *The importance of being place-friends: Discovering location-focused online communities*. Paper presented at WOSN 2012. New York, NY. doi: 10.1145/2342549.2342557

Cheng, Z., Caverlee, J., Lee, K., & Sui, D. Z. (2011). *Exploring millions of footprints in location sharing services*. Paper presented at ICWSM 2011. New York, NY. doi: 10.1.1.226.5324

Fortunato, S. (2010). Community detection in graphs. *Physics Reports*, *486*(3-5), 75–174. doi:10.1016/j.physrep.2009.11.002.

Gan, G., Ma, C., & Wu, J. (2007). *Data clustering: Theory, algorithms, and applications*. Philadelphia, PA: SIAM. doi:10.1137/1.9780898718348.

Girvan, M., & Newman, M. E. J. (2002). Community structure in social and biological networks. *Proceedings of the National Academy of Sciences of the United States of America*, *99*(12), 7821–7826. doi:10.1073/pnas.122653799 PMID:12060727.

Guo, B., Zhang, D., Wang, Z., Yu, Z., & Zhou, X. (2013). Opportunistic IoT: Exploring the harmonious interaction between human and the internet of things. *Journal of Network and Computer Applications*. doi:10.1016/j.jnca.2012.12.028.

Li, N., & Chen, G. (2009). *Analysis of a location-based social network*. Paper presented at International Conference on Computational Science and Engineering. New York, NY. doi: 10.1109/CSE.2009.98

McCallum, A. K. (2002). *MALLET: A machine learning for language toolkit*. Retrieved from http://mallet.cs.umass.edu.

Newman, M. E. J., & Girvan, M. (2004). Finding and evaluating community structure in networks. *Physical Review E: Statistical, Nonlinear, and Soft Matter Physics*, *69*(26), 113–127. doi: doi:10.1103/PhysRevE.69.026113.

Noulas, A., Scellato, S., Mascolo, C., & Pontil, M. (2011). *Exploiting semantic annotations for clustering geographic areas and users in location-based social networks*. Paper presented at ICWSM. New York, NY.

Orman, G. K., & Labatut, V. (2009). A comparison of community detection algorithms on artificial networks. *Lecture Notes in Artificial Intelligence*, *5808*, 242–256. doi: doi:10.1007/978-3-642-04747-3_20.

Pelleg, D., & Moore, A. (2000). X-means: Extending k-means with efficient estimation of the number of clusters. Paper presented at ICML 2000. New York, NY.

Scellato, S., Noulas, A., Lambiotte, R., & Mascolo, C. (2011). *Socio-spatial properties of online location-based social networks*. Paper presented at ICWSM 2011. New York, NY. doi: 10.1029/2011GC003824

Shi, J., & Malik, J. (2000). Normalized cuts and image segmentation. *IEEE Transactions on Pattern Analysis and Machine Intelligence, 22*(8), 888–905. doi:10.1109/34.868688.

Wang, Z., Zhang, D., Yang, D., Yu, Z., & Zhou, X. (2012). *Detecting overlapping communities in location-based social networks*. Paper presented at SocInfo 2012. New York, NY. doi: 10.1007/978-3-642-35386-4_9

Ye, M., Janowicz, K., Mulligann, C., & Lee, W. C. (2011). *What you are is when you are: The temporal dimension of feature types in location-based social networks*. Paper presented at GIS 2011. New York, NY. doi: 10.1145/2093973.2093989

Zhang, D., Guo, B., & Yu, Z. (2011). The emergence of social and community intelligence. *IEEE Computer, 44*(7), 21–28. doi:10.1109/MC.2011.65.

Chapter 8
Social Cars:
Sensing, Gathering, Sharing, and Conveying Social Cues to Road Users

Ronald Schroeter
Queensland University of Technology, Australia

Alessandro Soro
Queensland University of Technology, Australia

Andry Rakotonirainy
Queensland University of Technology, Australia

ABSTRACT

Intelligent Transport Systems (ITS) encompass sensing technologies, wireless communication, and intelligent algorithms, and resemble the infrastructure for ubiquitous computing in the car. This chapter borrows from social media, locative media, mobile technologies, and urban informatics research to explore three classes of ITS applications in which human behavior plays a more pivotal role. Applications for enhancing self-awareness could positively influence driver behavior, both in real-time and over time. Additionally, tools capable of supporting our social awareness while driving could change our attitude towards others and make it easier and safer to share the road. Lastly, a better urban awareness in and outside the car improves our understanding of the road infrastructure as a whole. As a case study, the authors discuss emotion recognition (emotions such as aggressiveness and anger are a major contributing factor to car crashes) and a suitable basis and first step towards further exploring the three levels of awareness, self-, social-, and urban-awareness, in the context of driving on roads.

INTRODUCTION

Intelligent Transport Systems (ITS) resembles the infrastructure for ubiquitous computing in the car. It encompasses a) all kinds of sensing technologies within vehicles as well as road infrastructure, b)

wireless communication protocols for the sensed information to be exchanged between vehicles (V2V) and between vehicles and infrastructure (V2I), and c) appropriate intelligent algorithms and computational technologies that process these real-time streams of information. As such, ITS

DOI: 10.4018/978-1-4666-4695-7.ch008

can be considered a game changer. It provides the fundamental basis of new, innovative concepts and applications, similar to the Internet itself.

The information sensed or gathered within or around the vehicle has led to a variety of context-aware in-vehicular technologies within the car. A simple example is the Anti-lock Breaking System (ABS), which releases the breaks when sensors detect that the wheels are locked. We refer to this type of context awareness as *vehicle/technology awareness*. V2V and V2I communication, often summarized as V2X, enables the exchange and sharing of sensed information amongst cars. As a result, the vehicle/technology awareness horizon of each individual car is expanded beyond its observable surrounding, paving the way to technologically enhance such already advanced systems.

In this chapter, we draw attention to those application areas of sensing and V2X technologies, where the human (driver), the human's behavior and hence the psychological perspective plays a more pivotal role. The focal points of our project are illustrated in Figure 1: In all areas, the vehicle first (1) gathers or senses information about the driver. Rather than to limit the use of such information towards vehicle/technology awareness, we see great potential for applications in which

this sensed information is then (2) fed back to the driver for an increased *self-awareness*. In addition, by using V2V technologies, it can also be (3) passed to surrounding drivers for an increased *social awareness*, or (4), pushed even further, into the cloud, where it is collected and visualized for an increased, collective *urban awareness* within the urban community at large, which includes all city dwellers.

In our view, these areas have been only little explored to date, although they bear great potentials. Technologies focusing on enhancing *self-awareness*, e.g., could positively influence driver behavior, not only in real-time, but also over time. Those technologies focusing on increasing our *social awareness* while driving could positively change our behavior towards others and make negotiating road use easier, friendlier and safer. Lastly, a better *urban awareness* in the context of the car enriches our understanding of the road infrastructure as a whole. We will demonstrate each of these potentials in more detail in the literature review of this chapter

Following the literature review, we discuss our initial case study experiment, which focuses on sensing driver emotion through facial expressions (cf., the first step (1) in Figure 1). Emotions such as aggressiveness and anger are regarded as

Figure 1. Focal points of our research

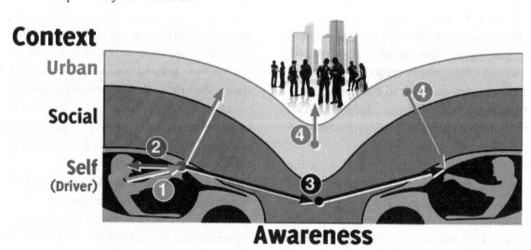

a major contributing factor to car crashes. This contribution is very difficult to quantify exactly, however aggressive driving is considered to be involved in a majority of car crashes (cf. AAAFoundation.org, 2009) and its effect on the driver is comparable to alcohol impairment in terms of probability of involvement in a car crash (Cook, Knight, & Olson, 2005). In addition to having a strong relevance to road safety, "emotion" is also a suitable basis and first step towards further exploring the three levels of awareness, self-, social and urban awareness (cf. Figure 1):

Firstly, one of our visions is to build applications that aim at increasing the *self-awareness* (cf. Figure 1) of our own negative emotions (i.e., those emotions that have been shown to have a negative impact on our safe driving ability) and in doing so, help to manage or mitigate them towards an overall safer driving behavior.

Secondly, emotions and facial expressions, or more accurately, the sharing of them, is also an important aspect of providing "social cues" to others (*social awareness*, cf. Figure 1). Social cues enrich the way we communicate and manage interactions in groups. One could argue that "interacting" with others to negotiate the use of the road as a shared resource is a major cause of crashes in itself. We will illustrate the potential future benefits that this type of sharing may offer in our literature review and we intend to explore them further using the base technology demonstrated in the latter part of this chapter.

Lastly, an increased *urban awareness* of crowdsourced, geo-tagged, emotion information of drivers allows us to, for example, create visualizations such as heat maps in order to more accurately identify the city's badly designed, dangerous road infrastructure that causes negative emotions such as aggression.

Previous works have mainly dealt with the issue of how a specific social cue can be sensed within the vehicle, and used for in-car systems like In-Vehicle Information Systems (IVIS) or Advanced Driver Assist Systems (ADAS) (vehicle awareness). Compared to these mostly technology focused application domains, current work around self-, social and urban awareness are vastly underexplored in the car context. Our contribution is a first step in overcoming these limitations. We show how we can borrow cues, inspiration, design guidelines and theories from social media, locative media, mobile technologies and urban informatics (Foth, 2009) research and apply them to the road safety domain.

AIMS

One aim of this chapter is to provide a big picture and future vision of ubiquitous computing in and around the car. This chapter will therefore review the literature on mobile and locative social media that is relevant to the automotive scenario, and set the context in relation to the research field of road safety. As an application scenario for UbiComp technologies, automotive presents additional challenges and constraints in terms of attention demands and severity of outcomes in case of malfunctioning.

After sketching the bigger picture, a case study is presented to provide a concrete example in the design and evaluation of an in-vehicle mobile application. The case study is an experiment in sensing facial expressions from road users. The ultimate goal is to understand how social information (such as mood, facial expressions and gestures) can help to positively influence the behavior of road users and ultimately improve road safety.

We will present and discuss methodology issues specific to the automotive context, which poses severe constraints to the designer of UbiComp technologies, e.g., how can new tools be evaluated without prejudice for the safety of the vehicle and its occupants?

The concluding remarks present further research trends and provide an outlook to the future of in-vehicle mobile/locative social media. The argument and examples presented in the chapter are generalized to show how road safety issues should be considered in the design of UbiComp technologies *at large*, in order to better exploit the opportunities they offer in the urban environment.

HUMAN-CENTERED UBICOMP IN THE CAR

Vehicle/Technology Awareness

The car is an important application area of ubiquitous computing, but also a broad one. A vast amount of work has been carried out in the fields of Intelligent Transport Systems (ITS), Advanced Driver Assist Systems (ADAS), Automotive User Interfaces (Automotive UI) and In-Vehicular Information Systems (IVIS).

ITS encompasses a) all kinds of sensing technologies within cars as well as road infrastructure, b) wireless communication protocols for the sensed information to be exchanged between vehicles (V2V) and between vehicles and infrastructure (V2I), and c) appropriate intelligent algorithms that process these real-time streams of information. Today, we can already experience real-world ITS applications on our daily drives in form of variable speed limit signs, dynamic traffic light sequencing, etc.

ITS will further improve ADAS, which sense the current state of the vehicle itself and its context, i.e., the environment, through sensors (speedometers, accelerometers, GPS, cameras, radar, laser, etc.), in order to help drivers with their primary driving task. To date, ADAS systems include ABS, intelligent parking assist systems or adaptive cruise control. ITS will enable future ADAS systems to expand their information horizon of the car's context, by retrieving it from other cars and infrastructure, which in turn enables systems such as advanced collision avoidance systems that can detect risks much earlier.

Automotive User Interfaces (Automotive UI) research focuses on the interface between driver and the car (human-machine or human-computer interaction) for tertiary tasks that do not concern the actual driving. Such tasks used to be simple, e.g., setting the volume or temperature. In todays world where drivers increasingly demand to stay digitally connected, IVIS systems now require more complex input tasks and output more complex information. The challenge of Automotive UI is to allow drivers to do this *safely* during the safety critical task of driving. This has led to the development of new in-car technologies to a) convey information via visual feedback (e.g., head-up displays), audio feedback (e.g., text-to-speech) and even haptic feedback (e.g., vibrating steering wheels), as well as b) to input information via steering wheel buttons, touch screens, speech, gestures and other more driver-friendly controllers.

The goal of any Automotive UI and IVIS is to provide the driver with the right amount of information at the right (safe) time and to ideally anticipate the driver's intent (Doshi, Morris, & Trivedi, 2011) to minimize input. To be able to calculate what the right amount of information is, it is essential to accurately sense the current driving context. Once again ITS plays a crucial role to improve this aspect, but note that there is a particular emphasis to sense the current *state of the driver*. The sensed information about the driver's facial expression, speech, skin conductivity, heart rate, eye gaze, etc., can be used to infer emotion, mood, fatigue, distractions, cognitive load, etc. (Figure 2). This information can then form the basis of smart, context aware systems inside the vehicle, such as recommender systems (Bader, Siegmund, & Woerndl, 2011), summarizers and even pairing warning systems[1] or in-car voice interfaces (Nass et al., 2005) to the driver's current emotion or mood.

The following sections draws attention to those type of technologies, where the human (driver),

Figure 2. Context, overview and focus (dotted rectangles) of this chapter

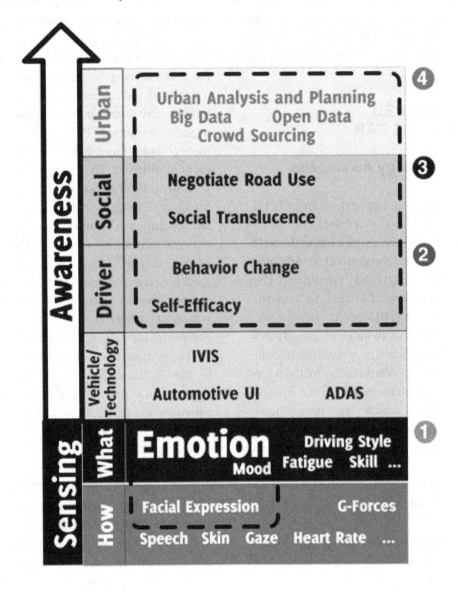

the human's behavior and hence the psychological perspective plays a more pivotal role. It further discusses future application areas of such technologies, their potentials and current gaps in the literature.

Self-Awareness

As mentioned in the introduction above, this section highlights related work in which information *about the driver* is (1) sensed and (2) somehow conveyed to the driver (cf. Figure 1) using Automotive UIs. The sensed information is either conveyed a) in real-time while driving, b) as a collected aggregate visualization, abstraction, etc., or c) both.

The first option - real-time - generally refers to real-time warning systems that warn us about current, potentially fatal states of driving. They include extreme speeding, tailgating (iOnRoad[2]) or driving unsafe while fatigued (CarSafe (You et al., 2012)) to name a few examples. In these instances, the warnings or alerts aim to positively influence our current driving decisions, e.g., to reduce speed, keep distance or take a break. In recent years, however, applications have expanded towards influencing less safety critical driving states, e.g., uneconomic driving behaviors, stress or frustration. These applications use various subtle, ambient or subliminal ways (tactile feedback, light, voice, music, etc.) to have a positive effect on the driver. Riener et al. (2010) provide subliminal vibro-tactile notifications about the current CO_2 economy. The AwareCar platform (Coughlin, Reimer, & Mehler, 2011) explores experimental implementations to constantly keep drivers within an optimal workload or stress range, between fatigue/inattention and overload/active distraction. It uses ambient lighting technologies to subtly alert or calm the driver. Harris and Nass (Harris & Nass, 2011) built a conversational interface providing voice appraisals after frustrating driving events. It was evaluated in a simulator study showing promising results towards a solution to prevent driver frustration. Jeon (2012) investigates the use of music to mitigate affective effects on the driving task.

The second option - collected aggregate visualizations and abstractions - is much less explored. As we will discuss in turn, there are untapped potentials and opportunities to build applications that aim to change our general driving behavior in a subtler, ambient way over a period of time by increasing the driver's self awareness.

Approximately 90% of drivers believe that they are "better than average" (Svenson, 1981). This illusory superiority is a cognitive bias that leads to drivers overestimating their positive qualities and driving abilities while underestimating their negative ones. This in turn may lead to driver aggression and consequently to risky driving behaviors, etc.

In order to change bad or risky driving behaviors, we can draw upon The Transtheoretical Model (Prochaska & Velicer, 1997) or "Stages of Change" model, an established model of behav-

ioral change processes, as well as Motivational Interviewing (MI) (Miller & Rollnick, 2002), which is a client-centered (read driver-centered) counseling style that aims to facilitate behavioral change. He et al (2010) provide a useful summary how to apply these models for technology designs that aim to change (bad) behavior. They note that behavior change is a lengthy process and that it includes several stages an individual generally has to move through: precontemplation; contemplation; preparation; action; maintenance, relapse, recycling (Prochaska & Velicer, 1997).

In precontemplation, individuals are unaware, uninformed, unwilling or discouraged to change a problem behavior. In contemplation, individuals acknowledge that their behavior is a problem and intend to change it. An increased *self-awareness*, therefore, is the basis of everything that is to follow, as it allows individuals to take that important first step in changing bad behaviors.

In addition, *motivation* is required for an individual to move through all stages (Miller & Rollnick, 2002). In order to elicit motivation from the driver himself, rather than through external factors such as fines, MI (He et al., 2010; Miller & Rollnick, 2002) suggests the following principles: a) build driver *self efficacy* (i.e., a measure of one's own competence to complete tasks and reach goals (Ormrod, 2010)), e.g., a log book); b) develop intrinsic attributions to successful driving behavior; and c) to visualize the differences between the driver's values, i.e., the self-expected ideal driving behavior, and the actual driving behavior.

The point here is that all these principles require that the current (driving) behavior is accurately sensed and measured in the first place. Within the safety conscious driving context, it is common sense that the sensing needs to be carried out in the least distracting and unobtrusive way. The accurate and unobtrusive recognition of the driver's current emotional state while driving is the focus of the case study presented in this chapter. Note, however, that this only forms *one of many* bases (cf. "Sensing" in Figure 2) of possible future technology interventions or applications aimed at positively changing bad driving behaviors.

Continuing this train of thought or vision, the development of such future in-car technology interventions can borrow design strategies from outside the driving context. Previous technologies, for example, have aimed at helping users to change behaviors in order to lose weight, eat better, exercise more, stop smoking, use less energy, recycle, etc. Their failures and successes have contributed towards the establishment of concrete design strategies (Consolvo, McDonald, & Landay, 2009). However, work that aims at evaluating such strategies in the context of the car is still in its infancy.

To date, some innovative applications were born for smartphones. Smartphone penetration in the western world is almost ubiquitous. They are also equipped with sensors (GPS, accelerometer, camera, etc.) and are easier to develop for than cars. Most of the work has focused on promoting a more economic driving behavior (Bergmans & Shahid, 2012; Meschtscherjakov, Wilfinger, Scherndl, & Tscheligi, 2009; Tulusan, Staake, & Fleisch, 2012). However, apps like Driver Feedback[3] (developed by car insurance company State Farm) use the phone's accelerometer to detect and log the driver's hard acceleration, deceleration and swerves to calculate a driving score, which aims to motivate drivers towards safer, less aggressive driving. While State Farm offers the app as a driver self evaluation tool, other insurance companies already offer policies with potential premium discounts that require the installation of black boxes in the car to monitor driving behavior. Another smartphone app, iOnRoad[4], logs tailgating or speeding events, displays them on a map and provides statistical trip summaries on a personal web dashboard, which the driver can access for self-efficacy.

These applications are just the beginning and will inevitably expand their functionalities as more sensing techniques become more accurate and more easily accessible by application developers. We argue that by applying The Transtheoretical Model, Motivational Interviewing techniques and design strategies put forward by the HCI community (Consolvo et al., 2009; He et al., 2010), these applications can become powerful tools to increase every drivers individual self-awareness, and by doing so, create safer roads in addition to all other safety technology advancements. *Fully* autonomous vehicles are unlikely going to exist in the near future and humans will continue to play a crucial role in operating the vehicle, even if this eventually consists of mostly monitoring largely automated systems (Coughlin et al., 2011). Hence, the driver-focused research will continue to be an important component of safe operation.

Social Awareness

When addressing the problem of road safety, focus is often on the fatal four: alcohol, fatigue, speed and unfastened seat belts. These are considered the main causes of a large proportion of road injuries and deaths worldwide.

Although these four factors contribute heavily to the number and seriousness of injuries, it must be recognized that *sharing* the use of the road in the first place is the cause of most crashes. As Elvik et al. state: "there is hardly any doubt that traffic volume is the single most important factor that influences the number of road accidents" (Elvik, Høye, Vaa, & Sørensen, 2009).

In this sense, the social aspects of driving, i.e., the way people plan and manage their road trips, and how they access and negotiate their use of the road as a shared resource, is a major contributor to crashes and a vast and rather unexplored research space. The way we communicate with other drivers sharing the road with us is often limited to honking the horn, flashing the lights or various hand gestures. Social scientists refer to cars as "semiprivate metal containers" (Leckie & Hopkins, 2002, p. 329) that isolate us from the outside world. In addition, cars provide a sense of anonymity, which has been shown to contribute towards driver aggression (Ellison-Potter, Bell, & Deffenbacher, 2001).

Consider the following scenario: what strikes many western newcomers of the Tokyo underground system is the amazing crowd of people walking at fast pace in any direction within the stations. If there is any order in chaos, it is not visible to the average eye. Even more amazingly, people seem to be able to (safely, if not easily) deal with such chaos quite well, when walking. One of the reasons why we cannot do this well when driving, is because we are missing crucial social cues. Social cues are verbal or non-verbal hints that guide our conversations and other social interactions. Examples of social cues include facial expressions, vocal tone, mood, direction of gaze, body posture, dress, proximity, orientation, and physical appearance.

In the context of communication technology systems, Erickson & Kellogg (2000) dubbed 'social translucence' the design approach that aims at making those socially relevant cues visible and persistent. Their work was motivated by noting that we are generally able to manage our group interaction gracefully in the physical world (face to face), but that such coherent interaction is difficult to achieve in online environments. There is a vast amount of literature targeting this challenge, specifically in the Computer Supported Cooperative Work (CSCW) domain.

However, only little work has been carried out towards overcoming limited social translucence in the traffic environment. One reason for this is that developing, deploying and evaluating such applications within the automotive context is more challenging than within computer-mediated communication, mainly because of its safety constraints. We still lack the underlying V2V infrastructure today that enables driver-to-driver communication from a technology perspective. This lack restricts such explorations to simulated environments, which are usually limited to only one driver/participant and therefore lack a natural

social setting. The challenge then is how to study the effects of an increased social awareness in an environment that is essentially not social.

Despite these challenges, there is some work targeting social awareness in the car. Healey et al. (2012), e.g., discuss preliminary results of a system that monitors the current state of the driver and communicates it to other cars. Note, that although their work focuses on sensing information about the driver, the information is not conveyed to the other drivers. Rather, they explore how exchanging information (through V2V) about the drivers' current distraction could be used as an additional data source for advanced modeling and prediction algorithms in (semi-) autonomous cars.

Rakotonirainy et al. (2009) did a simulator study to examine the effects on driving behavior when digital avatars representing the other driver's head and eye gaze were superimposed over other cars. The aim was to maximize a sense of social presence. They demonstrate the potential to improve social interactions between drivers, allow clearer collective decision-making between road users and reduce the incidence of antisocial behavior in the road environment.

Finally, Mitrevska et al. (2012) did an experimental study (through a Facebook driving game) that explored the effect on driving behavior when introducing technologies that reduce the anonymity between drivers. They used knowledge from the participants' social network to simulate common interests with other drivers and subjected them to driving scenarios that commonly trigger an angry response, such as honking or swearing. Their results showed a reduction in negative reactions and an increase in positive reactions, encouraging future research for such novel approaches.

In this chapter, we focus on the fundamental work that would allow the exchange of social cues between drivers in the future. Cues, such as mood, could be gathered from explicit, subjective user input, rather than sensed automatically and possibly more objectively. However, as Schroeter and Rakotonirainy (2012) note, in the context of driving, a more objective method of gathering drivers' state would be preferable. This further motivated our work on objectively sensing facial expressions and emotions in the car.

Urban Awareness

A plethora of new applications have been (or will be soon) made possible by the pervasive diffusion of personal mobile terminals, generally gathered under the umbrella of Location Based Services (LBS) and including geo-sensitive information, mobile social networking apps, and 'digital tapestries'. Going further, "data based on the location of mobile devices could potentially become one of the most exciting new sources of information for urban analysis." (Ratti, Williams, Frenchman, & Pulselli, 2006) Ratti and colleagues provide pertinent examples of mapping vehicle origins and destinations, understanding the patterns of pedestrian movements and spotting critical aspects of the urban infrastructure.

Besides highlighting the cost and effort of the 'traditional' approach to these issues (based on costly surveys and ad-hoc surveillance infrastructures), the authors point out how personal mobile technologies will allow to sense and represent these phenomena in real-time instead of simulating and estimating them.

Again there is strong emphasis on the self/social/urban perspective in terms of who benefits from such classes of applications. Ratti and colleagues distinguish among 'individuals as beneficiaries', e.g., in the case of navigation aids, and educational services; 'groups as beneficiaries' such as digital tapestries and location based gaming; 'third parties as beneficiaries', e.g., public safety applications and family security.

To give another example, Miluzzo et al. (2008) describe the architecture, performances and a user evaluation of a social networking application based on personal (mobile phone) sensing, and sharing. In their vision, people are at the same time the carriers of the sensing devices, as well as the final users and consumers of sensed events. Paulos et al. (2009) refer to this as 'citizen science', Campbell et al. (2008) dubbed such architectures 'People Centric Sensing'. While the terms differ, the concept is the same: Mobile applications are capable of sensing and sharing user location (via GPS), activity (via accelerometer) social context (inferred from the state of neighbors), and other parameters, such as air pollution, etc. Using this concept, Campbell et al. explore the technical challenges and opportunities that come from the availability of global infrastructure for sensing, learning and sharing data from personal devices.

The authors focus on the 'opportunistic' nature of the infrastructure, in which the owner of the device (the custodian) chooses to participate in the infrastructure by configuring his/her device, which then runs in the background sensing and pushing data up to the global infrastructure (as opposite to a 'participatory' approach, which requires the user to interactively and repeatedly accepting application requests). As the authors do not fail to point out, such unstructured and decentralized architecture present incredible technical challenges in terms of discovery and query of a sensor, interpretation of the raw result, privacy protection, etc.

Additionally, on a higher level of abstraction, merging and mining the potentially huge amount of data coming from heterogeneous sensors is a worthy research field of its own, as is the collaborative creation of appropriate training data for the classifiers and machine learning tool that will process the resulting features.

Particularly relevant to our approach, Campbell et al. (2008) distinguish the applications that can be built on top of the above two layers (sensing and learning) as having either a personal (i.e., focused on oneself), social (e.g., applications aimed at a given interest group) as or public (designed for the general use and addressing an higher, public benefit).

Sound theory is emerging to support the design of such infrastructure: Krause et al. (2008) propose a formalization of 'Community Sensing' in terms of demand and availability of sensors, as well as usage and preferences. Their case study shows that an application for traffic monitoring and prediction can be reliably build on top of community sensors while still respecting people's privacy.

While much research has focused on sensing and data mining, the panorama does not appear as rich on the application side, especially in the context of the car. IVIS and AutoUI research to date has largely focused on *how* a driver can safely interface (output/input) with various types of data or information (Schroeter, Rakotonirainy, & Foth, 2012). However, as Schroeter et al. point out, there appear to be great untapped potentials as to *what* such information can be, in particular considering the opportunities offered by the Urban Informatics research field (Foth, 2009).

A small number of applications started to hit the smartphone market, such as SignalGuru, PotHole or Waze. These apps rely on (semi-) automatic sensing based on camera, GPS, accelerometer, etc. Chatzimilioudis et al. (2012) provide an excellent overview of such current work, however, their impact on the urban awareness has not (to the best of our knowledge) been assessed to date, specifically in relation to road safety and in-vehicle use.

A CASE STUDY: EMOTION RECOGNITION

Background

A large part of human social skills is built on people's ability to guess other people's mood and feelings and react appropriately. Our motivation is to try to replicate, or at the very least to keep those skills in mind when we the design interactive systems.

Although intuitively emotion at the steering wheel can be regarded as a matter of pleasure and comfort (and hence material for marketing and advertising rather than for UbiComp research),

it must be remarked here that when driving, emotions such as anger and aggressive behavior are regarded as a major contributing factor to car crashes (cf. AAAFoundation.org, 2009), comparable to alcohol impairment (Cook et al., 2005)

More generally, being in a state of anger or excitement (as opposed to a neutral mood) while driving is known to decrease the drivers' performances in terms of lane adherence, steering wheel angle and sharpness of lane crossings (cf. Cai, Lin, & Mourant, 2007). This problem is even exacerbated by the obstruction caused by vehicle design and the physical and psychological distance between drivers, which makes the management of a driver's emotional arousal difficult (Deffenbacher, Lynch, Oetting, & Swaim, 2002).

The field of affective computing and emotion recognition in human computer interaction is not new, but it is still challenging today and also capable of provoking criticism (Picard, 2003). Although out of scope here, it should be mentioned that the very problem of defining what emotion is and how humans perceive and interpret emotion in themselves and in others is object of debate.

Despite the difficulties involved in the automatic recognition of emotion, techniques and tools exist that are capable of classifying the emotional state of a subject from (combinations of) streams of signals. Such signals include linguistic and paralinguistic cues in speech, physiological measures (e.g., of heart rate, blood pressure, galvanic skin response, respiration rate), facial expressions, gestures, body postures and more (Brave & Nass, 2003; Brave, Nass, & Hutchinson, 2005; Cowie et al., 2001). However, the automatic recognition of the emotional state of the driver, or more precisely, the classification of a suitable *proxy* for such emotional state, e.g., facial expressions, stress in the voice or a body postures, is still an open topic for research.

Within the car, several scenarios have been envisioned that rely on emotion recognition in order to, for example, improve drivers' productivity, well being or pleasure while keeping in mind drivers' safety (Eyben et al., 2010), which is discussed in more detail below. However, we see emotion recognition as an enabling technology for a much broader range of applications that span from self-evaluation and improvement, to social media, to traffic analysis and urban planning, which is illustrated across the personal/social/ urban context in Figure 2. Although most of the works described in turn have a rather techno- logical focus and avoid committing to a specific application, they do suggest some scenarios that allow us to frame them according to the schema shown in Figure 2.

Emotion recognition from speech recordings is an effective technique and has been applied with success in the car. Jones and Jonsson (2007) reported on experiments aimed at developing an emotionally responsive car. They evaluate para- linguistic cues in speech recordings taken during a simulated driving task by means of an automated system and compare the results to evaluations performed by human experts. In a subsequent refinement, the authors focused on older drivers with the aim of also assessing drivers' attitude towards a conversational/emotive interface (C. Jones & Jonsson, 2008). In their studies, the authors present challenging driving conditions to elicit a range of emotion in the test subjects, such as boredom, sadness/grief, frustration/anger, happiness or surprise. Results show an accuracy of about 70% in the automatic recognition system with respect to a human expert's classification.

The 'Emotionally Responsive Car' (C. Jones & Jonsson, 2008; C. M. Jones & Jonsson, 2005; Nass et al., 2005) is envisioned to *react* to the driver's sensed emotion by changing the driver- vehicle interface. Example reactions include be- coming 'less or more talkative depending on the mood of the driver' or changing 'the telematics, climate, music in the car in response the mood of the driver'. These examples clearly pertain to the bottom layers of the schema in Figure 2, as the information on the emotional state is consumed by an IVIS and/or an ADAS, and not fed back to the driver or pushed up to the social network.

Schuller et al. (2005) focus on recognizing emo- tional cues in spontaneous speech fragments that result from a wizard-of-oz study of an in-vehicle infotainment system. Later work further investi- gates the effect of noise on emotion recognition from speech (Grimm et al., 2007; Björn Schuller, Lang, & Rigoll, 2006). By overlaying the noise of 5 different car models in several driving condi- tions (such as highway, city, etc.) to the recordings of both professional and spontaneous speakers, such approach achieves remarkable recognition rates around 80 and 60% respectively. Grimm et al. (2007) as well as Schuller et al. (2006; 2005) subscribe to a similar perspective, although with little emphasis on a specific application domain, focusing instead on including the emotional aspect in the design of in-vehicle conversational interfaces.

MIT's SmartCar project (J. Healey & Picard, 2000) explored how an appropriate combination of sensors, capable of providing physiological data such as electromyogram, electrocardiogram, galvanic skin response and respiration can be fed to appropriate pattern recognition algorithm in order to predict driver's stress. In a naturalistic study, they compared the data gathered from sensors worn by the drivers to the level of stress self-reported by the participants, showing a fairly accurate (88.4%) rate of prediction for the mea- sures above. The application domain traced by J. Healey & Picard (2000) is the recognition of driver's stress, and hence comfort and well being. Again the authors focus on the technology rather than depicting an application scenario, although in the concluding remarks they sketch the pos- sible outcome of 'giving a quantified feedback to the individual about how life choices could be affecting their stress level and providing a new metric with which to make informed choices about their health and behavior; thus framing the possible interventions in the self-awareness domain (Figure 2). However, the use of intrusive technologies not acceptable in practice limited this study to controlled environments and their future work did not explore applications towards behavior change.

Hoch et al. (2005) exploit a fusion of audio and video modalities to classify the drivers' emotions according to three possible classes: neutral, positive, negative. They took audio and video recordings within a real car, but without motion (hence with little or no noise and relatively stable light). By doing so, they manage to achieve an average 90% recognition rate. The application domain they sketched is the improvement of human computer interaction in the car, for example, adapting the dialog strategies of the assistance and information systems (cf. vehicle awareness in Figure 2), reducing mental workload and distraction.

By now it should be clear to the reader that the design and implementation of emotion-aware applications for the car poses several major challenges, some of which are peculiar of the driving and road-safety context. As the main task for the 'user' will always be that of safely drive the vehicle, any application or interaction technique that adds to the cognitive load is plainly and simply not acceptable; at the same time, assessing and evaluating a new technology 'in the real world' can be dangerous, and is thus unethical.

A driving simulator, as the one described further below, can provide a suitable evaluation environment for certain classes of application and technologies, but is a rather expensive device and is not a panacea: Rouzikhah et al. (2010) review some studies on the validity of experiments carried out in driving simulators. They point out that many related works could demonstrate a 'relative validity', i.e., the simulator study shows an effect that goes in the same direction or has the same relative size as in reality. On the other hand, there is 'absolute validity', where the absolute size of the effect observed in the simulator is comparable to

the corresponding size of effect in the simulator. As an example, most simulator studies focusing on speed cannot demonstrate an absolute validity, mainly because of the low risk perception on the drivers' part. They conclude that the validity of any simulator study has to be considered carefully, especially when the tasks have a degree of risk. Additionally, the authors point out a lack of background for some important research topics, such as drunk/drug driving and driving while fatigued or while distracted.

As a result, a common limit of the studies found in literature is that the techniques proposed are not adequately evaluated in a real world experiment, i.e., while driving a real car through traffic. Some experiments, e.g., elicited speech artificially in the drivers through a particularly chatty in-vehicle information system. Others fail to consider noise (both in sound and video recordings) or occlusions caused by the drivers' looking into their mirrors, etc. All these conditions invariably emerge during a real-world test drive.

In this section, we give a brief overview of a simulator experiment aimed at assessing a novel algorithm for computer-vision based emotion recognition. Our aim is to point out the challenges arising from the design and evaluation of UbiComp technologies for the automotive domain.

The reason for us to focus on emotion recognition from facial expressions is that this appears to be a rather good compromise between accuracy and invasiveness. Additionally, personal mobile technologies such as smartphones are reaching the necessary computational power to be considered as the enabling technology, thus facilitating a potential deployment to *any* vehicle, not just newer, smarter ones. The next section provides an overview of the relevant literature on emotion recognition through facial expressions, a presentation of our technical approach, and a detailed description of the issues arising in the design and evaluation phases.

Developing and Testing an Emotion Recognition Device

Algorithms and techniques for facial expression recognition from images or video involve the isolation and subsequent processing of a variable number of regions (features) of the face, and a comparison with corresponding regions from other expressions (often the neutral expression) to determine changes in appearance or position of critical areas (see Fasel & Luettin (2003) for a comprehensive survey on this subject).

Changes in appearance, such as the onset of wrinkles on one's forehead when expressing surprise can be evidenced, for example, using (combinations of) Gabor filters (Lyons, Akamatsu, Kamachi, & Gyoba, 1998) and feeding the resulting representation into an appropriate classifier, typically a multilayer perceptron (such as described by Zhang et al. (1998)) or a support vector machine (Bartlett, Littlewort, Fasel, & Movellan, 2003).

Alternatively, geometry based approaches proceed recognizing meaningful features of the face (such as eyes, eyebrows, mouth shape) and comparing the relative size/position of such features between different expressions. Although such approaches tend to be computationally more demanding, they also appear to be more robust to changes in the position/orientation of the face in the frame (Zhang et al., 1998).

Our approach is then based on this latter category: after extracting face landmarks by means of active shape model fitting, we compute a small set of features as a ratio between specific areas of the face (e.g., mouth, eye+eyebrow, etc.) and the corresponding areas from a set of known examples of neutral expression.

Such regions are calculated as the polygons that enclose given sets of facial landmarks. Note that the polygons are not meant to form a mesh of the face based on the landmarks, but have been determined empirically based on the fact that a facial expression is determined by the contraction of muscles in the face and, for obvious reasons, results in highly visible and recognizable clues. The resulting feature vector is classified by means of a neural network, as described below.

Accurate landmarks, corresponding to the position of pupils, eye corners, mouth, nose, etc. in the image, can be obtained by fitting a statistical shape model: Active Shape Models (ASM) (Cootes, Taylor, Cooper, & Graham, 1995) represent an efficient and robust technique for matching a set of points that represent interesting features of a class of images to a new example of such class: ASMs have been applied to face landmarking with great success (Milborrow & Nicolls, 2008).

In essence, an ASM learns a statistical model of the shape of a face, starting from a training set of manually annotated images, and constructing a map of acceptable deformations and of the expected appearance of the image close to each landmark. Then, the fitting algorithm iteratively tries to optimize the match between the texture at each landmark's current position and the expected texture for that landmark by moving each landmark within a certain range.

In a controlled experimental environment this technique can achieve remarkable recognition rates. However, little evidence exists about how computer vision based facial expression recognition techniques can perform when used for in-vehicle interfaces in the context of a real drive.

This study explores in more depth some of the broader research issues mentioned above: What are the challenges in inferring a person's emotional state from facial expressions a) from a general technology perspective, and b) in the specialized context of the car?

Methodology

At the moment of writing, to the best of our knowledge, no dataset exists that provides annotated video footage from real drives suitable for automatic emotion recognition studies. The LISA-P Head Pose Database (Martin, Tawari,

Murphy-Chutorian, Cheng, & Trivedi, 2012) has not been released for public use yet and will only provide facial landmarks for eye corners, nose tip and nose corners, i.e., prominent features specifically chosen for being the least sensitive to facial expressions.

Gathering research data from naturalistic studies is problematic. Drivers are known to maintain a neutral mood for most of the time (cf. C. M. Jones & Jonsson, 2005). Key events in naturalistic studies that are likely to elicit emotional arousal, e.g., near escaped crashes, are (fortunately) unusual and cannot be recreated artificially for obvious reasons.

Analogously, it is not possible to ask the driver to enact the facial expressions during a real drive. This could be distracting and potentially dangerous, and even then, the validity of such non-spontaneous expressions would be arguable. It has been shown, that carefully designed driving conditions, e.g., obstacles in the road, other drivers, difficult road conditions and pedestrians, can indeed elicit spontaneous reactions of grief, excitement, etc. (C. Jones & Jonsson, 2008; C. M. Jones & Jonsson, 2007).

Driving simulators make it possible to recreate a realistic simulation of such dangerous or unusual driving conditions under which the researchers are then able to observe the drivers' reactions.

The Advanced Driving Simulator used in the presented research consists of a complete and fully functional vehicle body installed on top of computer controlled mobile platform (see Figure 3). All controls in the cabin, such as steering wheel, dashboard, pedals, electric windows, etc. are fully functional. All 5 seats are available for studies involving multiple occupants. A panoramic screen -composed from three 4x3m projected screens - provides 180 degrees of forward vision, while rear vision is simulated by means of small LCD screen that replace the 3 mirrors.

The cabin is mounted on top of a 6 Degrees of Freedom motion system that provides up to 700mm of motion in each direction, and up to 39 degrees of rotation in each direction. The motion system adds to the realism of the simulation providing shakes and a sense of acceleration consistent with the simulated drive.

Such complex setup can provide an immersive and fully interactive environment, including traffic and roadway environmental characteristics, and provide the driver with high-fidelity motion, visual, auditory, and force feedback cues.

The simulation is controlled from an adjacent control room (Figure 4), where the researchers and operator can monitor every aspect of the experiment, including the comfort of the participants.

Figure 3. The chassis, panoramic display and motion system of the Advanced Driving Simulator

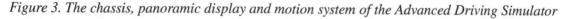

Figure 4. The control room of the Advanced Driving Simulator

Additional equipment can be installed for specific studies, including eye tracking hardware and software, EEG, ECG, Skin conductance sensors, body/head movements detectors, accelerometers or a head up display. State of the art data fusion algorithms then manage, record, synchronize or replay the output from these various data sources. For the present study the following equipment was installed in the simulator cabin:

- A night vision camera installed on the left end of the windshield provides a high quality side view of the driving seat and driver; the video is transmitted to a dedicated display in the control room;
- A USB video camera mounted on the dashboard provides a frontal view of the driver; the video is recorded and simultaneously streamed to the control room;
- A commercial smartphone running a custom software installed on the dashboard; it records a medium quality/low frame rate video of the driver;

The aim of the experiment is to record realistic (if not real) facial expressions of drivers during a simulated drive from the city center of Brisbane to the Brisbane international airport. Along the drive, the participants experience a number a preprogrammed events aimed at eliciting emotive reactions (summarized in Table 1)

1. Often the participant finds her/him self stuck into traffic or obstructed by slow vehicles; in one case the vehicle preceding the participant is specifically programmed to proceed slowly and obstruct the road, accelerating if the participant attempts to overtake.
2. Several intersections or roundabouts force the driver to stop and get into another traffic flow; the spacing between cars is initially small and increases gradually.
3. A number of potentially dangerous situations are programmed, including a vehicle drifting against the traffic as well as a car that pulls out of a blind intersection failing to give way.

Figure 5. A detail of the video recording equipment installed on board for monitoring and recording facial expressions

Table 1. The events programmed in the simultated drive in order to elicit emotional reactions on the drivers' part

1. Give way with gap acceptance test	6. Two slow leading cars, blocking the way	11. Left turn at roundabout with gap acceptance test
2. Turn left with cyclist passing	7. Right turn with pedestrian crossing	12. Oncoming car going against the traffic
3. Traffic light changes to amber	8. Pedestrian with child crossing	13. Slow moving car, partially blocks the road
4. Right turn with gap acceptance test	9. Leading car going slow, accelerates when trying to overtake	14. Parked car pulling out, failing to signal or give way
5. Traffic light changes to amber	10. Same car of point 9, then breaks unexpectedly and without visible reason	15. Car from far right not giving way, resulting in an almost unavoidable crash

From inside the control room, the research team monitored the reactions of the driver, taking note of the facial expressions, especially in coincidence with these key events. Additionally, immediately after the driving session, the subjects were invited to reflect upon the experience, with emphasis on their reactions to the key events. The video recordings of the facial expressions of the drivers were later used for training an automatic classifier as the one described above.

Data Analysis

The video recordings of the driving sessions resulted in about 130 minutes of video footage, or 250.000 frames of frontal images of facial

Figure 6. Several events are programmed in the simulated drive to elicit reactions from the drivers: a) stuck in the traffic; b) approaching a roundabout; c) oncoming car going against the traffic; d) a car pulls out of an intersection failing to give way

expressions. However, only a smaller part was suitable for training the automatic facial expression classifier, namely those frames in which the face of the driver appears clearly lighted, not covered by any occlusion (e.g., one hand kept in the line of sight of the camera) and from a frontal view, thus excluding those sequences in which the driver glances at the mirrors.

A small subset of 4000 outstanding examples of neutral and posed expressions was then manually selected from the video recordings and fed into the classifier as a training set. The performance of the classifier was then evaluated by running the classifier on a separate control set and checking the result against the evaluation of human experts.

It is customary to present the performances of automatic classifiers in the form of a *confusion matrix* that summarizes the positive results, as well as the error; the confusion matrix for the binary emotion classifier is presented in Table 1. Accord-

ing to these results, the classification technique adopted is very efficient in the specific context *when applied to images with ideal orientation and a neat, recognizable expression*. In these cases, the accuracy is as high as 99.6% for the neutral expression and 97.4% for peak expression.

But what can we say of the frames that were not included in the *outstanding* training set? Since the training set was composed of only 4000 (out of 250000) frames from the driving experiments, how is the technique described here going to perform on the average, unconstrained case?

Table 2. Confusion Matrix for the binary emotion automatic classifier

	Neutral	**Peak**
Neutral	**0.996**	0.004
Peak	0.026	**0.974**

Checking the effectiveness of the automatic classifier on the whole dataset collected would be an enormous amount of work and would not provide positive results for a number of reasons:

- Although large enough for the purpose of this work, the dataset is still a small picture when compared to a real drive in terms of variations in light, context, dressing (e.g., hats, eyeglasses), etc.
- Our small scale experiment was meant to expose and understand issues and opportunities related to the automatic recognition of the emotional state of the driver rather than to provide an accurate tool for recognizing and classifying emotions: as a consequence, other (perhaps more challenging) issues were left out of the picture, such as differences in gender, age, ethnicity, etc.
- Even humans (and among them, even trained experts) have sometimes difficulties in decoding and naming facial expressions. And it is even more difficult to guess what emotion is hidden behind an expression, although facial expressions are gener-

ally regarded as the more revealing social cues we have to this end (cf. Walther & D'Addario, 2001).

On the other hand, we wanted to see how the automatic classification correlates with the programmed events of the simulated drive. As a result, we used the automatic classifier to process all frames of the recorded drive, Figure 7 shows a graphical representation of the output:

The graph represents fragment of the timeline of the drive, time progresses from left to right. The two rugged bands are formed by the numerical output of the classifier for the neutral expression (lower band) and peak expression (upper band), while the hill-shaped area is an average value for the peak/neutral expression during the last 5 seconds. At first glance, it is clearly evident that the band for the neutral expression is more dense. This is coherent with similar results found in the literature that report that drivers show a neutral expression for the majority of their drive.

The numbers along the timeline of the graph indicate the occurrence of the 15 key events (see

Figure 7. Automatic classification of facial expressions. The 15 key event frequently correspond to gaps in the neutral expression and/or clusters in the peak expression classifier output.

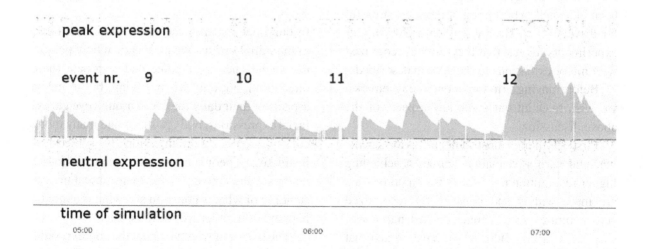

Table 1). It is evident that the interruptions in the neutral expression occur in coincidence with relevant events. Also, although the band that represents the peak expression is quite scattered and discontinuous, it is clear how in this example the largest clusters occur in coincidence with the most dangerous events number 12 in this fragment in which a vehicle coming from the opposite direction drifts from a curve, invading the lane.

Another such event is number 15 (see Table 1) in which a car pulls out from a side road at quite high speed, failing to give precedence. Both events happen quite suddenly within sections of the road in which the context of the simulation allows for quite high speeds and are very difficult to handle (several participants crashed in event 12 and/or event 15). Since in real life such events would result is serious outcomes, they almost invariably produced strong reactions that the system recognized with great consistence.

Gaps in the band of the neutral expression can also happen when the system fails to recognize the face of the driver. Although the system was not trained to recognize such events, these cases are clearly recognizable in the graph. They do not correspond to clear clusters in the peak expression (in the example depicted in Figure 3 events 1 and 4) and indicate that the driver is repeatedly glancing right and left at an intersection. Note that the tasks of giving way and lane merging have been indicated to be among of the most stressful for drivers (cf. J. Healey & Picard, 2000). Our experiments suggest that they can be recognized with minor extensions to the system described.

Before moving on to some concluding remarks, we wish to point out some key aspects of the above discussion:

Firstly, although most (if not all) efforts in the machine learning domain are aimed at achieving higher recognition rates for those emotions that are more widely and consistently recognized across cultures, such as anger, disgust, happiness, surprise, fear and sadness, we have argued that in the driving context these emotions make little sense, and efforts should instead be focused at distinguishing expressions (or moods) that are *desirable or not* when driving.

Secondly, we have shown that a carefully designed experiment can provide the necessary samples for training and testing an automatic recognition system. It became again apparent that the peculiarity of the driving context makes the collection of such data in a naturalistic setting very challenging. Besides the obvious ethical implications, the data collection is aimed at capturing reactions to events that are fortunately very unusual and rare. Even more, episodes of angry or reckless driving, or spontaneous reactions to unexpected events, could be mitigated and held back by the presence of the observing video camera during such naturalistic studies. A simulated environment, on the other hand, allows for the creation and planning of many challenging or dangerous driving conditions, which in turn increase the likelihood of providing useful material for the data analysis.

Overall, the design and tuning of sensors capable of recognizing the driver state and behavior is a necessary starting point for many of the applications that have been presented in the first part of this chapter.

CONCLUDING REMARKS

In our final remarks we would like to go back to the initial vision. We have shown how people use social cues to regulate and negotiate their interaction, not only when driving, but in many aspects of their daily routine. Through eye gazes, facial expressions, body postures and many more cues, sometimes sent intentionally, sometimes instinctively, people manage to create, reinforce, negotiate and actively shape their mutual understanding of what is going on and what is about to happen, or in other words, the context.

The matter of whether or not the context could be learnt and represented in a form that is suitable for automatic processing is subject to debate. The UbiComp community strongly supports the design of context aware technologies, while social scientist often subscribe to a different point of view, in which contextuality is a characteristic of embodied interaction (Dourish, 2004) that technology can either support or obstruct.

In this chapter we commit to a vision in which the future cars will monitor the driver in order to guess his/her state and react appropriately. We have reviewed a number of possible interventions aimed at improving the driver's self-awareness (by providing feedback), social awareness (by sharing such information with other drivers) and urban awareness (by pushing the information up to the public domain).

By focusing on the (human) driver, and especially on the human weakness par excellence, emotion, we consciously challenge the emerging trend that projects the proliferation of private autonomous vehicles to a not-so-far future. The availability of self-driving cars for the general public has been recently (perhaps optimistically) forecasted for the next 5-10 years, and there is quite good evidence that the necessary technology is reaching the stage of maturity for this to happen. However, even when autonomous vehicles will start moving through our cities, they will have to share the road with pedestrians, bikers, cyclists, and people that simply will not give up the pleasure of driving their old convertible to the beach on a sunny Sunday morning.

We therefore favor a scenario in which future cars will support the driver, facilitating the task of using, sharing and negotiating the road by gathering, interpreting, sharing and reacting appropriately to human peculiar signs and messages. We also chose to focus on emotion and facial expressions, as they appear to be a common motive along the three awareness dimensions.

For the driver, a system capable of sensing and reacting to emotional arousal can be a valu-able alarm, and it can help the user to manage and counteract such state before it escalates to road anger and aggressiveness. Several interesting applications are emerging that build on these principles, and some of them are hitting the market of personal mobile devices. However, little background exists to validate the real efficacy of these applications, or to assess their actual safety for in-car use.

One step further, communicating to the surrounding drivers the facial expressions can help in the safe negotiation of the shared road resource, and a system capable of sensing, recognizing and conveying emotional cues can counterbalance the loss of eye contact caused by the design of the vehicles.

Finally, pushed up to the public, urban domain, the information regarding the emotional state of drivers as a community can help to infer valuable information on the state of the traffic, efficiency of the infrastructure, occurrence of dangerous situations, and so on.

It must be noted, however, that in-vehicle applications for social and urban awareness represent, as of today, the cutting edge of research at the intersection between pervasive technologies, road safety and urban informatics, and many of the issues presented throughout this chapter are broadly open at the moment of writing.

We have presented a case study in order to illustrate the feasibility of emotion recognition from facial expressions in the car, and, more importantly, the additional complexity that must be faced in the design and evaluation of UbiComp technologies for the car. An advanced driving simulator, as the one described above, provides the driver with high-fidelity motion, visual, auditory, and force feedback cues, that help to recreate the experience of driving a real car, but in a carefully designed simulated world. In such a virtual world the researchers can generate dangerous intersections, challenging driving conditions, and even scary situations, that would be impossible, impracticable or unethical to recreate in real life. Yet, as we have shown, the driving simulator is not panacea, as the realism of the simulation can only go as far as the participants accept to be 'fooled' by a representation that they know is not real.

As a final remark, it is important to extend our considerations to different, though confining, domains, because drivers (and cars) are not the only 'users' of public roads, and among the many others, arguably the less vulnerable ones. For example, although little attention to road safety is paid in the design of personal mobile apps and technologies, distraction (e.g., from mobile phone use while walking) is becoming a threat for pedestrians (Nasar, Hecht, & Wener, 2008).

Our main goal in this chapter was to contribute a road safety perspective to the UbiComp research community. Intelligent Transport Systems can be regarded as the infrastructure for ubiquitous computing in the car, but with the compelling additional constraint of safety at all cost. Of course we are conscious of having barely scratched the surface of the vast and rather unexplored design space of affective and social computing in the car. At the same time, we hope to have provided enough cues to the reader that is eager to further delve into this fascinating new research topic.

REFERENCES

Bader, R., Siegmund, O., & Woerndl, W. (2011). A study on user acceptance of proactive in-car recommender systems. In *Proceedings of AutomotiveUI '11*. Salzburg, Austria: AutomotiveUI.

Bartlett, M. S., Littlewort, G., Fasel, I., & Movellan, J. R. (2003). Real time face detection and facial expression recognition: Development and applications to human computer interaction. In *Proceedings of Computer Vision and Pattern Recognition Workshop, 2003* (Vol. 5, p. 53). IEEE.

Bergmans, A., & Shahid, S. (2012). Drivers: An in-car persuasive system for making driving safe and fun. In A. Nijholt, T. Romão, & D. Reidsma (Eds.), *Advances in Computer Entertainment* (Vol. 7624, pp. 469–472). Berlin: Springer. doi:10.1007/978-3-642-34292-9_37.

Brave, S., & Nass, C. (2003). *The human-computer interaction handbook*. Hillsdale, NJ: L. Erlbaum Associates Inc..

Brave, S., Nass, C., & Hutchinson, K. (2005). Computers that care: Investigating the effects of orientation of emotion exhibited by an embodied computer agent. *International Journal of Human-Computer Studies*, *62*(2), 161–178. doi:10.1016/j.ijhcs.2004.11.002.

Cai, H., Lin, Y., & Mourant, R. R. (2007). Study on driver emotion in driver-vehicle-environment systems using multiple networked driving simulators. In *Proceedings of DSC 2007*. Iowa City, IA: DSC.

Campbell, A. T., Eisenman, S. B., Lane, N. D., Miluzzo, E., Peterson, R. A., & Lu, H. et al. (2008). The rise of people-centric sensing. *IEEE Internet Computing*, *12*(4), 12–21. doi:10.1109/MIC.2008.90.

Chatzimilioudis, G., Konstantinidis, A., Laoudias, C., & Zeinalipour-Yazti, D. (2012). Crowdsourcing with smartphones. *IEEE Internet Computing*, *16*(5), 36–44. doi:10.1109/MIC.2012.70.

Consolvo, S., McDonald, D. W., & Landay, J. A. (2009). Theory-driven design strategies for technologies that support behavior change in everyday life. In *Proceedings of CHI 2009*. Boston, MA: ACM.

Cook, L. J., Knight, S., & Olson, L. M. (2005). A comparison of aggressive and DUI crashes. *Journal of Safety Research*, *36*(5), 491. doi:10.1016/j.jsr.2005.10.010 PMID:16298395.

Cootes, T. F., Taylor, C. J., Cooper, D. H., & Graham, J. (1995). Active shape models-Their training and application. *Computer Vision and Image Understanding, 61*(1), 38–59. doi:10.1006/cviu.1995.1004.

Coughlin, J. F., Reimer, B., & Mehler, B. (2011). Monitoring, managing, and motivating driver safety and well-being. *IEEE Pervasive Computing/IEEE Computer Society [and] IEEE Communications Society, 10*(3), 14–21. doi:10.1109/MPRV.2011.54.

Cowie, R., Douglas-Cowie, E., Tsapatsoulis, N., Votsis, G., Kollias, S., & Fellenz, W. et al. (2001). Emotion recognition in human-computer interaction. *IEEE Signal Processing Magazine, 18*(1), 32–80. doi:10.1109/79.911197.

Deffenbacher, J. L., Lynch, R. S., Oetting, E. R., & Swaim, R. C. (2002). The driving anger expression inventory: A measure of how people express their anger on the road. *Behaviour Research and Therapy, 40*(6), 717–737. doi:10.1016/S0005-7967(01)00063-8 PMID:12051489.

Doshi, A., Morris, B. T., & Trivedi, M. M. (2011). On-road prediction of driver's intent with multimodal sensory cues. *IEEE Pervasive Computing/IEEE Computer Society [and] IEEE Communications Society, 10*(3), 22–34. doi:10.1109/MPRV.2011.38.

Dourish, P. (2004). What we talk about when we talk about context. *Personal and Ubiquitous Computing, 8*(1), 19–30. doi:10.1007/s00779-003-0253-8.

Ellison-Potter, P., Bell, P., & Deffenbacher, J. (2001). The effects of trait driving anger, anonymity, and aggressive stimuli on aggressive driving behaviour. *Journal of Applied Social Psychology, 31*(2), 431–443. doi:10.1111/j.1559-1816.2001.tb00204.x.

Elvik, R., Høye, A., Vaa, T., & Sørensen, M. (2009). *The handbook of road safety measures* (2nd ed.). Bingley, UK: Emerald Group Publishing Limited.

Erickson, T., & Kellogg, W. A. (2000). Social translucence: An approach to designing systems that support social processes. *ACM Transactions on Computer-Human Interaction, 7*(1), 59–83. doi:10.1145/344949.345004.

Eyben, F., Wöllmer, M., Poitschke, T., Schuller, B., Blaschke, C., & Färber, B. et al. (2010). Emotion on the road - Necessity, acceptance, and feasibility of affective computing in the car. In *Proceedings of Advances in Human-Computer Interaction, 2010*. IEEE. doi:10.1155/2010/263593.

Fasel, B., & Luettin, J. (2003). Automatic facial expression analysis: A survey. *Pattern Recognition, 36*(1), 259–275. doi:10.1016/S0031-3203(02)00052-3.

M. Foth (Ed.). (2009). *Handbook of research on urban informatics: The practice and promise of the real-time city*. Hershey, PA: IGI Global.

Foundation, A. A. A. (2009). *Aggressive driving: Research update*. Retrieved from http://www.aaafoundation.org

Grimm, M., Kroschel, K., Harris, H., Nass, C., Schuller, B., & Rigoll, G. et al. (2007). On the necessity and feasibility of detecting a driver's emotional state while driving. [LNCS]. *Proceedings of Affective Computing and Intelligent Interaction, 4738*, 126–138. doi:10.1007/978-3-540-74889-2_12.

Harris, H., & Nass, C. (2011). Emotion regulation for frustrating driving contexts. In *Proceedings of CHI 2011*. Vancouver, Canada: ACM.

He, H. A., Greenberg, S., & Huang, E. M. (2010). One size does not fit all: Applying the transtheoretical model to energy feedback technology design. In *Proceedings of CHI 2010*. Atlanta, GA: ACM.

Healey, J., & Picard, R. (2000). Smartcar: Detecting driver stress. In *Proceedings of ICPR 2000*. Barcelona, Spain: ICPR.

Healey, J., Wang, C.-C., Dopfer, A., & Yu, C.-C. (2012). M2m gossip: Why might we want cars to talk about us? In *Proceedings of AutomotiveUI '12*. Portsmouth, NH: AutomotiveUI. doi:10.1145/2390256.2390300.

Hoch, S., Althoff, F., McGlaun, G., & Rigoll, G. (2005). Bimodal fusion of emotional data in an automotive environment. In *Proceedings of ICASSP 2005*. ICASSP.

Jeon, M. (2012). A systematic approach to using music for mitigating affective effects on driving performance and safety. In *Proceedings of UbiComp 2012*. Pittsburgh, PA: UbiComp. doi:10.1145/2370216.2370455.

Jones, C., & Jonsson, I.-M. (2008). Using paralinguistic cues in speech to recognise emotions in older car drivers. [LNCS]. *Proceedings of Affect and Emotion in Human-Computer Interaction*, *4868*, 229–240. doi:10.1007/978-3-540-85099-1_20.

Jones, C. M., & Jonsson, I.-M. (2005). Automatic recognition of affective cues in the speech of car drivers to allow appropriate responses. In *Proceedings of OZCHI 2005*. Canberra, Australia: ACM.

Jones, C. M., & Jonsson, I.-M. (2007). Performance analysis of acoustic emotion recognition for in-car conversational interfaces. In *Proceedings of UAHCI 2007*. Beijing, China: UAHCI.

Krause, A., Horvitz, E., Kansal, A., & Zhao, F. (2008). Toward community sensing. In *Proceedings of IPSN 2008*. Washington, DC: IPSN.

Leckie, G. J., & Hopkins, J. (2002). The public place of central libraries: Findings from Toronto and Vancouver. *The Library Quarterly*, *72*(3), 326–372.

Lyons, M., Akamatsu, S., Kamachi, M., & Gyoba, J. (1998). Coding facial expressions with gabor wavelets. In *Proceedings of FG 1998*. Nara, Japan: FG.

Martin, S., Tawari, A., Murphy-Chutorian, E., Cheng, S. Y., & Trivedi, M. (2012). On the design and evaluation of robust head pose for visual user interfaces: Algorithms, databases, and comparisons. In *Proceedings of AutomotiveUI 2012*. Portsmouth, NH: AutomotiveUI. doi:10.1145/2390256.2390281.

Meschtscherjakov, A., Wilfinger, D., Scherndl, T., & Tscheligi, M. (2009). Acceptance of future persuasive in-car interfaces towards a more economic driving behaviour. In *Proceedings of AutomotiveUI '09*. Essen, Germany: AutomotiveUI. doi:10.1145/1620509.1620526.

Milborrow, S., & Nicolls, F. (2008). Locating facial features with an extended active shape model. In *Proceedings of ECCV 2008*. Marseille, France: ECCV.

Miller, W. R., & Rollnick, S. P. (2002). *Motivational interviewing: Preparing people for change*. New York, NY: The Guilford Press.

Miluzzo, E., Lane, N. D., Fodor, K., Peterson, R., Lu, H., & Musolesi, M. et al. (2008). Sensing meets mobile social networks: The design, implementation and evaluation of the cenceme application. In *Proceedings of Sensys 2008*. Raleigh, NC: Sensys. doi:10.1145/1460412.1460445.

Mitrevska, M., Castronovo, S., Mahr, A., & Müller, C. (2012). Physical and spiritual proximity: Linking Car2x communication with online social networks. In *Proceedings of AutomotiveUI '12*. Portsmouth, NH: AutomotiveUI. doi:10.1145/2390256.2390297.

Nasar, J., Hecht, P., & Wener, R. (2008). Mobile telephones, distracted attention, and pedestrian safety. *Accident; Analysis and Prevention*, *40*(1), 69–75. doi:10.1016/j.aap.2007.04.005 PMID:18215534.

Nass, C., Jonsson, I.-M., Harris, H., Reaves, B., Endo, J., Brave, S., et al. (2005). Improving automotive safety by pairing driver emotion and car voice emotion. In *Proceedings of CHI EA 2005*. Portland, OR: ACM.

Ormrod, J. E. (2010). *Educational psychology* (7th ed.). Upper Saddle River, NJ: Pearson.

Paulos, E., Honicky, R., & Hooker, B. (2009). Citizen science: Enabling participatory urbanism. In M. Foth (Ed.), *Handbook of Research on Urban Informatics: The Practice and Promise of the Real-Time City*. Hershey, PA: IGI Global.

Picard, R. W. (2003). Affective computing: Challenges. *International Journal of Human-Computer Studies*, *59*(1), 55–64. doi:10.1016/S1071-5819(03)00052-1.

Prochaska, J. O., & Velicer, W. F. (1997). The transtheoretical model of health behavior change. *American Journal of Health Promotion*, *12*(1), 38–48. doi:10.4278/0890-1171-12.1.38 PMID:10170434.

Rakotonirainy, A., Feller, F., & Haworth, N. (2009). In-vehicle avatars to elicit social response and change driving behaviour. *International Journal of Technology and Human Interaction*, *5*(4), 80–104. doi:10.4018/jthi.2009062505.

Ratti, C., Williams, S., Frenchman, D., & Pulselli, R. (2006). Mobile landscapes: Using location data from cell phones for urban analysis. *Environment and Planning. B, Planning & Design*, *33*(5), 727–748. doi:10.1068/b32047.

Riener, A., Ferscha, A., Frech, P., Hackl, M., & Kaltenberger, M. (2010). Subliminal vibro-tactile based notification of CO_2 economy while driving. In *Proceedings of AutomotiveUI 2010*. Pittsburgh, PA: AutomotiveUI.

Rouzikhah, H., King, M., & Rakotonirainy, A. (2010). The validity of simulators in studying driving behaviours. In *Proceedings of Australasian Road Safety Research, Policing and Education Conference 2012*. Canberra, Australia: ARSRPEC.

Schroeter, R., & Rakotonirainy, A. (2012). The future shape of digital cars. In *Proceedings of Australasian Road Safety Research, Policing and Education Conference 2012*. Wellington, New Zealand: ARSRPEC.

Schroeter, R., Rakotonirainy, A., & Foth, M. (2012). The social car: New interactive vehicular applications derived from social media and urban informatics. In *Proceedings of AutomotiveUI '12*. Portsmouth, NH: AutomotiveUI. doi:10.1145/2390256.2390273.

Schuller, B., Lang, M., & Rigoll, G. (2006). Recognition of spontaneous emotions by speech within automotive environment. *Tagungsband Fortschritte der Akustik*, *32*(1), 57–58.

Schuller, B., Reiter, S., Muller, R., Al-Hames, M., Lang, M., & Rigoll, G. (2005). Speaker independent speech emotion recognition by ensemble classification. In *Proceedings of ICME 2005*. Amsterdam, The Netherlands: ICME.

Svenson, O. (1981). Are we all less risky and more skillful than our fellow drivers? *Acta Psychologica*, *47*(2), 143–148. doi:10.1016/0001-6918(81)90005-6.

Tulusan, J., Staake, T., & Fleisch, E. (2012). Providing eco-driving feedback to corporate car drivers: What impact does a smartphone application have on their fuel efficiency? In *Proceedings of UbiComp 2012*. Pittsburgh, PA: UbiComp. doi:10.1145/2370216.2370250.

Walther, J. B., & D'Addario, K. P. (2001). The impacts of emoticons on message interpretation in computer-mediated communication. *Social Science Computer Review*, *19*(3), 324–347. doi:10.1177/089443930101900307.

You, C.-W., Montes-de-Oca, M., Bao, T. J., Lane, N. D., Lu, H., & Cardone, G. et al. (2012). CarSafe: A driver safety app. that detects dangerous driving behavior using dual-cameras on smartphones. In *Proceedings of UbiComp 2012*. Pittsburgh, PA: UbiComp. doi:10.1145/2370216.2370360.

Zhang, Z., Lyons, M., Schuster, M., & Akamatsu, S. (1998). Comparison between geometry-based and gabor-wavelets-based facial expression recognition using multi-layer perceptron. In *Proceedings of FG 1998*. Nara, Japan: FG.

ENDNOTES

[1] http://www.whatcar.com/car-news/future-toyotas-to-read-drivers-moods/262324

[2] http://www.ionroad.com/

[3] http://www.statefarm.com/mobile/driver-feedback/driverfeedback.asp

[4] http://www.ionroad.com/

Chapter 9
Challenges for Personal Data Stream Management in Smart Buildings

Dennis Geesen
University of Oldenburg, Germany

Marco Grawunder
University of Oldenburg, Germany

H. Jürgen Appelrath
University of Oldenburg, Germany

Daniela Nicklas
University of Oldenburg, Germany

ABSTRACT

Smart homes are equipped with multiple sensors and actuators to observe the residents and environmental phenomena, to interpret the situation out of that, and finally, to react accordingly. While the data processing for a single smart home is facile, the data processing for multiple smart homes in one smart building is more complex because there are different people (e.g., like several residents, administrators, or a property management) with different interests concerning the processed data. On that point, this chapter shows which kind of typical roles can be found in a smart building and what requirements and challenges they demand for managing and processing the data. Secondly, Data Stream Management Systems (DSMS) are introduced as an approach for processing and managing data in a smart building by presenting an appropriate architecture. Finally, the chapter discusses further concepts from DSMS and illustrates how they additionally meet and solve the requirements and the challenges.

INTRODUCTION

So-called smart homes have been envisioned since more than two decades now (Weiser, 1991), and we have seen more and more research projects, running prototypes, and even products that aim to make our everyday life easier, safer, more sustainable, or just to be more fun. However, since smart homes involve a number of microprocessors, sensors, networks, applications, and user interfaces to work together, and since users are still inexperienced in dealing with the technical

DOI: 10.4018/978-1-4666-4695-7.ch009

issues and the usage of such systems, many challenges remain. This is particularly true when we think not only of a single smart home, but of a smart building. For us, a smart building is a combination of two or more smart homes where each smart home has different residents like a block of flats. In contrast to a single smart home, where a family or friends live together, the tenants of flats tend to have more oppositional interests and share less common interests. This also holds for using pervasive computing within their smart home. For example, Martha is an older and calm woman, who uses the smart home for assistance in her daily living. Her neighbor Tom, on the other hand, is a young and trendy guy, who always wants the latest technical equipment. And their neighbor Jill wants to extend her smart home with her own new applications and hardware. Finally, there is Jerry, the property manager, who takes care about the whole building and wants to save resources, like energy and maintenance costs; in addition, Jerry aims for a high quality of living in all flats of this building, since by that, he can justify higher rents. In our scenario, we have a smart building with several apartments. Each apartment has a wide range of sensors and actuators. There are simple sensors to detect phenomena like temperature, motion, light, or weather. Furthermore, devices like a television or a telephone can also be seen as sensors, when they send their status or other data as events. A smart home uses all this data to detect certain states and calls some actuators by some predefined rules. Such a rule might be, for example, to turn on the light if the television is used. Although this approach works well for one certain person, it is not generalizable for everyone. That is why each of the residents has to define their own set of rules. For Tom this might be easy, but for Martha it is not practical. Because of that, the individual preferences can be automatically learned for each person by observing and detecting frequently emerging patterns that are derived from sensor events. Thus, such an approach provides a very adaptively processing for each resident, so

that the resident as well as the property manager does not need time consuming configurations. However, despite that learning is a very individual task; one system per person would be expensive: it needs additional configuration, maintenance, and resources like hardware and energy. Since all—or at least the most—sensors and actuators are part of the building and are managed by the property manager, it is recommended that they also provide a system where all processing is centrally managed. Since Jerry, the property manager, is interested in low costs and low energy consumption, he is sensible to use one single system for all processing. To keep also the individuality and independence of each resident, such a system has to support multiple users at once, where each user may not be able to influence other users. In this contribution, we present a conceptional architecture for an infrastructure for smart buildings. While previous work focused on middleware aspects (Garlan, Siewiorek, Smailagic, & Steenkiste, 2002; Roman & Campbell, 2000) or on model-driven approaches for the representation of the (physical) context (Lehmann, Bauer, Becker, & Nicklas, 2004; Wojciechowski & Wiedeler, 2012; Zhang, Gu, & Wang, 2005), they rely on human experts that configure, model, develop, and program smart home applications. A main aspect for creating personal awareness and individual applications is often neglected: the ability of systems to learn and predict patterns, to manage historical context information and the learned patterns, and to cope with concept drift. This has also been stated by a survey on context-aware architectures and applications by Baldauf et al. (2007):" Many of the systems store contextual information but none of them do not use learning techniques to provide context-aware service proactively". Furthermore, each new prototype mostly starts to design a completely new system, so that there are no standards and only few commercialized systems for home automation. Thus, we present an architecture that is based on one central system that provides learning and processing to multiple users while it is very adaptive, extensible and reusable. Similar to common and generally accepted database management systems (DBMS), we provide an approach that is based upon a data stream management system (DSMS). A DSMS is a system for general purposes and is designed for a flexible management of continuous and potential infinite data streams. The generic, flexible and standard compliant approach of DSMS and their availability from prototypes up to commercial systems may encourage that the processing and management of continuous data is not implemented up from the ground whenever a new smart home middleware is designed. Additionally, the main aspects of the proposed architecture are orthogonal to previous works in smart home architectures. We first present an overview of the architecture and show some user stories that the system covers. Afterwards, we present some challenges of the architecture and show what components and technologies can solve them.

ROLES AND REQUIREMENTS

Our focus within the infrastructure for a smart building is on the multi-tenancy management of sensor data. Since many people with different interests are involved in the smart building scenario, we introduce some representative roles and how they interact with the infrastructure in some exemplary scenarios.

Roles

Each interaction with the system relies on different rights and properties. Since there is usually more than one person who may have equal rights or properties, roles are used to define a certain set of rights and properties. This makes it possible to assign the same roles to different persons for an easier rights management. However, it may also be possible that one person may act the part of different roles. In the following, we define a set of common roles that may occur in a smart building,

- **Local User:** A local user is a resident of the smart building who interacts with applications. Since the local user lives inside of an apartment, he or she also influences the sensors, for example, by switching lights on or off. Thus, this role is taken by everyone within the flat, which are Martha, Tom and Jill in our example.

- **Local Administrator:** One of the local users must be able to decide which applications should be installed for one apartment. A local administrator may also grant access to data that is sensed in the apartment. Jill or Tom, for example, can and want decide for themselves which application they need and which not. However, Martha does not want to interact with any technical details, so that the local administrator is another person, who may install some assistive applications for Martha.

- **Property Manager:** A smart building is administrated by a property manager, who wants to provide high cost-effective smart homes. Thus, they try to keep the administration and maintenance as small as possible. The property manager is also responsible for all firmly installed sensors and actuators like windows, doors, lights, or weather sensors. Since these sensors and actuators are connected to a central control cabinet, it would be reasonable to handle all processing within one central system. So, the property management can act as a service provider, who offers their residents the possibility to process and compute their sensor data. Jerry fits into this role.

- **Global Administrator:** The property manager may provide the processing in a central system as part of the rent, so that the residents do not need to know special technical expertise to use such a system. However, the property manager needs to deploy a technician who administrates and configures the system. This administrator configures the system, runs tests or ensures the stability of the global system for all residents. In a small environment, this role could be also filled by a property manager like Jerry. In larger scopes, there would be dedicated persons for the global administration.

- **Application Developer:** An application developer is a person who uses the system and its interfaces for creating new personal-aware applications. Thus, a local administrator can extend the apartment with new appliances. An application developer could be a person like Jill, who wants to invent new applications for her own smart home. However, there could be also external application developers, which provide applications for downloading.

- **Remote User:** In addition to local users, who are usually residents, there might be remote users, who just want to observe certain sensor data or application results. A care attendant, for example, observes the vital signs of Martha, so that Martha must not take an exhausting way to the doctor. However, the local administrator of Martha must grant rights to the remote user.

Summarized, an appropriate infrastructure has different roles and should be customized for each resident to enable personal aware computing. Furthermore, all these involved persons of the smart building can be seen like a social network. They might be linked between themselves in different ways and they can—depending on their roles— grant or revoke rights on data and components to other persons. However, there are some requirements and challenges that we want to discuss in the following.

Requirements

In this section, we discuss a set of requirements for data management software for a smart building by using ISO/IEC 25010. This standard describes eight characteristics, where each has a set of attributes to describe the quality of the software. However, we omit the usability although it is considered by the standardization, because we focus on the data management level and not on user interfaces.

- **Functional Suitability:** The functionality of a system should be suitable so that each resident has a system that fits to its personal and individual needs. The admins or the property managers are interested in a *functional complete* system. Furthermore, each of the provided functionality should also be *functionally correct*. Users, for example, do not want applications that produce inaccurate and wrong results. Furthermore, the property manager may use the results for an energy management. Therefore, the results should be functionally correct for correct balancing energy accounts. However, each of the functionality should be *appropriate*, because on one hand, the user do not want a confusing and irritating functionality, which is normally not part of smart home systems. On the other hand, the property manager is interested in less functionality to keep down costs.

- **Performance Efficiency:** Efficiency in this context means a cost-efficient solution for the property manager, while the residents want to have a high performance level. The users, for example, are interested in the *time behavior*, because they want immediately results and therefore a fast processing. The property manager, however, is interested in small *resource utilization*, because fewer resources are more cost-effective. So, the system should also provide a high throughput so that a smaller system can receive more sensor data within a period of time. Furthermore, the property manager can only provide a system with limited *capacity*, but sensor data may be infinitely produced and the system may run for an infinite time.

- **Compatibility:** The compatibility considers the *co-existence* with other systems and the possibility to exchange information. According to efficiency, the system should be aware of resources, so it may run on the same system with other software. This is more economic for the property manager and application developers may also integrate their software even better. Additionally, the system should be highly *interoperable*, because it must receive sensor data, send data to actuators or should be interact with different applications. This allows an easier maintenance and fewer customizations for the administrators, which is also more economical for the property manager. Furthermore, an application developer has more possibilities to invent new programs, for example, by using novel sensors.

- **Reliability:** The reliability determines if the system can maintain its performance level under certain constraints for a certain time. In most cases, a system with a high *maturity* offers a stable and reliable system. This causes less administration and therefore also fewer costs. Furthermore, a mature system changes its interface extremely seldom, which is advantageous for application developers. Additionally, a reliable system should always be *available* for users. This is supported by a *fault tolerant* system; because wrong data may cause system errors and these may influence the availability. A fault tolerant system would also require less maintenance by adminis-

trators or property manager. This is also useful for application developers, because their software is subjected to fewer regulations. However, if the system interrupts, the administrators are interested in a *recoverable* system. This is also useful for application developers, who may hang-up the system during development.

- **Security:** Since the sensors (permanently) observe the residents, security and privacy for the personal data is crucial. The users, for example, are highly interested in *confidentiality*, because one resident or an administrator may not see any data of another resident. This also holds for the *integrity* of the system, because unauthorized persons should not be able to change any part of the system. The local administrator, for example, is only allowed to change settings for his or her apartment, but only the global administrator may change system internal settings. Furthermore, the property manager is interested in *non-repudiation*, so that they can prove the usage for each user, which may be used for invoicing. For this, *accountability*, which identifies an action of the system to a certain user, is also helpful. The *authenticity* is only partially important, because the system has no trustworthy parts.

- **Maintainability:** The maintainability describes how effective and efficient the system can be modified by maintainers, which are primarily the administrators and indirectly the property manager and application developers. The *modularity*, for example, allows the global administrator to change one component without influencing other components. This could increase the availability and also keeps down costs. The modularity also supports the *reusability*, because an enclosed module can be reused easier. For the one hand, reusing existing components is more cost-effective for the property manager. On the other hand, the development cycle for application developers is smaller. The administrators, however, are rather interested in an *analyzable* and *testable* system to find deficiencies or causes of failures. The analyzability is also needed by application developers, who want to analyze and test the impact of a new application to the system. Furthermore, developers are interested in a high *modifiable* and *extendable* system for a wide range of possibilities for new applications. Additionally, the administrators and the property manager are also interested in modifying and extending the system, although they focus more on maintain the running system or on integrating a new functionality.

- **Portability:** Since there is not only one smart building; the system should be easily portable to other smart buildings.

Therefore, the system should be *adaptable* and easily *installable* for new environments, including different sensors, actuators and hardware. This also allows an external developer to implement applications that are independent from certain buildings.

DATA STREAM MANAGEMENT

Since there are an increasing number of sensors that produce potential infinite sequences of data—so-called data streams, custom solutions for analyzing and processing of these data streams are mostly not practical anymore. Therefore, DSMS are developed for general purposes, which are quite similar to common DBMS and allows a flexible, reusable and adaptable processing of data streams. As illustrated in Figure 1, active sensors generate data that is continuously pushed into the DSMS.

Figure 1. Architecture of a data stream management system

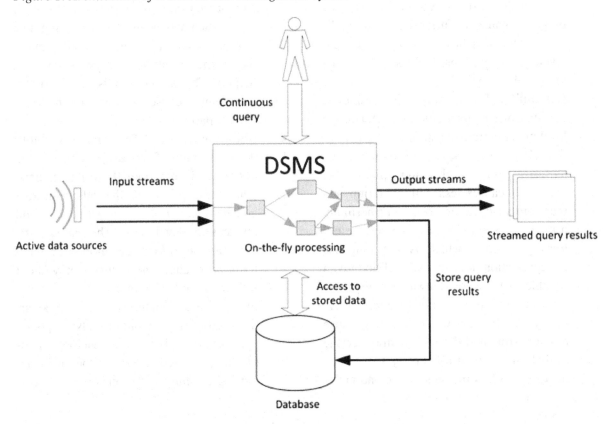

Based on a continuous query that is given by a user or an application and is permanently installed in the system, the DSMS processes the incoming data on-the-fly and continuously produces results. This resulting data streams can be either forwarded to applications or also be stored into a database. There are many DSMS with different approaches like STREAM (Arasu et al., 2003), TelegraphCQ (Chandrasekaran et al., 2003), Aurora (Abadi et al., 2003), Gigascope (Chakraborty & Singh, 2009), PIPES (J Krämer & Seeger, 2004), Borealis (Abadi et al., 2005), Stream Mill (Bai, Thakkar, Wang, Luo, & Zaniolo, 2006), System S (Gedik, Andrade, Wu, Yu, & Doo, 2008) or Odysseus (Appelrath et al., 2012). All systems use languages to describe continuous queries, so that the processing is not fixed code or hardwired and the system is not limited to special solutions. There are, for example, declarative approaches like CQL (Arasu, Babu, & Widom, 2006) and StreamSQL (StreamBase, 2006), or imperative approaches like a box-arrow-model (Abadi et al., 2005) or PQL (Appelrath et al., 2012). Therefore, a DSMS can be easily adapted and extended for a wide range of applications. Similar to database systems, a DSMS also offers some of the same benefits like a reduced application development time, because the query language allows a higher abstraction level for the developer (Elmasri & Navathe, 2006). Furthermore, the DSMS can provide a semantic and deterministic processing of continuous data so that the developer does not have to deal with limited resources, timing behavior or a correct data handling. A very similar approach is called complex event processing (CEP) where a data stream is seen as a sequence of events and CEP engines try to recognize pattern of events to generate new events (Etzion & Niblett, 2011). Although CEP and DSMS are often handled in different ways, they have a lot of common techniques and approaches, so that both fields move more and more together (Cugola & Margara, 2012). For example, some DSMS also integrate pattern matching techniques.

DATA STREAM MANAGEMENT FOR SMART BUILDINGS

Our vision of the management of continuous data in a smart building that addresses the requirements and challenges is built upon a DSMS, because it provides already a basis for an efficient processing of potentially unbounded data. The basis of the system is provided via a central server, which may be located in the technical room of the smart building. Each sensor and actuator of each smart home is connected to the central server, which also provides different interfaces through a local area network. The binding of one smart home—an apartment—to the central server is visualized in Figure 2.

Besides sensors that measure motions or the humidity, there might be sensors in a smart home, e.g. for doors which can detect persons or the state of the door. Furthermore, other devices like the TV, the stove or the washing machine can send their status as sensor data to the central server. The actuators are the counterparts to the sensors and are also connected to the central server. These are devices that can be influenced by the system. For example, a window or door can be opened or closed or lights can be turned off and on. Devices are also controllable by invoking commands like a start washing command for the washing machine. The data from sensors is received by the DSMS, which is the central system on the server and provides different layers. The first layer is an access control that uses a user management to authenticate the user and to check whether a user or its application can process or see the data. The next layer is used for load management. It guarantees the stability of the system

Figure 2. Architecture for a single smart home

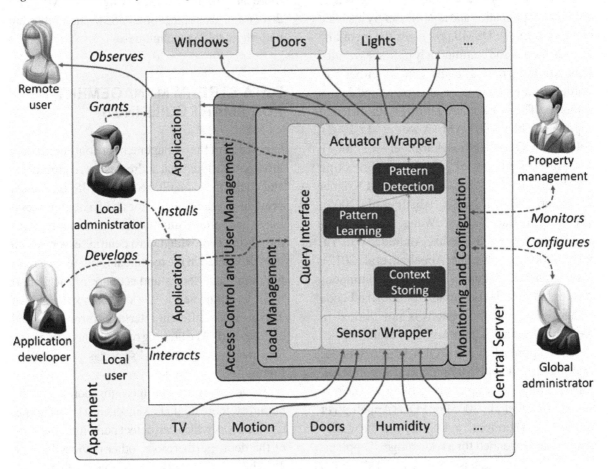

by controlling the incoming data as well as all commands that are passed by an application or a user. The monitoring and configuration provides an interface for global administrators. It has also a restricted access like the load management, but is not controlled by the load management itself. The global administrator or the property manager uses this component to monitor the current status of the system or, for example, to configure new users, to install updates or to add new features. The core of the DSMS processes the data and is a directed graph of operators that is connected between the incoming data from sensors and the outgoing data to the actuators. Such a directed graph is called query plan and is described by a query that was passed by an application through

the query interface. Besides basic operators for filtering, aggregating or combining data, there are also operators for learning patterns and for detecting learned patterns. This allows an adaptive processing. Furthermore, the system is context-aware so that e.g. the states of doors have to be stored for other operators. In addition to the DSMS, the central server also manages all related applications. An application is installed for a local user and uses the DSMS to process its data. For example, there is an application that handles the lights by observing the motions of local users and if a certain motion is recognized, a light is switched. A resident (the local administrator) installs this application to the central server. This application authenticates itself using the credentials of the resident and describes its query plan using a declarative query language. This query is received by the query interface of the DSMS and is initially checked by the load management. If the query can be installed without losing the performance level, the DSMS creates and connects a set of operators—which corresponds to the declarative query—between themselves and the wrappers for the motion sensors and the light actuators. If a motion sensor now detects a motion, it sends its data to the DSMS. The corresponding wrapper transforms the sensor specific data into the internal representation for the DSMS. Then, this event is processed by all connected operators from bottom to the top. If, for example, the query plan has a pattern detect operator that should match the certain motion, all motion data is pushed into this operator. If this operator recognize the given pattern (the motion), it produces a new event, which may be forwarded to the actuator wrapper for the lights. This wrapper invokes the respective switch for the light. Furthermore, the local administrator can also grant or revoke rights for applications or even sensor data. This is, for example, useful if a remote user like a doctor or care attendant wants to see some vital signs. An infrastructure for data management that is based on a DSMS has several advantages by using additional features and concepts. These concepts and how they can support such an infrastructure are explained in the following.

Flexible Processing and Fusing of Streams

Due to the flexible processing of sensor data by a DSMS, a query can be used to fuse several sensor data. This allows the combination of several semantic layers like they are used in most multi sensor data fusion systems (D.L. Hall & Llinas, 1997). Thus, a DSMS is able to process raw sensor data to information or to receive information and fuse this to a feature or can directly process features. These features are according to different processing levels, which are described by the most used JDL data fusion model (David L. Hall & McMullen, 2004). Also other fusion models like the Omnibus (Bedworth & O'Brien, 2000) or the Data-Feature-Decision (DFD) Model (Dasarathy, 1997) use equal levels. These levels, for example, are used for a pre-processing, feature extraction, pattern recognition and a decision making. As an example in a smart home, pre-processing would be used to calculate the average temperature within ten minutes. This is used to extract a feature, which would be something like cold or hot. The pattern recognition could try to match a rule like *"if it is cold, close the door"*. So, if the pattern is recognized with the temperature feature, the system decides to close the window and sends an appropriate command to the actuator. Since a DSMS is designed for general purposes, it fulfills already requirements like interoperability, adaptability or installability. For this, most systems are modular and modifiable. There are also concepts for reusability like query sharing (Sellis, 1988) where existing parts of the queries are reused if it is possible. Furthermore, Odysseus (Appelrath et al., 2012) as a framework for DSMS strives to be highly customizable and adaptive by offering an extendable, modifiable and modular architecture. Additionally, the key features of a DSMS—handling infinite data streams with limited resources—directly match the performance efficiency requirements.

Multi-User and Restricted Access

The user management within a DSMS allows a restricted access to any resources of the system. This allows that each resident and other person like the property manager has his or her own login data and can share the same system to save resources like in database systems (Elmasri & Navathe, 2006). With this login, a source in the DSMS, which corresponds to an incoming connection from a sensor, is exclusively accessible by one user. Therefore, other residents—or even the property manager or global administrators—may not be allowed to access specific sensor data from other residents. This also holds for queries that are installed by a resident or an application so that only a resident or its application can see the results of the query. However, a resident can grant or revoke an access to a source or query for other users. This is very helpful, when a resident is on vacation, an administrator checks the system or a doctor wants to control some vital signs. There are also additional security concepts for a DSMS. Security punctuations (Nehme, Rundensteiner, & Bertino, 2008), for example, are special events within the sensor data stream. They describe the access rights for the data stream. Security punctuations could grant a temporal access for ten minutes of sensor events to a doctor. Since, furthermore, all data is processed on-the-fly, normally no raw data is saved to a database (Geesen, Brell, Grawunder, Nicklas, & Appelrath, 2012). This leads to a higher protection of privacy and this to a better acceptance by users. The concept of multi-tenancy and roles are used to cover the security and privacy requirements. The restricted access to data or certain functionality ensures confidentiality, integrity, and accountability. Furthermore, it also supports fault tolerance and availability, because it prevents for an unauthorized access by intruders who want to shut down the system.

Connecting and Wrapping Sensors and Actuators

Since the system only processes data, the connection to sensors and actuators is an essential part of the DSMS. For the sensor, for example, there are a lot of techniques, protocols, and data formats that are in use. For example, there might be connections via LAN, WLAN, Powerline, Bluetooth or other transfer protocols. The data itself may also be formatted by different data protocols, for example, in XML using text files or tuples using a byte-based format. Therefore, a DSMS needs

sensor wrappers that are responsible for transforming the data into an internal representation. Equal to sources for sensors there must be outgoing connections for actuators. These actuators have also different transfer and data protocols, so that a command for an actuator must be transformed from the internal representation to the actuator-specific command. This could be a XML file that is transferred through a socket or a remote procedure call via a web service. Summarized, a wide range of supported data and transfer protocols for sensors and actuators is necessary. A multi-layered interface with different protocols, like it is part of most DSMS, is very useful to adapt the system to different environments or to extend the system with new sensors. This also includes often used protocols and methods of smart homes like KNX[1], ZigBee[2], or ZWave[3] to name a few. Furthermore, a multi-layered interface is directly advantageous for the portability as well as the compatibility requirement. To reduce the development time for sensor protocol wrappers, DSMS can be easily combined with model-based conversion methods like e.g. (Busemann & Nicklas, 2011).

Detecting Known Patterns

Current available solutions for smart homes are based upon rule-based engines. There are systems that are based upon different technologies like agents, ontologies or pattern recognition, for example, Gaia (Román et al., 2002), Nexus (Cipriani, Eissele, Brodt, Grossmann, & Mitschang, 2009), SOCAM (Gu, Pung, & Zhang, 2005), MAIS (Cappiello, Comuzzi, Mussi, & Pernici, 2006) or UniversAAL (Tazari et al., 2012), to name a few. However, in general, the resident can define rules like if rain is detected, then close the window. More precisely, such rules are based on the event-condition-action (ECA) paradigm. Compared to the DSMS approach, the event part, which triggers the rule, is similar to an incoming date from a sensor. The condition part, which is normally a test if the action should be performed, is similar to the query that is installed in the DSMS. If the query produces an output, it is forwarded to the actuator. This part corresponds to the action part of the rule. Thus, a DSMS can also be seen like a rule-based system. However, a DSMS can be extended with additional concepts for detecting patterns; although these concepts are also known as standalone CEP systems (cf. Flexible Processing and Fusing of Streams). For example, SASE+ (Gyllstrom, Agrawal, Diao, & Immerman, 2008), Cayuga (Demers et al., 2007), or CEDR (Barga & Caituiro-Monge, 2006) are systems that allow to match also sequences of events. This makes it possible to detect also a temporal behavior like trends. There are also some DSMS that integrate such pattern recognition approaches like MavEStream (Chakravarthy & Jiang, 2009) or Odysseus (Appelrath et al., 2012).

Learning New Patterns

Since the definition of patterns or rules like *"if temperature is high, open the window"* by the residents themselves is not feasible for everyone, there are two possible approaches. One possibility is a set of general rules that fit to most people and can be adjusted by simple sliders, for example, to set the threshold for the temperature. Another solution is to learn the special preferences of each person. For this, concepts of data stream mining like frequent pattern mining can be used to detect unknown patterns. In general, data stream mining (Gaber, Zaslavsky, & Krishnaswamy, 2005; Gama, 2007) focuses on applying data mining concepts to unbounded data streams. Thus, most solutions introduce concepts how an existing algorithm from traditional data mining can be used for data streams. For example, there is the VFDT (Domingos & Hulten, 2000) for classification by decision tree induction, single-pass k-means for clustering (MacQueen & others, 1967) or concepts for frequent pattern mining like FP-Stream (Giannella, Han, Pei, Yan, & Yu, 2003). There are already prototypes that combine data stream

management and data stream mining concepts, e.g. MAIDS (Cai et al., 2004), Odysseus (Appelrath et al., 2012) or Stream Mill Miner (Thakkar et al., 2011). Finally, if a system learned some new patterns, they can be automatically transformed into rules. These rules can be integrated as part of a pattern detection query (see Detecting Known Patterns). Since mining is not quite accurate, the resident should be able to deactivate unwanted rules, which is possible by removing or stopping the corresponding query. Thus, learning new patterns offers a high portability and maintainability.

Personal Awareness using Context Management

All incoming data, which is streamed by sensors, do not reflect a certain situation or person on its own. Therefore, most systems use additional information from static data sources that characterize the current situation. This is called context information (Dey, 2001) and is gathered in two different ways. On the one hand, there is state-oriented context of things like the window is closed or light is on. Although such information can be derived from sensor data, it is not really streaming information, because such context does not change rapidly. Since, for example, a window only communicates when it is opened or closed, but does not continuously sends its state, the system has to keep such states in mind. This is why all context information is hold as a consolidated context model, whose parts are updated when the corresponding context information changes. Other streaming data can access the context model by enriching each data stream element, e.g., with current state of the window. The second way for getting context information are external data sources like database systems or web services (Geesen et al., 2012). This context information can be something like current appointments or the actual weather and may also be enriched to each stream element. Although most DSMS already allow writing and reading from databases, there also approaches that focus of the combined querying over streaming archived static data at once like Moirae (Balazinska, Kwon, Kuchta, & Lee, 2007), DejaVu (Dindar, Fischer, Soner, & Tatbul, 2011), Latte (Tufte et al., 2007), TelegraphCQ (Chandrasekaran et al., 2003), or Stream Cube (Han et al., 2005).

Since the caching and enrichment of state-oriented or external data can be arbitrarily integrated into the query, the context model as well as the processed data can also consider different levels of context, e.g. raw data level, feature or situation level. This goes along with different fusion levels that are described before and are also used in typical context- or situation-aware systems (Coutaz, Crowley, Dobson, & Garlan, 2005; Dey, Abowd, & Salber, 2001).

Temporal and Spatial Context

In addition to state-oriented context, which is described in the previous section, there are is also a context that describes relations between events (Etzion & Niblett, 2011). The most common context is the temporal context, which makes it possible to process only data that temporally correlate. For example in a smart home, two events like an upcoming thunderstorm and closing a door should only be joined, if both measurements occur within, e.g. ten minutes. This time period is called a window and is also one concept of a DSMS to handle with unbounded data streams. There are different approaches to implement such windows. There are, for example, the time-interval approach (Jürgen Krämer & Seeger, 2009) or the positive/negative approach (Abadi et al., 2003), which implement a global window concept that is valid for the whole query or there are approaches like SPADE (Gedik et al., 2008) that implement local windows per operator. There are systems that do not consider any temporal behavior as well. Since most systems need incoming elements to produce outputs, some of their operators have a blocking behavior. One concept is to use punctua-

tions (Tucker, Maier, Sheard, & Fegaras, 2003), which are fixed points within the data streams that simply indicate the time progress of the stream. Therefore, punctuation can be used to unblock a waiting operator, if the data stream has no more elements. Since a few systems need a temporal ordered data streams, punctuation can be used instead, so that all elements between two punctuations could be unordered. This is also known as out-of-order processing (Li et al., 2008) and allows also a prioritization of important data stream elements (Jacobi, Bolles, Grawunder, Nicklas, & Appelrath, 2010).

Although two or more events are in the same temporal window, they are not necessarily in relation to each other when they focus on different areas. Therefore, sometimes events have also a spatial context that uses geospatial characteristics to describe, for example, the position or a distance to something else (Etzion & Niblett, 2011). Finally, both contexts together are also called a spatio-temporal processing (Mokbel & Aref, 2008) or moving objects (Patroumpas & Sellis, 2004). Besides functional completeness, all these concepts directly contribute to the performance efficiency requirements.

Reliability and Quality of Service

If more than one user uses the DSMS, the resources have to be shared. Although this reduces required resources, it also allows one user to influence the processing of another user. This happens, for example, if one resident installs a very complex and costly query so that the DSMS is nearly occupied with this query and the queries of other residents are starving. To avoid such things, a DSMS can adapt concepts from cloud computing (Franklin Jr, 2009) and provide virtualization, elasticity or, for example, an admission control that controls whether a new query can be added or not, for example, if it would require too much resources (Al Moakar et al., 2010). There are already some systems such as Nile (Hammad et al., 2004) or Odysseus (Appelrath et al., 2012), which contain cloud computing concepts. There are also other general concepts for handling overload situations like load shedding (Tatbul, Çetintemel, Zdonik, Cherniack, & Stonebraker, 2003), which discards certain objects to reduce the system load, or special scheduling approaches (Babcock, Babu, Motwani, & Datar, 2003; Carney et al., 2003). In order that the property manager does not configure the system to reject all queries of the residents, there must be an agreement that ensures a certain amount of resources for each resident. Thus, this architecture can also be seen as a platform as a service, or also called CEP as a service (Bilchev, 2008). In such a world, each resident would arrange a service level agreement (SLA) with the property manager for defining a certain quality of service (Chakravarthy & Jiang, 2009), which, e.g., could be paid as part of the rent. This SLA describes a set of warranties like a certain amount of sensor data that the service provider has to process for the resident in a given period of time. It also contains some penalties so that the property manager has to refund an amount, if it cannot satisfy the SLA.

DISCUSSION

To sum up, many different people have different roles in a smart building. Each role has its own set of requirements, where Table 1 shows a recommended comparison of roles and their requirements. This comparison is not a definite list, because the roles strongly depend on the building and how, for example, the property manager or the administration is organized. However, it shows that the design of personal sensor data management in smart building has many stakeholders with quite different requirements. We illustrate in the following section how an architecture could be designed that satisfied all these different requirements and roles.

It strongly depends on the role, which of the approaches that are described in the previous section has to be considered in designing a system. Therefore, Table 2 gives an advice which approach is useful for a certain role.

The flexible processing and fusing of streams is only attractive for application developers, because it strongly simplifies the development process. However, the usage of a user management with multiple users and restricted access is not that important for application developers, but local users as well as administrators want to protect their data and settings. Furthermore, the property manager may use users to distinguish between different residents for the monthly settlement. Another approach is to connect sensors and actuators. An easy binding and wrapping for new sensors and actuators would be kept down costs for the property manager. Additionally, it is easier for administrators and application developers to use new kinds of sensors or actuators, which would also reduce the maintenance. Although a user would indirectly benefit from pattern detection mechanisms, because it allows richer sets of applications, only the application developer may use these concepts directly while implementing new programs. However, learning new patterns would also be advantageous for administrators, because there is no detailed configuration of rules and initial settings needed. This also allows an easier adaption to new smart buildings for the property manager. The users are interested in personal awareness and in using temporal context, because it allows the system to distinguish between different users. This allows, for example, more individual patterns and therefore more personality for each user. The application developer may also use concepts for personal awareness or temporal contexts, because the developer may create other type of applications. Additionally, the temporal context reduces the complexity of applications for developers, because a time period limits the number of possible actions within the smart

Table 1. Roles and their Requirements

		Local User	Local Admin	Property Management	Global Admin	Application Developer	Remote User
Functional suitability	Functional complete	x	x	x	x	x	x
	Functional correct	x		x		x	x
	Functional appropriate	x	x	x	x	x	x
Performance efficiency	Time behavior	x					x
	Resource utilization			x			
	Capacity			x			
Com-pati-bility	Co-existence			x		x	
	Interoperability		x	x	x	x	
Reliability	Maturity		x	x	x	x	
	Availability	x					x
	Fault tolerance	x	x	x	x	x	x
	Recoverability		x		x	x	
Security	Confidentiality	x					
	Integrity		x	x	x		
	Non-repudiation			x	x		
	Accountability			x	x		
	Authenticity						
Maintainability	Modularity		x	x	x	x	
	Reusability			x		x	
	Analyzability		x	x	x	x	
	Modifiability		x	x	x	x	
	Testability		x	x	x	x	
	Extendibility		x	x	x	x	
Port-ability	Adaptability			x	x	x	
	Installability			x	x	x	

Table 2. Roles and useful approaches

	Local User	Local Admin	Property Manager	Global Admin	Application Developer	Remote User
Flexible processing					X	
Fusing of Streams					x	
Multi-user	x	x	x	x		
Restricted access	x	x	x	x		
Connecting sensors		x	x	x	x	
Detecting Patterns					x	
Learning patterns		x	x	x	x	
Personal awareness	x				x	x
Temporal context	x				x	x
Reliability and QoS	x	x	x	x		x

building. Finally, each role is interested in a reliable system, which also provides quality of services. While users benefit from a higher availability, the maintenance costs for administrators would be less. If the property manager offers a service level agreement, it would be also interested in a reliable system that does not break these agreements.

SUMMARY AND FUTURE WORK

In this contribution, we introduce an approach for the management of continuous data within a smart building. Based upon roles and their requirements, we present an architecture that uses DSMS. It allows a flexible processing of continuous data under limited resources for different tenants. Along with the advantages of common DSMS, we also present a bunch of additional concepts and technologies. These concepts can be used in cooperation with or integrated into a DSMS to solve several problems within a smart building like learning human preferences or processing context, to name a few. Further details of an implementation that use a DSMS as a base component within a smart home middleware is given in (Geesen et al., 2012).

Our goal is a comprehensive DSMS that integrated different concepts and technologies so that it can be used in a smart building. Therefore, we develop Odysseus (Appelrath et al., 2012), a framework for DSMS with the objective to offer a highly flexible, extendible and configurable system. To show these goals, we integrate the concepts and technologies that are mentioned in Section 4 into Odysseus. We evaluate new integrated concepts within a real world scenario of a smart home by using sensors and actuators, which can be also found in smart homes.

REFERENCES

Abadi, D., Ahmad, Y., Balazinska, M., Cetintemel, U., Cherniack, M., Hwang, J., et al. (2005). The design of the borealis stream processing engine. In *Proceedings of the Second Biennial Conference on Innovative Data Systems Research (CIDR 2005)*. CIDR.

Abadi, D., Carney, D., Çetintemel, U., Cherniack, M., Convey, C., & Lee, S. et al. (2003). Aurora: A new model and architecture for data stream management. *The VLDB Journal, 12*(2), 120–139. doi:10.1007/s00778-003-0095-z.

Al Moakar, L., Chrysanthis, P. K., Chung, C., Guirguis, S., Labrinidis, A., Neophytou, P., & Pruhs, K. (2010). Admission control mechanisms for continuous queries in the cloud. In Proceedings of Data Engineering (ICDE), (pp. 409–412). ICDE.

Appelrath, H., Geesen, D., Grawunder, M., Michelsen, T., Nicklas, D., et al. (2012). Odysseus: A highly customizable framework for creating efficient event stream management systems. In *Proceedings of the 6th ACM International Conference on Distributed Event-Based Systems* (pp. 367–368). ACM.

Arasu, A., Babcock, B., Babu, S., Datar, M., Ito, K., Nishizawa, I., et al. (2003). STREAM: The stanford stream data manager (demonstration description). In *Proceedings of the 2003 ACM SIGMOD International Conference on Management of Data* (p. 665). San Diego, CA: ACM. doi:10.1145/872757.872854

Arasu, A., Babu, S., & Widom, J. (2006). The CQL continuous query language: Semantic foundations and query execution. *The VLDB Journal, 15*(2), 121–142. doi:10.1007/s00778-004-0147-z.

Babcock, B., Babu, S., Motwani, R., & Datar, M. (2003). Chain: Operator scheduling for memory minimization in data stream systems. In *Proceedings of the 2003 ACM SIGMOD International Conference on Management of Data* (pp. 253–264). ACM.

Bai, Y., Thakkar, H., Wang, H., Luo, C., & Zaniolo, C. (2006). A data stream language and system designed for power and extensibility. In *Proceedings of the 15th ACM International Conference on Information and Knowledge Management* (pp. 337–346). ACM.

Balazinska, M., Kwon, Y. C., Kuchta, N., & Lee, D. (2007). Moirae: History-enhanced monitoring. In *Proceedings of the Third CIDR Conference*. CIDR.

Baldauf, M., Dustdar, S., & Rosenberg, F. (2007). A survey on context-aware systems. *International Journal of Ad Hoc and Ubiquitous Computing*, *2*(4), 263–277. doi:10.1504/IJA-HUC.2007.014070.

Barga, R., & Caituiro-Monge, H. (2006). Event correlation and pattern detection in CEDR. In Proceedings of Current Trends in Database Technology--EDBT 2006, (pp. 919–930). EDBT.

Bedworth, M., & O'Brien, J. (2000). The omnibus model: a new model of data fusion? *IEEE Aerospace and Electronic Systems Magazine*, *15*(4), 30–36. doi:10.1109/62.839632.

Bilchev, G. (2008). Complex event processing as a service. In Proceedings of Broadband Communications, Networks and Systems, 2008. BROADNETS.

Busemann, C., & Nicklas, D. (2011). *Converting conversation protocols using an {XML} based differential behavioral model*. Berlin: Springer. doi:10.1007/978-3-642-23091-2_27.

Cai, Y. D., Clutter, D., Pape, G., Han, J., Welge, M., & Auvil, L. (2004). MAIDS: Mining alarming incidents from data streams. In *Proceedings of the 2004 ACM SIGMOD International Conference on Management of Data* (pp. 919–920). ACM.

Cappiello, C., Comuzzi, M., Mussi, E., & Pernici, B. (2006). Context management for adaptive information systems. *Electronic Notes in Theoretical Computer Science*, *146*(1), 69–84. doi:10.1016/j.entcs.2005.11.008.

Carney, D., Çetintemel, U., Rasin, A., Zdonik, S., Cherniack, M., & Stonebraker, M. (2003). Operator scheduling in a data stream manager. In *Proceedings of the 29th International Conference on Very Large Data Bases* (pp. 838–849). VLDB.

Chakraborty, A., & Singh, A. (2009). A partition-based approach to support streaming updates over persistent data in an active datawarehouse. In *Proceedings of the IEEE International Symposium on Parallel & Distributed Processing* (pp. 1–11). IEEE.

Chakravarthy, S., & Jiang, Q. (2009). *Stream data processing: A quality of service perspective: modeling, scheduling, load shedding, and complex event processing*. Berlin: Springer.

Chandrasekaran, S., Cooper, O., Deshpande, A., Franklin, M. J., Hellerstein, J. M., Hong, W., et al. (2003). TelegraphCQ: Continuous dataflow processing. In *Proceedings of the 2003 ACM SIGMOD International Conference on Management of Data*. ACM.

Cipriani, N., Eissele, M., Brodt, A., Grossmann, M., & Mitschang, B. (2009). NexusDS: A flexible and extensible middleware for distributed stream processing. In *Proceedings of the 2009 International Database Engineering & Applications Symposium* (pp. 152–161). Cetraro - Calabria, Italy: ACM. doi:10.1145/1620432.1620448

Coutaz, J., Crowley, J. L., Dobson, S., & Garlan, D. (2005). Context is key. *Communications of the ACM, 48*(3), 49–53. doi:10.1145/1047671.1047703.

Cugola, G., & Margara, A. (2012). Processing flows of information: From data stream to complex event processing. *ACM Computing Surveys, 44*(3), 15. doi:10.1145/2187671.2187677.

Dasarathy, B. V. (1997). Sensor fusion potential exploitation-innovative architectures and illustrative applications. *Proceedings of the IEEE, 85*(1), 24–38. doi:10.1109/5.554206.

Demers, A., Gehrke, J., Panda, B., Riedewald, M., Sharma, V., White, W. M., et al. (2007). Cayuga: A general purpose event monitoring system. In *Proceedings of CIDR* (pp. 412–422). CIDR.

Dey, A. K. (2001). Understanding and using context. *Personal and Ubiquitous Computing, 5*(1), 4–7. doi:10.1007/s007790170019.

Dey, A. K., Abowd, G. D., & Salber, D. (2001). A conceptual framework and a toolkit for supporting the rapid prototyping of context-aware applications. *Human-Computer Interaction, 16*(2-4), 97–166. doi:10.1207/S15327051HCI16234_02.

Dindar, N., Fischer, P. M., Soner, M., & Tatbul, N. (2011). Efficiently correlating complex events over live and archived data streams. In *Proceedings of ACM DEBS Conference*. ACM.

Domingos, P., & Hulten, G. (2000). Mining high-speed data streams. In *Proceedings of the Sixth ACM SIGKDD International Conference on Knowledge Discovery and Data Mining* (pp. 71–80). ACM.

Elmasri, R., & Navathe, S. B. (2006). *Fundamentals of database systems* (5th ed.). Reading, MA: Addison Wesley. Retrieved from http://www.amazon.com/Fundamentals-Database-Systems-5th-Ed./dp/0321369572

Etzion, O., & Niblett, P. (2011). *Event processing in action*. Stamford, CT: Manning Publications.

Franklin, C. Jr. (2009). *Cloud computing: Technologies and strategies of the ubiquitous data center*. Boca Raton, FL: CRC.

Gaber, M. M., Zaslavsky, A., & Krishnaswamy, S. (2005). Mining data streams: a review. *SIGMOD Record, 34*(2), 18–26. doi:10.1145/1083784.1083789.

Gama, J. (2007). *Learning from data streams: Processing techniques in sensor networks*. Berlin: Springer. doi:10.1007/3-540-73679-4.

Garlan, D., Siewiorek, D., Smailagic, A., & Steenkiste, P. (2002). Project aura: Toward distraction-free pervasive computing. *IEEE Pervasive Computing / IEEE Computer Society [and] IEEE Communications Society, 1*(2), 22–31. doi:10.1109/MPRV.2002.1012334.

Gedik, B., Andrade, H., Wu, K.-L., Yu, P. S., & Doo, M. (2008). SPADE: The systems declarative stream processing engine. In *Proceedings of the 2008 ACM SIGMOD International Conference on Management of Data - SIGMOD '08*. New York, NY: ACM Press. doi:10.1145/1376616.1376729

Geesen, D., Brell, M., Grawunder, M., Nicklas, D., & Appelrath, H. J. (2012). Data stream management in the AAL: Universal and flexible preprocessing of continuous sensor data. *Ambient Assisted Living*, 213–228.

Giannella, C., Han, J., Pei, J., Yan, X., & Yu, P. (2003). Mining frequent patterns in data streams at multiple time granularities. In *Proceedings of Next Generation Data Mining*, (pp. 191–212). IEEE. Retrieved from http://citeseerx.ist.psu.edu/viewdoc/download?doi=10.1.1.14.2327&amp,rep=rep1&amp,type=pdf

Gu, T., Pung, H. K., & Zhang, D. Q. (2005). A service-oriented middleware for building context-aware services. *Journal of Network and Computer Applications*, *28*(1), 1–18. doi:10.1016/j.jnca.2004.06.002.

Gyllstrom, D., Agrawal, J., Diao, Y., & Immerman, N. (2008). On supporting kleene closure over event streams. In *Proceedings of 2008 IEEE 24th International Conference on Data Engineering*, (pp. 1391–1393). IEEE. doi:10.1109/ICDE.2008.4497566

Hall, D. L., & Llinas, J. (1997). An introduction to multisensor data fusion. *Proceedings of the IEEE*, *85*(1), 6–23. doi:10.1109/5.554205.

Hall, D. L., & McMullen, S. A. H. (2004). *Mathematical techniques in Multisensor data fusion*. Artech Print on Demand.

Hammad, M. A., Mokbel, M. F., Ali, M. H., Aref, W. G., Catlin, A. C., & Elmagarmid, A. K. et al. (2004). Nile: A query processing engine for data streams. In *Proceedings of Data Engineering, 2004*. IEEE. doi:10.1109/ICDE.2004.1320080.

Han, J., Chen, Y., Dong, G., Pei, J., Wah, B. W., Wang, J., & Cai, Y. D. (2005). Stream cube: An architecture for multi-dimensional analysis of data streams. *Distributed and Parallel Databases*, *18*(2), 173–197. doi:10.1007/s10619-005-3296-1.

Jacobi, J., Bolles, A., Grawunder, M., Nicklas, D., & Appelrath, H. J. (2010). A physical operator algebra for prioritized elements in data streams. *Computer Science-Research and Development*, *25*(3), 235–246. doi:10.1007/s00450-009-0102-8.

Krämer, J., & Seeger, B. (2004). PIPES: A public infrastructure for processing and exploring streams. In *Proceedings of the 2004 ACM SIGMOD International Conference on Management of Data* (pp. 925–926). ACM.

Krämer, J., & Seeger, B. (2009). Semantics and implementation of continuous sliding window queries over data streams. *ACM Transactions on Database Systems*, *34*(1), 1–49. doi:10.1145/1508857.1508861.

Lehmann, O., Bauer, M., Becker, C., & Nicklas, D. (2004). From home to world - Supporting context-aware applications through world models. In *Proceedings of the Second IEEE International Conference on Pervasive Computing and Communications*. IEEE.

Li, J., Tufte, K., Shkapenyuk, V., Papadimos, V., Johnson, T., & Maier, D. (2008). Out-of-order processing: A new architecture for high-performance stream systems. *Proceedings of the VLDB Endowment*, *1*(1), 274–288.

MacQueen, J., et al. (1967). Some methods for classification and analysis of multivariate observations. In *Proceedings of the Fifth Berkeley Symposium on Mathematical Statistics and Probability* (Vol. 1, p. 14). Berkeley, CA: IEEE.

Mokbel, M. F., & Aref, W. G. (2008). SOLE: Scalable on-line execution of continuous queries on spatio-temporal data streams. *The VLDB Journal*, *17*(5), 971–995. doi:10.1007/s00778-007-0046-1.

Nehme, R. V., Rundensteiner, E. A., & Bertino, E. (2008). A security punctuation framework for enforcing access control on streaming data. *Structure (London, England)*, 406–415. Retrieved from http://www.computer.org/portal/web/csdl/doi/10.1109/ICDE.2008.4497449.

Patroumpas, K., & Sellis, T. (2004). Managing trajectories of moving objects as data streams. In J. Sander & M. A. Nascimento (Eds.), *Proceedings of the Second Workshop on Spatio-Temporal Database Management*. Toronto, Canada: IEEE.

Roman, M., & Campbell, R. H. (2000). Gaia: Enabling active spaces. In *Proceedings of the 9th Workshop on ACM SIGOPS European Workshop: Beyond the PC: New Challenges for the Operating System* (pp. 229–234). ACM.

Román, M., Hess, C., Cerqueira, R., Ranganathan, A., Campbell, R. H., & Nahrstedt, K. (2002). Gaia: A middleware platform for active spaces. *ACM SIGMOBILE Mobile Computing and Communications Review*, 6(4), 65–67. doi:10.1145/643550.643558.

Sellis, T. K. (1988). Multiple-query optimization. *ACM Transactions on Database Systems*, 13(1), 23–52. doi:10.1145/42201.42203.

Tatbul, N., Çetintemel, U., Zdonik, S., Cherniack, M., & Stonebraker, M. (2003). Load shedding in a data stream manager. In *Proceedings of the 29th International Conference on Very Large Data Bases* (pp. 309–320). IEEE.

Tazari, M. R., Furfari, F., Valero, Á. F., Hanke, S., Höftberger, O., Kehagias, D., et al. (2012). The universAAL reference model for AAL. In Handbook on Ambient Assisted Living-Technology for Healthcare, Rehabilitation and Well-Being. AISE.

Thakkar, H., Laptev, N., Mousavi, H., Mozafari, B., Russo, V., & Zaniolo, C. (2011). SMM: A data stream management system for knowledge discovery. In *Proceedings of the IEEE 27th International Conference on Data Engineering (ICDE)* (pp. 757–768). IEEE.

Tucker, P. A., Maier, D., Sheard, T., & Fegaras, L. (2003). Exploiting punctuation semantics in continuous data streams. *IEEE Transactions on Knowledge and Data Engineering*, 15(3), 555–568. doi:10.1109/TKDE.2003.1198390.

Tufte, K., Li, J., Maier, D., Papadimos, V., Bertini, R. L., & Rucker, J. (2007). Travel time estimation using NiagaraST and latte. In *Proceedings of the 2007 ACM SIGMOD International Conference on Management of Data* (pp. 1091–1093). ACM.

Weiser, M. (1991). The computer for the 21st century. *Scientific American*, 265(3), 94–104. doi:10.1038/scientificamerican0991-94.

Wojciechowski, M., & Wiedeler, M. (2012). Model-based development of context-aware applications using the MILEO-context server. In *Proceedings of Pervasive Computing and Communications Workshops* (pp. 613–618). IEEE. doi:10.1109/PerComW.2012.6197588.

Zhang, D., Gu, T., & Wang, X. (2005). Enabling context-aware smart home with semantic technology. *International Journal of Human-Friendly Welfare Robotic Systems*, 6(4), 12–20.

ENDNOTES

1. http://www.knx.org
2. http://www.zigbee.org
3. http://www.z-wave.com

Chapter 10
News Recommendation for China Sina Weibo Microblog Service Based on User Social Behaviors

Zuo Yuchu
Sun Yat-sen University, China

You Fang
Sun Yat-sen University, China

Wang Jianmin
Sun Yat-sen University, China

Zhou Zhengle
Sun Yat-sen University, China

ABSTRACT

Sina weibo microblog is an increasingly popular social network service in China. In this work, the authors conducted a study of detecting news in Sina weibo microblog. They found the traditional definition for news can be generalized here. They first expanded the definition of news by conducting user surveys and quantitative analysis. The authors built a news recommendation system by modeling the users, classifying them into four different groups, and applying several heuristic rules, which derived from the generalized definition of news. By applying the new recommendation system, people got newsworthy information, while the funny and interesting tweets, which are popular in Sina weibo microblog, were put in the last ranking list. This study helps us achieve better understanding of heuristic rules about news. Some official organizations can also benefit from the work by supervising the most popular news around civilians.

1. RESEARCH BACKGROUND

As a new type of social media, Sina weibo microblog has become significantly popular in China nowadays. So far, considerable amount of work has been done in order to classify the tweets (or status) automatically. Current classification researches on Chinese microblog are mostly based on supervise learning (Alec Go, 2009; Dong Zhendong, 2011; Z. Liu, Yu, Chen, Wang, & Wu, 2010; Zitao, Wenchao, Wei, Shuran, & Fengyi, 2010) and semantic network (Okazaki & Matsuo,

DOI: 10.4018/978-1-4666-4695-7.ch010

2010), thus the tweets are classified into two categories—the positive and the negative(Qin, Xin, & Niu, 2010). Nevertheless, both supervise learning and semantic network are not so efficacious because of some inevitable shortcomings. For instance, supervise learning demands quite a large dataset while the constantly changing content in microblog makes it difficult to build a robust system. On the other hand, considering it has been noted that microblog possesses the attributes of news media (Kwak, Lee, Park, & Moon, 2010), it is necessary to classify it as news-worthy type and non-news-worthy type. As it was mentioned in (Kwak, et al., 2010), microblog is more of news media than social network, which can be justified by our basic motives of using microblog. (Java, Song, Finin, & Tseng, 2007) said a single user may have multiple intentions or may even play different roles in different communities. They may be an information source, a social relationship builder, an information seeker, or the one combining some intentions above. In Sina weibo microblog, users' intentions are quite the same with those of the Twitter's users since both have the same mechanism. Firstly, it's quite popular for us to raise and discuss issues or topics on microblog when news happens in the real world. Secondly, we pay attention to or "follow" celebrities who are "verified" as well as our friends in real life because we are eager to know what happen to them recently. Thirdly, we concern a special topic where our own interest lies and communicate with others in the common-interest communities. As a matter of fact, however, we are frequently harassed by piles of spam information, and unfortunately miss much news-worthy one. Hence, it's really imperative and significant for us to come up with one new microblog classification criteria and rule to optimize the microblog management and provide better user experience.

In this paper, we found that some user groups are more possible to post news-worthy content. They are verified-organizational user and unver-

ified-personal user. What's more, we are going to build a system to find these tweets out of piles of non-news-worthy content.

2. RELATED WORKS

In previous content-based classification researches which mainly center on the Chinese sentence structure and syntax analysis, we encountered such a fatal bottleneck: constantly newly-emerged words and usages. In fact, such a problem results from the complexity and flexibility of Chinese which is so different from English. Even some researchers solve this problem by building mathematical model (Abdullah & Wu, 2011), considering users' relations in social network(Magnani, Montesi, & Rossi, 2010), or combining social network with RSS feeds (Phelan, McCarthy, Bennett, & Smyth, 2011a, 2011b; Phelan, McCarthy, & Smyth, 2009) (though they only recommend RSS news by tweets, we can easily reverse the idea by recommending tweets by RSS feeds), a subtle problem which is omitted is that people use microblog not only for the news which would appear on every portal site, but also for some social purpose (Chen, Nairn, & Chi, 2011; Zhao & Rosson, 2009).

Apparently microblog is not a typical medium, and the traditional definition for "news" can be generalized here. As far as we know, this is the first study on finding the characters of the news-worthy content in microblog. We interviewed 37 Sina weibo microblog users, who have used Sina weibo microblog service over a year, and asked them the generalized definition for "news", which drove us to redefine "news" in the microblog-sphere. After that, we found evidences that can be used to decide whether a tweet is news-worthy. Back to previous research of (Guangxia, Hoi, Kuiyu, & Jain, 2010; Jansen, Zhang, Sobel, & Chowdury, 2009; Okazaki & Matsuo, 2010; Qin, et al., 2010), the existing classification method only focus on tweet contents and sentiment. We have tried to find out whether there is a tie linking the tweets' content with their being news-worthy, but little did we gain. So it is reasonable for us to suspect that, it is the non-content factor, such as some users' profiles and their corresponding characters, that decide whether a tweet is news-worthy, accompanying with the content(Zuo, You, Wang, & Wu, 2012). On the one hand, we found news-worthy tweets for users. On the other hand, which is more important, we give our definition for news according to some users' interviews and statistical analysis.

In the following parts we will give a detailed description of our study method in which three rules to determine whether a tweet is news-worthy are proposed and justified. In the fourth part, we will elaborate on how to tackle the problems aroused when taking the algorithm into practice, evaluate the result and discuss how well the rules work and what problems our approach may have. Besides, we will explore the potential applications of our approach and relevant significance.

3. HEURISTIC RULES FOR MICROBLOG SERVICE NEWS DEFINITION

3.1. Data Preparation

We have crawled a large amount of data for statistical analysis and all of them are available for cooperative research. As it is shown in Table 1, we got nearly all the verified users at Aug 2011

Table 1. Data description

	Verified Users	Unverified Users
#of Users	283482	264741
#of Tweets	18920412	8831727
#of Relations	111315515	83504541

according to some report of Sina(Sina, 2011), and all their tweets posted between Aug 20th 2011 and Sep 20th 2011. Noted that here 'verified' means the users are verified by Sina, while the word 'unverified' referred to the users who are not verified by Sina, or in general, who are not famous. We also stored all their friends and which we called relations here. On the other hand, we crawl an equivalent amount of unverified users randomly, and also their tweets posted between Aug 20th 2011 and Sep 20th 2011 and relations.

We built the network by using a node to represent a user, and a directed edge from node A to node B to represent that user A is following user B, which can also be illustrated as 'B is A's friend'. It is a conventional free-scale network by learning the degree of the network. The users with over 100 degree fit to a power law distribution according to Figure 1 with exponent of 1.69. However, according to the past research, followers' number from 100 to 10,000 fits to a power-law distribution with the exponent of 2.63[18]. Noted here degree means the number combined with followers and followings. The exponent is far lower than 2.63.

3.2. Interview with Microblog Users

To achieve a better understanding of what users demand on microblog, we have carried out some interviews. The interviews we conducted can be divided into two steps. First, we posted a questionnaire on "So-Jump"(http://www.sojump.com/), in order to get some basic information of the microblog users, and received 512 valid response. Second, 37 of them were interviewed what news on microblog is. In the first step, as it was shown in Figure 2, we found users in microblog are young. This result is exactly the same with some research done by EnfoDesk(EnfoDesk).

In the second step, we further choose 37 users to ask more about news on microblog. They were from IT, sales service, design industry,

Figure 1. Sina weibo microblog users degree distribution

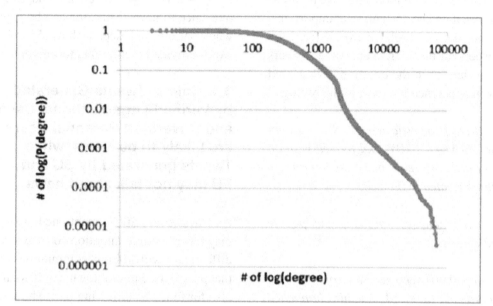

Figure 2. Age distribution of Sina weibo microblog users

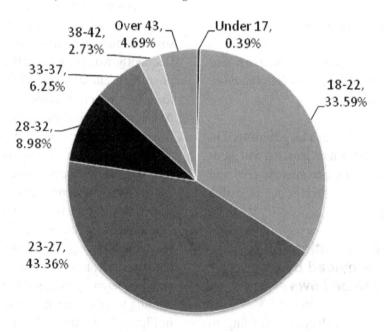

mechanical industry, 23.6 years old on average, and from 13 different cities. According to the answers from our interviewees, over 70% (26) of them are unconsciously influenced or distracted by entertaining tweets (such as tweets generated by "Selected Joke"). From serious news-related information to entertaining tweets, the general microblog users do have a wide range of interest in this new medium. However wide the range of interest can be, different users will have different focus. For those who are more attentive to news-related issues, it will be of significant importance to single out the news-related tweets from the general tweets for them. Here are some answers by the interviewees to the question "What kind of news you concerned the most in microblog?"

[@codingBreak]Domestic news, Li Shuangjiang (whose son drived a BMW, and fighted with an Audi driver days before we made the interview), and anything related to finance.

[@cnmpeach]Financial, political, and people livelihood's news.

[@mapleapple059]Tweets generated by my friend, which record their lives and something happened in specific area and time, which will not publish on any papers and magazines.

[@Hermione777] Entertainment news

[@Sophormore]Something happened around me; such as "@At Xi'an" may publish something happened around me.

Anyway, it shows news can be generalized in micro-blog-sphere. In the next part, we will summarize the opinions from our interviewees and re-defined "news" by several rules in a plausible and statistical way.

3.3. Rule 1: Tweets Hitting the Hourly Trends Provided by Sina are Likely to be Lews

Rule1 is naturally acknowledged according to traditional definition of news. Many people are concerning about finance news and political news every day, and can be easily found through the trend words provided by Sina weibo microblog. While Phelan using twitter to recommend RSS news in(Phelan, et al., 2011a, 2011b), here we are using some hot words, no matter who provided

them at this stage, to recommend tweets with relevance to news. This rule can be generalized when put into practice, such as absorbing some words provided by any other forums or RSS feeds.

3.4. Rule 2: Tweets Generated by Verified-Organizational Users and Unverified-Personal Users are Likely to be News, while Tweets generated by SU and FU may not talk about news

As (Java, et al., 2007) mentioned, a single user may have multiple intentions or may even serve different roles in different communities. We knew that people used microblog not only for news, but also for fun. The following parts showed people may follow someone who has little relevance with news, and seldom un-follow someone. According to the answer from our interviewees, over 70% of them are suffered from spam tweets. It means some account generated non-news-worthy tweets frequently. So considering that as the third-party microblog client, we can't check the group information of a user directly through Sina weibo API, it's not feasible for us to select representative tweets facing such unordered and clustered tweets.

However, when asked about why they follow the funny tweets generator, some of the answers may be representative: "they are funny sometimes", "they have so many followers" and "I followed it when I created my account". What may be interesting is the funny tweets generator, unfortunately, have a large amount of followers, and retweeted by others all over constantly. According to the data we crawled, as it was shown in Figure 3, the top 10 tweets generators generated many tweets and all of them have a large amount of followers.

As we mining the user profiles of the account appeared in Figure 3, we noticed that all of the so-called "funny makers" are not verified by Sina. However, it may not be perfect, we cannot simply acclaim that people who are verified tend to

Figure 3. Users of posting most tweets in a week

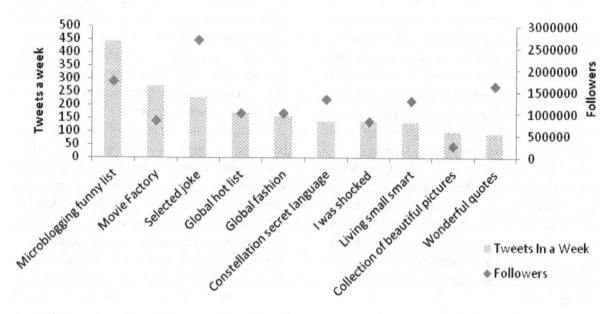

send news, since most of the users' friends are un-verified too. We have to introduce another parameter "frequency" to make our prediction more accurate.

We picked 150 users from our database to give an illustrative example, who are the friends of three different users, and classified them into four groups manually, as it is shown in Figure 4.

- **The First Group:** Verified organizational user, such as "China Daily" "New Weekly". We called them OU (Organizational User).

- **The Second Group:** Verified personal user, and they are stars such as "Ellen Degenerous" "Li Kaifu". We called them SU (Stars user). They are verified and personal users.

- **The Third Group:** Unverified personal user, typically they are our friends in daily life. We called them GU (General User).

- **The Fourth Group:** Unverified organizational user, typically they are users like "cold jokes"" Funny ranking". We called them FU (Funny User).

Figure 4. Illustrative example of user classification

	Organizational	Personal
Verified	China Daily	Stars in specific area (Ellen DeGeneres)
Unverified	Jokes, Funny Accounts	Friends (Common Interests or Classmates)

And we are going to demonstrate that, the Verified-Organizational user (OU) and the Unverified-Personal user (GU) are more likely to post "news" according to our generalized definition. Interviewees are then asked to judge who is likely to send news given these four types of users and their tweets respectively in our judge system (Figure 5). The result shows in Figure 6 that people are much more likely to prefer GU and OU.

So the rest of our work is to find the criterion for discriminating different user types. As we known verified users (OU and SU) and unverified user (GU and FU) can be easily clarified by taking a glance at their profiles to see whether they are verified. The most challenging work is to discriminate the personal users from the organizational ones.

We are going to distinguish the personal user from the organizational user by using behavior analysis. We have known that verified users may be different from the unverified ones when considering their behavior. However, at this stage we just assume that they have a same behavioral pattern and we just keep an eye on verified user to build our classifier. After we have built a qualified classifier, we will evaluate the performance of this classifier to see whether it performs well also for the unverified users.

Obviously, for the sake of studying users' behavior, we shall lay down a premise, which is that users do behave on the microblog. Here we eliminate the users who sent less than five original tweets during Aug 20th 2011 to Sep 20th 2011. Moreover, according to the policy of Sina (C. Sina, 2012), the user type should be between 0 and 7, while 0 represents a personal user and 1 to 7 represents different kinds of organizational users respectively. So it is reasonable for us to delete the user with a user type value of number lower than 0 or higher than 7, which may be caused by the system error. After that, we get 130809 users, 38811 of them are organizational users and 91998

Figure 5. "More likely to post news" judging system

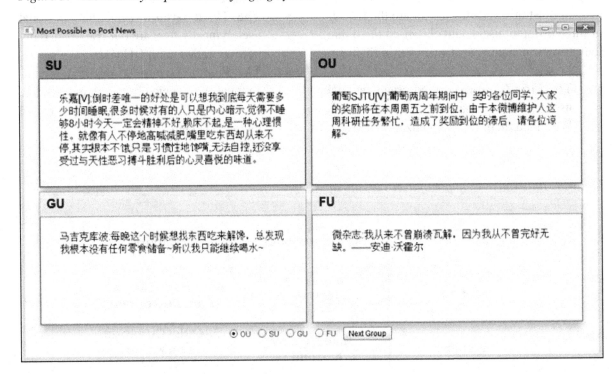

Figure 6. Result of the news judging system

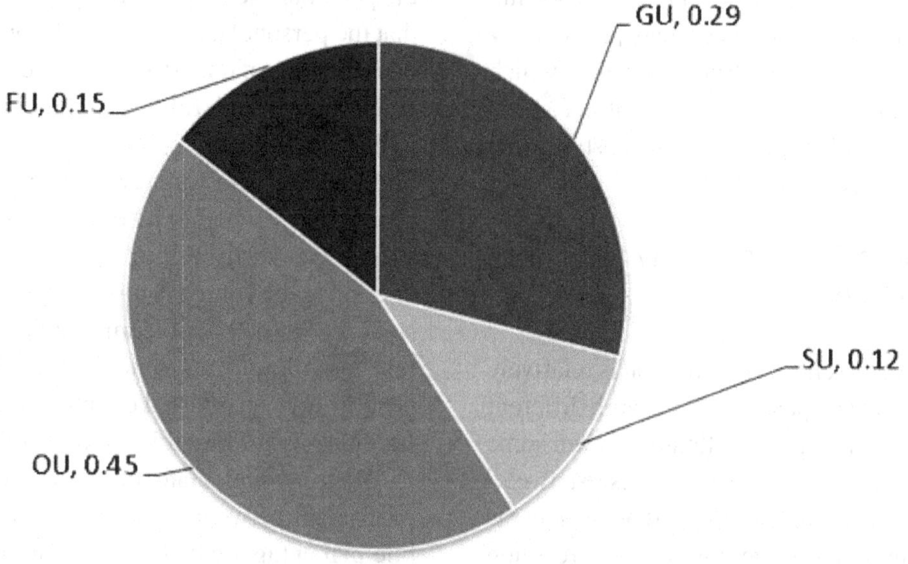

are personal ones. In our database, we use 0 to represent the personal user and 1 to represent the organizational user.

So we are going to mine the behavior a user performed. A user posts a tweet in a specific time, with a specific client, with some others being mentioned in his tweet, with or without a picture or a hyperlink, with certain number of characters. All these factors ought to be taken into consideration.

3.4.1. Posting Time Variety for Microblog Users

To measure some factors related to time by a value is not so eloquent sometimes, since most of the time series mining takes time series as a vector. From the aspect of information theory, it would lead to some kind of information loss. However, we still find some time-related parameter that is highly tied to the user's type. We define the earliest-tweet-time as the time, which calculated by minutes after the beginning of the day tweet in a day. We tend to think the organizational users are much more likely to have a close earliest-tweet-time, and it turns out to be right.

To address this issue statistically, first we sample from the whole dataset, and get 5000 organizational users and 5000 personal users, and all of them post over five original tweets during Aug 20th 2011 and Sep 20th 2011. Noted that this is the dataset we used to perform the statistical analysis in the following steps.

The Pearson correlation coefficient (usually being denoted by r) between user type and the standard deviation of earliest-tweet-time is -0.545(Table 2), which can be realized by the organizational users having a lower standard de-

Table 2. Pearson r and significance

	Pearson R
Avg. Content Length	0.513**
Mobile Percentage	-0.530**
Media Percentage	0.297**
Original Percentage	0.406**
Tweets Similarity	-0.444**
Std. Dev. Of Earliest-Tweet Time	-0.545**
**: Statistically significant at 0.01 level *: Statistically significant at 0.05 level	

viation of earliest-tweet-time. However, there are so many information we can get from the posting time, and what we do at this stage is just to show some character of posting time by a value, which can be recognized by a conventional classifier. We are going to learn more about posting time in Time-Series section.

3.4.2. Mobile Devices Variety for Microblog Service

When it comes to client, the situation is relatively diverse. People can post tweets through different clients, such as web page, cellphones, even some third party clients., For personal users, tweet-posting robots are seldom adopted as a client, as mobile client is more preferable, and we are going to justify that.

We select out the clients people used to post over 1000 tweets, and the number of tweets posted by personal and organizational users through respective clients. The o/p value is calculated by dividing the number of the organizational users' tweets posting using the specific client by that of the personal ones'. So a higher o/p value means this client is more possible being used by an organization while the higher p/o value denotes the personal users prefer the specific client. Note that the personal users surpass the organizational ones in terms of quantity. It can be easily deduced from Table 3 and Table 4 that they are inclined to different clients.

From the data we crawled from the API, we cannot know whether a certain client is a robot, but we can easily figure whether it is a mobile one, since the source is provided in the form like '<a href=http://weibo.com/mobile/android.php\ rel="nofollow" />', which shows this tweet is post through an android cellphone, the key word 'mobile' shows that it is a mobile client.

Then we calculate the Pearson correlation coefficient between user type(0, 1) and the mobile percentage, which means the probability of people posting tweets by their mobile devices like cellphones, panel computers, and the value is -0.530(Table 2), which means a personal user is much more possible to use a mobile device to send his tweet. Moreover, we can find that the mobile percentages of two groups are statistically significant under the independent sample T-test.

We can see that some tweeting robots are welcome by the organizational users, because they

Table 3. More preferred clients by organizational users

Client Name	O/P	# of o's Tweets	# of p's Tweets
Scheduled showone	20.09325	47621	2370
Time Machine	17.69568	72977	4124
Regular V	16.22798	33527	2066
Sina Pro. Edition	11.35509	316939	19105
Non-approved App.	6.654264	38628	5805
Micro-broad Com.	6.522362	41417	6350
Jigsaw puzzle game	6.211209	16292	2623
Pipi Time Machine	6.141289	303785	49466
Add Share Button	4.041834	10048	2486
Share Button	3.863474	58238	15074
P for personal user and O for organizational user			

Table 4. More preferred clients by personal users

Client Name	P/O	# of p's Tweets	# of o's Tweets
iPhone Client	20.05026	1838950	91717
Weico.iPhone	17.35376	173902	10021
S60 Client	14.93588	165863	11105
iPad Client	13.47001	273266	220287
Sina Mobile	13.19881	131381	9954
Motorola Smartphone	10.82	32460	3000
Android Client	10.72478	470689	43888
UCWeb	10.54042	71190	6754
Nokia 5230	9.023962	11298	1252
HTC Client	7.407672	16608	2242
P for personal user and O for organizational user			

would like to save their efforts in managing their microblog. However, the personal ones are more willing to use a mobile client.

3.4.3. Content Variety in Tweets

Generally speaking, the microblog limits each tweet's length to 140 characters, but it is obvious that a personal user would not like to type too many words on their mobile devices without a keyboard. We can see that the Pearson correlation coefficient between user type and the average content's length is quite high(0.513) from Table 2, which means an organizational user are more inclined to post a longer tweet.

As we know, people produced tweets in two ways. One is to create an original tweet, the other is to retweet the tweet made by others. We define 'original percentage' by the value of number of original tweets dividing the number of all the tweets he posts. A higher original percentage means the users are more inclined to post tweets originally. From Table 2 we can see the organizational user is more likely to make its own tweets(with r=0.406).

The third issue should be discussed about the content is the similarity between the tweets. We define similarity by the length of Longest Common Subsequence(LCS) of two tweets of the same user, i.e., if there are two tweets, '#Weather#sunny' and '#Weather#cloudy' respectively, their length of LCS is 11(by calculating the characters not the words). We tend to believe that some organizations post tweet in similar formats. Here we just take LCS as a way to measure the similarity of different tweets, it is simple and come out with a Pearson r value of 0.444(Table 2), which means the organizational users are posting 'similar' tweets exactly as we anticipated.

Most microblogs allow the user to post tweets with some media elements, such as hyper-links, pictures, or videos. We define such tweets as media tweets. At first we think the organizational users are more likely to send media tweets, however, it does not come out exactly as what we think. The r value is 0.297(Table 2), which means the organizational users are a little more likely to post media tweets. Considering that we restrict our attention solely to the verified users, this result is comprehensible.

Though not all the Pearson correlation coefficient values are high, all the parameters taken into consideration should be significant under independent sample T-test.

3.4.4. Co-Mention Behavior in Sina Weibo Microblog

As we know, people can mention someone in his tweet, but not all the mention behaviors are needed. For example, as it is shown in Figure 7 in Sina weibo microblog, A retweets C, C retweets E, E retweets F and F retweets G. However, in A's tweet, A is forced to mention C, D, E, F, G and H, who he may not know. So we try to find the one who people mention spontaneously. Here G mentioned C, F, H, and that is one of what we want. Moreover, we can use regular expressions to match the user before a double slash, and then we can find that A mentioned B and C mentioned D spontaneously. That is the other thing of what we want.

We primarily think that people of the same type would likely to mention each other, which means we tend to think A and B are of the same type. However, it turns out that we are wrong. Personal user would also like to mention the organizational one who shares the same interests. Moreover, many people mention accounts like 'Yangzi Evening' to report an event or incident happen in their daily life, and it is not a rare case. Then we try to focus on the people being mentioned simultaneously, as C, F and H in the example (Figure 7). A subtle relation behind this behavior is, if people mention two or more others in his tweet, the mentioned ones are highly related, meaning they possibly belong to the same community, share the same interest, and engage in the same professional realm. Noted that this is a really strict criterion, because most of the time, people would not mention over two others in one tweet. We got 600621 tweets that mentioned others spontaneously, however, only 133762 of them mentioned over one person at a time. Statistically speaking, if we use a tuple to represent two users ever being co-mentioned, we have 460555 tuples and only 77771(16.9%) of them are of two different types' users.

However, considering that we are discussing the type of user C, C is co-mentioned with user F and H. Though we have the priori knowledge that people are likely to be co-mentioned with the same type of the users, we do not know the type of user F and H at this stage. Fortunately, linear classifier provides the predict probability together with the predict value, and we can calculate how many of the co-mentioned users are personal ones approximately. Furthermore, we can predict the type of the user. For example, again we are trying to predict the type of user C who co-mentioned with F and H. F has the probability to be personal users

Figure 7. Co-mention example

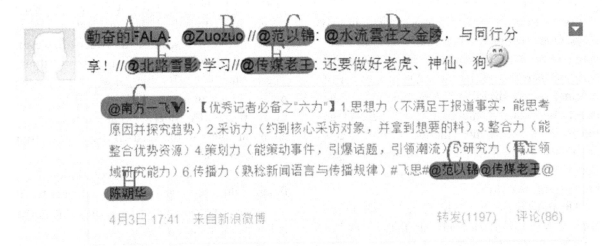

of p_f. H has the probability to be organizational user of ph. So we calculate that C co-occur with p_f personal users and p_h organizational users. Then we put them in another classifier together with the predict type and predict probability of the user C provided by the classifier in the previous section.

3.4.5. Bi-Relation

Bi-relation describes the reciprocated relation between two users. First we reckon that it is more likely to establish a reciprocated relationship between two users of same type. A personal user tends to build a reciprocated relation with another personal user according to Table 5, but considering that the number of the personal users is significantly larger than the organizational one, there is still a lot of work we should do to clarify the fact in the bi-relation.

We are going to prove that the organizational-bi-relation percentage, which means the proportion of organizational bi-relation in all his bi-relations, is statistically significant under independent sample T-test. There are 10000 users of each type and we calculate their organizational-bi-relation percentage. Clearly, they have a quite difference in average organizational-bi-relation-percentage(Table 6), and they are statistically significant.

3.4.6. Time-Series Pattern Detecting

We believe that people would like to post tweets in a specific period of time during a day. For example, since organizational users' tweets are posted by their

Table 5. Homogeneous bi-relation

Homogeneous Bi-Relation		Heterogeneous Bi-Relation
P-P Bi-Relation	O-O Bi-Relation	
6345581	1099674	1690302(18.5%)
P-P bi-relation: Bi-relation between personal users *O-O bi-relation: Bi-relation between organizational users*		

Table 6. Organizational-bi-relation-percentage of different users' type

	N	Mean
Personal User	10000	0.1164**
Organizational User	10000	0.5426**
**: Statistically significant at 0.01 level		

own staff, it is natural to suppose organizational users post the tweets during work time.

We calculate the number of tweets people sent in each hour of the day, then we get a vector of 24 dimensions, we called it posting-time-vector. The value in the first dimension represents the number of all the tweets a user post in 0 to 1 in the morning during a month. The rest of the problem is to classify the vectors we extract from the tweets post by users. (Yang & Leskovec, 2011)provides an efficient clustering method called K-Spectral Centroid(KSC) algorithm to cluster the time series, which is invariant to scaling and shifting, and outperforms K-means clustering algorithm in finding distinct shapes of time series.

But we still have to do a lot before we put this algorithm into use. Since we are trying to find out the feature of two types of users posting tweets in a day, we should make it sensitive to time shifting. For example, as it is shown in Figure 8, there are two users and one of them posts tweets only in 10 o'clock in the morning, the other only posts in the 3 o'clock in the afternoon. In the original K-SC algorithm, these two time series can be clustered into one cluster, while in our research, they should be treated differently.

We are starting to uncover the latent character of posting time of users. We enumerate 13000 users and 6500 of each type, and building their posting-time vector. Also we eliminate the users who post less than five tweets during Aug 20th 2011 to Sep 20th 2011 to make the result more perceivable. According to the findings in (Yang & Leskovec, 2011), we set the number of clusters to be 6.

Figure 8. Time series sampling

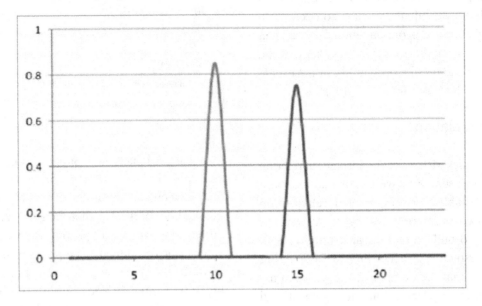

By Figure 10 we find that the organizational users are more likely to be the temporal pattern of 3,4,5,6 according to Figure 9. These four types of temporal pattern share the character that they seldom post tweets after eight o'clock in the eve-ning. It can be illuminated by the fact that it is the off work time. On the contrary, personal users would not stop posting tweets until one o'clock in the morning. The patterns of the specific time series are shown in Figure 9. We also find that a

Figure 9. Six time series patterns

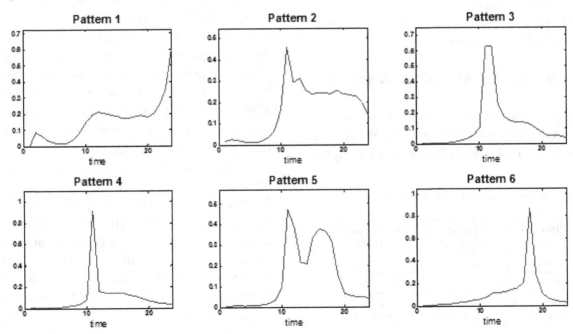

Figure 10 Users' aggregation of six time series patterns

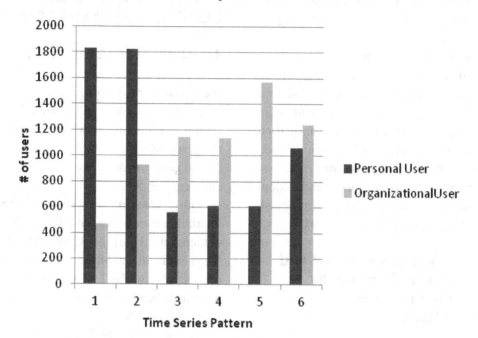

large number of organizational users belonging to the fifth pattern, which really confirms the assumption that they post tweets mostly during the work time. The third, fourth, and the sixth pattern can be illustrated by the fact that they like to post tweets in a certain time of a day.

First we should build features for every user. And the user's features of co-mention, bi-relation and time series of the specific user is descripted in detail above. As For algorithm of classification, actually, once we find enough and right parameters for the classifiers, the two types of users are separated naturally. We take standard deviation of the average content length, mobile percentage, media percentage, original tweets percentage, tweets similarity and standard deviation of earliest-tweet time of the user as the input parameters of the classifier. Then this classifier output the predicted user type and probability of the prediction. Once the probability is lower than 0.8 (we found most of the bad cases located in the probability range from 0.5 to 0.8), we fixed the prediction by considering the users co-mentioned with

them, the users built bi-relations with them, and also their time series patterns. The algorithm for the classifier is not even an essential factor because we found the accuracy floats slightly when we change the algorithm to Naive Bayes, Decision Tree or Logistic Regression. And below we will evaluate the result of the algorithm of logistic regression.

Another factor we should control is how many cases are used to train the classifier. Without loss of generality, we use 15% of the whole dataset for training, and all of the cases are used to evaluate. The ratio of precision and recall is shown in Table 7. The algorithm of logistic regression finally achieved an overall accuracy of 87.2%.

Table 7. Classifier evaluation

	PU(Actual)	**OU(Actual)**
PU(Predicted)	89.38%(82227)	*17.96(9771)*
OU(Predicted)	10.62%(6971)	*82.04%(31840)*
PU: Personal User OU: Organizational User		

So we have a classifier to determine whether a verified user is a organizational one or a personal one. Then we labeled over 5000 unverified users. Even though there are much more personal users than organizational users, we put 500 users of each type in the evaluating set. Then we found our classifier performs well and achieve an accuracy of 85.7%, which means the unverified users are not totally different from the verified users. And when we focus on the "bad case", we found that they are mostly spam users and seldom users follow them. After that we can distinguish the personal users and the organizational users.

3.5. Rule 3: Tweets Retweeted and Commented with Significantly Abnormal Frequency are Likely to be News

Rule 3 considers anomalous tweets. We asked our interviewees what are the possible reasons for a tweet being retweeted and commented much more times than the normal situation. The result can be summarized as follows by the interviews we conducted: 1. It is a piece of really shocking news. 2. Important changes in his friends. 3. It is really funny. 4. There is some prize if the tweet is retweeted.

Actually the first and the second situation is what the news we need. The third one can be eliminated by the previous work since it is usually sent by FU we have mentioned above. The fourth one is a phenomena in China. Vice president of a electronic products supplier sent a tweet to say "the one who retweet this tweet the most in five days can won a iPhone4S" in Oct, 16th, 2011 (Wenxiang, 2011), and this tweet was retweeted 148234 times finally. And this phenomena is even really common in micro-blog-sphere, since many corporation take microblog as a platform for marketing. We tend to think this kind of information, once retweeted abnormally, may be helpful for the account owner, while it was retweet and comment in a regular way, it can be eliminated when considering news.

4. NEWS RECOMMENDING SYSTEM DESIGN AND EVALUATION

4.1. Dataset for Evaluation

We should crawl some data to evaluate the performance of our algorithm. However we should not simply crawl the latest tweets of the given user when he logged on, for that the newly generate ones are not what we mainly concerned about.

Thirty-seven interviewees who use Sina weibo microblog over a year have shown that, only one of them said "I will check over 10 pages of tweets when I am really at leisure.", the average number of pages reviewed is 2.94, which is the first reason we crawl the tweets after the third page for the input of our system.

Though the research on twitter has shown that over sixty percent of the tweets are retweeted in 24 hours (86400 seconds), we still do some statistical analysis based on the data we crawled on Sina weibo microblog. 4962183 times of retweet and 4125198 comments have shown that the situation is quite the same in China. Half of the comments and retweet happened in twelve hours after the tweet sent. Since we have taken the retweet and comment count as parameters in our algorithm, and newly generated tweets have not been commented and retweeted completely, it is reasonable for us to observe the tweets generated twelve hours ago, which as Figure 11 shows, over half of the tweets are retweeted and commented completely. Our system crawled the tweets which are in accord with two criterions we listed above.

4.2. News Recommending System Architecture Design

The system architecture is shown in Figure 12. It crawl tweets and user profiles provided by Sina weibo microblog, and gets some trend words from a specific information source. Here we simply use

Figure 11. Time difference cumulative distribution function

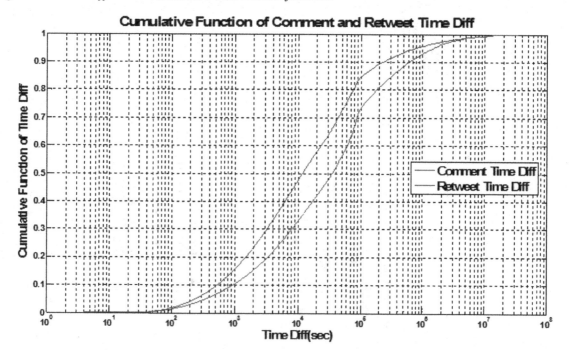

the trend words provided by Sina weibo microblog. Then we build a preference graph from the tweets and the user profiles.

We build a preference graph to rank the tweets. Here preference means, if there is an edge from Node A to Node B, B is more preferable than A. All the nodes in the preference graph represent the tweet. Then we will illustrate how we insert edges in the graph.

4.2.1. Add Trend Hitting Edge

Sina weibo microblog provide about 50 trend words a day, but according to (Kwak, et al., 2010) not all the trends should be considered as news and they can be classified into four classes (exogenous critical, exogenous subcritical, endogenous critical and endogenous subcritical).

We also crawled all the trends on Weibo.com from 2011 Aug 20th to 2011 Sep 20th. 150 topics are taken into consideration because they contain over 10000 tweets. We defined 'active period' exactly the same as (Kwak, et al., 2010), which no tweets on the topic in 24 hours means the topic

is inactive. Figure 13 shows situation is quite the same as twitter. Most of the topics have less than 2 active periods. When considered the duration of a topic in Figure 14, most of the topics (50%) cumulate 50% of the tweets in 3 days.

Since we cannot got a panorama view of a topic, i.e., we cannot know whether a topic is a news-worthy one or not during the active period of a topic, we regard a topic as a news – worthy one when it is in its first active period. We add these news-worthy words to our dictionary, create Lucence index(Apache) by using ICTCLAS(ICTCLAS, 2011) as the tokenizer for the tweets we need to rank. Finally we query the index with the trend words, and got a set Q of tweets which hit the trend word by a relatively high score over the value of ε. Then we add edge weights α from the tweets not in Q to the one in Q.

4.2.2. Add the User Preference Edge

We have previously demonstrated that user profiles have certain relevance with their tweets news

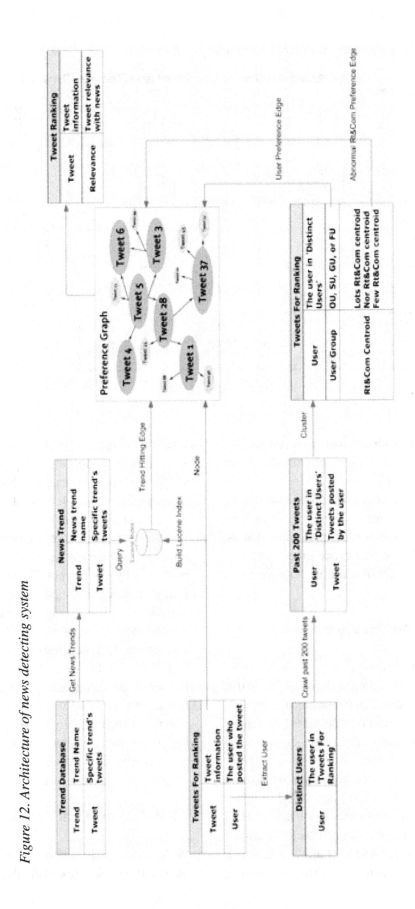

Figure 12. Architecture of news detecting system

Figure 13. Active period cumulative distribution function

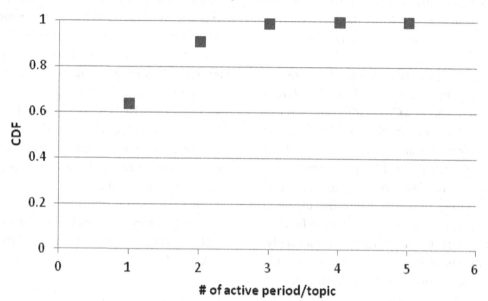

Figure 14. Topics complementary cumulative distribution function

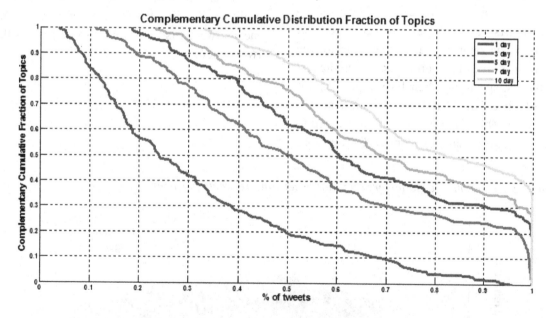

value. Based on the statistical analysis we have done, we can put the users into four sets: OU, SU, GU and FU. We got the tweets sender's last 200 tweets and user profiles to get the information we need. Finally we establish edges weight β from set $\{OU, GU\}$ to set $\{SU, FU\}$.

4.2.3. Add Abnormal Retweet and Comment Preference Edge

In this part we are going to discriminate a tweet is a normally Com&RT one or an abnormally one. According to some previous work our team have done in (Wu & Wang, 2011) and have shown in Figure 15, generally speaking, the more followers a user has, the more tweets and retweets he generates.

The first thing we have to is to cluster users' tweets into three classes, LotsCom&RT, NorCom&RT, and FewCom&RT. Here we use KMeans++ (Arthur & Vassilvitskii, 2007) as our clustering algorithm and cluster the microblog into three types list above. The specific tweet can be assigned to one cluster by calculating the Euclidean distance from the centroids of three clusters. The minimum distance one can be chosen as the specific tweet belongs to. Additionally, if the centroids of the clusters are not significantly diverse, we treated the two clusters as one.

However, how many tweets can decide the centroid of the three clusters? We have got last 200 posts by the specific users, but 200 is too much for clustering. We conduct our experiments by first randomly selecting 20 tweets out of 200 tweets sample to do a clustering for the OU, SU and GU, FU. Then we examined the rest 180 tweets, specifying their level types according to their counts of retweet or comment. We found over 90% of the tweet can be assigned to the NorCom&RT and FewCom&RT groups. To further confirm the LotsCom&RT ones are exactly the news, we picked out those anomalous tweets and showed them to people asking their opinion on whether they are news. In the survey, people had three choices: news, non-news, not sure. At last, we obtained a desirable result—over 80% of the "LotsCom&Re" tweets are judged to be news.

So 20 tweets Com&RT count is enough for clustering. We generate edges weight γ from the NorCom&RT and FewCom&RT groups to the LotsCom&RT group.

Here α, β, $\gamma > 0$. If the edge already exists, we are simply emerging them by plus two weights.

So the edge weight of tweet i and tweet j can be denoted as

$$\phi(i, j) = weight(i, j).$$

Preference function $P(i, j)$ shows the probability of jumping from tweet i to tweet j, which means tweet j is more likely to be a news than tweet i here.

$$P(i, j) = P(j \mid i) = \frac{e^{\phi(i,j)}}{\sum_{j=0}^{status\_size} e^{\phi(i,j)}} \quad (1)$$

Figure 15. The number of followers and that tweets and retweets per user

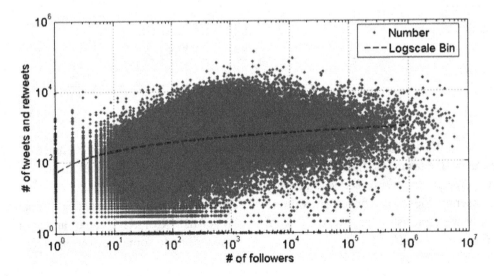

Performing EigenRank (N. N. Liu & Yang, 2008) and get the score of each tweet.

4.3. Evaluation

Ten users are selected from the 37 interviewees to evaluate the performance of our system. They are 23 years old on average, of 4 different professional backgrounds, coming from 8 different cities. We called the API and got 100 their tweets sent 12 hours ago, to see whether our agorithm performed well in different microblog account.

We simply set ε, which is the criterion to determine whether a tweet hit a trend word to be 0.5 and set the edge weight:

$$\alpha = 1, \beta = 0.8, \gamma = 0.8,$$

which are the probability of being news of each rule as what we have mentioned during the proof of the rules. To add abnormal retweet and comment preference edge, two clusters can be considered to be significantly diverse when the centroid points are 10 units apart.

First of all, we asked ten users to manually select the news from the 100 tweets. There are 37 tweets considered to be news on average, which also shows news is a big part of microblog but other information exist. Then we rank the tweets by different strategy, to see how different rules performed.

We evaluated different strategy by calculating the average news ranking. For instance, there is 3 pieces of news in all the tweets, they are in the first, second, and the fourth place by applying specific rules. The average ranking of news is (1+2+4)/3=2.3. So the lower value of average ranking denotes a better performance.

We can see when applying an single rule to our system, the rule defining by the relationship of user type and news relevance seems to perform well. However, the hot word hitting rule did not work well for a variety of reasons. One is that

there are not so many big news during we crawled the test set. But notice that once hit, the tweet is probably a piece of news. Another reason is exactly what we know microblog is not only publishing the news spreading all over the internet, but also news around us, which will not hit the trend words.

Figure 16 and Figure 17 shows when combining more and more rules, we can get a better and better result. We do not need to change the value of the parameters we used to achieved a much better result since it would lead to over fitting. We think we have found the answer.

5. DISCUSSION

As microblog has becoming more and more popular in China, an important task is to detecting useful information for the users. In this article we found most of the user easily suffered from funny maker since people seldom un-follow someone in China, and lost in the tweets they have generated. Since we found most of the users did not check the tweets over five pages, we have to find the useful information hidden by various tweets.

We re-defined the "news" to make it more precisely to meet the microblog users' demands based on the user survey. We successfully classified the user into four types, and we found the OU and GU seem to be welcomed when considering news. We found the abnormally RT&Com tweets tend to be news and have proved that. At last, we proposed to use EigenRank to rank the tweets according to their relevance to news, and it performs well.

Anyone who used microblog for several motivations can be benefit from our idea since they may follow some spam maker for fun but want some useful information sometimes. And it is meaningful for the third-party client because they cannot access the user groups' information by API provided by Sina weibo microblog, and

Figure 16. Single rule performance

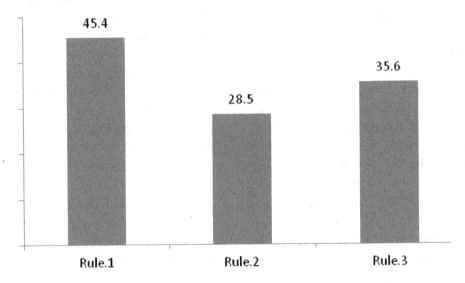

Figure 17. Combined rule performance

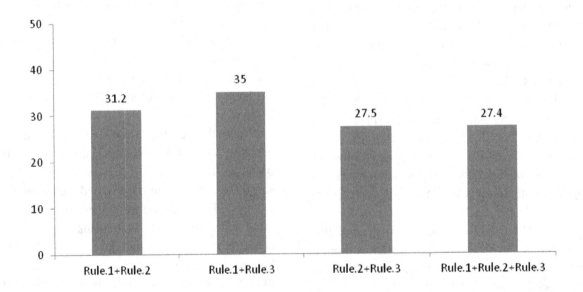

our algorithm just takes a few API callings. Some official organization will be benefit from our ideas to supervise what is going on in social network.

6. FUTURE WORK

By absorbing more precisely trend information we can get a better result. Moreover, if some sensors, like geo-location sensors are concerned, we can provide news with more relevance to location and meet more users' demands.

This is also some fundamental works for combining microblog, such a new media, with the traditional ones, such as TV and newspaper. The user modeling can also be used for spam user detecting, which is now becoming an increasingly serious problem for microblog.

ACKNOWLEDGMENT

This work was supported by the National Natural Science Foundation of China under Grant No.61073132 and 60776796; the Fundamental Research Funds for the Central Universities(101gpy33). Project 985 of Innovation Base for Journalism & Communication in the All-media Era, Sun Yat-sen University.

REFERENCES

Abdullah, S., & Wu, X. (2011). *An epidemic model for news spreading on Twitter*. Paper presented at the 23rd IEEE International Conference on Tools with Artificial Intelligence (ICTAI). New York, NY.

Apache. (2011). Retrieved from http://lucene.apache.org/

Arthur, D., & Vassilvitskii, S. (2007). *k-means++: The advantages of careful seeding*. Paper presented at the Proceedings of the Eighteenth Annual ACM-SIAM Symposium on Discrete Algorithms. New Orleans, LA.

Chen, J., Nairn, R., & Chi, E. (2011). *Speak little and well: Recommending conversations in online social streams*. Paper presented at the 2011 Annual Conference on Human Factors in Computing Systems. Vancouver, Canada. Retrieved from http://delivery.acm.org/10.1145/1980000/1978974/p217-chen.pdf?ip=113.108.133.51&CFID=42910813&CFTOKEN=50591669&__acm__=1316163901_3767d771ad065df8fe264f6de95d3a86

Guangxia, L., Hoi, S. C. H., Kuiyu, C., & Jain, R. (2010). *Micro-blogging sentiment detection by collaborative online learning*. Paper presented at the IEEE 10th International Conference on Data Mining (ICDM). New York, NY.

Jansen, B. J., Zhang, M., Sobel, K., & Chowdury, A. (2009). *Micro-blogging as online word of mouth branding*. Paper presented at the 27th International Conference Extended Abstracts on Human Factors in Computing Systems. Boston, MA. Retrieved from http://delivery.acm.org/10.1145/1530000/1520584/p3859-jansen.pdf?ip=113.108.133.51&CFID=42910813&CFTOKEN=50591669&__acm__=1316163961_848c3027a27643d729bec83158268224

Java, A., Song, X., Finin, T., & Tseng, B. (2007). *Why we Twitter: Understanding microblogging usage and communities*. Paper presented at the 9th WebKDD and 1st SNA-KDD 2007 Workshop on Web Mining and Social Network Analysis. San Jose, CA. Retrieved from http://delivery.acm.org/10.1145/1350000/1348556/p56-java.pdf?ip=113.108.133.51&CFID=38952822&CFTOKEN=89830532&__acm__=1315551300_38027b7e271e7a280970363cfd9dda70

Kwak, H., Lee, C., Park, H., & Moon, S. (2010). *What is Twitter, a social network or a news media?* Paper presented at the 19th International Conference on World Wide Web. Raleigh, NC. Retrieved from http://delivery.acm.org/10.1145/1780000/1772751/p591-kwak.pdf?ip=113.108.133.51&CFID=38952822&CFTOKEN=89830532&__acm__=1315549530_23d2d00b7553aebef4b6f8a5bb558ca4

Liu, N. N., & Yang, Q. (2008). *EigenRank: A ranking-oriented approach to collaborative filtering.* Paper presented at the 31st Annual International ACM SIGIR Conference on Research and Development in Information Retrieval. Singapore, Singapore. Retrieved from http://delivery.acm.org/10.1145/1400000/1390351/p83-liu.pdf?ip=113.108.133.48&acc=ACTIVE%20SERVICE&CFID=71306793&CFTOKEN=37355947&__acm__=1322880131_a2e-706ca2aeadef579437ac5c5a68771

Liu, Z., Yu, W., Chen, W., Wang, S., & Wu, F. (2010). *Short text feature selection for micro-blog mining.* Paper presented at the 2010 International Conference on Computational Intelligence and Software Engineering (CiSE). New York, NY.

Magnani, M., Montesi, D., & Rossi, L. (2010). *Friendfeed breaking news: Death of a public figure.* Paper presented at the IEEE Second International Conference on Social Computing (SocialCom). New York, NY.

Okazaki, M., & Matsuo, Y. (2010). *Semantic Twitter: Analyzing tweets for real-time event notification.* Paper presented at the 2008/2009 International Conference on Social Software: Recent Trends and Developments in Social Software. Cork, Ireland.

Phelan, O., McCarthy, K., Bennett, M., & Smyth, B. (2011a). *On using the real-time web for news recommendation &#38, discovery.* Paper presented at the 20th International Conference Companion on World Wide Web. Hyderabad, India. Retrieved from http://delivery.acm.org/10.1145/1970000/1963245/p103-phelan.pdf?ip=113.108.133.48&acc=ACTIVE%20SERVICE&CFID=55603221&CFTOKEN=33354824&__acm__=1322533158_61a344d4e4c752674fbe5b9f6139bfc6

Phelan, O., McCarthy, K., Bennett, M., & Smyth, B. (2011b). *Terms of a feather: Content-based news recommendation and discovery using Twitter.* Paper presented at the 33rd European Conference on Advances in Information Retrieval. Dublin, Ireland.

Phelan, O., McCarthy, K., & Smyth, B. (2009). *Using Twitter to recommend real-time topical news.* Paper presented at the Third ACM Conference on Recommender Systems. New York, NY. Retrieved from http://delivery.acm.org/10.1145/1640000/1639794/p385-phelan.pdf?ip=113.108.133.51&CFID=42910813&CFTOKEN=50591669&__acm__=1316163914_d2fb-c21a709a81ff8ad85e0ea37d5494

Qin, Z., Xin, M., & Niu, Z. (2010). *A content tendency judgment algorithm for micro-blog platform.* Paper presented at the 2010 IEEE International Conference on Intelligent Computing and Intelligent Systems (ICIS). New York, NY.

Sina. (2011). *Analysis for financial report of Sina in Q3 by Sina senior executives.* Retrieved from http://weibo.com/1800318967/xyuvFtm5z

Sina. (2012). *Get verified in Sina.* Retrieved from http://weibo.com/verify

Wenxiang, M. G. (2011). *Weibo*. Retrieved 12/2, 2011, from http://weibo.com/1649155730/xt1McBmP8

Wu, X., & Wang, J. (2011). *How about microblogging service in China: Analysis and mining on sina micro-blog*. Paper presented at the 1st International Symposium on From Digital Footprints to Social and Community Intelligence. Beijing, China. Retrieved from http://delivery.acm.org/10.1145/2040000/2030077/p37-wu.pdf?ip=113.108.133.48&acc=ACTIVE%20SERVICE&CFID=61317438&CFTOKEN=16074489&__acm__=1326088101_47810c63c0137404d8980674ad9b0aaa

Yang, J., & Leskovec, J. (2011). *Patterns of temporal variation in online media*. Paper presented at the Fourth ACM International Conference on Web Search and Data Mining. Hong Kong, China. Retrieved from http://delivery.acm.org/10.1145/1940000/1935863/p177-yang.pdf?ip=113.108.133.61&acc=ACTIVE%20SERVICE&CFID=95705915&CFTOKEN=94098446&__acm__=1333615850_74c77faf846e64dc5a61a5204c01ba21

Zhao, D., & Rosson, M. B. (2009). *How and why people Twitter: The role that micro-blogging plays in informal communication at work*. Paper presented at the ACM 2009 International Conference on Supporting Group Work. Sanibel Island, FL. Retrieved from http://delivery.acm.org/10.1145/1540000/1531710/p243-zhao.pdf?ip=113.108.133.51&CFID=38952822&CFTOKEN=89830532&__acm__=1315556372_d00df-09cb3a1059eb969e7d06a22d660

Zhendong, D. Q. (2011). *How net knowledge database*. Retrieved from http://www.keenage.com/

Zitao, L., Wenchao, Y., Wei, C., Shuran, W., & Fengyi, W. (2010). *Short text feature selection for micro-blog mining*. Paper presented at the Computational Intelligence and Software Engineering (CiSE). New York, NY.

Zuo, Y., You, F., Wang, J., & Wu, X. (2012). *User modeling driven news filtering algorithm for microblog service in China*. Paper presented at the 2012 IEEE/ACIS 11th International Conference on Computer and Information Science (ICIS). Shanghai, China.

KEY TERMS AND DEFINITIONS

Bi-Relation: People can follow others on any kind of microblog service. Once two microblog users follow each other, they build a Bi-Relation.

Co-Mention: When people post a piece of tweet, they can mention others in the tweet. Once two microblog users mentioned in one piece of tweet, they are co-mentioned.

Organizational User: A microblog account that is organized by a certain organization, cooperation or group.

Personal User: A microblog account that is organized by a certain human being.

Sina Weibo Microblog: Most popular microblog service in China. People can post messages, make comments, and retweet whenever they want. People can also follow some others in order to keep track of who he has followed.

Tweet: A piece of message on Twitter.

Verified User: A user who has great on his field usually would be verified by microblog service provider.

Section 4
Urban Awareness

Chapter 11
Human Mobility Patterns

Ali Diab
Al-Baath University, Syria & Ilmenau University of Technology, Germany

Andreas Mitschele-Thiel
Ilmenau University of Technology, Germany

ABSTRACT

It is well accepted that the physical world itself, including communication networks, humans, and objects, is becoming a type of information system. Thus, to improve the experience of individuals, communities, organizations, and societies within such systems, a thorough comprehension of collective intelligence processes responsible for generating, handling, and controlling data is fundamental. One of the major aspects in this context and also the focus of this chapter is the development of novel methods to model human mobility patterns, which have myriad uses in crucial fields (e.g. mobile communication, urban planning, etc.). The chapter highlights the state of the art and provides a comprehensive investigation of current research efforts in this field. It classifies mobility models into synthetic, trace-based, and community-based models, and also provides insight into each category. That is, well-known approaches are presented, discussed, and qualitatively compared with each other.

1. INTRODUCTION

Ubiquitous access to information anywhere, anytime and anyhow is one of the main features of future communication networks which experience a tremendous development including a wide variety of new services and broadband applications. The Internet itself emerges towards what is today known as "the Internet of things",

which assumes that each object is embedded with sensors and is able to communicate (Ovidiu et al., 2009). In other words, the physical world itself including communication networks, humans and objects is becoming a type of an information system. Thus, to improve the experience of individuals, communities, organizations and societies within such systems, a thorough comprehension of collective intelligence processes responsible

DOI: 10.4018/978-1-4666-4695-7.ch011

of generating, handling and controlling those data is fundamental. One of the major aspects in this context is the development of novel methods to model human mobility patterns, which have myriad uses in crucial fields, e.g. mobile communication research, urban planning, ecology, epidemiology, etc. The authors in (Gonzalez, Hidalgo & Barabasi, 2008) state that human mobility patterns are far from being random. They show a high degree of temporal and spatial regularity, thus, follow simple reproducible patterns. So, faithfully reproduction of the movements of real people significantly helps in answering crucial questions necessary to improve the experience of individuals, organizations, etc. For instance, an accurate reproduction of how people move around a city can help to evaluate if the installation of a specific sensing application on mobile devices would be able to reach the desired coverage, see (Isaacman et al., 2012).

The modeling of how large as well as small populations move within small, medium and metropolitan areas is the goal that various human mobility modeling techniques tried to achieve. Many studies have shown that individuals tend to spend the majority of their time at few places, e.g. work offices, homes, etc., see (Gonzalez et al., 2008), (Isaacman et al., 2011) and (Song, Qu, Blumm & Barabási 2010). Keep in mind that the reproduction of human density over time at various geographic scales helps in addressing essential societal issues like the environmental impact of home-to-work commutes for instance. Furthermore, different geographic distributions of communities, commercial centers, companies, etc. heavily affect human mobility patterns, which are affected by, and also must be reflected in, various factors such as transportation infrastructures, plans for cities growth, etc. Previous efforts have reported significant differences between cities in terms of metrics such as commute distances, for instance, see (Isaacman et al., 2011a), (Isaacman et al., 2010) and (Noulas, Scellato, Lambiotte, Pontil & Mascolo, 2012).

Models of human mobility patterns are categorized into three categories, namely synthetic, trace-based and community-based models, see (Musolesi & Mascolo, 2009), (Camp, Boleng & Davies, 2002) and (Ranjan Roy, 2011). Synthetic models are mathematical ones trying to capture the patterns of human movements by means of a set of equations. The key idea of trace-based models is the exploitation of available measurements and traces achieved in deployed systems to reproduce synthetic traces characterized by the same statistical properties of real traces. Community-based modeling of human movements depends on the fact stating that mobile devices are usually carried by humans, which implies that movement patterns of such devices are necessarily related to human decisions and socialization behaviors. So, human movement routines heavily affect the overall movement patterns resulting, e.g. people move daily morning from their houses to their offices and come back at the afternoon for instance. One of the major contributions in this context is the application of the social network theory to generate more realistic human movement patterns, see (Musolesi & Mascolo, 2009).

The chapter highlights the state of art and provides a comprehensive investigation of current research efforts in the field of human movement patterns. It is organized as follows: section 2 discusses synthetic mobility models. It overviews well-known approaches and summarizes with a qualitative comparison. The trace-based modeling of human movement patterns is handled in section 3. Section 4 discusses the third category of mobility models, namely the community-based. Following that, the chapter concludes in section 5 with the main results.

2. SYNTHETIC MODELING OF HUMAN MOBILITY PATTERNS

Synthetic models are largely preferred and widely applied to simulate mobile communication networks (Musolesi & Mascolo, 2009). These models are categorized into synthetic single node mobility models and synthetic group mobility models (Camp et al., 2002). The first category assumes that each user is allowed to move freely without caring of other users, while the second assumes that movements of each user relate to the movements of a group of users. Users, thus, are not allowed to move freely. This paragraph provides an insight into both categories and overviews well-known synthetic mobility models along with their strengths and weaknesses. The described models of each category will also be qualitatively compared with each other. Furthermore, the paragraph investigates the modeling of obstacles inside mobility scenarios, since users are not allowed to move in all directions in the reality.

2.1. Synthetic Single Node Mobility Models

These models are also referred to as synthetic individual/entity mobility models in the literature. The movement of each individual Mobile Node (MN) is considered based on the MN's speed, MN's direction, MN's transition length/time between two consecutive positions and the distribution of MNs' locations. Keep in mind that the movements of individuals do not relate to each other, more details are provided in the following.

2.1.1. Random Walk (RW) Mobility Model

The RW mobility model relates to the Brownian motion first described by Einstein in 1926 (Sanchez & Manzoni, 2001). This model simply mimics the statement: many individuals move in nature in extremely unpredictable ways (Davies, 2000). The operation of the RW mobility model is pretty simple and can be described as follows: MNs are first distributed in the area based on a specific distribution model. Each MN moves, following that, from its current location to a new one, selected randomly applying a uniform distribution from

the range , with a speed also selected randomly from a specific speeds' range applying a uniform or Gaussian distribution. Note that each movement occurs, in principle, after either a constant time interval () or a constant distance () traveled. Note also that there are no pause times between movements. When a MN reaches an area boundary, it bounces off the boundary with a specific angel determined by the incoming direction and continues moving along this path.

The RW mobility model is simple from the mathematical point of view. It generates memoryless movement patterns (Basu, Redi & Shurbanov, 2004), which in turn may lead to an oscillatory-type trajectory (moving forward and backward), see (Zonoozi & Dassanayake, 1997). The randomness in selecting the next direction as well as speed renders this type of motion completely unrealistic and unpredictable (movement patterns with sudden stops, sudden accelerations, sharp turns, etc.).

Although the RW model is widely used, it is insufficient to capture temporal dependencies of velocities as well as directions of MNs since no relations between current and future speeds as well as directions. Spatial dependencies of velocities and directions of MNs are also not possible. Note that due to the physical constraints of MNs and the surrounding environment, the speed/direction of a MN may be influenced by and/or correlated with the speeds/directions of specific or neighbor MNs. Concerning the geographic restrictions of movements, the RW mobility model does not consider such restrictions. As known, MNs are not allowed to move in arbitrary directions in real-life scenarios. For pause times restrictions, the RW model does not allow MNs to pause between movements. Sure, this does not reflect real-life scenarios, where MNs stop in specific places and move again to other ones.

2.1.2. Random Waypoint (RWp) Mobility Model

The RWp mobility model (Bettstetter & Wagner, 2002) is widely used to generate mobility patterns for MNs, especially for ad hoc networks. The model is simple and straightforward stochastic, see (Bettstetter, Hartenstein & Pérez-Costa, 2003). Similar to the RW model, each MN moves from its current location to a new one by randomly selecting a new location and speed. However, the MN additionally and also randomly selects a pause time duration. Upon reaching the new location, the MN waits for the selected pause time duration and repeats, following that, the process again. So, MNs move in completely unpredictable ways. That is, MNs directions as well as speeds at any given time are random and independent of past directions and speeds. Pause times between movements are random as well, without dependency on previous pause times. This implies that the RWp model is also a memory-less model. The randomness results, on one side, in an oscillatory-type trajectory and, on the other side, in unrealistic movement patterns with sudden stops, sharp turns, etc. The study of the stochastic parameters of the RWp model has shown that MNs in the RWp model tend to move back to the middle of the simulation area, see (Ranjan Roy, 2011), (Aschenbruck, Gerhards-Padilla & Martini, 2008) and (Bettstetter & Wagner, 2002). This effect is known as the density wave effect and results in the clustering of MNs in one part of the simulation area. MNs, therefore, appear to converge, disappear and converge again, and so on.

In spite of the wide usage of the RWp model, it is incapable of capturing temporal and spatial dependencies of the velocity and the direction (Bai, Sadagopan & Helmy, 2003). There are also no geographic restrictions of movements.

2.1.3. Probabilistic Mobility Model

The probabilistic mobility model (Diab, 2010) is adequate for generating movement patterns for MNs moving within the coverage area of cellular communication networks. This model relies on the statement saying: MNs restrict, in reality, their movements from a specific location to a location in their geographical neighborhood. The probabilistic mobility model considers movements between different locations, movements within the same location are not of interest. The locations are first determined, which express the locations of the base stations serving cellular cells. Following that, the transition probabilities between these locations are defined. MNs move then based on the transition probabilities provided. These probabilities can even be calculated based on measurements from real mobile communication networks.

The model is simple from a mathematical point of view. It significantly helps in mathematically analyzing communication protocols, services, etc., since it provides the probabilities of residing at the locations in the steady-state of the system. The transition probabilities defined are not time-depended in the model. They can, however, be extended to adapt to changes of day times. Of course, the density of MNs at the locations with higher residing probabilities will be higher than at other locations having less residing probabilities. Note that the speed of the MN is not of interest for the model, since the important is where the MN moves, not with which speed. Therefore, this model is not adequate for ad hoc networks. Concerning the limitations of the model, it cannot express temporal and spatial dependencies of the velocity and the direction. There are also no geographic restrictions of movements and no pause times restrictions.

2.1.4. Markovian Random Walk (MRW) Mobility Model

The MRW mobility model (Bettstetter & Wagner, 2002), (Bellavista, Corradi & Magistretti, 2005) mimics the following statement: people tend to continue moving in a semi-constant forward direction. They rarely turn suddenly back and retrace their steps. Moreover, they never move randomly hoping that they wind up somewhere toward their destinations. The model introduces, therefore, a probabilities matrix to determine the next position

() of a MN at the next time step. MNs are initially distributed within the simulation area. After that, each MN determines its new coordinates at the next time step based on the probabilities matrix introduced. The MN's speed is fixed during the simulation. Note also that there are no pause times between movements. The principles, the MRW model follows, produce probabilistic rather than purely random movement patterns. In fact, an accurate definition of the probabilities matrix heavily influences the mobility patterns produced.

The MRW model suffers from some limitations since it is incapable of expressing temporal and spatial dependencies of the velocity. Keep in mind that MNs' velocities are constant. There are also no dependencies between the location of any MN and the locations of other MNs, i.e. no spatial dependency of the direction. Furthermore, there exist no mechanisms to determine geographic restrictions of movements, e.g. obstacles, streets, etc., and restrictions of pause times. Concerning the temporal dependency of the direction, one notes the existence of such dependency between future and current locations.

2.1.5. Boundless Simulation Area (BSA) Mobility Model

The BSA mobility model relies on the fact that neither the locations nor the speeds of MNs are random. Future velocities and locations relate somehow to current ones (Haas, 1997). The model can be briefly described as follows: MNs are initially distributed in the simulation area. Initial directions and velocities are selected randomly. Each MN defines, following that, a velocity vector , where v is the current MN's speed and q is its current location. The speed vector is updated after each time steps using specific equations, see (Haas, 1997), and so on. The MN that reaches an area boundary continues moving and appears on the opposite side of the simulation area. This creates a torus-shaped simulation area.

The BSA model is not a memory-less model, this prohibits sudden stops, sharp turns, etc. However, speeds and also locations remain not predictable. This makes it impossible to pre-define streets or regions with specific mobility characteristics, i.e. geographic restrictions of movements are not possible. Moreover, the locations of MNs are not affected by each other. The same is true for the velocity. This means that there is a spatial dependency neither of the velocity nor of the direction. Pause times restrictions are also not possible since pause times between movements are not a part of the BSA model

2.1.6. City Section (CS) Mobility Model

The CS mobility model mimics the mobility of MNs inside cities. It relies on the fact that users (pedestrians, autos, etc.) move inside cities on streets with specific mobility characteristics including speeds limits (Davies, 2000). Users are not always allowed to move randomly in real-life scenarios. Thus, researchers define first the part of the city, where they want to simulate MNs' movements inside. Concrete, they define the streets with their speeds limits. MNs are then distributed on the streets defined. Each MN randomly selects a destination (a point on a street). The movement algorithm determines then the shortest path between the current and new location. Sure, the MN is allowed to move only on streets. Note also that the characteristics of the streets are considered while moving. Upon reaching the destination, the MN repeats the process again after a pause time and so on.

The CS model provides more realistic movement patterns inside cities for nomadic and vehicles. Obstacles are implicitly included in the model since MNs are allowed to move only on pre-defined streets. This, however, does not absolutely match the reality, since there are parts of cities where MNs are allowed to move freely, e.g. inside gardens, houses, etc. Additionally, there are not only speed limits on the streets. There exist accelerations and/or decelerations as well. Such behaviors are not possible when applying the CS mobility model.

Based on the discussion induced above, one notes that neither the future location nor the future velocity of any MN depends on previous values. So, a temporal dependency of the velocity as well as the direction does not exist. Locations and velocities of MNs are also not influenced by the locations and velocities of any specific/neighbor MNs. This means, there is no spatial dependency of the velocity and the direction. Geographic restrictions of movements and pause times restrictions are parts of the CS model.

2.1.7. Knowledge-Driven (KD) Mobility Model

The KD mobility model (Dobson, et al., 2006), (Handorean, Gill & Roman, 2004) (Sen, Handorean, Roman & Hackmann, 2004) depends on exploiting the knowledge of movement patterns and allows for a total freedom of MNs mobility. The basic idea is to exchange information among MNs about their intended movements and also services. So, the KD model deals with the mobility from two points of view, namely the mobility of users and services, see (Ranjan Roy, 2011). The KD model assumes a network of a finite set of MNs/hosts (), each operates a finite set of agents. Each agent is a piece of software with moving capability (Sen, Handorean, Roman & Hackmann, 2004). That is, agents may move from a MN/host to another. The KD model considers global clock synchronization and assumes that each MN/host is characterized by a motion profile and has knowledge . To obtain a global knowledge of the network, the profiles are exchanged between MNs/hosts using a gossiping protocol (Chandra, Ramasubramanian & Birman, 2001). Concerning the services, each service is also assigned a motion profile that, unlike motion profiles of MNs/hosts, cannot be defined arbitrary. Rather,

it is derived from services allocation profiles that define on which host the service will reside at which time. Keep in mind that both services motion and allocation profiles are constructed based on the service placement algorithm being operated, e.g. REplication in Dense MANet (RED-MAN) (Bellavista et al., 2005), Self-Organizing Network Density (SONDe) (Gramoli, Kermarrec & Merrer, 2008), etc. For more information, the readers are directed to (Ali, Mitschele-Thiel, Diab & Rasheed, 2010).

The KD model exploits the knowledge gathered from each MN/host and service instance. Thus, a pre-planning and proactively management tasks for the purpose of performance optimization are possible, see (Lopez-Nores, Garcia-Duque, Pazos-Arias, Blanco-Fernández & Diaz-redondo, 2008). Moreover, the selection of the service provider best suited to the client gets simpler. The deal with application-level services mobility in addition to the mobility of users is a main feature of the KD model that does not exist in another mobility model. The KD model considers the existence of global clock synchronization and accurate positioning capabilities. These make the model technology-depended and only applicable when all MNs/hosts have such capabilities. A global accurate synchronization in dynamic changing networks is a major problem and hard to be properly realized. The exchange of local knowledge among network nodes to build the global knowledge is a problem as well. For the limitations of the model, the KD mobility model does not define a specific mobility model, but accommodates an existing one. Thus, it inherits the limitations of the accommodated mobility model. Note that this will not be done primitively since some features and limitations of accommodated mobility models may disappear, others may emerge.

2.1.8. Summary

Table 1 sums up the survey we introduced in this section, and provides a qualitative comparison

Table 1. A qualitative comparison between the synthetic single node mobility models investigated

Model	Temporal Dependency		Spatial Dependency		Geographic Restrictions		Pause Time
	Velocity	Direction	Velocity	Direction	Paths, Streets, etc.	Obstacles	
RW model	N	N	N	N	N	N	N
RWp model	N	N	N	N	N	N	Y
Probabilistic model	N	Y	N	N	N	N	N
MRW model	N[1]	Y	N	N	N	N	N
BSA model	Y	Y	N	N	N	N	N
CS model	N	N	N	N	Y	N	Y
KD model	Mpd[2]	Mpd	Mpd	Mpd	Mpd	Mpd	Mpd

between the reviewed models. Concerning the temporal dependency, one notes that only the BSA and KD models are capable of providing a temporal dependency of the velocity and the direction. Remaining mobility models either provide a temporal dependency of the velocity or the direction or provide no temporal dependency at all. The provision of a spatial dependency of the velocity as well as the direction was not a focus of synthetic mobility models. There is only one mobility model that considered such dependency, namely the KD model.

For the geographical restrictions, one notices that streets, freeways, etc. are considered in mobility models developed especially to model movements in cities, e.g. the CS model.

2.2. Synthetic Group Mobility Models

Synthetic group mobility models are intended to investigate the motions of MNs where the communication is done among teams to cooperatively achieve a common goal. In such models there exist either a function that describes the behavior of the MNs' group, or MNs coordinate via a leader or a common target. This section provides more insight into these models and sums up with a qualitative comparison between the described models.

2.2.1. Reference Point Group (RVG) Mobility Model

The RPG mobility model (Hong, Gerla, Pei & Chiang, 1999) organizes MNs into groups based on their logical relationships. Each group is assigned a logical center termed "reference point", whose movement is followed by all members of the group. Members of the group are randomly/ uniformly distributed in the neighborhood of the reference point. Note that such scheme allows, in principle, for an independent random motion behavior of the group's members in addition to the motion of the group itself. Figure 1 illustrates how MNs move employing the RPG mobility model. As the figure shows, the scenario contains two groups, each has 5 members. First, the reference point of a group i randomly selects at time t_0 a new location with a motion vector $W_i(t)$. The new location of a member j of the group i is defined by adding a randomly selected motion vector deviation $M_{ij}(t)$ to the reference point. Note that the vector $M_{ij}(t)$ is an identically distributed random vector, whose length is independent of the previous location of the MN.

In fact, any synthetic single node mobility model can be applied to model the movements of groups' reference points. This enables generating

Figure 1. Motion vectors of two groups' members

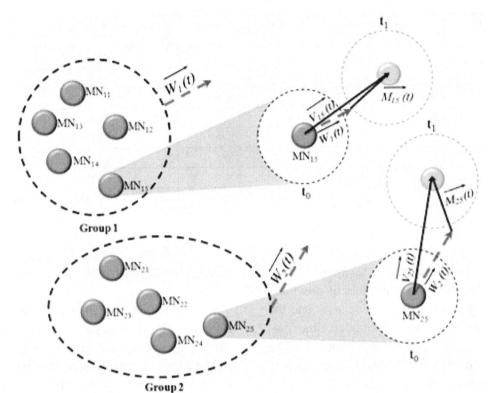

a wide range of mobility patterns. Concerning the limitations of the RPG model, it inherits the strengths and also drawbacks of the selected single node mobility model applied to model the movements of groups' reference points. Note, however, that because of the spatial dependency between each group's reference point and members, it is expected that the RPG model will behave somehow different from the synthetic single node mobility model applied. For groups' members, they are modeled, in principle, using the RW model. In spite of this, the limitations of the RW model are not inherited one to one. Concrete, there is a velocity as well as a location spatial dependency between the members of a group and their reference point, known hypothetically as a group leader. Geographic restrictions of movements are not possible. Note that groups' members do not pause between movements, although groups' leaders may do.

2.2.2. Reference Velocity Group (RVG) Mobility Model

The RVG mobility model (Wang & Li, 2002) is of a special interest for ad hoc networks where partitioning and merging are to be studied. The model extends the RPG model by additionally introducing a velocity representation of the groups, i.e. each group is characterized by its location and a mean group velocity $v=(v_x,v_y)$, where v_x and v_y where and are the velocity components in the x- and y-coordinates. Note that the velocity assigned to each group is the mean group velocity and it remains fixed during the simulation. Moreover, the coverage area of each group is set to a constant value. The members of the group are assigned velocities closed to the mean group velocity. This implies that the velocity of any group's member is characterized by two parameters, the velocity of the group and a local velocity deviation.

The model assumes a clustering algorithm to cluster MNs based on their velocities (Wang &Li, 2002). All MNs of a specific group will have speeds closed to the mean group velocity. So, it is not necessary to join members to groups. The groups will be formed automatically by grouping the MNs based on their speeds. Moreover, the model assumes that there is an omniscient observer that collects all information related to the mobility of MNs within the scenario. This enables to predict partitioning and merging before they occur. The RVG model allows for a random motion of the groups and their members. However, the speed of both groups and their members are not selected randomly. In fact, a synthetic single node mobility model (with light modification sometimes) is used to model the movements of groups and their members. The use of an omniscient observer with a global knowledge of the network is a drawback since this is impractical. A notable drawback of the RVG model is the assumption that the coverage area of each group is fixed, which is impractical. The assumption that groups' velocities do not change during the simulation is also not practical. The transformation of MNs representation from the physical to the velocity space can be seen as a weakness, consider for instance two groups with the same mean group velocity, however, with totally different mobility characteristics.

The RVG model inherits the strengths and weaknesses of the selected synthetic single node mobility model applied. Of course, strengths and weaknesses are not inherited one to one due to modifying the way applied to define the speed of all MNs in the scenario. As by the RPG model, there is no spatial and temporal dependency of the velocity and the direction between groups among each other and between members of each group (we assume the RW model). However, there is a velocity as well as location dependency between the members of a group and the group itself. Geographic restrictions of movements are not

possible. Concerning pause times, groups may stop between movements, however, members normally do not.

2.2.3. Reference Velocity and Acceleration Group (RVAG) Mobility Model

The RVAG mobility model (Chen & Chen, 2003) extends the RVG model by additionally using the acceleration to characterize mobility of MNs[3]. A key feature of the RVAG mobility model is the capability it has to predict ad hoc networks portioning by observing groups mobility patterns aggregated from MNs movements. Like the RVG model, a mean group velocity is assumed for each group. MNs are also grouped according to their logical relationships with the group's velocity. The velocities of group's members are chosen closed to the mean group velocity with a light deviation. In addition to the mean group velocity, a group acceleration is defined as a velocity-dependent random variable with a distribution of any arbitrary type. Due to the definition of the acceleration, more accurate modeling of the relationships between groups' members is possible. To accurately predict the partitioning time, each group (represents an ad hoc network) exchanges via a selected cluster head mobility parameters with its neighbor groups to calculate the overlapping area between them. The most important metric used is the acceleration, which represents the motion behavior of a group.

The RVAG model allows for a random motion of the groups and their members. The speed of both groups and their members are, however, not selected randomly. The mobility of groups can, in principle, be modeled using any synthetic single node mobility model (with light modification if necessary). A disadvantage of the RVAG model is the need for GPS-equipped devices to deliver locations information and devices with multiple interfaces to operate as clusters' heads. For the limitations, the model also inherits the limitations, advantages and disadvantages of the selected synthetic single node mobility model applied to model the movements of the groups and their members. Again, the inheritance is not one to one due to modifying the definition of the speed of all MNs in the scenario. As by the RPG and RVG models, there exist no spatial and temporal dependency of the velocity and the direction among groups and groups' members (we assume the RW model). However, there is a spatial dependency of the velocity and the direction between the members of a group and the group itself. There are also no geographic restrictions of movements. Concerning pause times, groups may stop between movements. However, groups' members do not stop.

2.2.4. Structured Group (SG) Mobility Model

The SG mobility model (Blakely & Lowekamp, 2004) aims at generating more realistic movement patterns for mobile communication networks, especially for ad hoc networks. The developers of the SG model state that inherent structures of groups are always apparent. Groups normally achieve common goals, which necessitate that groups' members must be aware of the goals rather than move randomly around groups' leaders. This also implies that the structures of the groups are known in advance and relate to the goals to be achieved. Moreover, it must be possible to define a hierarchical structure of groups, where members of main groups are allowed to construct groups by themselves. The SG model assigns no velocity vectors to individuals, whose locations are determined by distances and angular relationships to the reference points of their groups. The reference point of a group may be the geographical center of the group, the location of the group's leader or the group's center of mass. This point has a directional orientation of angle on a global coordination system regardless if the group moves

or not. Thus, the members of the group and also its sub-ordinate groups determine their positions and orient themselves based on .

Movements of the reference point are modeled by a specific single node mobility model. The movements of groups' members and sub-ordinate groups are then derived based on the relation to the reference point. The SG model is of a special importance for military scenarios and rescue actions in case of disasters. The SG mobility model parameterizes groups' structures dependencies aiming at generating traces closed to real-life observations as most as possible. Therefore, the SG model is marginally more complex than previous studied mobility models. Moreover, the derivation of movement traces when applying the SG model is also somewhat more complex than when using another model from the already studied ones. However, the simulation time the SG model consumes is insignificant despite the complexity mentioned (Ranjan Roy, 2011). A mean feature of the SG model is its capability to represent hierarchical organizations by allowing groups to have sub-ordinate groups. As known, such hierarchical organizations are common in real-life.

The SG model inherits the strengths and weaknesses of the synthetic single node mobility model used to model the movements of groups. There is a spatial dependency of the direction between groups among each other. Moreover, there is a spatial dependency of the direction between the members of each group and the group's leader. Concerning the spatial dependency of the velocity among groups, this depends on the synthetic single node mobility model applied. There is an implicit spatial dependency of the velocity between the groups' members and leaders, since the structures of the groups are maintained during the simulation. This means that the locations of individuals are maintained in relation to the location of the groups' leader, which also implies that velocities relate to each other somehow. For the temporal dependency, there is no temporal dependency of the direction and the velocity among groups' members. For the groups among each other, this depends of the mobility model applied to model their movements. Geographic restrictions of movements are possible neither among members nor between the members and groups. For pause times between movements, groups may stop. Consequently, groups' members may pause due to maintaining the relation to the groups' reference points.

2.2.5. Gathering Group (GG) Mobility Model

The GG mobility model (Borrel, De Amorim & Fdida, 2005) relies on a simple principle of dynamic networks, namely the preferential attachment (Barabási & Albert, 1999). It focuses on behavioral aspects of individuals and on interactions between them, i.e. MNs move independently, however, the resulting movement pattern exhibits a collective behavior. A main property of the GG model is its scale-free spatial distribution that makes it adequate for a population growth. This helps in solving many problems of large-scale mobile ad hoc networks. The GG developers stated that the population spatial density dynamics has not been properly considered. In real-life scenarios people form groups randomly, mimic others, etc. So, populations grow or diminish. The GG mobility model emphasizes that a common particular property is pertinent to human organizations, namely they are scale-free. This implies that human organizations follow a power law distribution (Barabási & Albert, 1999). A scenario, from the GG model point of view, consists of two components, individuals (MNs) and attractors. Attractors are the centers of interest, towards which individuals move. They appear for specific time duration, do not move and disappear following that. Individuals arrive, behave in cycles for a given time duration and then depart. A cycle consists of a displacement followed by pause duration.

The experiments done in (Borrel, De Amorim & Fdida, 2005) show that the GG mobility model produces bipartite graphs that have an equiprobable spatial distribution. Projections of the spatial distribution of individuals and attractors following the GG mobility model are depicted in Figure 2. The green points express individuals and the red circles stand for attractors. Note that attractors locate in the coordinates, where individuals converge. Although individuals do not belong explicitly to groups in the GG model, they evolve independently and exhibit a collective behavior resulting implicitly from the impacts of individuals and attractors on other individuals. Beside the benefits of the GG model, there are also several weaknesses since there is no possibility to represent rigid dedicated movements of groups or individuals, e.g. movements on streets, within gardens, etc. Moreover, no structures of groups can be maintained, this prohibits the usage of the GG mobility model for a wide range of applications. Concerning the limitations of the model, there is a spatial dependency of the location of individuals among each other and with attractors. There is, however, no temporal dependency of the location. Concerning the velocity, there is no temporal as well as spatial dependency of the velocity. There exist also no geographic restrictions of movements. For pause times, they are included between movements.

2.2.6. Summary

Table 2 summarizes the survey we introduced in this section and provides a qualitative comparison between the reviewed models with respect to the temporal and spatial dependency. When taking a look at the temporal dependency, one notes that no temporal dependency is supported when considering movements of groups' members. This is because all studied models assume the RW model as the standard model to be used. Concerning the temporal dependency of groups' movements, most studied mobility models support conditionally this

Figure 2. Two example spatial distributions of individuals and attractors generated by the GG mobility model in bounded (a) and boundless space (b) (Borrel, De Amorim & Fdida, 2005)

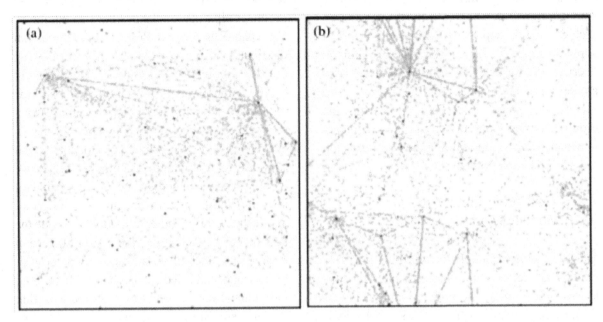

Table 2. A qualitative comparison between the synthetic group mobility models investigated with respect to the temporal and spatial dependency

Model	Temporal Dependency				Spatial Dependency			
	Groups' Members[4]		Groups		Groups' Members		Groups	
	Velocity	Direction	Velocity	Direction	Velocity	Direction	Velocity	Direction
RPG model	N	N	Mmd[5]		N	Between members and the reference point	Mmd	
RVG model	N	N	Mmd		Between members and the reference point		Mmd	
RVAG model	N	N	Mmd		Between members and the reference point		Mmd	
SG model	N	N	Mmd		Between members and the reference point		Y	Y
GG model	N	N	N	N	N	Yes (among individuals) Between individuals and attractors	N	N

dependency. In fact, this depends on the mobility model applied to model the movements of the groups. Exceptions are found in the GG model. Let us now consider the spatial dependency. Considering the movements of groups' members, one notes that there is in general no spatial dependency of the velocity. However, there is a spatial dependency of the direction between the members and the groups' leaders/reference points. For the movement of the groups themselves, the existence of a spatial dependency of the velocity as well as direction between groups depends on the mobility model applied to implement groups' movements. Exceptions exist, of course. The SG model supports such dependency, while the GG model does not.

Table 3 compares between the reviewed models with respect to the support of geographic restrictions and pause times. For geographic restrictions, one notes that the majority of the models do not support the definition of streets with specific mobility characteristics. There is, in general, no support of obstacles as well. Concerning pause times, the majority of the mobility models studied do not include pause times between movements of groups' members. However, pause times may exist between movements of groups. This depends, in fact, on the mobility model applied.

2.3. Obstacles Modeling

Another key issue heavily related to the modeling of mobility patterns is the modeling of obstacles. This problem is highly intertwined with the definition of realistic radio propagation models (Sarkar, Wicks, Salazar-Palma & Bonneau, 2004). Until now, there are very few mobility models that considered the modeling of obstacles by concept. The modeling of obstacles is, in fact, an open research issue that necessitates deeper researches and investigations. When taking a look at the survey we introduced above, one notes that all mobility models that introduce geographic restrictions on movements include somehow a definition of obstacles either explicitly or implicitly. One also notes that two main principles followed to express the existence of obstacles inside simulated scenarios.

1. **Implicit Definition of Obstacles:** here, obstacles are not clearly defined. Rather, the scenario introduces restrictions that affect the movements of MNs, so that an obstacle-like behavior results. This is done by:
   a. **Division of the Simulation Area into Adjacent/Overlapping Regions:** This is the weakest method applied, since it restricts somehow the movements of MNs.

Table 3. A qualitative comparison between the synthetic group mobility models investigated with respect to the support of geographic restrictions and pause times

Model	Geographic Restrictions				Pause Times	
	Groups' Members		Groups		Groups Members	Groups
	Paths, Streets, etc.	Obstacles	Paths, Streets, etc.	Obstacles		
RPG model	N	N	Mmd		N	Mmd
RVG model	N	N	Mmd		N	Mmd
RVAG model	N	N	Mmd		N	Mmd
SG model	N	N	Mmd		Y (only, if groups has pause times)	Mmd
GG model	N	N	N	N	Y	Y

b. **Definition of Tracks and Streets:** In this way, users are allowed to move only on streets or tracks. This implies that no movements are possible in areas where no streets/tracks are defined. Sure, these areas express then obstacles. The CS model is an example mobility model.

c. **Definition of Rules to Control the MNs' Movement Behavior:** The models that follow this method do not construct streets or regions with specific mobility characters. Rather, they determine movements' characteristics of MNs via rules or motion profiles. So, restrictions may be included in the rules or inside the motion profiles. The KD model is an example.

2. **Explicit Definition of Obstacles:** There are very few models that define obstacles explicitly. Well-known example mobility models include the Voronoi-based and the obstacle mobility models, see (Ranjan Roy, 2011).

3. TRACE-BASED MODELING OF HUMAN MOBILITY PATTERNS

Trace-based mobility models, also termed empirical models, characterize movement patterns based on connectivity information that represent the distribution of users' locations within the environment and the movements of humans carrying wireless devices. These models depend on traces gathered by already deployed cellular networks or GPS-enabled devices to obtain information about the locations of users. They refine existing mobility models based on the traces to make them more realistic (Kotz & Henderson, 2005) and capable of generating synthetic traces characterized by the same statistical properties of real ones.

3.1. Users Behavior in Mobility Traces

The authors in (Tang & Baker, 2000) analyzed a twelve-week trace of a building-wide Wireless Local Area Network (WLAN). The analysis focused on studying the overall user behavior and network traffic, in addition to, load characteristics. The authors have noted that most users access the network to surf the web, do session-oriented activities and chat with other users. In fact, there was a high number of chats, which showed that synchronous communication with others is preferred by users. Experienced peak throughput is usually caused by a single user and application. During the peak throughput duration, the outgoing traffic dominates incoming traffic. During other times, outgoing traffic is significantly less than incoming one. The main result says: users are divided into distinct location-based sub-communities, each has its own movements, activities, and usage characteristics.

To extend the understanding of users' behaviors, traces captured at the ACM SIGCOMM'01 conference, held at U.C. San Diego, August 2001, were investigated in (Balachandran, Voelker, Bahl & Rangan, 2002). The network is an IEEE 802.11b WLAN (IEEE. 802.11b/d3.0, 1999) with 4 APs installed in a large auditorium. The users monitored are 195 users, roughly 40% of the total attendees. The results of the analysis have shown that most sessions are relatively short. Although there are some longer sessions, however, they tend to be idle for the majority of the time. Dominant applications are the web surfing and secure shell applications. The authors also noted that average as well as peak bandwidth requirements of individual users are relatively small. This means that few APs are, in principle, adequate to serve relatively large number of users in such situations. An important result concerning the load distribution, namely the bandwidth is highly uneven and not well correlated with the number of users those APs serve. Concerning users' behavior, user arrivals into the network can be correlated according to a two-state Markov-modulated Poisson process. The distribution of the session time can be approximated to a general Pareto distribution.

The work presented in (Balazinska & Castro, 2003) provides the results obtained from a four week trace data collected in a large corporate environment (1366 users distributed in three buildings). The pattern used reflects a usual office environment traced during normal office work hours. The authors found that average user transfer-rates follow a power law distribution. Network load is unevenly distributed across APs. The variations in the number of users over time adherence the patterns of the underlying population. The results showed also that there are large differences in user movement patterns and data transfer rates. Usually, users spend a large fraction of their time at a single location, referred to as home location, and do not change their network usage when being a way of their home or when changing their location frequently. The authors, therefore, proposed to model users' mobility by means of a persistence and prevalence. The persistence determines how long users remain associated with the same AP, while the prevalence defines how often users visit various APs. The authors state that the probability distribution of both persistence and prevalence follows a power law distribution. The results of the investigation achieved in (Balazinska & Castro, 2003) were compared with other studies from the literature. The authors found similarities, especially to those observed at university campuses, offices, etc., see (Kotz & Essien, 2002), (Kotz & Essien, 2002a) and Tang & Baker, 2000). They found, however, differences compared to the results obtained from large-scaled scenarios such as dormitories (Kotz & Essien, 2002), (Kotz & Essien, 2002a) and public metropolitan networks (Tang & Baker, 2002).

An analysis of the usage of the Dartmouth College campus WLAN is provided in (Henderson, Kotz & Abyzov, 2004). This work analyzed more than 550 APs and 7000 users over seventeen weeks. A special important contribution of this study was the comparison of traces results to those taken from the same network direct after the initial deployment, two years ago. The authors found that the applications used in the network changed drastically. Initially, the network was mainly used for web surfing. After that, other applications started to appear and be widely used in the network, e.g. Peer-to-Peer (P2P), Voice over IP (VoIP) traffic, etc. VoIP traffic was mainly used on the wired network and calls were mainly short. Furthermore, the analysis of the devices used by clients has shown a considerable heterogeneity in the types of clients used including embedded devices, laptops, PDAs, etc.

Data about movement patterns were collected in (Leguay, Friedman & Conan, 2005) from traces measured in the Dartmouth WLAN between January 26th, 2004 and March 11th, 2004. The total number of tracked mobile users was 5,545 users. They were allowed to visit 536 locations, where each location is served by an AP. The authors noted that the distributions of the number of locations visited follow heavy tailed distribution, which implies that the majority of users have a low level of mobility, while a small amount of users move actively. Note that users with low level of mobility are those not often involved in data exchange or who prefer to remain or leave their wireless device in specific places for a long time. The mobility traces show that there is regularity in terms of the network usage. Note also that there are regular weekly cycles and approximately a constant number of active users per day in the traces. This simply means that users move based on a number of approximately constant habits. The analysis of the appearance of users in the network has shown that it is high probable that MNs will not disappear close to the beginning of the trace. Similarly, the probability that MNs will appear for the first time close to the end of the trace is also low. The appearance as well as disappearance of users is distributed over the whole time.

In brief, following results can be derived when abstracting the similarities between the traces we mentioned:

1. The variations in the number of users over time are proper representations of population patterns.
2. Users are divided into distinct location-based sub-communities, each has its own movements, activities, and usage characteristics.
3. The majority of users have a low level of mobility.
4. Users move based on approximately constant habits, which results in regular movement patterns.
5. Mobility characteristics are affected by the applications being running.
6. There is regularity in the network usage. There are even regular weekly cycles.
7. The load of the network is unevenly distributed across APs.
8. Dominant applications are web surfing and synchronous communications. The sessions users initiate are, in general, short.

3.2. WLAN Mobility Model

One of the first attempts to model users movements based on traces collected from already deployed networks is provided in (Tuduce & Gross, 2005). The authors measured mobility characteristics of users of a WLAN campus network of ETH Zurich. The WLAN monitored spread across 32 buildings with seminar and lecture rooms in addition to offices, however, without student dormitories. There were 166 APs installed, so that overlapping areas were minimized. Exceptions existed in seven heavily occupied lecture halls, where each hall was covered by more than one AP. Mobility data were gathered in two traces (each took nine weeks long) at different times (in 2003 and 2004). The first trace captured 3,073 users, who connected to the WLAN 97,575 times. The second trace captured 4,762 users, who connected to the WLAN 343,626 times. The authors noted that the number of users accessing the WLAN simultaneously tends to follow the weekly sociological trends expected. Users heavily access the network during working hours. There is a significant decrease in the number of users accessing the network at the weekends. Concerning daily routines, the number of connected users starts to increase at 6 am and diminishes slowly after 6 pm. Note that there is a slight decrease over lunch time.

The methodology the authors followed simply includes the analysis of mobility traces and the derivation of mobility model parameters. These parameters are applied, following that, to generate movement patterns for simulative studies. The mobility model from the authors point of view is seen as a collaboration between two processes, a spatial process () and a temporal process (). The result of this collaboration will be a trajectory in the described environment. The environment itself is described by the boundaries of the physical space, inside which users are allowed to move, together with restrictions on user movements, e.g. obstacles, the paths users must move on, etc. The spatial process defines the subset of points the user has to visit during the simulation, i.e. the user's trajectory. The temporal process determines the time, at which the user must be at his destination. That is, the temporal process implies the speed of the user.

Based on the analysis of mobility data traces, the topology of the network is derived. Based on the analysis of users movements in the traces, many transition probabilities and parameters are derived, e.g. the probability to move to a neighbor cell, remain in the same cell, etc. So as to capture the spatial as well as the temporal process, the authors analyzed the mobility of users based on two metrics, namely the prevalence and the persistence. The prevalence captures the spatial process, while the persistence captures the temporal process. The analysis of mobility traces has shown that the prevalence and persistence follow power-law distributions with low exponents. The distribution of prevalence values shows that the time durations users spend in different cells are unbalanced. Users spend the most of their time in one cell and move shortly to other cells.

Based on the analysis of mobility data traces, the authors decided to assign each user a set of cells to be visited during the simulation. The destination cell is selected randomly from this list and, following that, the user moves towards this cell. During the simulation, users follow inactive-active cyclic behavior. During the active phase, the user associates with a cell and actively uses the network, while during the inactive phase, the user will not be a part of the network, although he keeps moving. The temporal process can, therefore, be seen as a process invoking an active and inactive timer processes. The inactive phase duration is modeled using a uniform random distribution, while the active phase is generated using a general Pareto distribution. The parameters of these distributions are derived from mobility traces.

3.3. The Model T and Its Evolution, The Model T++

This work depends on the data collected from the WLAN of Dartmouth College (Kotz & Essien, 2002). The network had a dense topology with 586 APs in 161 buildings spread over approximately 200 acres. Each AP had an average number of 65 other APs in its neighborhood. The data collected represented a two-year long record of AP association, diassociation and re-association requests resulting from 6,202 users. Note that the collected data do not provide any exact geographical locations. Moreover, the associations with APs do not necessarily imply a physical movement of humans,

due to the existence of ping-pong effects. Another limitation in the data collected is the inaccuracy of the residence time before the user transits himself into an OFF state. Concerning the diassociation, it is not necessary that users diassociate themselves explicitly. Therefore, users that remain inactive for more than 30 minutes are considered diassociated. For more details, see (Kotz & Essien, 2002) and (Song, Kotz, Jain & He, 2004).

The authors first examined the traced data to better understand user behaviors and to extract the dominant features. Following that, the authors divided the traces into two disjoint sets, namely a training and a test data set. The training data set contains the data collected at the initial phase of the network installation, while the test data set includes the data collected after the network gets stable from the operation point of view. Based on the results obtained, the authors developed a statistical mobility model with few equations and parameters that are capable of characterizing the training data set. Following that, the authors generated synthetic mobility traces based on the developed statistical mobility model. The generated mobility traces are compared to the test data set for validation purposes. The results of these studies are the development of the Model T (Jain, Lelescu & Balakrishnan, 2005) and the Model T++ (Lelescu, Kozat, Jain & Balakrishnan, 2006) later on.

The Model T captures the spatial movements of users across the APs monitored. It shows that the observed patterns of user registrations exhibit a distinct two-level hierarchy. The APs of the WLAN of the Dartmouth College can be clustered based on a transition rate matrix. The distributions of clusters sizes are highly skewed. Moreover, intra-cluster transition probabilities and also trace lengths follow the heavy-tailed Weibull distribution. Inter-cluster transition probabilities have similar characteristics to intra-cluster ones. The popularities of APs are considered important factors. The main drawback of the Model T is the lack of a time model. The Model T states that any independent time model can simply be superimposed on the empirical mobility model developed, i.e. the Model T.

The authors compared the results of the Model T to those produced by the WLAN mobility model discussed earlier. The comparison results were, in fact, not surprising since different empirical models from different WLAN networks will significantly deviate from each other. Sure, this is not desirable and speaks against the generalization of empirical mobility models. The authors state that both models seem to well reflect the spatial mobility with a few parameters. However, they lack of a representation of the dependency between space and time aspects. Both models do not consider the changes in the velocity of users, which result from accelerations or decelerations due to present restrictions such as obstacles, paths' characteristics, etc. So as to express the correlation between space and time aspects, the authors have extended the Model T and developed the Model T++. The authors defined the concept of popularity gradient between different APs. They state that APs popularities and well-defined popularity gradients offer an effective way to reflect the relations between space and time. The AP popularity is defined as the number of visits the AP receives during the time duration defined for the study. So, the Model T++ is described as a joint time-space model that can regenerate the inter-dependence of time and space aspects by means of few methodical equations. The authors compared the Model T++ to the Model T and summarized that there is a small increase in the complexity. However, there are significant improvements and, thus, better capabilities to capture real mobility scenarios.

In spite of the great features of the Model T++, one must be cautious when using this model to generate mobility scenarios for ad hoc networks. This model is, in fact, not adequate for such networks. Another drawback is seen when geographical locations of users are necessary, since the model cannot reproduce such information.

3.4. Statistical Mobility Model (SMM)

The SMM (Yoon, Noble, Liu & Kim, 2006) combines between coarse-grained wireless traces (collected from the WLAN of Dartmouth College (Kotz, Henderson & Abyzov, 2012) and an actual map of the geographical space, where the traces were collected. Following a sequence of data processing steps including filtering of traces and mapping to real maps, the SMM constructs a probabilistic model that generates movement patterns to be used in simulations. First, the traces were filtered and a chronological list of "trips" taken by each user is generated. A trip includes an origin, destination and possibly intermediate positions, i.e. APs. The applied filtering process comprises various steps. First, discontinuous trips are separated. Following that, each trip is checked to filter undesired ping-pong handoffs. Finally, each trip is identified in a form of stationary and transient points, i.e. APs.

Following the filtering process, the route the user takes along his trip is inferred, i.e. the trip is converted to a geographical representation that is further converted to a graph with vertices (APs, buildings, etc.) and links (routes between the vertices). After the construction of the graph, the route users take on the graph must be inferred. First, the route candidates between each two points (APs) must be determined. In general, the shortest route is preferred. However, this is not an absolute rule. The SMM developers decided to use the distance as a metric to determine the preferred routes. Furthermore, they used an algorithm to find N shortest paths, see (Lawler, 1972) and (Lawler, 2001). After the generation of route candidates, the likelihood of using each of these candidates is derived. This step results in a route frequency statistics that are transferred to a set of transition probabilities associated with graph vertices. Note that this is done by modeling the mobility of users as a Markov chain. The last step one has to accomplish is the determination of the initial distribution of users, which in turn corresponds to the initial states distribution of the Markov model. This is done by determining the initial distribution of origins and destinations.

3.5. Work and Home Extracted REgions (WHERE) Mobility Model

WHERE (Isaacman et al., 2012) is a novel model attempting to model how large populations move. The model utilizes spatial and temporal probability distributions derived from large amount of empirical data representing real people living across wide geographic areas. The source of these distributions are the Call Detail Records (CDRs) taken from a cellular telephone network. The motivation behind the usage of CDRs are the results of many premium efforts, which depicted that the analysis of the data CDRs offer results in synthetic CDRs for a synthetic population, see (Gonzalez et al., 2008), (Isaacman et al., 2011), (Song et al., 2010) and (Bayir, Demirbas & Eagle, 2009). Note, however, that it is tempting to think that modeling human movement patterns based on CDRs is an easy task. It is correct that CDRs give an insight into population densities. However, they do not convey whether users' locations correspond to home, offices, etc. Keep also in mind that the spatial granularity of CDRs data is only accurate to the granularity of cells' towers spacing, while the temporal granularity is accurate only to users actively involved in communications.

The authors claim that their model makes a key contribution in overcoming the lack of semantic information and coarse granularity. It is nowadays widely accepted that there is a tight coupling between human movement patterns and the geographic of the city people live in, see (Isaacman et al., 2011a), (Isaacman et al., 2010) and (Noulas et al., 2012). The spatial data include the definition of important locations from users' point of view and also hourly population densities. The temporal data cover the calling patterns issued in the network. For important locations, the authors argue that a good accuracy is expected when only considering the probability distributions for the few locations, where users spend the majority of their time. Therefore, the authors decided to focus on the most important two locations, "work" and "home". So, the spatial home-work densities are first estimated. Following that, these densities are linked to temporal information. Note that in reality, heavily residential areas are likely to be more populated at night, while city centers and commercial locations are likely to be more populated during a day. Previous work (Isaacman et al., 2011a) has shown that cellular calls are an accurate representation of users' locations. Thus, when linking the calls to the towers handling them, one will be able to represent the density of users in the network. A step more is necessary to consider the time, namely the density is represented hourly.

The authors developed a two-place model and called it WHERE2. The WHERE2 utilizes the fact saying: people spend the majority of their time either at home or at work. Thus, synthetic CDR traces are generated in two stages, namely a user creation and movement stage. The user creation stage includes creating synthetic users and assigning a home to them. Following that, a commute distance is chosen for each synthetic user. Thereafter, possible work places are defined for each synthetic user. Finally, each user is assigned a calling pattern. In the second stage, the user moves between work and home according to the probability of being either at work or at home at that time of day. Note that a movement means making a call from either the work or the home. The authors further extended the WHERE2 to cover more than two places, see (Isaacman et al., 2012). A main advantage of WHERE is its application to metropolitan areas, since rarely we see models to represent movement patterns in such big areas. Another advantage is its privacy concerning real CDRs, since it necessitates anonymous CDRs to generate a wide range of synthetic CDRs for investigation purposes.

4. SOCIAL-BASED COMMUNITY MODELING OF MOBILITY PATTERNS

The aim of social-based community modeling is, as before, the generation of as realistic models as possible. Researchers have noted that existing mobility models generate movement patterns that are, in general, inhumane-like (Musolesi, Hailes & Mascolo, 2005), (Musolesi & Mascolo, 2007). The word 'human' is, in fact, the key. Mobile devices are usually carried by humans, so movement patterns of such devices are necessarily related to human decisions and socialization behavior. A social network is defined as a set of humans with some patterns of contacts or interactions among them (Scott, 2000). The first significant quantitative results were published in the 1950s and 1960s (Rapoport, 1957). The statistics of epidemic diffusion in populations characterized by different social structures are analyzed. In the same period, the interest in the graph theory was renewed and the so-called random graph was defined (Erdos & Renyi, 1959). These theoretical studies represented the beginning of the research in the complex network area and were applied to various disciplines, e.g. biology, sociology, etc. In the last decade, various studies have been conducted to assess the validity of these theories, especially for the analysis of social networks. One of the most interesting approaches is the so-called small world model (Watts, 1999). Researchers believe nowadays that the results of social networks analysis can be used to generate more realistic mobility models. The following gives more insight into.

4.1. Time-Variant Community (TVC) Mobility Model

The TVC mobility model (Hsu, Spyropoulos, Psounis & Helmy, 2007) relays on the concept of Community of Interest (CoI)-based[6] location preferences and time-dependent periodical appearance of MNs. There are Time Periods (TPs), each with a specific duration, see Figure 3. During each time period, there are some communities that represent geographical areas visited[7]. Sure, the number of communities may differ from a TP to another. Let us assume that is the community indexed with at time and the total number of communities at time is . Each community is presented in the figure as a square of edge length . Note that communities may overlap, be included in bigger communities, etc. Note also that TPs are arranged in a recursive sequence since they present a time schedule, e.g. daily, monthly, etc.

Thus, movements of MNs are sequences of epochs that reflect their behaviors during these periods. The TVC model assumes that MNs residing within each epoch randomly select their directions, speeds and movements' length. At the end of the epoch, MNs wait for a pause time duration selected also randomly and proceed, following that, to the next epoch. In this context, one notes similar behavior to that observed by the studied RW (within the community) and RWp (between communities) mobility models.

Great feature of the TVC model is the dynamic it allows for communities' structures, since their size, number and location can be dynamically changed during time. Moreover, the TVC model allows individuals to have different set of parameters including own TPs' structures. This also enables reflecting the time-dependent behavior of humans more accurately and enables describing heterogeneous environments with users having diverse mobility characteristics. Concerning the limitation of the model, it inherits the limitations of both the RW (within communities) and RWp (between communities) models.

4.2. Community-Based (CB) Mobility Model

The CB mobility model depends on social networks theory (Musolesi & Mascolo, 2006) and exploits social relationships present. It assumes that communities are associated with geographical

Figure 3. TVC mobility model illustration

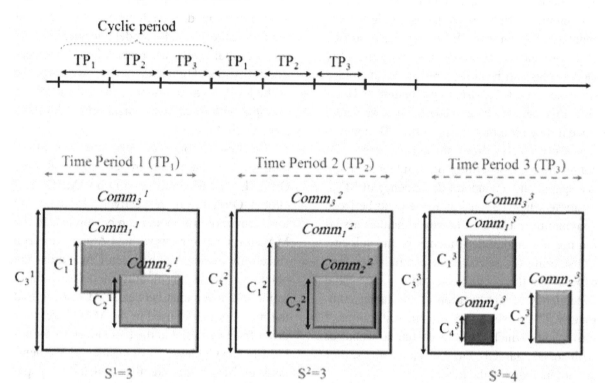

areas since humans with strong social links are often geographically co-located. Members of the same community are called friends, while those of different communities are named non-friends. Relations between MNs are modeled via social links with specific weights (Scott, 2000). The weights themselves refer to the social attractivity between MNs. When starting up, all friends have social links to each other. Links with non-friends are established according to a rewiring probability, which creates time-dependent changing communities structure. The interval time between such changes is an input parameter for the CB model.

MNs are placed within a grid that consists of cells, each represents a community. At each iteration, one of the MN's edges is rewired. The result will be a network composed of groups of MNs (communities). Concerning nodes' movements, they can be considered as a sequence of steps, where each step means a movement toward

a community and an association with a MN in this community. Note that MNs move toward their target cells gradually, where other MNs having strong interactions among them converge. This represents the behavior of most people, since they travel home every evening and join their families for instance.

An important feature of the CB mobility model is the avalanche effect resulting from movements of MNs. When a MN decides to move towards a target community, a probability termed remaining probability () is calculated. This probability is defined as the probability that no other members of the community will follow the MN moving. When approaches 0, at least one MN will follow the MN moving towards its target cell.

The CB model presents the reference point for social-aware community models. It is flexible and capable of matching a wide range of real applications. A great feature of the model is its dynamic behavior concerning the structures of communities, which helps in describing heterogeneous environments. However, the sequence of movements is not pre-defined as by the TVC model. This can be considered as an advantage since the scenario construction gets simpler. However, this can also be considered as a weakness since it may prohibit the use of the CB model to represent pre-defined movements between specific communities. Concerning the limitations, there is a spatial and a temporal dependency of MNs' locations when we consider movements between communities. There is, however, neither a spatial nor a temporal dependency of the velocity. Considering the selection of communities, one expects that there will be a temporal and spatial dependency of the location of the target community. There exist no geographic restrictions of movements, which prohibits designing scenarios with streets, gardens, etc. For pause times, they are not included in the model.

4.3. Orbit-Based (OB) Mobility Model

The OB mobility model (Ghosh, 2006), (Ghosh, Yoon, Ngo & Qiao, 2005), (Ghosh, Philip & Qiao,

2007), (Ghosh, Ngo & Qiao, 2006) is a semi-deterministic model that depends on macro-level sociological orbits. The model considers hierarchical orbital levels, where each level considers a mobility model best suited to the own purposes of the level. So as to illustrate the OB model, an example with three hierarchical orbital levels is provided in Figure 4.

The first, second and third hierarchical orbital levels in the figure are termed Local Area Orbit (LAO), Medium Area Orbit (MAO) and Global Orbit (GO), respectively. In the LAO level, any mobility model can be applied. In the MAO level, movements within LAOs are not seen since only movements between LAOs areas are of interest. Again, any mobility model can be used to model movements between LAOs. Note that the mobility model used in the MAO level may differ from that used in the LAO level. In a similar way, the GO level only considers movements between MAOs that are also modeled by a specific mobility model.

Initially, a specific number of LAOs is assigned to each MN to move between in the second level, i.e. the MAO. These LAOs present, in principle, the communities the MN is allowed to visit. It is

Figure 4. An example scenario generated by the OB mobility model

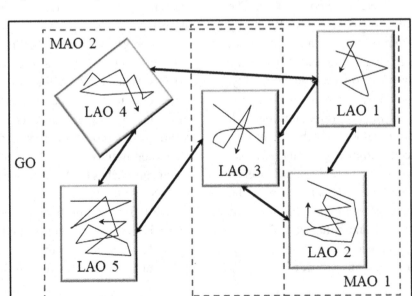

worth mentioning that an LAO is referred to as a hub as well. The MN locates initially inside a randomly selected LAO and starts moving based on the mobility model applied. Each LAO has its own speed range and timeout, which is determined as the time duration each visiting MN has to spend inside the LAO. When a given LAO timeout expires, the MN randomly selects another LAO from the LAOs it is allowed to move into, and starts moving towards the chosen LAO. This movement is controlled by the mobility model applied in the MAO level. Note that the MAO has also a timeout bounded, after which the MN has to change the MAO and to move in the GO level.

A great feature of the OB model is its capability to emulate existing mobility models, which enables modeling a wide range of applications and forming communities that interact with each other in specific patterns. Moreover and because the OB mobility model utilizes existing mobility models to model movements inside LAOs and among them and also between MAOs, it inherits the limitations of the applied mobility models.

4.4. Summary

Table 4 and table 5 sum up the survey we provided in this section and provide a qualitative comparison between the reviewed models. Note that only the OB mobility model is capable of implementing a temporal dependency of the velocity, direction and community selection. Concerning the spatial dependency and also geographical restrictions, the OB mobility model is also the model capable of representing all spatial dependencies studied and geographical restrictions.

Table 4. A qualitative comparison between the social-based community mobility models investigated with respect to the temporal dependency, spatial dependency and geographical restrictions

Model	Temporal Dependency			Spatial Dependency			Geographical Restrictions	
	Velocity	Direction	Community	Velocity	Direction	Community	Paths, Streets, etc.	Obstacles
TVC	No	No	Yes	No	No	Yes	No	No
CB	No	Yes	Yes	No	Yes	Yes	No	No
OB	Mmd	Mmd	Mmd	Mmd	Mmd	Mmd	Mmd	Mmd

Table 5. A qualitative comparison between the synthetic group mobility models investigated with respect to the individual MNs movements, group movements, direction, speed and pause times.

Model	Individual MNs Movements	Groups Movements	Direction	Speed	Pause Times
TVC	Based on CoI-based location preferences and time-dependent periodical appearance of MNs	Community-based, product of the decision of individual MNs	Uniformly distributed from the range	Uniformly distributed from a range	Partially (for movements between communities)
CB	Based on social attractiveness towards other MNs	Community-based (product of the decision of individual MNs)	Intrinsic (derived from the target attraction computation)	Uniformly distributed from a range	No
OB	Based on the mobility model applied in each orbital level	Community-based	Mobility model-dependent	Mobility model-dependent	Mobility model-dependent

5. CONCLUSION

The chapter has focused on the development of novel methods to model human mobility patterns, which have myriad uses in crucial fields. The chapter has stated that human mobility patterns are far from being random. They show regularity and are reproducible. Mobility models are categorized into synthetic, trace-based and community-based models. Synthetic models are largely preferred and widely applied to simulate mobile communication networks. They are mathematical models that try to capture movements' patterns by means of a set of equations. These models are traceable, however, not capable of generating realistic mobility patterns. The key idea of trace-based models is the exploitation of available measurements and traces to reproduce synthetic traces characterized by the same statistical properties of real ones. The measurements done have provided that users are in general non mobile. They spend the majority of their time at a limited amount of locations that have sociological relation to them. The variations in the number of users over time are proper representations of population patterns. Movement patterns and network usage show regularity. This regularity comes from the cyclic habits users follow in their life. The main drawback of trace-based models is the tight coupling between the empirical model developed and the traces collected, the network topology deployed and the geographic location. This is why the results of empirical models deviate clearly from each other.

Community-based modeling of human movements depends on the fact stating that mobile devices are usually carried by humans, which implies that movement patterns are necessarily related to human decisions and socialization behaviors. So, human movement routines heavily affect the overall movement patterns. One of the major contributions in this context is the application of social network theory to generate more realistic human movement patterns. The chapter has discussed the models depending on social communities and finalizes with a qualitative comparison between them.

REFERENCES

Ali, S., Mitschele-Thiel, A., Diab, V., & Rasheed, A. (2010). A survey of services placement mechanisms for future mobile communication networks. In *Proceeding of the 8th International Conference on Frontiers of Information Technology* (FIT'10). Islamabad, Pakistan. FIT.

Aschenbruck, N., Gerhards-Padilla, E., & Martini, P. (2008). A survey on mobility models for performance analysis in tactical mobile networks. *Journal of Telecommunication and Information Technology*.

Bai, F., Sadagopan, N., & Helmy, A. (2003). Important: A framework to systematically analyze the impact of mobility on performance of routing protocols for ad hoc networks. In *Proceeding of the 22th Annual Joint Conference of the IEEE Computer and Communications* (INFOCOM'03). San Francisco, CA: IEEE.

Balachandran, A., Voelker, G. M., Bahl, P., & Rangan, P. V. (2002). Characterizing user behavior and network performance in a public wireless LAN. In *Proceedings of the ACM SIGMETRICS International Conference on Measurement and Modeling of Computer Systems* (SIG-METRICS'02). New York, NY: ACM Press.

Balazinska, M., & Castro, P. (2003). Characterizing mobility and network usage in a corporate wireless local-area network. In *Proceedings of the 1st International Conference on Mobile Systems, Applications, and Services* (MobiSys'03). San Francisco, CA: ACM.

Barabási, A. L., & Albert, R. (1999). Emergence of scaling in random networks. *Science*, 286. PMID:10521342.

Basu, P., Redi, J., & Shurbanov, V. (2004). Coordinated flocking of UAVs for improved connectivity of mobile ground nodes. In *Proceeding of the Military Communications Conference* (MILCOM'04). BBN Technology.

Bayir, M. A., Demirbas, M., & Eagle, N. (2009). Discovering spatiotemporal mobility profiles of cellphone users. In *Proceeding of the 10th World of Wireless, Mobile and Multimedia Networks and Workshops* (WoWMoM'09). WoWMoM.

Bellavista, P., Corradi, A., & Magistretti, E. (2005). REDMAN: An optimistic replication middleware for read-only resources in dense MANETs. *Journal on Pervasive and Mobile Computing, 1*(3), 279–310. doi:10.1016/j.pmcj.2005.06.002.

Bettstetter, C., Hartenstein, H., & Pérez-Costa, X. (2003). *Stochastic properties of the random waypoint mobility model*. Dordrecht, The Netherlands: Kluwer Academic Publishers.

Bettstetter, C., & Wagner, C. (2002). The spatial node distribution of the random waypoint mobility model. In *Proceeding of 1st German Workshop on Mobile Ad Hoc Networks* (WMAN'02), (pp. 41-58). Ulm, Germany: ACM.

Blakely, K., & Lowekamp, B. (2004). A structured group mobility model for the simulation of mobile ad hoc networks. In *Proceeding of the ACM International Workshop on Mobility Management and Wireless Access Protocols* (MobiWac'04). ACM.

Borrel, V., De Amorim, M. D., & Fdida, S. (2005). A preferential attachment gathering mobility model. *IEEE Communications Letters, 9*(10). doi:10.1109/LCOMM.2005.10023.

Camp, T., Boleng, J., & Davies, V. (2002). A survey of mobility models for ad hoc network research. *Wireless Communication and Mobile Computing, 2*(5), 483–502. doi:10.1002/wcm.72.

Chandra, R., Ramasubramanian, V., & Birman, K. (2001). Anonymous gossip: Improving multicast reliability in mobile ad hoc networks. In *Proceeding of the 21st International Conference on Distributed Computing Systems* (ICDCS'01). Mesa, AZ: ICDCS.

Chen, W., & Chen, P. (2003). Group mobility management in wireless ad hoc networks. In *Proceeding of the 58th Vehicular Technology Conference* (VTC'03). Orlando, FL: VTC.

Davies, V. (2000). *Evaluating mobility models within an ad hoc network*. (Master's thesis). Colorado School of Mines. Retrieved from http://citeseerx.ist.psu.edu/viewdoc/summary?doi=10.1.1.18.4191

Diab, A. (2010). *Mobility management in IP-based networks: Analysis, design, programming and computer-based learning modules*. (Dissertation thesis). Ilmenau University of Technology, Ilmenau, Germany.

Dobson, S., et al. (2006). A survey of autonomic communications. *ACM Transactions on Autonomous and Adaptive Systems, 1*(2).

Erdos, P., & Renyi, A. (1959). On random graphs. *Publications Mathematicae, 6*, 290–297.

Ghosh, J. (2006). *Sociological orbit-based mobility profiling and routing for wireless networks*. (PhD Thesis). Department of Computer Science and Engineering, The State University of New York, Buffalo, NY.

Ghosh, J., Ngo, H. Q., & Qiao, C. (2006). Mobility profile-based routing within intermittently connected mobile ad hoc networks (ICMAN). In *Proceedings of the 2nd International Conference on Wireless Communications and Mobile Computing* (IWCMC'06). Vancouver, Canada: IWCMC.

Ghosh, J., Philip, S. J., & Qiao, C. (2007). Sociological orbit aware location approximation and routing (SOLAR) in MANET. *Ad Hoc Networks*, *5*(2), 189–209. doi:10.1016/j.adhoc.2005.10.003.

Ghosh, J., Yoon, S., Ngo, H. Q., & Qiao, C. (2005). *Sociological orbits for efficient routing in intermittently connected mobile ad hoc networks (UB CSE Technical Report)*. Buffalo, NY: Department of Computer Science and Engineering, University at Buffalo, The State University of New York.

Gonzalez, M. C., Hidalgo, C. A., & Barabasi, A.-L. (2008). Understanding individual human mobility patterns. *Nature Journal*, *453*, 779–782. doi:10.1038/nature06958 PMID:18528393.

Gramoli, V., Kermarrec, A. M., & Merrer, E. L. (2008). SONDe: A self-organizing object deployment algorithm in large-scale dynamic systems. In *Proceeding of the 7th Dependable Computing Conference* (EDCC'08). Kaunas, Lithuania: Vytautas Magnus University.

Haas, Z. (1997). A new routing protocol for reconfigurable wireless networks. In Proceeding of the IEEE International Conference on Universal Personal Communications (ICUPC'97), (pp. 562–565). IEEE.

Handorean, R., Gill, C., & Roman, G. C. (2004). Accommodating transient connectivity in ad hoc and mobile settings. *Lecture Notes in Computer Science*, *3001*, 305–322. doi:10.1007/978-3-540-24646-6_22.

Henderson, T., Kotz, D., & Abyzov, I. (2004). The changing usage of a mature campus-wide wireless network. In *Proceeding of the 10th Annual International Conference on Mobile Computing and Networking* (MobiCom'04), (pp. 187–201). New York, NY: ACM Press.

Hong, X., Gerla, M., Pei, G., & Chiang, C. C. (1999). A group mobility model for ad hoc wireless networks. In *Proceeding of the 2nd ACM International Workshop on Modeling, Analysis, and Simulation of Wireless and Mobile Systems* (MSWiM'99). Seattle, WA: MSWiM.

Hsu, W., Spyropoulos, T., Psounis, K., & Helmy, A. (2007). Modeling time-variant user mobility in wireless mobile networks. In *Proceeding of the 26th IEEE International Conference on Computer Communications* (INFOCOM'07). University of Florida.

IEEE 802.11b/d3.0 Wireless LAN Medium Access Control (MAC) and Physical Layer (PHY) Specification. (1999). Washington, DC: IEEE.

Isaacman, S., Becker, R., Cáceres, R., Kobourov, S., Martonosi, M., Rowland, J., & Varshavsky, A. (2011). Identifying important places in people's lives from cellular network data. In *Proceeding of the 9th International Conference on Pervasive Computing* (Pervasive'11). San Francisco, CA: Pervasive.

Isaacman, S., Becker, R., Cáceres, R., Kobourov, S., Martonosi, M., Rowland, J., & Varshavsky, A. (2011a). Ranges of human mobility in Los Angeles and New York. In *Proceeding of the 8th IEEE Workshop on Managing Ubiquitous Communications and Services* (MUCS' 11). Seattle, WA: IEEE.

Isaacman, S., Becker, R., Cáceres, R., Kobourov, S., Rowland, J., & Varshavsky, A. (2010). A tale of two cities. In *Proceeding of the 11th Workshop on Mobile Computing Systems and Applications* (HotMobile'10). HotMobile.

Isaacman, S., Becker, R., Cáceres, R., Martonosi, M., Rowland, J., Varshavsky, A., & Willinger, W. (2012). Human mobility modeling at metropolitan scales. In *Proceeding of the 10th International Conference on Mobile Systems* (MobiSys'12). ACM.

Jain, R., Lelescu, D., & Balakrishnan, M. (2005). Model T: An empirical model for user registration patterns in a campus wireless LAN. In *Proceeding of the 11th Annual International Conference on Mobile Computing and Networking* (MobiCom'05), (pp. 170–184). New York, NY: ACM.

Kotz, D., & Essien, K. (2002). Analysis of a campus-wide wireless network. In *Proceedings of the 8th Annual International Conference on Mobile Computing and Networking* (MobiCom'02). ACM Press.

Kotz, D., & Essien, K. (2002a). *Characterizing usage of a campus-wide wireless network* (Technical Report TR2002-423). Hanover, NH: Department of Computer Science, Dartmouth College.

Kotz, D., & Henderson, T. (2005). CRAWDAD: A community resource for archiving wireless data at Dartmouth. *IEEE Pervasive Computing / IEEE Computer Society [and] IEEE Communications Society, 4*(4), 12–14. doi:10.1109/MPRV.2005.75.

Kotz, D., Henderson, T., & Abyzov, I. (2012). *CRAWDAD trace Dartmouth*. Retrieved from http://crawdad.cs.dartmouth.edu

Lawler, E. L. (1972). A procedure for computing the K best solutions to discrete optimization problems and its application to the shortest path problem. *Management Science, 18*, 401–405. doi:10.1287/mnsc.18.7.401.

Lawler, E. L. (2001). *Combinatorial optimization: Networks and matroids*. New York: Dover Publications.

Leguay, J., Friedman, T., & Conan, V. (2005). *Evaluating mobility pattern space routing for DTNs*. Universite Pierre et Marie Curie, Laboratorie. Retrieved from http://arxiv.org/PS_cache/cs/pdf/0511/0511102v1.pdf

Lelescu, D., Kozat, U. C., Jain, R., & Balakrishnan, M. (2006). Model T++: An empirical joint space-time registration model. In *Proceeding of the 7th ACM International Symposium on Mobile Ad Hoc Networking and Computing* (MobiHoc'06), (pp. 61–72). New York, NY: ACM.

Lopez-Nores, M., Garcia-Duque, J., Pazos-Arias, J. J., Blanco-Fernández, Y., & Diaz-Redondo, R. P. (2008). Qualitative assessment of approaches to coordinate activities of mobile hosts in ad hoc networks. *IEEE Communications Magazine, 46*(12). doi:10.1109/MCOM.2008.4689216.

Musolesi, M., Hailes, S., & Mascolo, C. (2005). Social networks-based ad hoc mobility models. In *Proceeding of 3rd UK-UbiNet Workshop: Designing, Evaluating and Using Ubiquitous Computing Systems*. Bath, UK: University of Bath.

Musolesi, M., & Mascolo, C. (2006). A community-based mobility model for ad hoc network research. In *Proceeding of the 2nd International Workshop on Multi-Hop Ad Hoc Networks: From Theory to Reality* (RESLMAN'06). New York, NY: ACM.

Musolesi, M., & Mascolo, C. (2007). Designing mobility models based on social network theory. *ACM SIGMOBILE Mobile Computing and Communications Review Newsletter, 11*(3), 59–70. doi:10.1145/1317425.1317433.

Musolesi, M., & Mascolo, C. (2009). Mobility models for systems evaluation. In *Middleware for Network Eccentric and Mobile Applications*. Berlin: Springer. doi:10.1007/978-3-540-89707-1_3.

Noulas, A., Scellato, S., Lambiotte, R., Pontil, M., & Mascolo, C. (2012). A tale of many cities: Universal patterns in human urban mobility. *PLoS ONE*. Retrieved from http://www.plosone.org/article/info%3Adoi%2F10.1371%2Fjournal.pone.0037027

Ovidiu, V., Harrison, M., Vogt, H., Kalaboukas, K., Tomasella, M., & Wouters, K. ...Haller, S. (2009). Internet of things: Strategic research roadmap. *European Research Cluster: The European Research Cluster on the Internet of Things (IoT)*. Retrieved from http://www.internet-of-things-research.eu/pdf/IoT_Cluster_Strategic_Research_Agenda_2011.pdf

Ranjan Roy, R. (2011). Handbook of mobile ad hoc networks for mobility models. Berlin: Springer Science+Business Media. ISBN 978-1-4419-6048-1

Rapoport, A. (1957). Contribution to the theory of random and biased networks. *The Bulletin of Mathematical Biophysics*, (19): 257–277. doi:10.1007/BF02478417.

Sanchez, M., & Manzoni, P. (2001). Anejos: A java-based simulator for ad hoc networks. *Future Generation Computer Systems*, *17*(5), 573–583. doi:10.1016/S0167-739X(00)00040-6.

Sarkar, T. K., Wicks, M. C., Salazar-Palma, M., & Bonneau, R. J. (2004). A survey of various propagation models for mobile communication. *Smart Antennas*, 239-307.

Scott, J. (2000). *Social networks analysis: A handbook*. London: Sage Publications.

Sen, R., Handorean, R., Roman, G. C., & Hackmann, G. (2004). Knowledge-driven interactions with services across ad hoc networks. In *Proceedings of the 2nd International Conference on Service Oriented Computing* (ICSOC, '04). New York, NY: ICSOC.

Song, C., Qu, Z., Blumm, N., & Barabási, A.-L. (2010). Limits of predictability in human mobility. *Science*, 327. PMID:20167789.

Song, L., Kotz, D., Jain, R., & He, X. (2004). Evaluating next-cell predictors with extensive wi-fi mobility data. In *Proceeding of 23th IEEE International Conference on Computer Communications* (INFOCOM'04). Hong Kong, China: IEEE.

Tang, D., & Baker, M. (2000). Analysis of a local-area wireless network. In *Proceedings of the 6th Annual International Conference on Mobile Computing and Networking* (MobiCom'00). New York, NY: ACM Press.

Tang, D., & Baker, M. (2002). Analysis of a metropolitan-area wireless network. *Wireless Networks*, *8*(2/3), 107–120. doi:10.1023/A:1013739407600.

Tuduce, C., & Gross, T. (2005). A mobility model-based on WLAN traces and its validation. In *Proceeding of the 24th IEEE International Conference on Computer Communications* (INFOCOM'05), (pp. 19 – 24). IEEE.

Wang, K. H., & Li, B. (2002). Group mobility and partition prediction in wireless ad hoc networks. In *Proceeding of the IEEE International Conference on Communications* (ICC'02). New York: IEEE.

Watts, D. J. (1999). *Small worlds, the dynamics of networks between order and randomness*. Princeton, NJ: Princeton University Press.

Yoon, J., Noble, B. D., Liu, M., & Kim, M. (2006). Building realistic mobility models from coarse-grained traces. In *Proceeding of the 4th International Conference on Mobile Systems, Applications, and Services* (MobiSys'06), (pp. 177–190). New York, NY: ACM.

Zonoozi, M., & Dassanayake, P. (1997). User mobility modeling and characterization of mobility pattern. *IEEE Journal on Selected Areas in Communications*, *15*(7), 1239–1252. doi:10.1109/49.622908.

ENDNOTES

[1]   The new velocity is equal to the old one, since the velocity remains constant. So, there is no temporal dependency of the velocity.

[2]   Motion profiles-based

[3]   The RVG model characterizes the mobility of MNs by the velocity and the distance.

[4]   We assume here the RW model for groups' members. This is the most used model.

[5]   Mobility model-dependent

[6]   This concept simply means that MNs attach to the communities they are interested in, although there may exist many other communities.

[7]   These geographical areas represent, in principle, areas where specific social communities exist. Therefore, many communities may coexist beside each other in the same area.

Chapter 12
Spatial Relations in Contextual Information for Mobile Emergency Messaging

Alaa Almagrabi
Latrobe University, Australia & King Abdulaziz University, Saudi Arabia

Seng W. Loke
Latrobe University, Australia

Torab Torabi
Latrobe University, Australia

ABSTRACT

Responding to a disaster is a process that should take the least time with high-level information. It requires human decisions that could delay the whole process, thus putting more lives at stake. However, recent technological developments improve this process by facilitating decisions within the domain. Discovering the spatial relationship can help to clarify the spatial environment for the domain. In this chapter, the authors give an overview of using spatial modelling and spatial relations for context-aware messaging with emphasis on emergency situations. They utilize various existing spatial relations recognized within the field of spatial computing such as RCC8 and Egenhofer relations. The RCC8 and Egenhofer relations are examined besides a range of spatial relations using English phrases in Mona-ont emergency ontology. The Mona-ont emergency ontology is used to describe emergency scenarios. The Mona-ont emergency ontology is employed by the Mona Emergency System (MES) that generates alert messaging services to actors within a disaster area. The authors demonstrate the validity of the Mona-ont spatial relations in describing a (fictitious) flood situation in the Melbourne CBD area. They also prescribe the structure of such context-aware messages (i.e. their content and target description) for the MES system.

DOI: 10.4018/978-1-4666-4695-7.ch012

1. INTRODUCTION

Disasters are unavoidable, though modern science can predict the upcoming event, but the key to avoid such unfortunate episodes are yet to be discovered. The development of advanced technology for disaster management can offer benefit by decreasing the period of decision making (Bonham-Carter, 1994). Emergency management rests on three pillars: knowledge of history, an understanding of human nature expressed in the social sciences, and specialized technical expertise in response mechanisms (Canton, 2006). Emergency systems submit to the procedures that we establish in place in order to help us successfully deal with disasters (Berry, 1996). Advancement in technologies, changes in geographic scenarios and political differences, have made it mandatory for the deployment of an enhanced emergency management system. The evolving threats, the realities of global climate change and social, economic, and political environments demand further innovative approaches and management (Haddow, Bullock, & Coppola, 2010)

During disasters, many lives can be lost because of inefficiently managed rescue operations. In the case of any disaster, besides the government controlled rescue workers, many private or NGOs (Non Government Organizations) get involved in the rescue operation. Every rescue team operates using it's own independent communication system. This can slow the deliverance of protection to the victims, thereby creating complications in the entire operation. Emphasis should be put on coordination among all the different rescue teams. Usually, the rescue teams are monitored and controlled by a single leader. However, in order for the system to operate effectively, the system needs to be spatially aware about the individual contexts of personnel and systems, and the existence of other systems and their relations to each other. In their study Holzmann, and A. Ferscha, (2010) stated that spatial awareness is defined as follows: "Spatial awareness allows the system to determine and use

it's spatial properties to relate these properties to the spatial properties of other systems". Spatial awareness requires spatial contexts to be acquired via sensors, for such contexts to be represented and interpreted, and shared among diverse networked systems, as in context-aware applications (Dey, 2001) & (Salber, Dey, & Abowd, 1999)

Also, the level of abstraction of the representation of spatial context is important. For example, some systems using location information might only be concerned with high-level information like rooms and buildings instead of geographical coordinates. Many researchers have been addressing such symbolic representations of locations (Ferscha, C. Holzmann, & S. Oppl, 2004). For example, "left" or "near" can be a replacement for numeric angles or distances can be discovered, as in (Kortuem, Kray, & Gellersen, 2005). However, one of the fundamental problems of representing spatial data within a building is the need for it to be formally defined and standardized (Ekholm, & Fridqvist, 2000) . Furthermore, space can be formalized in a logical language using an ontology. An ontology is used to represent a particular situation or domain by determining the concepts that represent the domain and the relations between these concepts. Ontology allows knowledge to be shared and reused (Blomqvist & Öhgren, 2008).

The aim of this chapter is to review work on describing spatial modeling and spatial relationships especially with their usage in emergency systems in mind. The chapter will discuss the methodology to describe spatial relationships for context-aware messaging and apply it to an example emergency scenario. Furthermore, the chapter defines the spatial relations for our Mona-ont emergency ontology that operates in our Mona Emergency System (MES). The MES aims to disseminate alert messages to the user in the time of disasters using context information. In addition, we use selected existing spatial relations used and identified in the literature (e.g., RCC8 and Egenhofer relations[1]), with an interpretation for these notions, to describe the Mona-ont spatial relations. The Mona-and emergency ontology assists in describing and organizing spatial information within the emergency domain. The chapter illustrates our approach by describing an urban area in a virtual way in order to facilitate actors using the MES for messaging during rescue processes in a flood situation. MES spatial relations assist in structuring the message target and content, as represented using the EBNF format[2]. The MES uses the spatial relations to provide the actor with SMS messages. The SMS messages to survivors contain information about the path to the rescue team or to a safe area as well as the direction or a map.

2. BACKGROUND AND RELATED WORK

2.1 Background on Spatial Modeling and Spatial Relations

Spatial can be defined as involving, or having the nature of space. Moreover, spatial refers to an area such as country, mountain or building. In addition, spatial can be anything related to a particular area or space, not necessarily physical or geographic. In the old Latin language, the term "spatium" can mean different concepts like ''area'', ''room'', and ''interval of space or time'' (Webster's, 1995). Moreover, other dictionaries like Collins states that "space" can be defined in various ways

(McLeod, 1987). For instance, "space" can be described as the unrestricted three-dimensional span in which all material objects are located. Also, it can be seen as a gap of distance or time between two points, or objects. Every single description has a different understanding of space.

"Space" could be defined as a property of things, for example, the organization of buildings and their elements (Ekholm, & Fridqvist, 2000). Moreover, stating the spatial relationships can help define a region (Papadias, & Kavouras, 1994). A spatial relation is a common property of one or two or more things. It can be named as a separation relation; it does not affect the conditions of the related things themselves (Bunge, 1977). The idea is that spatial relations are properties of things that cannot be found separately from things; consequently, without things there are no spatial relations. The size of the space may depend on the relative position of the separated parts (see Figure 1).

Spatial relations usually contain topological relations, direction relations and distance relations. Furthermore, spatial relations play a central role in Geographic Information Science research. Current geographic information systems (GIS) integrate powerful tools to handle quantitative spatial relations, though their abilities in reasoning about qualitative spatial relations remain highly limited. Discovering the spatial relationships can help define the spatial environment for the domain. The topological relations illustrate

Figure 1. Space as a mutual property of a collective of things, and as an intrinsic property of a single thing (Ekholm, & Fridqvist, 2000)

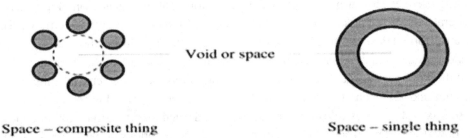

neighborhood and direction relations such as North and South, and distance relations such as near, far and others. Spatial relations are modeled by quantitative measurements or are represented qualitatively, depending on the requirements (Yao, & Thill, 2006). Moreover, spatial relations also comprise comparative or ordinal and fuzzy relations. The comparative or ordinal spatial relations describe inclusion or position such as "in" and "at", whereas fuzzy relations are such as "next to", and "close" (Pullar, & Egenhofer, 1988). Furthermore, spatial extension can be used along with the spatial relations to provide a full representation of an area.

There are two types of abstraction to represent spatial contexts. First, quantitative abstractions present an explanation for qualitative based queries. It enables qualitative spatial relations in tasks involving information query, retrieval, or even a data entry in geospatial information systems (Yao, & Thill, 2006). The spatial properties are represented with numerical values that are used to calculate the spatial relations between them. As a result, a model referred to as Zones-of-Influence has been given in (Ferscha et al., 2008). A Zone-of-Influence property represents a relevance geographic region that influences a spatial aware application. Technology rich-artifacts are linked with one or more Zones-of-Influence at a time, collectively representing the spatial knowledge. Second, qualitative abstraction which used to demonstrate the spatial relations in a way that the continuous relation values are quantized according to the requested accuracy and signified with discrete systems of symbols. Qualitative representations have concerned by researchers in the field of spatial reasoning (Cohn, & Hazarika, 2001). Once the spatial cognition of humans is involved, the qualitative approaches are regularly chosen. That is due to three main reasons. First, qualitative approaches are used to draw conclusions from common abstractions (Musto et al., 2000). Second, qualitative approaches are similar to natural language expressions and consequently

considered cognitively more sufficient (Renz, & Mitra, 2004). Third, qualitative abstractions are preferred with such systems that have limited computing resources or sensing capabilities (Gottfried, Guesgen, & Hubner, 2006)

One of the main existing challenges to propose spatial information systems is to prepare GISs to handle common sense geographic queries that are given by users without training in spatial technologies. The reason behind that is the view of the geographic world apprehended by the general public which is in the form of mental images or story descriptions, different from the digital forms stored in computer databases (Egenhofer, & Kuhn, 1998). The past decade has observed a rising flow of research on diverse aspects of qualitative spatial relations (Frank, 1992). Developing the capacity for handling natural language descriptions in general was a significant research area to enhance geographic information systems (GIS) user interfaces (Gould, 1989). Addressing the issue of accommodating common-sense geographic queries of the general public was embedded in many new geospatial information technologies and the notion of Naive Geography (Egenhofer, & Mark, 1995). The new face of geospatial applications can be represented easily with the spread of the World Wide Web, wireless communication and information technologies, and telematics technologies. User can query all sorts of space-related questions in their daily life using space-aware devices and location-based services which promise to offer users an abundance of information on their local environment in the field or on the street (Yao, & Thill, 2006).

2.2 Related Work on Spatial Data within Emergency Systems

With the accelerated increase in world population, there's an extreme demand for an advanced Emergency Management System. Effective emergency management requires the formulation of a new socio-technological system capable of coping with the situation at hand (Xiong, Liu, Liu, Zhu, & Shen, 2012). An effective emergency management system is supported by modern technology tools. However, there are certain restrictions for these tools. Frassl, Lichtenstern, Khider and Angermann (2010) stated that innovative tools have to be developed in order to handle diverse information in global disaster management operations. They present Disaster Management Tool (DMT) according to two types of requirements. First, the functional requirements illustrate the plan of the data management, user interface, device control and synchronization. Second, the nonfunctional requirements that relate to the situations in disaster management; these are usability, autonomy, reliability, integrity, interoperability and frugality. Here, we emphasize on the context aware messaging in terms of defining the content and the target of messages. We utilize the spatial relation in order to construct extra knowledge about an emergency situation. Also, we are talking about appropriate utilization and expert handling of computers and other devices in the entire rescue operation. In an event of natural calamity, though there could be much advancement in emergency systems, mismanagement and lack of communication may cause many losses.

In recent years, information technology has moved towards service-oriented architectures and distributed computing (Luo, 2009). The past disastrous events have compelled the authorities to consider induction of computer technologies into emergency management tactics. The success of the entire rescue operation is dependent on five factors; early warning, teams approaching the affected area in time, diagnosing the exact level of tragedy, aligning the rescue workers and developing good coordination. There is much research on minimizing a disaster's effect, being a serious concern.

Disasters fall into two categories; these are natural and human-caused disasters, both cases leading to destruction of life or property or both. For example, bush fires in Australia and Russia in the recent past are examples of disasters that call for adequate preparation measures. Similarly, flooding issues in various parts of the world are part of the increasing disaster incident. Destructive winds such as the hurricane Katrina also form part of unending misery. However, modern technological developments, and in particular, geospatial technology are catching up with some of these disasters by establishing methods of minimizing their effects. Measures that facilitate the prediction of the possibility of incidents are available. On the other hand, nature must take it's due course; so, establishing more mechanisms to address emerging issues become a priority. In particular, management by objectives promotes healthy relations among employees in emergency response centers while unity of command helps different groups to interact during such situations, and technology can help this.

For example, emergency systems are useful for enhancing response to disasters. It employs geospatial technology, enhances decision-making, facilitates adequate preparations, and assists in the evacuation process (Nakashima, Aghajan, & Augusto, 2009). Geospatial technology facilitates decision making through simulations and providing reliable alternatives in complex issues. The phases during emergencies are mitigation, preparation, response and recovery (Cohn, & Hazarika, 2001).

One of the most efficient emergency systems available in USA is the Incident Command System. The system has several features that include Management by Objectives, Unity of Command, Establishment and Transfer of Command, Organizational Flexibility, Unified Command, Span of Control, Common Terminology, Personnel Accountability, Integrated Communications, Resources Management, and the Incident Action Plan. All these feature work together to achieve the objectives of the organization (Bigley, & Roberts, 2001). However, the increasing use of geospatial technology in such emergency systems could make them more useful in responding to disasters.

Spatial data models and the use of geographic information system (GIS) in providing information concerning current events are increasingly attracting global interest in a number of fields. In the military, for instance, this technology is extremely useful particularly in enabling the industry to describe different positions, materials, and sites by making use of wireless devices and the satellite. The military uses this technology to monitor the changes in weather that may interfere with their activities such as flying jets and even managing disasters. Disaster management systems dealing with the civilians require similar techniques to facilitate the detection of emergencies in time (Sene, 2008). This will help in preparing an adequate response in time and designing the best plan of action to adopt in case an emergency arises. However, during an emergency situation, many government and private teams get involved in the rescue work.

One problem during an emergency for teams in the field and the command center is to get an overview about who is doing what and how it is related to other activities (e.g., in the Pervasive Emergency Response Process Management System) (Franke, Ulmer, & Charoy, 2010). A command and control centre is established to manage the whole operation; unfortunately, the centre is incapable of issuing proper directives to the teams if complete knowledge of the area and team's movement is not supplied to the center. Again, the blame goes to the weak communication network. To make communication more effective, a Process Management System can be used in emergency operations. It develops a chain link among the teams. In such a PMS, process schemas (in the form of Activity Diagrams) are defined, describing different aspects, such as task/activities, control and data flow, task assignment to services (coordinating Mobile Actors in Pervasive and Mobile Scenarios)]. Everyone is equipped with a wireless or cellular phone to allow the transfer of the current information to the base station. Utilizing a PMS, the same information is gathered in a

laptop or a PC; knowing the current team status and the team's position, a leader issues further action directives (de Leoni et al., 2008).

Exact location and shortest routes if given to the teams saves a lot of time. The context-aware emergency remedy system (CARE) has made it possible for the emergency teams to reach the affected areas in the shortest possible time. Based on GIS/GPS technologies, linked with the hospital, it enables the medical teams to give proper treatment to the survivals (Kung, Lin, Hsu, & Liu, 2005). In addition, modeling the emergency scenario will make it easy to use the available knowledge in an efficient way. Furthermore, the use of qualitative and quantitative spatial relations can help provide information to avoid tragedy.

3. MOTIVATING SCENARIO

In order to evaluate the MES system which uses spatial information in defining the Mona-ont ontology; we describe the following (fictitious) scenario about a flood at a Melbourne urban area (CBD), where there are many people around all the time (see Figure 2). We assumed that the flood started because of the heavy rain at the Yarra River. The flood is starting to take over the walking path between Queensbridge St and Kilda Rd from the Eureka Tower side where a lot of people walk. The water level is rising quickly, and people need to evacuate the area as soon as possible. However, the spatial environment is represented in MES via the Mona-and ontology allowing the MES system to categorize the CBD into several zones depending on the flood level and to inform people using messaging services about the flood such as direction, range and status of the situation at different times. Also, people can be given directions to the nearest point of interest (POI), i.e. high buildings, in the case of the flood. MES assists the rescue operation using spatial information such as "near", "far", and "next" to define the relations between actors and

Figure 2. Motivating Scenario snapshot
Copyright 2013 TerraMetrics, Inc. www.terrametrics.com

POIs within the flood situation. In addition, MES supplies the actors with quantitative information such as the distance to POIs and the range of the danger. For example, the MES informs Rechard who is located in the walking path at the front of the South Art and Leisure Precinct to go inside the building which is 30 meters away. Moreover, MES will inform Ahmed and David to run to the nearest POI. The MES can inform the survivors about all available information in order for them to avoid tragedy.

Moreover, the MES' real-time representation of the spatial environment (and its actors) via the Mona-ont Ontology provides a lot of knowledge

to the rescuer team about the survivors, such as the number of survivors within the area as well as other information where available, such as the health conditions of the survivors in order to perform the most suitable aid for them. In addition, the MES spatial environment supports representing unexpected events during flood times. For example, suppose that Mr. Smith is stuck somewhere because his wheelchair was broken on the way out of the flood area; the MES will send the medical team to assist him. Furthermore, representing the spatial environment allows the MES to apply priorities in the case of shortages in the number of rescuers. For example, Alaa who is young and fit, is located in the Red zone besides the Henry family. Both survivors will receive the alert message and will get some assistance. However, according to MES there is a policeman nearby. The MES will send the policeman towards Henry's family assuming that Alaa can handle the situation alone using the alert message he received. Moreover, the MES keeps updating the POI information and informs the survivors about alternative rescue plans, including directions to the new POI. The POI can be defined as a new building or a level in a building depending on the situation (such as water rising). The MES will update the rescuer team about any changes in the situation. Moreover, the MES is designed to support more complicated scenarios, where many survivors are in a danger area and the number of rescuer teams cannot handle the large number of survivors. For example, in the case of having one rescuer in the walking path between two survivors, the MES will offer the available information to the rescuer to help the rescuer assess the different priorities or urgency of the survivors. For example, Seth and Julia are located near a policeman but in different danger zones. Seth is in a yellow zone whereas Julia is in a red danger zone; so, the policeman will use this information to decide that Julia needs assistance first.

Furthermore, the use of social relations allows the MES system to inform actor's relatives or friends about their status within the hazard area. For example, the MES system can inform the Smith family that Smith is safe at the moment. Furthermore, MES keeps tracking the danger information and the POI status in order to inform the survivors about any change. For example, in the case of the water rising to a certain level, the MES will advise the survivors within the building to move towards higher levels. The MES uses available information for the decision making process. Furthermore, the MES provides information about the number of survivors in the risk area, the target of the first aid and types of assistance required. Additionally,

survivors need to have enough information about the current situation which includes the danger information and POI status, location and distance. Also, rescuers need to know practical and available information about the survivors, current dangers and points of interest status, all these information need to be updated in time, in order to make the best decision in the rescue process. In contrast, for all these scenarios the communication between the system's numerous actors must be organized and arranged. There is an urgent call for such a system that addresses these issues and to provide reliable useful timely information to the actors. In order to have a knowledge base that supports these functionalities, designing an efficient ontology to model the spatial environment is required.

4. MES MONA-ONT ONTOLOGY FOR URBAN AREA

An ontology is an organized knowledge structure that is understandable by humans and machines (Ezzell, Fishwick, & Cendan, 2011). An ontology describes a common vocabulary as well the meaning of it's terms and the relations between them (Gomez-Perez, 1999). An ontology can be described as a set of representative primitives that form knowledge about a domain (Gruber, 1993), and offers sharing and using of the available knowledge about the domain (Blomqvist, & Öhgren, 2008). There are five component types to distinguish the knowledge in an anthology such as taxonomy, relations, functions, axioms and instances (Araujo, Rocha, Campos., & Boukerche, 2008). An ontology assists in distributing the knowledge about an event. We developed Mona-ont ontology for context aware emergency messaging to capture, form and filter information about events and situation status within the emergency domain. The information is expressed by the use of context information involved in emergency domain to:

- Describe the targets/destinations/receivers for context-aware messaging.

- Support explaining events in the emerging domain.

- Help defining the emergency situation concepts and it's attributes.

- Express and discover the spatial relations that link emergency concepts (e.g., actors and POIs).

- Allow the spatial relations to be understandable by humans.

- Assist in building and modeling the emergency scenario.

- Define appropriate message contents for actors within the domain.

- Allow sharing information between concepts within the emergency scenario.

- Assist simulating the scenarios for context-aware messaging.

4.1 MES Mona-Ont Emergency Ontology Concept

The Mona-ont emergency ontology design was stimulated by TOVE ontologies (Gruninger, & Fox, 1995). The Mona-ont ontology was built according to several motivating scenarios (such as the one given earlier) and based on the concepts represented in one of the domain articles on emergency inspired by the Cyc method which is ontology and knowledge base of everyday common sense knowledge that allow reasoning (Elkan, & Greiner,1993). We use Protege[3] as the ontology editing tool to build Mona-ont in OWL. Mona-ont ontology can be used for ontology-based querying; allowing the actor to issue queries and obtains results over the ontology by employing reasoning services (Alberts, & Franconi, 2012).

The Mona-ont emergency ontology assists in describing common scenarios that may occur during emergency situations using ordinary language concepts, attributes and relations. It helps define the targets and the contents of messages. The Mo-

na-ont emergency ontology describes a scenario over a region covered by a disaster management unit. Also, the disaster management unit contains information about actors who are to be directed to points of interest (POI), which represent safe points, in order to survive. In addition, according to the danger information, the disaster management unit divides the region into surprise, depending on the level of the danger or the distance from the hazards such as the flood areas. Mona-ont aims to provide a schema to capture the knowledge in disaster situations, to be used by possibly different organizations and parties involved. Figure 3 shows the overview of the Mona-ont emergency general ontology, illustrating the relationships between the ontology's main concepts. It contains the concepts which will help in defining the targets in messages as well the contents of the messages. The Mona-ont emergency general ontology represents context information that will always be updated by the MES.

Figure 3 presents Mona-ont concepts and relations for general emergency situations. It shows the applied spatial relationships that connect the system's main entities and describes events during hazardous situations. The Mona-ont ontology has the following key concepts described as follows:

- **Disaster Management Unit:** It represents the unit that is responsible for overseeing and tracking emergency situations including actors, POI and the danger information in the region, and in acquiring contextual information, as well as servicing the actors. It represents any organization that uses the MES to deal with disasters.

- **Emergency Situation:** It represents an event that incorporates danger information such as type, range, direction and speed of the danger/hazard.

- **Region:** It represents the whole area where the actors, POI and the emergency situation reside, and it can be a small area, city,

Figure 3. Mon-ont ontology for General Emergency purposes

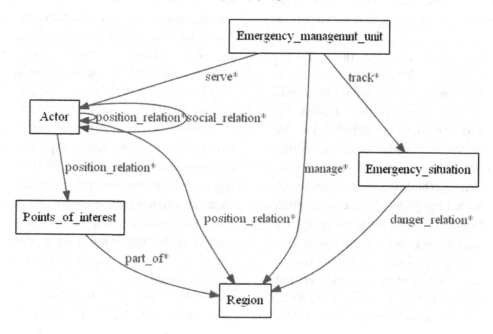

state or country. It is described by a status or condition of the area such as "destroyed" and "empty".

- **Actors:** Refers to the people within the region inside or outside the affected area(s) including survivor, rescuer and the user who are the actor social relation.

- **Points of Interest (POI):** It represents the geographical features (man-made or natural) that are part of the region that may influence the rescue operation. It is categorized according to the danger level that influences the POI, i.e., positive and negative POI. For example, in a flood situation, high buildings are considered as positive POI.

4.2 MES Mona-ont Emergency Ontology Spatial Relation

Mona-ont emergency ontology uses diverse types of spatial relations. Spatial relations connect Mona-ont general ontology concepts and are the key to constructing the alert messages. The

spatial relations to assist in querying and filtering the contextual knowledge used for messaging purposes during hazardous situations include the following:

- **Danger Relation:** Used to link the emergency situation and the region in order to describe the danger situation such as "closing in", "finished", "stopped", "moving towards", "end", "terminated within", "affecting", "changing direction", "spreading around", "taking over", "extend", "raise within", or "drop".

- **Position Relation:** Present geographic information that gives relative position information within the Mona-ont ontology, such as "near", "far", "next to", "close to" "away" and "in the neighborhood of". For example, such a relation spatially links an actor with POIs as well link actors with affected areas within the region, and also to describe the relative positions between the actors themselves.

We also use social relations together with spatial relations to define the spatial-social aspects within the region for the MES actors such as friend, colleague, parent, spouse, cousin, children and neighbor. These relations express the points of interest relation and actors within the spatial relation as well as categorization of areas. For example, suppose we need to use the MES to send a message to Mr. Smith who is inside the Blue zone and inform him that he is near the South Art and Leisure Precinct building. We need to identify an approach that integrates the use of quantitative and qualitative spatial relations in order to define the right message at the right time in terms of content and target. Spatial relations used in Mona-ont are based on existing spatial relations used and identified in the literature (e.g., RCC8 or Egenhofer relations) as shown in Table 1; MES translates existing RCC8 and Egenhofer quantitative spatial relations to measurable quantities as we show later. Note that such a translation might depend on the scale and actual application and hence Table 1 serves only as a practical example of what is possible.

Table 1 shows the development of the MES spatial relations based on RCC8 and Egenhofer relations for describing a situation. MES takes regions and points as fundamental notions. On the other hand, the RCC8 and Egenhofer relations are concerned about a region and it's relation to other regions instead of points. However, we can use these types of relations to describe regions as well as points within regions.

Furthermore, the Mona-ont ontology for an emergency situation can be expanded to cover different types of disasters and service different types of organizations. For example, Figure 4 shows the extended Mona-ont emergency ontology in a flood situation which includes more concepts to identify the context information within a flood situation, as well as spatial relations to connect these concepts.

Figure 4 gives an idea about extra context information in the form of concepts and relations that are used to describe flood emergency situations such as, the affected area where the danger occurs. It is divided into three different zones, the red, yellow and blue zones. The spatial relations assist in mapping, finding, and filtering target actors for messages within the emergency domain apart from being used for defining the content of the alert message. The following section dis-

Table 1. The development of MES spatial relations from RCC8 and Egenhofer relations

RCC8	Egenhofer	MES	Example	Explanation
DC (David, f)	disjoint	far, away from, distant	David away from f	David = survivor f = flood
EC (f, a)	meet	reach, coming towards, arrive at	f coming towards a	f = flood a = walking path
PO (f, C)	overlap	Overlap, cover some, entering	f entering c	f = flood c = CBD area
EQ (r, a)	equal	cover, same position, share	r cover a	r = red zone a = walking path
TPP (r, c)	covered by	part of, inside, within, in,	r within c	r = red zone c = CBD area
NTPPi (f, r)	contain	include, contain, have	c include t	c = CBD area t = towers
NTPP (Julia, a)	inside,	part of, inside, within	Julia inside r	Julia = survivor r = red zone
TPPi (a, r)	covers	include, contain, have	c have t	c = CBD area t = towers

Figure 4. Mon-ont flood emergency ontology

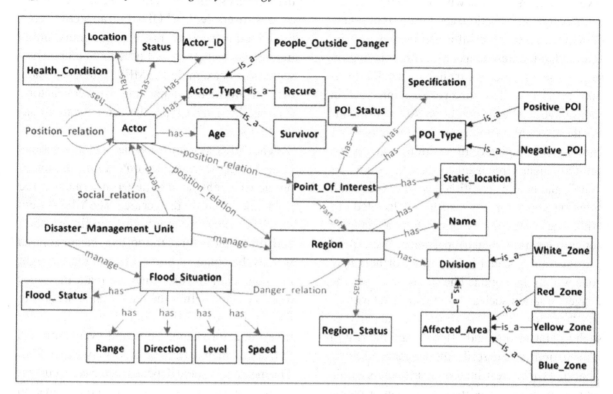

cusses the Mona Emergency System context information and techniques that are used in addressing flood situations.

5. MONA EMERGENCY SYSTEM SPATIAL RELATION MODEL AND TECHNIQUE

Mona Emergency System (MES) uses numerous context information related to elements within the system. The elements described in MES model are defined based on emergency scenarios, and include actor device, services, hazards information and points of interest. MES employs context in many ways to adjust the provided service to the mobile devices automatically or manually. The MES provide many services and functionalities which allow capturing and filtering information in emergency scenarios using spatial information.

Our approach uses spatial relations in the form of English expressions that are understandable by humans. These expressions assist in distributing the right message at the right time. Also, it supports addressing the message target and describing contents for the domain use context information.

There are two types of information that are used within the MES. First, the static information includes the geographic information that may available through the government agency such as the Department of Sustainability and Environment (DSE). Second, the dynamic information which includes the updated information such as the flood information as well as the actor status, condition and situation information. Moreover, flood information can be reported by survivor to the disaster management.

MES supports different types of interface adaptation using the context and the spatial relations. The design of the MES application depends on several contexts included within the region such as actor, danger information, and locations of points of interest. The context information involving the actor, which represents people within the region (e.g., survivor, rescuer), includes actor ID, location, status as well as some personal information such as age and health condition. Actor ID identifies the actor and location positions the actor using latitude and longitude. In addition, status is the actor's danger circumstance such as "stuck" or "safe", and health condition describes the health situation about the actor such as "disabled" or "fit". The context information about a "danger" contains location, status, type, range, level, speed and direction. Location is the position of the danger zone within the region. The status describes the danger situation such as "occurring", "starting", and "terminated". Type shows the danger type such as "bushfires" and "flood", and the rest of information are to describe the danger conditions. The points of interest, including safe points within the region, are described using context information such as location, status, name and specification. The POI name information help describes the POI such as "evacuation centre", "play grounds", "school", "hospital" and "hill" in a flood situation. The specification information may include information about certain buildings such as the number of levels. Furthermore, a POI is either a:

- **Positive Point of Interest:** That can be used to support the rescue operation; for example, in a flood scenario, Eureka Tower can be assigned by MES automatically as a refuge area where the survivors can be directed.
- **Negative Point of Interest:** This represents unsafe points that can delay or interrupt the rescue operation. For example, in a flood, a lake may be considered as an unsafe area.

The MES uses the POI's locations to assign to the POI its current danger zone, i.e. whether the POI is assigned a status label such as "lost" or "destroyed" (e.g., a POI within an area covered by a flood is labelled "lost"). This context information can change in real time in an emergency scenario. For example, the MES system generates the POI information depending on several factors, such as the danger type, the actor location and the POI status.

The MES system uses the spatial relations to deal with the available context information to provide the right message target and content at the right time during the danger area. The MES system matches the actor location with danger information and directs the actor to the correct danger zone as well as the points of interest by issuing the right message. The MES distribute automatic messages to every actor within the danger area according fixed time. Also, MES send the message every time the actor change zone and every time the POI status change from positive to negative POI. The message content depends on the actor current context information as well as the POI information and the danger context information. For example, in case of destroyed POI; the MES will direct the actor to new POI using the spatial relation. Also, the MES uses spatial relations to provide information about the nearest POI in order to assist the rescuing operation. It allows the rescue time to view the danger area using spatial relation. it assist in clustering the survivor information because it help grouping the actor depend on their context information and the spatial relation. For example, the rescue can target and message survivors near certain POI. Then, the MES disaster management server will generate the alert message depending on the available context information such as the survivor location, health condition, current danger information and the POI information. The MES keeps updating its scenario information until the flood is over (Almagrabi, Seng, & Torabi, 2012).

Spatial contexts can be represented qualitatively and so is much more human understandable and simpler for users or quantitatively so that this can be computed by the system, and there is a need to map between the two. Table 2 provides an example mapping between qualitative and quantitative spatial relations in the MES.

According to the motivating scenario as in Figure 2 during a flood situation at the Melbourne Yarra River, the system categorizes the danger areas depending on the threat level into three zones: red zone, yellow zone and blue zone. The MES applies the Haversine formula[4] to generate the danger zones. The formula allows the MES to manage the location information in the form of latitude and longitude for the danger and compares it to the actor and the POI location information. The MES uses a quantitative technique to assign an actor and POI into the correct danger zone by calculating and comparing their location coordinates with the danger zones' GPS information. The system uses qualitative techniques including danger relations, position relations and social relations in order that users can express spatial relationships in an understandable way. These expressions using these relations define the target and the content of the message. The alert message issued by MES to survivors includes information about the current danger zone and the available POIs in the surrounding area. The alert message issued by MES to rescuers includes information about the survivors within his/her range using position relations and the danger information.

Figure 5 gives a spatial view of the flood situation maintained by the MES during a flood scenario. The MES provides alert messages to actors who share the same position relation with certain negative POIs or certain danger zones. For example, MES messages survivors in the red zone about the way to avoid disaster.

Moreover, the MES system assigns flag-bearers for each group of survivors. The flag-bearer role is to receive the first alert message and spread it to its group of nearby survivors via any peer-to-peer communication method such as Bluetooth or Wi-Fi Direct. The flag-holder can monitor and assist with the evacuation process in this way. Also, the MES employs the social relations to discover the knowledge about actors' friends and relatives who may be concerned and would like to receive information about their relatives' or friends' current situation or provide social information to the rescue team to track family members within the affected area. The MES system keeps updating the danger zones depending on the observed danger information such as the direction and speed, and then, possibly redirects the actors to the right zones and informs them of up-to-date POI status and the actors' locations and status, accordingly. While we do not describe in detail how the MES maintains such information up-to-date, we note that such information about dangers can be obtained via crowd-sourcing by people sending in reports or by using sensors (e.g., water level sensors for a flood, or heat sensors for a bush fire).

Table 2. MES qualitative and quantitative spatial relations for emergency situation

Qualitative Spatial (Position Relation)	Quantitative Spatial
next to	less the 50m
close	less than 100m and more than 50m
near	more than 100m and less than 250m
far	more than 250m but still in the danger zone
away	more 500m outside the danger range

6. MESSAGE STRUCTURE USING EBNF FORMAT AND IMPLEMENTATION

This section describes the use of MES spatial relations in the Mona-ontology in defining the message target and content (expressed in EBNF format). There are two modes of MES messaging: automatic and manual.

Figure 5. The spatial view maintained by MES of the flooded Melbourne CBD area

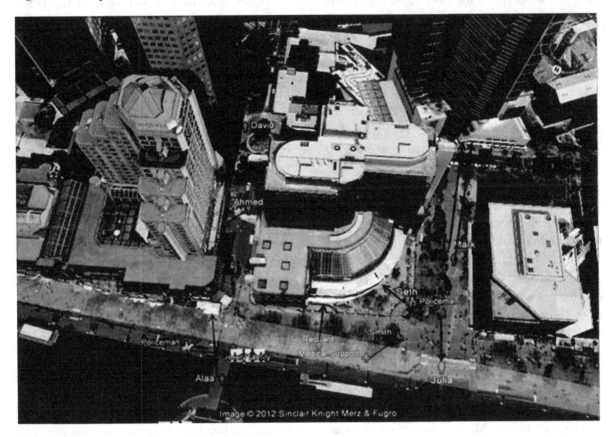

6.1 Message Target and Content Structure used in Automatic Mode

First, the automatic mode provides automatic messages to the survivors within the affected area in order to inform them about the danger information and the POI information to help them avoid tragedy. The MES server messages the survivors according to the danger zone levels, starting with red, then yellow, and then the blue. Every survivor will receive a different message according to his/her current location. The MES will stop sending the alert messages once the survivor is out of danger, or the danger is terminated. The MES uses the EBNF message structure shown in Box 1 in order to target the actor automatically.

According to the above format, every actor will receive the message during danger situation. Furthermore, the MES uses the EBNF format

shown in Box 2 in building and constructing the content message for the automatic and the manual mode that send to survivor.

For example, in the above scenario, the MES will inform the actor about the current position, danger and POI information. The current position information includes region information and the danger information such as "there is a flood and you are in the yellow zone". In addition, the POI information includes the closest POI name and distance. For example, the MES will message Ahmed who is at the Yarra river walking path and inside the yellow zone information such as "the WinBar is located in same area within 136 meters away". This information can be sent manually in the MES by a rescuer too.

The MES uses a different message content structure to inform the rescuers about available survivors in the range. Box 3 shows the contex-

Box 1.

```
<Message>:: =  <actor>⁺ <position_relation> <affected_area>⁺
        <actor>:: = "survivor_ID" | "rescuer_ID"
        <position_relation>:: = "near" | "far" | "next
          to" | "close to" | "away" | "in the neighborhood of" | "inside" |
          "outside" | "in" | "out"
        <affected_area>:: = "red_zone" | "yellow_zone" | "blue_zone"
    Note:
    (1) "survivor_ID" є <survivor>
    (2) "rescuer_ID" є < rescuer >
```

Box 2.

```
<message>::= <affected_area_name> <danger_type> <affected_area>
   <danger_distance> <POI_name> <POI_location> <POI_distance>
        <affected_area_name>::= "yarra_river_walking_path" |
          "crown_ plaza hotel" |"flinder_station"
        <danger_type>::=  "fire" | "flood" | "earthquake" |"nuclear_danger"
        <affected_area>::= "red_zone" | "yellow_zone" |"blue_zone"
        <danger_distance>::= "945" | "775" | "534"
        <POI_name>::= "lake" | "hospital" | "evacuation_center" | "school" |
          "playground" | "named_building".
        <POI_location>::= "yarra_river_walking_path" | "East Melbourne" |
          "South bank"|"Carlton"
        <POI_distance>::= "0.25" | "0.575" | "0.999"
```

tual information involve in such a message. The message structure describes the rescuer that will receive the message and also contains information about survivors and the current danger zone using the danger relations and the information about the related points of interest using the position relation.

For example, during the above scenario, the MES will inform the Policeman about Henry's family who are located in the red zone near the Southgate Art and Leisure Precinct building in order to assist them (see Figure 6)

Figure 6 shows the disaster management automatic messaging form, which offers additional services such as providing a list containing the survivor IDs who are located in the danger zone. Additionally, it shows a summary of the number of the survivors positioned in the different zones. Moreover, the form updates the actor context information automatically according to the danger zone using the update options (e.g., Messages containing location updates from actors, sent periodically). Also, the automatic form allows access to the manual form and URL link which view the scenario in a map that will be implanted in future work.

The disaster manger will inform the actors with different messages according to their context information see Figure 7. Moreover, the ac-

Box 3.

```
<Message>:: = <actor1>⁺ <poisitio_relation> <affected_area> <position_relation>
<POI_name> <actor1>:: = <Survivor_ID>⁺
          <position_relation>:: = "near" | "far" | "next to" |
             "close to" | "away" | "in the neighborhood of" | "inside" |
             "outside" | "in" | "out"
          <affected_area>::= "red_zone" | "yellow_zone" |"blue_zone"
          <position_relation>:: = "near" | "far" | "next to" |
             "close to" | "away" | "in the neighborhood of" | "inside" |
             "outside" |  "in" | "out"
          <POI_name>::= "lake" | "hospital" | "evacuation_center" | "school" |
             "playground" | "building".
     Note:
     (1) <Survivor_ID> e <Survivor>
```

Figure 6. Disaster manager for automatic messaging

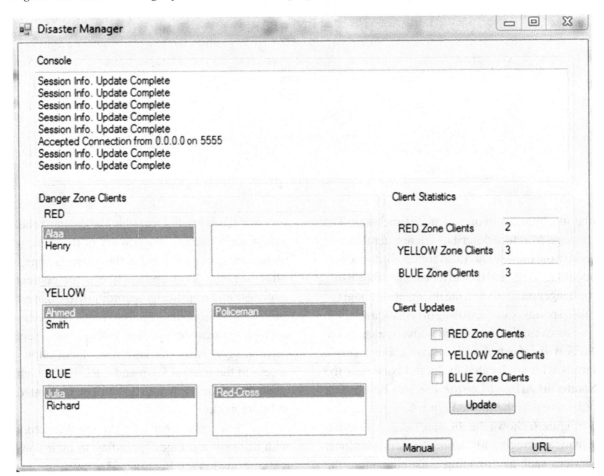

tor movement is represented by the use of GPS trace which contains the latitude and longitude coordinates:

The figure shows the diversity of the sent messages using the automatic mode. The MES server will send the messages depending on the reporting and the receiving conditions mentioned earlier. In addition, the MES informs the survivors in case of flooded POIs during the disaster in order to avoid mis-directing the survivors to such POIs. Finally, the MES will stop sending the automatic messages once the danger is terminated, or the survivor reaches the white zone where the danger does not exist.

6.2 Message Target and Content Structure used in Manual Mode

This section highlights one of the main features that the MES offers to the administrator at the server side. The message content structure using the manual mode is the same as that for the automatic mode but also has a field for a custom message to be included with the message (<custom_message>:: = STRING (e.g., "don't worry")). Moreover, the manual mode allows the use of the spatial relations for defining the target of the message in a dynamic and easy way using the position relation or the social relation. Moreover, the message target can be described as shown in Box 4; first, the system decides on the survivor(s) that are going to receive the message according to his/her (their) location(s) and his/her spatial relationships to the danger zone (e.g., message Ahmed and David about their current danger zone which is blue with the custom message to "walk away from that area").

In addition, the target can be defined also using the survivor's location and his/her POI spatial relation such as message survivors (Smith, Seth

Figure 7. The sent alert messages to Alaa and Ahmed

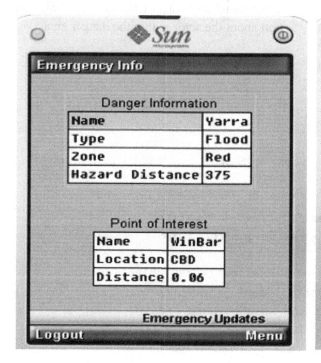
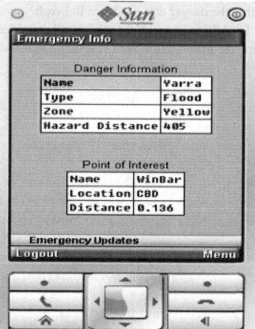

Box 4.

```
1)   <message>:: = <actor>⁺ <position_relation>:: <affected_area>
         <actor>:: = <survivor_ID >
         <position_relation>:: = "near" | "far" | "next to" |
            "close to" | "away" | "in the neighborhood of" | "inside" |
            "outside" | "in" | "out"
         <affected_area>:: = "red_zone" | "yellow_zone" |"blue_zone"
      Note:
      <survivor_ID> ∈ <survivor>
```

and Richard) who are located near the Southgate Arts and Leisure Precinct. Furthermore, the manual mode allows the MES to distribute the message using according to combination of position relation. For example, MES messages actors how share the same position relation with danger zone and the POI. The target of the message can be defined in EBNF as shown in Box 5.

Furthermore, the MES manual mode allows the use of social relations in addressing targets. For example, the MES can target the relatives of an actor to receive information about the relative within the danger area as shown in Box 6.

In addition, Figure 8 describes another service using the manual form such as sending a custom message only to one particular survivor, such as Henry who is located in the Red zone with message contents containing "Police coming". The figure shows that only one survivor receives the custom message while the others keep receiving the automatic messages from the server.

The figure shows the MES's ability to send the message using spatial relations, which in this case is the position relation "Close". Furthermore, the MES manual mode allows the use of social relations in messaging services, the MES can target the relatives of an actor, to receive information about the actor within the danger area.

Box 5.

```
2) <message>::=<actor>⁺ [<position_relation><affected_area>]<POI_position>
      <POI_name>
         <actor>:: = <survivor_ID >
         <position_relation>:: = "near" | "far" | "next to" |
            "close to" | "away" | "in the neighborhood of" |
            "inside" | "outside" | "in" | "out"
         <affected_area>:: = "red_zone" | "yellow_zone" |"blue_zone"
         <position_relation>:: = "near" | "far" | "next to" |
            "close to" | "away" | "in the neighborhood of" |
            "inside" | "outside" | "in" | "out"
         <POI_name>::= "lake" | "hospital" | "evacuation_center" |
            "school" | "playground" | "named_building".
```

Box 6.

```
3) <Message>:: = <actor_relative>+ <social_relation> <actor>+
        <actor1>+:: =  <actor_relative>
        <social_relative>+:: = "parent" | "children" |
           "neighbor"|" friend" | "spouse" |"cousin" | "colleague"|
        <actor>:: = <Survivor_ID > | <Rescuer_ID>
```

Figure 8. Only Henry receives the custom message

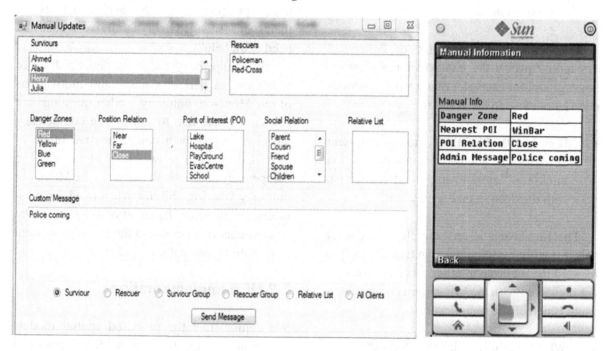

7. EVALUATION

We evaluate our approach in two ways. First, proposing a range of key competency question which can be answered by the Mona-ont ontology that shows the expressiveness of Mona-ont. Second, we used the Mona-ont ontology as part of the implementation of the Mona Emergency messaging system developed to assist in rescue operations during flood situation as shown in Section 6.

7.1 Competency Questions

We use competency questions to demonstrate that Mona-ont ontology can be used to represent and organizes knowledge that addresses key questions in emergency settings, as well as illustrating a comprehensive range of queries that can be answered by Mona-ont.

- How does the Mona-ont ontology organize information about people based on context?

The Mona-ont ontology organizes actors in varying ways such as grouping actors according to whether they share the same POI relationships or grouping actors within the same danger zones; for example, Figure 7 shows that two people share the same danger zone.

- How does a policeman refer to a group of people near certain POI in order to send a message to them?

The Mona-ont ontology allows the Policeman to capture/specify the context of the message target group; for example, figure 8 demonstrates that Henry close to the WinBar.

- How does the Mona-ont ontology represent the case of ad hoc network communication in case of actors losing direct connection with the disaster emergency unit?

The flag-bearer is an example of a cluster head for ad-hoc communication that allows it to forward the message to other survivors who are not registered with the ME system (for instance, using Bluetooth communication).

- What happens if a danger affects POI?

First, the Mona-ont ontology allows this POI to be labelled as negative, i.e. a POI to avoid; the ME system would send messages to direct survivors to avoid that POI, and then inform rescuers about the status and location of that POI.

- What type of relation is used to describe situations within Mona-ont?

First, the Mona-ont ontology uses spatial relations, for example, the Danger_relation such as "in", "out" and "with" to describe the danger locations in the region. Also, the Mona-ont ontology uses the Position_relation such as "near", "far" and "close" to locate actors and POIs in

the affected area as well as to locate actors with respect to other actors in the affected area.

- How can we know if someone is stuck somewhere in the danger area?

Mona-ont allows representation of the status of actors, and so, the ME system can update the survivor location and status which can help identify the positions of the actors at certain times and their status (such as "Henry family were stuck and need extra help").

The competency questions described above illustrates, in part, the scope and motivations of our Mona-ont ontology – other questions are not shown here due to space. The competency questions represent a comprehensive range of queries that can be answered by Mona-ont. The competency questions also express the Mona-ont ontology filtering abilities when used for messaging by allowing the target of messages to be contextually described and the message content to contain contextual knowledge.

7.2 MES Implementation

We demonstrate the proposed spatial models within the implementation of the MES as described in section 6. In addition, further demonstration and implementation of the MES approach is available within the MES for fire scenario (Almagrabi, Seng, & Torabi, 2012).

8. SUMMARY

This chapter highlights the use of spatial modeling and spatial relations for context-aware messaging within emergency situation. The understanding of the spatial environment assists constructing the domain ontology which organizes the available knowledge. This approach helps describe the alert messages structure during flood scenario using the MES. The MES uses the message structure in order to define the message target and content.

We evaluate the MES approach using two ways. First, implementing the MES by applying the Mona-ont ontology for flood emergency situation. Second, using the competency questions that give an overview about the Mona-ont concepts and spatial relation scope.

9. CONCLUSION

During disaster emergency situations, many government and private teams gets involve in the rescue work. However, the lack of coordination between teams makes the rescue command centre unable to deliver effective directives. Also, without getting detailed status of the disaster, the command centre becomes ineffective. There is a need for an effective communication system that makes the rescue operations more reliable and effective. Emergency Management requires coordination of a wide range of organizations and activities, public and private (Wamsley, 1993). To make communication more effective, describing the spatial relations between the emergency parties is essential. In this paper, we describe the spatial relations for the Mona-ont emergency ontology which is used to link the information about concepts within an emergency situation, such as a flood scenario within Melbourne CBD area. We described the Mona-ont emergency ontology based on existing spatial relations such as RCC8 and Egenhofer relations. We define Mona-ont emergency spatial relations using English expressions. The spatial relation assists in defining the message target and content for the MES. The MES provides alert messages to actors within emergency situations.

ACKNOWLEDGMENT

I am very thankful to the Departments of Faculty of Computing and Information Technology, King Abdul-Aziz University Jeddah, Saudi Arabia to sponsor this project.

REFERENCES

Alberts, R., & Franconi, E. (2012). An integrated method using conceptual modelling to generate an ontology-based query mechanism. In *Proceedings of OWL: Experiences and Directions Workshop.* OWL.

Almagrabi, A., Seng, W. L., & Torabi, T. (2012). MES: A system for location-aware smart messaging in emergency situations. In *Proceeding of MOBIQUITOUS 2012, 9th International Conference on Mobile and Ubiquitous Systems: Computing, Networking and Services*. Beijing: ACM.

Araujo, R. B., Rocha, R. V., Campos, M. R., & Boukerche, A. (2008). *Creating emergency management training simulations through ontologies integration*. New York: Academic Press. doi:10.1109/CSEW.2008.52.

Berry, J. K. (1996). *Spatial reasoning for effective GIS*. New York: Wiley.

Bigley, G. A., & Roberts, K. H. (2001). The incident command system: High-reliability organizing for complex and volatile task environments. *Academy of Management Journal, 44*, 1281–1299. doi:10.2307/3069401.

Blomqvist, E., & Öhgren, A. (2008). Constructing an enterprise ontology for an automotive supplier. *Engineering Applications of Artificial Intelligence, 21*, 386–397. doi:10.1016/j.engappai.2007.09.004.

Bonham-Carter, G. (1994). *Geographic information systems for geoscientists: Modelling with GIS*. London: Pergamon Press.

Bunge, M. (1977). *The furniture of the world*. Dordrecht, The Netherlands: Academic Press.

Canton, L. G. (2006). *Emergency management: concepts and strategies for effective programs*. New York: Wiley-Interscience. doi:10.1002/0470119764.

Cohn, A. G., & Hazarika, S. M. (2001). Qualitative spatial representation and reasoning: An overview. *Fundamenta Informaticae, 46,* 1–29.

de Leoni, M., Marrella, A., Mecella, M., Valentini, S., & Sardina, S. (2008). *Coordinating mobile actors in pervasive and mobile scenarios: An AI-based approach.* New York: Academic Press. doi:10.1109/WETICE.2008.30.

Dey, A. K. (2001). Understanding and using context. *Personal and Ubiquitous Computing, 5,* 4–7. doi:10.1007/s007790170019.

Egenhofer, M., & Mark, D. (1995). Naive geography. *Spatial Information Theory A: Theoretical Basis for GIS,* 1-15.

Egenhofer, M. J. & Kuhn, W. (1998). *Beyond desktop GIS.* Lisbon: GIS PlaNET.

Ekholm, A., & Fridqvist, S. (2000). A concept of space for building classification, product modelling, and design. *Automation in Construction,* 315–328. doi:10.1016/S0926-5805(99)00013-8.

Elkan, C., & Greiner, R. (1993). Building large knowledge-based systems: Representation and inference in the CYC project: DB Lenat and RV Guha. *Artificial Intelligence, 61,* 41–52. doi:10.1016/0004-3702(93)90092-P.

Ezzell, Z., Fishwick, P., & Cendan, J. (2011). *Linking simulation and visualization construction through interactions with an ontology visualization.* New York: Academic Press. doi:10.1109/WSC.2011.6147995.

Ferscha, A., Hechinger, M., & Riener, A. et al. (2008). Peer-it: Stick-on solutions for networks of things. *Pervasive and Mobile Computing, 4,* 448–479. doi:10.1016/j.pmcj.2008.01.003.

Ferscha, A., Holzmann, C., & Oppl, S. (2004). *Context awareness for group interaction support.* New York: Academic Press.

Frank, A. U. (1992). Qualitative spatial reasoning about distances and directions in geographic space. *Journal of Visual Languages and Computing, 3,* 343–371. doi:10.1016/1045-926X(92)90007-9.

Franke, J., Ulmer, C., & Charoy, F. (2010). *Pervasive emergency response process management system.* New York: Academic Press.

Frassl, M., Lichtenstern, M., Khider, M., & Angermann, M. (2010). Developing a system for information management in disaster relief—Methodology and requirements. In *Proceedings of the 7th International ISCRAM Conference.* Seattle, WA: ISCRAM.

Gomez-Perez, G. (1999). Ontological engineering: A state of the art. *Expert Update: Knowledge Based Systems and Applied Artificial Intelligence, 2,* 33–43.

Gottfried, B., Guesgen, H., & Hubner, S. (2006). Spatiotemporal reasoning for smart homes. *Designing Smart Homes,* 16-34.

Gould, M. D. (1989). *Human factors research and its value to GIS user interface design.* New York: Academic Press.

Gruber, T. R. (1993). A translation approach to portable ontology specifications. *Knowledge Acquisition, 5,* 199–220. doi:10.1006/knac.1993.1008.

Gruninger, M., & Fox, M. S. (1995). *Methodology for the design and evaluation of ontologies.* New York: Academic Press.

Haddow, G., Bullock, J., & Coppola, D. P. (2010). *Introduction to emergency management.* London: Butterworth-Heinemann.

Holzmann, C., & Ferscha, A. (2010). A framework for utilizing qualitative spatial relations between networked embedded systems. *Pervasive and Mobile Computing, 6*, 362–381. doi:10.1016/j.pmcj.2010.03.001.

Kortuem, G., Kray, C., & Gellersen, H. (2005). *Sensing and visualizing spatial relations of mobile devices*. New York: Academic Press. doi:10.1145/1095034.1095049.

Kung, H. Y., Lin, M. H., Hsu, C. Y., & Liu, C. N. (2005). Context-aware emergency remedy system based on pervasive computing. In *Proceedings of Embedded and Ubiquitous Computing* (pp. 775–784). Academic Press. doi:10.1007/11596356_77.

Luo, Q. (2009). Advancing computing. In *Communication, Control and Management*. Berlin: Springer.

Musto, A., Stein, K., & Eisenkolb, A. et al. (2000). From motion observation to qualitative motion representation. *Spatial Cognition, 2*, 115–126. doi:10.1007/3-540-45460-8_9.

Nakashima, H., Aghajan, H., & Augusto, J. C. (2009). *Handbook of ambient intelligence and smart environments*. Berlin: Springer.

Papadias, D., & Kavouras, M. (1994). *Acquiring, representing and processing spatial relations*. New York: Academic Press.

Pullar, D., & Egenhofer, M. (1988). *Towards formal definitions of topological relations among spatial objects*. New York: Academic Press.

Renz, J., & Mitra, D. (2004). Qualitative direction calculi with arbitrary granularity. *Lecture Notes in Computer Science*, 65–74. doi:10.1007/978-3-540-28633-2_9.

Salber, D., Dey, A. K., & Abowd, G. D. (1999). *The context toolkit: Aiding the development of context-enabled applications*. New York: Academic Press. doi:10.1145/302979.303126.

Sene, K. (2008). *Flood warning, forecasting and emergency response*. Berlin: Springer. doi:10.1007/978-3-540-77853-0.

Wamsley, G. L. (1993). *Coping with catastrophe: Building an emergency management system to meet people's needs in natural & manmade disasters*. New York: DIANE Publishing.

Xiong, G., Liu, Z., Liu, X., & Shen, D. (2012). *Service science, management, and engineering: Theory and applications*. New York: Academic Press.

Yao, X., & Thill, J. C. (2006). Spatial queries with qualitative locations in spatial information systems. *Computers, Environment and Urban Systems, 30*, 485–502. doi:10.1016/j.compenvurbsys.2004.08.001.

KEY TERMS AND DEFINITIONS

Emergency Context: Any information that are related to emergency situation.

Mona Emergency System (MES): It is an emergency system that based on understanding the emergency environment and the Mona-Ont emergency ontology.

Ontology: Is an organized knowledge structure that is understandable by humans and machines.

Qualitative Spatial Representation: Qualitative abstractions present an explanation for qualitative based queries. It enables qualitative spatial relations in tasks involving information query, retrieval, or even a data entry in geospatial information systems.

Quantitative Spatial Representation: Quantities used to describe the spatial relations in a way that they are quantized according to the requested accuracy.

Spatial Information: Spatial information can be anything related to a particular area or space, not necessarily physical or geographic.

Spatial Relations: It is relation that link the spatial concepts It usually contain topological relations, direction relations and distance relations.

ENDNOTES

[1] http://www.w3.org/2005/Incubator/geo/XGR-geo-ont-20071023/

[2] www.cs.man.ac.uk/~pjj/farrell/comp2.html#EBNF

[3] http://protege.stanford.edu/

[4] http://www.movable-type.co.uk/scripts/latlong.html

Chapter 13
Understanding Urban Dynamics from Taxi GPS Traces

Lin Sun
TELECOM SudParis, France

Chao Chen
TELECOM SudParis, France

Daqing Zhang
TELECOM SudParis, France

ABSTRACT

The GPS traces collected from a large taxi fleet provide researchers novel opportunities to inspect the urban dynamics in a city and lead to applications that can bring great benefits to the public. In this chapter, based on a real life large-scale taxi GPS dataset, the authors reveal the unique characteristics in the four different trace stages according to the passenger status, study the urban dynamics revealed in each stage, and explain the possible applications. Specifically, from passenger vacant traces, they study the taxi service dynamics, introduce how to use them to help taxis and passengers find each other, and reveal the work shifting dynamics in a city. From passenger occupied traces, they introduce their capabilities in monitoring and predicting urban traffic and estimating travel time. From the pick-up and drop-off events, the authors show the passenger hotspots and human mobility patterns in a city. They also consider taxis as mobile GPS sensors, which probe the urban road infrastructure dynamics.

1. INTRODUCTION

With the recent advances of sensing, computing, networking and storage, the digital footprints left by people while interacting with the cyber-physical world are accumulating at an unprecedented rate.

The abundance and richness of large scale digital traces collected from huge groups of individuals provide us new opportunities to understand the collective human behaviors and probe various aspects about our society, showing great potential to revolutionize the services in various areas

DOI: 10.4018/978-1-4666-4695-7.ch013

ranging from public safety, urban planning and monitoring, to transportation management and so on (Paulos, Honicky, & Hooker, 2009, Zhang, Guo & Yu, 2011). In this chapter, as an illustrative study we try to investigate the urban dynamics by exploiting the taxi GPS traces collected from a large taxi fleet running in a real city.

Nowadays in many modern cities, taxis are equipped with GPS devices for navigation and dispatch, which report the status of the vehicle, such as the GPS location, speed, orientation and passenger status, to a central sever via telecommunication network in a real time manner. Generally speaking, the operation of taxis is under many physical constraints in the city, such as the road infrastructure, traffic situations and passenger demand distributions. And thus the collected GPS traces potentially reflect many aspects about the city, revealing its status and dynamics over time. For example, the running taxis generally follow the traffic flow on the road, and their speeds well represent the real time traffic situations (Giannotti et al. 2011, Schäfer, Thiessenhusen & Wagner, 2002, Wen, Hu, Guo, Zhu & Sun, 2008). And by gathering the real time speeds from a large taxi fleet, we can obtain a comprehensive picture about the traffics in a city. Besides, as taxis are running on the roads, their GPS traces are able to describe the road infrastructure in a city and thus can be used to detect the road network changes, such as the newly built, opened, or blocked road segments. Meanwhile, the large collections of the pick-up and drop-off events directly tell the human dynamics in a city, showing the high transportation demand areas (*i.e.*, those pick-up hotspots) and human mobility among them.

If we look further inside the taxi GPS traces, we will find that, unlike private vehicle, taxis have unique characteristics at different passenger status. Specifically, in passenger finding process, the target of the drivers is to efficiently find the passengers to achieve high profits. They are under the influences of passenger distributions, competitions from other taxis, traffic situations

and so on. They may hunt around the city, following whatever routes they prefer, or wait at some hotspots. Besides, they also serve the passenger requests broadcasted from the dispatch center. While in passenger delivery process, their targets shift to the efficient delivery of the passengers to their destinations. They try to avoid the jammed roads. Additionally, a few dishonest taxi drivers commit fraudulent driving, mainly detours, to charge more money. Meanwhile, the passenger status changes between occupied to vacant denote pick-up and drop-off events, which directly tell the transportation demands in a city. All these characteristics provide useful clues for us to understand the urban dynamics.

In this chapter, we separate the taxi GPS traces into 4 stages according to the passenger status, study the urban dynamics revealed in each stage and explain the possible applications. Besides, we also consider taxis as mobile GPS sensors, which probe the urban road infrastructure dynamics. Before going to the detail, we first introduce the scopes of the urban dynamics studied in this chapter. Then we introduce the taxi GPS traces and its intrinsic characteristics with a real life dataset collected from thousands of taxis in Hangzhou, China for one year.

1.1 Urban Dynamics

Urban dynamics (also called as city dynamics) describes the evolvement about various aspects of the functioning of a city, ranging from urban land use[1], human mobility, traffic flow, to the evolvement of energy consumptions, environment, economics[2], public services, and so on. The aspects which state-of-the-art work already explored based on the taxi GPS traces can be summarized in the following groups:

1. **Urban Human Dynamics:** Which describes the human mobility happened in a city. Specifically, it tells that at different time periods of day, how people move around

the city, going from one area to another. For example, normally people go from the residential areas to their working places in the morning, and come back in the evening. And the traffic demands in the main railway station fluctuate with the arrival of the trains. Urban human dynamics is one of the main considerations for urban planning, such as designing public transportation services and planning the development of settlements and communities.

2. **Urban Traffic Dynamics:** Which depicts the spatial-temporal evolvement of the traffics in a city. It includes the real time traffic flow in a city, the spatial-temporal traffic patterns and sudden breaks due to traffic accidents or human factors. Urban traffic dynamics is critical for the route planning. It's critical for taxi drivers to avoid heavy routes when delivering passengers.

3. **Urban Road Infrastructure Dynamics:** Which describes the road network change in a city, such as the opening and closing of certain road segments. It greatly influences the urban traffic dynamics, causing traffic fluctuations in the related road segments. Newly built roads can relieve the traffic loads of the parallel road segments and provide new possible ways for the path planning. On the contrary, the closing of a road segment will stop all the traffic loads it bears and force drivers to find other possible roads.

4. **Urban Public Transportation Dynamics:** Which reveals the dynamics in the public transportation service. Public transportation includes the transportation services provided to the public, such as buses, subway and taxis. The public transportation service is highly influenced by two factors, the "demand", which is decided by the human mobility in the city, and the "supply", which is decided by the capacity of the public transportation.

5. **Urban Land Use:** Which comprises two parts, the nature of land use in a city, which relates to which activities are taking place where, and the level of spatial accumulation, which indicates their intensity and concentration[3]. The areas in a city serve various types of functions in a city, such as the residential areas, the retailing (supermarkets, shopping malls), entertainment, and so on. And the various nature of the activities conducted in different function areas may produce different transportation demand. For example, the residential areas normally have high demand for taxis in the morning as people need to go to work, while for night entertainment areas, the demands occur at night.

In this chapter we are going to show how taxi GPS traces are used to reveal the urban dynamics in the above aspects. First of all, we introduce how taxi GPS traces are collected and what they are.

1.2 Taxi GPS Traces Introduction

For efficient dispatching, in many modern cities taxis have been deployed with GPS-embedded devices, which report the taxi ID, longitude, latitude, speed, orientation, occupation status and timestamp (some examples are shown in Table 1) to a data center via telecommunication networks (such as 3G) with a sampling rate of once in a few minutes (2~5 minutes in Beijing reported in (Luo et al., 2009) and one minute in Hangzhou reported in (Li et al. 2011). We will use the same GPS dataset with (Li et al. 2011) as an example to demonstrate the related topics. It's collected from thousands of taxis serving in Hangzhou, China during about one year time period. With such a large taxi fleet, huge number of GPS reports is accumulated. For example, in March 2010 there are about 441 million GPS packets collected from about 7600 taxis, which recorded about 7.35 million passenger delivery events.

The accumulated records reveal the location traces of taxis during their business process. In Figure 1 we visualize a real life digital trace of a

Table 1. Examples of GPS packets

ID	Longitude	Latitude	Speed	Ori.	Occupa.	Year	Mon.	Day	Hour	Min.	Sec.
9970	120.157762	30.259317	3.7	280	Vacant	2011	11	12	13	2	20
1120	120.258423	30.365834	27	120	occupied	2011	11	12	13	2	50
7869	123.340354	30.289732	18.3	340	Vacant	2011	11	12	13	3	5

Figure 1. Visualization of a real life taxi digital trace during about 1 hour time period. Black represents occupied status while red represents vacant.

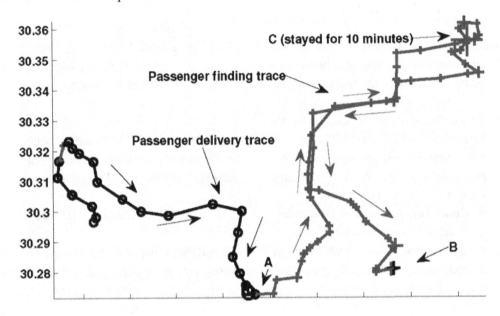

taxi during about 1 hour time period. The markers are the sampling points and their size reflects the waiting time duration with a default size for non-waiting status. The black trace denotes the passenger delivery processes while the red for passenger finding processes. The changes of status from red to black and from black to red imply passenger pick-up and drop-off events respectively. We can see that, the driver dropped off passengers at location A and drove to location C for finding passengers. After staying there for 10 minutes, he failed to find them and then decided to go to place B, where it succeeded. It can be seen that, the difference between passenger finding process and passenger delivery process is that, normally passenger delivery processes are efficient because the aim is to deliver passengers to

their destinations as quick as possible, while passenger finding processes may wander around for finding passengers.

1.3 Perspectives of Studying Taxi GPS Traces

The digital traces of a taxi can be separated into a business cycle according to the passenger status, which generally contains four stages, *i.e.*, *Vacant*, *Pick-up*, *Delivery*, and *Drop-off* (shown in Figure 2). As aforementioned, each stage has its unique characteristics, which potentially reveal certain aspects about the urban dynamics.

During *Vacant* stage, in order to achieve high profit, taxi drivers normally try to find appropriate passengers in efficient ways. They run over

Figure 2. Different stages of the taxi GPS traces and the possible applications

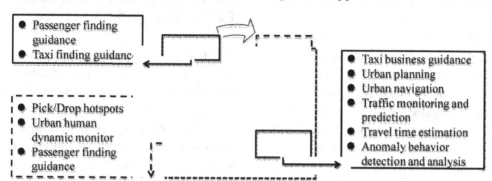

the road infrastructure, causing different passenger finding possibilities in the road segments for the vacant taxis and taxi finding possibilities for passengers. Besides, there are various hot locations, where vacant taxis stop to wait for passengers. The extraction of such information provides necessary guidance for passengers to find the taxi service. Please note that, *Vacant* stage doesn't necessarily imply passenger finding behaviors. It also includes other behaviors, such as the daily work shifting of the day driver and night driver of the taxi.

The *Pick-up* stage is detected by the state change from vacant to occupied. The aggregation of pick-up events from all taxis reveals the taxi demands in different areas in a city throughout different time periods of a day. Together with the *Drop-off* events which are revealed by the state change from occupied to vacant, we can observe the mobility patterns among different regions of a city in different time period of day, which is valuable for taxi drivers to find passengers and for city planners to design public transportation routes.

After picking up passengers, the *Delivery* process begins. Taxi drivers normally choose the clear traffic routes to deliver passengers in the possible fastest speed, as the charge is mainly decided by the traveling distance. So the speed collected in this stage generally reflects the traffic situations on the road. And thus the speeds of a taxi fleet can be used to estimate the traffics in

a city. Meanwhile, based on the historical traffic record, we can extract patterns to represent the hidden rules of the evolvement of traffic in different contexts and use it to predict the traffics in the future. After dropping off passengers at their destinations, taxis enter the *Vacant* stage again and form a business process circle.

Besides the above four stages, we can also simply treat the taxis as mobile GPS sensors running over the road network, without the distinctions about the passenger status. Their traces can be used to build the road network map, and detect the road network change in a promote way. In the following sections, we are going to introduce the urban dynamic topics studied in the above four stages and the perspective of taxis as sensor separately.

2. INFERRING TAXI SERVICE DYNAMICS FROM PASSENGER VACANT TRACES

As an important public transportation system, taxi service dynamics greatly influences the cost to find taxis for passengers and vice versa. For most cases, vacant taxis hunt around the city or wait at certain locations for finding passengers. They seek the potential passengers while facing the competition from other adversaries. It is a dynamic process, as the "good" locations for find passengers will soon attract the taxis in the "poor" locations and cause the redistribution of them. Besides, passenger vacant traces may also record the process of shifting work or having meals and so on. And the daily work shifting dynamics of all taxis greatly affects the taxi services.

Here we mainly introduce three types of taxi service dynamics based on the passenger vacant traces with the direct applications. Firstly, with large number of historical locations of vacant taxis, we introduce how to use the location dynamics to help passengers to find taxis. Secondly, based on the taxi service dynamics, we elaborate how to help taxis to efficiently finding passengers. Lastly, we demonstrate how to find taxi work shifting dynamics based on the historical traces, and we reveal the spatial and temporal distribution to see its influences.

2.1 Vacant Taxi Location Dynamics and Taxi Finding Service

Knowing where vacant taxis are and will be helps people to find taxis. Considering the context of time of the day, day of the week and weather condition, Phithakkitnukoon, Veloso, Bento, Biderman and Ratti (2010) presented a predictive model, which, based on the prior probability distribution of vacant taxis inferred from historical dataset, predicts the number of vacant taxis in given areas. Such a target can be fulfilled by the following steps. Firstly, the city map can be decomposed into square grid cells and a day into different time slots. Then the number of vacant taxis can be predicted in each cell in the given time slot by methods like simply averaging the historical records under the same context. Due to the variance of vacant taxi number in each day, after, mathematical ways can be introduced to reduce the predicting errors, such as the negative feedback control. In real practice, the predict result can be provided to people to help them to go to these locations in order to have higher chances to get a taxi delivery.

2.2 Taxi Service Dynamics and Passenger Finding Service

The research about passenger finding guidance from the vacant trajectories of taxis is mainly from two perspectives. One is to build statistical models based on the passenger finding possibilities in each action of the taxi drivers, such as the traveling through an area or a road segment, waiting at a certain location for certain time period. Yuan, Zheng, Zhang, Xie and Sun (2011) presented a recommender from this perspective, which provides taxi drivers with some locations and route to these locations, towards which they are more likely to get passenger and thus maximize the profit.

The other perspective is to directly learn the passenger finding techniques from the observation of the passenger finding behaviors of a taxi fleet and their profitability. The performance of a driver is influenced by a variety of "time-evolving" objective factors, such as the passenger distributions and their potential travel lengths, and the vacant taxi distributions, which are the demand and supply respectively, and the traffic situations. Meanwhile, it's also influenced by other more "stable" factors such as the hunting cost, which is mainly decided by the cost of fuel and elapsed time, the need to shift work and etc. Moreover, subjectively it's also highly influenced by the driver's awareness of these objective factors (*i.e.* mainly decided by one's experiences), and his reactions accordingly, such as whether hunting nearby, or going to distant hot locations after dropping off passengers, which area to serve, which route to take to avoid the heavy traffic and so on. In (Li et al. 2011) we presented a primary study about learning good and bad passenger finding strategies based on the behaviors of good and normal drivers. Different from the other perspectives, we intend to learn the good and bad taxi serving strategies from the behaviors of a community of taxi drivers revealed in their digital traces, *i.e.* to learn the hidden human intelligence during the business process. Since taxi drivers already consider the influencing factors and their actions lead to different revenue levels, we intend to learn the good and bad behaviors from them by considering the relations between the behaviors and the revenues in a community of drivers, and provide this information back to them for improving their performance. Here we present the general logic about learning the passenger finding strategies from the taxi GPS traces.

The drivers' serving strategies can be viewed from three aspects: passenger finding preference, service area preference and passenger delivery skills. In particular, in passenger finding strategies we are interested in the preference of going distant, hunting locally or waiting locally right after dropping off passengers and their preference in hunting or waiting before picking up passengers. And for passenger service areas, we study their preference of serving at each area. And for passenger delivery technique, we study their average passenger delivery speed, which implicitly reflects the drivers' ability to choose unobstructed route when delivering passengers.

Similar as passenger finding strategies, we decompose the city into square grid cells and a day into different time slots. For each combination of them, we formulate the strategy preference of a particular strategy by examining the possibility of committing it under the circumstance for a driver. Then we can form a feature matrix, in which each row for a taxi and each column for a particular strategy.

There are two perspectives to learn the strategies, i.e., learning from the behaviors of good taxi drivers and evaluating each strategy by its correlation with taxi revenue.

Learning from Good Taxi Drivers

In a given location and time context, we want to learn the strategy which is mostly preferred by good drivers. To measure the preference of a particular

strategy in a group of drivers, we have to consider not only the preference of each driver, but also their profitability level, which is measured as the hourly revenue rate, and their experience, which is measured by the number of drop-off events in the corresponding location and time context. The learned strategies are the ones generally followed by good drivers in given location and time contexts. However, it's certain that if they are strictly followed by all the drivers, they will become bad ones because of the competition among the drivers. In real life, how much degree a driver follows these strategies depends on their experiences and may be one key influencing factor of the revenue performance. So we need to investigate how the degree of following one strategy influences the performance.

Learning from Correlation with Revenue

We evaluate each individual strategy by calculating the correlation value of the feature dimension with the corresponding drivers' profitability. A positive correlation value implies that, generally when drivers prefer more to this strategy, they earn more. So for the drivers with lower preferences of the strategy, they'd better increase it. On the contrary, with small negative correlation value, the drivers with greater preference should decrease it.

2.3 Taxi Work-Shifting Dynamics

In China, all taxis are managed by a few big taxi companies, who rent taxis to drivers. To obtain high profit, most taxis are served by two drivers, one during the daytime and the other during the nighttime. Each day these two drivers shift work twice, once in the early morning and once in the afternoon. The location and time of the work shifting are negotiated beforehand and serve as an agreement for daily shifting. The morning work shifting events happen around 6:00AM while the afternoon work shifting happens between 4:30PM and 6:30PM. As taxis may not be close to the shifting location, the drivers normally start to go to the work shifting location half an hour earlier, which reduces their ability to serve for passenger requests with reverse directions and causes difficulties for passengers to find a taxi during this time period. The work shifting event happens within a few minutes (some drivers say that it takes about 10 minutes) for handing over the vehicle.

The detection of the work shifting events can be divided into the following two steps. Firstly, we detect the work shifting locations by searching whether there is a location where a taxi goes routinely in the same time period of every day. Then we identify the daily work shifting events and separate daily taxi GPS traces accordingly. The detection of the work shifting location is based on the following three facts:

1. The taxi parks in the work shifting place for a while as drivers need some time to shift the vehicle;

2. For most of the days, the taxi usually visits the work shifting place within a fixed short time period of day while vacant;

3. By expanding the time slot to a larger range, we are able to find the work shifting events which are delayed or in advance.

The process of detecting the work shifting location of a taxi is elaborated as follows. Firstly we collect all the vacant trajectories and extract the parking locations inside them. The general idea of detecting the work shifting location is that, if a taxi stays inside a small area for time duration long enough, we consider it as a parking location.

After, we split the city into equal-sized grid cells, with each one *50m×50m* large grid cells and separate a day into half-overlapping 20-minute-long time window. In each time window, we record the days that a taxi has parking records in each grid. In case the work shifting place is on the

edge of a grid, the shifting events may scatter in different grids. To overcome this problem, when counting the number of days a taxi parked in a grid, we also count the days of the neighboring grids. If the number of the parked days in a grid is bigger than 70% of the total number of days, we will keep it as a possible work shifting candidate location. Then we expand the time window one hour ahead and one hour later, to include the days corresponding to the delayed and ahead shifting.

Since we count the neighboring grids, the same work shifting events will make the nearby grids look like possible candidates. Practically we can combine those candidates into one as they are based on the same work shifting logs. In real life, there are some rare occasions that the driver changes the work shifting location temporarily for possible reasons like personal issues or occasionally blocked roads. So we may not be able to get the visiting records of everyday. In practice, for a taxi, if there is one and only one grid achieves 90% of the total number of days within 15:00~19:00, we say it's the afternoon work shifting place, and if it's within 3:00~8:00, we say it's the morning work shifting place. In case there is more than one candidate, we consider it as an uncertain (failed) case. With the 6863 taxis, we successfully find the work shifting locations for 4773 taxis. Besides, there are 27 taxis having more than 1 candidate location in the afternoon shifting and 100 taxis in the morning shifting. The rest taxis don't have candidates and exhibit chaos parking patterns, and they are believed to be served only by one driver.

After obtaining the work shifting location, we can detect the daily work shifting events for a taxi. We collect the work shifting locations and time slots of all the 4773 taxis and analyze their characteristics in spatial and temporal distribution. We partition the city into *2.4km×2.4km* grid cells and count the number of taxis that shift work in each grid to get the spatial distribution. The work shifting location distributions for morning and

Figure 3. Distribution of work shifting places: (a) Morning work shifting; (b) Evening work shifting

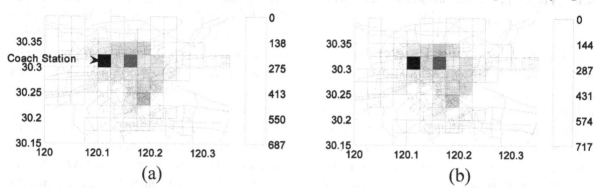

(a)   (b)

evening are shown in Figure 3 (a) and (b) respectively. It can be easily seen that both distribution are very similar and most of the morning shifting places locate outside of top hot areas. It's surprising to see that lots of drivers choose to shift near the coach station, perhaps because the drivers can easily take transportation before or after the work shifting.

The shifting time distribution is revealed in Figure 4, in which (a) is for the morning shifting time and (b) is for the evening. The morning work shifting time generally distribute between 4:00~7:20 evenly, while the evening shifting mainly happen between 16:40~17:20, which is the one of the major reasons why people feel hard to get taxis around that time period. In order to alleviate the problem, policies can be adopted to help the drivers to shift work evenly instead of concentrating together.

3. DERIVING TRAFFIC DYNAMICS AND TAXI SERVICE DYNAMICS FROM PASSENGER OCCUPIED TRACES

As explained earlier, the speeds in the collected records of passenger occupied trajectories reflect the traffic dynamics in a city. Here we summarize the current studies about the urban traffic monitoring, predicting and traveling time estimation based on the historical passenger occupied trajectories.

Besides, since passenger delivery traces reveal the passenger delivery behaviors in the taxi service, we are interested in monitoring the anomalous passenger delivery behaviors in the taxi service dynamics, for purposes such as inspecting the ongoing anomalous behaviors and uncovering areas with high detour possibilities in citywide. Based on large collections of anomalous passenger

Figure 4. Distribution of work shifting time: (a) Morning work shifting; (b) Evening work shifting

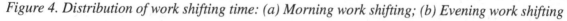

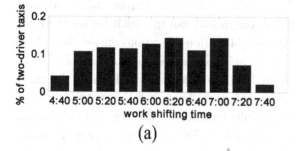

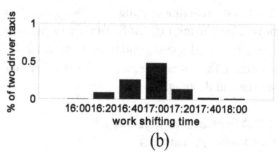

(a)   (b)

delivery behaviors, we provide analysis about their general characteristics in a city.

3.1 Traffic Monitoring, Prediction and Traveling Time Estimation

The collective movements of vehicles in a city cause different congestion levels in the road network throughout different time periods of a day. Knowing traffic dynamics is helpful for researches such as improving taxi business and smart navigation. The traffics generally follow regular patterns during the day. Much research work has been studied the patterns to better understand the traffic dynamics. With the synergies of hundreds of GPS-embedded taxis which send GPS positions to the head quarter once per minute, Schäfer, Thiessenhusen and Wagner (2002) presented a system which reported the real time traffic information. Wen Hu Guo, Zhu, and Sun (2008) measured the traffic changes in Beijing around the Olympic game time period based on GPS-equipped taxis. Giannotti et al. (2011) found traffic jams by detecting groups of vehicles that move slowly together. Yuan, Zheng, Xie and Sun (2011) inferred the traffic condition at a future time of the landmark graph built from historical data and real-time traffic flow calculated based on recently received taxi trajectories.

Given that taxi drivers are continuously delivering passengers around the city, the collected passenger delivery traces are a natural source for estimating the traveling time and distance between two points. Balan, Nguyen & Jiang (2011) described a real time trip information system and proved that using taxi GPS data for estimating travel time and speed conditions is practical by averaging the collected similar trips with similar source and destination.

3.2 Anomalous Passenger Delivery Dynamics

Generally speaking, anomalous passenger delivery behaviors are those behaviors that aren't often seen in the passenger delivery process. Such behaviors may be caused by reasons like fraud driving, blocked or newly built roads or required detours from passengers (For instance, a passenger needs to detour to one place to pick up a friend, and then go to the destination). Currently we propose two methods to detect such behaviors inside the taxi GPS traces. One is named *iBAT* (Zhang et al. 2011), which is able to detect the anomaly of a completed trajectory. The other is named *iBOAT* (Chen et al. 2011), which can detect the exact anomalous segments inside an anomalous passenger delivery trace (For the details of these two algorithms, please refer to the cited papers). With *iBOAT*, we monitor all the ongoing anomalous passenger delivery trajectories in a city (Schäfer et al. 2002). Moreover, we analyze the anomalous passenger delivery trajectories to give more insights about their characteristics.

As in different time periods of day and day of week, the traffics are quite different and thus the normal routes change from time to time. We divide a week into working and non-working days, and separate each day into 4 different time slots: night (0:00~6:59), morning (7:00~11:59), afternoon (12:00~16:59) and evening (17:00~23:59). By combining the type of day and time slots, we get 8 different combinations, which we encode as WN (Working day Night), WM (Working day Morning), WA (Working day Afternoon), WE (Working day Evening), NWN (Non-Working day Night), NWM (Non-Working day Morning), NWA (Non-Working day Afternoon), and NWE (Non-Working day Evening). There are about 7.35 million passenger delivery trajectories in the whole month, out of which we successfully obtain 0.44 million anomalous ones with *iBOAT*.

For each anomalous trajectory, we obtain the anomalous sub-trajectories inside with the exact starts and ends. From this large collection of anomalous trajectories, we intend to understand the anomalous behaviors, extracting common characteristics of anomalous behaviors and uncovering the motivations behind. We thus conduct the analysis aiming to answer the following questions.

- What percentage of all trips is anomalous?
- Out of the anomalous trajectories, what percentage of them travels longer distance than necessary?
- What statistical "tendencies" can we discern from the detected anomalous trajectories?

We aim to discover what the common characteristics in the anomalous driving behaviors are. Although we can't know the exact motives behind anomalous behaviors, these analysis provide clues for these motives, and can potentially increase the detection rate of future anomaly detection methods, as they provide the most pertinent conditions that exist when anomalous behaviors occur.

The first aspect we consider is how many anomalous sub-trajectories occur in one trip. We plot these results for the different time segments in Figure 5. And we can see that for all time slots

the grand majority of anomalous trips have only one anomalous sub-trajectory.

Inspecting at what point during the trip the anomalous behavior began and ended will help us to understand the motives for the anomalous behaviors. We split the trips into thirds and examine where each anomalous sub-trajectory begins and ends. These results are displayed in Table 2, and we can see that anomalous sub-trajectories usually don't start and begin in the same third, and most begin in the first or second third. Although this does not clarify the motivations behind the anomalous behaviors, it does suggest that the anomalous behaviors are occurring as a result of a conscious decision, and not by "accident": if drivers had inadvertently left their intended route, they would generally return to it immediately. In fact, out of all anomalous trajectories, 27% of them remain in an anomalous state until they reach the destination, further reinforc-

Figure 5. Number of anomalous sub-trajectories per trip

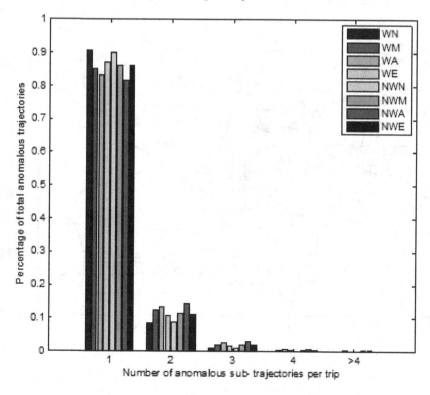

Table 2. Starting and ending positions of anomalous sub-trajectories

Start	End			
	1st third	**2nd third**	**3rd third**	**Total**
1st third	10%	19%	16%	46%
2nd third	N/A	12%	24%	36%
3rd third	N/A	N/A	18%	18%
Total	10%	31%	58%	

ing the belief that these anomalous behaviors are not occurring by "accident".

This is further supported by Figure 6, where we display the areas where most of the anomalous trips began. We can see that many of the places are bus stations, where tourists would generally arrive. It is not surprising that they are responsible for a large fraction of the anomalous trajectories. This further confirms our previous claim that anomalous behaviors are conscious decisions.

4. REVEALING URBAN HUMAN DYNAMICS FROM PICK-UP AND DROP-OFF EVENTS

The ability to detect dynamics of the most frequented locations in a city can be useful for urban planning, public transportation route design, tourism agencies, and security agencies, amongst others. Taxis provide a precise indication of people's desired destinations, and they can well reveal the

Figure 6. Areas where most of the anomalous trips begin

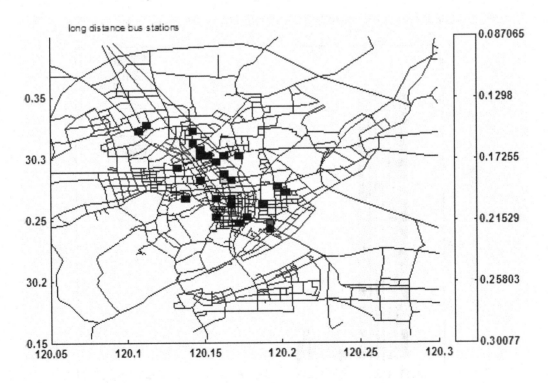

pulse of the human dynamic in a city. In this section we discuss detecting a city's "hotspots" using the end-points information of the taxi GPS trace. "Hotspots" is often associated with certain context, such as the time, the origins, and the destinations.

4.1 Extracting Hotspots

With taxi data sets, we know with reasonable accuracy where passengers have been picked up and dropped off. This information is very useful as it can be used to directly detect places of interest. However, even the passengers are picked up or dropped off at the same place, their reported GPS points are not exactly the same. Close points can be clustered to form a dynamic area, or we just partition the whole city into different fixed areas in advance. In this chapter, we partition the whole city into fixed equal grid cell. By simply counting the number of drop-offs at different grid cells, we can directly compare the importance of different destinations. Meanwhile, by counting the number of pick-ups, we can see the density of different origins. More meaningful results can be uncovered if we add further contextual information such as time of day, season of the year, weather conditions, etc.

Hot Origins/Destinations

We partition Hangzhou metropolitan area (longitude [120.0, 120.5], latitude [30.15, 30.4]) into *40×20* grid cells with equal intervals (see Figure 7). We count all the pick-up and drop-off events during the selected 15 days in each region and select the top 99 busiest regions as the hotspots and the rest as non-hot area. The locations and functions of the hotspot are numbered as shown in Figure 7. The far away isolated region 99 is the international airport. The railway station, commercial zones, residential zones, and the main campus of Zhejiang University surrounding the West Lake are the top hotspots.

The skeleton of Hangzhou metropolitan area can be outlined by all the pick-up/drop-off points as shown in Figure 8. We can see that the drop-off points (blue) are more scattered than the pick-up points (red) since people usually catch a taxi on main roads while get off anywhere. We count the pickup/drop-off points in each region at 6 equal time slots (sub-captions in Figure 8). We plot the top 10 pick-up/drop-off hotspots on the background of pick-up/drop-off point cloud in Figure 8. Most of the top 10 pick-up/drop-off regions are surrounding the West Lake across different time

Figure 7. Left: Hangzhou metropolitan area partition. Two spots are the railway station (left) and the airport (right), respectively. Right: Density map of Hangzhou metropolitan area. Different label colors indicate different region functions.

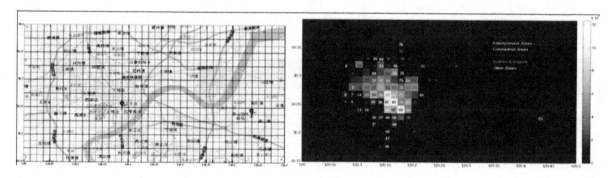

slots. The top 10 pick-up/drop-off hotspots also depend on the time. The railway station is among the top 10 pick-up/drop-off hotspots across the whole day. During mid-night (00h~04h), as expected, the drop-off locations are almost located in residential zones while the pick-up locations are mainly in the railway station and entertainment zones. During rush hours (04h~08h), the pick-up locations are mainly in residential zones while the drop-off locations are mainly in commercial zones. As seen from Figure 8(b), the airport is among top 10 hotspots only during the early morning. The reason may be that passengers are inclined to take airport shuttle buses in daytime since it is cheaper. While during the early morning people turn to take taxis since airport shuttle buses are out of services.

Hot Origin-Destination Pairs

We are also interested in the hot Origin-Destination (OD) pairs around the city. This kind of hotspots

Figure 8. Top 10 pick-up/drop-off hotspots (marked with 'o/x' at different time slots in Hangzhou metropolitan area. The background point clouds are plotted by using all the pick-up points (red) and drop-off points (blue) at the same time slot.

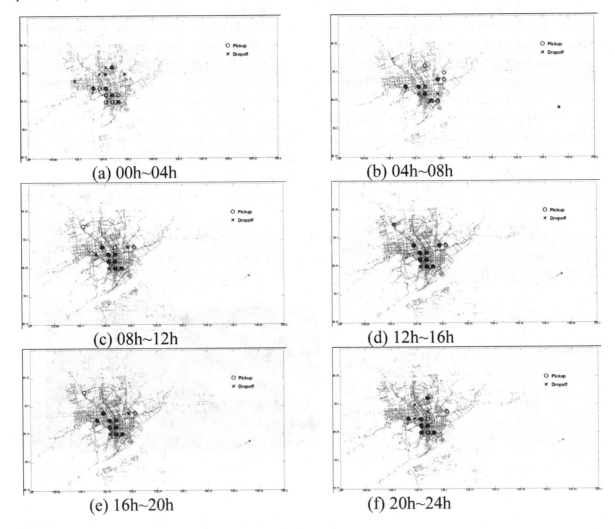

(a) 00h~04h

(b) 04h~08h

(c) 08h~12h

(d) 12h~16h

(e) 16h~20h

(f) 20h~24h

shows the highly preferred trips between regions, which provide useful insights to urban planners. To be specific, open new bus line or increase the bus frequency to the existed bus line may be necessary to OD pairs where people travel very frequently but with relative low public transportation resource. Another possible application is to suggest bus routes which connect several hot OD pairs. Two hot OD pairs can be connected if one of OD pair starts from the destination of the other OD pair. Additional constraints can be also added (*i.e.* the time constraints).

4.2 Human Mobility Pattern

Total number of pick-up and drop-off events can reveal the human movement intensity. The higher the value is, the more intensively that human travel around the city. This value is equal to the total passenger-delivering trips. Careful analysis of its temporary characteristics can help to understand the mobility pattern better and deeper.

Workdays vs. Non-Workdays

Workdays are the exception days of weekends and holidays. The New Year holidays begin 1st January and end 3rd January. Figure 9(left) shows the total number of trips of the whole Hangzhou city in the first month of 2010. The maximal value happens on the first day of January, while the minimal value takes place on the first workday after New Year holiday. Maybe the high number of pick-ups/drop-offs is caused by the tourists from other cities. An evident tendency could be seen from Figure 9(left) is that people travel more during non-workdays than workdays. Moreover, the value of the first day of non-workdays (Saturday) is almost the peak one among its respected week. A reasonable explanation is that people turn to travel around once after a week's work. Saturday is always associated with the peak value while Monday is often associated with valley value. There is no significant regular pattern among weeks; this may be due to the "noise" caused by the bad weather, low/high temperatures, and tourists from other cities or countries, etc..

Time of a Day

The number of pick-ups and drop-offs at different time periods of a day generally correspond to people's mobility patterns in a city. In Figure 9(right) we display the number of the pick-ups/drop-offs in each quarter of a day. The quietest time of a day is the early morning, from about 4am to 6am, while the busiest time is the nighttime, from about 20PM to 22PM. It is surprising to see that the busiest time is not the rush time. It may because that the poor traffic conditions during rush hour would increase the travel time of each trip, resulting in the decrease of the total

Figure 9. Temporary characteristic. Left: workdays vs. non-workdays; Right: different time of a day.

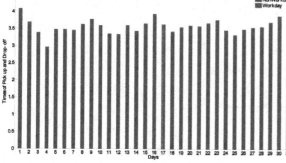
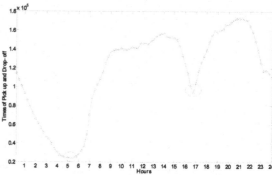

passenger-delivering trips. We can further infer that people who travel for entertainments during nighttime begin at about 19PM and such a pattern lasts to the next day.

Two representative time slots (22h~24h and 0h~4h) are selected when considering several types of "noise" can be safely excluded (the traffic conditions, tourists from outside, etc.). They are two time periods respected to people who work or fun late. Figure 10 shows the number of pick-ups/drop-offs during these two time slots. Much more regular period pattern can be seen. People travel more on Friday late night than the other workdays; while less people travel during the very earlier morning. The reason why the pattern on Fridays is similar as non-workdays is mainly because that more people travel out for pleasure on Friday night after a week's work. Human presents non-workday pattern a little earlier. The total number of trips at morning time on Saturday is the biggest of that on other different days. It may be because that people have fun at night and go back home later than other days. People prefer to stay at home under cold temperature which is evidenced by the fact that the value of pick-ups and drop-offs is extremely low on 25th. The temperature of that time is about -6°C, the coldest day of that year.

Land Use

By investigating the temporal pick-up/drop-off characteristic of a given area, it's possible to find its function in a city, such as whether it's a residential area or a working area. Qi et al. (2011) measured the relationship between social functions of city regions and the pick-up/drop-off characteristics of taxis there, and found that, the temporal pick-up/drop-off characteristic is tightly related with the land use of the area. Firstly, they extract the regions of a city with a DBSCAN-based method. Then they extract 6 pick-up/drop-off features to for the land use classification, including the daily pick-up feature, the daily drop-off feature, the pick-up/drop-off difference feature, the pick-up/drop-off ratio feature, the weekly pick-up feature and the weekly drop-off feature. After, they use classification methods to classify 8 types of land use, including station, campus, hospital, scenic spot, commercial district and entertainment district.

5. DETECTING ROAD INFRASTRUCTURE DYNAMICS FROM TAXI GPS TRACES

Taxis can be generally considered as mobile GPS sensors running on the roads, and the collected GPS can well reflect the road infrastructure dynamics in a city. The real time GPS traces are useful source to detect the road network changes, such as the blocked or newly-built road segment. Generally speaking, the road network change causes the vanishing or emerging of travel patterns in the corresponding places. Here we present an easy

Figure 10. Temporary characteristic: two representative time slots; 22h~24h (left) and 0h~4h (right)

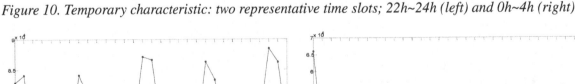

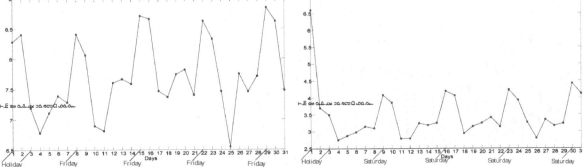

complementary method to isolate the road network change areas, whereafter the road map construction task focuses only on the network changes.

We first use grid decomposition to partition the city into a grid cell matrix (the dashed grids in Figure 12). A grid cell has 8 orientations as shown in the grid decomposition in Figure 11. For each grid cell, we count the visiting frequency, i.e., the number of trips that traverse through it, in each orientation. For a block road segment, as illustrated in Figure 12(a), the visiting frequencies of the grids along with the road direction, which cover the changed road segment, will change from a big number to zero. On the contrary, they change from zero to a big number for a new road segment (shown in Figure 12(b)). So by checking the visiting frequency change, we can easily isolate the road network change.

After isolating the road network changes, if the road is blocked, we can simply updating it into the road map. Otherwise, it's the newly opening road. In this case, we can build the road segments in the road network change areas by methods like proposed in (Cao and Krumm, 2009), which proposed a method to build a routable road map from the collected traces.

6. CONCLUSION

The large collections of taxi GPS traces provide us great opportunities to inspect the urban dynamics, revealing many aspects about the human mobility, traffics, road infrastructure, public transportation and land use. In this chapter we separate the taxi GPS traces into four stages, *i.e.*, *Vacant*, *Pick-up*,

Figure 11. Orientations of the grid cell and the road segment

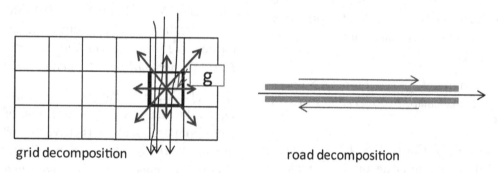

grid decomposition   road decomposition

Figure 12. Examples of isolating road network change: (a) blocked road segment; (b) new road segment

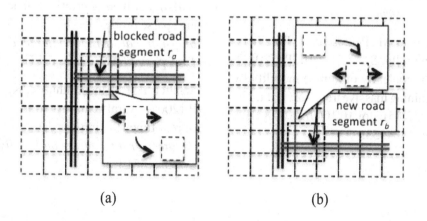

(a)   (b)

Delivery, Drop-off, according to the passenger status. Each stage has its unique characteristics and reflects different urban dynamics. From passenger vacant traces, we study the taxi service dynamics, introduce how to use them to help taxis and passengers to find each other, and reveal the work shifting dynamics of in a city. While from passenger occupied traces, we introduce their capabilities in monitoring and predicting the urban traffics and estimating the traveling time. From the pick-up and drop-off events, we show the passenger hotspots and human mobility patterns in a city. Beside, taxis can also be considered as mobile GPS sensors, which detect the road infrastructure dynamics.

REFERENCES

Balan, R. K., Nguyen, K. X., & Jiang, L. (2011). Real-time trip information service for a large taxi fleet. In *Proceedings of the 9th International Conference on Mobile Systems, Applications, and Services*. IEEE.

Cao, L., & Krumm, J. (2009). From GPS traces to a routable road map. In *Proceedings of GIS 2009*. GIS.

Chen, C., Zhang, D., Castro, P. S., Li, N., Sun, L., & Li, S. (2011). Real-time detection of anomalous taxi trajectories from GPS traces. In *Proceedings of the 8th International ICST Conference on Mobile and Ubiquitous Systems*. ICST.

Giannotti, F., Nanni, M., Pedreschi, D., Pinelli, F., Renso, C., Rinzivillo, S., & Trasarti, R. (2011). Unveiling the complexity of human mobility by querying and mining massive trajectory data. *The VLDB Journal, 20*(5). doi:10.1007/s00778-011-0244-8 PMID:21804753.

Li, B., Zhang, D., Sun, L., Chen, C., Li, S., Qi, G., & Yang, Q. (2011). Hunting or waiting? Discovering passenger-finding strategies from a large-scale real-world taxi dataset. In *Proceedings of the IEEE International Conference on Pervasive Computing and Communications Workshops* (PERCOM Workshops). IEEE.

Lou, Y., Zhang, C., Zheng, Y., Xie, X., Wang, W., & Huang, Y. (2009). Map-matching for low-sampling-rate GPS trajectories. In *Proceedings of the 17th ACM SIGSPATIAL International Conference on Advances in Geographic Information Systems*. ACM.

Paulos, E., Honicky, R., & Hooker, B. (2009). Citizen science: Enabling participatory urbanism. In M. Foth (Ed.), *Handbook of Research on Urban Informatics: The Practice and Promise of the Real-Time City*. Hershey, PA: IGI Global.

Phithakkitnukoon, S., Veloso, M., Bento, C., Biderman, A., & Ratti, C. (2010). Taxi-aware map: Identifying and predicting vacant taxis in the city. In *Proceedings of Ambient Intelligence: First International Joint Conference*. IEEE.

Qi, G., Li, X., Li, S., Pan, G., Wang, Z., & Zhang, D. (2011). Measuring social functions of city regions from large-scale taxi behaviors. In *Proceedings of the 9th IEEE International Conference on Pervasive Computing and Communications*. IEEE.

Ryan, H., Aude, H., Pieter, A., & Alexandre, B. (2010). Estimating arterial traffic conditions using sparse probe data. In *Proceedings of the 13th International IEEE Conference on Intelligent Transportation Systems*. IEEE.

Schäfer, R. P., Thiessenhusen, K. U., & Wagner, P. (2002). A traffic information system by means of real-time floating-car data. In *Proceedings of the 9th World Congress on Intelligent Transport Systems*. IEEE.

Sun, L., Zhang, D., Chen, C., Castro, P. S., Li, S., & Wang, Z. (2012). Real time anomalous trajectory detection and analysis. *Mobile Networks and Applications*.

Wen, H., Hu, Z., Guo, J., Zhu, L., & Sun, J. (2008). Operational analysis on Beijing road network during the olympic games. *Journal of Transportation Systems Engineering and Information Technology*, *8*(6). doi:10.1016/S1570-6672(09)60003-9.

Yuan, J., Zheng, Y., Xie, X., & Sun, G. (2011). Driving with knowledge from the physical world. In *Proceedings of the 17th ACM SIGKDD International Conference on Knowledge Discovery and Data Mining, KDD '11*. ACM.

Yuan, J., Zheng, Y., Zhang, L., Xie, X., & Sun, G. (2011). Where to find my next passenger? In *Proceedings of the 13th ACM International Conference on Ubiquitous Computing*. ACM.

Zhang, D., Guo, B., & Yu, Z. (2011). *The emergence of social and community intelligence*. IEEE Computer. doi:10.1109/MC.2011.65.

Zhang, D., Li, N., Zhou, Z. H., Chen, C., Sun, L., & Li, S. (2011). iBAT: Detecting anomalous taxi trajectories from GPS traces. In *Proceedings of the 13th ACM International Conference on Ubiquitous Computing*. ACM.

ENDNOTES

[1]   http://landcover.usgs.gov/urban/intro.php

[2]   http://research.microsoft.com/en-us/projects/urbancomputing/urbancomputing_1h.pdf

[3]   http://people.hofstra.edu/geotrans/eng/ch6en/conc6en/ch6c2en.html

Chapter 14
User–Centric Social Interaction for Digital Cities

Kåre Synnes
Luleå University of Technology, Sweden

Juwel Rana
Luleå University of Technology, Sweden

Matthias Kranz
University of Passau, Germany

Olov Schelén
Luleå University of Technology, Sweden

ABSTRACT

Pervasive computing was envisioned by pioneers like Mark Weiser but has yet to become an everyday technology in our society. The recent advances regarding Internet of Things, social computing, and mobile access technologies converge to make pervasive computing truly ubiquitous. The key challenge is to make simple and robust solutions for normal users, which shifts the focus from complex platforms involving machine learning and artificial intelligence to more hands on construction of services that are tailored or personalized for individual users. This chapter discusses Internet of Things together with Social Computing as a basis for components that users in a "digital city" could utilize to make their daily life better, safer, etc. A novel environment for user-created services, such as social apps, is presented as a possible solution for this. The vision is that anyone could make a simple service based on Internet-enabled devices (Internet of Things) and encapsulated digital resources such as Open Data, which also can have social aspects embedded. This chapter also aims to identify trends, challenges, and recommendations in regard of Social Interaction for Digital Cities. This work will help expose future themes with high innovation and business potential based on a timeframe roughly 15 years ahead of now. The purpose is to create a common outlook on the future of Information and Communication Technologies (ICT) based on the extrapolation of current trends and ongoing research efforts.

1. INTRODUCTION

By the end of 2008 a milestone was reached, there was now more people living in the cities than outside. This has of course affected and will even more affect people's life in the future. A higher density of people creates its challenges, problems and needs.

Today's society and economy is totally depending on a working and always accessible Internet 24/7. This fact changes and creates opportunities among people in cities and elsewhere. In the cities

DOI: 10.4018/978-1-4666-4695-7.ch014

there is a high density of almost everything and therefore the need of services is special - citizen centric services.

Early 2010 the topic Smart Cities was not very much known in the research community of Future Internet (FI). So far FI had focused on the next generation Internet, building large-scale test-beds, having in mind that this is a 30 year old design. Visions like 50 billion connected devices by the year 2020 (Ericsson), Internet of things creates new opportunities.

The last ten years another topic called Living Labs, sometimes also described as open user driven innovation, entered the European research scene. Methods, tools and processes have been developed in how to involve users as co-creators and this in parallel to FI research. Today there are tools ready to be used involving end users, many end users, to participate in the development of new services and products as co-creators. Not in the end of the product development cycle but early, for, with and by, the users of the new services/products. These new services can be developed by the end-users in the cities (citizens).

Up to now many services that already from the start didn't attract a huge amount of potential customer was never created. Phenomena like the entry of the iPhones and Android mobile phones completely changed the game plan in the telecom world. Services for a very small group of users was possible to develop to a small cost and by the users of their own. Still though, you have to be a rather skilled 'programmer' to create a mobile 'app' or service so the challenge today is to lower the threshold, the barriers of becoming a 'programmer'.

By providing the users, the citizens with tools in order to make their own mobile services the expectation is booming regarding potential new needs to be solved by citizens developing their own services. Internet of things, 50 billion connected devices, open and accessible public data, both from static servers in the city but also by dynamic sensor data in the street will create a totally new scenario about a more intelligent use of smart technology creating a better quality of life and entrepreneurship in cities.

One definition of a Smart City is 'We believe a city to be smart when investments in human and social capital and traditional (transport) and modern (ICT) communications infrastructure fuel sustainable economic growth and a high quality of life, with a wise management of natural resources, through participatory governance' (Caragliu et al, 2009).

The trend is to allow anybody to become a developer of services, even for a small target group usually not in focus by telecom operators and thereby contribute to a better society in many aspects, step by step. Smart Cities is very close to the thematic research area of Digital Cities and the importance of citizen centric services can not enough be seen as a strong driver of new services, products and companies but to reach full effect, there is also a need to lower the threshold, provide the tools, and utilize peoples creativity and the cities advantage as a multicultural melting pot driving societal changes will reach its full potential.

This book discusses the creation of personal, social, and urban awareness through pervasive computing. Although pervasive computing services are foreseen as potentially revolutionary, there is yet little adaption in industry. This paradox is similar to the predicted potential of artificial intelligence and later machine learning, which are successfully applied within a few applications, but which are not generally adopted. Though, this topic recently received again a lot of attention within the context of embodied AI, that is AI within technical systems. The reason for the lack of real-world adoption of pervasive computing for social interaction is potentially due to the inherit complexity of such systems that needs to span both heterogeneous networks and organizations. There are also inherent usability problems in pervasive systems (Drugge et al, 2004). How can then pervasive computing succeed better? The authors of this chapter believe that there are clear incentives, which will be discussed further later in this chapter. It however builds on three pillars: access to open data, novel interaction techniques and enabling end-users to visually compose mobile/pervasive components.

In the following, we introduce in Section 2 the characteristics for grid architectures for Internet of Things, which enables citizen-centric services based on open data. Section 3 presents a discussion of Social Web of Things. Section 4 presents initial work on a framework of social components enabling citizens to easily create their own mobile social apps. Section 5 summaries the chapter, highlights the trends, identifies future challenges and presents recommendations based on the presented work.

2. GRID ARCHITECTURES FOR THE INTERNET OF THINGS

There are several proposed architectures for storing, indexing and presenting large scale sensor (ESNA, 2009)(Sensei, 2008)(Smart Santander, 2008)(Castellani et al, 2010)(Enokido et al, 2010) (Krantz et al, 2010). However, there is more research needed to fully exploit the Internet of Things (IoT) and Crowd scenario across wireless domain and a distributed cloud of multiple players in providing application services. Experiences from these earlier architectures should be considered.

Earlier results in real-time and client-server scenarios should be reused. There are systems focusing on real-time streaming of sensor data to sinks (Schneidman et al, 2004). More recently there is a trend towards advanced sensor nodes that have capabilities to act as servers providing their data through lightweight RESTFUL approaches (Tsiftes et al, 2011). Methods for advertising and discovering data are needed (Aloisio et al, 2006) (Botts et al, 2009). Protocols for communications in resource-constrained environments are developed in the IETF (McGregor et al, 2012).

The objective would be to provide technology and infrastructure for an open business environment of both free data (Yuriyama et al, 2010) and data provided commercially on equal terms. Security considerations must be explored (Kapadia et al, 2010)(Poolsappasit et al, 2011).

Grid Architectures for Internet of Things and Future Media

The Internet of Things is expected to grow quickly to 50 billion devices and beyond (Ericson IoT, 2012)(Ericsson 2020, 2012). The solutions will include sensor networks and machine-to-machine communication. Applications may range over dynamic services in smart cities, advanced annotated media, supporting industrial and business processes, etc. In such networks, sensors and other input-devices will produce vast amounts of data that need to be collected, disseminated, stored, classified and indexed in a scalable way for various application purposes. Sensor data must in some cases be provided in real-time to large numbers of receivers and in some cases be stored and indexed for retrieval of large numbers of applications.

Research has emerged on the above-described aspects but most proposals are point solutions for specific scenarios, requirements, and problem domains. Consequently, the objective of this focus area is to support more research on scalable solutions for Internet of Things scenarios. This includes supporting crowd services where the crowd can be both producers and consumers of data. Besides meeting technical requirements, a clear objective is to promote open and generic distributed cloud solutions where a diversity of players can interact on reasonable and equal business terms to jointly provide unprecedented end services.

Research direction includes generative grid architectures that can scale over the data collection domain and application domain involving multiple users and organizations cooperating for the common objectives. Some specific research issues are mentioned in the following sections and at the end some related work is listed.

Security (Authentication, Authorization, Encryption)

The solutions must be completely open and promote equal opportunities (e.g. business terms) to different players, however this does not necessarily mean that all data is free and available to anyone. Therefore authentication, authorization and encryption are essential elements that need to be researched in this context.

Performance and Scalability

The vast number of producers and consumers where many entities will assume both roles, require specific research on performance and scalability in this context. The scalability solutions must be applied across all other requirements as here listed.

Decentralization, Open Interfaces, Business Interfaces

A key objective is that there must be an open market place with open interfaces and open business terms. Much data may be free and unrestricted (possibly funded by advertisements), but diversity of players that refine data and services is normally increasing if there is support to charge for and protect access to such data.

Wireless Aspects

Wireless devices may be the norm in Internet of Things and crowd scenarios. The architecture must support efficient resource usage (e.g. battery and power) and some degree of service continuity in scenarios where mobile devices (producers or consumers of data) only have occasional connectivity.

Resource Discovery

The vast amount of data provided must be discoverable by entities that want to use them. It is expected that data offered in the crowd scenario may in some cases be hard to find and in some cases be very redundant. In either case it is a matter of resource efficiency and service availability to be able to determine how and where to retrieve data.

Storage, Classification and Indexation

Large-scale (big data) storage of information in Internet of Things networks is a critical issue. For data that is timeless or of typical historical value this is a natural issue. However, even for typical real-time data it may be desirable to store some history for following up on failures etc. Existing data store technologies may need adaptation for effective storage and indexation of such data. Also, machine generated data from multiple sources is often hard to combine and interpret for humans. Automated methods to interpret data and classify it into real-world status and events are essential.

Applications

The key drivers for Internet of Things grid networks come from specific and creative applications in smart city scenarios, both addressing citizens and organizations/enterprises. Besides bringing clear values, the technologies mentioned previously should be evaluated both quantitatively and qualitatively in such application scenarios.

3. SOCIAL WEB OF THINGS

The on-going connection of appliances, the increasing adoption of smartphones, and emerging instrumentation of items with QR-codes and RFID provide the basis for a comprehensive layer of connectedness to objects, products, things and people. People are becoming part of digital social networks driven by personal interests and aspiration. The feeling of belonging to a community and the perpetual drive of getting connected from real life find it continuation in digital networks.

Both the digital integration of things and people starts to embrace our daily lives and enables for new interaction, new experiences and new behaviors. We can remotely query and control appliances of a smart home, we can participate in the experiences and opinions of our friends about product while shopping, and we can share our activities, our preferences instantly? (Michahelles et al, 2012) (Kranz et al, 2013)

The technological developments with respect to computing power, sensing systems, communication technologies, identification systems, middleware systems and infrastructure have resulted in a large number of uniquely identifiable systems and objects allow the sensing and actuation of real world phenomena on a large scale, not possible before. These embedded systems and the information embedded therein (Schmidt et al, 2004) is mainly designed for machine-to-machine communication (M2M), but also facilitate human-machine communication (M2H), also called human-computer interaction (HCI).

This provides novel chances for future services, especially with respect to the integration into people's everyday life. Technology becomes, as envisioned by Weiser, part of it, indistinguishable and woven into the fabric of everyday life: *'In the 21st century the technology revolution will move into the everyday, the small and the invisible'* (Weiser, 1991). In the following text we discuss the novel challenges and potentials of the proliferation of these developments, just entering our environment and emerging markets.

Private and Public Sensing as Basis for Open Data and Big Data

Networked sensing systems on all scales are on the verge of entering different environments of public and private life: intelligent power grids, vehicular communication systems such as vehicle-to-vehicle (V2V) and vehicle-to-infrastructure communication (V2I) (Schmidt et al, 2008)(Schmidt et al, 2010)(Rusu et al, 2006), smart home sensing, or crowd-sourced data, both acquired explicitly (manually inputted or automatically acquired) and implicitly (e.g. such as the traffic data generated by GSM base station changes from travellers using navigation services, such as TomTom HD traffic) or by explicitly incorporating the smartphone of the user (Diewald et al, 2011). This data is complemented by the release of governmental data, such as geo-referenced data sets (e.g. maps, pollution data, air quality data, health information) or other institutional data. This data is shared, online (e.g. using services such as former Pachube) or offline, in near-real time or even real time. The data originates from both public (e.g. governmental institutions, research agencies) and private sources (companies, private persons). This can be use to create novel socio-technical networks optimizing e.g. personal mobility (Diewald et al, 2012).

Solutions making use of the data will not only be required to make sense of all the sensing (such as employing techniques from machine learning), but also will need to handle this big data (immense amount of potentially heterogeneous data sources and data types that need processing, potentially in short periods of time). This requires novel tools and methods, especially novel middleware solutions (Roalter et al, 2010)(Atzori et al, 2010) (Rusu et al, 2006). While current social networks and social interaction platforms such as Facebook feature 1,000,000,000 users, the amount of sensor systems will be several magnitudes higher, assuming 50 to 100 devices per person will result in 50,000,000,000 to 100,000,000,000 data sources and sinks that produce data, at several Herz per second, and potentially of high dimension (multiple sensors per device) or size (full HD imagery).

The availability of data, provided that privacy and other legal issues are appropriately addressed, forms the basis for novel business models, services and markets by the end of 2020.

Embedded Interaction: Distributed Sensor and Actuator Systems

Technological advances and new usage models can cause computing to undergo a stark transformation. Automatic object identification (such as RFID or Near Field Communication, and visual markers), ubiquitous connectivity, improved processing and storage capabilities, various new display technologies, sensor device availability, and decreasing hardware costs all lay the foundation for a new computing era. We can now build vehicles, devices, goods, and everyday objects to become a part of the Internet of Things. (Kranz et al, 2010).

The resulting artifacts are equipped with sensors and actuators that let users seamlessly manipulate digital information and data in the context of real-world usage. This means data is not only sensed, but also used for control purposes (such as intelligent heating and climate control (HVAC – heating, ventilation, air conditioning)). This development does not only increasingly show in the process industry (which, according to today's standards and the state of research is in urgent need for applied solutions to increase efficiency and environmental balance), but also the private and public sector. The control might occur automatically in many cases (e.g. based on machine-to-machine (M2M) communication) to control and steer systems, but it will often enough involve human users that want to modify their environment according to their social needs and social contexts (Kranz et al, 2010).

This sensing and actuation will more increasingly be done via embedded systems and embedded devices. This trend is already immanent, looking e.g. at CPU sales where embedded CPUs have already by far outnumbered classical CPUs for desktop or enterprise computing. These embedded devices and systems will, in addition to their use in automated systems, become important points of interaction between humans and the environment, both in the private domain and in the public space. Miniaturization does not only allow us already to include technology e.g. in clothing (so-called wearables), but to further decrease the costs for a constant amount of computing power. The technological development of the ten recent years has made it possible to transfer this from prototypical objects (Kranz et al, 2005) used in research into smart products for the mass market. This results in networked embedded systems being deployed in public infrastructure, from waste containers, to parks, public spots, etc., allowing data exchange not only with an a-priori known central infrastructure, but spontaneously with e.g. mobile devices of users, both via network-only connection, but also by more natural means such as public-private interaction. These services will be available citywide and moving and following their human users. Further research will be necessary on how to develop, deploy and maintain these large-scale services for citizens (Möller et al, 2012).

We expect, given the existence of initial field studies and case in 2012 (such as in the city of Oulu, Finland, public data sets from smart cities like Amsterdam, Netherlands, and several others), the availability of first citywide interactive services, enabled by embedded interaction sensor-actuator systems, by 2025 or even thereafter. One major issue to be resolved will be the legal framework that ensures privacy and the algorithms for ensuring trust (between service providers and consumers – both technical and human). An example for a challenge in this dimension is, e.g. ensuring or detecting the trustworthiness of sensor data as basis for calculations.

Crowd City Services

A governance infrastructure is the collection of technologies, people, policies, practices, resources, social norms, and information that interact to support governing activities. Smart governance infrastructures augment society's ability to orga-

nize, interact, and govern. Novel instances of smart governance infrastructures already exist and are regularly emerging in distributed organizations and online (social) communities. (Johnston, 2005)

The governments of Europe aim at integrating their citizens more directly in all administrative and governance processes. This trend, fostering community and social interaction, will not be limited to governance, but also be extended to all parts of the daily life. We in the following sketch some ideas for services that could evolve in future smart cities, given the current trends and potential future developments foresighted in this report.

The availability of distributed, networked sensor-actuator system will allow for a novel level of participation and social interaction in future smart cities (Erickson, 2010). This poses the question how future participatory systems need, from a methodological point of view, need to be designed to integrate with the societal goals and digital cities.

Future participatory services will, by combining both machine and human intelligence, allow for a faster and more efficient than the information systems and electronic services today (King et al, 2005). We distinguish between services using information push (to the citizen) and information pull (from the citizen).

Classical participatory services for eliciting information are e.g. MobileWorks[1] (e.g. used for large-scale research studies to overcome the current limitations of user-involvement in research projects (Kranz et al, 2013), or Amazon's Mechanical Turk[2] where not only pure information is solicited, but 'artificial intelligence' is simulated, e.g. to overcome the limitations of current machine learning systems (e.g. when Steve Fosset's plane crashed, satellite imagery was bought, put online, and participants asked to find potential crash sites and respective reports were financially awarded).

Further examples of current solutions for crowd sourcing and participatory sensing are shortly presented here: The service Waze[3] uses user-generated geo-references movement data to build up maps e.g. of street networks and to generate and maintain additional information, such as the traffic information. User-contributed content is elicited in a gamified approach where points are awarded e.g. based on the type of data and its novelty (a road that hundreds of people have taken results in less points than a road only few have taken). WheelMap[4] uses also a user-based approach to generate information on accessibility of transportation networks (such as public sidewalks, places, etc.). The service EyeQuest[5] aims at providing up-to-date, on-demand imagery of physical locations. An example could be to ask the community about a photo of places to be visited soon. Users then take pictures of the desired spots and share them. The project 'Kleinwassersensor'[6] democratizes environmental and pollution sensing (today still a domain for the public authorities), at the example of water quality sensing. Finally, services like FixMyStreet[7] or SeeClickFix[8] try to include the user in identifying potentially problematic issues in the city and to raise awareness of the authorities to them. These services today do not 'match' to still pre-dominant governance style. Additionally, they usually lack integration in today's ICT systems. Future digital cities might very well benefit from these and similar services – if the challenges and hurdles can be overcome: lack of middleware and data exchange, lack of trust models of public and user generated/sensed data, scalability (e.g. of public responses to thousands of reports), etc., and finally a model how this more efficient reporting can result in more efficient solutions (demanding for cheaper fixes to the problems).

Data from future networked sensor-actuator systems will demand for an in-depth research on what value-added services can be composed, by e.g. providing the data and eliciting information from the citizen. This might, in a simple case be, e.g. the display of a picture of a spot in the city and the annotation of pollution.

But different data will put different demands on the users, some information will be harder to generate (and potentially not be possible to elicit from everyone), so novel approaches will be needed to develop these services. Gamification might be one of many possible solutions. This methodological research will be required prior to the availability of the digital city's data, so that to-be-identified day0 use cases can be implemented and further speed up development, acceptance and proliferation of these services.

Additional research questions will include a formalized development methodology, an identification of key parameters of these services (from input to output, users, fields of applications, etc.), and finally the societal, economical and social goals that shall be supported, from increasing social interaction if potentially anonymous mega cities, to increased community perception and awareness, well-being and health, citizen-involving governance, or many other possible goals. We are currently, after more then a decade of research, only in the beginning towards and understanding of future digital cities (Ishida, 2000)(Ishida, 2002).

The challenge includes finding methods, tools and approaches that e.g. increasing social interaction in society, by linking data from the digital city (digital networks), to e.g. Facebook (social networks) to physical human 'ad-hoc' networks (find a group to solve, in a community approach, specific problems, community networks).

As Virtanen and Malinen formulate the problem: "there is a growing interest to use online communities to support social interaction also in geography-based communities" (Virtanen et al, 2008).

How could these extensions of current social networks be achieved with the goal of fostering and increasing social interactions in the real world (and not decreasing it by the introduction of technology and data)?

Personal User-Configured Services

Large-scale deployments and large scale sensing solutions are enabled and supported by the expected technological developments. But the resulting services will need more than ever before be able to adapt to situations, contexts, and user-preferences. One size fits all solutions will no longer be adequate – we see here the same trend away from the 'personal computer' to 'ubiquitous computing' where users have multiple computational devices, probably even one device per task.

Personalization and Individualization: Individualization of the Society

Successful services will have to support end-user composition (see below in this report) and end-user configuration of the services, allowing the user to personalize the data, service and user interface. The need for personalization is driven by the societal trend of individualization of the particular members of our society. The larger mega cities become, the more mass production and consumption are at the centre, the more important it becomes for the people to live their individuality. This trend, so far, is at least visible in the western societies and in the growing generation E.

Many anthropologists state that there are great generational differences that can be forseen today, where the new generation is intrinsically accustomed to computers and mobile technologies. Ida Hult, CEO of Trendethnography, defines these as 'Moklofs' or 'Mobile kids with lots of friends'. This Generation E is used to getting rapid feedback on their opinions and actions, through a big flora of tools[9].

Those ages 8 to 18 spend more than 7,5 hours a day with such devices, compared with less than 6,5 hours 5 years ago, when the study was last conducted. And that does not count the 1,5 hours that youths spend texting, or the 0,5 hour they talk on their cell phones. And because so many of them are multitasking – say, surfing the Internet while listening to music – they pack on average nearly 11 hours of media content into that 7,5 hours. (Kevin Drum, MotherJones.com)

The challenges include to develop novel tools that allow the development of these services, the education of users to compose their own services, and the development of mental models for end-users that foster the understanding of the underlying processes. Understanding will be a crucial part of the acceptance of the services, and in turn also of the acquisition of the underlying data. Shared ownership will be crucial and important to achieve for the stakeholders, the citizens, of future digital cities.

From Personalized and Individualized Production to Personalized and Individualized Consumption: Example for Novel Services

We currently see the personalization of mass production. The hot topics are how to facilitate one-of production scenarios (instead of mass market), that is, efficiently (with respect to resource and machine usage) produce one customized item for one customer after each other. Instead of producing the same product or service after another, one different service or product will follow another different product or service. This, as we currently see it, requires immense changes in the manufacturing industry, process optimization to facilitate cheap one-of production in generalized plants and fabrication; networked manufacturing (from initial production of raw materials, to refinement, to production, to delivery), etc., and includes the complete supply and manufacturing chain until the delivery of the good or service.

We see this individualization or socialization of production also in the rise of novel tools, allowing already the individual to produce his own goods: laser cutters, 3D printers, fab labs, etc. are getting more and more popular. Today, individuals have access to highly sophisticated manufacturing equipment. This trend in physical production is accompanied by first approaches to deliver personalized and contextualized services. Though, today's technology is not able to reliably sense or infer human contexts outside the laboratory yet.

Given current trends of e.g. cloud computing and the commercial availability of compute services for individuals (e.g. Amazon's Elastic Compute Cloud (Amazon EC2)) and extrapolating this, in several years it will be possible and economically feasible to reliably enough determine citizens' contexts and combine this with the data from the smart city. Socializing e.g. consumption (my quarter, my town) using e.g. social network data and open data, could result in a socialization again that in he end might result in more awareness. Other future trends will very certain include personal robotics, both as e.g. household helpers, but also as facilitators of social interaction. An other example could be unmanned aerial vehicles (UAV) that e.g. substitute current bike messengers, for both delivering physical goods (e.g. mail, pizza, ...) and virtual goods (e.g. call a movie – where a projector equipped UAV delivers the movie and the presentation service). In these examples again, the computational demands will be lifted to the cloud and combined there with the data from the networked distributed sensor-actuator systems.

4. SOCIAL COMPONENTS FOR APP DEVELOPMENT BY EMPOWERED CITIZENS

This part presents a framework of social components for the Satin app development environment (Satin2, 2012), which provides a systematic way of designing, developing and deploying social components, e.g. for social network applications. We discuss the life cycle of developing social apps (that is information applications designed for a great number of users and personalized towards specific social target groups), where the social app development environment is targeting end-users. We consider here persons that have no dedicated programming skills and more specifically have not programmed using languages such as HTML5, JavaScript or other similar scripting languages. As proof-of-concept, several social components have been deployed to the Satin Editor, which can be used to compose mobile social apps. We report on the specific results of this deployment, and extrapolate trends for social interaction in future digital cities.

Social Media

At present, there is a huge interest from the users in social media such as Facebook[10], LinkedIn[11], Google+[12], YouTube[13], Twitter[14], and others (Faloutsos et al, 2012). Smartphones are becoming more and more apps driven, with people using apps as specialized front end to different data sources and sinks. One of the major areas of apps development is social media, which covers different kind of communication and media distribution needs (Böhmer et al, 2011)(Cui et al, 2011). Moreover, popular social networking services such as Facebook, Twitter, Google+ are offering developer-oriented APIs to produce new apps on basis of these platforms.

End-users, though, are due to their lack of expert-level programming skills, excluded from 'developing' novel applications or personalizing existing services to their needs. This excludes an immense number of people (with other skills than programming) from contributing to social applications and services. Comparing 1,000,000,000 Facebook users to several thousand active developers highlights this imbalance. We argue that, next to user empowerment, including these people in a structured, self-driven development process can leverage an immense potential.

Social web-based mash-ups are a means allowing for end-user to compose mash-up applications without programming dedicated knowledge (Liu et all, 2007)(Wong, 2007). In our proposed component-based social apps development framework,

we aim to minimize this gap between traditional application developer and non-technical users with the goal to enable these end-users to develop social apps in a drag-and drop manner. For example, a component could retrieve a user's friends' birthday, process the information and e.g. compute an action, and eventually another component could send a SMS with personalized birthday wishes. By combining these components, a user is able to form, from existing components, a novel and personalized app for this purpose. Social components show important aspects of social apps composition by offering new ways of managing contacts and initiating communication. For example, based on social components, users will be able to generate mash-ups to visualize global contacts (e.g. across several independent social networks), forming groups of people by adapting to contexts and by connecting participants, e.g. to organize a group video chat on a special topic (such as organizing a birthday present for the aforementioned friend).

Software structures are, also in other areas, evolving towards component-based architectures that support dynamic, high-level composition through wrapping and adaptors. We expect that open component libraries will be available for end-users that enable individual components to be reusable for visual end-user composition.

Another important problem in this context (Rana et al, 2009, 2010, 2012) is communication and social data aggregation. There are few theoretical models proposed to access social data generated from heterogeneous data sources in a unified manner. However, the proposed solutions do not cover appropriate cases where social data aggregation is essential and appropriate apps on that. By the proposed component based social apps creation framework, now it's being possible for the end-user to fuse social and communication data from different sources and develop attractive apps out of it. For example, collaborative social apps creation where collaborators from different networks need to be invited was complicated due to partition in social networking mechanism. However, compose-able component of such networks may cross that partition and invite each other to perform collaboration.

Social data is increasingly available in more and more areas of our daily life, which makes this data interesting for app developers. Data from these apps and their usage is also fed back to (groups in) social networks. Creating your own personalized apps based on the available social data by visual editing will, in the future, be offered by several platforms.

Note that the notion of a dynamic group can be used for many of these social components for media distribution (Rana et al, 2009)(Hallberg et al, 2007). These dynamic groups could be created at need or be managed over time, and be used to control access to real-time collaborative applications (Parnes et al, 1999). Making components that are easily included in mobile apps support otherwise complex user management in a good way.

Social media distribution is often time critical (posing real-time demands on the delivery) and usually unpredictable beforehand (except examples e.g. from the sports domain, e.g. on a final baseball game). These circumstances inflict that it is complicated to handle, even for (temporary) homogenous social groups. Even despite the availability of a-priori knowledge on the sharing interest similarity allowing to generate patterns that define when and how users generally share content (Gilbert et al, 2009). Therefore, frequently access to a user's real-time content is very resource demanding in terms of data-capturing, or computational complexity of data processing. The research problem addressed here is: 'How does a framework support social components to capture social data and utilize those components for real-time social apps composition?'

Related Work on Social App Development and End-User Service Composition

The literature lists several graphical tools (Rana et al, 2009, 2012)(Roalter et al, 2011) where user can create different kind of (desktop) applications or (mobile) apps without any programming knowledge. In most cases, users can, by using the 'Drag-and-Drop' metaphor, or by simply connecting (e.g. by clicking via a direct manipulation interface such as a mouse or a tangible user interface) different visual or physical objects to create the desired apps. The source code of the components is shielded from the user, the functionality of the components are embedded within these visual or physical objects.

Liu et al (2007) have proposed a mash-up creation architecture by extending a mash-up creating SOA models. In this architecture, they present a mash-up component model allowing the user to create own services by the composition of individual, smaller components.

Wong presented 'MARMITE', a visual tool that offers different kinds of graphical objects and allows users with no programming knowledge to create one's own mash-ups (Wong, 2007). Required programming scripts and logic are here, again, embedded within these graphical objects.

Web technology giants like Yahoo[15] and Microsoft[16] also provide environments for creating mash-ups by the end users. Using 'Yahoo Pipes' or 'Microsoft Popfly', end-users (with no programming knowledge) can create mash-ups. Both tools provide graphical editors where the user can drag and drop and interconnect the individual component to create the resulting mash-ups. Microsoft Popfly provides a platform where user can create apps ranging from games to small applications and eventually share these again. Ennals et al (2007) presents the 'Intel Mash Maker' that is the web extension of the user's existing web browser. It allows the user to expand the current page that the user browsed to with additional information from other websites (which potentially poses security risks e.g. due to cross-site scripting etc.). A user can create a new mash-up and add it to the current web site with the 'Intel Mash Maker' tool. After learning about the new mash-up, 'Intel Mash Maker' suggests this new mash-up to other users. 'Intel Mash Maker' provides a platform for building and exchanging these new mash-ups. 'Intel Mash Maker' depends on the developer community who will 'teach' it about the structure and semantics of web pages (supported of course by the structuring HTML/XHTML/XML elements embedded in the pages).

Jung and Park proposed an ontology-based mash-up creation system that uses different kinds of web data sources to construct mash-ups by end-users without any programming knowledge (Jung et all, 2011). This system proposed a 'mash-up rule language'. This system gets parameters from the users and uses a rule-based language to construct new mash-ups.

Berners-Lee and et al. proposed a platform called 'Tabulator' which links RDF data with the semantic web browser in order to create new applications based on the RDF data sources

(Berners-Lee et al, 2008). 'Tabulator' allows users to search a RDF graph in a tree structure and to browse nodes to find more information about them. An outliner mode is used which enables 'Tabulator' to create tables, Google maps, calendars, timelines, etc. Morbidoni et al (2008) present 'Semantic Web Pipes' which is a tool to create RDF based mash-ups. This tool aggregates and manipulates the content from different RDF data. This Semantic Web Pipe' can perform operations starting from straightforward aggregation to complex collaborative editing and filtering of distributed graphs.

Social Apps Development Lifecycle

This section describes a potential social apps development life cycle. The life cycle consists of four different conceptual steps of the component development process, namely the business model, the component development model, the composition model and evaluation model. Figure 1 depicts the iterative development flow of the proposed life cycle, which is similar to life-cycles for general system development but has an increased focus on the interaction between component developers and users/composers of apps (such as their creation of business models).

Figure 1. Social application development life cycle

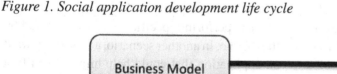

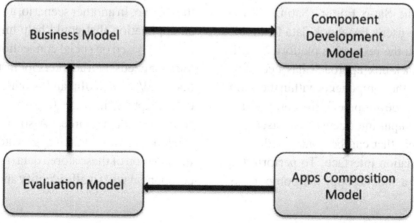

Business Model

There are different categories of mobile apps available in the various apps stores. We identified, based upon a qualitative investigation, a list of components from representative example apps in these app stores. Without loss of generalization we assume that comparable apps exist for all major platforms (such as Google's Android or Apple's iOS). When it comes specifically to social apps, their components have a lot of importance in user-centric mobile apps development. These components might include means to manipulate and process the users' social information, contact information, and communication history, and by utilizing this information, provide a means to create more personalized and contextualized mobile applications for improved communication experiences. An appropriate business model could help component developer and apps developer to understand the need for useful apps development and make use for a commercialization (e.g. by respective advertisement, or just by providing more appropriate services to the user).

Component Development Model

Components, within the context of this work, are considered as a building blocks of program logic or program code that performs a specific task in the context of social apps development. For example, a Facebook data aggregator is a component in the Satin Editor (Satin2, 2012) that captures the user's Facebook data from this platform through the respective platform's API. In general, a black-box approach has been followed to develop the components within the Satin context. After the development, the components provide inputs/output interfaces to the users via a graphical object that can be configured using a direct manipulation interface. To perform the composition of a mobile app, the components

need to be connected via their input/output labels of the components in a graphical editor. All of the processing is hidden to the end-user. The details of the component development framework are discussed to the next section.

Apps Composition Model

The apps composition model describes how various components can be used for creating different kind of social applications. The individual social components could be used for different purposes in order to create various social apps that fulfill the user's specific requirements. A component can be composed through input/output interfaces. During the building session, the composition provides a web link to access the apps. In our apps composition model, there are several components that can be used for capturing social data, while there are other components for representing and filtering social data and finally there exist other components for visualizing data.

Figure 2 shows a high-level composition of an app for providing alerts for coffee breaks, where the blocks represent different single components. The 'Group Former' is a social data collector component that gathers and creates groups from a user's social connections based on a given context. 'Context' represents a supporting component that provides an input option for the apps user. The other three components 'Calendar', 'Alert' and 'Timer' performs specific tasks, as indicated by their name. In another scenario, a user might want an application that could help him to identify a location based on social connections. In this task, the user needs data adapters for instance for Facebook and/or LinkedIn (and/or other social network data adapters) in order to gather his social data from these data sources. A social data aggregator component will then aggregate the necessary information of these stored data. A data analyzing component will finally identify and sort the user's

Figure 2. Apps composition

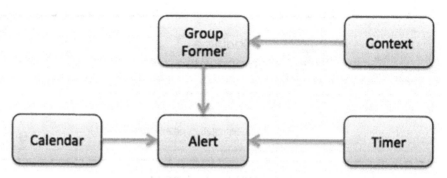

specific locations (e.g. Europe) based on the user's friends connected in different social networks and eventually suggest a location, e.g. to meet.

Evaluation Model

The evaluation model allows the users to study or provide feedback based on the app creation. The user's experiences of the app creation using these components will be collected here with the goal to improve the components in terms of compatibility, composition with other components, scalability, and simplicity. Moreover, in the evaluation model we have included some validation parameters. Evaluation for the proposed components will be carried out based on these parameters. Selected validation parameters are listed below:

- **Social Acceptance:** A user could evaluate if the social component based apps are acceptable from a societal point of view.
- **Positive Affect:** A user could evaluate if the social components allow for composition of any useful apps that make users' life more comfortable.
- **Quality of Experience:** A user could evaluate if the social apps are more useful and/or user friendly compared to commercial apps available.
- **Control:** A user could evaluate if he feels in control over the apps composition process.

- **Ownership:** A user could evaluate if the ownership of the newly generated apps remains with the user itself (and not with the platform provider).

Social Component Framework

Figure 3 shows a generalized, high-level framework for social components. It contains different layers of the social components development model that we previously described. In the lower layer, social data sources are connected to fetch the users' social networking data such as (e.g. Facebook, Twitter, LinkedIn, etc.). The middle layer provides a temporary storage of the users' social data, performs initial analysis on the data to offer different extended functionalities in the components placed on the top layer. Social data aggregation and analysis are performed in the middle layer. The social components itself constitute from the top layer.

During the component development, it is well recognized that different components have different levels of complexity (such as varying rights to use the contained data, richness of the data types and models, etc). A challenge is to express the components such that they can adapt to varying data sources, where the adoption naturally needs to be done per individual component. In the case of social components, most of the components are based on internal or external web APIs of social networks and social services (some

Figure 3. Social component framework

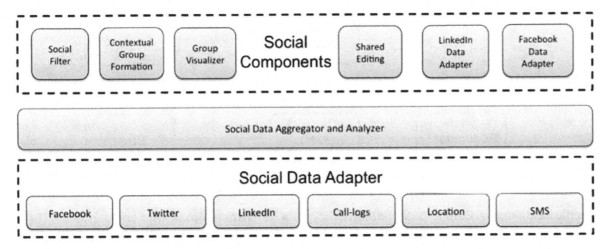

of these APIs are based on open standards, such as OpenSocial). Therefore, we find it crucial to start with the identification what class of social components we need to develop. Primarily, two groups of components have been identified, which we call core components and supporting components (c.f. Figure 4).

Core components are the main social components such as social filters, social data adapter and so on. Many of these components have been implemented and deployed for illustration and research purposes in the Satin Editor. There are also some components that support these core components, e.g. in triggering or labeling of web apps, which we therefore called supporting components. We find it important to provide a classification of the components to help social apps developers in assessing what is there and by providing a joint naming scheme. The classification is illustrated in Figure 4. The different types of core components that would be suitable for social apps creation are as follows:

- **Social Data Adapter:** This class of components adapts social data from the social networking sites (which are made available through the users' credentials). The data is

stored in a (computational) cloud for context reasoning.

- **Social Data Connector:** This class of components provides an interface to communicate between data sources and other components that utilize data.
- **Social Data Processing:** These components apply unified data representation to enhance data mining within social data components.
- **Social Data Reasoning:** These components implement different program logic or semantic functions on the social data for the user's desired apps.
- **Visualization:** Visualization components display different forms of social data. For example, if a processing and reasoning component forms a social group based on the user's social data, the visualization components can show this group in e.g. a grid view or a graphical tree view.
- **Smart Object:** Smart object components provide interfaces for lightweight devices with messaging and web connectivity functionalities.
- **Messaging:** These components provide different options of sending and receiving

Figure 4. A classification of components for social apps development

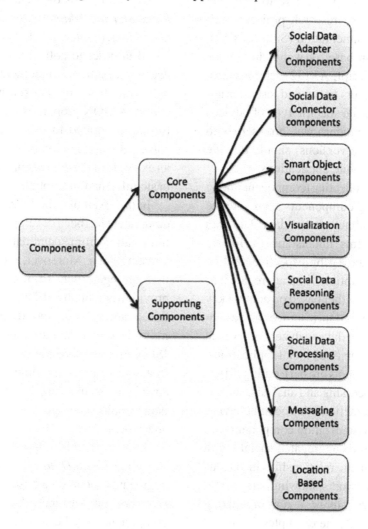

messages such as email, posting to social networks, SMS, and so on.

- **Location:** These components use the location APIs and social networks location-based services, such as Checkin.

Implementation

As discussed above, different kinds of core social components along with some supporting components have been developed towards a fully working prototype in an explorative and constructive approach to investigate this important research field. The users' social data is embedded within a social data component and deployed in a platform that allows our target groups (end users without any programming knowledge) to create their own social application.

Additionally, other social components embed 'intelligence' that can exploit the social data to create social applications to provide novel services. In our case, the so-called Satin Editor is used as the test-bed for simulating and evaluating the proposed social component-based application creation environment. As the background and details of the Satin Editor are beyond the scope of this work, we would like to refer the interested reader to the research project's web site with the full documentation (Satin2, 2012). Social components are based on web technologies (i.e., HTML5, JavaScript, AXIS2 web Services, etc.), which enable users to run and test their applications regardless the specific type of devices used. Therefore any modern web browser (both in desktop and mobile versions) should be able to run Satin-based mobile applications.

Data adapting (or collecting) components along with other supporting components aggregate the users' different social network(s) data. The data aggregating components 'understand' the format of the stored social data (e.g. by respective XML or similar resource descriptions) and aggregate it as a single data resource either based on context key or as a whole. Later, this data resource can be analyzed and reused by the data analyzer component in order to create personalized social applications. Data analyzer components are performing different kinds of data processing and analysis, such as the user's social interaction, his social behavior, interests, etc. Data visualization components are used to show e.g. user's aggregated social graph (a graph created from the relationships in various independent social networks, showing persons that e.g. have a temporary interest, e.g. as organizing a birthday present - c.f. the examples discussed above) either as graphical form or text form.

Different kinds of social data adapters (e.g., *LinkedIn Data Adapter*, *Facebook Data Adapter*, *Gmail Log Adapter*, etc.) have been developed and tested in order to collect users' data from these data sources. In the implementation, all collected data from different data sources are stored in as common JSON properties. The same JSON data format is applied to other data-sources to e.g. solve data aggregation problem. Figure 5 shows an example of the data format of profiling friend's basic information through social components.

In this example, the *JSON properties Reader* component has been developed to parse important information from social data and developing interesting apps. Moreover, there are components that aggregate data from different sources and provide a personalized data source. To implement this, a new indexing based upon user's access in multiple social data sources is conducted. The JSON properties of the index file are then used to associate users multiple social identities and social data sources are shown in figure 6. Social data visualizer component could be used to visualize social data.

Another social component was created which we called *Social Data Filter*, which filters users, aggregates social data based on the filtering parameters. For instance this *Social Data Filter* component could be used to create group with the users social connections based on users' interest.

Figure 5. JSON properties for profiling friends basic information

```
{
        "Friendsname": "abc" , "userid": 519817106, "username": "ab.c",
        "birthdate": "0",
        "email": "ab.c@facebook.com",
        "profileurl": "https ://www.1212121/ab.c", "movies": "",
        "interests": "",
        "picture": "https://a.akamaihd.net/hp/3 t.jpg",
        "contextkey": "p,q,r,s,t,u"

}
```

Figure 6. JSON properties for associating user's identities in multiple social data sources

{"index":[{"asguser":"1323732759" ,"data":
{"username":"1323732759" ,"socialIDs":
{"facebookId":"1323732759" ,
"linkedinId " : "UQxEWbiYX5" ,
"googlePlusId " : " 10957021022352334209 " } ,
"socialDataPaths"
{"facebook":"../../jsonfiles/facebook/1323732759",
"linkedin":"../../jsonfiles/linkedin/UQxEWbiYX5",
"googleplus":"../../jsonfiles/googleplus/109570"}}}
]
}

There are also other social components that are used to share user social resources with his/her connections.

Figure 7 shows the composition of an application in the Satin Editor. In this example one supporting component is used with three social components such as *Facebook Data Adapter*, *JSON Reader* and *Social Data Viewer*. Users can drag and drop the components in the canvas of the Satin Editor and compose the application. This application is used to collect the user's Facebook friend's data and view the whole collected data

to analyze it further or to use this information with other components to create further apps. In a similar way, users can use different social data collector components to amass his/her social connections' information from different social data sources.

Evaluation

The ultimate aim of this work is that any user after a 15-20 minutes introduction should be able to easily create simple social apps on their

Figure 7. Sample social apps composition in the Satin Editor

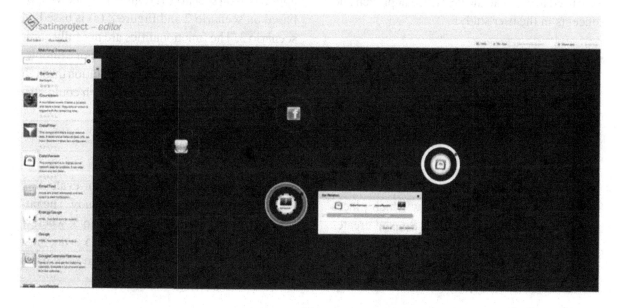

own. The objective of this study was however to indicate whether this would be achievable at all, as even visual composition can be challenging for normal users as data paths and sequential dependencies still are hard to understand, and thus provide feedback on social apps development for the next iteration of the Satin Editor. A small user study was therefore initiated, which was based on the evaluation model and which was limited to 10 users with some prior knowledge of mobile apps (they were for instance required to at least have used apps before). The limited set of users and their a-priori knowledge makes the results no more than indicative, but they are still very valuable as feedback for the next generation of the Satin Editor. To conduct the study, we prepared three different scenarios (described below) of apps development. Before the users start with the app composition, the available components for social apps were introduced to the users by providing written descriptions of the components, as well as demonstrating apps composition using the Satin Editor. In this subsection, description of the scenarios is presented.

Scenarios

The following three scenarios of app compositions were used to evaluate the described approach and concepts in the user study:

Scenario 1: Bob is planning an outdoor party in a newly explored and interesting place. He wants to invite all his Facebook friends to join the party from wherever they are. Thus, Bob intends to publish an app to his Facebook timeline in order to invite his friends, as well as a to provide a map to direct them to the party place in a comfortable way.

Scenario 2: Alice wants to know which places are of most interest to her. So, she creates an app that automatically logs her current location if she stays at a place for more that 30 minutes. At the end of the month, she is provided information about her most frequently visited places and potentially a respective visualization.

Scenario 3: Charlie is going for a coffee break, and he would like to send an alert message to his co-workers so that they can have the break at the same time.

Data Collection

The following parameters have been taken into consideration during the test for data collection:

- **App Composition Time:** The time that a user has spent to compose an app on a given scenario.
- **Number of Components:** The number of components that have been selected to perform the final composition.
- **App Formation:** The user is able to build an apps and able to run the apps
- **App Functionality:** Logs whether the app that are composed by the users is functioning correctly with respect to the scenarios described above.

Figure 8 shows the snapshot of the apps generated during the user tests. Figure 8 (a) shows the apps based on scenario 1. Figure 8 (b) shows apps based on scenario 2 and Figure 8 (c) is based on scenario 3. The functionalities are not fully compliant with the described scenarios. For example, apps for the scenario 1 share the invitation through the Facebook 'Like' operation, which could also be done with other options.

Evaluation Results

Figure 9 shows the users' ratings for evaluating social apps as gathered in the user study. The ratings are taken within the scale of 1 to 5, where 1 is the most negative response while 5 is the most positive response. In general, from most of users we received positive responses.

Figure 8. Social apps generated by the Satin users for scenarios 1 to 3

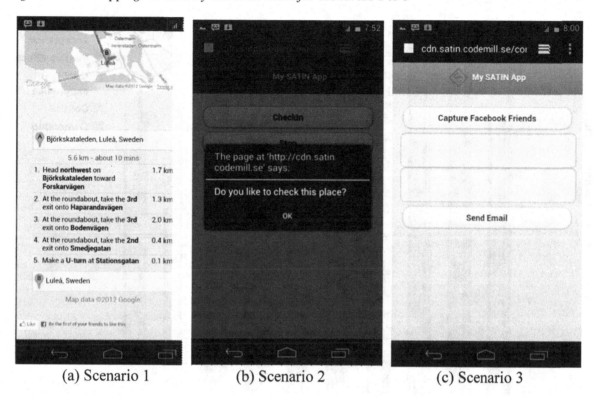

(a) Scenario 1   (b) Scenario 2   (c) Scenario 3

Figure 10 shows time durations for social apps composition. Although there are significant amount of assistance have been given before or during apps composition to the users, however the time duration varies highly from user to user. Average time is calculated to 29.3 minutes required per user to compose apps based on the given scenarios.

Moreover, we collected the users' individual opinions based on the described parameters from the evaluation model such as social acceptance, positive affect, quality of experience, control and ownership. Some of the general problems that we have identified are common amongst most of users during apps development. As of now, they are not comfortable enough with the editor environment, and they need more support to identifying appropriate components to accomplish functionalities. However, those are not directly connected with social components, but valid com-

ments to fix those before re-running the study for larger user group and a more mature version of the Satin Editor. The positive impact that we got that after being to able successfully apps creation, the users are being relaxed and appreciates the environment as well as apps. Overall, the approach has been validated as effective and the participants of the user study have rated the concept positively.

Discussion and Future Work

We have proposed components for social app development environment via a high-level, four-phase social app development life cycle. Each of the phases of life cycle has been briefly discussed. The business model does not provide any technological challenges, however it describes the social components from the business and usability point of view. The business model is important,

Figure 9. Users' rating for evaluating social apps

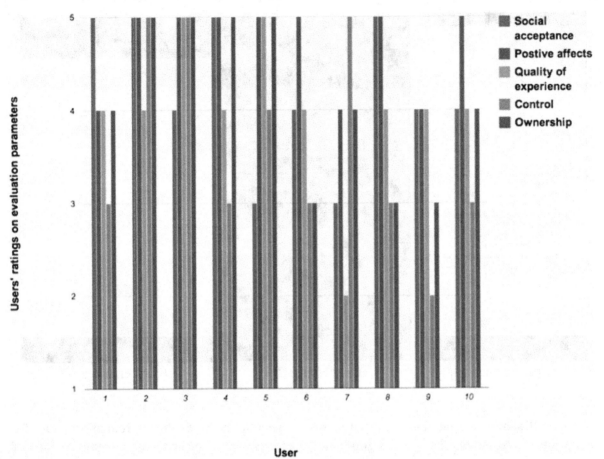

Figure 10. Time durations for social apps composition

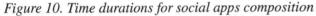

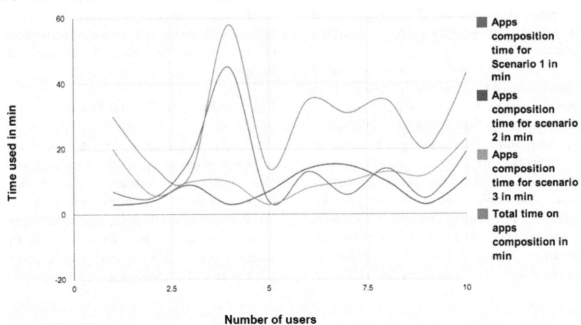

as it will help to understand the users' needs and wishes and thus be an important driving factor.

The component development model mainly addresses social aspects of the app development. It identifies different core components and supporting components to compose social apps. We also provided a classification of components to provide developers with an overview of what kind of components that could add value to the mobile apps development environment. We argue that there are huge domains of components that need to be developed and classified for diverse apps development, and that is one of the targets for the future work.

From the user study we identified the users' difficulties to understand the composition scheme of the Satin Editor, however having initial support from a instructors, users could soon get proficient in app composition. By our validation model, we achieved useful feedback from the users even though the scale of user study was limited.

The research question addressed in this work ('How can be the user's social and communication data captured from the social and communication data sources be utilized to compose real-time social apps?') considers social data as one of the important area of component development. Facebook and LinkedIn data components got users attractions as they being able to develop social components based on those. We have shown that the social component framework provides a standard way of developing social components to capture data from social media sources. It also shows different kinds of social data collector components developed in Satin platform. The framework could be used as model for other social component developer and could adapt our JSON properties to make their components possible to compose with Satin-based social data components. Thus, new component developers may be benefitted to design and implement their social component in Satin environment. Another aspect of future works is to cover different domains of

apps developments such as games, mobile OS based native apps, and so on.

The challenge will be creating an open platform for components-based visual design of apps requires standardization or an industrial de-facto. For user-composed and personalized services to become ubiquitous, the challenge is to create such an open platform based on recognized (de-facto) standards.

Due to use of smart devices, social apps are becoming part of everyday life. Social apps could be very beneficial in social media distribution, group formation, lightweight collaboration and so on. If users being able to adapt social components to build their own apps, then it will open up a new and efficient way of social development. The user of the Satin Editor logically does not require any programming knowledge to develop mobile apps. From the user study and deployed social components in the Satin Editor, it show that proposed social component development framework could be used to develop social component using different kind of social networks and social media data. The social component development life cycle and classification of component may help other developer to develop useful components to generate not only social components but also diverse type of mobile apps in general.

A key technological challenge is to manage to link openly available software components with smart devices and tangible artifacts. This challenge builds on open and standardized APIs.

Our recommendation is to study component-based visual editing of apps that utilize open data, social data and personal preferences, such that personalized apps can be easily constructed by any end-user for use with a smart device.

5. SUMMARY AND DISCUSSION

We have presented three areas of research necessary to achieve personal, social and urban awareness through pervasive computing. The argument made is that pervasive computing services are likely to be driven by user-needs, where three pillars enable these services. These are free access to open data, novel interaction techniques based on the social web of things and the vast potential behind end-users able to easily visually compose mobile/pervasive apps. In other words, that awareness is accomplished by personalizing apps through easy visual composition of components based on open (urban) data connected to social facets that allows for effective filtering, prioritization and recommendation of information and services. What drives the next age of computing is then highly personalized services that harness information from the social web of things.

The vision of pervasive computing is thus likely to be achieved, at least in part, not by inherent complex architectures and services but on simple building blocks that just about anyone can combine into useful services. These services are naturally first deployed in mobile devices, but is likely later also deployed into smart environments when available. Techniques such as tangible computing may then bloom from the few applications available today, to a full range of personalized applications applied to various areas of society such as teaching tools for children, smart homes for elder care, environments for social and tangible communication, etc.

The path towards this development can be plotted by currents trends in this area, which also highlight challenges to overcome and thus recommendations for how to achieve the vision above. A few trends, challenges and recommendations based on the work above is identified in the following sections.

Trends

- Software structures are constantly evolving towards component-based architectures that support dynamic high-level composi-

tion through wrapping and adaptors. By 2016, open component libraries will be available that enable single components to be reused for visual end-user composition.

- Social data is increasingly interesting for app developers, so is feeding back information to (groups in) social networks. By 2018, creating your own personalized apps based on social data by visual editing will be offered by several platforms.

- Personalized Physical and Digital Services: Individualization of the members of the society will further increase the demand for personalized services, extending significantly the current services that are designed for the mass.

- The amount of data sensed (and available for control) will grow exponentially. This trend is mainly grounded in the development of the so-called Internet of Things and results in many challenges regarding capturing, filtering, storing, managing and utilizing Big Data.

Challenges

- Creating an open platform for components-based visual design of apps requires standardization or an industrial de-facto. For user-composed and personalized services to become ubiquitous, the challenge is to create such an open platform based on recognized (de-facto) standards.

- A key technological challenge is to manage to link openly available software components with smart devices and tangible artifacts. This challenge builds on open and standardized APIs.

- Provision of a European-wide legal framework for sensing and open data: future smart cities will be providing and collecting a lot data to and on their citizens. Before this data can be used as basis for novel services, clear rules have to be defined on the extent this data may be used and how e.g. the privacy of the digital citizens can be ensured.

- **Physical and Digital Rural Depopulation:** The size of cities will further grow. Today already more than half of the population lives in cities. In the future, more and more people will live in connected mega cities. The rural areas will need to develop services that, if not stopping this trend, make it at least convenient and possible for the remaining population to stay there. This will most probably concern elderly people that are more reluctant to move, but have special needs and demands, such as connected healthcare.

- The trend for individualization of inhabitants of mega cities requires the society to take countermeasures against a future 'digital loneliness'. The data and digital cities will need to use the digital data to create spaces that foster physical real cooperation, co-living and interaction. This can potentially also support virtual communities, sprung from a common need or understanding, that can offer the benefits of smaller communities in a mega city (digital villages).

- Social interaction and responsibility should, using the available data of the connected artifacts, be employed to increase the participation of the digital citizens in all social and societal issues, e.g. co-governance or to-be-developed services like FixMyDigitalCity 2.0.

Recommendations

- Study component-based visual editing of apps that utilize open data, social data and personal preferences, such that personalized apps can be easily constructed by any end-user for use with a smart device.

- Use Sweden, due its leading position with respect to widespread availability of high-bandwidth internet connectivity (esp. in rural areas), the availability of electronic IDs for digital services, and spearhead projects for digital cities, like in Skellefteå, Sweden, as a test-bed for Europe due to the widespread acceptance and adoption of new technology

- The lack of a common legal framework across the borders of the EU member states will be hindering the development of future digital city services. As can be foreseen now, most probably it will be multinational companies that will be developing these novel services, due to the challenges from big data and the from the Internet of Things. The associated costs are higher due to the different existing legislative frameworks. A 'legal standardization' will both provide security for the investments and also be valuable for the citizens as users as clear rules will have to ensure their rights, esp. privacy.

- Standardization of middleware and service APIs allowing the interconnection of services, data, etc., while ensuring trust, authenticity and privacy. Application areas benefitting from this range from e-government, citizen service, social interaction to novel business opportunities. This will include the need for modeling and developing a 'transparency' layer for open/big/user centric data in future digital cities and economies.

6. CONCLUSION

End-users in Digital Cities able to compose personalized services within a short span of time through component-based visual composition will drive the development of truly pervasive computing services, first deployed in smart phones and later in smart environments. Components will leverage of open data from both urban and private environments as well as on the advent of novel interaction techniques such as tangible interaction devices. Personal, social and urban awareness through pervasive computing is thus accomplished by a wide variety of novel personalized services, based on users' needs.

REFERENCES

Aloisio, G., Conte, D., Elefante, C., Epicoco, I., Marra, G. P., Mastrantonio, G., & Quarta, G. (2006). Sensorml for grid sensor networks. In *Proceedings of the 2006 International Conference on Grid Computing & Applications, GCA 2006*. Las Vegas, NV: CSREA Press.

Atzori, L., Iera, A., & Morabito, G. (2010). The internet of things: A survey. *Computer Networks, 54*(15), 2787–2805. doi:10.1016/j.comnet.2010.05.010.

Berners-Lee, T., Hollenbach, J., Lu, K., Presbrey, J., Prud'hommeaux, E., & Schraefel, M. M. C. (2008). Tabulator redux: Browsing and writing linked data. In *Proceedings of CEUR Workshop*. CEUR-WS.

Böhmer, M., Hecht, B., Schöning, J., Krüger, A., & Bauer, G. (2011). Falling asleep with angry birds, Facebook and Kindle: A large scale study on mobile application usage. In *Proceedings of the 13th International Conference on Human Computer Interaction with Mobile Devices and Services* (MobileHCI '11). ACM.

Botts, M., & Robin, A. (2009). *Sensor model language (SensorML)*. Retrieved from http://www.ogcnetwork.net/SensorML

Caragliu, A., Del Bo, C., Kourtit, K., & Nijkamp, P. (2009). *Performance of smart cities in the north sea basin*. Retrieved from http://www.smartcities.info/files/13%20-%20Peter%20Nijkamp%20-%20Performance%20of%20Smart%20Cities.pdf

Castellani, A. P., Bui, N., Casari, P., Rossi, M., Shelby, Z., & Zorzi, M. (2010). Architecture and protocols for the internet of things: A case study. In *Proceedings of PerCom 2010 Workshops*. Mannheim, Germany: PerCom. doi:10.1109/PERCOMW.2010.5470520.

Cui, Y., & Honkala, M. (2011). The consumption of integrated social networking services on mobile devices. In *Proceedings of the 10th International Conference on Mobile and Ubiquitous Multimedia, MUM '11*. ACM.

Diewald, S., Möller, A., Roalter, L., & Kranz, M. (2011). Mobile device integration and interaction in the automotive domain. In *Proceedings of AutoNUI: Automotive Natural User Interfaces Workshop at the 3rd International Conference on Automotive User Interfaces and Interactive Vehicular Applications* (AutomotiveUI 2011). AutomotiveUI.

Diewald, S., Möller, A., Roalter, L., & Kranz, M. (2012). MobiliNet: A social network for optimized mobility. In *Proceedings of the 4th International Conference on Automotive User Interfaces and Interactive Vehicular Applications* (AutomotiveUI 2012). AutomotiveUI.

Drugge, M., Nilsson, M., Liljedahl, U., Synnes, K., & Parnes, P. (2004). Methods for interrupting a wearable computer user. In *Proceedings of ISWC 2004, the Eighth International Symposium on Wearable Computers*. IEEE.

Ennals, R., Brewer, E., Garofalakis, M., Shadle, M., & Gandhi, P. (2007). Intel mash maker: Join the web. *SIGMOD Record, 36*(4), 27–33. doi:10.1145/1361348.1361355.

Enokido, T., Xhafa, F., Barolli, L., Takizawa, M., Uehara, M., & Durresi, A. (Eds.). (2010). *The 13th international conference on network-based information systems* (NBiS 2010). Takayama, Japan: IEEE.

Erickson, T. (2010). *Geocentric crowdsourcing and smarter cities: Enabling urban intelligence in cities and regions.* Paper presented at the 1st International Workshop on Ubiquitous Crowd-sourcing. New York, NY.

Ericsson 2020. (2012). *Vision 2020 – 50 billion connected devices.* Retrieved from http://www. slideshare.net/EricssonFrance/vision-2020-50-billion-connected-devices-ericsson

Ericsson IoT. (2012). *The internet of things comes alive through smart objects interoperability.* Retrieved from http://labs.ericsson.com/

ESNA. (2009). *European sensor network architecture (ESNA).* Retrieved from https://www.sics.se/esna/

Faloutsos, C., & Kang, U. (2012). Managing and mining large graphs: Patterns and algorithms. In *Proceedings of SIGMOD Conference.* ACM.

Gilbert, E., & Karahalios, K. (2009). Predicting tie strength with social media. In *Proceedings of the SIGCHI Conference on Human Factors in Computing Systems* (CHI '09). ACM.

Hallberg, J., Norberg, M. B., Kristiansson, J., Synnes, K., & Nugent, C. (2007). Creating dynamic groups using context-awareness. In *Proceedings of the 6th International Conference on Mobile and Ubiquitous Multimedia* (MUM '07). ACM.

Ishida, T. (2000). Understanding digital cities. In *Digital Cities, Technologies, Experiences, and Future Perspectives.* Berlin: Springer-Verlag. doi:10.1007/3-540-46422-0_2.

Ishida, T. (2002). Digital city Kyoto. *Communications of the ACM, 45*(7), 76–81. doi:10.1145/514236.514238.

Johnston, E. W. (2010). Governance infrastructures in 2020. *Public Administration Review, 70*(1), 122–128. doi:10.1111/j.1540-6210.2010.02254.x.

Johnston, E. W., & Hansen, D. L. (2005). Design lessons for smart governance infrastructures. In *American Governance 3.0: Rebooting the Public Square?* National Academy of Public Administration.

Jung, H., & Park, S. (2011). Mash-up creation using a mash-up rule language. *J. Inf. Sci. Eng., 27*(2), 761–775.

Kapadia, A., Myers, S., Wang, X., & Fox, G. (2010). Secure cloud computing with brokered trusted sensor networks. In *Proceedings of CTS.* IEEE.

King, S. F., & Brown, P. (2007). Fix my street or else: using the internet to voice local public service concerns. In *Proceedings of the 1st International Conference on Theory and Practice of Electronic Governance* (ICEGOV '07). ACM.

Kranz, M., Murmann, L., & Michahelles, F. (2013). Research in the large: Challenges for large- scale mobile application research - A case study about NFC adoption using gamification via an app. store. *International Journal of Mobile Human Computer Interaction.* doi:10.4018/jmhci.2013010103.

Kranz, M., Roalter, L., & Michahelles, F. (2010). Things that Twitter: Social networks and the internet of things. In *Proceedings of the What can the Internet of Things do for the Citizen (CIoT) Workshop at The Eighth International Conference on Pervasive Computing* (Pervasive 2010). IEEE.

Kranz, M., & Schmidt, A. (2005). Prototyping smart objects for ubiquitous computing. In *Proceedings of the International Workshop on Smart Object Systems in Conjunction with the Seventh International Conference on Ubiquitous Computing*. ACM.

Kranz, M., Schmidt, A., & Holleis, P. (2010). Embedded interaction: Interacting with the internet of things. *IEEE Internet Computing, 14*(2), 46–53. doi:10.1109/MIC.2009.141.

Liu, X., Hui, Y., Sun, W., & Liang, H. (2007). Towards service composition based on mashup. In *Proceedings of IEEE SCW*. IEEE.

McGregor, A., & Bormann, C. (2012a). *Constrained RESTful environments (CoRE) (Tech. rep.). Internet Engineering Task Force*. IETF.

McGregor, A., & Bormann, C. (2012b). *IPv6 over low power wireless personal area networks (Tech. rep.). Internet Engineering Task Force*. IETF.

Michahelles, F., Kranz, M., & Mandl, S. (2012). *Social networks for people and things (SoNePT)*. Retrieved from http://www.theinternetofthings.eu/social-networks-people-and-things-sonept

Möller, A., Michahelles, F., Diewald, S., Roalter, L., & Kranz, M. (2012). Update behavior in app. markets and security implications: A case study in Google play. In *Proceedings of the 3rd International Workshop on Research in the Large*. ACM.

Morbidoni, C., Le Phuoc, D., Polleres, A., Samwald, M., & Tummarello, G. (2008). Previewing semantic web pipes. In *Proceedings of the 5th European Semantic Web Conference on the Semantic Web: Research and Applications* (ESWC'08). Berlin: Springer-Verlag.

Parnes, P., Synnes, K., & Schefström, D. (1999). Real-time control and management of distributed applications using IP-multicast. In *Proceedings of Integrated Network Management, Distributed Management for the Networked Millennium*. IEEE. doi:10.1109/INM.1999.770730.

Poolsappasit, N., Kumar, V., Madria, S., & Chellappan, S. (2011). Challenges in secure sensor-cloud computing. In *Proceedings of the 8th VLDB International Conference on Secure Data Management, SDM'11*. Springer-Verlag.

Rana, J., Kristiansson, J., Hallberg, J., & Synnes, K. (2009). Challenges for mobile social networking applications. In *Proceedings of First international ICST Conference on Communications, Infrastructure, Systems and Applications in Europe* (EuropeComm 2009). London, UK: EuropeComm.

Rana, J., Kristiansson, J., Hallberg, J., & Synnes, K. (2009). An architecture for mobile social networking applications. In *Proceedings of the First International Conference on Computational Intelligence, Modelling and Simulation* (CSSim 2009). IEEE.

Rana, J., Kristiansson, J., & Synnes, K. (2010a). Enriching and simplifying communication by social prioritization. In *Proceedings of ASONAM 20110, the International Conference on Advances in Social Network Analysis and Mining*. ASONAM.

Rana, J., Kristiansson, J., & Synnes, K. (2010b). Modeling unified interaction for communication service integration. In *Proceedings of UBICOMM 2010, The Fourth International Conference on Mobile Ubiquitous Computing, Systems, Services and Technologies*. IARIA.

Rana, J., Kristiansson, J., & Synnes, K. (2012a). Supporting ubiquitous interaction in dynamic shared spaces through automatic group formation based on social context. In *Proceedings of SCI 2012, the ASE International Conference on Social Informatics*. IEEE.

Rana, J., Kristiansson, J., & Synnes, K. (2012b). Dynamic media distribution in ad-hoc social networks. In *Proceedings of the 2nd International Conference on Social Computing and its Applications* (SCA2012). IEEE.

Roalter, L., Kranz, M., & Möller, A. (2010). A middleware for intelligent environments and the internet of things. [LNCS]. *Proceedings of Ubiquitous Intelligence and Computing, 6406*, 267–281. doi:10.1007/978-3-642-16355-5_23.

Roalter, L., Möller, A., Diewald, S., & Kranz, M. (2011). Developing intelligent environments: A development tool chain for creation, testing and simulation of smart and intelligent environments. In *Proceedings of the 7th International Conference on Intelligent Environments (IE)*. IE.

Röckl, M., Gacnik, J., Schomerus, J., Strang, T., & Kranz, M. (2008). Sensing the environment for future driver assistance combining autonomous and cooperative appliances. In *Proceedings of the Fourth International Workshop on Vehicle-to-Vehicle Communications (V2VCOM)*. V2VCOM.

Rusu, R. B., Maldonado, A., Beetz, M., Kranz, M., Mösenlechner, L., Holleis, P., & Schmidt, A. (2006). Player/stage as middleware for ubiquitous computing. In *Proceedings of the 8th Annual Conference on Ubiquitous Computing* (Ubicomp 2006). ACM.

Satin. (2012). *SATIN editor*. Retrieved from http://satinproject.eu/

Schmidt, A., Kranz, M., & Holleis, P. (2004). Embedded information. In *Proceedings of Workshop Ubiquitous Display Environments at UbiComp 2004*. ACM.

Schmidt, R. K., Leinmüller, T., & Böddeker, B. (2008). V2x kommunikation. In *Proceedings of 17th Aachener Kolloquium*. Academic Press.

Schmidt, R. K., Leinmüller, T., Schoch, E., Kargl, F., & Schäfer, G. (2010). Exploration of adaptive beaconing for efficient intervehicle safety communication. *IEEE Network Magazine, 24*, 14–19. doi:10.1109/MNET.2010.5395778.

Sensei. (2008). *SENSEI - Integrating the physical with the digital world of the network of the future*. Retrieved from http://www.ict-sensei.org/

Shneidman, J., Pietzuch, P., Ledlie, J., Roussopoulos, M., Seltzer, M., & Welsh, M. (2004). *Hourglass: An infrastructure for connecting sensor networks and applications (Tech. rep.)*. Harvard.

Smart Santander. (2008). *Smart santander - Future internet research & experimentation*. Retrieved from http: //www.smartsantander.eu/

Tsiftes, N., & Dunkels, A. (2011). A database in every sensor. In *Proceedings of the 9th ACM Conference on Embedded Networked Sensor Systems* (SenSys '11). ACM.

Virtanen, T., & Malinen, S. (2008). Supporting the sense of locality with online communities. In Proceedings of MindTrek 2008, International Digital Media & Business Festival. MindTrek.

Weiser, M. (1991). The computer for the 21st century. *Scientific American, 265*(3), 66–75. doi:10.1038/scientificamerican0991-94 PMID:1754874.

Wong, J. (2007). Marmite: Towards end-user programming for the web. In *Proceedings of VL/HCC*. IEEE.

Wong, J., & Hong, J. I. (2007). Making mash-ups with marmite: Towards end-user programming for the web. In *Proceedings of CHI*. ACM.

ENDNOTES

[1] https://www.mobileworks.com

[2] http://www.mturk.com

[3] http://www.waze.com

[4] http://www.wheelmap.org/

[5] http://www.eyequest.de/

[6] http://kleinwassersensor.com/

[7] http://www.fixmystreet.com/

[8] http://www.seeclickfix.com/

[9] Dagens Nyheter 2010-06-15 "Generation E går sin egen väg?" http://www.dn.se/insidan/insidan-hem/generation-e-gar-sin-egen-vag

[10] https://www.facebook.com/

[11] https://www.linkedin.com/

[12] https://plus.google.com/

[13] https://www.youtube.com/

[14] https://www.twitter.com/

[15] http://pipes.yahoo.com/pipes/

[16] http://www.popfly.ms/

Section 5
Conclusion

Chapter 15
Research Challenges for Personal and Collective Awareness

Daniele Riboni
University of Milano, Italy

Rim Helaoui
University of Mannheim, Germany

ABSTRACT

The "big data" explicitly produced by people through social applications, or implicitly gathered through sensors and transaction records, enables a new generation of mining and analysis tools to understand the trends and dynamics of today's interconnected society. While important steps have been made towards personal, urban, and social awareness, several research challenges still need to be addressed to fully realize the pervasive computing vision. On the one hand, the lack of standard languages and common semantic frameworks strongly limit the possibility to opportunistically acquire available context data, reason with it, and provide proactive services. On the other hand, existing techniques for identifying complex contextual situations are mainly restricted to the recognition of simple actions and activities. Most importantly, due to the unprecedented quantity of digital traces that people leave as they go about their everyday lives, formal privacy methods and trust models must be enforced to avoid the "big data" vision turning into a "big brother" nightmare. In this chapter, the authors discuss the above-mentioned research issues and highlight promising research directions.

DOI: 10.4018/978-1-4666-4695-7.ch015

THE BIG DATA CHALLENGE

Currently, people leave an unprecedented quantity of digital traces, which describe their life and mind under several dimensions:

- **Activities, Location and Movements:** Can be inferred based on data produced by sensors integrated in mobile phones, GPS navigation system, transaction records, surveillance systems, pictures and videos posted on social media sites.
- **Moods and Opinions:** Can be derived based on blog posts, Twitter messages, search engine queries, sensor data from personal devices.
- **Social Relationships:** Can be revealed by social network connections, digital contacts, frequent co-occurrence in specific places.

The combined analysis of the above dimensions can reveal further details, such as lifestyle, purchase habits, health issues, political affiliations, religious beliefs, and many others. One of the greatest challenges of today's world is how to understand the dynamics of our interconnected society from the "big data" originated by the single persons, in order to improve both the existence of individuals, and the fairness of societies. This is the intriguing vision of a *planetary nervous system* (Giannotti, et al., 2012), which necessarily starts from achieving personal, urban, and social awareness. However, several research challenges still need to be faced to realize this vision.

At the level of personal awareness, a plethora of sensors are available today, to recognize individual activities, sentiments, and other context data at both fine- and coarse-grained levels. Unfortunately, the recognition of high-level context data like complex activities is still not sufficiently realized, due to different technical issues and limitations of existing approaches. On the one hand, the lack of interoperability and integration limits the quantity of data available for context inference, claiming for the definition of novel methods for opportunistic data acquisition and reasoning. On the other hand, existing statistical learning methods for activity recognition are mainly restricted to simple actions.

At the level of collective awareness, we are overwhelmed by massive amounts of data fed to social networks, mobile carriers, communication and transaction systems: one of the most challenging issues is how to extract useful information from these data, without violating the privacy of individuals.

OPEN CHALLENGES AND RESEARCH DIRECTIONS

In this section, we discuss some of the most challenging open issues to realize personal and collective awareness, and highlight promising research directions.

Opportunistic Context Data Acquisition and Reasoning

Given the multifaceted nature of people's activities and interactions, a wide spectrum of context data should be acquired from different context data sources (including sensors, mobile apps, and social network sites) to fully characterize the personal context. The availability of these sources is highly dynamic: for instance, during a day, a person can move from indoor environments in which a plethora of sensors is available, to outdoor environments in which the sensor infrastructure is limited. Ideally, a pervasive computing system should be able to proactively discover the available context sources, get the needed data based on user's activities and goals, and activate reasoning algorithms to recognize the current high-level context, in order to take appropriate decisions. Of course, this vision requires:

- A common infrastructure layer to proactively discover sources of interest;
- Opportunistic reasoning algorithms to infer high-level context data based on available knowledge;
- A semantic layer to integrate the context data coming from heterogeneous sources, and evaluate their provenance and quality.

Integration, Proactive Discovery, and Opportunistic Reasoning

Unfortunately, current sensor systems, produced by different vendors, lack integration: they employ different communication protocols and data representation formalisms, and are not supported by shared annotations to express the semantics of the data. This contradicts with the *Sensor Web* vision, in which heterogeneous context sources can be seamlessly searched and queried, as people are used to do with traditional Web resources. In order to pursue this vision, the Open Geospatial Consortium (OGC) is carrying on the Sensor Web Enablement initiative, which essentially consists in the definition of a suite of standard specifications for describing sensor systems, encoding measurements, and supporting publishing and subscribe to sensor events. In particular, the *Sensor Model Language* (SensorML) is an XML Schema for representing the functional model of a sensor system, in order to enable sensor discovery and on-demand processing of sensor measurements.

An architecture for opportunistic context discovery and reasoning has been proposed in (Riboni, Pareschi, & Bettini, 2010). That architecture, illustrated in Figure 1, adopts a lightweight broker, hosted by a personal mobile device, to dynamically match the data requirements of context reasoners with the capabilities of available context sources, in order to enable proactive reasoning. Context sources, such as sensors, broadcast their capabilities through SensorML documents (*Spec*

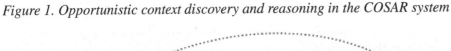

Figure 1. Opportunistic context discovery and reasoning in the COSAR system

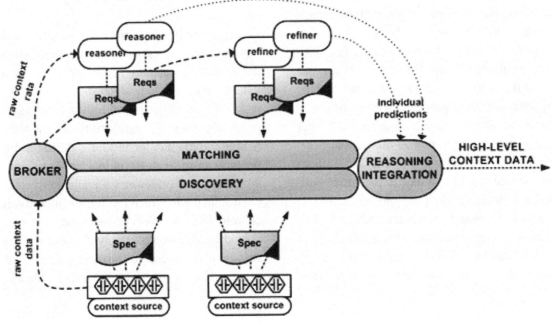

in Figure 1). The data requirements of reasoners (*Reqs*) are represented in a custom XML format. A hybrid intelligent system is in charge of integrating the inference methods of the different context reasoners in order to derive higher-level context data, solving possible conflicts and inconsistencies through a refining and filtering mechanism. A prototype system was developed, in which physical activities are continuously recognized through different configurations of sensors, such as positioning systems, and accelerometers worn at different body locations.

Opportunistic high-level context recognition is also the objective of the Opportunity European project (Roggen, et al., 2013). Opportunity envisions an *adaptive recognition chain*, in which interconnected signal processing and inference modules exchange atomic context data to cooperatively derive higher-level context abstractions, in particular, complex human activities. Sensors broadcast their basic characteristics (e.g., "the sensor measure 3-axis acceleration"), as well as the recognition task they can contribute to (e.g., "recognizing human posture"), the required positioning (e.g., "at the belt"), the required reasoning elements and features, and the corresponding accuracy. The framework is not based on static assumptions about the available sensors and reasoners. Instead, the whole context inference process seamlessly adapts to changes in sensors configurations, exploiting domain knowledge expressed through ontologies to choose the proper configuration based on the recognition goal.

While opportunistic context recognition is still in its infancy, and is not adequately supported by off the shelf sensor systems, this approach offers clear advantages with respect to today's static context recognition systems. Several research challenges remain open and deserve further investigation. In particular, how to dynamically integrate separate reasoning algorithms to achieve accurate recognition of high-level context abstractions, and how to devise trust models and privacy-preserving

methods to enhance sharing of context data acquired by personal sensors.

Context Provenance and Quality

Context data provided to pervasive computing systems are characterized by variable levels of accuracy and reliability; indeed, they are derived through different reasoning methods based on heterogeneous and possibly inaccurate sensor measurements. Hence, a desirable feature of context-aware systems is a mechanism to assess the quality of context information based on its *provenance*; i.e., *"the derivation history of a data product starting from its original sources"* (Simmhan, Plale, & Gannon, 2005). Several methods have been proposed to track the provenance of data in workflow and database systems, in order to document the complex process chain that determined the computation of a data product, and to evaluate its quality. However, since context data are extremely dynamic, and are often computed in open and heterogeneous environments, they claim for a specific provenance model.

In (Chowdhury, Falchuk, & Misra, 2010), context data has been used as provenance information, to describe the user's situation at the time of higher-level context recognition in an e-health application. More recently, a specific provenance model for context data acquired and processed in ambient intelligence systems has been presented in (Riboni & Bettini, 2012). That model adopts a graph-based formalism to represent the process chain that led to the derivation of the context data. For instance, Figure 2 represents the context provenance graph of a person's activity, recognized in a smart-home scenario. Ellipses represent context data, rectangles represent processes that produce context data, hexagons represent sensors, and labeled arcs represent the relations among those entities. In this example, the user's activity has been derived by a Hidden Markov Model reasoner based on a vector of observations produced by a sensor data aggregation module of the smart-home system. That module acquired lower-level context data from 14 change-sensing sensors attached to different home appliances. The context provenance graph is mapped to an ontological description, in order to automatically check the consistency of provenance information, and to enhance interoperability. The model copes with uncertainty and temporal aspects by means of a mechanism for time-dependent data confidence revision. The mechanism considers the time instant at which

the context value has been produced, and applies an ageing function that represents the temporal decay of confidence. Since context data may be used in context-aware access control systems, context provenance must be protected against accidental corruption or malicious forgery; thus, cryptographic methods are used to ensure the integrity of context provenance.

Depending on the actual application, context provenance may be manually observed by domain

Figure 2. Context provenance for user's activity

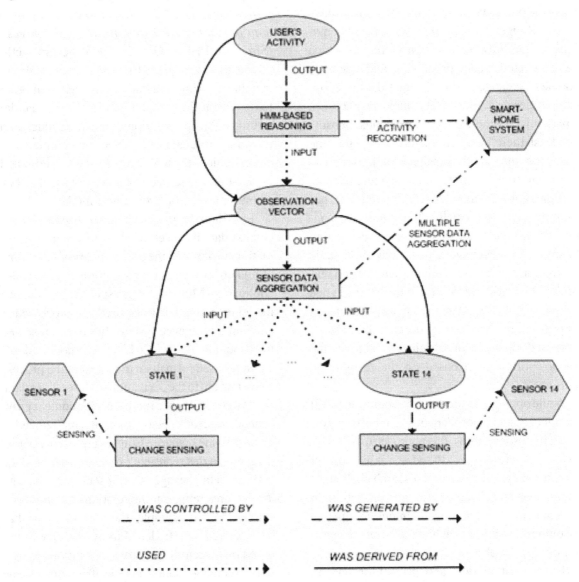

experts, or automatically processed by software modules. For instance, in (Riboni & Bettini, 2012), context provenance is exploited to enhance the reliability of a smart-home system. Many other applications may benefit from context provenance, including access control systems, context reasoners, reporting, and decision support systems.

Obviously, the provenance of context information determines the quality of the context data. The issue of modeling and quantifying the *quality of context* has been extensively studied in the literature. In particular, (Sheikh, Wegdam, & van Sinderen, 2008) propose five quality indicators: precision, temporal freshness, spatial resolution, temporal resolution, and probability of correctness. Since context data must be usually handled by software modules, it is necessary to devise effective mechanisms for automatically deriving the quality of context based on its provenance. Existing proposals in this sense, as the one presented in (Riboni & Bettini, 2012) to update confidence based on temporal features, provide only a partial solution to this challenging research issue, which deserves further investigation.

Recognition of Complex Context Data

As mentioned above, context information can be acquired from different sensing sources and modalities. The goal of gathering this context data is to develop context-aware applications to support personalization, adaptability and anticipation. This requires retrieving and interpreting high-level information from the collected data to understand the current situation of the users and their environment. Especially, activity recognition is becoming determinant for a number of real-world problems such as surveillance, healthcare applications and proactive service provision. Further efforts towards the enrichment of high-level context information have led to the emergence of novel disciplines such as emotion detection and social context recognition. Currently, several

challenges are facing these research fields. In this section, we discuss some of these challenges and open issues.

Complex Activity Recognition

To give an overview of the major limitations and opportunities in the development of sensor-based activity recognition approaches, we distinguish between data-driven and knowledge-driven methods. The first are bottom up approaches which employ probabilistic or statistical methods to predict the ongoing activities from sensor observations such as Hidden Markov Models (Patterson, Fox, Kautz, & Philipose, 2005) Bayesian networks and Conditional Random Fields (Buettner, Prasad, Philipose, & Wetherall, 2009). The second exploit prior knowledge and domain expertise to construct top-down activity recognition models. These include Ontology-based approaches and Logic-based approaches such as event calculus (Chen, et al., 2008) and Plan recognition (Bouchard, Bouzouane, & Giroux, 2006). While data-driven approaches require large datasets and suffer from the "cold start" problem, knowledge-driven approaches also necessitate a significant prior knowledge and modeling effort.

Each of them is capable of addressing some challenges of activity recognition systems but fails in others. Indeed knowledge-driven paradigms are semantically clear and usually present a better scalability, extensibility and re-usability. Unlike data-driven methods, however, they are weak in handling uncertainty and temporal information, two crucial aspects underlying human activities.

Fulfilling all these requirements has been the concern of recent works that opted for hybrid knowledge representation formalisms for activity recognition. They attempt to bridge the gap between purely symbolic approach and supporting uncertainty. For instance, Knox *et al.* (Knox, Coyle, & and Dobson, 2010) use vectors of sensor observations to apply a case base approach to activity recognition. Their case base is semantically extended through the extraction ontological relationships between sensors, locations and activities.

Similarly, Yamada *et al.* (Yamada, et al., 2007) try to exploit semantic information to handle unlearned object and improve their recognition system. Ontological reasoning has been also exploited by Riboni and Bettini (Riboni & Bettini, COSAR: hybrid reasoning for context-aware activity recognition, 2011) to refine the prediction of statistical learning methods based on the current context. Helaoui *et al.* (Helaoui, Niepert, & Stuckenschmidt, Recognizing interleaved and concurrent activities using qualitative and quantitative temporal relationships, 2011) applied Markov Logic Networks which unites both logical statements as well as probabilistic ones in one single framework. In a more recent work (Helaoui, Riboni, Niepert, Bettini, & Stuckenschmidt, 2012), the authors have approached activity recognition using probabilistic DLs.

Despite the increasing interest in complex activity recognition, there are still several open issues that need to be solved. The majority of the proposed systems have been tested under laboratory settings. The executed activities are usually simplistic and sequential while real life activities are often interleaved, concurrent or even interrupted. Moreover, realistic scenarios usually involve composite and multi-level activities and can often engage more than one person simultaneously.

Thus, further investigation of hybrid system capable of addressing uncertainty as well as rich inter- and intra- temporal relationships of the activities are urged. Ideally, these system should inherent the complex modeling potentials of knowledge-driven approaches using standard formalisms such as Description Logics. This is especially relevant to achieve portability and reusability under other settings and with different users. Evaluating activity recognition systems under real world deployment would also be of a great benefit to the community and an important step towards functional context-aware applications. Finally,

although the majority of existing researches focus on recognizing ongoing human activities, forecasting future activities might significantly contribute to novel pro-active application.

Emotion Detection and Social Context Recognition

Widespread low-cost and portable devices did not only open new avenues to activity recognition but also to further relevant context components. Appealing ideas and novel solutions have appeared to automatically recognize the user's emotions and social context. These emerging disciplines are very promising but not yet adequate for realistic applications (Wagner, Kim, & André, 2005).

Several challenges are still facing these highly interdisciplinary research fields. Indeed, unlike activities, emotions are uncontrollable. Thus, collecting training data require a proper stimulation of the required emotions. This is usually done by means of music, films and affective pictures. Further, representing and modeling emotions is not straightforward. The most common representations so far are: "Emotion description models" and "dimensional description models". The majority of works have followed the first, which refers to recognizing discrete emotion categories. Mapping emotions into categories, however, could range between different degrees of granularity such as coarse grained "positive", "negative" or "neutral" emotions or finer-grained classes like "anger" and "fear" (Schuller, Batliner, Steidl, & Seppi, 2011). The dimensional description of emotions is simpler and bases on two physiological states- Valence (negative, positive) and arousal (high-low). For example, anger has high arousal and neutral valence (Jerritta, Murugappan, Nagarajan, & Wan, 2011).

Recognizing and understanding human emotions have been approached in two ways. Either by analyzing speech data or based on physiological changes. The most common physiological sensors for emotion recognition systems are: Heart Rate

Variability (HRV), Skin conductivity (SC), Electromyography (EMG) and breathes per minute. Researchers have used these vital signals to extract classification features and applied supervised learning algorithms to recognize the corresponding emotion. Despite the multiplied efforts, the reported recognition results are still unsatisfactory especially under realistic and user-independent setting. Moreover, extracting adequate classification features at the instant of emotion elicitation is not straightforward, mainly that changes in physiological signals can be observed for a very small time interval (3-15 seconds) (Jerritta, Murugappan, Nagarajan, & Wan, 2011).

Similarly, speech-based emotion recognition depends on specific characteristics such as intonation, speaking rate as well as acoustic and linguistic aspects. There, more and more sophisticated statistical approaches are employed. Nonetheless, the proposed systems and applications are also still operating in un-realistic conditions using non-naturalistic "acted" data (Schuller, Batliner, Steidl, & Seppi, 2011). As an example, we cite the work of Taleb *et al.* (Taleb, Bottazzi, & Nasser, 2010) which proposes a speaker dependent system under lab settings. The system recognizes five standard broader emotion groups including "happy, sad, fear, anger and neutral" using the GMM classifier.

Interestingly, recent works have attempted to combine emotion recognition with activity recognition for a better context acquisition such as in the work of Tacconi *et al.* (Tacconi, et al., 2008). The system aims at supporting early diagnosis of psychiatric diseases, yet remains closer to feasibility study rather than an operable application.

The recent proliferation of personal and collaborative publishing services such as blogs and wikis as well as the increasing popularity of social networks have boosted information and opinion exchanges on different topics. Since emotions are subjective feelings and thoughts, they are considered as closely related to opinions. Hence, several researchers have tried to detect them in textual data. To do so, two tasks are required: information retrieval and classification into target categories.

Usually, features like the employed terms, their frequency and Part of Speech information are used to classify the retrieved information into positive and negative sentiments. Supervised learning methods such as Support Vector Machine and Naïve Bayes are the most common methods applied in the community (Xia & Zong, 2010). Other works have highlighted the importance of domain knowledge and the general structure of the text to the classification results. As examples, Zhang et al. (Zhang, Yoshida, & Tang, 2008) have employed Ontologies to integrate background knowledge in their model, while Zirn et al. have applied Markov Logic Networks (Zirn, Niepert, Stuckenschmidt, & Strube, 2011).

Sentiment analysis and opinion mining have multi-faceted open challenges. Since product reviews are especially rich in opinion information, most of the researchers have focused on them neglecting more complicated documents such as discussions and forums. Subsequently, the resulting systems and proposed solutions cover a small range of domains such as electronic products, hotels and restaurants. Furthermore, some types of sentences have not been addressed thoroughly. Indeed, expressions with opposite opinions such as "I still have hope in this desperate world", or comparative and superlative sentences are still critical cases. Another limitation of opinion and emotion mining is due to the highly noisy nature of the available data. This usually includes grammatical and spelling errors which burden the use of NLP tools and impose a lot of pre-processing effort. Spamming is also an important restriction affecting the retrieved data. Due to the importance of the opinion's financial and social impact, this phenomenon is growing without receiving enough attention (Liu, 2012).

Compared to the context components "activities" and "emotion", far less effort has been dedicated to acquire and understand the user's social environment. Controversially, social context can offer significant clues about the overall high-level situation. It can provide collective assistance and services and help attain collaborative and common social goals. The majority of the existing works have opted for ontologies to model and manage the user's surrounding social interactions and structure (Biamino, 2011) and (Kabir, Han, Yu, & Colman, 2012). Based on social networks and other social web applications, different types of relationships, interactions and roles are retrieved and fed into the model.

Obviously, privacy related issues are a heavy obstacle towards accessing the required sources and populate the model. Privacy also raises some concerns related to other information sources mentioned above such as recorded speech data. This aspect is discussed in the following section.

Privacy for Personal and Collective Awareness

Personal and collective awareness involve a variety of sensitive data describing individuals and communities. In wrong hands, these data could be misused to perpetrate discrimination and violate civil rights. Hence, it is necessary to devise formal models and technical tools to ensure privacy, while preserving the utility of the data for context-awareness purposes.

Privacy preservation techniques have been extensively studied in the fields of databases and data mining, in order to release sanitized versions of sensitive micro-data, or aggregated information extracted from large repositories. More recently, similar techniques have been used to preserve the privacy of Location Based Service (LBS) users (Bettini, Jajodia, Samarati, & Wang, 2009) against untrusted service providers. Location data introduce novel challenges with respect to the protection of traditional data bases. Indeed, the dynamic nature of users' location, as well as the necessity to sanitize data on-the-fly, claim for the use of *online* methods, while traditional database

views are sanitized offline. Moreover, location data are characterized by a strong degree of correlation. Think, for instance, at the recurrent request that an individual on the move issues at an LBS provider. Even if the exact location of each request issuer is generalized to include many other possible issuers, an adversary having access to (even partial) information about users' location may reconstruct the actual issuer by observing the requests during a sufficiently long period of time. A technique to protect against this threat, which combines both location generalization and obfuscation of the other request parameters, has been proposed in (Riboni, Pareschi, Bettini, & Jajodia, Preserving Anonymity of Recurrent Location-based Queries, 2009). Many other defense methods based on location generalization or obfuscation have been proposed, which counteract different kinds of attacks, under different assumptions about the external knowledge available to adversaries (Bettini, Jajodia, Samarati, & Wang, 2009).

However, the availability of additional context information may enable new kinds of attacks, which cannot be contrasted by the above techniques. For instance, in (Riboni, Pareschi, & Bettini, Shadow Attacks on Users' Anonymity in Pervasive Computing Environments), it is shown how an adversary observing the *behavior* of individuals (such as their activities) may be able to reconstruct the actual issuer of requests sanitized by location anonymity methods. The increasing availability of context data claims for the definition of specific defense methods for context-aware systems, which are reviewed in (Riboni, Pareschi, & Bettini, Privacy in Georeferenced Context-aware Services: A Survey, 2009). The most relevant approaches can be classified as follows.

- **Secure Communication Protocols:** Are used to protect against malicious third parties that may intercept the communication of private context data to a trusted entity; as a consequence, they do not protect against untrusted service providers.

- **Private Information Retrieval:** Makes use of cryptographic techniques to hide both request parameters and service responses from the service provider. This approach provides strong privacy guarantees. However, it is applicable only to a restricted set of context-aware services, like response to LBS queries (Ghinita, Kalnis, Khoshgozaran, Shahabi, & Tan, 2008). Moreover, it incurs high overhead, both in terms of computation and communication costs, at the client and server side.

- **Obfuscation Techniques:** Are based on the generalization, or partial suppression, of context data, in order to limit the disclosure of sensitive information (Wishart, Henricksen, & Indulska, 2007). For instance, while the exact location of an individual may be sensitive, its generalization at the level of *city* may be insensitive. However, this approach does not provide a complete solution. Indeed, while a single obfuscated context data may be insensitive when considered in isolation, a privacy violation may occur when it is matched with other obfuscated context data, or with background information about the subject.

- **Identity Anonymity Techniques:** Aim at hiding the identity of an individual in a sufficiently large set of candidates (Bettini, Mascetti, & Wang, 2008). Anonymity is enforced by generalizing those context data that, matched with external knowledge, may help an adversary in reconstructing the identity of an individual. The main limitation of these methods is that they rely on strict assumptions about the external knowledge available to possible adversaries: if an adversary actually has more knowledge than assumed by the defender, anonymity may be easily broken.

A different approach is taken by *privacy-preserving data mining*: starting from a set of sensitive data, the trusted data curator releases sanitized statistics, such that an observer cannot reconstruct the original sensitive micro-data. In particular, Differential Privacy (Dwork, 2006) ensures that the probability distribution of released statistics is essentially the same, irrespective of whether a data of a single individual is present or absent from the original data set. This property is enforced by adding random noise to the exact statistics. Differential privacy has been used in a mobile recommender system of points of interest (Riboni & Bettini, 2012), in which recommendations are provided based on the private check-ins of a community of users. This technique guarantees that an adversary issuing fictitious queries to the system cannot reconstruct the places visited by a target individual. The advantage of differential privacy is that it does not rely on strict assumptions about the external knowledge available to adversaries. However, it can only be applied to context-aware applications based on aggregated data. How to provide strong privacy guarantees for the release of micro-data, irrespective of the adversary's knowledge, is still an open research challenge.

Furthermore, the increasing success of Geo-Social networks poses additional privacy threats to the preservation of both individual and collective privacy. These threats arise not only from social relationships such as *friend* or *follower*, but also from the possibility of geo-tagging multimedia resources such as pictures, and annotate them with related people (for instance, the persons appearing in a picture). This issue has been recently studied in (Ruiz Vicente, Freni, Bettini, & Jensen, 2011). In particular, the authors study the *co-location* privacy issue, in which the presence of two or more specific individuals in the same place at the same time is considered sensitive. At the time of writing, the most popular Geo-Social Network services do not offer protection against this kind of threat. In general, most people are still unaware of the privacy issues involved in the use of context-aware social networks. Hence, open research issues include not only the definition of formal protection mechanisms, but also the development of automatic tools to help the user assessing the privacy risk determined by her online activity, and user-friendly interfaces to guide the definition of personal privacy policies.

CONCLUSION

Important steps have been made towards the realization of personal and collective awareness. Sensor-based activity recognition and emotion detection tools promise to improve the lives of elderly people at home, support work and training, and enable new forms of gaming and entertainment. Personal awareness enables proactive services based on an individual's context, needs and goals. Novel social and urban applications are enabled by community detection and opinion mining tools. The big data produced by people, sensors and transaction records are more and more exploited to understand structures and trends in our societies, to improve the collective life. Nevertheless, personal and collective awareness is still in its infancy, and several research challenges need to be addressed, including how to improve interoperability, recognize complex contextual situations, and preserve the privacy of individuals and communities.

REFERENCES

C. Bettini, S. Jajodia, P. Samarati, & X. S. Wang (Eds.). (2009). *Trends, privacy in location-based applications: Research issues and emerging.* Berlin: Springer. doi:10.1007/978-3-642-03511-1.

Bettini, C., Mascetti, S., & Wang, X. (2008). Privacy protection through anonymity in location-based services. In *Handbook of Database Security: Applications and Trends* (pp. 509–530). Berlin: Springer. doi:10.1007/978-0-387-48533-1_21.

Biamino, G. (2011). Modeling social contexts for pervasive computing environments. In Proceedings of Pervasive Computing and Communications Workshops (PERCOM Workshops), (pp. 415-420). PERCOM.

Bouchard, B., Bouzouane, A., & Giroux, S. (2006). A smart home agent for plan recognition. In *Proceedings of the Fifth International Joint Conference on Autonomous Agents and Multiagent Systems*, (pp. 320-322). ACM.

Buettner, M., Prasad, R., Philipose, M., & Wetherall, D. (2009). Recognizing daily activities with rfid-based sensors. [ACM.]. *Proceedings of Ubicomp, 09*, 51–60. doi:10.1145/1620545.1620553.

Chen, L., Nugent, C., Mulvenna, M., Finlay, D., Hong, X., & Poland, M. (2008). Logical framework for behaviour reasoning and assistance in a smart home. *International Journal of ARM*.

Chowdhury, A. R., Falchuk, B., & Misra, A. (2010). A provenance-aware remote health monitoring middleware. In *Proceedings of the Eight Annual IEEE International Conference on Pervasive Computing and Communications (PerCom)* (pp. 125-134). IEEE Computer Society.

Coloberti, M., Lombriser, C., Roggen, D., Troester, G., Guarneri, R., & Riboni, D. (2008). Service discovery and composition in body area networks. In *Proceedings of the Third International Conference on Body Area Networks (BodyNets).* BodyNets.

Dwork, C. (2006). Differential privacy. In *Proceedings of Automata, Languages and Programming (ICALP)* (pp. 1–12). Berlin: Springer. doi:10.1007/11787006_1.

Ghinita, G., Kalnis, P., Khoshgozaran, A., Shahabi, C., & Tan, K. (2008). Private queries in location based services: Anonymizers are not necessary. In *Proceedings of ACM SIGMOD International Conference on Management of Data (SIGMOD)* (pp. 121-132). ACM.

Giannotti, F., Pedreschi, D., Pentland, A., Lukowicz, P., Kossmann, D., Crowley, J., & Helbing, D. (2012). A planetary nervous system for social mining and collective awareness. *The European Physical Journal. Special Topics*, *214*, 49–75. doi:10.1140/epjst/e2012-01688-9.

Helaoui, R., Niepert, M., & Stuckenschmidt, H. (2011). Recognizing interleaved and concurrent activities using qualitative and quantitative temporal relationships. In *Proceedings of Pervasive and Mobile Computing* (pp. 660–670). IEEE. doi:10.1016/j.pmcj.2011.08.004.

Helaoui, R., Riboni, D., Niepert, M., Bettini, C., & Stuckenschmidt, H. (2012). Towards activity recognition using probabilistic description logics. In *Proceedings of AAAI Workshops*. AAAI.

Jerritta, S., Murugappan, M., Nagarajan, R., & Wan, K. (2011). Physiological signals based human emotion recognition: A review. In Proceedings of Signal Processing and its Applications (CSPA), (pp. 410-415). CSPA.

Kabir, M. A., Han, J., Yu, J., & Colman, A. W. (2012). SCIMS: A social context information management system for socially-aware applications. In *Proceedings of CAiSE*, (pp. 301-317). CAiSE.

Knox, S., Coyle, L., & Dobson, S. (2010). Using ontologies in case-based activity recognition. In *Proceedings of FLAIRS'10*. FLAIRS.

Liu, B. (2012). *Sentiment analysis and opinion mining*. New York: Morgan & Claypool Publishers.

OGC. (n.d.). Retrieved from http://www.open-geospatial.org/

Patterson, D. J., Fox, D., Kautz, H., & Philipose, M. (2005). Fine-grained activity recognition by aggregating abstract object usage. [ISWC.]. *Proceedings of ISWC*, *05*, 44–51.

Riboni, D., & Bettini, C. (2011). COSAR: Hybrid reasoning for context-aware activity recognition. In Proceedings of Personal and Ubiquitous Computing, (pp. 271-289). ACM.

Riboni, D., & Bettini, C. (2012). Context provenance to enhance the dependability of ambient intelligence systems. *Personal and Ubiquitous Computing*, *16*(7), 799–818. doi:10.1007/s00779-011-0448-3.

Riboni, D., & Bettini, C. (2012). Private context-aware recommendation of points of interest: An initial investigation. In *Proceedings of the Workshops of the Tenth Annual IEEE International Conference on Pervasive Computing and Communications (PerCom)* (pp. 584-589). IEEE Computer Society.

Riboni, D., Pareschi, L., & Bettini, C. (2009). Privacy in georeferenced context-aware services: A survey. In S. J. C. Bettini (Ed.), *Privacy in Location-Based Applications: Research Issues and Emerging Trends*. Berlin: Springer. doi:10.1007/978-3-642-03511-1_7.

Riboni, D., Pareschi, L., & Bettini, C. (2010). Towards the adaptive integration of multiple context reasoners in pervasive computing environments. In *Proceedings of the Eighth Annual IEEE International Conference on Pervasive Computing and Communications Workshops* (pp. 25-29). IEEE Computer Society.

Riboni, D., Pareschi, L., & Bettini, C. (n.d.). Shadow attacks on users' anonymity in pervasive computing environments. *Journal of Pervasive and Mobile Computing, 4*(6), 819-835. doi:10.1016/j.pmcj.2008.04.008

Riboni, D., Pareschi, L., Bettini, C., & Jajodia, S. (2009). Preserving anonymity of recurrent location-based queries. In *Proceedings of the 16th International Symposium on Temporal Representation and Reasoning (TIME-2009)* (pp. 62-69). IEEE Computer Society.

Roggen, D., Tröster, G., Lukowicz, P., Ferscha, A., Millán, J., & Chavarriaga, R. (2013). Opportunistic human activity and context recognition. *IEEE Computer*, *46*(2), 36–45. doi:10.1109/MC.2012.393.

Ruiz Vicente, C., Freni, D., Bettini, C., & Jensen, C. S. (2011). Location-related privacy in geo-social networks. *IEEE Internet Computing*, *15*(3), 20–27. doi:10.1109/MIC.2011.29.

Schuller, B., Batliner, A., Steidl, S., & Seppi, D. (2011). Recognising realistic emotions and affect in speech: State of the art and lessons learnt from the first challenge. *Speech Communication*, 1062–1087. doi:10.1016/j.specom.2011.01.011.

SensorML. (n.d.). Retrieved from http://www.opengeospatial.org/standards/sensorml

Sheikh, K., Wegdam, M., & van Sinderen, M. (2008). Quality-of-context and its use for protecting privacy in context aware systems. *Journal of Software*, *3*(3), 83–93. doi:10.4304/jsw.3.3.83-93.

Simmhan, Y., Plale, B., & Gannon, D. (2005). A survey of data provenance in e-science. *SIGMOD Record*, *34*(3), 31–36. doi:10.1145/1084805.1084812.

Tacconi, D., Mayora, O., Lukowicz, P., Arnrich, B., Kappeler-Setz, C., Tröster, G., & Haring, C. (2008). Activity and emotion recognition to support early diagnosis of psychiatric diseases. In *Proceedings of 2nd International Conference on Pervasive Computing Technologies for Healthcare (Pervasive Health)*, (pp. 100-102). ACM.

Taleb, T., Bottazzi, D., & Nasser, N. (2010). A novel middleware solution to improve ubiquitous healthcare systems aided by affective information. *IEEE Transactions on Information Technology in Biomedicine*, 335–349. doi:10.1109/TITB.2010.2042608 PMID:20659832.

Wagner, J., Kim, J., & André, E. (2005). From physiological signals to emotions: Implementing and comparing selected methods for feature extraction and classification. In *Proceedings of ICME*, (pp. 940-943). ICME.

Wishart, R., Henricksen, K., & Indulska, J. (2007). Context privacy and obfuscation supported by dynamic context source discovery and processing in a context management system. In *Proceedings of the 4th International Conference on Ubiquitous Intelligence and Computing (UIC)* (pp. 929-940). Springer.

Xia, R., & Zong, C. (2010). Exploring the use of word relation features for sentiment classification. In *Proceedings of COLING (Posters)*, (pp. 1336-1344). COLING.

Yamada, N., Sakamoto, K., Kunito, G., Isoda, Y., Yamazaki, K., & Tanaka, S. (2007). Applying ontology and probabilistic model to human activity recognition from surrounding things. *IPSJ Digital Courier*, 506-517.

Zhang, W., Yoshida, T., & Tang, X. (2008). Text classification based on multi-word with support vector. *Knowledge-Based Systems*, 879–886. doi:10.1016/j.knosys.2008.03.044.

Zirn, C., Niepert, M., Stuckenschmidt, H., & Strube, M. (2011). fine-grained sentiment analysis with structural features. *IJCNLP*, 336-344.

Compilation of References

Abadi, D., Ahmad, Y., Balazinska, M., Cetintemel, U., Cherniack, M., Hwang, J., et al. (2005). The design of the borealis stream processing engine. In *Proceedings of the Second Biennial Conference on Innovative Data Systems Research (CIDR 2005)*. CIDR.

Abadi, D., Carney, D., Çetintemel, U., Cherniack, M., Convey, C., & Lee, S. et al. (2003). Aurora: A new model and architecture for data stream management. *The VLDB Journal*, *12*(2), 120–139. doi:10.1007/s00778-003-0095-z.

Abdennadher, S. M. A. (2007). BECAM tool a semi-automatic tool for bootstrapping emotion corpus annotation and management. *European Conference on Speech and Language Processing (EUROSPEECH '07)*, (pp. 946–949).

Abdullah, S., & Wu, X. (2011). *An epidemic model for news spreading on Twitter*. Paper presented at the 23rd IEEE International Conference on Tools with Artificial Intelligence (ICTAI). New York, NY.

Abercrombie, D. (1967). *Elements of general phonetics*. Chicago: University of Chicago Press.

Adomavicius, G., & Tuzhilin, A. (2011). Context-aware recommender systems. In F. Ricci, L. Rokach, B. Shapira, & P. B. Kantor (Eds.), *Recommender Systems Handbook* (pp. 217–253). Berlin: Springer. doi:10.1007/978-0-387-85820-3_7.

Agneessens, A., Bisio, I., Lavagetto, F., Marchese, M., & Sciarrone, A. (2010). Speaker Count application for smartphone platforms. *Wireless Pervasive Computing (ISWPC), 2010 5th IEEE International Symposium on*, (pp. 361-366). Modena.

Ahmed, S., Sharmin, M., & Ahmed, S. I. (2005). A smart meeting room with pervasive computing technologies. In *Proceedings of SNPD/SAWN*. SNPD/SAWN.

Ahn, Y. Y., Bagrow, J. P., & Lehmann, S. (2010). Link communities reveal multi-scale complexity in networks. *Nature*, *466*(7307), 761–764. doi:10.1038/nature09182 PMID:20562860.

Aiello, M., Aloise, F., Baldoni, R., Cincotti, F., Guger, C., & Lazovik, A. et al. (2011). Smart homes to improve the quality of life for all. In *Proceedings of Engineering in Medicine and Biology Society* (pp. 1777–1780). IEEE. doi:10.1109/IEMBS.2011.6090507.

Al Moakar, L., Chrysanthis, P. K., Chung, C., Guirguis, S., Labrinidis, A., Neophytou, P., & Pruhs, K. (2010). Admission control mechanisms for continuous queries in the cloud. In Proceedings of Data Engineering (ICDE), (pp. 409–412). ICDE.

Alberts, R., & Franconi, E. (2012). An integrated method using conceptual modelling to generate an ontology-based query mechanism. In *Proceedings of OWL: Experiences and Directions Workshop*. OWL.

Ali, S., Mitschele-Thiel, A., Diab, V., & Rasheed, A. (2010). A survey of services placement mechanisms for future mobile communication networks. In *Proceeding of the 8th International Conference on Frontiers of Information Technology* (FIT' 10). Islamabad, Pakistan. FIT.

Almagrabi, A., Seng, W. L., & Torabi, T. (2012). MES: A system for location-aware smart messaging in emergency situations. In *Proceeding of MOBIQUITOUS 2012, 9th International Conference on Mobile and Ubiquitous Systems: Computing, Networking and Services*. Beijing: ACM.

Aloisio, G., Conte, D., Elefante, C., Epicoco, I., Marra, G. P., Mastrantonio, G., & Quarta, G. (2006). Sensorml for grid sensor networks. In *Proceedings of the 2006 International Conference on Grid Computing & Applications, GCA 2006*. Las Vegas, NV: CSREA Press.

Ang, J. R. D. (2002). Prosody-based automatic detection of annoyance and frustration in human computer dialog. *Proc. Int. Conf. Spoken Language Processing (ICSLP '02)*, (pp. 2037-2040).

Antonakaki, P., Kosmopoulos, D., & Perantonis, S. J. (2009). Detecting abnormal human behavior using multiple cameras. *Signal Processing*, *89*(9), 1723–1738. doi:10.1016/j.sigpro.2009.03.016.

Antoniou, G., & Harmelen, F. V. (2009). Web ontology language: Owl. In *Handbook on ontologies* (pp. 91–110). Berlin: Springer. doi:10.1007/978-3-540-92673-3_4.

Apache Zookeeper. (2010). Retrieved 2013, from http://zookeeper.apache.org/

Apache. (2011). Retrieved from http://lucene.apache.org/

Appelrath, H., Geesen, D., Grawunder, M., Michelsen, T., Nicklas, D., et al. (2012). Odysseus: A highly customizable framework for creating efficient event stream management systems. In *Proceedings of the 6th ACM International Conference on Distributed Event-Based Systems* (pp. 367–368). ACM.

Arasu, A., Babcock, B., Babu, S., Datar, M., Ito, K., Nishizawa, I., et al. (2003). STREAM: The stanford stream data manager (demonstration description). In *Proceedings of the 2003 ACM SIGMOD International Conference on Management of Data* (p. 665). San Diego, CA: ACM. doi:10.1145/872757.872854

Arasu, A., Babu, S., & Widom, J. (2006). The CQL continuous query language: Semantic foundations and query execution. *The VLDB Journal*, *15*(2), 121–142. doi:10.1007/s00778-004-0147-z.

Araujo, R. B., Rocha, R. V., Campos, M. R., & Boukerche, A. (2008). *Creating emergency management training simulations through ontologies integration*. New York: Academic Press. doi:10.1109/CSEW.2008.52.

Arnott, I. M. (1993). Toward the simulation of emotion in synthetic speech: a review of the literature on human vocal emotion. *The Journal of the Acoustical Society of America*, *93*, 1097–1108. doi:10.1121/1.405558 PMID:8445120.

Arthur, D., & Vassilvitskii, S. (2007). *k-means++: The advantages of careful seeding*. Paper presented at the Proceedings of the Eighteenth Annual ACM-SIAM Symposium on Discrete Algorithms. New Orleans, LA.

Aryananda, C. B. (2002). Recognition of affective communicative intent in robot-directed speech. *Autonomous Robots*, *2*, 83–104.

Aschenbruck, N., Gerhards-Padilla, E., & Martini, P. (2008). A survey on mobility models for performance analysis in tactical mobile networks. *Journal of Telecommunication and Information Technology*.

Atal, B. S. (1974). Effectiveness of linear prediction characteristics of the speech wave for automatic speaker identification and verification. *The Journal of the Acoustical Society of America*, *55*(6), 1304–1312. doi:10.1121/1.1914702 PMID:4846727.

Atzori, L., Iera, A., & Morabito, G. (2010). The internet of things: A survey. *Computer Networks*, *54*(15), 2787–2805. doi:10.1016/j.comnet.2010.05.010.

Babcock, B., Babu, S., Motwani, R., & Datar, M. (2003). Chain: Operator scheduling for memory minimization in data stream systems. In *Proceedings of the 2003 ACM SIGMOD International Conference on Management of Data* (pp. 253–264). ACM.

Badder, F., & Nutt, W. (2003). Basic description logics. In F. Badder, D. Calvanese, D. McGuinness, D. Nardi, & P. Patel-Schneider (Eds.), *The Description Logic Handbook: Theory, Implementation, and Applications* (pp. 41–90). New York: Cambridge University Press.

Bader, R., Siegmund, O., & Woerndl, W. (2011). A study on user acceptance of proactive in-car recommender systems. In *Proceedings of AutomotiveUI '11*. Salzburg, Austria: AutomotiveUI.

Bai, F., Sadagopan, N., & Helmy, A. (2003). Important: A framework to systematically analyze the impact of mobility on performance of routing protocols for ad hoc networks. In *Proceeding of the 22th Annual Joint Conference of the IEEE Computer and Communications* (INFOCOM'03). San Francisco, CA: IEEE.

Bai, Y., Thakkar, H., Wang, H., Luo, C., & Zaniolo, C. (2006). A data stream language and system designed for power and extensibility. In *Proceedings of the 15th ACM International Conference on Information and Knowledge Management* (pp. 337–346). ACM.

Balachandran, A., Voelker, G. M., Bahl, P., & Rangan, P. V. (2002). Characterizing user behavior and network performance in a public wireless LAN. In *Proceedings of the ACM SIGMETRICS International Conference on Measurement and Modeling of Computer Systems* (SIGMETRICS'02). New York, NY: ACM Press.

Balan, R. K., Nguyen, K. X., & Jiang, L. (2011). Real-time trip information service for a large taxi fleet. In *Proceedings of the 9th International Conference on Mobile Systems, Applications, and Services*. IEEE.

Balazinska, M., & Castro, P. (2003). Characterizing mobility and network usage in a corporate wireless local-area network. In *Proceedings of the 1st International Conference on Mobile Systems, Applications, and Services* (MobiSys'03). San Francisco, CA: ACM.

Balazinska, M., Kwon, Y. C., Kuchta, N., & Lee, D. (2007). Moirae: History-enhanced monitoring. In *Proceedings of the Third CIDR Conference*. CIDR.

Baldauf, M., Dustdar, S., & Rosenberg, F. (2007). A survey on context-aware systems. *International Journal of Ad Hoc and Ubiquitous Computing, 2*(4), 263–277. doi:10.1504/IJAHUC.2007.014070.

Bao, L., & Intille, S. S. (2004). Activity recognition from user-annotated acceleration data. *Lecture Notes in Computer Science, 3001*, 1–17. doi:10.1007/978-3-540-24646-6_1.

Barabasi, A. L., Jeong, H., Neda, Z., Ravasz, E., Schubert, A., & Vicsek, T. (2002). Evolution of the social network of scientific collaborations. *Statistical Mechanics and its Applications, 311*(3–4), 590–614. doi: 10.1016/S0378-4371(02)00736-7

Barabási, A. L., & Albert, R. (1999). Emergence of scaling in random networks. *Science*, 286. PMID:10521342.

Barga, R., & Caituiro-Monge, H. (2006). Event correlation and pattern detection in CEDR. In Proceedings of Current Trends in Database Technology--EDBT 2006, (pp. 919–930). EDBT.

Bartlett, M. P. (2007). Machine Analysis of Facial Expressions. In K. D. Grgic, Face Recognition (pp. 377-416). I-Tech Education and Publishing.

Bartlett, M. S. G. L. (2005). Recognizing Facial Expression: Machine Learning and Application to Spontaneous Behavior. *Proc. IEEE Int'l Conf. Computer Vision and Pattern Recognition (CVPR '05)*.

Bartlett, M. S., Littlewort, G., Fasel, I., & Movellan, J. R. (2003). Real time face detection and facial expression recognition: Development and applications to human computer interaction. In *Proceedings of Computer Vision and Pattern Recognition Workshop, 2003* (Vol. 5, p. 53). IEEE.

Basu, P., Redi, J., & Shurbanov, V. (2004). Coordinated flocking of UAVs for improved connectivity of mobile ground nodes. In *Proceeding of the Military Communications Conference* (MILCOM'04). BBN Technology.

Batliner, A. C. H. (2004). "You stupid tin box" - children interacting with the AIBO robot: A crosslinguistic emotional speech corpus. *Proc. Language Resources and Evaluation (LREC '04)*. Lisbon.

Bayir, M. A., Demirbas, M., & Eagle, N. (2009). Discovering spatiotemporal mobility profiles of cellphone users. In *Proceeding of the 10th World of Wireless, Mobile and Multimedia Networks and Workshops* (WoWMoM'09). WoWMoM.

Bedworth, M., & O'Brien, J. (2000). The omnibus model: a new model of data fusion? *IEEE Aerospace and Electronic Systems Magazine, 15*(4), 30–36. doi:10.1109/62.839632.

Bellavista, P., Corradi, A., & Magistretti, E. (2005). REDMAN: An optimistic replication middleware for read-only resources in dense MANETs. *Journal on Pervasive and Mobile Computing, 1*(3), 279–310. doi:10.1016/j.pmcj.2005.06.002.

Bell, M. (2008). Toward a definition of ``virtual worlds''. *Journal of Virtual Worlds Research, 1*(1), 1–5.

Benford, S., Crabtree, A., Flintham, M., Drozd, A., Anastasi, R., & Paxton, M. (2006). Can you see me now? *ACM Transactions on Computer-Human Interaction, 13*(11).

Benford, S., Flintham, M., Drozd, A., Anastasi, R., Rowland, D., Tandavanitj, N., & Sutton, J. (2004). *Uncle Roy all around you: Implicating the city in a location-based performance*. ACM Advanced Computer Entertainment.

Benford, S., Magerkurth, C., & Ljungstrand, P. (2005). Bridging the physical and digital in pervasive gaming. *Communications of the ACM, 48*(3), 54–57. doi:10.1145/1047671.1047704.

Benzeghiba, M., R. D. (2007). Automatic speech recognition and speech variability: A review. *Speech Communication, 49*.

Bergmans, A., & Shahid, S. (2012). Drivers: An in-car persuasive system for making driving safe and fun. In A. Nijholt, T. Romão, & D. Reidsma (Eds.), *Advances in Computer Entertainment* (Vol. 7624, pp. 469–472). Berlin: Springer. doi:10.1007/978-3-642-34292-9_37.

Berners-Lee, T., Hollenbach, J., Lu, K., Presbrey, J., Prud'hommeaux, E., & Schraefel, M. M. C. (2008). Tabulator redux: Browsing and writing linked data. In *Proceedings of CEUR Workshop*. CEUR-WS.

Berry, J. K. (1996). *Spatial reasoning for effective GIS*. New York: Wiley.

Bettini, C., Brdiczka, O., Henricksen, K., Indulska, J., Nicklas, D., & Ranganathan, A. et al. (2010). A survey of context modelling and reasoning techniques. *Pervasive and Mobile Computing, 6*(2), 161–180. doi:10.1016/j.pmcj.2009.06.002.

C. Bettini, S. Jajodia, P. Samarati, & X. S. Wang (Eds.). (2009). *Trends, privacy in location-based applications: Research issues and emerging*. Berlin: Springer. doi:10.1007/978-3-642-03511-1.

Bettini, C., Mascetti, S., & Wang, X. (2008). Privacy protection through anonymity in location-based services. In *Handbook of Database Security: Applications and Trends* (pp. 509–530). Berlin: Springer. doi:10.1007/978-0-387-48533-1_21.

Bettstetter, C., & Wagner, C. (2002). The spatial node distribution of the random waypoint mobility model. In *Proceeding of 1st German Workshop on Mobile Ad Hoc Networks* (WMAN'02), (pp. 41-58). Ulm, Germany: ACM.

Bettstetter, C., Hartenstein, H., & Pérez-Costa, X. (2003). *Stochastic properties of the random waypoint mobility model*. Dordrecht, The Netherlands: Kluwer Academic Publishers.

Beywatch. (2008). Retrieved 2013, from http://www.beywatch.eu/

Biamino, G. (2011). Modeling social contexts for pervasive computing environments. In Proceedings of Pervasive Computing and Communications Workshops (PERCOM Workshops), (pp. 415-420). PERCOM.

Bigley, G. A., & Roberts, K. H. (2001). The incident command system: High-reliability organizing for complex and volatile task environments. *Academy of Management Journal, 44*, 1281–1299. doi:10.2307/3069401.

Bilchev, G. (2008). Complex event processing as a service. In Proceedings of Broadband Communications, Networks and Systems, 2008. BROADNETS.

Bisio, I. F. (2011). Context-Aware Smartphone Services. In *Pervasive Computing and Communications Design and Deployment: Technologies, Trends, and Applications*. IGI Global. doi:10.4018/978-1-60960-611-4.ch002.

Blake, M. B., Bleul, S., Weise, T., Bansal, A., & Kona, S. (2009). *Web services challenge*. Retrieved February 21, 2013, from http://ws-challenge.georgetown.edu/wsc09

Blakely, K., & Lowekamp, B. (2004). A structured group mobility model for the simulation of mobile ad hoc networks. In *Proceeding of the ACM International Workshop on Mobility Management and Wireless Access Protocols* (MobiWac'04). ACM.

Blake, M. B., Cabral, L., König-Ries, B., Küster, U., & Martin, D. (2012). *Semantic web services: Advancement through evaluation*. Berlin: Springer. doi:10.1007/978-3-642-28735-0.

Bliek, F., van den Noort, A., Roossien, B., Kamphuis, R., de Wit, J., van Der Velde, J., et al. (2010). PowerMatching city, a living lab smart grid demonstration. In *Proceedings of Innovative Smart Grid Technologies Conference Europe (ISGT Europe)* (pp. 1-8). IEEE.

Blomqvist, E., & Öhgren, A. (2008). Constructing an enterprise ontology for an automotive supplier. *Engineering Applications of Artificial Intelligence, 21*, 386–397. doi:10.1016/j.engappai.2007.09.004.

Blondel, V. D., Guillaume, J. L., Lambiotte, R., & Lefebvre, E. (2008). Fast unfolding of communities in large networks. *Journal of Statistical Mechanics*. doi:10.1088/1742-5468/2008/10/P10008.

Bo, C., Xiuquan, Q., Budan, W., Xiaokun, W., Ruisheng, S., & Junliang, C. (2012). *RESTful web service mashup based coal mine safety monitoring and control automation with wireless sensor network.* Paper presented at IEEE 19th International Conference on Web Services (ICWS), (pp. 620-622). IEEE.

Böhmer, M., Hecht, B., Schöning, J., Krüger, A., & Bauer, G. (2011). Falling asleep with angry birds, Facebook and Kindle: A large scale study on mobile application usage. In *Proceedings of the 13th International Conference on Human Computer Interaction with Mobile Devices and Services* (MobileHCI '11). ACM.

Bollen, J., Pepe, A., & Mao, H. (2009). *Modeling public mood and emotion: Twitter sentiment and socio-economic phenomena.* Paper presented at the meeting of WWW 2009 Conference. Madrid, Spain.

Bonham-Carter, G. (1994). *Geographic information systems for geoscientists: Modelling with GIS.* London: Pergamon Press.

Borrel, V., De Amorim, M. D., & Fdida, S. (2005). A preferential attachment gathering mobility model. *IEEE Communications Letters, 9*(10). doi:10.1109/LCOMM.2005.10023.

Bottazzi, D., Montanari, R., & Toninelli, A. (2007). Context-aware middleware for anytime, anywhere social networks. *IEEE Intelligent Systems, 22*(5), 23–32. doi:10.1109/MIS.2007.4338491.

Botts, M., & Robin, A. (2009). *Sensor model language (SensorML).* Retrieved from http://www.ogcnetwork.net/SensorML

Bouchard, B., Bouzouane, A., & Giroux, S. (2006). A smart home agent for plan recognition. In *Proceedings of the Fifth International Joint Conference on Autonomous Agents and Multiagent Systems,* (pp. 320-322). ACM.

Bouchard, K., Bouchard, B., & Bouzouane, A. (2011). Qualitative spatial activity recognition using a complete platform based on passive RFID tags: Experiments and results. In *Proceedings of 9th International Conference on Smart Homes and Health Telematics (ICOST)*. Montreal, Canada: ICOST.

Brave, S., & Nass, C. (2003). *The human-computer interaction handbook.* Hillsdale, NJ: L. Erlbaum Associates Inc..

Brave, S., Nass, C., & Hutchinson, K. (2005). Computers that care: Investigating the effects of orientation of emotion exhibited by an embodied computer agent. *International Journal of Human-Computer Studies, 62*(2), 161–178. doi:10.1016/j.ijhcs.2004.11.002.

Breslin, J. G., Passant, A., & Decker, S. (2009). *The social semantic web.* Berlin: Springer. doi:10.1007/978-3-642-01172-6.

Broll, W., Ohlenburg, J., Lindt, I., Herbst, I., & Braun, A. K. (2006). *Meeting technology challenges of pervasive augmented reality games.* Paper presented at the 5th ACM SIGCOMM Workshop on Network and System Support for Games (NetGames'06). New York, NY.

Brown, C., Nicosia, V., Scellato, S., Noulas, A., & Mascolo, C. (2012). *The importance of being place-friends: Discovering location-focused online communities.* Paper presented at WOSN 2012. New York, NY. doi:10.1145/2342549.2342557

Buettner, M., Prasad, R., Philipose, M., & Wetherall, D. (2009). Recognizing daily activities with RFID-based sensors. In *Proceedings of the 11th International Conference on Ubiquitous Computing (Ubicomp)*. Ubicomp.

Buettner, M., Prasad, R., Philipose, M., & Wetherall, D. (2009). Recognizing daily activities with rfid-based sensors.[ACM.]. *Proceedings of Ubicomp, 09*, 51–60. doi:10.1145/1620545.1620553.

Bunge, M. (1977). *The furniture of the world*. Dordrecht, The Netherlands: Academic Press.

Burger, S. V. M. (2002). The ISL Meeting Corpus: The Impact of Meeting Type on Speech Style. *Proc. 8th Int'l Conf. Spoken Language Processing (ICSLP)*.

Burkhardt, F. v. (2005). *An emotion-aware voice portal*. Proc. Electronic Speech Signal Processing ESSP.

Busemann, C., & Nicklas, D. (2011). *Converting conversation protocols using an {XML} based differential behavioral model*. Berlin: Springer. doi:10.1007/978-3-642-23091-2_27.

Byrne, J. E., Stergiou, N., Blanke, D., Houser, J., Kurz, M. J., & Hageman, P. A. (2002). Comparison of gait patterns between young and elderly women: An examination of coordination. *Perceptual and Motor Skills, 94*(1), 265–280. doi:10.2466/pms.2002.94.1.265 PMID:11883574.

Cai, H., Lin, Y., & Mourant, R. R. (2007). Study on driver emotion in driver-vehicle-environment systems using multiple networked driving simulators. In *Proceedings of DSC 2007*. Iowa City, IA: DSC.

Cai, Y. D., Clutter, D., Pape, G., Han, J., Welge, M., & Auvil, L. (2004). MAIDS: Mining alarming incidents from data streams. In *Proceedings of the 2004 ACM SIGMOD International Conference on Management of Data* (pp. 919–920). ACM.

Cairns, D., J. H. (1994). Nonlinear analysis and detection of speech under stressed conditions. *The Journal of the Acoustical Society of America, 96*(6), 3392–3400. doi:10.1121/1.410601.

Calabrese, F., & Ratti, C. (2006). Real time Rome. *Networks and Communications Studies, 20*(3-4), 247–258.

Callaghan, V., Clarke, G., Colley, M., Hagras, H., Chin, J. S., & Doctor, F. (2004). Inhabited intelligent environments. *BT Technology Journal, 22*(3), 233–247. doi:10.1023/B:BTTJ.0000047137.42670.4d.

Campbell, A. T., Eisenman, S. B., Lane, N. D., Miluzzo, E., & Peterson, R. A. (2006). *People-centric urban sensing*. Paper presented at the 2nd Annual International Workshop on Wireless Internet. Boston, MA.

Campbell, A. T., Eisenman, S. B., Lane, N. D., Miluzzo, E., Peterson, R. A., & Lu, H. et al. (2008). The rise of people-centric sensing. *IEEE Internet Computing, 12*(4), 12–21. doi:10.1109/MIC.2008.90.

Camp, T., Boleng, J., & Davies, V. (2002). A survey of mobility models for ad hoc network research. *Wireless Communication and Mobile Computing, 2*(5), 483–502. doi:10.1002/wcm.72.

Canton, L. G. (2006). *Emergency management: concepts and strategies for effective programs*. New York: Wiley-Interscience. doi:10.1002/0470119764.

Cao, L., & Krumm, J. (2009). From GPS traces to a routable road map. In *Proceedings of GIS 2009*. GIS.

Capodieci, N., Pagani, A., Cabri, G., & Aiello, M. (2011). Smart meter aware domestic energy trading agents. In *Proceedings of the 2011 Workshop on E-Energy Market Challenge* (pp. 1-10). ACM.

Cappiello, C., Comuzzi, M., Mussi, E., & Pernici, B. (2006). Context management for adaptive information systems. *Electronic Notes in Theoretical Computer Science, 146*(1), 69–84. doi:10.1016/j.entcs.2005.11.008.

Capra, M., Radenkovic, M., Benford, S., Oppermann, L., Drozd, A., & Flintham, M. (2005). *The multimedia challenges raised by pervasive games*. Paper presented at the 13th Annual ACM International Conference on Multimedia. New York, NY.

Caragliu, A., Del Bo, C., Kourtit, K., & Nijkamp, P. (2009). *Performance of smart cities in the north sea basin*. Retrieved from http://www.smartcities.info/files/13%20-%20Peter%20Nijkamp%20-%20Performance%20of%20Smart%20Cities.pdf

Carney, D., Çetintemel, U., Rasin, A., Zdonik, S., Cherniack, M., & Stonebraker, M. (2003). Operator scheduling in a data stream manager. In *Proceedings of the 29th International Conference on Very Large Data Bases* (pp. 838–849). VLDB.

CASAS. (2008). Retrieved 2013, from http://ailab.wsu.edu/casas/

Castellani, A. P., Bui, N., Casari, P., Rossi, M., Shelby, Z., & Zorzi, M. (2010). Architecture and protocols for the internet of things: A case study. In *Proceedings of PerCom 2010 Workshops*. Mannheim, Germany: PerCom. doi:10.1109/PERCOMW.2010.5470520.

Castelli, G., Rosi, A., Mamei, M., & Zambonelli, F. (2006). The W4 model and infrastructure for context-aware browsing the world. In *Proceedings of the 7th WOA Workshop*. WOA.

Cauldwell, R. (2000). Where did the anger go? The role of context in interpreting emotion in speech. *Proceedings of the ISCA ITRW on Speech and Emotion*, (pp. 127–131).

Chakraborty, A., & Singh, A. (2009). A partition-based approach to support streaming updates over persistent data in an active datawarehouse. In *Proceedings of the IEEE International Symposium on Parallel & Distributed Processing* (pp. 1–11). IEEE.

Chakravarthy, S., & Jiang, Q. (2009). *Stream data processing: A quality of service perspective: modeling, scheduling, load shedding, and complex event processing*. Berlin: Springer.

Chalmers, M., Bell, M., Brown, B., Hall, M., Sherwood, S., & Tennent, T. (2005). *Gaming on the edge: Using seams in ubicomp games*. Paper presented at the 2005 ACM SIGCHI International Conference on Advances in Computer Entertainment Technology. Valencia, Spain.

Chandra, R., Ramasubramanian, V., & Birman, K. (2001). Anonymous gossip: Improving multicast reliability in mobile ad hoc networks. In *Proceeding of the 21st International Conference on Distributed Computing Systems (ICDCS'01)*. Mesa, AZ: ICDCS.

Chandrasekaran, S., Cooper, O., Deshpande, A., Franklin, M. J., Hellerstein, J. M., Hong, W., et al. (2003). TelegraphCQ: Continuous dataflow processing. In *Proceedings of the 2003 ACM SIGMOD International Conference on Management of Data*. ACM.

Chang, M., Krahnstoever, N., & Ge, W. (2011). Probabilistic group-level motion analysis and scenario recognition. In *Proceedings of IEEE International Conference on Computer Vision (ICCV)*. Barcelona, Spain: IEEE.

Charif, H. N., & Mckenna, S. (2006). Tracking the activity of participants in a meeting. *Machine Vision and Applications*, *17*(2), 83–93. doi:10.1007/s00138-006-0015-5.

Chatzigiannakis, I., Mylonas, G., Akribopoulos, O., Logaras, M., Kokkinos, P., & Spirakis, P. (2010). The hot potato case: Challenges in multiplayer pervasive games based on AdHoc mobile sensor networks and the experimental evaluation of a prototype game. *CoRR abs/1002.1099*.

Chatzigiannakis, I., Mylonas, G., Kokkinos, P., Akribopoulos, O., Logaras, M., & Mavrommati, I. (2011). Implementing multiplayer pervasive installations based on mobile sensing devices: Field experience and user evaluation from a public showcase. *Journal of Systems and Software*. doi:10.1016/j.jss.2011.06.062 PMID:21532969.

Chatzimilioudis, G., Konstantinidis, A., Laoudias, C., & Zeinalipour-Yazti, D. (2012). Crowdsourcing with smartphones. *IEEE Internet Computing*, *16*(5), 36–44. doi:10.1109/MIC.2012.70.

Chen, A. (2005). *Context-aware collaborative filtering system: Predicting the user's preference in the ubiquitous*. Paper presented at the International Workshop on Location and Context-Awareness. New York, NY.

Chen, C., Zhang, D., Castro, P. S., Li, N., Sun, L., & Li, S. (2011). Real-time detection of anomalous taxi trajectories from GPS traces. In *Proceedings of the 8th International ICST Conference on Mobile and Ubiquitous Systems*. ICST.

Chen, J., Nairn, R., & Chi, E. (2011). *Speak little and well: Recommending conversations in online social streams*. Paper presented at the 2011 Annual Conference on Human Factors in Computing Systems. Vancouver, Canada. Retrieved from http://delivery.acm.org/10.1145/1980000/1978974/p217-chen.pdf?ip=113.108.133.51&CFID=42910813&CFTOKEN=50591669&__acm__=1316163901_3767d771ad0 65df8fe264f6de95d3a86

Chen, L., Nugent, C., Mulvenna, M., Finlay, D., Hong, X., & Poland, M. (2008). Logical framework for behaviour reasoning and assistance in a smart home. *International Journal of ARM*.

Chen, W., & Chen, P. (2003). Group mobility management in wireless ad hoc networks. In *Proceeding of the 58th Vehicular Technology Conference* (VTC'03). Orlando, FL: VTC.

Cheng, Z., Caverlee, J., Lee, K., & Sui, D. Z. (2011). *Exploring millions of footprints in location sharing services*. Paper presented at ICWSM 2011. New York, NY. doi: 10.1.1.226.5324

Chen, L., Hoey, J., Nugent, C., Cook, D., & Yu, Z. (2012). Sensor-based activity recognition. *IEEE Transactions on Systems, Man, and Cybernetics. Part C, 42*(6), 790–808. doi: doi:10.1109/TSMCC.2012.2198883.

Chen, L., & Khalil, I. (2011). Activity recognition: Approaches, practices and trends. In L. Chen, C. D. Nugent, J. Biswas, & J. Hoey (Eds.), *Activity Recognition in Pervasive Intelligent Environments* (pp. 1–31). Atlantis Press. doi:10.2991/978-94-91216-05-3_1.

Chen, L., Nugent, C. D., Cook, D., & Yu, Z. (2011). Knowledge-driven activity recognition in intelligent environment. *Pervasive and Mobile Computing, 7*(3), 285–286. doi:10.1016/j.pmcj.2011.05.001.

Chen, L., Nugent, C. D., & Wang, H. (2012). A knowledge-driven approach to activity recognition in smart homes. *IEEE Transactions on Knowledge and Data Engineering, 24*(6), 961–974. doi:10.1109/TKDE.2011.51.

Cheok, A. D., & Khoo, E. T. (2006). Age Invaders: Intergenerational mixed reality family game. *The International Journal of Virtual Reality, 5*(2), 45–50.

Cheok, A. D., Sreekumar, A., Lei, C., & Thang, L. M. (2006). Capture the flag: Mixed-reality social gaming with smart phones. *IEEE Pervasive Computing / IEEE Computer Society [and] IEEE Communications Society, 5*(2), 62–63. doi:10.1109/MPRV.2006.25.

Childress, M., & Braswell, R. (2006). Using massively multiplayer online role-playing games for online learning. *Distance Education, 27*(2), 187–196. doi:10.1080/01587910600789522.

Cho, Y., Nam, Y., Choi, Y., & Cho, W. (2008). SmartBuckle: Human activity recognition using a 3-axis accelerometer and a wearable camera. In Proceedings of HealthNet. HealthNet.

Chodorow, K., & Dirolf, M. (2010). *MongoDB: The definitive guide*. Sebastopol, CA: O'Reilly Media.

Choudhury, T., Consolvo, S., Harrison, B., Hightower, J., Lamarca, A., & LeGrand, L. et al. (2008). The mobile sensing platform: An embedded activity recognition system. *IEEE Pervasive Computing / IEEE Computer Society [and] IEEE Communications Society, 7*(2), 32–41. doi:10.1109/MPRV.2008.39.

Chowdhury, A. R., Falchuk, B., & Misra, A. (2010). A provenance-aware remote health monitoring middleware. In *Proceedings of the Eight Annual IEEE International Conference on Pervasive Computing and Communications (PerCom)* (pp. 125-134). IEEE Computer Society.

Christensen, E., Curbera, F., Meredith, G., & Weerawarana, S. (2001). *Web services description language (WSDL)*. Retrieved February 21, 2013, from http://www.w3.org/TR/wsdl

Cipriani, N., Eissele, M., Brodt, A., Grossmann, M., & Mitschang, B. (2009). NexusDS: A flexible and extensible middleware for distributed stream processing. In *Proceedings of the 2009 International Database Engineering & Applications Symposium* (pp. 152–161). Cetraro - Calabria, Italy: ACM. doi:10.1145/1620432.1620448

Clavel, C. I. V. (2004). Fiction database for emotion detection in abnormal situations. *Proc. Int. Conf. Spoken Language Process. (ICSLP '04)*, (pp. 2277–2280). Korea.

Cloud Business Apps Integration – CloudWork. (2013). Retrieved February 21, 2013, from https://cloudwork.com/

Cohn, A. G., & Hazarika, S. M. (2001). Qualitative spatial representation and reasoning: An overview. *Fundamenta Informaticae, 46*, 1–29.

Coloberti, M., Lombriser, C., Roggen, D., Troester, G., Guarneri, R., & Riboni, D. (2008). Service discovery and composition in body area networks. In *Proceedings of the Third International Conference on Body Area Networks (BodyNets)*. BodyNets.

Connelly, K., Siek, K. A., Mulder, I., Neely, S., Stevenson, G., & Kray, C. (2008). Evaluating pervasive and ubiquitous systems. *IEEE Pervasive Computing / IEEE Computer Society [and] IEEE Communications Society, 7*(3), 85–88. doi:10.1109/MPRV.2008.47.

Connolly, C. I., Burns, J. B., & Bui, H. H. (2008). *Recovering social networks from massive track datasets.* Paper presented at the Meeting of the IEEE Workshop on Applications of Computer Vision. Copper Mountain, CO.

Consolvo, S., McDonald, D. W., & Landay, J. A. (2009). Theory-driven design strategies for technologies that support behavior change in everyday life. In *Proceedings of CHI 2009.* Boston, MA: ACM.

Cook, D., Feuz, K. D., & Krishnan, N. (2012). *Transfer learning for activity recognition: A survey.* Retrieved from http://eecs.wsu.edu/~cook/pubs/kais12.pdf

Cook, D. J. (2009). Multi-agent smart environments. *Journal of Ambient Intelligence and Smart Environments, 1*(1), 51–55.

Cook, D. J., & Das, S. K. (2007). How smart are our environments? An updated look at the state of the art. *Pervasive and Mobile Computing, 3*(2), 53–73. doi:10.1016/j.pmcj.2006.12.001.

Cook, L. J., Knight, S., & Olson, L. M. (2005). A comparison of aggressive and DUI crashes. *Journal of Safety Research, 36*(5), 491. doi:10.1016/j.jsr.2005.10.010 PMID:16298395.

Cootes, T. F., Taylor, C. J., Cooper, D. H., & Graham, J. (1995). Active shape models-Their training and application. *Computer Vision and Image Understanding, 61*(1), 38–59. doi:10.1006/cviu.1995.1004.

Cornelius, R. C. (2003). Describing the Emotional States that are Expressed in Speech. *Speech Communication, 40,* 5–32. doi:10.1016/S0167-6393(02)00071-7.

Cosm - Internet of Things Platform Connecting Devices and Apps for Real-Time Control and Data Storage. (2012). Retrieved February 21, 2013, from https://cosm.com

Coughlin, J. F., Reimer, B., & Mehler, B. (2011). Monitoring, managing, and motivating driver safety and well-being. *IEEE Pervasive Computing / IEEE Computer Society [and] IEEE Communications Society, 10*(3), 14–21. doi:10.1109/MPRV.2011.54.

Coutaz, J., Crowley, J. L., Dobson, S., & Garlan, D. (2005). Context is key. *Communications of the ACM, 48*(3), 49–53. doi:10.1145/1047671.1047703.

Cowan, M. (2006). *Pitch and intensity characteristics of stage speech.* Arch. Speech.

Cowie, R., Douglas-Cowie, E., Tsapatsoulis, N., Votsis, G., Kollias, S., Fellenz, W., & Taylor, J. (2001, Jan). Emotion recognition in human-computer interaction. *Signal Processing Magazine, IEEE, 18*(1), 32–80. doi:10.1109/79.911197.

Cranshaw, J., Toch, E., Hong, J., Kittur, A., & Sadeh, N. (2010). *Bridging the gap between physical location and online social networks.* Paper presented at the Meeting of ACM Conference on Ubiquitous Computing. Copenhagen, Denmark.

Cugola, G., & Margara, A. (2012). Processing flows of information: From data stream to complex event processing. *ACM Computing Surveys, 44*(3), 15. doi:10.1145/2187671.2187677.

Cui, Y., & Honkala, M. (2011). The consumption of integrated social networking services on mobile devices. In *Proceedings of the 10th International Conference on Mobile and Ubiquitous Multimedia, MUM '11.* ACM.

Darwin, C. (1872). *The Expression of the Emotions in Man and Animals.* John Murray. doi:10.1037/10001-000.

Dasarathy, B. V. (1997). Sensor fusion potential exploitation-innovative architectures and illustrative applications. *Proceedings of the IEEE, 85*(1), 24–38. doi:10.1109/5.554206.

Das, S. K., Cook, D. J., Battacharya, A., Heierman, E. O. III, & Lin, T.-Y. (2002). The role of prediction algorithms in the MavHome smart home architecture. *IEEE Wireless Communications, 9*(6), 77–84. doi:10.1109/MWC.2002.1160085.

Davies, V. (2000). *Evaluating mobility models within an ad hoc network.* (Master's thesis). Colorado School of Mines. Retrieved from http://citeseerx.ist.psu.edu/viewdoc/summary?doi=10.1.1.18.4191

Davitz, J. R. (1964). Personality, perceptual, and cognitive correlates of emotional sensitivity. In J. R. Davitz (Ed.), *The Communication of Emotional Meaning.* New York: McGraw-Hill.

Davitz, J. R. (1964). *The Communication of Emotional Meaning.* New York: McGraw-Hill.

de Leoni, M., Marrella, A., Mecella, M., Valentini, S., & Sardina, S. (2008). *Coordinating mobile actors in pervasive and mobile scenarios: An AI-based approach*. New York: Academic Press. doi:10.1109/WETICE.2008.30.

Deffenbacher, J. L., Lynch, R. S., Oetting, E. R., & Swaim, R. C. (2002). The driving anger expression inventory: A measure of how people express their anger on the road. *Behaviour Research and Therapy, 40*(6), 717–737. doi:10.1016/S0005-7967(01)00063-8 PMID:12051489.

Dellaert, F. T. P. (1996). Recognizing emotion in speech. *Proceedings of the International Conference on Spoken Language Processing (ICSLP '96)*, (pp. 1970–1973). Philadelphia, PA.

Demers, A., Gehrke, J., Panda, B., Riedewald, M., Sharma, V., White, W. M., et al. (2007). Cayuga: A general purpose event monitoring system. In *Proceedings of CIDR* (pp. 412–422). CIDR.

Devillers, L. V. (2005). *Detection of real-life emotions in call centers* (pp. 1841–1844). Proc. Eurospeech.

Dey, A. K. (2001). Understanding and using context. *Personal and Ubiquitous Computing, 5*(1), 4–7. doi:10.1007/s007790170019.

Dey, A. K., Abowd, G. D., & Salber, D. (2001). A conceptual framework and a toolkit for supporting the rapid prototyping of context-aware applications. *Human-Computer Interaction, 16*(2-4), 97–166. doi:10.1207/S15327051HCI16234_02.

Dey, A. K., Sohn, T., Streng, S., & Kodama, J. (2006). iCAP: Interactive prototyping of context-aware applications.[]. Berlin: Springer.]. *Proceedings of Pervasive Computing, 3968*, 254–271. doi:10.1007/11748625_16.

Diab, A. (2010). *Mobility management in IP-based networks: Analysis, design, programming and computer-based learning modules*. (Dissertation thesis). Ilmenau University of Technology, Ilmenau, Germany.

Diewald, S., Möller, A., Roalter, L., & Kranz, M. (2011). Mobile device integration and interaction in the automotive domain. In *Proceedings of AutoNUI: Automotive Natural User Interfaces Workshop at the 3rd International Conference on Automotive User Interfaces and Interactive Vehicular Applications* (AutomotiveUI 2011). AutomotiveUI.

Diewald, S., Möller, A., Roalter, L., & Kranz, M. (2012). MobiliNet: A social network for optimized mobility. In *Proceedings of the 4th International Conference on Automotive User Interfaces and Interactive Vehicular Applications* (AutomotiveUI 2012). AutomotiveUI.

Dindar, N., Fischer, P. M., Soner, M., & Tatbul, N. (2011). Efficiently correlating complex events over live and archived data streams. In *Proceedings of ACM DEBS Conference*. ACM.

Ding, Z., Lei, D., Yan, J., Bin, Z., & Lun, A. (2010). *A web service discovery method based on tag*. Paper presented at International Conference on Complex, Intelligent and Software Intensive Systems (CISIS). New York, NY.

Dobson, S., et al. (2006). A survey of autonomic communications. *ACM Transactions on Autonomous and Adaptive Systems, 1*(2).

Domingos, P., & Hulten, G. (2000). Mining high-speed data streams. In *Proceedings of the Sixth ACM SIGKDD International Conference on Knowledge Discovery and Data Mining* (pp. 71–80). ACM.

Doozer. (2011). Retrieved 2013, from http://github.com/ha/doozer

Dorman, K., Yahyanejad, M., Nahapetian, A., Suh, M., Sarrafzadeh, M., McCarthy, W., & Kaiser, W. (2010). Nutrition monitor: A food purchase and consumption monitoring mobile system. *Mobile Computing, Application, and Services, 35*. doi:10.1007/978-3-642-12607-9_1.

Doryab, A., & Togelius, J. (2012). Activity recognition in collaborative environments. In *Proceedings of IEEE World Congress on Computational Intelligence (WCCI)*. Brisbane, Australia: IEEE.

Doshi, A., Morris, B. T., & Trivedi, M. M. (2011). On-road prediction of driver's intent with multimodal sensory cues. *IEEE Pervasive Computing / IEEE Computer Society [and] IEEE Communications Society, 10*(3), 22–34. doi:10.1109/MPRV.2011.38.

Douglas-Cowie, E., N. C. (2003). Emotional speech: Towards a new generation of databases. *Speech Communication, 40*(1–2), 33–60. doi:10.1016/S0167-6393(02)00070-5.

Dourish, P. (2004). What we talk about when we talk about context. *Personal and Ubiquitous Computing, 8*(1), 19–30. doi:10.1007/s00779-003-0253-8.

Drugge, M., Nilsson, M., Liljedahl, U., Synnes, K., & Parnes, P. (2004). Methods for interrupting a wearable computer user. In *Proceedings of ISWC 2004, the Eighth International Symposium on Wearable Computers*. IEEE.

Dwork, C. (2006). Differential privacy. In *Proceedings of Automata, Languages and Programming (ICALP)* (pp. 1–12). Berlin: Springer. doi:10.1007/11787006_1.

e-Diana. (2009). Retrieved 2013, from http://www.artemis-ediana.eu/

Egenhofer, M. J. & Kuhn, W. (1998). *Beyond desktop GIS*. Lisbon: GIS PlaNET.

Egenhofer, M., & Mark, D. (1995). Naive geography. *Spatial Information Theory A: Theoretical Basis for GIS*, 1-15.

Eisenman, S. B., Miluzzo, E., Lane, N. D., Peterson, R. A., Ahn, G.-S., & Campbell, A. T. (2007). *The bikenet mobile sensing system for cyclist experience mapping*. Paper presented at the Meeting of ACM Conference on Embedded Networked Sensor Systems. Sydney, Australia.

Ekholm, A., & Fridqvist, S. (2000). A concept of space for building classification, product modelling, and design. *Automation in Construction*, 315–328. doi:10.1016/S0926-5805(99)00013-8.

Ekman, P. F. W. (1971). Constants across cultures in the face and emotion. In Journal of Personality and Social Psychology. Elsevier.

Ekman, P. (1994). Strong evidence for universals in facial expressions: A reply to Russell's mistaken critique. *Psychological Bulletin, 115*, 268–287. doi:10.1037/0033-2909.115.2.268 PMID:8165272.

Elkan, C., & Greiner, R. (1993). Building large knowledge-based systems: Representation and inference in the CYC project: DB Lenat and RV Guha. *Artificial Intelligence, 61*, 41–52. doi:10.1016/0004-3702(93)90092-P.

Ellison-Potter, P., Bell, P., & Deffenbacher, J. (2001). The effects of trait driving anger, anonymity, and aggressive stimuli on aggressive driving behaviour. *Journal of Applied Social Psychology, 31*(2), 431–443. doi:10.1111/j.1559-1816.2001.tb00204.x.

Elmasri, R., & Navathe, S. B. (2006). *Fundamentals of database systems* (5th ed.). Reading, MA: Addison Wesley. Retrieved from http://www.amazon.com/Fundamentals-Database-Systems-5th-Ed./dp/0321369572

Elvik, R., Høye, A., Vaa, T., & Sørensen, M. (2009). *The handbook of road safety measures* (2nd ed.). Bingley, UK: Emerald Group Publishing Limited.

Ennals, R., Brewer, E., Garofalakis, M., Shadle, M., & Gandhi, P. (2007). Intel mash maker: Join the web. *SIGMOD Record, 36*(4), 27–33. doi:10.1145/1361348.1361355.

Enokido, T., Xhafa, F., Barolli, L., Takizawa, M., Uehara, M., & Durresi, A. (Eds.). (2010). *The 13th international conference on network-based information systems* (NBiS 2010). Takayama, Japan: IEEE.

EnPROVE. (2013). Retrieved 2013, from http://www.enprove.eu/

Erdos, P., & Renyi, A. (1959). On random graphs. *Publications Mathematicae, 6*, 290–297.

Erickson, T. (2010). *Geocentric crowdsourcing and smarter cities: Enabling urban intelligence in cities and regions*. Paper presented at the 1st International Workshop on Ubiquitous Crowdsourcing. New York, NY.

Erickson, T., & Kellogg, W. A. (2000). Social translucence: An approach to designing systems that support social processes. *ACM Transactions on Computer-Human Interaction, 7*(1), 59–83. doi:10.1145/344949.345004.

Ericsson 2020. (2012). *Vision 2020 – 50 billion connected devices*. Retrieved from http://www.slideshare.net/EricssonFrance/vision-2020-50-billion-connected-devices-ericsson

Ericsson IoT. (2012). *The internet of things comes alive through smart objects interoperability*. Retrieved from http://labs.ericsson.com/

ESNA. (2009). *European sensor network architecture (ESNA)*. Retrieved from https://www.sics.se/esna/

Etzion, O., & Niblett, P. (2011). *Event processing in action*. Stamford, CT: Manning Publications.

Evrythng. (2012). Retrieved February 21, 2013, from http://www.evrythng.com

Eyben, F., Wöllmer, M., Poitschke, T., Schuller, B., Blaschke, C., & Färber, B. et al. (2010). Emotion on the road - Necessity, acceptance, and feasibility of affective computing in the car. In *Proceedings of Advances in Human-Computer Interaction, 2010*. IEEE. doi:10.1155/2010/263593.

Ezzell, Z., Fishwick, P., & Cendan, J. (2011). *Linking simulation and visualization construction through interactions with an ontology visualization*. New York: Academic Press. doi:10.1109/WSC.2011.6147995.

Faloutsos, C., & Kang, U. (2012). Managing and mining large graphs: Patterns and algorithms. In *Proceedings of SIGMOD Conference*. ACM.

Fasel, B., & Luettin, J. (2003). Automatic facial expression analysis: A survey. *Pattern Recognition*, *36*(1), 259–275. doi:10.1016/S0031-3203(02)00052-3.

Fernandez, R., & Picard, R. (2003). Modeling drivers' speech under stress. *Speech Communication*, *40*, 145–159. doi:10.1016/S0167-6393(02)00080-8.

Ferscha, A., Hechinger, M., & Riener, A. et al. (2008). Peer-it: Stick-on solutions for networks of things. *Pervasive and Mobile Computing*, *4*, 448–479. doi:10.1016/j.pmcj.2008.01.003.

Ferscha, A., Holzmann, C., & Oppl, S. (2004). *Context awareness for group interaction support*. New York: Academic Press.

Fischer, K. (1999). *Annotating emotional language data*. Tech. Rep. 236, Univ. of Hamburg, Hamburg.

Fischer, J., Lindt, I., & Stenros, J. (2006). *Final crossmedia report (part II) – Epidemic menace II evaluation report*. Integrated Project on Pervasive Gaming.

Flintham, M., Anastasi, R., Benford, S., Drozd, A., Mathrick, J., Rowland, D., & Sutton, J. (2003). *Uncle Roy all around you: Mixing games and theatre on the city streets*. Paper presented at the 1st International Conference on Digital Games Research Association (DIGRA'03). New York, NY.

Foley, D., Ancoli-Israel, S., Britz, P., & Walsh, J. (2004). Sleep disturbances and chronic disease in older adults: Results of the 2003 national sleep foundation sleep in America survey. *Journal of Psychosomatic Research*, *56*(5), 497–502. doi:10.1016/j.jpsychores.2004.02.010 PMID:15172205.

Fonagy, I. (1981). Emotions, voice and music. In J. Sundberg, Research Aspects on Singing (pp. 51–79). Royal Swedish Academy of Music no. 33

Fonagy, I. (1978). A new method of investigating the perception of prosodic features. *Language and Speech*, *21*, 34–49. PMID:692241.

Fortunato, S. (2010). Community detection in graphs. *Physics Reports*, *486*(3-5), 75–174. doi:10.1016/j.physrep.2009.11.002.

M. Foth (Ed.). (2009). *Handbook of research on urban informatics: The practice and promise of the real-time city*. Hershey, PA: IGI Global.

Foundation, A. A. A. (2009). *Aggressive driving: Research update*. Retrieved from http://www.aaafoundation.org

France, D. J., R. G. (2000). Acoustical properties of speech as indicators of depression and suicidal risk. *IEEE Transactions on Bio-Medical Engineering*, *7*, 829–837. doi:10.1109/10.846676 PMID:10916253.

Frank, A. U. (1992). Qualitative spatial reasoning about distances and directions in geographic space. *Journal of Visual Languages and Computing*, *3*, 343–371. doi:10.1016/1045-926X(92)90007-9.

Franke, J., Ulmer, C., & Charoy, F. (2010). *Pervasive emergency response process management system*. New York: Academic Press.

Franklin, C. Jr. (2009). *Cloud computing: Technologies and strategies of the ubiquitous data center.* Boca Raton, FL: CRC.

Frassl, M., Lichtenstern, M., Khider, M., & Angermann, M. (2010). Developing a system for information management in disaster relief—Methodology and requirements. In *Proceedings of the 7th International ISCRAM Conference.* Seattle, WA: ISCRAM.

Freeman, L. C. (2004). *The development of social network analysis: A study in the sociology of science.* Empirical Press.

Frick, R. W. (1986). The prosodic expression of anger: differentiating thread and frustration. *Aggressive Behavior, 12*, 121–128. doi:10.1002/1098-2337(1986)12:2<121::AID-AB2480120206>3.0.CO;2-F.

Fujiki, Y., Kazakos, K., Puri, C., Buddharaju, P., Pavlidis, I., & Levine, J. (2008). NEAT-o-games: Blending physical activity and fun in the daily routine. *ACM Computers in Entertainment, 6*(2). doi:10.1145/1371216.1371224.

Fusier, F., Valentin, V., Bremond, F., Thonnat, M., Borg, M., Thirde, D., & Ferryman, J. (2007). Video understanding for complex activity recognition. *Machine Vision and Applications, 18*(3), 167–188. doi:10.1007/s00138-006-0054-y.

Gaber, M. M., Zaslavsky, A., & Krishnaswamy, S. (2005). Mining data streams: a review. *SIGMOD Record, 34*(2), 18–26. doi:10.1145/1083784.1083789.

Gama, J. (2007). *Learning from data streams: Processing techniques in sensor networks.* Berlin: Springer. doi:10.1007/3-540-73679-4.

Gan, G., Ma, C., & Wu, J. (2007). *Data clustering: Theory, algorithms, and applications.* Philadelphia, PA: SIAM. doi:10.1137/1.9780898718348.

Garg, N. P., Favre, S., Salamin, H., Dilek, H. T., & Vinciarelli, A. (2008). *Role recognition for meeting participants: An approach based on lexical information and social network analysis.* Paper presented at the Meeting of ACM International Conference on Multimedia. Vancouver, Canada.

Garlan, D., Siewiorek, D., Smailagic, A., & Steenkiste, P. (2002). Project aura: Toward distraction-free pervasive computing. *IEEE Pervasive Computing / IEEE Computer Society [and] IEEE Communications Society, 1*(2), 22–31. doi:10.1109/MPRV.2002.1012334.

Gavalas, D., & Economou, D. (2011). Development platforms for mobile applications: Status and trends. *IEEE Software, 28*(1), 77–86. doi:10.1109/MS.2010.155.

Gavalas, D., & Kenteris, M. (2011). A pervasive web-based recommendation system for mobile tourist guides. *Personal and Ubiquitous Computing, 15*(7), 759–770. doi:10.1007/s00779-011-0389-x.

Gaver, W., Beaver, J., & Benford, S. (2003). *Ambiguity as a resource for design.* Paper presented at the SIGCHI Conference on Human Factors in Computing Systems. Ft. Lauderdale, FL.

Gavrila, D. M. (1999). The visual analysis of human movement: A survey. *Computer Vision and Image Understanding, 73*(1), 82-98. doi: 10.1.1.131.2072

Gawinecki, M. (2009). *WSColab: Structured collaborative tagging for web service matchmaking.* Retrieved February 21, 2013, from http://www.ibspan.waw.pl/~gawinec/wss/wscolab.html

Gawinecki, M., Cabri, G., Paprzycki, M., & Ganzha, M. (2010). WSColab: Structured collaborative tagging for web service matchmaking. In *Proceedings of the 6th International Conference on Web Information Systems and Technologies (WEBIST 2010),* (pp.70-77). Valencia, Spain: INSTICC Press.

Gawinecki, M., Cabri, G., Paprzycki, M., & Ganzha, M. (2012). Evaluation of structured collaborative tagging for web service matchmaking. In *Semantic Web Services Advancement through Evaluation* (pp. 173–189). Berlin: Springer. doi:10.1007/978-3-642-28735-0_11.

Gedik, B., Andrade, H., Wu, K.-L., Yu, P. S., & Doo, M. (2008). SPADE: The systems declarative stream processing engine. In *Proceedings of the 2008 ACM SIGMOD International Conference on Management of Data - SIGMOD '08.* New York, NY: ACM Press. doi:10.1145/1376616.1376729

Geesen, D., Brell, M., Grawunder, M., Nicklas, D., & Appelrath, H. J. (2012). Data stream management in the AAL: Universal and flexible preprocessing of continuous sensor data. *Ambient Assisted Living*, 213–228.

Gellersen, H. W., Schmidt, A., & Beigl, M. (2002). Multi-sensor context-awareness in mobile devices and smart artefacts. *Mobile Networks and Applications*, 7(5). doi:10.1023/A:1016587515822.

Georgievski, I., Degeler, V., Pagani, G. A., Nguyen, T. A., Lazovik, A., & Aiello, M. (2012). Optimizing energy costs for offices connected to the smart grid. *IEEE Transactions on Smart Grid*, 3, 2273–2285. doi:10.1109/TSG.2012.2218666.

Gerhard, D. (2003). *Pitch extraction and fundamental frequency: History and current technique*. Technical Report TR-CS.

Ghinita, G., Kalnis, P., Khoshgozaran, A., Shahabi, C., & Tan, K. (2008). Private queries in location based services: Anonymizers are not necessary. In *Proceedings of ACM SIGMOD International Conference on Management of Data (SIGMOD)* (pp. 121-132). ACM.

Ghosh, J. (2006). *Sociological orbit-based mobility profiling and routing for wireless networks*. (PhD Thesis). Department of Computer Science and Engineering, The State University of New York, Buffalo, NY.

Ghosh, J., Ngo, H. Q., & Qiao, C. (2006). Mobility profile-based routing within intermittently connected mobile ad hoc networks (ICMAN). In *Proceedings of the 2nd International Conference on Wireless Communications and Mobile Computing* (IWCMC'06). Vancouver, Canada: IWCMC.

Ghosh, J., Philip, S. J., & Qiao, C. (2007). Sociological orbit aware location approximation and routing (SOLAR) in MANET. *Ad Hoc Networks*, 5(2), 189–209. doi:10.1016/j.adhoc.2005.10.003.

Ghosh, J., Yoon, S., Ngo, H. Q., & Qiao, C. (2005). *Sociological orbits for efficient routing in intermittently connected mobile ad hoc networks (UB CSE Technical Report)*. Buffalo, NY: Department of Computer Science and Engineering, University at Buffalo, The State University of New York.

Giannella, C., Han, J., Pei, J., Yan, X., & Yu, P. (2003). Mining frequent patterns in data streams at multiple time granularities. In *Proceedings of Next Generation Data Mining*, (pp. 191–212). IEEE. Retrieved from http://citeseerx.ist.psu.edu/viewdoc/download?doi=10.1.1.14.2327&amp,rep=rep1&amp,type=pdf

Giannotti, F., Nanni, M., Pinelli, F., & Pedreschi, D. (2007). *Trajectory pattern mining*. Paper presented at the Meeting of ACM SIGKDD International Conference on Knowledge Discovery and Data Mining. San Jose, CA.

Giannotti, F., Nanni, M., Pedreschi, D., Pinelli, F., Renso, C., Rinzivillo, S., & Trasarti, R. (2011). Unveiling the complexity of human mobility by querying and mining massive trajectory data. *The VLDB Journal*, 20(5). doi:10.1007/s00778-011-0244-8 PMID:21804753.

Giannotti, F., Pedreschi, D., Pentland, A., Lukowicz, P., Kossmann, D., Crowley, J., & Helbing, D. (2012). A planetary nervous system for social mining and collective awareness. *The European Physical Journal. Special Topics*, 214, 49–75. doi:10.1140/epjst/e2012-01688-9.

Gilbert, E., & Karahalios, K. (2009). Predicting tie strength with social media. In *Proceedings of the SIGCHI Conference on Human Factors in Computing Systems* (CHI '09). ACM.

Girvan, M., & Newman, M. E. J. (2002). Community structure in social and biological networks. *Proceedings of the National Academy of Sciences of the United States of America*, 99(12), 7821–7826. doi:10.1073/pnas.122653799 PMID:12060727.

Gomez-Perez, G. (1999). Ontological engineering: A state of the art. *Expert Update: Knowledge Based Systems and Applied Artificial Intelligence*, 2, 33–43.

Gong, M., Zhang, L., Ma, J., & Jiao, L. (2012). Community detection in dynamic social networks based on multiobjective immune algorithm. *Journal of Computer Science and Technology*, 27(3), 455–467. doi:10.1007/s11390-012-1235-y.

Gonzalez, M. C., Hidalgo, C. A., & Barabasi, A. L. (2008). Understanding individual human mobility patterns. *Nature*, 453(5), 779–782. doi:10.1038/nature06958 PMID:18528393.

Gottfried, B., Guesgen, H., & Hubner, S. (2006). Spatiotemporal reasoning for smart homes. *Designing Smart Homes*, 16-34.

Gould, M. D. (1989). *Human factors research and its value to GIS user interface design*. New York: Academic Press.

Gramoli, V., Kermarrec, A. M., & Merrer, E. L. (2008). SONDe: A self-organizing object deployment algorithm in large-scale dynamic systems. In *Proceeding of the 7th Dependable Computing Conference* (EDCC'08). Kaunas, Lithuania: Vytautas Magnus University.

Gray, A. J. G., Castro, R. G., Kyzirakos, K., Karpathiotakis, M., Calbimonte, J. P., Page, K., et al. (2011). A semantically enabled service architecture for mashups over streaming and stored data. In *Proceedings of the 8th Extended Semantic Web Conference on the Semantic Web: Research and Applications*, (pp. 300-314). Berlin: Springer.

GreenerBuildings. (2013). Retrieved 2013, from http://www.greenerbuildings.eu/

Grimm, M., Kroschel, K., Harris, H., Nass, C., Schuller, B., & Rigoll, G. et al. (2007). On the necessity and feasibility of detecting a driver's emotional state while driving.[LNCS]. *Proceedings of Affective Computing and Intelligent Interaction, 4738*, 126–138. doi:10.1007/978-3-540-74889-2_12.

Grosky, W. I., Kansal, A., Nath, S., Liu, J., & Zhao, F. (2007). SenseWeb: An infrastructure for shared sensing. *IEEE MultiMedia, 14*(4), 8–13. doi:10.1109/MMUL.2007.82.

Gruber, T. R. (1993). A translation approach to portable ontology specifications. *Knowledge Acquisition, 5*, 199–220. doi:10.1006/knac.1993.1008.

Gruninger, M., & Fox, M. S. (1995). *Methodology for the design and evaluation of ontologies*. New York: Academic Press.

Guangxia, L., Hoi, S. C. H., Kuiyu, C., & Jain, R. (2010). *Micro-blogging sentiment detection by collaborative online learning*. Paper presented at the IEEE 10th International Conference on Data Mining (ICDM). New York, NY.

Guinard, D. (2009). *Towards the web of things: Web mashups for embedded devices*. Paper presented at 2nd Workshop on Mashups, Enterprise Mashups and Lightweight Composition on the Web MEM 2009. Madrid, Spain.

Guo, B., He, H., Yu, Z., Zhang, D., & Zhou, X. (2012). *GroupMe: Supporting group formation with mobile sensing and social graph mining*. Paper presented at the Meeting of International Conference on Mobile and Ubiquitous Systems: Computing, Networking and Services (MobiQuitous'12). Beijing, China.

Guo, B., Zhang, D., & Yang, D. (2011). *Read more from business cards: Toward a smart social contact management system*. Paper presented at the Meeting of IEEE/WIC/ACM International Conference on Web Intelligence (WI-11). Lyon, France.

Guo, B., Zhang, D., Yu, Z., & Zhou, X. (2012). *Hybrid SN: Interlinking opportunistic and online communities to augment information dissemination*. Paper presented at the Meeting of IEEE International Conference on Ubiquitous Intelligence and Computing. Fukuoka, Japan.

Guo, B., Fujimura, R., Zhang, D., & Imai, M. (2012). Design-in-play: Improving the variability of indoor pervasive games. *Multimedia Tools and Applications, 59*(1), 259–277. doi:10.1007/s11042-010-0711-z.

Guo, B., Zhang, D., & Imai, M. (2010). Enabling user-oriented management for ubiquitous computing: The meta-design approach. *Computer Networks, 54*(16), 2840–2855. doi:10.1016/j.comnet.2010.07.016.

Guo, B., Zhang, D., & Michita, I. (2011). Toward a cooperative programming framework for context-aware applications. *Journal of Personal and Ubiquitous Computing, 15*(3), 221–233. doi:10.1007/s00779-010-0329-1.

Guo, B., Zhang, D., Wang, Z., Yu, Z., & Zhou, X. (2013). Opportunistic IoT: Exploring the harmonious interaction between human and the internet of things. *Journal of Network and Computer Applications*. doi:10.1016/j.jnca.2012.12.028.

Guo, B., Zhang, D., Yu, Z., Liang, Y., Wang, Z., & Zhou, X. (2012). *From the internet of things to embedded intelligence*. World Wide Web Journal. doi:10.1007/s11280-012-0188-y.

Gu, T., Pung, H. K., & Zhang, D. Q. (2005). A service-oriented middleware for building context-aware services. *Journal of Network and Computer Applications*, *28*(1), 1–18. doi:10.1016/j.jnca.2004.06.002.

Gu, T., Wang, L., Wu, Z., Tao, X., & Lu, J. (2011). A pattern mining approach to sensor-based human activity recognition. *IEEE Transactions on Knowledge and Data Engineering*, *23*(9), 1359–1372. doi:10.1109/TKDE.2010.184.

Gyllstrom, D., Agrawal, J., Diao, Y., & Immerman, N. (2008). On supporting kleene closure over event streams. In *Proceedings of 2008 IEEE 24th International Conference on Data Engineering*, (pp. 1391–1393). IEEE. doi:10.1109/ICDE.2008.4497566

Gyorbíró, N., Fábián, Á., & Hományi, G. (2009). An activity recognition system for mobile phones. *Mobile Networks and Applications*, *14*(1), 82–91. doi:10.1007/s11036-008-0112-y.

Haas, Z. (1997). A new routing protocol for reconfigurable wireless networks. In Proceeding of the IEEE International Conference on Universal Personal Communications (ICUPC'97), (pp. 562–565). IEEE.

Haddow, G., Bullock, J., & Coppola, D. P. (2010). *Introduction to emergency management*. London: Butterworth-Heinemann.

Hallberg, J., Norberg, M. B., Kristiansson, J., Synnes, K., & Nugent, C. (2007). Creating dynamic groups using context-awareness. In *Proceedings of the 6th International Conference on Mobile and Ubiquitous Multimedia* (MUM '07). ACM.

Hall, D. L., & Llinas, J. (1997). An introduction to multisensor data fusion. *Proceedings of the IEEE*, *85*(1), 6–23. doi:10.1109/5.554205.

Hall, D. L., & McMullen, S. A. H. (2004). *Mathematical techniques in Multisensor data fusion*. Artech Print on Demand.

Hammad, M. A., Mokbel, M. F., Ali, M. H., Aref, W. G., Catlin, A. C., & Elmagarmid, A. K. et al. (2004). Nile: A query processing engine for data streams. In *Proceedings of Data Engineering, 2004*. IEEE. doi:10.1109/ICDE.2004.1320080.

Handorean, R., Gill, C., & Roman, G. C. (2004). Accommodating transient connectivity in ad hoc and mobile settings. *Lecture Notes in Computer Science*, *3001*, 305–322. doi:10.1007/978-3-540-24646-6_22.

Han, J., Chen, Y., Dong, G., Pei, J., Wah, B. W., Wang, J., & Cai, Y. D. (2005). Stream cube: An architecture for multi-dimensional analysis of data streams. *Distributed and Parallel Databases*, *18*(2), 173–197. doi:10.1007/s10619-005-3296-1.

Hannamari, S., Kuittinen, J., & Montola, M. (2007). *Insectopia evaluation report*. Integrated Project on Pervasive Gaming.

Hansen, H. J. (1999). Speech under stress conditions: Overview of the effect of speech production and on system performance. *Proc. Int. Conf. Acoustics, Speech, and Signal Processing (ICASSP '99)*, *4*, pp. 2079–2089. Phoenix.

Hansen, M. R. (2002). Frequency band analysis for stress detection using a Teager energy operator based feature. *Proc. Int. Conf. Spoken Language Processing (ICSLP '02)*, (pp. 2021–2024).

Hansen, S. B.-G. (2000). A comparative study of traditional and newly proposed features for recognition of speech under stress. *IEEE Transactions on Speech and Audio Processing*, *8*(4), 429–442. doi:10.1109/89.848224.

Harris, H., & Nass, C. (2011). Emotion regulation for frustrating driving contexts. In *Proceedings of CHI 2011*. Vancouver, Canada: ACM.

Harth, A., & Maynard, D. (2012). *Semantic web challenge*. Retrieved February 21, 2013, from http://challenge.semanticweb.org

Hartmann, B. (2011). *Human worker activity recognition in industrial environments*. (PhD thesis). KIT. Retrieved from http://uvka.ubka.uni-karlsruhe.de/shop/download/1000022235

Hay, S., & Harle, R. (2009). *Bluetooth tracking without discoverability*. Paper presented at the 4th International Symposium of Location and Context Awareness (LoCA'2009). New York, NY.

He, H. A., Greenberg, S., & Huang, E. M. (2010). One size does not fit all: Applying the transtheoretical model to energy feedback technology design. In *Proceedings of CHI 2010*. Atlanta, GA: ACM.

He, Z., Liu, Z., Jin, L., Zhen, L., & Huang, J. (2008). Weightlessness feature - A novel feature for single tri-axial accelerometer based activity recognition. In *Proceedings of 19th International Conference on Pattern Recognition (ICPR)*. Tampa, FL: ICPR.

Headon, R., & Curwen, R. (2002). Movement awareness for ubiquitous game control. *Personal and Ubiquitous Computing*, 6(5-6), 407–415. doi:10.1007/s007790200045.

Healey, J., & Picard, R. (2000). Smartcar: Detecting driver stress. In *Proceedings of ICPR 2000*. Barcelona, Spain: ICPR.

Healey, J., Wang, C.-C., Dopfer, A., & Yu, C.-C. (2012). M2m gossip: Why might we want cars to talk about us? In *Proceedings of AutomotiveUI '12*. Portsmouth, NH: AutomotiveUI. doi:10.1145/2390256.2390300.

Helaoui, R., Riboni, D., Niepert, M., Bettini, C., & Stuckenschmidt, H. (2012). Towards activity recognition using probabilistic description logics. In *Proceedings of AAAI Workshops*. AAAI.

Helaoui, R., Niepert, M., & Stuckenschmidt, H. (2011). Recognizing interleaved and concurrent activities using qualitative and quantitative temporal relationships. In *Proceedings of Pervasive and Mobile Computing* (pp. 660–670). IEEE. doi:10.1016/j.pmcj.2011.08.004.

Henderson, T., Kotz, D., & Abyzov, I. (2004). The changing usage of a mature campus-wide wireless network. In *Proceeding of the 10th Annual International Conference on Mobile Computing and Networking* (MobiCom'04), (pp. 187–201). New York, NY: ACM Press.

Herbst, I., Braun, A.-K., McCall, R., & Broll, W. (2008). *TimeWarp: Interactive time travel with a mobile mixed reality game*. Paper presented at the 10th International Conference on Human Computer Interaction with Mobile Devices and Services. New York, NY.

Herlocker, J. L., Konstan, J. A., & Riedl, J. (2000). *Explaining collaborative filtering recommendations*. Paper presented at the ACM Conference on Computer Supported Cooperative Work. New York, NY.

Hillard, D., Ostendorf, M., & Shriberg, E. (2003). Detection of agreement vs. disagreement in meetings: Training with unlabeled data. In *Proceedings of HLT-NAACL*. HLT-NAACL.

Hirschberg, J. S. B. (2005). Distinguishing Deceptive from Non-Deceptive Speech. *Proc. 9th European Conf. Speech Comm. and Technology (INTERSPEECH '05)*, (pp. 1833-1836).

Hobold, G. C., & Siqueira, F. (2012). *Discovery of semantic web services compositions based on SAWSDL annotations*. Paper presented at IEEE 19th International Conference on Web Services (ICWS). New York, NY.

Hoch, S., Althoff, F., McGlaun, G., & Rigoll, G. (2005). Bimodal fusion of emotional data in an automotive environment. In *Proceedings of ICASSP 2005*. ICASSP.

Hoey, J., Bertoldi, A., Poupart, P., & Mihailidis, A. (2010). Assisting persons with dementia during handwashing using a partially observable Markov decision process. In *Proceedings of the 5th International Conference on Computer Vision Systems (ICVS)*. ICVS.

Holzmann, C., & Ferscha, A. (2010). A framework for utilizing qualitative spatial relations between networked embedded systems. *Pervasive and Mobile Computing*, 6, 362–381. doi:10.1016/j.pmcj.2010.03.001.

Hong, X., Gerla, M., Pei, G., & Chiang, C. C. (1999). A group mobility model for ad hoc wireless networks. In *Proceeding of the 2nd ACM International Workshop on Modeling, Analysis, and Simulation of Wireless and Mobile Systems* (MSWiM'99). Seattle, WA: MSWiM.

Hsiao, T., & Yuan, S. (2005). Practical middleware for massively multiplayer online games. *IEEE Internet Computing*, 9(5), 47–54. doi:10.1109/MIC.2005.106.

Hsu, W., Spyropoulos, T., Psounis, K., & Helmy, A. (2007). Modeling time-variant user mobility in wireless mobile networks. In *Proceeding of the 26th IEEE International Conference on Computer Communications* (INFOCOM'07). University of Florida.

Hu, D. H., & Yang, Q. (2011). Transfer learning for activity recognition via sensor mapping. In *Proceedings of the 22nd International Joint Conference on Artificial Intelligence*. Barcelona, Spain: IEEE.

Huber, R. E. N. (1998). You beep machine–emotion in automatic speech understanding systems. *Proceedings of the Workshop on Text, Speech, and Dialog*, (pp. 223–228).

Hu, D. H., Zheng, V. W., & Yang, Q. (2011). Cross-domain activity recognition via transfer learning. *Pervasive and Mobile Computing*, 7(3), 344–358. doi:10.1016/j.pmcj.2010.11.005.

IAD. (2011). *Urban defender*. Retrieved from http://iad.zhdk.ch/en/node/157

IBM WebSphere Portal. (2013). Retrieved February 21, 2013, from http://www-01.ibm.com/software/websphere/portal/

iDorm. (2002). Retrieved 2013, from http://cswww.essex.ac.uk/iieg/idorm.htm

IEEE 802.11b/d3.0 Wireless LAN Medium Access Control (MAC) and Physical Layer (PHY) Specification. (1999). Washington, DC: IEEE.

IFTTT - If This Then That. (2013). Retrieved February 21, 2013, from https://ifttt.com

Inomata, T., Naya, F., Kuwahara, N., Hattori, F., & Kogure, K. (2009). Activity recognition from interactions with objects using dynamic bayesian network. In *Proceedings of ACM International Workshop on Context-Awareness for Self-Managing Systems (CASEMANS)*. Nara, Japan: ACM.

Inooka, H., Ohtaki, Y., Hayasaka, H., Suzuki, A., & Nagatomi, R. (2006). Development of advanced portable device for daily physical assessment. In *Proceedings of SICE-ICASE International Joint Conference*. Busan, Korea: SICE-ICASE.

Intrepidus. (2010). *NFC and RFID-enabled smartphones and mobile devices are coming*. Retrieved from http://intrepidusgroup.com/insight/2010/12/nfc-rfid-enabled-smartphones-and-mobile-devices-are-coming/

Isaacman, S., Becker, R., Cáceres, R., Kobourov, S., Martonosi, M., Rowland, J., & Varshavsky, A. (2011). Identifying important places in people's lives from cellular network data. In *Proceeding of the 9th International Conference on Pervasive Computing* (Pervasive'11). San Francisco, CA: Pervasive.

Isaacman, S., Becker, R., Cáceres, R., Kobourov, S., Martonosi, M., Rowland, J., & Varshavsky, A. (2011). Ranges of human mobility in Los Angeles and New York. In *Proceeding of the 8th IEEE Workshop on Managing Ubiquitous Communications and Services* (MUCS' 11). Seattle, WA: IEEE.

Isaacman, S., Becker, R., Cáceres, R., Kobourov, S., Rowland, J., & Varshavsky, A. (2010). A tale of two cities. In *Proceeding of the 11th Workshop on Mobile Computing Systems and Applications* (HotMobile'10). HotMobile.

Isaacman, S., Becker, R., Cáceres, R., Martonosi, M., Rowland, J., Varshavsky, A., & Willinger, W. (2012). Human mobility modeling at metropolitan scales. In *Proceeding of the 10th International Conference on Mobile Systems* (MobiSys'12). ACM.

Ishida, T. (2000). Understanding digital cities. In *Digital Cities, Technologies, Experiences, and Future Perspectives*. Berlin: Springer-Verlag. doi:10.1007/3-540-46422-0_2.

Ishida, T. (2002). Digital city Kyoto. *Communications of the ACM*, 45(7), 76–81. doi:10.1145/514236.514238.

Istrate, D., Castelli, E., Vacher, M., Besacier, L., & Serignat, J. (2006). Information extraction from sound for medical telemonitoring. *IEEE Transactions on Information Technology in Biomedicine*, 10(2), 264–274. doi:10.1109/TITB.2005.859889 PMID:16617615.

Izard, C. E. (1977). *Human emotions*. New York: Plenum Press. doi:10.1007/978-1-4899-2209-0.

Jacobi, J., Bolles, A., Grawunder, M., Nicklas, D., & Appelrath, H. J. (2010). A physical operator algebra for prioritized elements in data streams. *Computer Science-Research and Development*, 25(3), 235–246. doi:10.1007/s00450-009-0102-8.

Jaimes, A., & Sebe, N. (2007). Multimodal human-computer interaction: A survey. *Computer Vision and Image Understanding, 108*(1-2), 116–134. doi:10.1016/j.cviu.2006.10.019.

Jain, R., Lelescu, D., & Balakrishnan, M. (2005). Model T: An empirical model for user registration patterns in a campus wireless LAN. In *Proceeding of the 11ᵗʰ Annual International Conference on Mobile Computing and Networking* (MobiCom'05), (pp. 170–184). New York, NY: ACM.

James, W. (1884). What Is an Emotion? *Mind*. doi:10.1093/mind/os-IX.34.188.

Jansen, B. J., Zhang, M., Sobel, K., & Chowdury, A. (2009). *Micro-blogging as online word of mouth branding*. Paper presented at the 27th International Conference Extended Abstracts on Human Factors in Computing Systems. Boston, MA. Retrieved from http://delivery.acm.org/10.1145/1530000/1520584/p3859-jansen.pdf?ip=113.108.133.51&CFID=42910813&CFTOKEN=50591669&__acm__=1316163961_848c3027a27643d729bec83158268224

Java, A., Song, X., Finin, T., & Tseng, B. (2007). *Why we Twitter: Understanding microblogging usage and communities*. Paper presented at the 9th WebKDD and 1st SNA-KDD 2007 Workshop on Web Mining and Social Network Analysis. San Jose, CA. Retrieved from http://delivery.acm.org/10.1145/1350000/1348556/p56-java.pdf?ip=113.108.133.51&CFID=38952822&CFTOKEN=89830532&__acm__=1315551300_38027b7e271e7a280970363cfd9dda70

Jegers, K. (2004). *Usability of pervasive games*. Paper presented at the 1st International Workshop on Pervasive Gaming Applications (PerGames'2004). New York, NY.

Jegers, K. (2007). Pervasive game flow: Understanding player enjoyment in pervasive gaming. *Computers in Entertainment, 5*(1).

Jegers, K. (2009). Pervasive GameFlow: Identifying and exploring the mechanisms of player enjoyment in pervasive games. Umea, Sweden: Department of informatics, Umeå University.

Jegers, K., & Wiberg, M. (2006). Pervasive gaming in the everyday world. *IEEE Pervasive Computing / IEEE Computer Society [and] IEEE Communications Society, 5*(1), 78–85. doi:10.1109/MPRV.2006.11.

Jeon, M. (2012). A systematic approach to using music for mitigating affective effects on driving performance and safety. In *Proceedings of UbiComp 2012*. Pittsburgh, PA: UbiComp. doi:10.1145/2370216.2370455.

Jerritta, S., Murugappan, M., Nagarajan, R., & Wan, K. (2011). Physiological signals based human emotion recognition: A review. In Proceedings of Signal Processing and its Applications (CSPA), (pp. 410-415). CSPA.

Johns-Lewis, C. (1986). Prosodic differentiation of discourse modes. In *C. Johns-Lewis, Intonation in Discourse* (pp. 199–220). San Diego: College-Hill Press.

Johnson, W. F., R. N. (1986). Recognition of emotion from vocal cues. *Arch. Gen. Psych, 43*, 280–283. doi:10.1001/archpsyc.1986.01800030098011 PMID:3954549.

Johnston, E. W., & Hansen, D. L. (2005). Design lessons for smart governance infrastructures. In American Governance 3.0: Rebooting the Public Square? National Academy of Public Administration.

Johnston, E. W. (2010). Governance infrastructures in 2020. *Public Administration Review, 70*(1), 122–128. doi:10.1111/j.1540-6210.2010.02254.x.

Jones, C. M., & Jonsson, I.-M. (2005). Automatic recognition of affective cues in the speech of car drivers to allow appropriate responses. In *Proceedings of OZCHI 2005*. Canberra, Australia: ACM.

Jones, C. M., & Jonsson, I.-M. (2007). Performance analysis of acoustic emotion recognition for in-car conversational interfaces. In *Proceedings of UAHCI 2007*. Beijing, China: UAHCI.

Jones, C., & Jonsson, I.-M. (2008). Using paralinguistic cues in speech to recognise emotions in older car drivers. [LNCS]. *Proceedings of Affect and Emotion in Human-Computer Interaction, 4868*, 229–240. doi:10.1007/978-3-540-85099-1_20.

Jung, H., & Park, S. (2011). Mash-up creation using a mash-up rule language. *J. Inf. Sci. Eng.*, *27*(2), 761–775.

Kabir, M. A., Han, J., Yu, J., & Colman, A. W. (2012). SCIMS: A social context information management system for socially-aware applications. In *Proceedings of CAiSE*, (pp. 301-317). CAiSE.

Kaiser, A., Achir, N., & Boussetta, K. (2009). *Multiplayer games over wireless ad hoc networks: Energy and delay analysis.* Paper presented at the International Conference on Ultra Modern Telecommunications & Workshops (ICUMT'09). New York, NY.

Kaiser, J. (1993). Some useful properties of Teager's energy operators. *Acoustics, Speech, and Signal Processing, 1993. ICASSP-93., 1993 IEEE International Conference on*, (pp. 149-152).

Kaiser, L. (1962). Communication of affects by single vowels. *Synthese, 14*, 300–319. doi:10.1007/BF00869311.

Kao, E.-C., Liu, C.-C., Yang, T.-H., Hsieh, C.-T., & Soo, V.-W. (2009). Towards Text-based Emotion Detection A Survey and Possible Improvements. *Information Management and Engineering, 2009. ICIME '09. International Conference on*, (p. 70).

Kapadia, A., Myers, S., Wang, X., & Fox, G. (2010). Secure cloud computing with brokered trusted sensor networks. In *Proceedings of CTS*. IEEE.

Kasteren, T. L. M., Englebienne, G., & Krose, B. J. A. (2010). Transferring knowledge of activity recognition across sensor networks. In *Proceedings of the 8th International Conference on Pervasive*. IEEE.

Kawaguchi, N., Terada, T., Inoue, S., et al. (2012). HASC-2012corpus: Large scale human activity corpus and its application. In *Proceedings of International Conference on Information Processing in Sensor Networks (IPSN)*. Beijing, China: IPSN.

Kawahara, Y., Ryu, N., & Asami, T. (2009). Monitoring daily energy expenditure using a 3-axis accelerometer with a low-power microprocessor. *International Journal of Human-Computer Interaction, 1*, 145–154.

Kern, N., Schiele, B., & Schmidt, A. (2003). Multi-sensor activity context detection for wearable computing. *Lecture Notes in Computer Science, 2875*, 220–232. doi:10.1007/978-3-540-39863-9_17.

Khan, S. M., & Shah, M. (2005). Detection group activities using rigidity of formation. In *Proceedings of the 13th Annual ACM International Conference on Multimedia (MM)*. ACM.

Khan, A. M., Lee, Y., Lee, S. Y., & Kim, T. (2010). A triaxial accelerometer-based physical-activity recognition via augmented-signal features and a hierarchical recognizer. *IEEE Transactions on Information Technology in Biomedicine, 14*(6), 1166–1172. doi:10.1109/TITB.2010.2051955 PMID:20529753.

Kiefer, P., Matyas, S., & Schlieder, C. (2006). *Systematically exploring the design space of location-based games.* Paper presented at the 4th International Conference on Pervasive Computing (Pervasive'2006). New York, NY.

Kim, E., Helal, S., & Cook, D. (2010). Human activity recognition and pattern discovery. *IEEE Pervasive Computing / IEEE Computer Society [and] IEEE Communications Society, 9*(1), 48–53. doi:10.1109/MPRV.2010.7 PMID:21258659.

King, S. F., & Brown, P. (2007). Fix my street or else: using the internet to voice local public service concerns. In *Proceedings of the 1st International Conference on Theory and Practice of Electronic Governance* (ICEGOV '07). ACM.

Kiukkonen, N., Blom, J., Dousse, O., & Laurila, J. K. (2010). Towards rich mobile phone datasets: Lausanne data collection campaign. In *Proceedings of 7th ACM International Conference on Pervasive Service (ICPS)*. Berlin: ICPS.

Klusch, M. (2012). *Semantic service selection (S3) contest.* Retrieved February 21, 2013, from http://www-ags.dfki.uni-sb.de/~klusch/s3/index.html

Klusch, M., Kapahnke, P., & Zinnikus, I. (2009). SAWS-DL-MX2: A machine-learning approach for integrating semantic web service matchmaking variants. In *Proceedings of Web Services* (pp. 335–342). IEEE. doi:10.1109/ICWS.2009.76.

Knox, S., Coyle, L., & Dobson, S. (2010). Using ontologies in case-based activity recognition. In *Proceedings of FLAIRS'10*. FLAIRS.

Koenig-Ries, B., Opasjumruskit, K., Nauerz, A., & Welsch, M. (2012). *MERCURY: User centric device & service processing*. Paper presented at Mensch & Computer Workshopband (MKWI). Braunschweig, Germany.

Koike, H., Nagashima, S., Nakanishi, Y., & Sato, Y. (2004). Enhanced table: Supporting a small meeting in ubiquitous and augmented environment. In *Proceedings of 5th Pacific Rim Conference on Multimedia Information Application (PCM)*. Tokyo, Japan: PCM.

Kortuem, G., Kray, C., & Gellersen, H. (2005). *Sensing and visualizing spatial relations of mobile devices*. New York: Academic Press. doi:10.1145/1095034.1095049.

Kotz, D., & Essien, K. (2002). Analysis of a campus-wide wireless network. In *Proceedings of the 8th Annual International Conference on Mobile Computing and Networking* (MobiCom'02). ACM Press.

Kotz, D., & Essien, K. (2002). *Characterizing usage of a campus-wide wireless network* (Technical Report TR2002-423). Hanover, NH: Department of Computer Science, Dartmouth College.

Kotz, D., Henderson, T., & Abyzov, I. (2012). *CRAW-DAD trace Dartmouth*. Retrieved from http://crawdad.cs.dartmouth.edu

Kotz, D., & Henderson, T. (2005). CRAWDAD: A community resource for archiving wireless data at Dartmouth. *IEEE Pervasive Computing/IEEE Computer Society [and] IEEE Communications Society, 4*(4), 12–14. doi:10.1109/MPRV.2005.75.

Kovatsch, M., Lanter, M., & Duquennoy, S. (2012). Actinium: A RESTful runtime container for scriptable internet of things applications. In *Proceedings of the 3rd International Conference on the Internet of Things (IoT)*, (pp. 135-142). IoT.

Krahnstoever, N., Rittscher, J., Tu, P., Chean, K., & Tomlinson, T. (2005). Activity recognition using visual tracking and RFID. In *Proceedings of IEEE Workshop on Applications of Computer Vision*. Breckenridge, CO: IEEE.

Krämer, J., & Seeger, B. (2004). PIPES: A public infrastructure for processing and exploring streams. In *Proceedings of the 2004 ACM SIGMOD International Conference on Management of Data* (pp. 925–926). ACM.

Krämer, J., & Seeger, B. (2009). Semantics and implementation of continuous sliding window queries over data streams. *ACM Transactions on Database Systems, 34*(1), 1–49. doi:10.1145/1508857.1508861.

Kranz, M., & Schmidt, A. (2005). Prototyping smart objects for ubiquitous computing. In *Proceedings of the International Workshop on Smart Object Systems in Conjunction with the Seventh International Conference on Ubiquitous Computing*. ACM.

Kranz, M., Roalter, L., & Michahelles, F. (2010). Things that Twitter: Social networks and the internet of things. In *Proceedings of the What can the Internet of Things do for the Citizen (CIoT) Workshop at The Eighth International Conference on Pervasive Computing* (Pervasive 2010). IEEE.

Kranz, M., Murmann, L., & Michahelles, F. (2013). Research in the large: Challenges for large- scale mobile application research - A case study about NFC adoption using gamification via an app. store. *International Journal of Mobile Human Computer Interaction*. doi:10.4018/jmhci.2013010103.

Kranz, M., Schmidt, A., & Holleis, P. (2010). Embedded interaction: Interacting with the internet of things. *IEEE Internet Computing, 14*(2), 46–53. doi:10.1109/MIC.2009.141.

Krassing, G., Tantinger, D., Hofmann, C., Wittenberg, T., & Struck, M. (2010). User-friendly system for recognition of activities with an accelerometer. In *Proceedings of 4th International Conference on Pervasive Computing Technologies for Healthcare (PervasiveHealth)*. Munich, Germany: PervasiveHealth.

Krause, A., Horvitz, E., Kansal, A., & Zhao, F. (2008). Toward community sensing. In *Proceedings of IPSN 2008*. Washington, DC: IPSN.

Krishnan, N. C., Juillard, C., & Colbry, D. (2009). Recognition of hand movements using wearable accelerometers. *Journal of Ambient Intelligence and Smart Environments, 1*(2), 143–155.

Kung, H. Y., Lin, M. H., Hsu, C. Y., & Liu, C. N. (2005). Context-aware emergency remedy system based on pervasive computing. In *Proceedings of Embedded and Ubiquitous Computing* (pp. 775–784). Academic Press. doi:10.1007/11596356_77.

Kusznir, J., & Cook, D. J. (2010). Designing lightweight software architectures for smart environments. In *Proceedings of the 6th International Conference on Intelligent Environments* (pp. 220-224). IEEE.

Kwak, H., Lee, C., Park, H., & Moon, S. (2010). *What is Twitter, a social network or a news media?* Paper presented at the 19th International Conference on World Wide Web. Raleigh, NC. Retrieved from http://delivery.acm.org/10.1145/1780000/1772751/p591-kwak.pdf?ip=113.108.133.51&CFID=38952822&CFTOKEN=89830532&__acm__=1315549530_23d2d00b7553aebef4b6f8a5bb558ca4

Kwapisz, J. R., Weiss, G. M., & Moore, S. A. (2010). Activity recognition using cell phone accelerometers. *ACM SIGKDD Explorations Newsletter*, *12*(2), 74–82. doi:10.1145/1964897.1964918.

Ladd, D. R. K. S. (1986). An integrated approach to studying intonation and attitude. In C. Johns-Lewis, Intonation in Discourse (pp. 125–138). San Diego: College-Hill Press.

Lakshman, A., & Malik, P. (2009). Cassandra: A structured storage system on a P2P network. In *Proceedings of the 21st Annual Symposium on Parallelism in Algorithms and Architectures*. ACM.

Lane, N. D., Xu, Y., Lu, H., Hu, S., Choudhury, T., Campbell, A. T., & Zhao, F. (2011). Enabling large-scale human activity inference on smartphones using community similarity networks (CSN). In *Proceedings of the 13th International Conference on Ubiquitous Computing (Ubicomp)*. Beijing, China: UbiComp.

Lankoski, P., Heliö, S., Nummela, J., Lahti, J., Mäyrä, F., & Ermi, L. (2004). *A case study in pervasive game design: The songs of north*. Paper presented at the Third Nordic Conference on Human-Computer Interaction. Tampere, Finland.

Lassila, O., & Swick, R. R. (1998). *Resource description framework (RDF) model and syntax specification*. World Wide Web Consortium.

Lavier, J. D. (1968). Voice Quality and Indexical Information. *Department of Phonetics and Linguistics. University of Edinburgh*, *3*(1), 43–54.

Lavín-Mera, P., Torrente, J., Moreno-Ger, P., & Fernández-Manjón, B. (2009). *Mobile game development for multiple devices in education*. Paper presented at the 4th International Conference on Interactive Mobile and Computer-Aided Learning. New York, NY.

Lawler, E. L. (1972). A procedure for computing the K best solutions to discrete optimization problems and its application to the shortest path problem. *Management Science*, *18*, 401–405. doi:10.1287/mnsc.18.7.401.

Lawler, E. L. (2001). *Combinatorial optimization: Networks and matroids*. New York: Dover Publications.

Leckie, G. J., & Hopkins, J. (2002). The public place of central libraries: Findings from Toronto and Vancouver. *The Library Quarterly*, *72*(3), 326–372.

Lee, M., Khan, A. M., Kim, J., Cho, Y. S., & Kim, T. S. (2010). A single tri-axial accelerometer-based real-time personal life log system capable of activity classification and exercise information generation. In *Proceedings of 2010 Annual International Conference of the IEEE Engineering in Medicine and Biology Society*. IEEE.

Lee, C. M., & Narayanan, S. S. (2005). Toward detecting emotions in spoken dialogs. *IEEE Transactions on Speech and Audio Processing*, *13*(2), 293–303. doi:10.1109/TSA.2004.838534.

Lee, R., Wakamiya, S., & Sumiya, K. (2011). Discovery of unusual regional social activities using geo-tagged microblogs. *World Wide Web (Bussum)*, *14*(4), 321–349. doi:10.1007/s11280-011-0120-x.

Leguay, J., Friedman, T., & Conan, V. (2005). *Evaluating mobility pattern space routing for DTNs*. Universite Pierre et Marie Curie, Laboratorie. Retrieved from http://arxiv.org/PS_cache/cs/pdf/0511/0511102v1.pdf

Lehmann, O., Bauer, M., Becker, C., & Nicklas, D. (2004). From home to world - Supporting context-aware applications through world models. In *Proceedings of the Second IEEE International Conference on Pervasive Computing and Communications*. IEEE.

Lelescu, D., Kozat, U. C., Jain, R., & Balakrishnan, M. (2006). Model T++: An empirical joint space-time registration model. In *Proceeding of the 7th ACM International Symposium on Mobile Ad Hoc Networking and Computing* (MobiHoc'06), (pp. 61–72). New York, NY: ACM.

Li, B., Zhang, D., Sun, L., Chen, C., Li, S., Qi, G., & Yang, Q. (2011). Hunting or waiting? Discovering passenger-finding strategies from a large-scale real-world taxi dataset. In *Proceedings of the IEEE International Conference on Pervasive Computing and Communications Workshops* (PERCOM Workshops). IEEE.

Li, M., Wang, H., Guo, B., & Yu, Z. (2012). *Extraction of human social behavior from mobile phone sensing*. Paper presented in the meeting of International Conference on Active Media Technology (AMT-12). Macau.

Li, N., & Chen, G. (2009). *Analysis of a location-based social network*. Paper presented at International Conference on Computational Science and Engineering. New York, NY. doi: 10.1109/CSE.2009.98

Liang, Y., Zhou, X., Guo, B., & Yu, Z. (2012). *Understanding the regularity and variability of human mobility from geo-trajectory*. Paper presented at the Meeting of the 2012 IEEE/WIC/ACM International Conference on Web Intelligence (WI-12). Macau.

Liang, Y., Zhou, X., Yu, Z., Guo, B., & Yang, Y. (2012). Energy efficient activity recognition based on low resolution accelerometer in smart phones. In *Proceedings of 7th International Conference on Grid and Pervasive Computing (GPC)*. Hong Kong: GPC.

Liang, Y., Zhou, X., Yu, Z., Wang, H., & Guo, B. (2012). A context-aware multimedia service scheduling framework in smart homes. *EURASIP Journal on Wireless Communications and Networking, 67.* doi: doi:10.1186/1687-1499-2012-67.

Li, J., Tufte, K., Shkapenyuk, V., Papadimos, V., Johnson, T., & Maier, D. (2008). Out-of-order processing: A new architecture for high-performance stream systems. *Proceedings of the VLDB Endowment, 1*(1), 274–288.

Lindley, C. A. (2004). *Trans-reality gaming*. Paper presented at the Annual International Workshop in Computer Game Design and Technology. New York, NY.

Lindley, C. A., & Eladhari, M. (2005). *Narrative structure in trans-reality role-playing games: Integrating story construction from live action, table top and computer-based role-playing games*. Paper presented at the Digital Games Research Conference (DiGRA'2005). New York, NY.

Lin, W., Sun, M., Poovendran, R., & Zhang, Z. (2010). Group event detection with a varying number of group members for video surveillance. *IEEE Transactions on Circuits and Systems for Video Technology, 20*(8), 1057–1067. doi:10.1109/TCSVT.2010.2057013.

Litman, K. F.-R. (2004). Predicting Emotion in Spoken Dialogue from Multiple Knowledge Sources. *Proc. Human Language Technology Conf. North Am. Chapter of the Assoc. Computational Linguistics (HLT/NAACL)*.

Liu, L., Biderman, A., & Ratti, C. (2009). *Urban mobility landscape: Real time monitoring of urban mobility patterns*. Paper presented at the 11th International Conference on Computers in Urban Planning and Urban Management. Hong Kong.

Liu, N. N., & Yang, Q. (2008). *EigenRank: A ranking-oriented approach to collaborative filtering*. Paper presented at the 31st Annual International ACM SIGIR Conference on Research and Development in Information Retrieval. Singapore, Singapore. Retrieved from http://delivery.acm.org/10.1145/1400000/1390351/p83-liu.pdf?ip=113.108.133.48&acc=ACTIVE%20SERVICE&CFID=71306793&CFTOKEN=37355947&__acm__=1322880131_a2e706ca2aeadef579437ac-5c5a68771

Liu, X., Hui, Y., Sun, W., & Liang, H. (2007). Towards service composition based on mashup. In *Proceedings of IEEE SCW*. IEEE.

Liu, Z., Yu, W., Chen, W., Wang, S., & Wu, F. (2010). *Short text feature selection for micro-blog mining*. Paper presented at the 2010 International Conference on Computational Intelligence and Software Engineering (CiSE). New York, NY.

Liu, B. (2012). *Sentiment analysis and opinion mining*. New York: Morgan & Claypool Publishers.

Li, X., Cao, H., Chen, E., & Tian, J. (2012). Learning to infer the status of heavy-duty sensors for energy efficient context-sensing. *ACM Transactions on Intelligent Systems and Technology, 3*(2). doi:10.1145/2089094.2089111.

Loke, S. (2006). *Context-aware pervasive systems: Architectures for a new breed of applications.* Auerbach Publications. doi:10.1201/9781420013498.

López-de-Ipiña, D., Almeida, A., Aguilera, U., Larizgoitia, I., Laiseca, X., Orduña, P., et al. (2008). Dynamic discovery and semantic reasoning for next generation intelligent environments. In *Proceedings of the 4th International Conference on Intelligent Environments* (pp. 1-10). IET.

Lopez-Nores, M., Garcia-Duque, J., Pazos-Arias, J. J., Blanco-Fernández, Y., & Diaz-Redondo, R. P. (2008). Qualitative assessment of approaches to coordinate activities of mobile hosts in ad hoc networks. *IEEE Communications Magazine, 46*(12). doi:10.1109/MCOM.2008.4689216.

Lou, Y., Zhang, C., Zheng, Y., Xie, X., Wang, W., & Huang, Y. (2009). Map-matching for low-sampling-rate GPS trajectories. In *Proceedings of the 17th ACM SIGSPATIAL International Conference on Advances in Geographic Information Systems.* ACM.

Lövheim, H. (2012, Feb). A new three-dimensional model for emotions and monoamine neurotransmitters. *Medical Hypotheses, Elsevier, 78*(2), 341–348. doi:10.1016/j.mehy.2011.11.016 PMID:22153577.

Lu, Z., Wen, Y., & Cao, G. (2013). *Community detection in weighted networks: Algorithms and applications.* Paper presented at the Meeting of PerCom'13. New York, NY.

Lugger, M. B. Y. (2006). Robust estimation of voice quality parameters under real world disturbances. *Proc. IEEE ICASSP.*

Lukowicz, P., Ward, J. A., Junker, H., Stager, M., Troster, G., Atrash, A., & Starner, T. (2004). Recognizing workshop activity using body worn microphone and accelerometers. In *Proceedings of Pervasive Computing(Pervasive).* Vienna, Austria: IEEE. doi:10.1007/978-3-540-24646-6_2.

Luo, Q. (2009). Advancing computing. In *Communication, Control and Management.* Berlin: Springer.

Lyons, M., Akamatsu, S., Kamachi, M., & Gyoba, J. (1998). Coding facial expressions with gabor wavelets. In *Proceedings of FG 1998.* Nara, Japan: FG.

MacQueen, J., et al. (1967). Some methods for classification and analysis of multivariate observations. In *Proceedings of the Fifth Berkeley Symposium on Mathematical Statistics and Probability* (Vol. 1, p. 14). Berkeley, CA: IEEE.

Magdics, I. F. (1963). Emotional patterns in intonation and music. Z. *Phonetik, 16*, 293–326.

Magerkurth, C., Cheok, A. D., Mandryk, R. L., & Nilsen, T. (2005). Pervasive games: Bringing computer entertainment back to the real world. *Computers in Entertainment, 3*(3), 1–19. doi:10.1145/1077246.1077257.

Magnani, M., Montesi, D., & Rossi, L. (2010). *Friendfeed breaking news: Death of a public figure.* Paper presented at the IEEE Second International Conference on Social Computing (SocialCom). New York, NY.

Maleshkova, M., Kopeck, J., & Pedrinaci, C. (2009). Adapting SAWSDL for semantic annotations of RESTful services. In *Proceedings of the Confederated International Workshops and Posters on On the Move to Meaningful Internet Systems,* (pp. 917-926). Berlin: Springer.

Mannini, A., & Sabatini, A. M. (2010). Machine learning methods for classifying human physical activity from on-body accelerometers. *Sensors (Basel, Switzerland), 10*(2), 1154–1175. doi:10.3390/s100201154 PMID:22205862.

Martin, D., Paolucci, M., & Wagner, M. (2007). Bringing semantic annotations to web services: OWL-S from the SAWSDL perspective. In *Proceedings of the 6th International the Semantic Web and 2nd Asian Conference on Asian Semantic Web Conference,* (pp. 340-352). Berlin: Springer.

Martin, D., Paolucci, M., Mcilraith, S., Burstein, M., Mcdermott, D., Mcguinness, D., et al. (2004). Bringing semantics to web services: The OWL-S approach. In *Proceedings of the First International Workshop on Semantic Web Services and Web Process Composition (SWSWPC 2004),* (pp. 26-42). Berlin: Springer.

Martin, S., Tawari, A., Murphy-Chutorian, E., Cheng, S. Y., & Trivedi, M. (2012). On the design and evaluation of robust head pose for visual user interfaces: Algorithms, databases, and comparisons. In *Proceedings of AutomotiveUI 2012.* Portsmouth, NH: AutomotiveUI. doi:10.1145/2390256.2390281.

Mathias, S. (2006). *Low-power sound-based user activity recognition.* (PhD thesis). Swiss Federal Institute of Technology, Zurich, Switzerland. Retrieved from http://e-collection.library.ethz.ch/eserv/eth:29348/eth-29348-02.pdf

Mathie, M. J., Celler, B. G., Lovell, N. H., & Coster, A. C. (2004). Classification of basic daily movements using a triaxial accelerometer. *Medical & Biological Engineering & Computing, 42*(5), 679–687. doi:10.1007/BF02347551 PMID:15503970.

Mattern, F., & Floerkemeier, C. (2010). From the internet of computers to the internet of things. *Lecture Notes in Computer Science, 6462. On{X} – Automate Your Life.* (2012). Retrieved February 21, 2013, from https://www.onx.ms

MavHome. (2003). Retrieved 2013, from http://ailab.wsu.edu/mavhome

McCallum, A. K. (2002). *MALLET: A machine learning for language toolkit.* Retrieved from http://mallet.cs.umass.edu.

McCallum, A., Wang, X., & Corrada-Emmanuel, A. (2007). Topic and role discovery in social networks with experiments on Enron and academic email. *Journal of Artificial Intelligence Research, 30*(1), 249–272.

McGilloway, S. R. C.-C. (2000). Approaching automatic recognition of emotion from voice: A rough benchmark. *Proc. ISCA Workshop Speech Emotion,* (pp. 207-212).

McGregor, A., & Bormann, C. (2012). *Constrained RESTful environments (CoRE) (Tech. rep.). Internet Engineering Task Force.* IETF.

McGregor, A., & Bormann, C. (2012). *IPv6 over low power wireless personal area networks (Tech. rep.). Internet Engineering Task Force.* IETF.

McRoberts, M. S. (2003). Babyears: A recognition system for affective vocalizations. *Speech Communication, 39,* 367–384. doi:10.1016/S0167-6393(02)00049-3.

Mermelstein, S. D. (1980). Comparison of Parametric Representations of Monosyllabic Word Recognition in Continuously Spoken Sentences. *IEEE Transactions on Acoustics, Speech, and Signal Processing, 28*(4), 357–366. doi:10.1109/TASSP.1980.1163420.

Meschtscherjakov, A., Wilfinger, D., Scherndl, T., & Tscheligi, M. (2009). Acceptance of future persuasive in-car interfaces towards a more economic driving behaviour. In *Proceedings of AutomotiveUI '09.* Essen, Germany: AutomotiveUI. doi:10.1145/1620509.1620526.

Michahelles, F., Kranz, M., & Mandl, S. (2012). *Social networks for people and things (SoNePT).* Retrieved from http://www.theinternetofthings.eu/social-networks-people-and-things-sonept

Michele, C., Fosca, G., & Dino, P. (2011). A classification for community discovery methods in complex networks. *Journal of Statistical Analysis and Data Mining, 4*(5), 512–546. doi:10.1002/sam.10133.

Mihailidis, A., Boger, J. N., Craig, T., & Hoey, J. (2008). The COACH prompting system to assist older adults with dementia through handwashing: An efficacy study. *BMC Geriatrics, 8*(28). doi: doi:10.1186/1471-2318-8-28 PMID:18992135.

Milborrow, S., & Nicolls, F. (2008). Locating facial features with an extended active shape model. In *Proceedings of ECCV 2008.* Marseille, France: ECCV.

Miller, W. R., & Rollnick, S. P. (2002). *Motivational interviewing: Preparing people for change.* New York, NY: The Guilford Press.

Miluzzo, E., Cornelius, C. T., Ramaswamy, A., Choudhury, T., Liu, Z., & Campbell, A. T. (2010). *Darwin phones: The evolution of sensing and inference on mobile phones.* Paper presented at the Meeting of MobiSys '10. San Francisco, CA.

Miluzzo, E., Lane, N. D., Fodor, K., Peterson, R., Lu, H., & Musolesi, M. et al. (2008). Sensing meets mobile social networks: The design, implementation and evaluation of the cenceme application. In *Proceedings of Sensys 2008.* Raleigh, NC: Sensys. doi:10.1145/1460412.1460445.

Mitrevska, M., Castronovo, S., Mahr, A., & Müller, C. (2012). Physical and spiritual proximity: Linking Car2x communication with online social networks. In *Proceedings of AutomotiveUI '12.* Portsmouth, NH: AutomotiveUI. doi:10.1145/2390256.2390297.

Mizuno, H., Nagai, H., Sasaki, K., Suginoto, C., Khalil, K., & Tatsuta, S. (2007). Wearable sensor system for human behavior recognition. In *Proceedings of 4th International Conference on Solid-State Sensors, Actuators and Microsystems*. Lyon, France: IEEE.

Moataz El Ayadi, M. S. (2011, March). Survey on speech emotion recognition: Features, classification schemes, and databases. *Pattern Recognition, 44*(3), 572–587. doi:10.1016/j.patcog.2010.09.020.

Moeslund, T. B., Hilton, A., & Kruger, V. (2006). A survey of advances in vision-based human motion capture and analysis. *Computer Vision and Image Understanding, 104*(2), 90–126. doi:10.1016/j.cviu.2006.08.002.

Mokbel, M. F., & Aref, W. G. (2008). SOLE: Scalable on-line execution of continuous queries on spatio-temporal data streams. *The VLDB Journal, 17*(5), 971–995. doi:10.1007/s00778-007-0046-1.

Möller, A., Michahelles, F., Diewald, S., Roalter, L., & Kranz, M. (2012). Update behavior in app. markets and security implications: A case study in Google play. In *Proceedings of the 3rd International Workshop on Research in the Large*. ACM.

Montola, M. (2005). *Exploring the edge of the magic circle: Defining pervasive games*. Paper presented at the Digital Arts and Culture (DAC'2005). New York, NY.

Montola, M., Stenros, J., & Waern, A. (2009). *Pervasive games: Theory and design*. San Francisco, CA: Morgan Kaufmann Publishers Inc..

Morbidoni, C., Le Phuoc, D., Polleres, A., Samwald, M., & Tummarello, G. (2008). Previewing semantic web pipes. In *Proceedings of the 5th European Semantic Web Conference on the Semantic Web: Research and Applications* (ESWC'08). Berlin: Springer-Verlag.

Morency, C., Trépanier, M., & Agard, B. (2007). Measuring transit use variability with smart-card data. *Transport Policy, 14*(3), 193-203. doi: 10.1.1.156.2090

Morrison, D., R. W. (2007). Ensemble methods for spoken emotion recognition in call-centres. *Speech Communication, 49*(2), 98–112. doi:10.1016/j.specom.2006.11.004.

Mun, M., Reddy, S., Shilton, K., Yau, N., Burke, J., & Estrin, D. … Boda, P. (2009). *PEIR: The personal environmental impact report as a platform for participatory sensing systems research*. Paper presented at the Meeting of MobiSys. Krakow, Poland.

Musolesi, M., & Mascolo, C. (2006). A community-based mobility model for ad hoc network research. In *Proceeding of the 2nd International Workshop on Multi-Hop Ad Hoc Networks: From Theory to Reality* (RESLMAN'06). New York, NY: ACM.

Musolesi, M., Hailes, S., & Mascolo, C. (2005). Social networks-based ad hoc mobility models. In *Proceeding of 3rd UK-UbiNet Workshop: Designing, Evaluating and Using Ubiquitous Computing Systems*. Bath, UK: University of Bath.

Musolesi, M., & Mascolo, C. (2007). Designing mobility models based on social network theory. *ACM SIGMOBILE Mobile Computing and Communications Review Newsletter, 11*(3), 59–70. doi:10.1145/1317425.1317433.

Musolesi, M., & Mascolo, C. (2009). Mobility models for systems evaluation. In *Middleware for Network Eccentric and Mobile Applications*. Berlin: Springer. doi:10.1007/978-3-540-89707-1_3.

Musto, A., Stein, K., & Eisenkolb, A. et al. (2000). From motion observation to qualitative motion representation. *Spatial Cognition, 2*, 115–126. doi:10.1007/3-540-45460-8_9.

Nadeu, J. H. (1997). Linear prediction of the one-sided autocorrelation sequence for noisy speech recognition. *IEEE Transactions on Speech and Audio Processing, 5*(1), 80–84. doi:10.1109/89.554273.

Nakashima, H., Aghajan, H., & Augusto, J. C. (2009). *Handbook of ambient intelligence and smart environments*. Berlin: Springer.

Nakatsu, R. N. T. (1999). Emotion recognition and its application to computer agents with spontaneous interactive capabilities. *Proceedings IEEE workshop on multimedia signal processing*, (pp. 439–444).

Nasar, J., Hecht, P., & Wener, R. (2008). Mobile telephones, distracted attention, and pedestrian safety. *Accident; Analysis and Prevention, 40*(1), 69–75. doi:10.1016/j.aap.2007.04.005 PMID:18215534.

Nass, C., Jonsson, I.-M., Harris, H., Reaves, B., Endo, J., Brave, S., et al. (2005). Improving automotive safety by pairing driver emotion and car voice emotion. In *Proceedings of CHI EA 2005*. Portland, OR: ACM.

Nathan, E., & Alex, P. (2005). Social serendipity: mobilizing social software. *IEEE Pervasive Computing / IEEE Computer Society [and] IEEE Communications Society*, *4*(2), 28–34. doi:10.1109/MPRV.2005.37.

Nathan, E., Alex, P., & David, L. (2009). Inferring social network structure using mobile phone data. *Proceedings of the National Academy of Sciences of the United States of America*, *106*(36), 15274–15278. doi:10.1073/pnas.0900282106 PMID:19706491.

Nehme, R. V., Rundensteiner, E. A., & Bertino, E. (2008). A security punctuation framework for enforcing access control on streaming data. *Structure (London, England)*, 406–415. Retrieved from http://www.computer.org/portal/web/csdl/doi/10.1109/ICDE.2008.4497449.

Neil, M. F., Derek, A. T. C., Christophe, F., James, C. C., Philip, C. C., & Donald, S. B. (2006). Strategies for mitigating an influenza pandemic. *Nature*, *442*(7101), 448–452. doi:10.1038/nature04795 PMID:16642006.

Newman, M. E. J., & Girvan, M. (2004). Finding and evaluating community structure in networks. *Physical Review E: Statistical, Nonlinear, and Soft Matter Physics*, *69*(26), 113–127. doi:doi:10.1103/PhysRevE.69.026113.

Ngan, L. D., Kirchberg, M., & Kanagasabai, R. (2010). *Review of semantic web service discovery methods*. Paper presented at IEEE 6th World Congress on Services (SERVICES-1). New York, NY.

Nguyen, N. P., Dinh, T. N., Tokala, S., & Thai, M. T. (2011). *Overlapping communities in dynamic networks: Their detection and mobile applications*. Paper presented at the Meeting of Mobile Computing and Networking. Las Vegas, NV.

Nguyen, T. A., & Aiello, M. (2012). Energy intelligent buildings based on user activity: A survey. *Energy and Buildings*.

Nicholson, J., & Noble, B. D. (2008). *Bread crumbs: Forecasting mobile connectivity*. Paper presented at the Meeting of Mobile Computing and Networking. San Francisco, CA.

Ni, H., Abdulrazak, B., Zhang, D., Wu, S., Yu, Z., Zhou, X., & Wang, S. (2012). Towards non-intrusive sleep pattern recognition in elder assistive environment. *Journal of Ambient Intelligence and Humanized Computing*, *3*(2), 167–175. doi:10.1007/s12652-011-0082-y.

Ning, H., Xu, W., Chi, Y., Gong, Y., & Huang, T. (2007). *Incremental spectral clustering with application to monitoring of evolving blog communities*. Paper presented in the Meeting of SIAM International Conference on Data Mining. Minneapolis, MN.

Nogueiras, A. A. M. (2001). Speech Emotion Recognition Using Hidden Markov Models. EUROSPEECH-2001, (pp. 2679-2682).

Noulas, A., Scellato, S., Lambiotte, R., Pontil, M., & Mascolo, C. (2012). A tale of many cities: Universal patterns in human urban mobility. *PLoS ONE*. Retrieved from http://www.plosone.org/article/info%3Adoi%2F10.1371%2Fjournal.pone.0037027

Noulas, A., Scellato, S., Mascolo, C., & Pontil, M. (2011). *Exploiting semantic annotations for clustering geographic areas and users in location-based social networks*. Paper presented at ICWSM. New York, NY.

Nwe, T., S. F. (2003). Speech emotion recognition using hidden Markov models. *Speech Communication*, *41*, 603–623. doi:10.1016/S0167-6393(03)00099-2.

O'Toole, A. J. (2005). A Video Database of Moving Faces and People. *IEEE Transactions on Pattern Analysis and Machine Intelligence*, *27*(5), 812–816. doi:10.1109/TPAMI.2005.90 PMID:15875802.

OGC. (n.d.). Retrieved from http://www.opengeospatial.org/

Okazaki, M., & Matsuo, Y. (2010). *Semantic Twitter: Analyzing tweets for real-time event notification*. Paper presented at the 2008/2009 International Conference on Social Software: Recent Trends and Developments in Social Software. Cork, Ireland.

Opasjumruskit, K., Exposito, J., Koenig-Ries, B., Nauerz, A., & Welsch, M. (2012) *MERCURY: User centric device and service processing – Demo paper*. Paper presented at 19th Intl. Workshop on Personalization and Recommendation on the Web and Beyond, Mensch & Computer 2012. Konstanz, Germany.

Orman, G. K., & Labatut, V. (2009). A comparison of community detection algorithms on artificial networks. *Lecture Notes in Artificial Intelligence, 5808*, 242–256. doi: doi:10.1007/978-3-642-04747-3_20.

Ormrod, J. E. (2010). *Educational psychology* (7th ed.). Upper Saddle River, NJ: Pearson.

Ovidiu, V., Harrison, M., Vogt, H., Kalaboukas, K., Tomasella, M., & Wouters, K. …Haller, S. (2009). Internet of things: Strategic research roadmap. *European Research Cluster: The European Research Cluster on the Internet of Things (IoT)*. Retrieved from http://www.internet-of-things-research.eu/pdf/IoT_Cluster_Strategic_Research_Agenda_2011.pdf

Papadias, D., & Kavouras, M. (1994). *Acquiring, representing and processing spatial relations*. New York: Academic Press.

Pappis, C. P., & Siettos, C. I. (2005). Fuzzy reasoning. In E. K. Burke, & G. Kendall (Eds.), *Search Methodologies* (pp. 437–474). Springer. doi:10.1007/0-387-28356-0_15.

Paraimpu - The Web of Things is More Than Things in the Web. (2012). Retrieved February 21, 2013, from http://paraimpu.crs4.it/

Parnes, P., Synnes, K., & Schefström, D. (1999). Real-time control and management of distributed applications using IP-multicast. In *Proceedings of Integrated Network Management, Distributed Management for the Networked Millennium*. IEEE. doi:10.1109/INM.1999.770730.

Parrott, W. (2001). *Emotions in Social Psychology*. Psychology Press.

Patroumpas, K., & Sellis, T. (2004). Managing trajectories of moving objects as data streams. In J. Sander & M. A. Nascimento (Eds.), *Proceedings of the Second Workshop on Spatio-Temporal Database Management*. Toronto, Canada: IEEE.

Patterson, D. J., Fox, D., Kautz, H., & Philipose, M. (2005). Fine grained activity recognition by aggregating abstract object usage. In *Proceedings of the 9th International Symposium on Wearable Computers (ISWC)*. Osaka, Japan: ISWC.

Patterson, D. J., Fox, D., Kautz, H., & Philipose, M. (2005). Fine-grained activity recognition by aggregating abstract object usage.[ISWC.]. *Proceedings of ISWC, 05*, 44–51.

Paulos, E., Honicky, R., & Hooker, B. (2009). Citizen science: Enabling participatory urbanism. In M. Foth (Ed.), *Handbook of Research on Urban Informatics: The Practice and Promise of the Real-Time City*. Hershey, PA: IGI Global.

Peitz, J. (2006). Game design document - Insectopia. *Integrated Project on Pervasive Gaming, Deliverable D9.8B*.

Peitz, J., Saarenpää, H., & Björk, S. (2007). *Insectopia: Exploring pervasive games through technology already pervasively available*. Paper presented at the International Conference on Advances in Computer Entertainment Technology. Salzburg, Austria.

Peitz, J., & Björk, S. (2007). INSECTOPIA using the real world as a game resource. In *Space Time Play* (pp. 294–295). Basel: Birkhäuser.

Pelleg, D., & Moore, A. (2000). X-means: Extending k-means with efficient estimation of the number of clusters. Paper presented at ICML 2000. New York, NY.

Pereira, C. (2000,). Dimensions of emotional meaning in speech. *Proceedings of the ISCA ITRW on Speech and Emotion*, (pp. 25–28). Newcastle, Belfast.

Perianu, M., Lombriser, C., Amft, O., Havinga, P., & Troster, G. (2008). Distributed activity recognition with fuzzy-enabled wireless sensor networks. In *Proceedings of the 4th IEEE International Conference on Distributed Computing in Sensor Systems (DCOSS)*. Santorini Island, Greece: DCOSS.

Petrushin, V. A. (2000). Emotion recognition in speech signal: Experimental study, development, and application. *Proceedings of 6th international conference on spoken language processing (ICSLP '00)*.

Phelan, O., McCarthy, K., & Smyth, B. (2009). *Using Twitter to recommend real-time topical news*. Paper presented at the Third ACM Conference on Recommender Systems. New York, NY. Retrieved from http://delivery.acm.org/10.1145/1640000/1639794/p385-phelan.pdf?ip=113.108.133.51&CFID=42910813&CFTOKEN=50591669&__acm__=1316163914_d2fb-c21a709a81ff8ad85e0ea37d5494

Phelan, O., McCarthy, K., Bennett, M., & Smyth, B. (2011). *On using the real-time web for news recommendation &#38, discovery*. Paper presented at the 20th International Conference Companion on World Wide Web. Hyderabad, India. Retrieved from http://delivery.acm.org/10.1145/1970000/1963245/p103-phelan.pdf?ip=113.108.133.48&acc=ACTIVE%20SERVICE&CFID=55603221&CFTOKEN=33354824&__acm__=1322533158_61a344d4e4c752674fbe5b9f6139bfc6

Phelan, O., McCarthy, K., Bennett, M., & Smyth, B. (2011). *Terms of a feather: Content-based news recommendation and discovery using Twitter*. Paper presented at the 33rd European Conference on Advances in Information Retrieval. Dublin, Ireland.

Philipose, M., Fishkin, K. P., Perkowitz, M., Patterson, D. J., Fox, D., Kautz, H., & Hahnel, D. (2004). Inferring activities from interactions with objects. *IEEE Pervasive Computing / IEEE Computer Society [and] IEEE Communications Society, 3*(4), 50–57. doi:10.1109/MPRV.2004.7.

Phithakkitnukoon, S., Veloso, M., Bento, C., Biderman, A., & Ratti, C. (2010). Taxi-aware map: Identifying and predicting vacant taxis in the city. In *Proceedings of Ambient Intelligence: First International Joint Conference*. IEEE.

Phuoc, D. L., & Hauswirth, M. (2009). Linked open data in sensor data mashups. In *Proceedings of the 2nd International Workshop on Semantic Sensor Networks (SSN09) in Conjunction with ISWC 2009*, (pp. 1-16). ISWC.

PhysicalComp. (2009). *Physical computing: Urban defender*. Retrieved from http://iad.projects.zhdk.ch/physicalcomputing/seminare/embodied-interaction-hs-2009/projektgruppen/nino-dondi-philipp/

Picard, R. W. (2003). Affective computing: Challenges. *International Journal of Human-Computer Studies, 59*(1), 55–64. doi:10.1016/S1071-5819(03)00052-1.

Piccardi, H. G. (2006). A Bimodal Face and Body Gesture Database for Automatic Analysis of Human Nonverbal Affective Behavior. *Proc. 18th Int'l Conf. Pattern Recognition (ICPR '06)*, (pp. 1148-1153).

Pieraccini, C. L. (2002). Combining acoustic and language information for emotion recognition. *Proceedings of the ICSLP, 02*, 873–876.

PK. (2011). *Parallel kingdom*. Retrieved from http://www.parallelkingdom.com

Plutchik, R. (2001). The nature of emotions (Vol. 89, No. 4. ed.). American Scientist.

PM. (2011). *Pac Manhattan*. Retrieved from http://www.pacmanhattan.com/about.php

Pollack, M. E. (2005). Intelligent technology for an aging population: The use of AI to assist elders with cognitive impairment. *AI Magazine, 26*(2), 9–24.

Poolsappasit, N., Kumar, V., Madria, S., & Chellappan, S. (2011). Challenges in secure sensor-cloud computing. In *Proceedings of the 8th VLDB International Conference on Secure Data Management, SDM'11*. Springer-Verlag.

Preuveneers, D., & Novais, P. (2012). A survey of software engineering best practices for the development of smart applications in ambient intelligence. *Journal of Ambient Intelligence and Smart Environments, 4*(3), 149–162.

Prochaska, J. O., & Velicer, W. F. (1997). The transtheoretical model of health behavior change. *American Journal of Health Promotion, 12*(1), 38–48. doi:10.4278/0890-1171-12.1.38 PMID:10170434.

Pronovost, G. F. (1939). An experimental study of the pitch characteristics of the voice during the expression of emotion. *Speech Monograph, 6*, 87–104. doi:10.1080/03637753909374863.

Pullar, D., & Egenhofer, M. (1988). *Towards formal definitions of topological relations among spatial objects*. New York: Academic Press.

Qi, G., Li, X., Li, S., Pan, G., Wang, Z., & Zhang, D. (2011). Measuring social functions of city regions from large-scale taxi behaviors. In *Proceedings of the 9th IEEE International Conference on Pervasive Computing and Communications*. IEEE.

Qin, Z., Xin, M., & Niu, Z. (2010). *A content tendency judgment algorithm for micro-blog platform*. Paper presented at the 2010 IEEE International Conference on Intelligent Computing and Intelligent Systems (ICIS). New York, NY.

Rakotonirainy, A., Feller, F., & Haworth, N. (2009). In-vehicle avatars to elicit social response and change driving behaviour. *International Journal of Technology and Human Interaction*, 5(4), 80–104. doi:10.4018/jthi.2009062505.

Rana, J., Kristiansson, J., & Synnes, K. (2010). Enriching and simplifying communication by social prioritization. In *Proceedings of ASONAM 20110, the International Conference on Advances in Social Network Analysis and Mining*. ASONAM.

Rana, J., Kristiansson, J., & Synnes, K. (2010). Modeling unified interaction for communication service integration. In *Proceedings of UBICOMM 2010, The Fourth International Conference on Mobile Ubiquitous Computing, Systems, Services and Technologies*. IARIA.

Rana, J., Kristiansson, J., & Synnes, K. (2012). Supporting ubiquitous interaction in dynamic shared spaces through automatic group formation based on social context. In *Proceedings of SCI 2012, the ASE International Conference on Social Informatics*. IEEE.

Rana, J., Kristiansson, J., & Synnes, K. (2012). Dynamic media distribution in ad-hoc social networks. In *Proceedings of the 2nd International Conference on Social Computing and its Applications* (SCA2012). IEEE.

Rana, J., Kristiansson, J., Hallberg, J., & Synnes, K. (2009). An architecture for mobile social networking applications. In *Proceedings of the First International Conference on Computational Intelligence, Modelling and Simulation* (CSSim 2009). IEEE.

Rana, J., Kristiansson, J., Hallberg, J., & Synnes, K. (2009). Challenges for mobile social networking applications. In *Proceedings of First international ICST Conference on Communications, Infrastructure, Systems and Applications in Europe* (EuropeComm 2009). London, UK: EuropeComm.

Ranjan Roy, R. (2011). Handbook of mobile ad hoc networks for mobility models. Berlin: Springer Science+Business Media. ISBN 978-1-4419-6048-1

Rapoport, A. (1957). Contribution to the theory of random and biased networks. *The Bulletin of Mathematical Biophysics*, (19): 257–277. doi:10.1007/BF02478417.

Ratti, C., Williams, S., Frenchman, D., & Pulselli, R. (2006). Mobile landscapes: Using location data from cell phones for urban analysis. *Environment and Planning. B, Planning & Design*, 33(5), 727–748. doi:10.1068/b32047.

Ravi, N., Dander, N., Mysore, P., & Littman, M. L. (2005). Activity recognition from accelerometer data. In *Proceedings of the 17th Conference Innovative Applications of Artificial Intelligence (IAAI)*. Pittsburgh, PA: IAAI.

Reinisch, C., Kofler, M. J., & Kastner, W. (2010). ThinkHome: A smart home as digital ecosystem. In *Proceedings of the 4th IEEE International Conference on Digital Ecosystems and Technologies (DEST)* (pp. 256-261). IEEE.

Renz, J., & Mitra, D. (2004). Qualitative direction calculi with arbitrary granularity. *Lecture Notes in Computer Science*, 65–74. doi:10.1007/978-3-540-28633-2_9.

Riboni, D., & Bettini, C. (2011). COSAR: Hybrid reasoning for context-aware activity recognition. In Proceedings of Personal and Ubiquitous Computing, (pp. 271-289). ACM.

Riboni, D., & Bettini, C. (2012). Private context-aware recommendation of points of interest: An initial investigation. In *Proceedings of the Workshops of the Tenth Annual IEEE International Conference on Pervasive Computing and Communications (PerCom)* (pp. 584-589). IEEE Computer Society.

Riboni, D., Pareschi, L., & Bettini, C. (2010). Towards the adaptive integration of multiple context reasoners in pervasive computing environments. In *Proceedings of the Eighth Annual IEEE International Conference on Pervasive Computing and Communications Workshops* (pp. 25-29). IEEE Computer Society.

Riboni, D., Pareschi, L., & Bettini, C. (n.d.). Shadow attacks on users' anonymity in pervasive computing environments. *Journal of Pervasive and Mobile Computing*, 4(6), 819-835. doi:10.1016/j.pmcj.2008.04.008

Riboni, D., Pareschi, L., Bettini, C., & Jajodia, S. (2009). Preserving anonymity of recurrent location-based queries. In *Proceedings of the 16th International Symposium on Temporal Representation and Reasoning (TIME-2009)* (pp. 62-69). IEEE Computer Society.

Riboni, D., & Bettini, C. (2012). Context provenance to enhance the dependability of ambient intelligence systems. *Personal and Ubiquitous Computing, 16*(7), 799–818. doi:10.1007/s00779-011-0448-3.

Riboni, D., Pareschi, L., & Bettini, C. (2009). Privacy in georeferenced context-aware services: A survey. In S. J. C. Bettini (Ed.), *Privacy in Location-Based Applications: Research Issues and Emerging Trends*. Berlin: Springer. doi:10.1007/978-3-642-03511-1_7.

Ricci, F. (2011). Mobile recommender systems. *Information Technology & Tourism, 12*(3), 205–231. doi:10.3727/109830511X12978702284390.

Riener, A., Ferscha, A., Frech, P., Hackl, M., & Kaltenberger, M. (2010). Subliminal vibro-tactile based notification of Co2 economy while driving. In *Proceedings of AutomotiveUI 2010*. Pittsburgh, PA: AutomotiveUI.

Risberg, A. O. (1986). The identification of the mood of a speaker by hearing impaired listeners. *Speech Transmission Lab.*[Stockholm.]. *Quarterly Progress Status Report, 4*, 79–90.

Roalter, L., Möller, A., Diewald, S., & Kranz, M. (2011). Developing intelligent environments: A development tool chain for creation, testing and simulation of smart and intelligent environments. In *Proceedings of the 7th International Conference on Intelligent Environments (IE)*. IE.

Roalter, L., Kranz, M., & Möller, A. (2010). A middleware for intelligent environments and the internet of things. [LNCS]. *Proceedings of Ubiquitous Intelligence and Computing, 6406*, 267–281. doi:10.1007/978-3-642-16355-5_23.

Robertson, N., & Reid, I. (2006). A general method for human activity recognition in video. *Computer Vision and Image Understanding, 104*(2), 232–248. doi:10.1016/j.cviu.2006.07.006.

Röckl, M., Gacnik, J., Schomerus, J., Strang, T., & Kranz, M. (2008). Sensing the environment for future driver assistance combining autonomous and cooperative appliances. In *Proceedings of the Fourth International Workshop on Vehicle-to-Vehicle Communications* (V2VCOM). V2VCOM.

Rodrigo, O., Cherubini, M., & Oliver, N. (2010). MoviPill: Improving medication compliance for elders using a mobile persuasive social game. In *Proceedings of 12th International Conference on Ubiquitous Computing (Ubicomp)*. Beijing, China: UbiComp.

Roggen, D., Tröster, G., Lukowicz, P., Ferscha, A., Millán, J., & Chavarriaga, R. (2013). Opportunistic human activity and context recognition. *IEEE Computer, 46*(2), 36–45. doi:10.1109/MC.2012.393.

Roisman, G. I., J. L. (2004). The Emotional Integration of Childhood Experience: Physiological, Facial Expressive, and Self-Reported Emotional Response during the Adult Attachment Interview. *Developmental Psychology, 40*. PMID:15355165.

Roman, M., & Campbell, R. H. (2000). Gaia: Enabling active spaces. In *Proceedings of the 9th Workshop on ACM SIGOPS European Workshop: Beyond the PC: New Challenges for the Operating System* (pp. 229–234). ACM.

Roman, D., Keller, U., Lausen, H., Bruijn, J. D., Lara, R., & Stollberg, M. et al. (2005). Web service modeling ontology. *Applied Ontology, 1*(1), 77–106.

Román, M., Hess, C., Cerqueira, R., Ranganathan, A., Campbell, R. H., & Nahrstedt, K. (2002). Gaia: A middleware platform for active spaces. *ACM SIGMOBILE Mobile Computing and Communications Review, 6*(4), 65–67. doi:10.1145/643550.643558.

Rong, J., G. L.-P. (2009). Acoustic feature selection for automatic emotion recognition from speech. *Information Processing & Management, 45*, 315–328. doi:10.1016/j.ipm.2008.09.003.

Ross, T. J. (2004). Properties of membership functions, fuzzification and defuzzification. In T. J. Ross (Ed.), *Fuzzy Logic with Engineering Applications* (2nd ed., pp. 90–119). New York: John Wiley & Sons.

Rothney, M. P., Neumann, M., Beziat, A., & Chen, K. (2007). An artificial neural network model of energy expenditure using nonintegrated acceleration signals. *Journal of Applied Physiology, 103*(4), 1419–1427. doi:10.1152/japplphysiol.00429.2007 PMID:17641221.

Rouzikhah, H., King, M., & Rakotonirainy, A. (2010). The validity of simulators in studying driving behaviours. In *Proceedings of Australasian Road Safety Research, Policing and Education Conference 2012*. Canberra, Australia: ARSRPEC.

Ruch, N., Rumo, M., & Mader, U. (2011). Recognition of activities in children by two uniaxial accelerometers in free-living conditions. *European Journal of Applied Physiology*, *111*(8), 1917–1927. doi:10.1007/s00421-011-1828-0 PMID:21249388.

Ruiz Vicente, C., Freni, D., Bettini, C., & Jensen, C. S. (2011). Location-related privacy in geo-social networks. *IEEE Internet Computing*, *15*(3), 20–27. doi:10.1109/MIC.2011.29.

Rusu, R. B., Maldonado, A., Beetz, M., Kranz, M., Mösenlechner, L., Holleis, P., & Schmidt, A. (2006). Player/stage as middleware for ubiquitous computing. In *Proceedings of the 8th Annual Conference on Ubiquitous Computing* (Ubicomp 2006). ACM.

Ryan, H., Aude, H., Pieter, A., & Alexandre, B. (2010). Estimating arterial traffic conditions using sparse probe data. In *Proceedings of the 13th International IEEE Conference on Intelligent Transportation Systems*. IEEE.

Ryu, N., Kawahara, Y., & Asami, T. (2008). A calorie count application for a mobile phone based on METS value. In *Proceedings of 5th Annual IEEE Communications Society Conference on Sensor, Mesh and Ad Hoc Communications and Networks(SECON)*. IEEE.

Sakaki, T., Okazaki, M., & Matsuo, Y. (2010). *Earthquake shakes Twitter users: Real-time event detection by social sensors*. Paper presented at the Meeting of WWW 2010 Conference. Raleigh, NC.

Salber, D., Dey, A. K., & Abowd, G. D. (1999). *The context toolkit: Aiding the development of context-enabled applications*. New York: Academic Press. doi:10.1145/302979.303126.

Salen, K., & Zimmerman, E. (2004). *Rules of play: Game design fundamentals*. Cambridge, MA: MIT Press.

Samovskiy, D. (2008). *Introduction to AMQP messaging with RabbitMQ*.

Sánchez, D., Tentori, M., & Favela, J. (2008). Activity recognition for the smart hospital. *IEEE Intelligent Systems*, *23*(2), 50–57. doi:10.1109/MIS.2008.18.

Sanchez, M., & Manzoni, P. (2001). Anejos: A java-based simulator for ad hoc networks. *Future Generation Computer Systems*, *17*(5), 573–583. doi:10.1016/S0167-739X(00)00040-6.

Sandor Dornbush, K. F. (2005). XPod a human activity and emotion aware mobile music player. *Proceedings of the International Conference on Mobile Technology, Applications and Systems*.

Sanfilippo, S., & Noordhuis, P. (2011). *Redis*. Retrieved from http://redis.io

Sarkar, T. K., Wicks, M. C., Salazar-Palma, M., & Bonneau, R. J. (2004). A survey of various propagation models for mobile communication. *Smart Antennas*, 239-307.

Satin. (2012). *SATIN editor*. Retrieved from http://satinproject.eu/

Scellato, S., Noulas, A., Lambiotte, R., & Mascolo, C. (2011). *Socio-spatial properties of online location-based social networks*. Paper presented at ICWSM 2011. New York, NY. doi: 10.1029/2011GC003824

Schäfer, R. P., Thiessenhusen, K. U., & Wagner, P. (2002). A traffic information system by means of real-time floating-car data. In *Proceedings of the 9th World Congress on Intelligent Transport Systems*. IEEE.

Schafer, J. B., Frankowski, D., Herlocker, J., & Sen, S. (2007). Collaborative filtering recommender systems. *The Adaptive Web*, *4321*, 291–324. doi:10.1007/978-3-540-72079-9_9.

Schafer, L. R. (1978). *Digital Processing of Speech Signals*. Englewood Cliffs, New Jersey: Prentice-Hall.

Scherer, K. R. (1996). Adding the affective dimension: a new look in speech analysis and synthesis. *Proceedings of the International Conference on Spoken Language Processing (ICSLP 1996)*. Philadelphia, PA.

Scherer, F. J. (1986). Effects of experimentally induced stress on vocal parameters. *Journal of Experimental Psychology. Human Perception and Performance*, *12*(3), 302–313. doi:10.1037/0096-1523.12.3.302 PMID:2943858.

Scherer, K. R. (1994). *Vocal Affect Expression: A Review and a Model for Future Research*. Psychology and Biology of Emotion.

Scherer, K. R. (2003). Vocal communication of emotion: a review of research paradigms. *Speech Communication, 40*, 227–256. doi:10.1016/S0167-6393(02)00084-5.

Scherer, R. B. (1996). Acoustic profiles in vocal emotion expression. *Journal of Personality and Social Psychology, 70*, 641–636.

Scherer, T. J. (2000). Vocal communication of emotion. In J. H. M. Lewis (Ed.), *Handbook of emotion* (pp. 220–235). New York: Guilford.

Schmidt, A., Kranz, M., & Holleis, P. (2004). Embedded information. In *Proceedings of Workshop Ubiquitous Display Environments at UbiComp 2004*. ACM.

Schmidt, R. K., Leinmüller, T., & Böddeker, B. (2008). V2x kommunikation. In *Proceedings of 17th Aachener Kolloquium*. Academic Press.

Schmidt, R. K., Leinmüller, T., Schoch, E., Kargl, F., & Schäfer, G. (2010). Exploration of adaptive beaconing for efficient intervehicle safety communication. *IEEE Network Magazine, 24*, 14–19. doi:10.1109/MNET.2010.5395778.

Scholtz, J., & Consolvo, S. (2004). Toward a framework for evaluating ubiquitous computing applications. *IEEE Pervasive Computing / IEEE Computer Society [and] IEEE Communications Society, 3*(2), 82–88. doi:10.1109/MPRV.2004.1316826.

Schroeter, R., & Rakotonirainy, A. (2012). The future shape of digital cars. In *Proceedings of Australasian Road Safety Research, Policing and Education Conference 2012*. Wellington, New Zealand: ARSRPEC.

Schroeter, R., Rakotonirainy, A., & Foth, M. (2012). The social car: New interactive vehicular applications derived from social media and urban informatics. In *Proceedings of AutomotiveUI '12*. Portsmouth, NH: AutomotiveUI. doi:10.1145/2390256.2390273.

Schuette, R., & Rotthowe, T. (1998). *The guidelines of modeling – An approach to enhance the quality in information models*. Paper presented at the 17th International Conference on Conceptual Modeling (ER'98). New York, NY.

Schuller, B. S. R.-H. (2005). Speaker independent speech emotion recognition by ensemble classification. *IEEE International Conference on Multimedia and Expo (ICME '05)*, (pp. 864–867).

Schuller, B., Reiter, S., Muller, R., Al-Hames, M., Lang, M., & Rigoll, G. (2005). Speaker independent speech emotion recognition by ensemble classification. In *Proceedings of ICME 2005*. Amsterdam, The Netherlands: ICME.

Schuller, B., Batliner, A., Steidl, S., & Seppi, D. (2011). Recognising realistic emotions and affect in speech: State of the art and lessons learnt from the first challenge. *Speech Communication*, 1062–1087. doi:10.1016/j.specom.2011.01.011.

Schuller, B., Lang, M., & Rigoll, G. (2006). Recognition of spontaneous emotions by speech within automotive environment. *Tagungsband Fortschritte der Akustik, 32*(1), 57–58.

Scott, J. (2000). *Social networks analysis: A handbook*. London: Sage Publications.

Sebe, N. M. S. (2004). Authentic Facial Expression Analysis. *Proc. IEEE Int'l Conf. Automatic Face and Gesture Recognition (AFGR)*.

Sellis, T. K. (1988). Multiple-query optimization. *ACM Transactions on Database Systems, 13*(1), 23–52. doi:10.1145/42201.42203.

Sen, R., Handorean, R., Roman, G. C., & Hackmann, G. (2004). Knowledge-driven interactions with services across ad hoc networks. In *Proceedings of the 2nd International Conference on Service Oriented Computing* (ICSOC, '04). New York, NY: ICSOC.

Sene, K. (2008). *Flood warning, forecasting and emergency response*. Berlin: Springer. doi:10.1007/978-3-540-77853-0.

Sensei. (2008). *SENSEI - Integrating the physical with the digital world of the network of the future*. Retrieved from http://www.ict-sensei.org/

SensorML. (n.d.). Retrieved from http://www.opengeo-spatial.org/standards/sensorml

Sheikh, K., Wegdam, M., & van Sinderen, M. (2008). Quality-of-context and its use for protecting privacy in context aware systems. *Journal of Software, 3*(3), 83–93. doi:10.4304/jsw.3.3.83-93.

Sheth, A. (2009). Citizen sensing, social signals, and enriching human experience. *IEEE Internet Computing, 13*(4), 87–92. doi:10.1109/MIC.2009.77.

Sheth, A. (2010). Computing for human experience – Semantics-empowered sensors, services, and social computing on the ubiquitous web. *IEEE Internet Computing, 14*(1), 88–97. doi:10.1109/MIC.2010.4.

Shi, J., & Malik, J. (2000). Normalized cuts and image segmentation. *IEEE Transactions on Pattern Analysis and Machine Intelligence, 22*(8), 888–905. doi:10.1109/34.868688.

Shneidman, J., Pietzuch, P., Ledlie, J., Roussopoulos, M., Seltzer, M., & Welsh, M. (2004). *Hourglass: An infrastructure for connecting sensor networks and applications (Tech. rep.)*. Harvard.

Siler, W., & Buckley, J. J. (2004). *Fuzzy expert systems and fuzzy reasoning*. Hoboken, NJ: John Wiley & Sons, Inc. doi:10.1002/0471698504.

Simmhan, Y., Plale, B., & Gannon, D. (2005). A survey of data provenance in e-science. *SIGMOD Record, 34*(3), 31–36. doi:10.1145/1084805.1084812.

Sina. (2011). *Analysis for financial report of Sina in Q3 by Sina senior executives*. Retrieved from http://weibo.com/1800318967/xyuvFtm5z

Sina. (2012). *Get verified in Sina*. Retrieved from http://weibo.com/verify

Skinner, E. R. (1935). A calibrated recording and analysis of the pitch, force and quality of vocal tones expressing happiness and sadness. *Speech Monogr., 2*, 81–137. doi:10.1080/03637753509374833.

SM4All. (2008). Retrieved 2013, from http://sm4all-project.eu/

Smart Santander. (2008). *Smart santander - Future internet research & experimentation*. Retrieved from http://www.smartsantander.eu/

SmartLab. (2006). Retrieved 2013, from http://www.smartlab.deusto.es/

Smith, J. D., & Graham, T. C. N. (2006). Use of eye movements for video game control. In *Proceedings of ACM SIGCHI International Conference on Advances in Computer Entertainment Technology (ACE)*. ACM.

Song, L., Kotz, D., Jain, R., & He, X. (2004). Evaluating next-cell predictors with extensive wi-fi mobility data. In *Proceeding of 23th IEEE International Conference on Computer Communications* (INFOCOM'04). Hong Kong, China: IEEE.

Song, C., Qu, Z., Blumm, N., & Barabási, A.-L. (2010). Limits of predictability in human mobility. *Science, 327*. PMID:20167789.

Sotamma, O. (2002). *All the world's a botfighter stage: Notes on location-based multi-user gaming*. Paper presented at the Computer Games and Digital Cultures Conference. New York, NY.

Soylu, A., Causmaecker, P., & Desmet, P. (2009). Context and adaptivity in pervasive computing environments: Links with software engineering and ontological engineering. *Journal of Software, 4*(9), 992–1013. doi:10.4304/jsw.4.9.992-1013.

Spanoudakis, N. I., & Moraitis, P. (2006). Agent based architecture in an ambient intelligence context. In *Proceedings of the 4th European Workshop on Multi-Agent Systems (EUMAS'06)* (pp. 1-12). Lisbon: EUMAS.

Stenros, J., Montola, M., Waern, A., & Jonsson, S. (2007). Momentum evaluation report. *IPerG Deliverable D11.7*.

Stevens, C. W. (1972). Emotions and speech: Some acoustical correlates. *The Journal of the Acoustical Society of America, 52*(4), 1238–1250. PMID:4638039.

Stiefmeier, T., Roggen, D., Tröster, G., Ogris, G., & Lukowicz, P. (2008). Wearable activity tracking in car manufacturing. *IEEE Pervasive Computing / IEEE Computer Society [and] IEEE Communications Society, 7*(2), 42–50. doi:10.1109/MPRV.2008.40.

Sumi, Y., & Mase, K. (2001). Digital assistant for supporting conference participants: An attempt to combine mobile, ubiquitous and web computing. In *Proceedings of International Conference on Ubiquitous Computing (Ubicomp)*. Atlanta, GA: UbiComp.

Sun, L., Zhang, D., Chen, C., Castro, P. S., Li, S., & Wang, Z. (2012). Real time anomalous trajectory detection and analysis. *Mobile Networks and Applications.*

Svenson, O. (1981). Are we all less risky and more skillful than our fellow drivers? *Acta Psychologica, 47*(2), 143–148. doi:10.1016/0001-6918(81)90005-6.

Szewczyk, R., Osterweil, E., Polastre, J., Hamilton, M., Mainwaring, A., & Estrin, D. (2004). Habitat monitoring with sensor networks. *Communications of the ACM, 47*(6), 34–40. doi:10.1145/990680.990704.

Tacconi, D., Mayora, O., Lukowicz, P., Arnrich, B., Kappeler-Setz, C., Tröster, G., & Haring, C. (2008). Activity and emotion recognition to support early diagnosis of psychiatric diseases. In *Proceedings of 2nd International Conference on Pervasive Computing Technologies for Healthcare (Pervasive Health)*, (pp. 100-102). ACM.

Talantikite, H. N., Aissani, D., & Boudjlida, N. (2009). Semantic annotations for web services discovery and composition. *Computer Standards & Interfaces, 31*(6), 1108–1117. doi:10.1016/j.csi.2008.09.041.

Taleb, T., Bottazzi, D., & Nasser, N. (2010). A novel middleware solution to improve ubiquitous healthcare systems aided by affective information. *IEEE Transactions on Information Technology in Biomedicine*, 335–349. doi:10.1109/TITB.2010.2042608 PMID:20659832.

Tang, D., & Baker, M. (2000). Analysis of a local-area wireless network. In *Proceedings of the 6ᵗʰ Annual International Conference on Mobile Computing and Networking (MobiCom'00)*. New York, NY: ACM Press.

Tang, J., Jin, R. M., & Zhang, J. (2008). *A topic modeling approach and its integration into the random walk framework for academic search*. Paper presented at the Meeting of 2008 IEEE International Conference on Data Mining. Pisa, Italy.

Tang, J., Lou, T., & Kleinberg, J. (2012). *Inferring social ties across heterogeneous networks*. Paper presented at the Meeting of Web Search and Data Mining. Seattle, WA.

Tang, D., & Baker, M. (2002). Analysis of a metropolitan-area wireless network. *Wireless Networks, 8*(2/3), 107–120. doi:10.1023/A:1013739407600.

Tang, L., Zhou, X., Yu, Z., Liang, Y., Zhang, D., & Ni, H. (2011). MHS: A multimedia system for improving medication adherence in elderly care. *IEEE System Journal, 5*(4), 506–517. doi:10.1109/JSYST.2011.2165593.

Tapia, E. M., Intille, S. S., & Larson, K. (2004). Activity recognition in the home using simple and ubiquitous sensors. *Pervasive Computing, 3001*, 158–175. doi:10.1007/978-3-540-24646-6_10.

Tatbul, N., Çetintemel, U., Zdonik, S., Cherniack, M., & Stonebraker, M. (2003). Load shedding in a data stream manager. In *Proceedings of the 29th International Conference on Very Large Data Bases* (pp. 309–320). IEEE.

Tazari, M. R., Furfari, F., Valero, Á. F., Hanke, S., Höftberger, O., Kehagias, D., et al. (2012). The universAAL reference model for AAL. In Handbook on Ambient Assisted Living-Technology for Healthcare, Rehabilitation and Well-Being. AISE.

Teager, H. a. (1990). Evidence for Nonlinear Sound Production Mechanisms in the Vocal Tract. In W. J. Hardcastle, Speech Production and Speech Modelling. Springer Netherlands.

Tentori, M., & Favela, J. (2008). Activity-aware computing for healthcare. *IEEE Pervasive Computing / IEEE Computer Society [and] IEEE Communications Society, 7*(2), 51–57. doi:10.1109/MPRV.2008.24.

TexasInstr. (2011). *Texas instruments brings ZigBee home automation to smartphones & tablets*. Retrieved from http://www.cocoontech.com/portal/articles/news/17-zigbee/432-texas-instruments-brings-zigbee-home-automation-to-smartphones-a-tablets

Thakkar, H., Laptev, N., Mousavi, H., Mozafari, B., Russo, V., & Zaniolo, C. (2011). SMM: A data stream management system for knowledge discovery. In *Proceedings of the IEEE 27th International Conference on Data Engineering (ICDE)* (pp. 757–768). IEEE.

Tomkins, S. S. (1962). *Affect, Imagery, Consciousness.* Springer.

Tran, V. X., Puntheeranurak, S., & Tsuji, H. (2009). *A new service matching definition and algorithm with SAWSDL.* Paper presented at 3rd IEEE International Conference on Digital Ecosystems and Technologies (DEST '09). New York, NY.

Trudgill, P. (1983). *Sociolinguistics: An Introduction to Language and Society.* London: Penguin.

Tsiftes, N., & Dunkels, A. (2011). A database in every sensor. In *Proceedings of the 9th ACM Conference on Embedded Networked Sensor Systems* (SenSys '11). ACM.

Tucker, P. A., Maier, D., Sheard, T., & Fegaras, L. (2003). Exploiting punctuation semantics in continuous data streams. *IEEE Transactions on Knowledge and Data Engineering, 15*(3), 555–568. doi:10.1109/TKDE.2003.1198390.

Tuduce, C., & Gross, T. (2005). A mobility model-based on WLAN traces and its validation. In *Proceeding of the 24th IEEE International Conference on Computer Communications* (INFOCOM'05), (pp. 19 – 24). IEEE.

Tufte, K., Li, J., Maier, D., Papadimos, V., Bertini, R. L., & Rucker, J. (2007). Travel time estimation using NiagaraST and latte. In *Proceedings of the 2007 ACM SIGMOD International Conference on Management of Data* (pp. 1091–1093). ACM.

Tulusan, J., Staake, T., & Fleisch, E. (2012). Providing eco-driving feedback to corporate car drivers: What impact does a smartphone application have on their fuel efficiency? In *Proceedings of UbiComp 2012.* Pittsburgh, PA: UbiComp. doi:10.1145/2370216.2370250.

Twitter Storm. (2013). Retrieved 2013, from http://storm-project.net/

Varshavsky, A., & Patel, S. (2010). Location in ubiquitous computing. In J. Krumm (Ed.), *Ubiquitous Computing Fundamentals* (pp. 285–319). Boca Raton, FL: CRC Press.

Vasilescu, L. D. (2004). Reliability of Lexical and Prosodic Cues in Two Real-Life Spoken Dialog Corpora. *Proc. 4th Int. Conf. Language Resources and Evaluation (LREC).*

Vergetis, E., Guerin, R., Sarkar, S., & Rank, J. (2005). Can bluetooth succeed as a large-scale Ad Hoc networking technology? *IEEE Journal on Selected Areas in Communications, 23*(3), 644–656. doi:10.1109/JSAC.2004.842544.

Ververidis, D. K. (2003). A review of emotional speech databases. *PCI 2003, 9th Panhellenic Conf. on Informatics,* (pp. 560-574). Thessaloniki, Greece.

Virtanen, T., & Malinen, S. (2008). Supporting the sense of locality with online communities. In Proceedings of MindTrek 2008, International Digital Media & Business Festival. MindTrek.

Wagner, J., Kim, J., & André, E. (2005). From physiological signals to emotions: Implementing and comparing selected methods for feature extraction and classification. In *Proceedings of ICME,* (pp. 940-943). ICME.

Waibel, T. P. (2000). Emotion-sensitive human-computer interfaces. *Proc. ISCA Workshop Speech and Emotion,* (pp. 201–206). 2000.

Wakita, K., & Tsurumi, T. (2007). Finding community structure in mega-scale social networks. Paper presented in the meeting of WWW'07. Alberta, Canada.

Walther, B. K. (2005). *Notes on the methodology of pervasive gaming.* Paper presented at the 4th International Conference on Entertainment Computing. Sanda, Japan.

Walther, B. K. (2005). Atomic actions -- Molecular experience: Theory of pervasive gaming. *Computers in Entertainment, 3*(3), 1–13. doi:10.1145/1077246.1077258.

Walther, B. K. (2007). Pervasive game-play: Theoretical reflections and classifications. *Matrix (Stuttgart, Germany), 1.*

Walther, J. B., & D'Addario, K. P. (2001). The impacts of emoticons on message interpretation in computer-mediated communication. *Social Science Computer Review, 19*(3), 324–347. doi:10.1177/089443930101900307.

Wamsley, G. L. (1993). *Coping with catastrophe: Building an emergency management system to meet people's needs in natural & manmade disasters.* New York: DIANE Publishing.

Wang, K. H., & Li, B. (2002). Group mobility and partition prediction in wireless ad hoc networks. In *Proceeding of the IEEE International Conference on Communications (ICC'02)*. New York: IEEE.

Wang, X., Rosenblum, D., & Wang, Y. (2012). Context-aware mobile music recommendation for daily activities. In *Proceedings of the 20ᵗʰ ACM International Conference on Multimedia (MM)*. Nara, Japan: ACM.

Wang, Y., Lin, J., Annavaram, M., Jacobson, Q. A., Hong, J., Krishnamachari, B., & Sadeh, N. (2009). A framework of energy efficient mobile sensing for automatic user state recognition. In *Proceedings of 7ᵗʰ International Conference on Mobile Systems, Applications, and Services (MobiSys)*. Kraków, Poland: ACM.

Wang, Z., Zhang, D., Yang, D., Yu, Z., & Zhou, X. (2012). *Detecting overlapping communities in location-based social networks*. Paper presented at SocInfo 2012. New York, NY. doi: 10.1007/978-3-642-35386-4_9

Want, R., Hopper, A., Falcão, V., & Gibbons, J. (1992). The active badge location system. *ACM Transactions on Information Systems, 10*(1), 91–102. doi:10.1145/128756.128759.

Ward, J. A., Lukowicz, P., Gerhard, T., & Starner, T. E. (2006). Activity recognition of assembly tasks using body-worn microphones and accelerometers. *IEEE Transactions on Pattern Analysis and Machine Intelligence, 28*, 1553–1566. doi:10.1109/TPAMI.2006.197 PMID:16986539.

Wasserman, S., & Faust, K. (1994). *Social network analysis: Methods and applications*. Cambridge, UK: Cambridge University Press. doi:10.1017/CBO9780511815478.

Watts, D. J. (1999). *Small worlds, the dynamics of networks between order and randomness*. Princeton, NJ: Princeton University Press.

Wei, Y. L. (2005). Speech emotion recognition based on HMM and SVM. *Proc. of Int. Conf. on Machine Learning and Cybernetics, 8*, pp. 4898- 4901.

Wei, D., Wang, T., Wang, J., & Bernstein, A. (2011). SAWSDL-iMatcher: A customizable and effective semantic web service matchmaker. *Web Semantics: Science. Services and Agents on the World Wide Web, 9*(4), 402–417. doi:10.1016/j.websem.2011.08.001.

Weiser, M. (1991). The computer for the 21ˢᵗ century. *Scientific American, 265*(3), 66–75. doi:10.1038/scientificamerican0991-94 PMID:1754874.

Weiss, M., & Guinard, D. (2010). Increasing energy awareness through web-enabled power outlets. In *Proceedings of the 9th International Conference on Mobile and Ubiquitous Multimedia* (pp. 20). ACM.

Wen, H., Hu, Z., Guo, J., Zhu, L., & Sun, J. (2008). Operational analysis on Beijing road network during the olympic games. *Journal of Transportation Systems Engineering and Information Technology, 8*(6). doi:10.1016/S1570-6672(09)60003-9.

Wenxiang, M. G. (2011). *Weibo*. Retrieved 12/2, 2011, from http://weibo.com/1649155730/xt1McBmP8

Wetzel, W., Blum, L., McCall, R., Oppermann, L., Broeke, T.S., & Szalavári, Z. (2009). Final prototype of timewarp application. *IPCity*.

Whissel, C. M. (1989). *The dictionary of affect in language*. New York: Academic.

White, T. (2012). *Hadoop: The definitive guide*. Sebastopol, CA: O'Reilly Media.

Whitney, A. (2010). *Traverse a fantastic virtual world within the real world with parallel kingdom-age of emergence*. Retrieved from http://www.examiner.com/video-games-in-wichita-falls/traverse-a-fantastic-virtual-world-within-the-real-world-with-parallel-kingdom-age-of-emergence

Wishart, R., Henricksen, K., & Indulska, J. (2007). Context privacy and obfuscation supported by dynamic context source discovery and processing in a context management system. In *Proceedings of the 4th International Conference on Ubiquitous Intelligence and Computing (UIC)* (pp. 929-940). Springer.

Wojciechowski, M., & Wiedeler, M. (2012). Model-based development of context-aware applications using the MILEO-context server. In *Proceedings of Pervasive Computing and Communications Workshops* (pp. 613–618). IEEE. doi:10.1109/PerComW.2012.6197588.

Wong, J. (2007). Marmite: Towards end-user programming for the web. In *Proceedings of VL/HCC*. IEEE.

Wong, J., & Hong, J. I. (2007). Making mash-ups with marmite: Towards end-user programming for the web. In *Proceedings of CHI*. ACM.

Wu, X., & Wang, J. (2011). *How about micro-blogging service in China: Analysis and mining on sina micro-blog*. Paper presented at the 1st International Symposium on From Digital Footprints to Social and Community Intelligence. Beijing, China. Retrieved from http://delivery.acm.org/10.1145/2040000/2030077/p37-wu.pdf?ip=113.108.133.48&acc=ACTIVE%20SERVICE&CFID=61317438&CFTOKEN=16074489&__acm__=1326088101_47810c63c0137404d8980674ad9b0aaa

Xia, R., & Zong, C. (2010). Exploring the use of word relation features for sentiment classification. In *Proceedings of COLING (Posters)*, (pp. 1336-1344). COLING.

Xie, J., Stephen, K., & Boleslaw, K. S. (2013). Overlapping community detection in networks: The state of the art and comparative study. *ACM Computing Surveys*, *45*(4). doi:10.1145/2501654.2501657.

Xiong, G., Liu, Z., Liu, X., & Shen, D. (2012). *Service science, management, and engineering: Theory and applications*. New York: Academic Press.

Xu, R., & Wunsch, D. (2005). Survey of clustering algorithms. *IEEE Transactions on Neural Networks*, *16*(3), 645–678. doi:10.1109/TNN.2005.845141 PMID:15940994.

Yamada, N., Sakamoto, K., Kunito, G., Isoda, Y., Yamazaki, K., & Tanaka, S. (2007). Applying ontology and probabilistic model to human activity recognition from surrounding things. *IPSJ Digital Courier*, 506-517.

Yang, J., & Leskovec, J. (2011). *Patterns of temporal variation in online media*. Paper presented at the Fourth ACM International Conference on Web Search and Data Mining. Hong Kong, China. Retrieved from http://delivery.acm.org/10.1145/1940000/1935863/p177-yang.pdf?ip=113.108.133.61&acc=ACTIVE%20SERVICE&CFID=95705915&CFTOKEN=94098446&__acm__=1333615850_74c77faf846e64dc5a61a5204c01ba21

Yang, J., Lee, J., & Choi, J. (2011). Activity recognition based on RFID object usage for smart mobile devices. *Journal of Computer Science and Technology*, *26*, 239–246. doi:10.1007/s11390-011-9430-9.

Yao, X., & Thill, J. C. (2006). Spatial queries with qualitative locations in spatial information systems. *Computers, Environment and Urban Systems*, *30*, 485–502. doi:10.1016/j.compenvurbsys.2004.08.001.

Yatani, K., & Truong, K. N. (2012). BodyScope: A wearable acoustic sensor for activity recognition. In *Proceedings of the ACM Conference on Ubiquitous Computing (Ubicomp)*. Pittsburgh, PA: ACM.

Ye, M., Janowicz, K., Mulligann, C., & Lee, W. C. (2011). *What you are is when you are: The temporal dimension of feature types in location-based social networks*. Paper presented at GIS 2011. New York, NY. doi:10.1145/2093973.2093989

Yick, J., Mukherjee, B., & Ghosal, D. (2008). Wireless sensor network survey. *Computer Networks*, *52*(12), 2292–2330. doi:10.1016/j.comnet.2008.04.002.

Yilmaz, A., Javed, O., & Shah, M. (2006). Object tracking: A survey. *ACM Computing Surveys*, *38*(4). doi:10.1145/1177352.1177355.

Yoon, J., Noble, B. D., Liu, M., & Kim, M. (2006). Building realistic mobility models from coarse-grained traces. In *Proceeding of the 4th International Conference on Mobile Systems, Applications, and Services* (MobiSys'06), (pp. 177–190). New York, NY: ACM.

You, C.-W., Montes-de-Oca, M., Bao, T. J., Lane, N. D., Lu, H., & Cardone, G. et al. (2012). CarSafe: A driver safety app. that detects dangerous driving behavior using dual-cameras on smartphones. In *Proceedings of UbiComp 2012*. Pittsburgh, PA: UbiComp. doi:10.1145/2370216.2370360.

Youngblood, G. M., Cook, D. J., & Holder, L. B. (2004). *The MavHome architecture*. Arlington, TX: Department of Computer Science and Engineering University of Texas at Arlington.

Yu, Z., Liang, Y., Xu, B., Yang, Y., & Guo, B. (2011). *Towards a smart campus with mobile social networking*. Paper presented at the Meeting of IEEE International Conference on Internet of Things. Dalian, China.

Yuan, J., Zheng, Y., Xie, X., & Sun, G. (2011). Driving with knowledge from the physical world. In *Proceedings of the 17th ACM SIGKDD International Conference on Knowledge Discovery and Data Mining, KDD '11*. ACM.

Yuan, J., Zheng, Y., Zhang, L., Xie, X., & Sun, G. (2011). Where to find my next passenger? In *Proceedings of the 13th ACM International Conference on Ubiquitous Computing*. ACM.

Yu, Z., & Nakamura, Y. (2010). Smart meeting systems: A survey of state-of-the-art and open issues. *ACM Computing Surveys, 42*(2). doi:10.1145/1667062.1667065.

Yu, Z., & Xie, X. (2011). Learning travel recommendations from user-generated GPS traces. *ACM Transactions on Intelligent Systems and Technology, 2*(1). doi: doi:10.1145/1889681.1889683.

Yu, Z., Yu, Z., Aoyama, H., Ozeki, M., & Nakamura, Y. (2010). Capture, recognition, and visualization of human semantic interactions in meetings. In *Proceedings of Pervasive Computing and Communications (Percom)*. Mannheim, Germany: Percom. doi:10.1109/PERCOM.2010.5466987.

Yu, Z., Yu, Z., Zhou, X., Becker, C., & Nakamura, Y. (2012). Tree-based mining for discovering patterns of human interaction in meetings. *IEEE Transactions on Knowledge and Data Engineering, 24*(4), 759–768. doi:10.1109/TKDE.2010.224.

Yu, Z., Zhou, X., Yu, Z., Park, J. H., & Ma, J. (2008). iMuseum: A scalable context-aware intelligent museum system. *Computer Communications, 31*(18), 4376–4382. doi:10.1016/j.comcom.2008.05.004.

Yu, Z., Zhou, X., Zhang, D., Chin, C., Wang, X., & Men, J. (2006). Supporting context-aware media recommendations for smart phones. *IEEE Pervasive Computing/IEEE Computer Society [and] IEEE Communications Society, 5*(3), 68–75. doi:10.1109/MPRV.2006.61.

Zappi, P., Lombriser, C., Stiefmeier, T., Farella, E., Roggen, D., Benini, L., & Troster, G. (2008). Activity recognition from on-body sensors: Accuracy-power trade-off by dynamic sensor selection. In *Proceedings of 5th European Conference on Wireless Sensor Networks (EWSN)*. Bologna, Italy: EWSN.

Zappi, P., Stiefmeier, T., Farella, E., Roggen, D., Benini, L., & Troster, G. (2007). Activity recognition from on-body sensors by classifier fusion: Sensor scalability and robustness. In *Proceedings of the 3rd International Conference on Intelligent Sensors, Sensor Networks and Information (ISSNIP)*. Melbourne, Australia: ISSNIP.

Zeng, Z., M. P. (2009). A survey of affect recognition methods: audio, visual and spontaneous expressions. *IEEE Transactions on Pattern Analysis and Machine Intelligence, 31*(1), 39–58. doi:10.1109/TPAMI.2008.52 PMID:19029545.

Zhang, D., Li, N., Zhou, Z. H., Chen, C., Sun, L., & Li, S. (2011). iBAT: Detecting anomalous taxi trajectories from GPS traces. In *Proceedings of the 13th ACM International Conference on Ubiquitous Computing*. ACM.

Zhang, Z., Lyons, M., Schuster, M., & Akamatsu, S. (1998). Comparison between geometry-based and gabor-wavelets-based facial expression recognition using multi-layer perceptron. In *Proceedings of FG 1998*. Nara, Japan: FG.

Zhang, D., Guo, B., & Yu, Z. (2011). The emergence of social and community intelligence. *IEEE Computer, 44*(7), 21–28. doi:10.1109/MC.2011.65.

Zhang, D., Gu, T., & Wang, X. (2005). Enabling context-aware smart home with semantic technology. *International Journal of Human-Friendly Welfare Robotic Systems, 6*(4), 12–20.

Zhang, W., Yoshida, T., & Tang, X. (2008). Text classification based on multi-word with support vector. *Knowledge-Based Systems*, 879–886. doi:10.1016/j.knosys.2008.03.044.

Zhao, D., & Rosson, M. B. (2009). *How and why people Twitter: The role that micro-blogging plays in informal communication at work*. Paper presented at the ACM 2009 International Conference on Supporting Group Work. Sanibel Island, FL. Retrieved from http://delivery.acm.org/10.1145/1540000/1531710/p243-zhao.pdf?ip=113.108.133.51&CFID=38952822&CFTOKEN=89830532&__acm__=1315556372_d00df-09cb3a1059eb969e7d06a22d660

Zhendong, D. Q. (2011). *How net knowledge database.* Retrieved from http://www.keenage.com/

Zhou, S., Chu, C., Yu, Z., & Kim, J. (2012). A context-aware reminder system for elders based on fuzzy linguistic approach. *Expert Systems with Applications*, *39*(1), 9411–9419. doi:10.1016/j.eswa.2012.02.124.

Zhu, F., Mutka, M. W., & Ni, L. M. (2005). Service discovery in pervasive computing environments. *IEEE Pervasive Computing / IEEE Computer Society [and] IEEE Communications Society*, *4*(4), 81–90. doi:10.1109/MPRV.2005.87.

Zirn, C., Niepert, M., Stuckenschmidt, H., & Strube, M. (2011). fine-grained sentiment analysis with structural features. *IJCNLP*, 336-344.

Zitao, L., Wenchao, Y., Wei, C., Shuran, W., & Fengyi, W. (2010). *Short text feature selection for micro-blog mining.* Paper presented at the Computational Intelligence and Software Engineering (CiSE). New York, NY.

Zonoozi, M., & Dassanayake, P. (1997). User mobility modeling and characterization of mobility pattern. *IEEE Journal on Selected Areas in Communications*, *15*(7), 1239–1252. doi:10.1109/49.622908.

Zuo, Y., You, F., Wang, J., & Wu, X. (2012). *User modeling driven news filtering algorithm for microblog service in China.* Paper presented at the 2012 IEEE/ACIS 11th International Conference on Computer and Information Science (ICIS). Shanghai, China.

About the Contributors

Bin Guo is an associate professor from Northwestern Polytechnical University, China. He received his Ph.D. degree in computer science from Keio University, Tokyo, Japan, in 2009. During 2009-2011, he was a post-doctoral researcher at Institut TELECOM SudParis in France. His research interests include ubiquitous computing, mobile social networking, and cross-community mining. Dr. Guo has served as an editor of *IEEE Communications Magazine, ACM/Springer Personal and Ubiquitous Computing* (PUC), and guest editor of *ACM Transactions on Intelligent Systems and Technology* (TIST). He has served as the general chair of the SCI-11, the publicity chair of UIC'12, ICTH'13, the workshop chair of iThings'13, and the TPC member for a number of conferences. He has published over 50 scientific papers in referred journals, conferences, and book chapters. He won the best paper award of AMT'2012 and GPC'2012.

Daniele Riboni is a Research Fellow at the Department of Computer Science of the University of Milano, where he is member of the EveryWare Laboratory. He received his PhD in Computer Science from the University of Milano in 2007 with a thesis on "Techniques, Algorithms, and Architectures for Adaptation in Mobile Computing." His research interests are in the areas of context-awareness and adaptation, pervasive and mobile computing, and privacy. He participated in several research projects, and during his research activity, he actively collaborated with various Italian and foreign partners, both from industry and academia. He has published over 40 scientific papers and his contributions appeared in the proceedings of major conferences and in leading journals of his research fields. He belongs to the program committee of various conferences and workshops.

Peizhao Hu is a Senior Research Engineer at NICTA (Australia's centre for research excellence). His research interests include mobile application development, context-aware and pervasive computing, autonomic computing, and wireless mesh networking. Dr. Hu had served as technical program committee and organising committee for a number of conference and workshops, including PerCom, LCN, AINA, UIC. He has (co)authored more than twenty journal and conference papers in his research expertise.

* * *

Alaa Omran Almagrabi is a PhD candidate in the Department of Computer Science and Computer Engineering, La Trobe University. He completed his Master in Information Technology from the same University and BSc in Computer Science from King Abdul Aziz University Saudi Arabia. His research interest is as follows: Context Aware Computing, Mobile Computing, Ontology, and Networking.

Hans-Jürgen Appelrath is professor of practical computer science at University of Oldenburg, Germany. He studied and received his doctorate at the University of Dortmund and was assistant professor at ETH Zürich. Prof. Dr. Dr. h.c. Hans-Jürgen Appelrath is on the board of OFFIS, on the advisory board of various research institutes and member of the supervisory board of several companies. In 2007, he was awarded the honorary doctorate from the TU Braunschweig.

Igor Bisio was born in Novi Ligure (Alessandria), Italy in 1978. He got his "Laurea" degree in Telecommunication Engineering at the University of Genoa, Italy, in 2002, and his Ph.D. degree in 2006. He is currently Assistant Professor and he is member of the Digital Signal Processing (DSP) and Satellite Communications and Networking (SCNL) Laboratories research staffs at the University of Genoa. He is the Chair of the IEEE Satellite and Space Communications Technical Committee. He is the recipient of several best paper awards and author of about 70 scientific papers including international journals, international conferences, and book chapters. His main research activities concern Resource Allocation and Management for Satellite and Space Communication systems, Signal Processing over Portable Devices such as Smartphones, Context and Location Awareness, Adaptive Coding Mechanisms, Indoor Localization, Security, and e-health Applications.

Chao Chen received the B.Sc. and M.Sc. degrees in control science and control engineering from Northwestern Polytechnical University, Xi'an, China, in 2007 and 2010, respectively. He is currently working toward the Ph.D. degree with Pierre and Marie Curie University, Paris, France, and with Institut Mines-Télécom/Telecom SudParis, Evry, France. In 2009, he worked as a Research Assistant with Hong Kong Polytechnic University, Kowloon, Hong Kong. His research interests include pervasive computing, social network analysis, and data mining from large-scale taxi data.

Viktoriya Degeler received her B.Sc. degree in applied mathematics from National Polytechnical University Kh.P.I., Kharkiv, Ukraine, in 2005, and the M.Sc. degree in intelligent systems design from Chalmers University of Technology, Gothenburg, Sweden, in 2007. She is currently working toward the PhD degree at the University of Groningen, The Netherlands. Her research interests include AI techniques for reasoning and decision making in intelligent pervasive systems, constraint satisfaction, optimization, context modeling, and representation, with particular interest in intelligent buildings automation.

Alessandro Delfino was born in Milan, Italy, in 1984. He got his B.Sc in Telecommunication Engineering in 2007 from University of Genoa. He got his M.Sc in Telecommunication Engineering in 2010 from University of Genoa with a thesis on Audio Fingerprinting. In 2010 he worked on MAC protocols for Cognitive Radio at European funded Joint Research Center (JRC) of Ispra, Italy. He is currently Ph.D Student of the Digital Signal Processing Laboratory of University of Genoa and his main research activity concerns: Emotion Recognition, Audio Fingerprinting and Audio Information Retrieval, Cognitive Radio.

Ali Diab received the B.E. degree in Electronic Engineering from the Damascus University, Damascus, Syria, in 1999, and the Diploma degree in Computer Science and Automation from the same university in 2000. After that, he obtained his Dr.-Ing. Title from the Ilmenau University of Technology, Faculty of Computer Science in 2010. His dissertation focused on mobility management in IP-based networks. Currently, he is pursuing his postdoctoral degree at the Ilmenau University of Technology on the topic "Self-Organized Future Mobile Communication Networks."

Damianos Gavalas received his BSc degree in Informatics from the University of Athens, Greece, in 1995, and his MSc and PhD degree in Electronic Engineering from University of Essex, UK, in 1997 and 2001, respectively. Currently, he is an Assistant Professor in the Department of Cultural Informatics, University of the Aegean, Greece. He has served as TPC member in several leading conferences and guest-editor in highly ranked journals in the field of mobile and wireless communications. He has co-authored over 100 papers published in international journals, conference proceedings and edited books. His research interests currently include mobile and pervasive computing, wireless sensor networks, and optimization algorithms.

Dennis Geesen received his diploma degree in computer science in 2010 at the University of Oldenburg, Germany, where he is currently research associate in the database and information systems group of Prof. Dr. Dr. h.c. Hans-Jürgen Appelrath. His research interests are in the fields of data stream management, complex event processing and machine learning for context-aware environments.

Marco Grawunder leads the Software Labor at the University of Oldenburg, Germany, where he received his PhD in 2005. His current research focuses on data stream systems, especially adaptive execution of continuous queries. He also investigates cloud concepts for data stream processing.

Rim Helaoui is a researcher and a PhD candidate at the research group data and Web science of the University of Mannheim in Germany. She graduated with a computer science diploma from the Karlsruher Institute for Technology (KIT) in 2008. Her research field is pervasive and mobile computing and, in particular, sensor-based activity recognition and context-aware healthcare applications. During the last four years, she worked in several research projects and collaborated with researchers from different institutions and companies. In addition to her scientific publications, she contributed to the reviewing process of several conferences and journals.

Vlasios Kasapakis received his BSc degree from the Cultural Technology and Communication Dept (University of the Aegean, Greece) in 2007 and his MSc degree in Cultural Informatics and Communication from the same department. Currently, he is pursuing PhD studies in the field of Pervasive Gaming. He has served as Adjunct Professor in the Athens School of Fine Arts in 2010-2011 and has also lectured several Game Design and Development seminars in the AKTO Art and Design Institute of Athens in 2011-2012. His research interests currently lie in the fields of game technologies and mobile and pervasive computing.

Birgitta König-Ries holds the Heinz-Nixdorf Endowed Chair of Distributed Information Systems at the University of Jena, Germany. Prior to this, she has worked with the Technical University of Munich, Florida International University, the University of Louisiana at Lafayette, and the University of Karlsruhe. Birgitta holds both a diploma and a PhD from the latter. Her research is focused on the transparent integration of both information and functionality. In particular, her group is working on Semantic Web services and portal technology and on applying these technologies to research data management.

Matthias Kranz, PhD, is a full professor in Pervasive Computing at the University of Passau, Germany. He conducts research in the areas of Ubiquitous Computing, Intelligent Environments, Pervasive and Mobile Computing, Human-Computer Interaction, Automotive User Interfaces, and Vehicle-to-X Communication. Matthias Kranz lead the Distributed Multimodal Information Processing Group at Technische Universität München after his PhD and has also been an Associate Professor at Luleå University of Technology.

Fabio Lavagetto was born in Genoa on August 6, 1962. He is currently full professor in Telecommunications at the DITEN Department of the University of Genoa. Since 2008, he is Vice-Chancellor with responsibility for Research and Technology Transfer at the University of Genoa. Since 2005, he is Vice-Chair of the Institute for Advanced Studies in Information Technology and Communication. Since 1995, he is the head of research of the Digital Signal Processing Laboratory of the University of Genoa. He was General Chair of several international scientific conferences. He is the recipient of several best paper awards and has authored over 100 scientific publications in international journals and conferences.

Alexander Lazovik is an assistant professor at Distributed Systems group at University of Groningen (NL), after being ERCIM fellow at CWI (NL) and INRIA (F), intern at IBM TJ Watson. He obtained the PhD in computer science from the University of Trento (I) in 2006. His research interests are in the areas of service-oriented and distributed computing, including service composition, business process validation and execution, diagnosis and automated repair. His expertise and research interests center around these application problems and methods for solving them (e.g., automated planning and constraint-solving). Over the last few years, he is also actively interested in pervasive computing, smarter environments, energy-aware systems, where he mainly applies results from his research in service-oriented computing.

Yunji Liang received the M.S. degree in computer science and technology in 2011. He is currently pursuing the Ph.D. degree from the School of Computer Science, Northwestern Polytechnical University, Shaanxi, China. From 2012 to 2014, he is a visiting scholar in Management of Information System (MIS), Eller College, University of Arizona, USA. His current research interests include pervasive computing, social computing and intelligent information system.

Seng Loke is a Reader and Associate Professor at the Department of Computer Science and Computer Engineering in La Trobe University. He is leading the Pervasive Computing Group at La Trobe, and has authored *Context-Aware Pervasive Systems: Architectures for a New Breed of Applications* published by Auerbach (CRC Press), Dec 2006. He has (co-)authored more than 220 research publications including 40 journal papers, 10 book chapters, and over 150 conference/workshop papers, with numerous work on context-aware computing, and mobile and pervasive computing. He has been on the program committee of numerous conferences/workshops in the area, including Pervasive'08 and Percom'10 (and 2011). His research has been published in journals such as *IEEE Pervasive, Knowledge Engineering Review, Elsevier's Pervasive and Mobile Computing Journal, IEEE Transactions on SMC, MONET, Future Generation Computer Systems, Journal of Systems and Software*, and *Theory and Practice of Logic Programming*. Loke has also published in leading conferences in the pervasive, middleware, and services computing areas.

Mario Marchese was born in Genoa, Italy, in 1967. He got his "Laurea" degree cum laude at the University of Genoa, Italy in 1992, and his Ph.D. degree in "Telecommunications" at the University of Genoa in 1997. From 1999 to 2004, he worked with the Italian Consortium of Telecommunications (CNIT), by the University of Genoa Research Unit, where he was Head of Research. Since February 2005, he has been Associate Professor at the University of Genoa. He was the Chair of the IEEE Satellite and Space Communications Technical Committee from 2006 to 2008. He is the author of the book *Quality of Service over Heterogeneous Networks*, John Wiley & Sons, Chichester, 2007, and author/co-author of more than 200 scientific works, including international magazines, international conferences and book chapters. His main research activity concerns: Satellite and Radio Networks, Quality of Service over Heterogeneous Networks, Emulation and Simulation of Telecommunication Networks, DTN Networks, Energy Aware Signal Processing for Mobile Devices, and Context Aware Systems.

Jesús Exposito Marquina holds a diploma with honors in Computer Science at the Central University of Venezuela. Currently, Jesús is pursuing his PhD degree at the University of Jena. There he is part of the Mercury CAS Research Project, where one of his main tasks is research on how interconnect heterogeneous devices and services together. Prior to this, he worked in the area of telecommunications, computer networks, design and Web/software development.

Andreas Mitschele-Thiel is a full professor at the Ilmenau University of Technology, Germany, and head of the Integrated Communication Systems lab. In addition, he is the head of the International Graduate School on Mobile Communications of the University. From 2005 to 2009, he also served as Dean for the Faculty for Computer Science and Automation. In addition, he is co-founder and scientific director of two research spin-offs of the university, Cuculus and IDEO Labs. He received a Diploma in Computer Engineering from the Fachhochschule Esslingen in 1985, a M.S. in Computer and Information Science from The Ohio State University in 1989, and a Doctoral degree in Computer Science from the University of Erlangen in 1994. He completed his habilitation in Computer Science at the University of Erlangen in 2000. Andreas Mitschele-Thiel has held various positions in development, research, and management at Alcatel and Lucent Bell Labs. His research focuses on the engineering of telecommunication systems. Special interests are in mobile communication networks, especially self-organization in next generation mobile networks, and IP-based mobile communication systems.

Andreas Nauerz holds a PhD in Computer Science. He is currently working as Lead Architect at the IBM Laboratories in Boeblingen, Germany. There he is the technical head of the Mercury CAS Research Project, a joint effort between the IBM Labs and the University of Jena. Andreas has been co-organizer, committee member, and reviewer for various conferences, workshops, and journals.

Daniela Nicklas is junior professor for database and Internet technologies at the Universität Oldenburg and member of the Member of Executive Board in the Transportation division at the OFFIS institute for computer science. Before that, she had a PostDoc position at the Universität Stuttgart where she also obtained her PhD, working on the integration of large-scale spatial context models for mobile applications. Her research interests are computer systems that bridge the gap between the physical world and the digital world. She focuses on the continuous management of data from sensors and other active data sources and their incorporation in so-called context-aware applications. Currently, she works on data stream management technologies. She applies these technologies to the domains of pervasive computing, intelligent transportation systems, and situational awareness.

Kobkaew Opasjumruskit is a researcher and PhD candidate at Heinz-Nixdorf Endowed Chair of Distributed Information Systems at the University of Jena, Germany. She holds a master degree in Electrical Engineering at Chulalongkorn University, Thailand. As a software engineer, her work experiences related to embedded system and context analyzing domains. Since September 2011, she has joined the Mercury CAS Research Project, and her focus is on user-context adaptive discovery of sensor and service.

Andry Rakotonirainy directs the Intelligent Transport System Human factor research program within CARRS-Q. He is also a program leader for operations Safety in the Cooperative Research Center for rail innovation (RailCRC). He has 25 years of research experience in computer science, road safety, and context-aware systems.

Juwel Rana is a PhD student in Pervasive and Mobile Computing at Luleå University of Technology, Sweden. He conducts research in the areas of Social Network Analysis, Ego-Centric Graphs, and Multimedia Communication. Juwel Rana is conducting his research in close collaboration with Ericsson Research, where he has been an intern both in Luleå and San Jose.

Olov Schelén, PhD, is an Assistant Professor in Computer Communications at Luleå University of Technology, Sweden. He conducts research in the areas of IP Multimedia Networking, Policy Control (PCRF/RACS/PS), IMS/SIP/NGN Control Plane Architectures, IP routing, Ethernet Switching, and Real-time Systems. Olov Schelén was the founder of Operax, which was acquired by NetSocket, and is currently the CEO of Xarepo.

Ronald Schroeter completed his PhD at the Urban Informatics Research Lab in 2011. His research investigated forms of in-place digital augmentation, which refer to the ability to enhance the experiences of citizens in physical spaces through digital technologies that are directly accessible within that space. In particular, he developed mobile phone and public screen for public civic engagement of local citizens, in particular young citizens. As part of his study, he has developed "Discussions in Space," a fun, fast paced, short-text platform for collective expression and public discourse, for which he also received the National iAwards Merit. He is currently a PostDoctoral Research Fellow at the Centre for Accident Research and Road Safety – Queensland (CARRS-Q), where his main research interests are to translate Urban Informatics and HCI concepts into innovative in-vehicular information systems and interfaces that promote road safety.

Alessandro Soro got his a post-doctoral research fellow at the Centre for Accident Research and Road Safety – Queensland (CARRS-Q), where he investigates technical and human factors of in-vehicle intelligent user interfaces. His research interests include human-computer interaction and computer supported cooperative work, focused on the design of in-vehicle intelligent interfaces. In the past he has explored several aspects of social, collaborative and ubiquitous computing, focusing on the design of multi-touch interactive surfaces (tables and walls) and their applications, such as, to name a few, collaborative information retrieval, exploration of multimedia databases, collaborative software engineering.

Lin Sun received the Ph.D. degree from Université Pierre and Marie Curie and TELECOM SudParis, Paris, France, in 2012. He received his B.Sc. and M.Sc. degrees from School of Computer Science and Technology, Northwestern Polytechnical University, Xi'an, China, in 2005 and 2008, respectively. His research interests include pervasive/ ubiquitous computing and context-aware systems, particularly in activity recognition with multimodality sensors and reality mining from large-scale real- life taxi Global Positioning System data.

Kåre Synnes, PhD, is an Associated Professor in Pervasive and Mobile Computing at Luleå University of Technology, Sweden. He conducts research in the areas of Multimedia Communication and Ubiquitous Computing, in particular for Smart Environments, Digital Cities, and Ambient Assisted Living. Kåre Synnes is also a cofounder of the IST Prize winner Marratech AB, which was acquired by Google in May 2007 to form the basis for Google Talk and Google+ Hangouts.

Torab Torabi is Senior Lecturer at Department of Computer Science and Computer Engineering. He is the head of Software Engineering Interest Group, and with Dr Seng Loke organizing the Pervasive Computing Interest Group in La Trobe University. He has (co)authored more than forty journal and conference papers in Software Engineering and Mobile Computing. His research interests include Software Engineering, CASE Tools, Process Modeling, Software Quality, XML and Metadata, Location-Based Services, Context-Aware Mobile Services, Integration of Mobile Services, Model Driven Specification, and Component-Based Simulation. Dr. Torabi serves in editorial board of number of journals, and he has served in program committee and organization of number of conferences and workshops in his research expertise. Dr Torabi has been involved in number of research projects including a project with Air services Australia. In 2007, Dr Torabi received both Vice Chancellor's and Dean's Awards for Teaching Excellence.

Jian-Min Wang graduated with Ph.D from Sun Yat-sen University in 2003. With more than 30 scientific publications and 40 patents, he is a staff of the Institute of computer application, and fellow of National Engineering Research Center of Digital Life, China. He has won a number of awards on research papers and scholarships. His research interests cover network analysis, embedded media technology, Interaction design.

Zhu Wang is a Ph.D student from the School of Computer Science, Northwestern Polytechnical University, China. He received the B.Sc. and M.Sc. degrees in Computer Science and Technology from the same university, in 2006 and 2009, respectively. During Nov. 2010 to Apr. 2012, he worked as a visiting student at Institut TELECOM SudParis in France. His research interests mainly include pervasive computing, mobile social networking, and context-aware computing.

Martin Welsch is Chief Technology Advisor at the IBM Germany Research & Development Laboratory Böblingen near Stuttgart. He holds an honorary professorship for Computer Science at the Friedrich Schiller University Jena and a PhD in Physics from the Philips University in Marburg. Martin joined IBM in 1984 and has since held various positions in hardware and software development. His current research interests are in application of context and semantics to portal and Web technologies.

Fang You is an associate professor and director of Digital Media Research Center of School of Communication and Design of Sun Yat-sen University from 2005. Her mainly research interesting is User behaviors and Interaction Design, Ubiquitous Computing, Mobile Computing, Computer Animation, and Game Design. She has published more than 20 scientific publications and 13 patents.

Zhiwen Yu is currently a professor and vice-dean at the School of Computer Science, Northwestern Polytechnical University, China. He has worked as an Alexander Von Humboldt Fellow at Mannheim University, Germany from Nov. 2009 to Oct. 2010, a research fellow at Kyoto University, Japan from Feb. 2007 to Jan. 2009, and a post-doctoral researcher at Nagoya University, Japan in 2006-2007. He serves as associate editor or guest editor for a number of international journals, such as *ACM/Springer Personal and Ubiquitous Computing, ACM Transactions on Intelligent Systems and Technology* (TIST), etc. He is the Program Chair of UIC 2010, Workshop Chair of UbiComp 2011, Publicity Chair of PerCom 2010 and PERVASIVE 2008. Dr. Yu has published around 80 scientific papers in refereed journals and conferences (e.g., *ACM Computing Surveys*, IEEE TKDE, *IEEE Pervasive Computing*, etc.). His research interests cover pervasive computing, context-aware systems, human-computer interaction, and personalization.

Daqing Zhang is a professor from Institut Mines-TELECOM/TELECOM SudParis, France. He obtained his Ph.D. from University of Rome "La Sapienza," Italy in 1996. Dr. Zhang has organized a dozen of international conferences/workshops as General Chair or Program Chair. He is the associate editor for four journals including *ACM Transactions on Intelligent Systems and Technology, Journal of Ambient Intelligence and Humanized Computing* (Springer), etc. He also served in the technical committee for conferences such as UbiComp, Pervasive, PerCom, etc. Dr. Zhang's research interests include ubiquitous computing, context-aware computing, big data analytics, social computing and service-oriented computing. He has published more than 170 papers in referred journals, conferences and books.

Xingshe Zhou is a professor from the School of Computer Science, Northwestern Polytechnical University, China. He is the director of Shaanxi Key Laboratory of Embedded System Technology. He has published more than 100 academic papers (e.g., IEEE TKDE, IEEE TSMC Systems, *IEEE Pervasive Computing*, etc.). He has served as general chair or program chair for a number of conferences, such as ICOST 2007 and UIC 2010. His research interests include embedded computing, distributed real-time computing, and pervasive computing. He is a member of the IEEE and the IEEE Computer Society.

Zhengle Zhou received his B.Eng. degree in Computer Science from Hunan University of Technology, Zhuzhou, China, in 2007. He worked as a Software Engineer in Huawei corporation from Oct. 2008 to May 2010. He is currently pursuing the M.Eng degree in the Computer Science and Technology Department, the Sun Yat-sen University. His research interests are in Information Retrieval, Data Mining, and Recommender System.

Yuchu Zuo has received his bachelor degree in the School of Electronic and Information Engineering from Xi'an Jiaotong University in 2010. He is currently pursuing his master degree in the School of Information Science and Technology in Sun Yat-sen University, Guangzhou, China. His mayor is human-computer interaction and usability engineering now. He has already published two papers on the International Conference on Computer and Information Science and International Conference on Advances in Social Networks Analysis and Mining. His research interests include social network analysis, information retrieval, data mining, machine learning and recommender system.

Index

U

V

W